The Persistence of the Palestinian Question

How is the Jewish Question related to the …

Images of horror from Israel and the Oc… familiar to Western readers but the meaning … of the flood of competing analyses, remains … erudite and unsettling series of essays, renowned Col… Professor Joseph Massad asks and answers the key questions: Wh… been the main achievement of the Zionist movement? What accounts for the failure of the Palestinian National Movement to win its struggle against Israel? What do anti-Semitism, colonialism, and racism have to do with the Palestinian/Israeli "conflict"?

Dr Massad here proposes more than the usual review of the ideological and political histories of Zionism and Palestinian nationalism. It is not in de-linking the Palestinian Question from the Jewish Question that a resolution can be found but by linking them as one and the same question. All other proposed solutions, the author argues, are bound to fail.

The book analyzes the failure of the "peace process" and proposes that a solution to the Palestinian Question will not be found unless settler-colonialism, racism, and anti-Semitism are abandoned as the ideological framework for a resolution. Individual essays further explore the struggle over Jewish identity in Israel and the struggle among Palestinians over what constitutes the Palestinian Question today.

This book will delight and discomfort many, offering a radical departure from mainstream analysis in order to expose the causes for the persistence of the "Palestinian Question." Deeply researched and documented, *The Persistence of the Palestinian Question* is essential reading for those with interests in Middle East politics, Jewish studies, colonialism, and nationalism.

Joseph A. Massad is Associate Professor of Modern Arab Politics and Intellectual History at Columbia University. He is the author of *Colonial Effects: The Making of National Identity in Jordan* (2001).

The Persistence of the Palestinian Question

Essays on Zionism and the Palestinians

Joseph A. Massad

Routledge
Taylor & Francis Group
LONDON AND NEW YORK

First published 2006
by Routledge
2 Park Square, Milton Park, Abingdon, Oxon OX14 4RN

Simultaneously published in the USA and Canada
by Routledge
270 Madison Ave, New York, NY 10016

Reprinted 2007 (twice)

Routledge is an imprint of the Taylor & Francis Group, an informa business

Typeset in Times New Roman by
Newgen Imaging Systems (P) Ltd, Chennai, India
Printed and bound in Great Britain by
Cromwell Press Ltd, Trowbridge, Wiltshire

British Library Cataloguing in Publication Data
A catalogue record for this book is available
from the British Library

Library of Congress Cataloging in Publication Data
A catalog record for this book has been requested

ISBN10: 0–415–77009–2 (hbk)
ISBN10: 0–415–77010–6 (pbk)

ISBN13: 9–78–0–415–77009–5 (hbk)
ISBN13: 9–78–0–415–77010–1 (pbk)

For Fayez

Contents

Acknowledgments

"The 'post-colonial' colony: time, space, and bodies in Palestine/Israel," first appeared in *The Pre-Occupation of Post-Colonial Studies*, edited by Fawzia Afzal-Khan and Kalpana Seshadri-Crooks (Durham, NC: Duke University Press, 2000). Reprinted by permission of Duke University Press, copyright (2000).

"Conceiving the masculine: gender and Palestinian nationalism," first appeared in *Middle East Journal* (Summer 1995) Vol. 49(3), 467–483. Reprinted by permission of *Middle East Journal*.

"Zionism's internal others: Israel and the Oriental Jews," first appeared in *Journal of Palestine Studies* (Summer 1996) No. 100, 53–68. Reprinted by permission of California University Press, copyright (1996).

"Palestinians and the limits of racialized discourse," first appeared in *Social Text* (Spring 1993) No. 34, 94–114. Reprinted by permission of Duke University Press, copyright (1993).

"Repentant terrorists or settler-colonialism revisited: the PLO–Israeli agreement in perspective," first appeared in *Found Object* (Spring 1994) No. 3, 81–90. Reprinted by permission of the Center for the Study of Culture, Technology and Work, City University of New York, copyright (1994).

"Political realists or comprador intelligentsia: Palestinian intellectuals and the national struggle," first appeared in *Critique* (Fall 1997), 23–35, http://www.tandf.co.uk. Reprinted by permission of Taylor and Francis, copyright (1997).

"Return or permanent exile? Palestinian refugees and the ends of Oslo," first appeared in *Critique* (Spring 1999) No. 14, 5–23, http://www.tandf.co.uk. Reprinted by permission of Taylor and Francis, copyright (1999).

"Palestinians and Jewish history: recognition or submission?" first appeared in *Journal of Palestine Studies* (Fall 2000) No. 117, 52–67. Reprinted by permission of California University Press, copyright (2000).

"The ends of Zionism: racism and the Palestinian struggle," first appeared in *Interventions* (2003) Vol. 5(3), 440–451, http://www.tandf.co.uk. Reprinted by permission of Taylor and Francis, copyright (2003).

"History on the line: Joseph Massad and Benny Morris discuss the Middle East," Debate with Israeli historian Benny Morris, first appeared in *History Workshop Journal* (Spring 2002) 205–216. Reprinted by permission of Oxford University Press, copyright (2002).

"The persistence of the Palestinian Question," first appeared in *Cultural Critique* (Winter 2005) No. 59, 1–23. Copyright (2005) by the Regents of the University of Minnesota. Reprinted by permission of the University of Minnesota Press.

Introduction

The opposite of terror

Terror is a name that is never assumed but always tendered. The taxonomy that transforms it from a practice into an identity is always particular. State power designates certain practices as terror and christens those who commit them as terrorists. Yet all subjects thus named do not accept their State-tendered names, and do not identify with them (there is, e.g. no Irish Terrorist Army, no African Terrorist Congress, and no Palestine Terror Organization). If the condition of identity is its having subjective and objective components (internalization and interpellation), terrorist identities remain contested terrains, controlled by an enemy who is in power and who controls the means of representation. While all subjective identities (sexual, racial, national, etc.) posit a self and an other as its opposite, objective identities are constituted similarly but from another's subject position. In the case of the terrorist, it is the other, the enemy, and not the self, who defines the identity of the "terrorist," specifying its self and its other. Since the State itself as enemy of terror defines the terrorist's self, does it posit itself as the terrorist's other? This applies just as much to the Superpower State that designates groups and weaker states as "terrorists." Is this process nothing less than Nietzsche's "slave-morality" at work, or is it the Hegelian telos of the journey of self-consciousness toward "absolute freedom and terror," or, is it of a different order altogether? What exactly is the opposite of terror as a practice? Indeed, what is the opposite of the terrorist as identity?

In order to investigate these questions, I have found the Palestinian–Israeli case instructive, especially so as both the Zionist colonial settlers and the Palestinian natives have been interpellated as terrorists—the Zionists by the British Empire and by the Palestinians, and the Palestinians by the British Empire, the US Empire, and the Israeli settler-colony. The history of this identitarian designation and its deployment in the case of Palestine/Israel may provide some answers.

Zionist colonial practices under the British Mandate, which lasted from 1921 and ended on May 14, 1948 with the establishment of the settler-colony, were characterized by different strategies. While the Zionists' main project, which was sponsored by the British Empire, was to acquire the lands of the Palestinians, drive the peasants off that land, and establish an exclusive Jewish economy based on what they termed "pure Hebrew Labor," early Palestinian resistance (punctuated by occasional violence) mostly took the form of legal appeals to the British, organizing and mobilizing the population against land sales to Zionists, and appealing to international actors to help in obtaining national independence. As this proved ineffective, by 1936, Palestinian resistance erupted into an all-out revolt, which lasted from 1936 to 1939. The revolt included strikes, demonstrations, and guerrilla action taken against the British and the Jewish colonial settlers. British response was massive and included the re-invasion of the country, killing over 5,000 Palestinians, and wounding 15,000, exiling and executing the Palestinian leadership, and organizing joint British–Zionist death squads (known as the Special Night Squads) that attacked Palestinian villages at night and shot and killed numerous Palestinians.[1] In this context David Ben-Gurion, the leader of the colonial settlers understood that the revolt of the Palestinians had civilizational dimensions that were definitional of both Palestinian identity and that of the Jewish colonists. He asserted in 1936, a few months after the eruption of the Palestinian Revolt, that Zionist strategy would be different from that of the Palestinians on civilizational grounds:

> We are not Arabs, and others measure us by a different standard... our instruments of war are different from those of the Arabs, and only our instruments can guarantee our victory. Our strength is in defense... and this strength will give us a political victory if England and the world know that we are defending ourselves rather than attacking.[2]

While Ben-Gurion's group would form death squads under a British commander (Charles Orde Wingate[3]) and thus maintained what he believed to be a civilized and thus legitimate form of violence, other Zionists opted for a different kind of organized violence that would soon be termed "terrorism." Those Zionists began to use new methods to suppress the Palestinian revolt, including the blowing up of cafés with grenades (in Jerusalem, e.g. on March 17, 1937), and placing electrically timed mines in crowded market places, first used against Palestinians in Haifa on July 6, 1938. When following the suppression of the Palestinian revolt, the British had to limit their support for the Zionist project, Zionist attacks turned against them. This was going to be a defining moment for the British and the Zionists. The Zionist response included blowing up a ship with civilian passengers in Haifa in November 1940, killing 242 Jewish civilians and a number of British police personnel, assassination of British government officials, taking British citizens hostages, blowing up government offices and killing employees and civilians, blowing up the British embassy in Rome (1946), exploding car bombs parked next to government buildings, killing hostages as reprisal for government actions, sending letter bombs and parcel bombs to British politicians in London, among others.[4] Menachem Begin, the future prime minister of Israel, was the mastermind behind many of these attacks, especially the market and café bombings as well as the car bombs. It was in light of such acts that Zionist groups like the Irgun and later Stern would be called "terrorist" by the British.

Menachem Begin however was unconvinced that the actions of his group and those of other Zionist groups constituted "terrorism." Begin who headed the Irgun

Zvai Leumi, the military organization that committed many of these violent and murderous acts protested the label that the British government and the British and American media bestowed on him. Following his group's massacre of 100 unarmed Palestinians at the village of Dayr Yasin in April 1948, his name had become synonymous with terrorism. Albert Einstein and Hannah Arendt, among others, were so offended by Begin that they objected to the welcome accorded the latter while on a fund-raising trip in the United States in December 1948. Einstein and Arendt stressed to the *New York Times* in a letter to the editor that Begin's group, the Irgun, was not only "a terrorist rightwing, chauvinist organization," but that the political party to which the Irgun had given birth was "closely akin in its organization, methods, political philosophy and social appeal to the Nazi and Fascist parties." Decrying Begin's rhetoric and that of his party as dissimulation, Einstein and Arendt insisted that "It is in its actions that the terrorist party betrays its real character."[5] It is, however, Arendt and Einstein's letter that betrays a strong liberal belief in the category "terrorist" as having an objective character. Menachem Begin begged to differ. His response to such descriptions was sophisticated and clear-headed. He insisted on deconstructing the term "terrorism" and on historicizing it. In his famed autobiography, published in 1951, he begins by dissociating his group from the term:

> Our enemies called us terrorists. People who were neither friends nor enemies, like the correspondents of the *New York Herald-Tribune*, also used this Latin name, either under the influence of British propaganda or out of habit . . . They called us "terrorists" to the end. And yet, we were not terrorists.

Begin proceeded to provide a history of the use of the term "terrorism" from the French Revolution to the Russian Revolution. He was astute enough to appreciate that "terrorism" is not an objective term that is agreed upon by all parties, but rather a rhetorical strategy used by unequal enemies for political ends:

> Thenceforward the word "terror" came to define the acts of revolutionaries or counter-revolutionaries, or fighters for freedom and oppressors. It all depends on who uses the term. It frequently happens that it is used by both sides in their mutual exchange of compliments . . . . The historical and linguistic origins of the political term "terror" prove that it cannot be applied to a revolutionary war of liberation. A revolution may give birth to what we call "terror," as happened in France. Terror may at times be its herald, as happened in Russia. But the revolution itself is not terror and terror is not the revolution. A revolution, or a revolutionary war, does not aim to instil fear. Its object is to overthrow a regime and to set up a new regime in its place . . . The sole aim on the one side is the overthrow of armed tyranny; on the other side it is the perpetuation of that tyranny.

Having explained this rhetorical strategy which he attempts to reinscribe into a discourse of objectivity, wherein "terror" cannot describe or apply to certain situations objectively, Begin proceeds to give an objective account of what his group was engaged in, and to insist that terrorism *has* an objective meaning outside its rhetorical uses:

> But what has a struggle for the dignity of man, against oppression and subjugation, to do with "terrorism"? Our purpose, in fact, was precisely the reverse of "terrorism." The whole essence of our struggle was the determination to free our people of its chief affliction—fear . . . We . . . arose therefore to rebel and fight, not in order to instil fear but to eradicate it. But historically we were not "terrorists." We were anti-terrorists.[6]

Here Begin seems to grasp what is at stake in the identitarian appellation "terrorist" and therefore declares the identity of his group as "anti-terrorists." Thus, the Irgun, was engaged not in terrorism but in its opposite, its reverse: anti-terrorism. In this, Begin is claiming for his group the very same identity that the British authorities chose for themselves and was designating them as "terrorists" instead. If objectivity is established as an inter-subjective agreement on terms and concepts that constitute objective reality, it would seem that neither terrorists nor anti-terrorists agree as to who belongs to each of their communities. If the community is interchangeable, then it surely becomes superfluous to insist on an identitarian binary with everyone wanting to belong only to one of its terms. Here, terrorism seems to function as a moral identity, akin to the binary of good and evil, where everyone wants to be on one side of the binary and *not* the other. In the present time, George W. Bush's "Axis of Evil," for example, remains an involuntary coercive club that no one has joined and whose virtual members are all forced into it against their will by the peremptory power of US diktat.

But, if the anti-terrorist is the opposite and the reverse of the terrorist, then there is no identity between the terrorist and the anti-terrorist, rather what exists between them is radical alterity, or so we would assume. Again the Zionist case is instructive in this regard. Speaking of Palestinian resistance in 1923, Vladimir Jabotinsky, the founder of Revisionist Zionism, who was later succeeded by Menachem Begin, had asserted that:

> Any native people—it's all the same whether they are civilized or savage—views their country as their national home, of which they will always be the complete masters. They will not voluntarily allow, not only a new master, but even a new partner. And so it is for the Arabs. Compromisers in our midst attempt to convince us that the Arabs are some kind of fools who can be tricked . . . [and] who will abandon their birth right to Palestine for cultural and economic gains. I flatly reject this assessment of the Palestinian Arabs. Culturally they are 500 years behind us, spiritually they do not have our endurance or our strength of will, but this exhausts all of the internal differences . . . They look upon Palestine with the same instinctive love and true fervour that any Aztec looked upon his Mexico or any Sioux looked upon the

> prairie...this childish fantasy of our "Arabo-philes" comes from some kind of contempt for the Arab people...[that] this race [is] a rabble ready to be bribed or sell out their homeland for a railroad network.[7]

Jabotinsky understood well that the Palestinians "are not a rabble but a nation."[8] As a fascist who admired Mussolini, he did not allow his racism against the Palestinians to blind him to the conditions on the ground, which is precisely why he sought to fight the Palestinians and subject them to Zionist rule and expulsion. Jabotinsky however did not identify with the Palestinians although he attempted to equalize them with European Jews (mutatis mutandis) at the level of nationalism and the use of violence to defend their country. Other Zionists would go further than he. Ben-Gurion himself understood Palestinian nationalism fully and identified with it, even though he was committed to crush it. This is how he expressed his identification:

> If I was an Arab leader, I would never make terms with Israel. That is natural; we have taken their country. Sure, God promised it to us, but what does that matter to them? Our God is not theirs. We come from Israel, it's true, but that was two thousand years ago, and what is that to them? There has been antisemitism, the Nazis, Hitler, Auschwitz, but was that their fault? They only see one thing: we have come and stolen their country. Why should they accept that?[9]

This, however, has not prevented Israeli policy-makers from proceeding with the destruction of Palestinian society and to introduce violent methods that they would identify as terrorism if emulated by the Palestinians. While the Zionists might have introduced car bombs and market and café bombings to the Middle East, Israel would introduce plane hijackings to the world as early as December 12, 1954 when it hijacked a Syrian airliner and forced it to land in Israel.[10] The Israeli Air Force would often seize flying civilian airliners in international skies and divert them to Israel, subject the passengers to inspection, interrogation, as well as incarceration. Indeed, Israel remains the only party in the Middle East who shot down a civilian airliner, as it did on February 21, 1973, when it downed a Libyan passenger plane, killing 108 passengers on board, an act reminiscent of the Zionist blowing up of the passenger ship in the 1940. Israeli government officials would, on occasion, use the term "terror" to describe some of their own policies, but not the term "terrorism." In 1976, Israel Koenig, advisor to the Israeli Knesset, wrote in the now infamous Koenig Memorandum regarding government policy toward Palestinian citizens of Israel that "We must use terror, assassination, intimidation, land confiscation, and the cutting of all social services to rid the Galilee of its Arab population."[11]

Such linguistic lapses aside, Zionist leaders continued to identify with Palestinians as "terrorists." Indeed, if Ben-Gurion was able to identify with the Palestinians, then, as terrorists, the Palestinians do not function as *other* at all to the Zionist self being constructed. Such an identification is made more strongly in fact by former Prime Minister Ehud Barak. Barak was member of an Israeli death squad commando unit dispatched to Beirut in 1973 to kill three Palestinians (he is said to have locked eyes with Palestinian poet Kamal Nasser before he shot him in the mouth to punish him literally for being a Palestine Liberation Organization (PLO) spokesman). Like Menachem Begin before him, Barak posits a national theory of terrorism. In an interview with Israeli newspaper *Ha'Aretz*, he asserted that "If I were a Palestinian, I'd also join a terror group."[12] Barak's identification with terrorist Palestinians is unreserved, although unlike Begin before him, he does not seem to understand that as far as Palestinians are concerned they never join "terror" groups but rather "liberation" groups. Still, he seems to grasp that in the Palestinian case, nationality is the condition of legitimacy for violence, which is precisely the moment that he identifies with Palestinians as "terrorists." Here, Leah Rabin, widow of the late Yitzhak Rabin who had fought in the 1948 war, was more astute in deploying her identification with the Palestinians than all other Zionist leaders. She asserted in 1997 that "We [the Jews] used terrorism to establish our state. Why should we expect the Palestinians to be any different?"[13] Palestinians therefore seem to be the same as Jews and not other at all. Sure enough, Leah Rabin's identification with the Palestinians is developmentalist in nature, but it is still one that differentiates them along the axis of time not essence, which is deployed as identical.

This is not however the way Zionism and Israel normally construct Palestinians. In fact, not only is Israel committed officially to identifying Palestinians as terrorist, it is also intent on forcing Palestinians to ventriloquize Zionism in their very self-definition. Take this example of an interrogation by an Israeli radio broadcaster of a Palestinian "terrorist" prisoner, interviewed on Israel's Arabic language radio service for Palestinians to hear:

I.B.: Tell me Mr. Abu Leil, to which terrorist organization do you belong?

PAL.: I belong to the Popular Front for the Liberation [tahrir]—I mean Terrorization [takhrib]—of Palestine.[14]

I.B.: And when did you get involved in the terrorists' organization?

PAL.: When I first became aware of terrorism.

I.B.: And what was your mission in South Lebanon?

PAL.: My mission was terrorism... In other words, we would enter villages and just terrorize. And whenever there were women and children, we would terrorize. Everything and all what we did was terrorism.

I.B.: And did you practice terrorism out of belief in a cause or simply for money?

PAL.: No, by God, just for money. What kind of cause is this anyway? Why? Is there still a cause? We sold out a long time ago.

. . .

I.B.: What's your opinion of the way the Israel Defense Forces have conducted themselves?

PAL.: On my honor, we thank the Israel Defense Forces for their good treatment to each terrorist.[15]

The prisoner's miming of the narrative given to him by his Israeli torturers, notwithstanding, his declarations are engineered by the Israelis to shift the terrorist identity from an objective to a subjective identification. The Israelis seem to believe that the only way Palestinians can repudiate terrorism is by internalizing it as their identity first, which the example of the interrogation hoped to facilitate. If Palestinians refuse the designation as one that is self-chosen, then they will have the same objective power as the Israelis in identifying who the real terrorist is. This also applies to enemies of US power. It is in this context that Edward Said identified the functional importance of the counter-terrorism industry, which extends from Tel Aviv to Washington, and keeps churning out experts, studies, documents, a veritable "science" of terrorology:

> This has justified Israeli mass terror against even the idea of Palestinian nationalism, joined in by air force, army, navy, administrative rhetoric, and scholarship, on a scale so large it caricatures our actual strength. The distortion recalls Swift's abrupt juxtaposition of large and small in the first and second voyages of *Gulliver's Travels*. Thus the dismissible terrorist is Lilliputian on the one hand; on the other hand, the efforts at dehumanization and miniaturization are so obsessive they inflate the threat unimaginably. The Palestinian as resident of Brobdingnag.[16]

A very popular recent song by the Israeli Palestinian rap group Dam is titled: "Who is the terrorist?" The refrain asks in colloquial Palestinian rhymed verse:

> Who is the terrorist?
> Me, the terrorist?
> How am I a terrorist
> When I am living in my own homeland?
> Who is the terrorist?
> You are the terrorist.
> You have eaten me up
> While I am living in my own homeland
> You are killing me now,
> Like you have killed my forefathers[17]

Palestinian refusal and resistance to concede the objective power of naming the terrorist continues to undermine Israeli efforts to subjectify the designation.

An important dimension of the discourse on terror is that it is a discourse not about the victims of "terrorism" but rather about the "perpetrators." The terrorist is not an actor who targets civilians and/or military and government personnel, as state armies can target the very same victims and not be referred to as "terrorist." Therefore, it is not the act of "terror" that designates the actor as "terrorist" but the opposite, the perpetrator's conferred identity as "terrorist" is what defines his/her act as "terrorist" in nature.

Terror therefore seems to have no opposite. If the opposite of the terrorist is the terrorist, and the opposite of terror is terror, both discursively and materially, then it is a term that folds unto itself, stripping itself of any identitarian dimension.

Yet, its rhetorical deployment is indeed of the identitarian variety, albeit in the sense of mirror reflection. If the identity "terrorist" is used only by enemies of those designated terrorist against one another, or, as Menachem Begin asserted, it is "used by both sides in their mutual exchange of compliments," then it becomes nothing less than a projected fantasy, with each party holding up a mirror to the other so that whatever one party says reflects back onto it. In this sense "terrorism" as identity functions exactly as Nietzsche's slave-morality: "You are a terrorist, therefore I am an anti-terrorist." At the level of discourse, it is the anti-terrorist who creates the "terrorist," not the other way around. Yet what the discourse of terror achieves is a radical relativism and a Nietzschean perspectivalism that forecloses any discussion of the materiality of colonial conquest and anti-colonial resistance, which are reduced by the most "objective" observers to a neutral "cycle of violence."

But if terrorism is the discourse of identity and equalization between Colonial State violence and those who resist it among the colonized, it remains remarkable that terrorism is identified not as the weapon of the strong, but ironically as the weapon of the weak. Terror then is a discourse about a colonial identity that needs to differentiate itself but always fails. What the discourse on terror seeks is the erasure of power relations as the central problematic of violence. It is here that I find Saint Augustine's famous tale about Alexander not much of a radical departure from this liberal approach, although, unlike the latter, it does posit power relations as essential: Alexander the Great is said to have captured a pirate and then began to interrogate him: "What is your idea in infesting the sea?" he asked. The pirate's response questioned Alexander's imperial taxonomy: "The same as yours in infesting the earth! But because I do it with a tiny craft, I'm called a pirate; because you have a mighty navy, you're called an emperor."[18] Augustine's pirate seems to agree with Alexander that the moral difference between them is quantitative. In this colonial discourse which essentializes terrorism, terror is indeed the opposite of terror. The Zionist–Palestinian case, however, demonstrates that "terrorism" functions in powerfully shifting dialectical terms. At the level of argument then, the opposite of the discourse on terror is nothing less than historical materialism, which is the only antidote to such musings.

***

This book is a collection of essays on Zionism and Palestinian nationalism that were published over a period of one decade or so, starting in 1993. The essays analyze the ideological underpinnings and political alliances of Zionism since its inception in order to explain its historical record on European Jews, Asian and African Jews, and on the Palestinian people. It is my hope that through providing a genealogy, a history, and an analysis of what came to be constituted as the Palestinian–Israeli "conflict," these essays will shed some light on how the discourse of terrorism constructs its subjects and objects. The essays focus on Zionism's conception of culture and race as central to its ideological and practical aims as well as its policies toward all the groups over whom it exercises dominion, whether Jewish or Arab. Based on this analysis, which is fully or partially explored in Chapters 1, 3, 4, and 8–11, the other essays analyze Palestinian nationalism, the peace process begun in 1991, and the latter's transformation of Palestinian politics. These essays (Chapters 2 and 4–9) explicate the effect of the peace process on Palestinian intellectuals, as well as on the Palestinian national agenda, as regards the questions of Palestinian refugees, Israel's racialism, and the relationship of the Palestinian people to Jewish history, especially the Jewish holocaust. The final essay's analysis of the Palestinian question harks back to the first essay but has a different focus, namely the centrality of the Jewish question to the Palestinian question, and their overlap, wherein resolving one leads to resolving the other.

The book is divided into two sections: Part I includes essays on Zionist ideology and Palestinian nationalism, while Part II includes essays on the origins of the "Peace Process" and its transformation of the Palestinian political field. The essays were published in academic journals (and in one case in an edited book) and are all pertinent to the ongoing tragedy of the Palestinian encounter with Zionism. Some repetitions of argument are unavoidably present in some of the different essays, as they were all published independently of each other, but in situations where this is the case, the focus is different and the arguments are deployed to make other (albeit related) points. I have done some minor editing of the chapters to minimize unnecessary repetition.

I have also included a debate with Israeli historian Benny Morris that he and I had in July 2001 (Chapter 10). The exchange, which was mediated by an editor of the *History Workshop Journal* (where the text was published), centered on the core issues of Zionism's encounter with the Palestinians. It is significant that this debate signalled for the first time the more recent public transformation in Morris's political commitments. He would flesh them out in a later interview with the Israeli newspaper *Ha'Aretz*.[19] I responded to him in *Al-Ahram Weekly*.[20]

Part I

Zionist ideology and Palestinian nationalism

1 The "post-colonial" colony*,[1]

Time, space, and bodies in Palestine/Israel

"Colonial" and "post-colonial" are terms that are generally used to designate a historical trajectory of the beginning and end of the process of colonialism and the ushering of a new era. A territory and people who are colonized and inhabit a colonial order transform themselves and are transformed into inhabiting a post-colonial order, both spatially and temporally. The diachronic aspect of this process is guaranteed by the logical imperative of the process of colonialism itself: in order to decolonize oneself, one has to have been colonized first. Consequently, colonialism's end, it is said, brings about post-colonialism.

Aside from ignoring the material relations of colonial and post-colonial rule and rendering these terms limited to the discursive realm, this diachronic presentation of the history of colonialism has ignored the potential if not actual synchronicity of these "two" eras in different contexts. Settler-colonialism, being a variant of colonialism, presents us with different spatialities and temporalities as regards a diachronic schema of "colonialism-then-post-colonialism." The Rhodesian "Unilateral Declaration of Independence" in 1965, the formation of the Union of South Africa in 1910, the American Revolution in 1776, or the Declaration of the Establishment of the State of Israel in 1948 are some examples where settler-colonists declared themselves "independent" while maintaining colonial privileges for themselves over the conquered populations. The United States, Rhodesia, South Africa, and Israel, for example, instituted themselves as post-colonial states, territories and spaces, and instituted their political status as "independent" in order to render their present a post-colonial era. Yet, the conquered peoples of these territories continue (including the people of Zimbabwe following "independence"[2] and South Africa following the "end" of apartheid) to inhabit these spaces as colonial spaces, and to live in eras that are thoroughly colonial. Given such a situation, how can one determine the coloniality and/or post-coloniality of these spaces or times? The perspectival answers to such questions ignore the commonality of these particular spaces and histories. Whereas an Ashkenazi Jew after May 1948 would view her/himself as living in a post-colonial space and era, Palestinians would view themselves as still living in a colonized space and in a colonial era. Mizrahi Jews

* This essay was first published in 2000.

would have a more difficult task characterizing the nature of the space and time they inhabit due to their dual status of being (internally) colonized *vis-à-vis* the Ashkenazim with colonizer privileges *vis-à-vis* the Palestinians. The commonality of this space and time, then, at least in its abstract appellation, Palestine or Israel, renders its status a combinational one. The very naming of this space is, in fact, a process of historicizing it. To call it Palestine is to refer to it as a colonized space in both the pre-1948 and the post-1948 periods and to signal its continued appellation as such for a postcolonial period still to come. To call it Israel is to refer to it in the post-1948 period after the coming to fruition of the Zionist project forestalling any notion of a post-Israel Palestine. Naming, therefore, functions as locating in history, as temporalizing, and ultimately as asserting power as colonial domination or as anti-colonial resistance.

The synchronicity of the colonial and the post-colonial (as discursive and material relations) in Palestine/Israel as one era is not a situation that exists only in reference to the different national groups and their relationship to this common space and time, but also to the same national group. The Zionist movement was and presented its project of creating a Jewish State through colonization as part of the European colonizing world, while "socialist" variants of it were presenting the Zionist project as one assisting in combating imperialism and the world capitalist order. Later, the Zionist establishment itself which had initially presented its project as colonial was presenting itself as a movement of national liberation constituting its project as anticolonial in nature, albeit one established through colonization but not colonialism![3] The synchronic presentation of the Zionist project as colonial and anti-colonial coupled with the diachronic process of transforming its explicitly colonial heritage as anti-colonial show the palimpsestic nature of current Zionist historiography. Moreover, the dual status of Mizrahi Jews as colonizer and colonized renders the national space and time within and during which they live as colonial/postcolonial synchronically. What is then this space and time called Israel? What constitutes the difficulty in naming it in relation to colonialism? Can one determine the coloniality of Palestine/Israel without noting its "post-coloniality" for Ashkenazi Jews? Can one determine the post-coloniality of Palestine/Israel without noting its coloniality for Palestinians? Can one determine both or either without noting the simultaneous colonizer/colonized status of Mizrahi Jews? How can all these people inhabit a colonial/postcolonial space in a world that declares itself living in a post-colonial time?[4] This chapter will chart the ideological history of the Zionist movement with an emphasis on its epistemological underpinnings, and how it was/is conceived by its agents in an attempt to begin to answer the above questions.

Colonial Zionism, Jewish and Gentile

Since its prehistory, Zionism, in both its Jewish and gentile versions, was incorporated within colonial thought. Non-Jewish Zionism was propagated for the first time within European colonial projects by Napoleon Bonaparte during his Egyptian campaign. By the closing years of the nineteenth century, French and British colonial officials were explicitly advancing the idea of European Jewish colonization of Palestine as part of the construction of a permanent imperial order in the region. Sharing a colonial project, the interests of European Jewish proponents of Zionism and its gentile advocates converged, leading to collaboration among them.[5] The convergence of interests between Jewish and non-Jewish Zionists was a result of their shared views on anti-Semitism. Like European anti-Semites, Zionism viewed the presence of Jews among gentiles as the main cause for gentile anti-Semitism. Whereas Herzl had initially considered the option of converting Jews to Christianity as a solution to anti-Semitism, he, and his disciples after him, opted for a second solution, namely, the removal of Jews from gentile societies, that is, from Europe (a solution long advocated by anti-Semitic Christian Zionists). Removing Jews from gentile societies and "normalizing" them by creating a state for them would be, the Zionists argued, the only way to end anti-Semitism. Thus, Zionism and anti-Semitism had a unified goal—the removal of Jews from Europe—which became the basis for their shared imperial vision.

In France, Ernest Laharanne, private secretary of Napoleon III, wrote in 1860 *La Nouvelle Question d'Orient: Reconstruction de la Nationalité Juive*. In his book, Laharanne emphasized the economic gains that could accrue to Europe if European Jews were to settle Palestine. He spoke highly of the Jewish people who were "to open new highways and byways to European civilization."[6] Such views of Jews as transmitters of European civilization to the uncivilized were also espoused by the father of Jewish Zionism, Theodor Herzl. In his *Der Judenstaat* (which contrary to common translations means *The State of the Jews* not *The Jewish State*—which in German is *Der Jüdische Staat*[7]) Herzl saw his proposed state as "the portion of the rampart of Europe against Asia, an outpost of civilization as opposed to barbarism."[8] Laharanne's work also influenced one of the earliest Jewish Zionists, Moses Hess, who used Laharanne's book extensively while writing his *Rome and Jerusalem* in 1862. The collusion with European imperialism was so central to the Zionist project that Hess notes in his book to those unpersuaded in the practicality of Zionist aims: "Do you still doubt that France will help the Jews to found colonies which may extend from Suez to Jerusalem and from the banks of the Jordan to the coast of the Mediterranean?"[9]

On the British front, Lord Palmerston, who became Britain's foreign minister in 1830, was an advocate of Jewish "restoration" to Palestine. The context of Palmerston's Zionism was to provide support to a teetering Ottoman Empire against Muhammad Ali's defiance of the Ottoman Sultan. For Palmerston, a Jewish presence in Palestine was a key element in supporting the Sultan against "any future evil designs of Mahomet Ali or his successor."[10] British Zionist designs, like their French counterparts, were to coincide later with the rise of Jewish Zionism. Meeting with the kings and leaders of European empires (from the Italian King to the German Kaiser, Czarist Russian ministers, the Ottoman Sultan *et al.*), Herzl finally settled on Britain as the "Archimidean point where the lever can be applied."[11] In his opening address to the Fourth Zionist Congress, taking place in London in 1900, Herzl proclaimed: "From this place the Zionist movement will take a higher and higher flight... England the great, England the free, England with her eyes on the seven seas, will understand us."[12] In his negotiations with the British, the quid pro quo that Herzl had offered Joseph Chamberlain and Lord Lansdowne, the foreign secretary, in return for British imperial sponsorship of Jewish colonization was that Jews will

> wear England in their hearts if through such a deed it becomes the protective power of the Jewish people. *At one stroke England will get ten million secret but loyal subjects* active in all walks of life all over the world...As at a signal, all of them will place themselves at the service of the magnanimous nation that brings long-desired help. England will get ten million agents for her greatness and her influence. And the spread of this sort of thing usually spreads from the political to the economic. It is surely no exaggeration to say that a Jew would rather purchase and propagate the products of a country that has rendered the Jewish people a benefaction than those of a country in which the Jews are badly off... May the English government recognize what value there is in gaining the Jewish people [emphasis added].[13]

Chamberlain offered the Zionists El Arish in Sinai, which they readily accepted. The project, however, did not materialize in light of the impracticality of its settlement (due to the arid conditions in the area and the lack of water resources), a conclusion that was reached by Zionist envoys to the region. Chamberlain immediately located another possible territory for Jewish colonization, Uganda. He reassured Herzl that although "[i]t's hot on the coast,... farther inland the climate becomes excellent, *even for Europeans* [emphasis added]."[14] The offer was to be later rejected at the Sixth Zionist Congress in 1903 in favor of Palestine. The priority of Palestine, however, did not prevent Herzl from asserting that "our base must be in or near Palestine. Later we could also settle in Uganda, for we have masses of people ready to emigrate."[15] Whereas by 1903, Palestine was the primary candidate for the Jewish settler-colony, this was not always the case. Herzl himself spoke of Argentina in his *Der Judenstaat* as a possible location for the Jewish colony. He even pursued other African locations as late as 1903, namely Mozambique. He had met with the Portuguese ambassador, Count Paraty, requesting of him that he "inquire of his government whether it was willing to give us a Charter for an adequate territory."[16] In a follow-up letter to the ambassador, Herzl explained to him that "the preliminary question to submit to the Minister is the following: Is there a territory *sufficiently habitable and cultivable by Europeans*? [emphasis added]."[17] Other solicited territories included Herzl's request during a meeting with the Italian King for Tripolitania (Libya) as a territory for Jewish colonization. But as in the case of Uganda, Tripolitania was not intended to be the primary territory for the Jewish state, rather its function was "de déverser le trop plein de l'immigration juive en Tripolitaine sous les lois et institutions libérales de l'Italie."[18] The King responded with surprise due to Herzl's earlier declaration that the Zionist movement did not want to send many Jews to Palestine before insuring that the country would be theirs. For "[o]ur project means investments and improvements, and I don't want them undertaken as long as the country isn't ours."[19] Seeing the parallel with Palestine, the King responded to the Tripolitania proposal by saying "Ma é ancora casa di altri."[20]

Herzl assured the King that "the partition of Turkey is bound to come, Your Majesty."[21]

Herzl's requested territorial concessions for his State of the Jews, it is important to stress, were always located in the colonized world. It was never suggested by Jewish or gentile Zionists that a location for a state for the Jews be in Europe—in the Pale of Settlement,[22] for example. Such a proposal would never have been considered by the European empires, who would never have agreed to the displacement of gentile Europeans for the purposes of erecting a Jewish state. Similarly, Stalin's Birobidzhan project of an autonomous Jewish region was located in the far reaches of Asia, far, that is, from Soviet Europe. What is noteworthy, however, is that such a proposal was never entertained by the Zionist movement at any time in its history. This was not the result of an implicit understanding of the impracticality of a Zionist project that would require displacing white Christian people, but, rather, an understanding of European race politics that was quite explicit in the minds of Zionist leaders. In the context of his negotiations with Joseph Chamberlain (in which Herzl suggested Cyprus, El Arish, and the Sinai Peninsula as possible territories in the vicinity of Palestine), Herzl commented in his diaries that "[i]n fact, if I could show him a spot in the English possessions *where there were no white people as yet*, we could talk about that [emphasis added]."[23]

Other Zionist thinkers who preceded and succeeded Herzl had a similar understanding of Zionist goals. Leo Pinsker, an assimilationist, who was converted to Zionism by the pogroms of 1881, wrote in his well-known 1882 book *Auto-Emancipation* that the "auto-emancipation of the Jewish people as a nation [would take place through] the foundation of a colonial community belonging to the Jews, which is some day to become our inalienable home, our fatherland."[24] He understood that "of course, the establishment of a Jewish refuge cannot come about without the support of [European] governments."[25] A similar sentiment was expressed by Herzl when in a conversation with Chamberlain, in which Chamberlain wondered about the survivability of the Jewish state in the absence of Britain and in the presence of European power rivalry over the Ottoman Empire, he stated that "I believe that our chances then would be even better. For we shall be used as small *buffer-state. We shall get it not from the good will, but from the jealousy of the powers! And once we are at El Arish under the Union Jack, then Palestine too will fall into the British sphere of influence* [emphasis added]."[26] Such a sentiment was to be echoed again fifteen years later by the British War Office: "The Creation of a buffer Jewish State in Palestine, though this state will be weak in itself, is strategically desirable for Britain."[27]

As the above references to Jews-as-colonists indicate, European Jews and gentiles alike viewed European Jews as "Europeans" (only) insofar as they were/are undertaking a colonial venture. Theodor Herzl, in his opening address to the First Zionist Congress asserts this self-perception of Jews qua Europeans in stating that "[i]t is more and more to the interest of the civilised nations and of civilisation in general that a cultural station be established on the shortest road to Asia. Palestine is this station and we Jews are the bearers of culture who are ready to give our property and our lives to bring about its creation."[28] Such sentiments were already characteristic of the early directors of Jewish agricultural settlements in Palestine as they were "in the mould of the French *service colonial* and imbued with their share of *la mission civilisartrice*."[29] Asserting the coloniality of the European Jewish presence in Palestine, Chaim Weizmann stated in 1930 that "[w]e wish to spare the Arabs as much as we can of the sufferings which every backward race has gone through on the coming of another, more advanced nation."[30]

Even self-styled socialist Zionists like Ber Borochov, who had to deal with the presence of the Palestinian people, advocated solidarity with them while stressing the practical tasks of Jewish colonization which were being carried out at the Palestinians' expense. Embarrassed by the argument that Zionism oppresses the Palestinians, Borochov responded in 1917 by stating that thanks to the new working methods, "there will be sufficient land to accommodate both the Jews and the Arabs. *Normal* relations between the Jews and Arabs will and must prevail [emphasis added]."[31]

Anti-colonial Zionism, a new strategy

In the 1930s, some Zionists were beginning to suggest a change in the ideological vocabulary of their colonial-settler project. F.H. Kisch, the chairman of the Zionist Executive, noted in his diary in 1931 that he was

> striving to eliminate the word "colonization" in this connection [Jewish agricultural settlement in Palestine] from our phraseology. The word is not appropriate from our point of view since one does not set up colonies in a homeland but abroad: e.g. German colonies on the Volga or Jewish colonies in the Argentine, while from the point of view of Arab opinion the verb to "colonize" is associated with imperialism and aggressiveness.[32]

This was not only an expression of political shrewdness but also a reflection of the real ambivalence characteristic of Zionist thinking in relation to Palestine. On the one hand, Zionists claimed Jews were a Semitic people who originated in Palestine, while on the other hand, they viewed Jews as modern Europeans participating in colonial endeavors.

This trend was consolidated after the Zionists could no longer rely fully on British support. This transformation in Zionist–British relations was a result of the 1939 British-issued White Paper restricting Jewish immigration to Palestine, which was in response to the anti-colonial Palestinian Revolt of 1936–1939. Many of the British-armed Zionists whose weapons until then were used against Palestinian resistance to Jewish colonization, now were turning their weapons also against their British sponsors. Many anti-British terrorist attacks took place throughout the forties culminating in the assassination of the British High Commissioner for the Middle East, Lord Moyne, in 1944.[33] Other terrorist attacks and massacres were to be committed against the Palestinians in the mid and late forties as the date for British withdrawal from the country neared. The 1946 bombing of the King David Hotel by Menachem Begin's Irgun Zvai Leumi killing 100 Palestinians, Jews and Britons, the assassination of the UN envoy Count Bernadotte by Yitzhak Shamir's Lehi[34] and the 1948 savage massacres of hundreds of Palestinian civilians including children at Al-Dawayimah by the mainstream Zionist army, the Haganah,[35] and at Dayr Yasin by Begin's Irgun[36] became features of either Zionist "anti-colonial resistance" or the Zionist "struggle for independence" depending on the ideological preference.[37]

Following the Zionists' unilateral "Declaration of the Establishment of the State of Israel" on May 14, 1948, five Arab armies intervened in Palestine to reverse the establishment of the Jewish settler-colony or to safeguard the portion allocated to the Arab State. The Israeli victory in the war which gave the Israelis control over 77 percent of Palestine resulted in the Zionist expulsion of close to a million Palestinians and the subsequent destruction of 418 Palestinian villages.[38] This war became known in Israeli ideological pronouncements as the "War of Independence" and the officially named "Declaration of the Establishment of the State of Israel" was to be renamed in popular discourse (although never officially) as the "Declaration of Independence." It must be noted that the Declaration did not proclaim Israel a sovereign independent state, rather it proclaimed it a "Jewish State."[39] This was done not as an oversight but as an explicit rejection of adding the words "sovereign independent" when an amendment to that effect was proposed. Thus, Israel was declared the state of Jews worldwide and not of its citizens (165,000 Palestinians remained in the territories of the State of Israel). Nevertheless, the "Declaration of Independence" and its derivative correlate the "War of Independence" became the operative terminology in popular parlance as well as in the ideological discourse of apologist politicians and academics. Independence from whom, however, remains unclear. After all, the British had already left voluntarily without being party to the war. The Arab armies had not been in occupation of any Palestinian land prior to the Zionist "Declaration." The Palestinian people had no regular army and were being bombarded by the mainstream Zionist forces leading to their expulsion beginning as early as December 1947. From whom then were the Zionists declaring their independence? They could not have declared independence from imperial sponsorship as they had continued to be supported by the European Empires, including Britain. Such sponsorship and alliance, it may be recalled, was to lead to the tripartite Israeli–French–British invasion of Egypt in 1956 and the Israeli occupation of the Sinai peninsula following Gamal Abdul-Nasir's nationalization of the Suez Canal Company. Therefore, renaming the "Declaration of the Establishment of the State of Israel" as the "Declaration of Independence" had a more important meaning in the ideological not the practical realm. Israel's establishment in 1948 followed and coincided with the independence of many formerly colonial territories. Naming the "Declaration of the Establishment of the State of Israel" as the "Declaration of Independence" is then to be seen as an attempt to recontextualize the new Zionist territorial entity as one established *against* not *via* colonialism. Also, given the waning of the European empires, this renaming was equally an attempt *to rehistoricize the new Zionist era as a post-colonial one.*

New arguments had to be amassed for the new line of Zionist apologia. Although there is no need to rehash here all the Zionist arguments and the anti-Zionist responses,[40] the following is important to point out in this context. Self-styled Zionist socialists and their friends in the West were deploying the ideological weight of the slogan of socialism as a defense against the Zionism-is-colonialism argument. As Maxime Rodinson has argued, however,

> this socialist outlook can neither logically nor sociologically be used as an argument to deny the colonial character of the Yishuv. Those who do use it this way are, whether they are aware of it or not, following the traditional line of thinking in European socialism that the only kind of relations a socialist society can possibly have with other societies are those motivated by the most deeply-rooted altruism. This is ideological juggling of the worst kind... This approach [which followed from a certain interpretation of the Young Marx]... acquired more or less theoretical shape from Stalinism. The theoreticians of Jewish nationalist socialism paid very little attention to the societies their project threatened to hurt or destroy... they naively thought that a renewal of the Jewish community could have only a beneficial effect on these societies and that as a result it was pointless to deal concretely with the question of what relations should be established with them. The analogy with the mental attitude of the French colonizers, imbued with the democratic ideology of the French Revolution, is obvious. It was for their own good that the Algerians and the Tonkinese were subjugated. In this way they would be prepared little by little for the day when later—much later—they would understand the Declaration of the Rights of Man and when, still later, it could be applied to them too.[41]

Responding to the Zionist argument that unlike colonial conquests, Zionism did not seek to exploit the native population thanks to its doctrine of pure *'Avodah 'Ivrit* (Hebrew Labor), Rodinson answers back stating that

> if direct exploitation of the native population occurs frequently in the colonial world, it is not necessarily always a characteristic of it. It was an exception to the rule for the English colonists settling the territory that was to become the United States to have native Indians working for them. The English in the East Indies were not land-owners who exploited peasants, any more than they were in Australia or New Zealand.... Are there those who would, as a result, entertain the idea that British expansion into all these territories was not colonial in nature?[42]

Moreover, whereas the Zionist ideology of "Hebrew Labor" did not seek to exploit native Palestinians, it had no qualms about importing cheap Arab Jewish labor from Yemen in 1910 (and later the rest of the Middle East and North Africa) since their Jewishness did not compromise the "Hebrewness" of the ideology.[43]

Many, however, continue to defend the creation ("independence" in Zionist-speak) of Israel as no different than the independence of India. Isaac Deutscher, for example, one of the most important luminaries among Marxist historians, who had been an anti-Zionist "based on a confidence in the European labour movement, or more broadly in European society and civilization, which that society and civilization have not justified" decided to abandon his anti-Zionism.[44] In a tirade defense of Israel's raison d'être, he still says that "[e]ven now... I am not a Zionist."[45] Not being a Zionist, however, did not prevent Deutscher from asserting that what happened to the Palestinian people as a result of Zionist colonialism cannot "in fairness" be blamed on the Jews. "People pursued by a monster and running to save their lives cannot help injuring those who are in the way and cannot help trampling over their property."[46] Deutscher, it would seem, never stopped to consider that European Jews could have still fled the monster as refugees without becoming colonists.[47] He never investigated the en route (from Europe to Palestine) transformation of the status of European Jews from refugees to colonists. Palestinian resistance to European Jewish presence in Palestine was on account of their arrival as invading colonists. Had European Jews arrived as refugees, no national threat would have been perceived by the Palestinians who had accommodated other refugee populations, like the Armenians, before. In another piece that he wrote on Israel's tenth anniversary, Deutscher describes how Israelis are celebrating the creation of their state by

> recollect[ing] with intense pride the heroism with which, in the spring of 1948, their men and women took up arms and wrested independence and statehood from the Arabs, the British, and the hesitant and intriguing diplomacies of the Great Powers... The emergence of Israel is indeed... a phenomenon unique in its kind, a marvel and a prodigy of history, before which Jew and non-Jew alike stand in awe and amazement, wondering over its significance. This is the stuff of which in earlier epochs the great heroic myths and legends were created, such as the legends of Thermopylae and of the Maccabees.[48]

A legend it indeed was in the minds of Zionist leaders. This "heroic" legend was described by Chaim Weizmann, Israel's first president, in the context of the Palestinian anti-colonial revolt of 1936–1939, as follows: "On one side, the forces of destruction, the forces of the desert, have arisen, and on the other side stand firm the forces of civilization and building. It is the old war of the desert against civilization, but we will not be stopped."[49]

Although Deutscher proceeds to criticize Israel in its conceit over its neighbors, he continues to portray the colonizer and the colonized with a kind of liberal parity uncharacteristic of his Marxist thinking on other issues. In his classic essay, "The non-Jewish Jew," Deutscher concludes by lamenting that in a world of nation-states the Jews were forced to establish one. The Marxist anti-nationalist that he was, however, Deutscher viewed the development of nation-states as a stage in world history, and was aware of how the progressive nature of national liberation becomes regressive after liberation takes place:

> Even those young nation-states that have come into being as the result of a necessary and progressive struggle waged by colonial and semi-colonial

> peoples for emancipation—India, Burma, Ghana, Algeria, and others—cannot preserve their progressive character for long. They form a necessary stage in the history of some peoples; but it is a stage that those peoples too will have to overcome in order to find wider frameworks for their existence. In our epoch any new nation-state, soon after its constitution, begins to be affected by the general decline of this form of political organization; and this is already showing itself in the short experience of India, Ghana, and Israel.[50]

Note that Israel is not compared to South Africa, the United States, Rhodesia, or Australia, lest it be mistaken for a settler-colony. It is "appropriately" listed with India and Ghana, which several lines earlier were identified as countries who "have come into being as a result of a necessary and progressive struggle waged by colonial and semi-colonial peoples for emancipation." Nevertheless, even Deutscher, his ideological acrobatics aside, could not help but refer to Israel's Kibbutzniks approvingly as "Israel's Pilgrim Fathers."[51]

Unlike many of Israel's apologists, however, the self-declared non-Zionist Deutscher was to continue his critiques of what he termed Zionist nationalist conceit. His mild critiques of 1958 multiplied in light of the 1967 Arab/Israeli war. It was in that context that he shifted away from liberal notions of parity between the two "contending" sides. He states that:

> On the face of it, the Arab–Israeli conflict is only a clash of two rival nationalisms, each moving within the vicious circle of its self-righteous and inflated ambitions. From the viewpoint of an abstract internationalism nothing would be easier than to dismiss both as equally worthless and reactionary. However, such a view would ignore the social and political realities of the situation. The nationalism of the people in semi-colonial or colonial countries, fighting for their independence, must not be put on at the same moral–political level as the nationalism of conquerors and oppressors. The former has its historic justification and progressive aspect which the latter has not. Clearly Arab nationalism, unlike the Israeli, still belongs to the former category.[52]

The implication being that Israeli nationalism, at some point, had also belonged to the former category.

Whereas until the 1960s and 1970s Zionist apologia had to defend its new claim of being anti-colonial, by the eighties it only needed to assert its claim as incontestable fact. A more recent example where Israel is grouped with former colonies and where its colonial-settler project is presented as anti-colonial is Joel Migdal's *Strong Societies and Weak States*. Migdal, a mainstream political scientist in the US academy, wrote his book as part of the 1980s political science research agenda exploring state–society relations with emphasis on the state. His book, which critiques the state-centered approach in studying the "Third World," is considered to be one of the seminal contributions to the field. In discussing the effect of colonialism on the strength and/or weakness of the post-colonial state, Migdal begins with a theoretical framework that he applies to Egypt, Sierra Leone, and Israel. In his narrative, Israel's alleged anti-colonial and post-colonial character is stated in a matter-of-fact way, presenting it to be as uncontroversial as the anti-colonial and post-colonial character of India. For example, he would casually state that, compared to Sierra Leone, a

> far less demure sort of excitement gripped India and Israel upon their independence in 1947 and 1948...Also, mutual admiration was much less the order of the day between the British and their former subjects. Both Israelis and Indians felt they had realized their dreams despite the British, not because of them, and the long bitter struggles were not easily put aside.[53]

In describing the events leading to Israel's creation, Migdal, in the tradition of other pro-Israeli apologists, refers to the official "Declaration of the Establishment of the State of Israel," as the "declaration of independence."[54] Furthermore, in discussing the Zionist movement and its efforts to recruit European Jews to settle in Palestine, Migdal, in a typically colonial fashion, states that "[p]robably close to 100,000 Jews immigrated to Palestine in those years [by WWI], but more than half left shortly after their arrival in that *desolate Asian outpost* [emphasis added]."[55]

Migdal is proceeding in an Israeli propagandistic tradition that, as we saw earlier, extends back to the thirties. Unlike earlier pro-Israeli apologists, however, which include among them the mainstream Jewish American social scientist Seymour Martin Lipset and the left-wing Tunisian Sephardi Jew Albert Memmi,[56] Migdal no longer has to come up, as they did, with arguments to refute the "Zionism-is-colonialism" claim. That argument, for Migdal, has been settled. He and many in the Israeli and Western academies need only assert that Israel was indeed established through anti-colonial struggle for that to become fact.

Zionist-speak has become so hegemonic that even scholars from the formerly colonized world who are associated with critiques of colonialism participate in its discourse. Kwame Anthony Appiah's book, *In My Father's House*,[57] is a case-in-point. In discussing the racialist basis of some strands of African and African-American nationalist thought, Appiah compares Pan-Africanism and Zionism:

> The two major uses of race as a basis for moral solidarity that are most familiar both in Africa and in Europe and America are varieties of Pan-Africanism and Zionism. In each case it is presupposed that a "people," Negroes or Jews, has the basis for a shared political life in their being of a single race. There are varieties of each form of "nationalism" that make the basis lie in shared traditions, *but however plausible this may be in the case of Zionism, which has in Judaism, the religion, a realistic candidate for a common and nonracial focus for nationality*, the peoples of Africa have a good deal less culturally in common than is usually assumed [emphasis added].[58]

He adds that:

> Judaism—the religion—and the wider body of Jewish practice through which the various communities of the Diaspora have defined themselves allow for a cultural conception of Jewish identity that cannot be made plausible in the case of Pan-Africanism. As evidence of this fact, I would simply cite the way the fifty or so rather disparate African nationalities in our present world seem to have met the nationalist impulses of many Africans, while Zionism has, of necessity, been satisfied by the creation of a single state.[59]

Note the matter-of-fact way in which Pan-Africanism, a movement that calls for the unification of Africa and does so as a nationalist anti-colonial movement, is rendered similar to Zionism, which calls for the unification of world Jewry in a colonial-settler state in Palestine. The fact that West European Jews differed markedly in their cultures and traditions (including religious traditions and practice) from East European Jews (the "Ostjuden") and that both groups were traditionally, culturally and religiously different from Asian and African Jews who also differed among themselves, is not factored in in Appiah's analysis. For him, the Jew is the universal European Jew invented by Zionism.

Appiah proceeds to voice his concern by noting that the fact that there were:

> Jewish racialists in the early story of modern Zionism…is important in the practical world of politics because a racialized Zionism continues to be one of the threats to the moral stability of Israeli nationalism; as witness the politics of the late Rabbi Meir Kahane.[60]

In the tradition of Zionist liberalism, Kahane, who in fact had never advocated a practice against Palestinians that had not already been committed or advocated by the different variants of the Zionist movement and successive Israeli governments, is portrayed by Appiah as an exceptional threat to an as yet uncontaminated morality of Israeli nationalism. The racist colonial history of Zionism is thus obliterated by Appiah whose central concern is the preservation of the alleged "morality" of Israeli nationalism.

This portrayal of Israel as anti-colonial is not limited to political debates and academic polemics but to all realms of Western culture. An illustrative example of this is the political thinking of the actor and pop culture figure, Marlon Brando. Brando, a known human rights activist and defender of Native American rights, stated, when pressed by a journalist about "what is it the Indians want from the [US] government," that "[t]hey want nothing more and nothing less than what the Jews have in Israel."[61] Brando's financial support for Begin's Irgun in the forties[62] and his continued defense of the European Jewish settler colony were never in contradiction with his championing of Native American rights in the US. For him, the two cases were the same. In this narrative, it is the Palestinians who are seen as the colonists who have taken over this ancient Jewish land. In an ironic twist of anti-Semitic logic, Brando, like many anti-Jewish racists who believe that Jews control all the governments of the world, believed in 1982 that "Palestinians ran the Middle East" (p. 175). This belief is invoked as the Palestinians and Lebanese were being killed in the thousands under Israeli bombardment throughout the seventies and early eighties leading to the June 1982 second Israeli invasion of that country in four years.

This new line of propaganda portraying Palestinians as the actual colonizers of the Jewish homeland was ratified by the scurrilous book *From Time Immemorial* by Joan Peters,[63] which argued that Palestinians had in fact immigrated to Palestine in the mid-to-late nineteenth century and in the first decades of the twentieth century seeking a better economic climate which was brought about by European Jewish colonization. The book went through at least ten printings as major US Jewish and gentile scholars endorsed it.[64] What is important about these arguments, however, is not whether they are supported by doctored documents to prove them (as Peters' book was), but rather the *subtext* which makes them credible. The subtext of these arguments is the stuff Zionist ideology had relied on since its very inception, namely, the Zionist (il)logic that: (i) Modern European Jews are the direct descendants of the ancient Hebrews; (ii) The ancient Hebrews had exclusive rights to Palestine in which they lived alone; and (iii) European Jews have the right to claim the homeland of their alleged ancestors 2,000 years later. It is with these Zionist axioms as subtext that Palestinians become the colonizers of Jewish land and their expulsion becomes nothing but part of the European Jewish anti-colonial struggle for the restoration of Palestine to its true inheritors. In this logic, Brando's likening European Jews to Native Americans is treated as an uncontroversial assertion that is never questioned by his interviewer who himself referred to the Zionist project as the "Jewish struggle for independence."[65] In this regard, Edward Said described how the Zionists related to Palestine:

> The colonization of Palestine proceeded always as a fact of repetition: The Jews were not supplanting, destroying, breaking up a native society. That society was itself the oddity that had broken the pattern of a sixty-year Jewish sovereignty over Palestine which had lapsed for two millennia. In Jewish hearts, however, Israel had always been there, an actuality difficult for the natives to perceive. Zionism therefore reclaimed, redeemed, repeated, replanted, realized Palestine, and Jewish hegemony over it. Israel was a return to a previous state of affairs, even if the new facts bore a far greater resemblance to the methods and successes of nineteenth century European colonialism than to some mysterious first-century forebears.[66]

Israeli clinical psychologist Benjamin Beit-Hallahmi agrees:

> Zionism as a colonialist movement offered the world the most original and unique defence for such an enterprise. The justification in this case was based not on a civilizing mission, or on commercial interests [although as we saw earlier this was also the case]. Unlike settlers anywhere else in the world,

> Zionist settlers claimed they were not moving to a new country, but simply coming home after an extended stay abroad; the apparent natives were actually the real foreigners. Theirs was an act of repatriation.[67]

Consequently, it is pre-Israel Palestine that represents a colonial era in Zionist discourse with Israel being its post-colonial successor.

Having presented a history of the ideological acrobatics of the Zionist project, I want to turn now to how this national/colonial project mapped out the bodies of European Jews whom it posited as its agents. Like all nationalist projects, colonial and anti-colonial alike, Zionism's own *embodiment* as a project was to take place through a specific figuration of those European Jewish bodies it recruited. The following section will trace this transformation of European Jewish bodies from their diasporic condition to their new Zionist condition as this was/is conceived by Zionism.

Colonizing the body, or the signifying penis

Zionism, as a movement, did not only seek to transplant Jews into a new territory and usher them into a new period of history through establishing for them a state. Zionism was also going to make available to European Jewry a whole range of economic/physical activity denied it in Europe (especially in the agricultural realm). Hence, the objective of the Zionist movement was not simply to transplant European Jews into a new geographical area, but also to transform the very nature of European Jewish society and identity as it had existed in the diaspora until then. The locus of this transformation was the European Jew's body.

As early as 1903, Max Nordau, one of Herzl's closest associates, wrote his article "Jewry of muscle."[68] Nordau sought a pre-diasporic model of Jewish male bodies to be emulated by Jewish men for a post-diasporic Jewish body-type to emerge. He asserted at the 1901 Zionist Congress in Basle: "We must think of creating a Jewry of muscles." He was to add later that

> history is our witness that such a Jewry had once existed . . . For too long, all too long have we been engaged in the mortification of our own flesh. Or rather, to put it more precisely—others did the killing of our flesh for us. . . . But now [1903], all coercion has become a memory of the past, and at least we are allowed space enough for our bodies to live again. Let us take up our oldest traditions; let us once more become deep-chested, sturdy, sharp-eyed men.[69]

Bar Kochba, the hero of the last Jewish revolt against the Romans,[70] became the new model for Nordau, who back in 1898, along with Max Mandelstamm, had established the Bar Kochba gymnastic club in Berlin to promote the physical fitness of Jewish youth. Soon after, similar clubs were established throughout Europe. Nordau concludes his article with the following wish: "May the Jewish gymnastic club flourish and thrive and become an example to be imitated in all the centers of Jewish life!" The transformation of Jewish men from "Schlemiels" into what Paul Breines calls "tough Jews" had just begun.[71]

The new post-diasporic Jewish man, unlike his "feminine" predecessor, would engage in agriculture, war, and athletics. The first two, at least, were areas of activity denied most European Jews at varying times of their residence in Europe. As Breines has explained, "statelessness, according to Zionism, is the cause of meekness, frailty, passivity, humiliation, pogroms, futile appeals to reason and dialogue—in short, Jewish weakness and gentleness."[72] These views characterizing European Jews as "feminine" are derived from the then dominant anti-Semitic discourse that posited Jews as the racial/feminine other.[73] The Masada Jewish man (in reference to the anti-Roman Jewish revolt at Masada in 73 AD[74]) thus becomes the Israeli colonist–explorer in touch with the land/nature and is able to defend himself—an image that is ubiquitous in early Israeli films.[75] The Masada Jewish man becomes, in fact, the model for the Mossad agent,[76] the Israeli soldier, the very essence of the militarized and masculine Israeli Sabra,[77] thus realizing Zionist plans of rendering post-diasporic Jews as settler-soldiers.

The rewriting of the Jewish body and of Jewish history by Zionism has infiltrated all Western cultural productions including films made outside Israel. *Europa Europa* is one such film. Although this film is only one document among many, it is emblematic of how Zionism rewrites Jewish bodies. An analysis of this film will help to illustrate Zionism's interpretation of pre-diasporic Jewish bodies and its plans to transform them.

In her highly acclaimed film *Europa Europa*[78] based on the *Memoirs of Solomon Perel*, the European director Agnieszka Holland tells the true story of a German Jewish boy, Solomon (Solek) Perel played by Marco Hofschneider, and his tragic life under Nazi rule. The film's focus is the Jewish adolescent's male body. In fact, the film begins and ends with his body. *Europa Europa* opens with Solomon's circumcision, his Covenant of the flesh with God, with the camera soon moving to Solomon's nude adolescent body as he is beginning to take a bath. The story is of a German Jewish boy who is caught by the Nazis. Aided by his "European" features, he pretends to be a German gentile so well that he is accepted as such, and is subsequently sent to a Nazi military school for education and training. The entire film revolves around Solomon's (now Josef Peters) success or failure in concealing his circumcised penis from public view. The circumcised penis functions in the film as the only signifying mark of the Jew. Nazi genealogies of family histories, physical and anatomical descriptions including phrenological measurements, although mentioned in the film, fall by the wayside, giving room to the circumcised penis as the only practical way of identifying Jews (Solomon was able to circumvent the Nazi inquiry into his parentage by lying and presenting himself to be a gentile German from Grodnok whose papers had been lost, and Nazi facial profiles and phrenological measurements of Solomon concluded that he was an "authentic Aryan"). It would seem that, according to this narrative, Jewish women could not have been identified as Jews by the Nazis had they had Solomon's skill, luck, and, above all, his features. Since the difference between the ability of "European"-looking Jews and "Semitic"-looking Jews to pass as gentiles is never explored by the film (since the nineteenth century, the "blackness" of Jewish skin was one of the important constructed markers of Jews posited by the scientific racialist discourse of anti-Semitism[79]), the only practical way of identifying Jews, in the film, becomes one of identifying only the males among them by inspecting their penises. Through this construction, the Jew, for Holland and Perel, is always already the male Jew. In fact, an Armenian man "accused" of being Jewish by the Nazis exposes his uncircumcised penis as proof of his "innocence" (one wonders what an Albanian or a Bosnian Muslim man, let alone woman, "accused" of being Jewish would have done in a similar situation).

Although the film begins with an anti-Jewish attack by Nazi youth in which Solomon's sister, Bertha, is killed, during the attack, the camera, ignoring Bertha, is too busy following Solek's nude body as he jumps out of the bathroom window covering his penis with his hands. He remains in hiding in a back-alley barrel until the pogrom is over. A gentile neighbor provides him with her brother's Nazi military coat marked by the swastika to cover himself as he makes his way back to the house. In the coat, Solek looks indistinguishable from Aryan Nazis, thus rendering Nazi symbols as a pharmakon—both responsible for marking Jews out, *revealing* them, and for hiding/erasing their identity, *concealing* them, simultaneously. In fact, Nazi symbology is presented as a pharmakon throughout the film. What the narrative of *Europa Europa* enacts is precisely this tension between the two opposite/complementary functions of Nazism as pharmakon. Bertha's death, which is the only Jewish death on the hands of the Nazis that the film portrays close-up, remains an unexplained phenomenon, since she has no "explicit" Jewish markings allowed by the film. Her only possible marking as a Jew may have been, perhaps, her spatial proximity to Jewish men and/or, as Solek himself affirms, her "jealousy" of him, for "she wanted to be the boy." It would seem that Solek's own self-hatred and identification with the Nazis are unconsciously projected onto his sister.

However, Holland is at pains to show that despite the fact that Jewish men are marked by the Jewish penis, this does not make them less desirable to German women and men. In fact, Solek's penis is the object of desire of German gentile women as well as German gentile men. However, Solek's penis, the film asserts, is a heterosexual one. The pleasure it gave to a German Nazi woman, who had seduced the adolescent Solek, is evidenced by her orgasmic expression in the darkness of a train car. Of course, the Nazi woman's excitement is over her assumption that it was a Nazi German gentile penis that gave her that pleasure. Her excitement was made even greater when she found out that Solek was born on the same day as the Führer, April 20. Solek's excitement over the loss of his virginity with her drives him to put his head out of the train window and yell with triumphant pleasure, with the wind caressing his hair and his newly acquired manly smile. At the military school, where Solek meets a German gentile civilian woman who adheres to Nazi ideology and hates Jews (a sentiment that landed her a powerful slap from Solek), Solek is scared of sleeping with her lest he be discovered. The young woman's impatience with Solek's insistent celibacy (for she wanted to bear Aryan babies for the Third Reich), which was exacerbated by his slapping her, pushes her to call him "limp dick"—a castrating comment that distresses him greatly. Other women, a Polish woman and a Soviet Russian Komsomol leader, were also desirous of the young Solek, as was a German homosexual soldier. As for the homosexual German gentile soldier, he discovers Solek's Jewishness while in hot sexual pursuit of his nude bathing body. As a result of the "discovery," they become allies and platonic friends until the soldier's death in battle. The film makes clear that while Solek's penis is available for the penetration of gentile women who desire it (except when self-preservation is at stake), his heterosexual penis is unavailable to other desirous men, although he is flattered by the attention. The bathing motif (which as we saw earlier recorded Solek's first direct experience with the Nazis), with its attendant risks of vulnerability to Nazi discovery, would seem to be unconciously related by Perel to the anti-Semitic image of the "dirty" Jew. Due to Solek's identification with the Nazis, his recounting of the bathing scenes indicates, as it were, his obsessive compulsion with bodily cleanliness in order that he not be confused with "dirty" Jews.

While serving with Nazi soldiers under the guise of his gentile identity, Solek was confused by their kindness to him. He exclaims about what separates him from them: "a simple foreskin?" Like Hellenized Jewish circus fighters who used to undergo surgical procedures to hide their circumcision due to their sense of shame when fighting in the nude with the Romans, Solek, in his Nazi school, out of terror of being discovered, attempts to push his foreskin by tying it with a thread in a desperate attempt to reverse his circumcision. His attempt fails. In disappointment, Solek despairingly states "I couldn't escape my own body"—wherein his body is standing in metonymically for the circumcised penis.

Solek had many nightmares at the Nazi school in which he is pursued by the Nazis and is trying to hide from them. In one such dream, Solek's sister Bertha pushes him in the closet to hide him from the Nazis. In the closet, Solek finds the Führer with both hands on his crotch in an attempt to hide his penis. Bertha tells Solek that the Führer is also Jewish. This conflation of identities, in Solek's dream, between himself and the Führer, with whom he shares the same birthday, the same closet, and the same circumcised penis, is brought to the fore with their success in passing as Nazis. Solek's ambivalent Jewishness (he tells us earlier how he hated Passover because eating eggs dipped in salt-water made him nauseous) and his ambivalent identification with the Nazis resolves itself in this context, wherein all Nazis including the Führer himself, are, like him, closet-Jewish men who pass as Aryans. This fantastic move not only consolidates Solek's (who is nicknamed by his class mates "Jupp," short for Josef) political choices in rendering Jews the real Nazis, thus alleviating his sense of guilt about betraying his family and his Jewishness, but also consolidates his newly found Aryan manhood. In fact, Solek is so manly that he excels in his military training at school coming out first in competitions with his authentic Aryan classmates.

The final act of liberation by the Soviets brings with it the climactic moment of the film. In it, Solek and his long lost brother, the less "European"-looking (where European is always already gentile) Isaac, whose inability to pass rendered him confined to one of Hitler's death camps, whip out their penises and urinate in full view of their surroundings (but with their backs to the camera). This scene is to be contrasted with an earlier scene when Solek was attempting to urinate away from German Nazi soldiers but was almost discovered by them. Liberation from the Nazis has finally allowed the Jew, as man, to whip his circumcised penis out of the closet without fear. This staging of the circumcised penis as spectacle is engineered to meet the gentile gaze head-on as an assertion of a recovered Jewish masculinity. The real Solek narrating the story, tells us that he moved to Palestine after the war. He states that "when I had boys, I barely hesitated to circumcise them." The film ends with the real Solomon Perel, now an old man, appearing with the caption: "Solomon Perel is now living in Israel."

The shame of the circumcised penis had occupied the thoughts of Max Nordau. In his "Jewry of muscle" mentioned earlier, Nordau stresses that:

> Our new muscle-Jews have not yet regained the heroism of our forefathers who in large numbers eagerly entered the sport arenas in order to take part in competition and to pit themselves against the highly trained Hellenistic athletes and the powerful Nordic barbarians. But morally, even now the new muscle-Jews surpass their ancestors, for the ancient Jewish circus fighters were ashamed of their Judaism and tried to conceal the sign of the Covenant by means of a surgical operation, . . . while the members of the "Bar Kochba" club loudly and proudly *affirm their national loyalty* [emphasis added].[80]

The memoirs of Perel on which *Europa Europa* is based, it must be remembered, are written from Perel's new geographic and ideological location, that of Israel and Zionism. His new positionality seems to be quite influential in his reinterpreting of his unique Jewish experience under the Nazis. Solomon Perel, like Nordau's muscle-Jews, was able to affirm his "national loyalty" by urinating in public, thus showing the mark of his Jewishness, his *brit mila*, or Covenant of the Flesh, a mark, he makes certain, is passed on to his Israeli sons. Given this Zionist rewriting of the holocaust experience, it is not surprising that Israel and the Zionist American Jewish establishment welcomed the film lavishing it with praise and prizes. Agnieszka Holland (born to a Catholic Polish mother and a Jewish Polish father), however, had a harder time in Europe. Claude Lanzman, the director of the Holocaust documentary *Shoah*, called her an "anti-Semite." Lanzman stated: "It's no coincidence if Agnieszka Holland . . . chose this one Jew as the hero of 'Europa Europa' a movie that would make anyone vomit."[81] His conclusion was not only based on *Europa Europa*, but also on Holland's previous film *Korczak* which tells yet another real story, this time of a Jewish doctor, Janusz Korczak, who struggled in vain to save 200 Jewish children living in his Warsaw Ghetto orphanage. The final scene of the film shows a cattle car crammed with Jewish children heading for a concentration camp. In slow motion, the car uncouples from the train and comes to a stop. The children and Korczak then come out of the car skipping away happily under a flag emblazoned with the Star of David. As they recede, a caption appears on the screen: "Korczak and the children were gassed at Treblinka in 1942." In Israel, the film's final scene was hailed as symbolizing the birth of the Jewish State. In France, Jewish intellectuals condemned it as anti-Semitic, since the real children it depicted were killed in the holocaust, a fate quite different from those Jews who survived and colonized Palestine. Holland's response to these charges was simply that these Jewish intellectuals along with Lanzman are "viscerally anti-Polish."[82]

Europa Europa, however, is no more guided by anti-Semitic views of European Jews than Zionist thought itself is. The film participates in the discursive construction of Jews as "indistinguishable" from gentile Europeans except by their circumcised penises, in an attempt to preempt the civilizing mission European Jews were undertaking in Palestine. Consonant with predominant anti-Semitic and Zionist views, this reduction of European Jews to phallic men who are always already marked by the sign of the Covenant is the prerequisite for Holland's presenting of the Jewish penis as the only site/mark of Jewish identity that led Jews to the death camps. Based on this privileging, Holland posits the same Jewish-marked penis as the necessary mark for Jewish liberation. In that, her anti-Semitism is no more horrific than the overall Zionist discursive construction of Jews as "responsible" for their own victimization due to their insistence on remaining in the diaspora with their Jewish markings intact, rather than transforming these Jewish markings into new ones in the context of a colonial-settler nation-state.

In line with this denigration of diaspora Jews qua victims is the popular modern Hebrew term for "sissy," the word "sabon" or soap. The term appeared in the wake of the Second World War when stories circulated about Jews being made into soap by the Nazis.[83] Like Zionism, Holland presents the solution of the colonial-settler nation-state as the only way to Jewish liberation which can preserve the Jewish-marked penis without fear of annihilation/castration (the two being the same thing in Holland's symbolic order). This is made clear in *Korczak*, where Polish Jews (including assimilating Jewish children who were being taught to speak Polish by Dr Korczak) were to perish in the death camps, in contrast with Zionist Jews who, at the beginning of the film, were portrayed as "free," evidenced by the products of their agricultural labor—Dr Korczak's assistant Stefa brought "Jewish-grown" oranges from her trip to Palestine to demonstrate to non-Zionist Jews, Korczak included, Jewish "freedom." In Holland's *Korczak* narrative, Zionist Jewish colonial settlers, unlike non-Zionist Polish Jews, assimilated and unassimilated alike, survived the holocaust due to the "liberating" Zionist project.

The image of castrated Jewish manhood was part of the European anti-Semitic arsenal against which Zionism responded by asserting its own cult of Sabra masculinity. The Jew as castrated man represented the terror of castration for anti-Semitic gentile men. According to Freud, the

> castration complex is the deepest unconscious root of anti-Semitism; for even in the nursery little [gentile] boys hear that a Jew has something cut off his penis—a piece of his penis they think—and this gives them a right to despise Jews. And there is no stronger unconscious root for the sense of

> superiority over women . . . and from that standpoint what is common to Jews and women is their relation to the castration complex.[84]

Hence the Jewish penis becomes the site of reinterpretation of Jewish masculinity by Zionism. The only way Jewish men can rejoin the world of (gentile) men after the Nazi annihilation, the film suggests, is through a spectacular exposure of their circumcised penises as a visual assertion of phallicity against a discursively and materially castrating order.

The new Israeli Sabra is by Zionist design nothing like the pre-Israel European Jew. "He" and his penis are "normalized" by Zionist achievements (the Jewish penis could only be the norm in an exclusively Jewish nation-state). In this regard, Benjamin Beit-Hallahmi states that the:

> Israeli ethos, like the dominant American one, is one of identifying with winners, and showing no feeling for the losers. Never identify with the weak, because you don't want to be like them . . . So Israelis have two reasons for not identifying with victims: first, victimhood isn't part of their experience; second, it is contrary to the ideal of being tough.[85]

By "returning" Jewish men's bodies to their pre-diasporic selves and improving on them through the creation of the Israeli *Sabra*, Zionism has sought to "decolonize" European Jewish men's bodies from gentile control to which these bodies had been subjected since the beginning of the Jewish diaspora. Different Jewish experiences that contradict Zionist accounts of diaspora experience are quickly rewritten within the Zionist narrative. A major example of such rewriting is Zionism's attempt to reinscribe the death of 200,000 Soviet Jewish soldiers who fell in the Second World War as having fallen in the struggle for the Jewish state. Israel erected a monument for these soldiers in its central military cemetery in Jerusalem. In commenting about the monument, Israeli historian Tom Segev states that a

> memorial to them here, among the graves of Israeli soldiers, seems to appropriate them posthumously into the Israeli army and into the Zionist movement. It proclaims, in a way, that they fell not in defense of the Soviet Union in its war against the Nazis but in defense of the Jewish people and for the establishment of the state of Israel. For this reason, they are worth being remembered among Israel's heroes, on the memorial mountain, alongside the fathers of Zionism and national leaders.[86]

Zionist colonial discourse, like its European gentile counterparts, viewed Palestine as the motherland to which European Jews were "returning," and a virgin land which the post-diasporic masculinized Jew will deflower and refecundate with post-diasporic Jewish seed.[87] The image of the land as mother is linked inherently to the sexual and reproductive project of colonial-settler nationalism.

As psychoanalyst Melanie Klein points out:

> In the explorer's unconscious mind, a new territory stands for a new mother. He [*sic*] is seeking the "promised land"—the "land flowing with milk and honey."... The child's early aggression [against its mother] stimulated the drive to restore and to make good, to put back into his [*sic*] mother the good things he had robbed her of in phantasy, and these wishes to make good merge into the later drive to explore, for by finding new [*sic*] land the explorer gives something to the world at large and to a number of people in particular. In his pursuit the explorer actually gives expression to both aggression and the drive to reparation. We know that in discovering a new country aggression is made use of in the struggle with the elements, and in overcoming difficulties of all kinds. But sometimes aggression is shown more openly; especially was this so in the former times when ruthless cruelty against native populations was displayed by people who not only explored, but conquered and colonized... The wished-for restoration, however, found full expression in repopulating the country with people of their own nationality.[88]

The new Sabra, like the American Adam,[89] proud of his Covenant, will be the deflowerer and inseminator of this mother/virgin land. (In this vein, note the oranges that resulted from the reproductive union of Zionist settler-soldiers and the mother/virgin land portrayed in Holland's *Korczak*.) When a Polish Jew, upon returning from Palestine in 1920, reported that "the bride is beautiful, but she has got a bridegroom already," Golda Meir retorted by saying: "And I thank God every night that the bridegroom was so weak, and the bride could be taken away from him."[90] The fact that in modern Hebrew, the word *Zayin* is the root word for both weapon and penis[91] simply lends more credibility to this Zionist Weltanschauung, whose views of Jewish bodies are almost entirely borrowed from anti-Semitism. (It must be noted that Hebrew is not alone in deploying patriarchal and militaritistic notions in its vocabulary. This is a tradition that pervades most languages. Note, for example, the vernacular use in English of a man "shooting his load" to signify ejaculation. This is also consistent with the infamous US Marines training song which Marines, while grabbing their rifles in one hand and their penises in the other, sing: "This is my rifle, this is my gun, this is for killing, and this is for fun)."[92] The penis as a sign of liberation is transformed by Zionist atrocities into one of oppression. Like its use in all colonizing and oppressive societies, the penis is used literally and metaphorically as a weapon of oppression. From the colonial conquests of the Americas in which the rape of Native American women by European conquerors was ubiquitous, the institution of raping black women in the United States by their white masters from the time of slavery and beyond,[93] to the US military strategy for its soldiers to rape Vietnamese women by "searching" them with their penises as an anti-communist weapon,[94] the penis as a colonial instrument is institutionalized in international relations.[95] The coincidence of the Zionist reinterpretation of diasporic Jewish experience with a post-diasporic Israeli colonial discourse, and the latter being part of European colonial discourse more generally introduce a new dimension to this signifying penis. As part of a universal patriarchal tradition, it would seem that the rape of Palestinian women by Israeli soldiers in 1948[96] and today's Israeli soldiers' not-so-uncommon practice of exposing their genitalia to Palestinian women on the streets of the *still* Occupied West Bank and Gaza Strip are giving new meaning to Nordau's vision of the affirmation of European Jewish national loyalty in the specular economy of Israel's occupation.

This Zionist penis-pride (to borrow Melanie Klein's term) was interestingly shared by none other than Zionism's "father" Theodor Herzl. When in Law School, the 20-year-old Herzl had contracted a venereal disease (possibly gonorrhea). We know of the story through a letter that Herzl had written to a close male friend, Heinrich Kana. In the letter, Herzl tells his friend that he has put the syringe aside, and that his next attack of "xxx" will be cured by zinc sulphate. He proceeds to inform Kana how he had commissioned a penis linen sheath from a high class ladies' fancy goods shop, making up all kinds of lies to the seamstresses to avoid embarrassment. Unfortunately, the

> said sheath is a little too tight for my penis.... I can only get him in when he is being quite quiet, like a peaceful trouser-burgher. But that is extremely seldom, for bold German–Austrian as he is... he rebels against my sheath regulation. So I got them to make a second underpants pocket for me... however, this second apparatus also has its defects. It is true that I can get the [young] candidate for knighthood into the linen shaft, but either he feels himself confined or he is now slipping out—you see what erection dilemma fills my mind—Should I perhaps strip him of the whole hair shirt?—All right, but you must not forget, much dripping liquid flows down. What would the washerwoman think?! Perhaps she would despise me. Should I risk it?[97]

Herzl's exhibitionist penis-pride, as Peter Lowenberg notes, is manifested through his recounting to his friend "the size of his organ, its erective power, [and] the wide experience of his 'young knight' in the pursuit of women."[98] In identifying his penis as a German–Austrian, Herzl is asserting the masculine characteristics of such a nationality. He could not have identified it/him as Jewish, since that would have signified something feminine, or at least effeminate, and certainly not "bold." Sharing predominant anti-Semitic views of the time which characterized Jewish men as effeminate, Herzl's assimilation of his penis into gentile Austro-Germanness ensures for him that such a fate would not befall him. His apparent fear of discovery by the seamstresses and by the washerwoman, moreover, seems to be an expression of an exhibitionist fantasy projected onto these women.

Exposing the penis, which according to Zionist reading signified Jewish (men's) liberation from the Nazis, now functions as an assertion of Israeli European Jewish power and authority. In Zionist discourse, however, since *all* Jews are conceived as always already survivors of the holocaust living in an anti-Semitic world, the exhibitionism of Israeli male soldiers remains part and parcel of a

Zionist discourse which defines such an action as "liberation." In this vein, the fact that many Israelis refer to the Occupied Territories as "liberated territories" is not incidental. As for Jewish women (Ashkenazi and Mizrahi alike), the Israeli state has relegated their bodies to the important task of national reproduction of new "de"colonized Jewish male bodies.[99]

Zionist plans for Mizrahi Jewish and Palestinian bodies were quite different from those for European Jewish bodies. While the utility or lack of utility of Mizrahi Jewish women's and men's bodies was discussed as early as the first decade of this century with Zionism's attempt to bring to Palestine Yemeni Jews to replace Palestinian workers, the utility and dispensability of Palestinian women's and men's bodies have been constant hallmarks of Zionist thinking throughout. While idealistic concepts, like *'Avodah 'Ivrit* (Hebrew Labor), had kept Palestinian workers out of some Kibbutzim and other colonial settlements for a while, Zionism had to rely on their bodies for different periods in its history, including its present. Kibbutzim, however, have kept their ideals—they employ Palestinian workers as cheap labor while denying them membership in the exclusively Jewish (and mostly Ashkenazi) collectives. The reproduction of Palestinian bodies had become such a concern for Israel in the 1960s and 1970s that former Israeli Prime Minister Golda Meir could not sleep worrying about how many Palestinians were being conceived or were born every night.[100] In order to feel better about this appalling situation, Meir had to repress the existence of Palestinian bodies. In 1969, she informed the *London Sunday Times* that "It was not as though there was a Palestinian people in Palestine considering itself as a Palestinian people and we came and threw them out and took their country away from them. They did not exist."[101]

As for those, like Moshe Dayan, who still acknowledged the existence of the Palestinians to the Israeli public, they emphasized the new toughness of Jews:

> Let us not today fling accusations at the murderers. Who are we that we should argue against their hatred? For eight years now they sit in their refugee camps in Gaza, and before their very eyes, we turn into our homestead the land and the villages in which they and their forefathers have lived. *We are a generation of settlers, and without the steel helmet and the cannon we cannot plant a tree and build a home*. Let us not shrink back when we see the hatred fermenting and filling the lives of hundreds of thousands of Arabs, who sit all around us. Let us not avert our gaze, so that our hand shall not slip. This is the fate of our generation, the choice of our life—*to be prepared and armed, strong and tough*—or otherwise, the sword will slip from our fist, and our life will be snuffed out [emphasis added].[102]

Dayan's emphasis on the complementarity of war and agriculture in the context of the Jewish state is important to stress in light of the initial Zionist goals of making these activities available to post-diasporic Jews. It is these activities which, as Zionism contended in its pre-state era, would transform the feeble bodies of Jewish men into "tough" Sabras.

Naming as geography

The renaming of Palestine as Israel was part of the spatial reorganization of the people who would inhabit it. It is important to remember here that "Israel" in the pre-Zionist period referred to the Jewish people not to a state (*Bnei Yisrael* or the Children of Israel, with Israel being the name given to Jacob who fought the angel of God, hence the literal meaning of Israel as the struggler with God). Israel was how the Jewish God addressed His people. The conflation/collapse of the Jewish people into a Jewish state is by Zionist design an attempt to render the Jewish people non-existent except in the confines of a Zionist time/space called the Jewish state.

Moreover, the renaming of Palestine as Israel by the European Jewish settler colonists was not only of symbolic value, rather it involved (and still involves) a geographic overhauling of the entire country. Archaeology became the guiding principle of Israel's transformation of Palestine. The spatial regeneration of the ancient Hebrews' land was to go hand in hand with the transformation of Jewish and Palestinian histories and their rewriting according to Zionist dicta. In a reminder to the younger generation of Israelis, Moshe Dayan explained the process of creating geographic simulacra which informs Israeli state policies:

> Jewish villages were built in the place of Arab villages. You don't even know the names of these Arab villages, and I don't blame you, because these geography books no longer exist. Not only do the books not exist, the Arab villages are not there either. Nahalal arose in the place of Mahlul, Gvat in the place of Jibta, Sarid in the place of Haneifa, and Kfar-Yehoshua in the place of Tel-Shaman. There is not one single place built in this country that did not have a former Arab population.[103]

This renaming process was not arbitrary, rather it was institutionally organized since before Israel was founded. An important part of Zionist institutions in the pre-Israel era was the Jewish National Fund's "Place-Names Committee." After 1948, it was replaced by the "Israel Place-Names Committee."[104] Both Committees suggested and/or approved all the new names given to streets, towns, cities, Kibbutzim, Moshavim and other colonial-settlements. Zionist renaming continued unabated upon Israel's occupation of the West Bank and the Gaza Strip.[105] Whereas the West Bank was renamed (with the pre-diasporic names of) Judea and Samaria, the Land of Israel Movement took it upon itself to change the names of the streets in Palestinian East Jerusalem (not to mention Palestinian towns and cities). Expunging the Arabic signs, they renamed the streets with more appropriate names—Suleiman the Magnificent Street, for example, became Paratroop Street.[106]

Nationalist movements' attempt to "retrieve" the memory of the "nation" was analogized by Freud to a person's childhood memories.

> This is often the way in which childhood memories originate. Quite unlike conscious memories from the time of maturity, they are not fixed at the moment of being experienced and afterwards repeated, but are only elicited

> at a later age when childhood is already past; in the process they are altered and falsified, and are put in the service of later trends, so that generally speaking they cannot be sharply distinguished from phantasies.

Freud proceeds to explain how nations come to write their histories:

> Historical writing, which had begun to keep a continuous record of the present, now also cast a glance back to the past, gathered traditions and legends, interpreted the traces of antiquity that survived in customs and usages, and in this way created a history of the past. It was inevitable that this early history should have been an expression of present beliefs and wishes rather than a true picture of the past; for many things had been dropped from the nation's memory, while others were distorted, and some remains of the past were given the wrong interpretation in order to fit in with contemporary ideas. Moreover people's motive in writing history was not objective curiosity but a desire to influence their contemporaries, to encourage and inspire them, *or to hold a mirror up before them* [emphasis added].[107]

The importance of this mirror was not missed by Jacques Lacan. Like the child whose fragmented self is unified in an inverted image represented by the child's reflection in the mirror, the reconstructed historical memory of the nation provides such a function. Lacan saw the mirror stage in a child "*as an identification*."[108] This is exactly how historical memory as mirror *identifies* the nation's subject by unifying its fragmented self. It is through this Zionist identificatory mirror that the "Jew" is imaged/imagined (based on a specific figuration of a Jewish European experience) as a universal category that assimilates all other Jewish experiences into it as one and the same. It is through this mirror that a Yemeni Jew, a German Jew, a Polish Jew, a Libyan Jew, an Iraqi Jew, an Ethiopian Jew, *et al.* become the national subjects of the Zionist enterprise.

The very naming of the children of European Jewish immigrants who were born in Palestine as "Sabras" is underwritten by Zionism's program of charting a new land-based Jewish identity. The word Sabra[109] is the Arabic word for the native Palestinian cactus fruit or prickly pear (Tsabar in Hebrew). Zionists "adopted" it as the name of the new Palestine-born Jews of European parentage after the First World War. According to Georges Friedmann, the term originated in the Tel Aviv school of Herzlia, where the immigrant European children did better academically than the Palestine-born children of European-Jewish immigrants. In order to make up for the inferiority feelings that resulted, they would challenge the star pupils to peel a prickly pear and get to the sweet fruit under its thorny exterior without getting the thorns in their hands—something the Palestine-born Jews were able to do easily.[110] Thus, the new Israeli, while having a tough exterior when fighting his enemies, is tender on the inside, especially with his loved ones.[111] The naming of the New Jew (Beit-Hallahmi refers to the "new Jew" as the "anti-Jew"[112]) as "Sabra" is consistent with Zionism's interest in nature and geography. The New Jew is not only a hard fruit to pick, *he* also grows in the desert, the product of a new geography. *His* mother is nature and the "Land of Israel." *His* name is part and parcel of the geographic, historical, and cultural appropriation of Palestine by Zionism. That the very name of the New Jew is Arabic is no more of an inconsistency than the future Israeli cultural theft and appropriation of Falafil and Hummus (traditional Palestinian and Levantine Arab dishes) as Israeli Jewish dishes, or Dabkah (traditional Palestinian and Levantine Arab line-dancing) as Israeli Jewish folk dancing.[113]

This collective renaming of the children of European Jewish colonial-settlers born in Palestine went hand in hand with the actual renaming of all European Jewish colonial-settlers and their children individually.[114] European Jewish last names such as Rosenthal, Goldstein, Schwartz, or Shapiro were changed to Galili and Golan (after the Galilee and the Golan Heights), and Even (stone), Sella (rock), Shamir (rock), Peled (steel), and Nir (furrow) to reflect the new relationship to nature, political geography, and tough masculinity. Even ancient Jewish last names like Cohen (priest) and Levi (a Levite, member of the priesthood) were on many occasions changed into Keidan (spear) and Lavi (Lion). First names were also changed according to the Zionist plan. Benjamin Beit-Hallahmi asserts that for the past 2,000 years "there was no Jewish Amos, no Yoram (the names of two Biblical kings who 'did evil in the sight of the Lord'). Only names rejected by the Jewish tradition now became acceptable, as the guiding principle became a rejection of that tradition."[115] In this vein, David Ben-Gurion who was born in Plonsk in 1886 as David Grun, found his new name, upon arrival in Palestine in 1906, in Talmudic reports about the Great Rebellion against the Romans in 66 AD.

Zionism's revival of Jewish history was in fact a revival of Hebrew geography. Jewish historical memory (Ber Borochov used to refer to Palestine as the "land of memories") was transfigured through Zionist hermeneutic filters into geographic memory. The Zionist celebration of the ancient Hebrew kings rather than the Hebrew prophets was not accidental. It is, after all, the Hebrew kings, not prophets, who conquered land and expanded the territory which Zionism now claims as its own. It is this collapse of Jewish history into Hebrew geography that prefigures Zionism's self-legitimating claims. In fact, some of the reconstructed figures of the ancient Hebrew's past have acquired an opposite valuation from that given to them by the diasporic tradition. Bar Kochba (son of star) was actually called Bar Koziba (son of lie) by the pre-Zionist Jewish tradition in reference to his false claim as a Messiah and as one who had forsaken God leading to his defeat. In the Zionist tradition, he is the last Jewish "president" or nasi' (as Yigael Yadin, modern Israel's first military chief of staff and leading archaeologist in the 1950s, called him),[116] nay the "last chief of staff of the historical armies of Israel."[117] Here, what is crucial to grasp is not only the shift of emphasis from what diaspora Jewishness and Judaism considered important in the Hebrew past to what modern Zionists excavate as important, but the very active invention of ancient Israel, an Israel that had never existed as such before Zionism's fantastic fabrications.[118]

For Palestine to become "the desert that European Jews would make bloom," the Israelis undertook the destruction of any signifying traces left by the expelled

Palestinians, including 418 Palestinian villages.[119] In this regard, Israel Shahak wrote that:

> The truth about Arab settlement which used to exist in the area of the State of Israel before 1948, is one of the most guarded secrets of Israeli life. No publication, book or pamphlet gives either [the] number [of Arab villages] or their location. This of course is done on purpose, so that the accepted official myth of "an empty country" can be taught and accepted in the Israeli schools and told to visitors . . . This falsification is specially grave in my opinion, as it is accepted almost universally, outside the Middle East, and because the destroyed villages were—in almost all cases—destroyed completely, with their houses, garden-walls, and even cemeteries and tombstones, so that literally a stone does not remain standing, and visitors are passing and being told that "it was all desert."[120]

For Palestine to be "a land without people for a people without land," the Israelis expelled the majority of the Palestinians to render their vision a reality.[121] As for the history of the Palestinians in Palestine, Zionism undertook its rewriting. As a result, the war between the European Jewish colonists and the colonized Palestinians extended to the realm of cartography and archaeology with Israeli maps showing all of historic Palestine as Israel and Palestinian maps showing all of historic Palestine to be an occupied country. As for archeology, the Israelis, who have a monopoly on it, are in a constant search for archeological "proofs" of pre-diasporic Hebrew "settlement" in all parts of historic Palestine to further authenticate European Jewish claims to Palestinian/Israeli space and time. One Israeli scholar characterizes archeology as a "national sport" for Israelis.[122] On many occasions the military and archeologists combine forces for important finds. On the occasion of uncovering letters written by Bar Kochba, the Israeli army's chief of staff called for "an all-out archeological offensive."[123]

Parallel to this geographic transformation of Palestine, juridical efforts were under way to delimit the nature of bodies with access to this newly transformed space. It is these efforts which resulted in the confiscation of the lands of both the expelled and the remaining Palestinians.[124] After the establishment of the Jewish State, Zionism required the exclusivity of Jewish accessibility to what that state encompassed, both spatially and temporally. Whereas temporally, Israel's history became the history of European Jews, spatially, Israel had to create new *faits accomplis*. In that regard 93 percent of the now Israeli lands (Jews only owned 6.5 percent of the land before the establishment of Israel with the rest of the land being confiscated after 1948[125]) were placed in the custody of the Jewish National Fund with the legal stipulation that the lands could only be leased to, lived on and worked on by Jews (although the best lands and resources went and still go to Ashkenazi Jews).[126]

The geographic transformation of Palestine was in fact an attempt to complete the epistemological transformation of how it is to be apprehended by European Jews not only spatially and temporally but also corporeally. The Zionist condition is characterized by what David Harvey has called in a different context a space–time compression.[127] The spatial–temporal Zionist condition is one inhabited by post-diasporic Jewish bodies. The corporeal self-perception of the Israeli Sabra is always already delimited within this space–time compression outside of which "he" cannot exist. Israel as a colonial/"post-colonial" space–time, however, allows the existence of new post-diasporic Jewish bodies only as holograms (virtual images as in mirror reflections). If they exit (in the Zionist lexicon "descend from") the Israeli space–time continuum, these bodies lose their new corporeality and revert back to their pre-Israel diasporic condition—the mirror reflection as an organizing principle of national subjectivity shatters.[128] This occurrence results from the epistemological shattering of self-perception whose anchorage was lost with the changes in the material conditions of power and domination in which these bodies were embedded (as dominating and powerful tough Sabras) in the Israeli space–time, and which do not apply in the same way outside it. Like the *holodeck* on *Star Trek*'s spaceship "Enterprise," where people can program the deck (which has the capacity to rearrange matter) to recreate any time, space, and bodies according to the programmer's specifications, and where the programmer enters the *holodeck* with an identity commensurate with the space, time, and bodies s/he programmed, Palestine was/is Zionism's *holodeck*. On the Enterprise's *holodeck*, recreated bodies, even if they become conscious of their *holodeck* condition, cannot exist outside it. In fact, they disappear into oblivion if they attempt to exit the holodeck's perimeter. Similarly, the Israeli Sabra with—almost always—"his" new body can only exist *within* the Israeli space–time outside of which "he" reverts to being the "feminine *schlemiel*" that he was before. The establishment of the Jewish settler-colony makes it possible for post-diasporic Jewish male bodies to be "de"colonized *only* within it. These new Jewish bodies are actually imprisoned within this Zionist-created space–time—a space–time whose coloniality is rendered discursively "post-colonial." Israel, as a "*post-colonial*" *colony*, can *only* exist in this temporal–spatial–corporeal limitation. Palestinian and Mizrahi bodies resisting this Zionist condition are simply attempting to chip away at its hegemony. The hegemony of Zionist discourse, however, is so pervasive, that signs of Palestinian and Mizrahi agency are explained by Zionism—to continue with the *Star Trek* analogy—as simple program malfunctions and glitches which need only be corrected through Zionist reprogramming.

2 Conceiving the masculine*

Gender and Palestinian nationalism[1]

Palestinian nationalism like other nationalisms is influenced in its philosophy by Enlightenment and post-Enlightenment Romantic thought. Enlightenment philosophy underlies a variety of nationalisms in Europe and, through European colonialism, the rest of the world. In an embattled situation, the colonized view European Enlightenment thought as the only available discourse (under the time constraints of anti-colonial resistance) for mobilizing people against colonial hostility and onslaughts. This extension of nationalist thought to the colonial world, however, was an enterprise fraught with contradictions. One of the most obvious underpinnings of anti-colonial nationalisms is the combining of modernization and tradition. While one of anti-colonial nationalism's dual goals is the achievement of technological modernization in the Western sense, its other goal is the assertion of a traditional national culture.

In the European political arena, nationalism is expressed through gendered narratives. Although anti-colonial nationalist agency defines itself in opposition to European nationalism, it does not escape implication in the same narrative. In responding to a Western colonial discourse that negates the possibility of nationalist agency in the colonies, anti-colonial nationalists had to deal with how Western modernization fits in their identitarian project. The nationalist project, which is predicated on the creation of a national identity, posits this very identity as the locus of negotiating the relation of the traditional to the modern.[2] The metaphor of the nation as a mother- or fatherland, the practice of defending and administering it with homosocial institutions like the military and the bureaucracy, and the gendered strategies of reproducing not only the nation and its nationalist agents but also the very national culture defining it, were all constitutive of nationalist discourse.[3] Kumari Jayawardena identifies the gender objectives of nationalist reformers across Asia as two-fold:

> to establish in their countries a system of stable, monogamous nuclear families with educated and employable women such as was associated with capitalist development and bourgeois ideology; and yet to ensure that women would retain a position of traditional subordination within the family.[4]

* This essay was first published in 1995.

In putting this project into effect, the nationalists' combining of European and existing gender norms does not result in cultural syncretism; rather, it is a process whereby European norms sublate traditional ones. The new gender norms are modern inventions dressed up in traditional garb to satisfy nationalism's claim of a national culture for which it stands. These new ideals are not so much traditional as they are *traditionalized*.[5]

In the Arab East, as in the rest of Asia[6] national identity and nationalist agency were the sites of negotiating not only East and West as conceptual anchoring categories, but as importantly the foundational ruse of gendered citizenship. The respective responsibilities of men and women to the nation emerged as epistemic cornerstones of nation building. Arguing that masculinity was always the identitarian pole of European nationalist thought, I will examine how Palestinian nationalism conceives (of) the masculine in defining Palestinian nationalist agency. In so doing, the category of masculinity will be shown to have certain attributes as it is embedded within a temporal schema—that of post-Enlightenment modernity, a class schema—that of bourgeois entrepreneurs, and a geocultural schema—that of European colonial culture as a paradigm through which tradition is (re)interpreted. My objective here is not so much to describe the unfolding of a masculine-based nationalism, rather to show the process through which masculinity itself is lived within the modality of nationalism, indeed how masculinity is *nationalized*. I maintain that the mobilizing metaphors of nationalist movements are not only metaphors. They reflect the fundamental assumptions of nationalist thought, which establishes the future gender constitution and gender roles of nationalist agents. History shows that other revolutions have foundered on a "nation first, women after" strategy; it is not too soon to ask this question of Palestinian nationalism and its plans for a post-colonial future.

For a decade following the establishment of the state of Israel in May 1948 and the expulsion of close to a million Palestinians, the Palestinian people remained without a national leadership. As a result, the majority of the Palestinians looked to Arab governments in the region to help them retrieve Palestine from the Zionists and return them to their homes. When no such development occurred, guerrilla groups began emerging in the late fifties in the refugee camps and among Palestinian university students. This development threatened the Arab régimes who by then had reached a modus vivendi with the decade-old Israeli state.

As a response to this rising tide of Palestinian nationalist agitation, and in an attempt to control and restrict it, the Palestine Liberation Organization was created in 1964 by a number of Arab governments.[7] In the wake of the 1967 Israeli occupation of the remainder of Palestine (and the expulsion of hundreds of thousands more Palestinians), Palestinian guerrilla groups intensified their military attacks on Israel and their ideological attacks on Arab governments. This situation culminated in a sort of coup d'état in 1969 ousting Ahmad Shuqayri from his position as head of the PLO and replacing him with Yasser Arafat. Arafat, who had been the leader of the independent Palestinian Liberation Movement (Fateh), along with the leaders of the other major guerrilla groups, became members of the executive committee of the PLO.

This development coincided with other changes in the social and economic fortunes of the Palestinian bourgeoisie in the diaspora. In Lebanon, an alliance of the different elements of the Lebanese bourgeoisie against the rising fortunes of bourgeois Palestinians manifested itself in the 1965 successful attempt to break the Palestinian-owned Intra Bank, the largest Arab-owned bank in the Middle East at the time.[8] By the late 1960s, Arab countries of the Gulf, who had opened their borders earlier to the Palestinian intelligentsia and to Palestinian entrepreneurs, were now restricting such entry in order to forestall future competition between Palestinians and the increasingly better-educated national populations of these countries.[9] In 1970, civil war broke out in Jordan between the Jordanian army and PLO guerrillas culminating in the latter's expulsion from that country a year later after the Jordanian army's slaughter of thousands of guerrillas.[10] These developments help to explain the sudden nationalist fervor emanating from the diaspora Palestinian bourgeoisie who, until the 1960s, had remained quiet.[11] By 1974, the Palestinian bourgeoisie, backing Arafat's liberal Fateh, was successful in enlisting the support of the Arab League to recognize the PLO as the sole legitimate representative of the Palestinian people. That same year, Arafat addressed the United Nations (UN) General Assembly on behalf of the Palestinian people, a development eliciting world recognition (the United States and Israel excepted) of the legitimacy of the Palestinian struggle.[12]

In the Palestinian case, as with all nationalist movements, the project of gendering inevitably starts with the very establishment of the nationalist movement. In their pioneering collection *Nationalisms and Sexualities*, Andrew Parker *et al.* argue that in "the same way that 'man' and 'woman' define themselves reciprocally (though never symmetrically), national identity is determined not on the basis of its own intrinsic properties but as a function of what it (presumably) is not."[13] Thus the important task for anti-colonial nationalists is not only to define gender roles in relation to each other (female–male), but also to define both in relation to the nationalist project, and in doing so dissociating national identity from any colonial contamination.

Territory versus paternity: determining palestinian identity

The first two documents issued by the PLO were the Palestinian National Charter (al-Mithaq al-Watani al-Filastini) and the Palestinian Nationalist Charter (Al-Mithaq al-Qawmi al-Filastini). These Charters functioned as a sort of constitution defining Palestinian political goals, Palestinian rights, indeed Palestinianness itself. They were the founding documents of the new generation of Palestinian nationalists. An analysis of these texts gives us some indication of how post-1948 Palestinian nationalism was articulated by its architects.

In the introduction to the *Palestinian Nationalist Charter*, the Zionist conquest of Palestine is presented as a rape of the land.[14] It views Palestinians as the children of Palestine, which is portrayed as a mother. The Zionist enemy is clearly seen as masculine, and the wrong committed by this enemy to Palestinians is considered metaphorically to be of a violent sexual nature.[15]

This view is in full concert with early Zionist discourse that viewed the role of Zionists as fertilizing the virgin land. For Zionists, as elucidated in Chapter 1, Palestine was both the motherland to which Jews needed to return, and the virgin-land which the Zionists needed to fertilize and fecundate. As Ella Shohat has shown, the Zionist view was in turn borrowed from European colonial discourse especially in relation to the "New World." The Israeli Sabra, like the American Adam but unlike the "feminine" diaspora Jew,[16] was a new masculine pioneer impregnating the virgin/mother land with new life. This pregnancy was to result in the reproduction of the "new Jew."[17] Zionism's gendered discourse echoes Orientalist discourse—Orientalists described the Orient "as feminine, its riches as fertile, its main symbols the sensual woman, the harem, and the despotic—but curiously attractive—ruler."[18]

These masculine-centric discursive axioms constituted European nationalism from its inception. Both Benedict Anderson[19] and George Mosse[20] argue that nationalism favors a distinctly homosocial form of male bonding. Mosse argues that "[European] nationalism had a special affinity for male society and together with the concept of respectability legitimized the dominance of men over women."[21] For Anderson, the "nation is always conceived as a deep, horizontal comradeship. Ultimately, it is this *fraternity* [emphasis added] that makes it possible, over the past two centuries, for so many millions of people, not so much to kill, as willingly to die for such limited imaginings."[22] In *Imagined Communities*, Anderson observes that "in the modern world everyone can, should, will 'have' a nationality, as he or she 'has' a gender."[23] This development is part and parcel of the advent of modernity and the specifically modern ways of classifying people. However, this naturalization of national identity, like the naturalization of gender and sexual identities that are synchronous with it, has a history which I will try to chart in the Palestinian case.

Article 4 of the *Palestinian National Charter* defines Palestinian identity as "a genuine, inherent and eternal trait and is transmitted from *fathers to sons*."[24] Article 5 states that "Palestinians are those Arab citizens who used to reside... in Palestine until 1947,... *and everyone who is born of an Arab Palestinian father* after this date—whether inside Palestine or outside it—is a Palestinian [emphasis added]."[25] What is interesting in this definition is that Palestinian identity is defined differently depending on the historical period. While until 1947, that is until the "rape" (which is viewed as having been legitimated by the 1947 UN Partition Plan), Palestinians are defined as those who lived in Palestine, that is, those who lived on the land which was already defined as a mother; after 1947, this is no longer the case. In the post-1947 period, Palestinians, whether still in historic Palestine or live outside its borders, no longer fit the earlier definition. This spatial–temporal prerequisite for Palestinianness and its metaphorical stress on maternity become directly linked, after the "rape," to the issue of reproducing the nation. In nationalist discourse, this is to be carried out through physiological and metaphorical paternity. It is being born to a Palestinian father that now functions as the prerequisite for Palestinianness. A father, it is important to note, whose very Palestinianness is established through his residence in the motherland before the "rape." Revealing the importance of eugenics in nationalist logic, this definition carries itself to future generations, whereby it is the sons of these fathers who will continue the reproduction of the Palestinian people. In sum, while the land as mother was responsible for the reproduction of Palestinians until 1947, the rape disqualified her from this role. It is now fathers who will reproduce the nation. Territory was replaced by paternity.

The disqualification of the land as mother in her national reproductive role, in the Charter, does not deny that the land, as mother, can produce children, but rather that, since the rape, it can no longer be relied upon to reproduce *legitimate* Palestinian children. Within this metaphoric schema, women clearly cannot be agents of nationality. Their role, thus, becomes secondary and supportive in the narrative of nationalism. As anti-colonial nationalism is derived from the European Enlightenment, so are the laws demarcating nationhood in the now independent former colonies derived from the laws of European nations. The PLO Charter is hardly an exception in this regard. The establishment of paternity as the source of nationhood has been enshrined in the exemplary case of British nationality laws since the nineteenth century.[26]

In his 1974 address to the UN General Assembly, PLO chairman Yasser Arafat again uses metaphors of sexual violence to describe the Zionists' use of colonial methods to "rape the Palestinian homeland and to exploit and disperse its people."[27] Arafat stresses that Israel's international alliance with the colonial powers and the US against Third World liberation and independence gives a clearer picture of our enemy "who raped our country" and illustrates the "honor" of the struggle which we are launching against it.[28] The rape image is invoked again in the November 1988 Political Communiqué issued by the Palestine National Council. Reasserting the continuing perception of the Zionist occupation as sexual in its symbology, it said that "Israel showed its real self to be a fascist, racist, colonial-settler country that exists through raping/usurping Palestinian land and through exterminating the Palestinian people."[29] Thus, liberation is staged as a transaction between men over the honor of a woman–mother whose ownership passes through paternity.

This discourse has its own momentum. Explaining the refusal of the Palestinian people to accept the UN partition plan of 1947, wherein the United Nations "partitioned what it had no right to divide—the land of the indivisible homeland," Arafat, in his 1974 UN address, compares the Palestinian people to the natural/true mother in the King Solomon story: "when we rejected that decision, our position corresponded to that of the true mother who refused Solomon's division of her child when another woman claimed it."[30] This reversal of roles is interesting to note; for in the Palestinian case, it is Palestine's true children, men and women living there, who refused the UN division of their mother. This indicates how Palestinian men and women were engaged in the defense of their mother against what was later referred to as the rape. Note how the mother's agency in Solomon's story is transferred to the children by Arafat, with Palestine, as mother, retaining only the position of victim. For Arafat, Palestinian nationalist agency, in 1947, was characterized by the children's defense. But unlike the mother in Solomon's story whose stance convinced Solomon to give her back her child, the defense of their mother by Palestine's true children failed. The rape took place.

Conceiving and mothering the masculine

Twenty years after the Israeli occupation of the West Bank (including East Jerusalem) and the Gaza Strip, the Palestinians revolted against colonialism for the second time in half a century. More intense than the last revolt which lasted from 1936 to 1939, the Palestinian intifada which erupted in 1987 continued until Arafat, through the Oslo Accords, terminated it in 1993. The intifada led to the emergence of a new Palestinian leadership that began organizing demonstrations, strikes, and other acts of resistance to the occupation. The Unified National Leadership of the Uprising (UNLU) was later joined by the diaspora-headquartered PLO in providing leadership and financial support to the resisting population. Key in mobilizing the population were the UNLU- and PLO-issued communiqués, and the Palestinian Declaration of Independence, issued by the PLO in November 1988 from its Tunis headquarters.

In his 1974 UN speech, Yasser Arafat described the Palestinian people as the "trustworthy guardian" of the holy places of their homeland.[31] The November 1988 Declaration of Independence, in addition to bestowing the adjective "courageous" on the Palestinian woman, describes her as being "the *guardian* of our survival and our lives, the *guardian* of our perennial flame."[32] The way Palestinian women are perceived to guard Palestinian survival and lives is to be found in the Communiqués of the Unified National Leadership of the Uprising.[33]

Communiqué no. 29, titled "The Call of the Wedding of the Palestinian Independent State," which celebrates the Declaration of Independence, congratulates women, in their role as mothers. The communiqué salutes "the *mother of the martyr* and her celebratory ululations, for she has ululated twice, the day her son went to fight and was martyred, and the day the state was declared [emphasis added]."

Communiqué no. 5 describes Palestinian mothers, sisters, and daughters as "Manabit,"[34] or the soil on which "manhood, respect and dignity" grow. Women are being referred to here in biologically and socially relational terms to men. The communiqué calls on women to "work together side by side with their husbands, sons and brothers…." Whereas mothers, sisters, and daughters are described as the producing soil of manhood, respect, and dignity,[35] a later communiqué describes the Palestinian people, conceived in the masculine, as the "*makers* of glory, respect, and dignity." The discrepancy is central to the conception of Palestinian nationalist agents as masculine. While men actively create glory, respect, and dignity, women are merely the soil on which these attributes, along with manhood, grow. It is as soil that they are the "guardians" of Palestinian lives and survival.[36]

The UNLU, which issued the intifada communiqués, seems at times ambivalent, while at others, fully complicit in continuing the earlier tradition in conceiving the masculine. In some communiqués,[37] women are listed with occupational groups like merchants, peasants, students, and workers. This gives the impression that these occupational groups include men only, or that women, unlike men, constitute an occupational group, taking for granted women's roles as housewives without giving it the dignity of an occupation. In other communiqués,[38] women are mentioned together with vulnerable sectors of the population,[39] mainly children and old people, positioning women within the life cycle. Women are listed with men only in the context of resistance and struggle, thus recognizing men's agency as their *only* defining attribute, with women (who are not mothers) as possessing limited agency.[40]

The specificity of Palestinian women's bodies is significant in these texts only when reproduction is considered. This conception of the body defines the Palestinian that the UNLU has in mind, when it declares that the intifada consists of "the children and young men of the stones and Molotov cocktails, it is the thousands of women who miscarried as a result of poison gas and tear gas grenades, and those women whose sons and husbands were thrown in the Nazi prisons."[41] Palestinian women are mentioned in their reproductive capacities (when they miscarry) or in their social roles as mothers (when their sons are imprisoned).

Women's reproductive roles appear everywhere in the communiqués of the first year of the intifada. Their suffering at the hands of the occupier is exemplified in miscarriages—their failure to reproduce nationalist agents.[42] Yet, they are commended as mothers throughout. It is in recognition of their reproductive capacity that the UNLU sends women its love,[43] salutes them,[44] addresses them as the mothers of "the martyrs, the detainees, and the wounded [all males],"[45] and congratulates them on the martyrdom of their sons,[46] and sympathizes with them as "wailing widows and thakala [mothers who lost their sons]."[47]

Women, in those communiqués, are also viewed outside the context of their reproductive roles. They are saluted as detainees of the occupation authorities,[48] and mourned when they, along with children and old people, are killed by the Israelis.[49] Women are described as martyrs, however, in their role as daughters, at which point they are listed with sons.[50] They are also referred to, along with children and young and old people, as the "makers of the intifada,"[51] and are singled out to perform activities that the UNLU views as their responsibility.[52] These "responsibilities" include the commemoration of March 8, International Women's Day, with demonstrations against the occupation. Women are praised for subordinating gender issues to national ones, and are being asked implicitly *to transfer the legitimacy of their cause against sexual oppression to the national struggle*.[53] Although the women's committees' (who are attached to the different branches of the national movement) March 8 Communiqué addressed more directly the different facets of women's activities during the intifada, the committees did not articulate a clear gender agenda. Women's activities, as elaborated by the women's committees, "remained an extension of [women's] traditional roles in such fields as education and social services."[54]

In 1989, in contrast to the tone of previous communiqués, the UNLU saluted the Palestinian woman and declared its "admiration for her heroism in the national struggle."[55] In 1990, the UNLU named its communiqué "The Woman's Call," where a special section was devoted to women who were presented again in relational terms to men.

> Progressive nations celebrate International Women's Day on 8 March as a day of struggle for the world's women's masses. While celebrating this great

> day, in the name of all the sons of our people, we congratulate the world's women's masses and the masses of the Palestinian women's movement and its vanguard organizations, hailing every working woman, woman struggler, and housewife, and especially our imprisoned strugglers. We also pay tribute to the struggling role of the Palestinian uprising's women's movement, to every mother who has lost a son, daughter, husband, or brother, and to every woman who meets with a struggling daughter or a heroic son from behind the Bastille of the Zionist enemy.

The communiqué proceeds to praise the Palestinian people for making history "through the blood of their sons."[56]

The UNLU Communiqués implicitly analogize the intifada to a pregnancy. While the intifada is referred to as *entering* its, eighth, ninth, or twelfth month,[57] the enemy's attempt to repress it is constantly referred to as the enemy's attempt to *abort* it.[58] Palestinian independence is clearly seen as the ultimate birth of the intifada's pregnancy (see the Declaration). The intifada is also viewed as "the Palestinian wedding," the apogee of heterosexual love.[59] It seems that the outcome of the intifada's pregnancy is both a birth and a wedding, in the sense that weddings inaugurate a new reproductive cycle—the reproduction of the next generation. This places the heterosexual reproduction of the family at the center of the nationalist project. The parties to the wedding seem to be none other than the Palestinians as nationalist agents, who are always already masculine, and Palestine, the mother/woman/land. Once independence takes place, however, it is not clear whether Palestine, the mother, would be trusted again to conceive/reproduce the Palestinian people. In the meantime, it is the Palestinian man who is the conceiver/reproducer of the nation. In this vein, Yasser Arafat himself (who on some occasions is referred to as a "brother") is described as the "symbolic father" of the nation.[60]

Mapping out Palestinian masculinity

Establishing a new model of anti-colonial masculinity was a much more complicated endeavor than its colonial counterpart. In European nationalist discourses, as Chandra Mohanty argues, it was always European white masculinity that defined nationalist agency at home. In the colonies, it was that same white colonial masculinity, made normative through European colonialism, which reigned supreme in dealing with the natives.[61] In adapting European nationalist thought to local conditions, anti-colonial nationalists were faced with the task of defining not only the roles of men and women in the nationalist project, but also what a non-European nationalist masculinity would look like, and what kind of performances would guarantee it. In this vein, Palestinian nationalism, like other anti-colonial nationalisms, set itself similar tasks.

Article 7 of the Palestinian National Charter refers to the Palestinian "individual" in a typically contract theory fashion, and is thus less gender-specific than the rest of the Charter. Article 7 states that it is a Palestinian "national duty" to raise this "individual in an Arab and revolutionary way and... all means of education and consciousness-raising [will be used] to acquaint the Palestinian with his [*sic*] homeland." The article describes the national duty of the Palestinian individual, who, after being raised according to the recommendations of Article 7 rendering him "qualified [to launch] armed struggle," to be the "sacrific[ing] of his life and his money in the interest of retrieving his homeland until liberation."[62] This appeal to Palestinians includes not only the masculine ability to launch armed struggle but also of having a bourgeois economic status. The appeal is made in the context of the Palestinian diaspora, where most of the Palestinian bourgeoisie now lives.

The trajectory of this discourse's metaphors serves to produce a gendered mindset of agency with its own momentum. Speaking in 1974 at the UN about diaspora Palestinians, Arafat states that Palestinian sons, educated in the diaspora where they worked and contributed to the construction and development of neighboring countries, earned income which they used to help their younger and older relatives who could not leave the refugee camps. He emphasizes that

> the brother paid for the education of his brother and sister, and took care of his parents and raised his children but continued to dream in his heart of returning to Palestine. He remained Palestinian attached to his homeland with unrelenting loyalty, unweakened will and untempered enthusiasm.[63]

Like all other political ideologies, nationalism is derived from its own social construction. In this vein, it is important to note the performative aspect of nationalist agency in Arafat's text, whereby it is the brother's paying for the education of his brother and sister, taking care of "his" parents, raising "his" children, dreaming in "his" heart of returning to Palestine which characterize the agency of the Palestinian nationalist agent. Following Judith Butler, it is clear that the substantive effect of nationalist agency, like sexual and gender identities, is performatively produced and compelled by the regulatory practices of the coherence of the category of nationalist agency itself.[64] Given that nationalism, like all political positions, is perforce performative, nationalist agency proves to be performatively constituted by the very expressions that are said to be its results. As the above quote illustrates, nationalist agency is constituted through gender-specific performances whose meanings are always already paired up with nationalism. A nationalist performance would seem to be then imbricated with masculine performances which guarantee its definitional coherence and without which it would become impossible. Here, it is interesting to contrast the performativity of nationalist agency with Palestinian identity itself, which is constituted through interpellation in the Althusserian sense. The interpellatory constitution of Palestinian identity is asserted by the definitional fiat of the National Charter, in which Palestinians are hailed *as* "Palestinians."[65] Consequently, whereas men and women are interpellated as Palestinians, thus assuming Palestinian identity tout court, only masculine performativity defines Palestinian nationalist agency.

Clearly, when referring to Palestinians, a slippage occurs in the text of Arafat's speech. "Palestinians" at times means, both men and women; at others "Palestinians" slips into men. What is important here is the context of this slippage. It is in defining the Palestinian nationalist agent and this agent's commitment to Palestine, that this agent slips from the ostensibly ungendered universal into the clearly masculine realm. This is not an uncharacteristic slip. Rather, as I will show later, it is a reflection of how the masculine and the feminine are conceived within Palestinian nationalist thought.

While the Charter's call on bourgeois Palestinians to sacrifice their money is made in the mid-1960s, Arafat's view of the Palestinian nationalist agent is informed by the economic improvement in the life of many Palestinians, inside the Occupied Territories and in the diaspora, over the next decade. Arafat's Palestinian nationalist agent is working hard and obtaining money to support "his" family and educate "his" brothers and sisters. "He" is able to do this as a result of the economic opportunities opened up in the Gulf. These economic developments provide Arafat with the context to portray the Palestinian nationalist agent, not only as masculine, but also as bourgeois-in-the-making. In this regard, it is important to note that while the future national status of the second brother is secured through his following in the footsteps of (performing like) the first older brother, who educated him, the future national status of the sister, for whose education the Palestinian nationalist agent pays, is uncontemplated by Arafat. In her autobiography, Leila Khaled, one of the better-known Palestinian guerrilla fighters of the 1960s and 1970s, agrees with Arafat on one count. Like him, she expects Palestinian men to follow a certain code of behavior. When the money, that her revolutionary brother Mohamad promised to send her in order to register at the American University of Beirut, was late in reaching her, she did not doubt her brother. He, "like all good Arab men, honored his promises."[66] Like a "good" Arab woman herself, Khaled accepts her dependence on her brother.

In confronting the occupation in the context of the intifada, the nationalist agent's body becomes the crucial instrument. One communiqué, for example, speaks to (male) students as follows: "you are the stronger body, you are the continuously pulsating artery among our people."[67] The comparative adjective "stronger" implicitly contrasts the Palestinian nationalist agent's body with the body of its male enemy. It is the nationalist agent's arm/hand, however, that is constantly invoked when describing the agent's body. Women, for example, are supposed to stand side by side with men, "in one line, and with one hand."[68] The UNLU states that "your [a masculine pronoun] strong arms which shake the foundations of the Zionist occupation are the same arms which will build the independent Palestinian state."[69] "Gaza's sons," in the thousands, the UNLU states, "went out of their den confronting with *their bodies* the occupier's machines [of destruction]."[70]

The UNLU, however, conceives (of) the Palestinian people as one body, a man's body. It describes the Palestinian people's body as being a "giant [which] has *erected* itself and will not *bow* [emphasis added]."[71] Calls for the Palestinian people to rise up in a unified way are expressed by the UNLU's call on them to "rise as one man" in the face of siege,[72] to defend the right of the people to struggle.[73] In this context, the battles against the enemy in which Palestinian children are killed are nothing but the "battles of *honor*, heroism and sacrifice."[74] The Palestinian nationalist agent, in addition to being masculine and bourgeois-in-the-making, is young and able-bodied—free from the physical vulnerabilities of old age. "He" conceives (of) himself in terms of a group identity unifying him along with the *shabibah* (male youth), with whom he struggles against the occupation. The self-masking of many Palestinian young men (and some women), when confronting their occupiers (for fear of being identified and punished by the Israelis), contributes to the erasure of their individual identities and the emergence of a strong collective one. The mask itself is usually the Palestinian *hatta* (the male head scarf or "kufiyyah"), the symbol of Palestinian identity. Thus, struggling against the Israeli occupiers and colonizers is not only an affirmation of Palestinian nationalist agency, it is also a masculinizing act enabling the concrete pairing of nationalist agency and masculinity (the two being always already paired conceptually) and their logical inseparability within the discourse of nationalism. *Thus, resisting occupation can be used to stage masculine acts as it performs nationalist ones*. Through this national anti-colonial resistance, a new figuration of masculine bodies is mapped out on the terrain of the national struggle, one that becomes the model for Palestinian nationalist agency itself.[75]

Toward a "post-colonial" future[76]

Having examined the gender underpinnings of Palestinian nationalist thought, the following will look at how these impact the experience of Palestinian women in the intifada, and women's prospects for liberation in a Palestinian independent state-to-be. My study stops at the signing of the Oslo agreement, but subsequent developments have made little conceptual change in nationalist thinking on gender.

During the intifada, Palestinian women's freedom of movement, dress, and behavior became highly restricted in Gaza as a result of the collaboration between the secular and religious strands of Palestinian nationalism. The secular nationalists assured women that this is a temporary arrangement, and that after liberation, women too will be free. This was not a tactical mistake that the secular leadership later declaredly regretted.[77] It was rather a political move that compromised very little nationalist ideology. It, in fact, follows directly from how nationalist thought has always conceived the feminine and the masculine. It is within this context of nationalist thought as always already gendered that Ann McClintock underscores that "if nationalism is not deeply informed by an analysis of gender power, the nation-state will remain a repository of male hopes, male aspirations, and male privilege."[78]

Given the experience of Palestinian women in the intifada, this view is shared by many a Palestinian woman activist and intellectual.[79] A Union of Palestinian Working Women's Committees' (UPWWC) activist stated that "men are still making the decisions... it will take a long time of struggle [to achieve equality], and we won't automatically get our rights as women when we get our state."[80] Another activist emphasized that

> [w]e realize that if we don't raise issues now, we won't be able to push them later on, and we'll be abused by the national movement. We are struggling for independence, but we don't want to compromise our role as women. The issue has come up now because we have realized through our work in the intifada how important our role really is. This has given us confidence.[81]

The intifada created a new discursive space in which Palestinian women could challenge the dominant conception of Palestinian nationalist agency. Unfortunately, however, the strength and resilience of the masculinist axioms buttressing Palestinian nationalist thought are yet to be dented in any major way.[82]

Despite the masculinist logic of Palestinian nationalist thought, Palestinian feminist Hanan Mikhail-Ashrawi expresses, with some skepticism, a belief that Palestinian women will be able to free themselves within the framework of Palestinian nationalism.[83] She implies this by asserting that Palestinian feminists are "on the right track."[84] Hoping to avoid replicating the defeat of Algerian women after the revolution, Ashrawi observed that Palestinian feminists "are trying to create a place for ourselves, to take part in the decision-making process,"[85] an eventuality, given the discursive axioms of Palestinian nationalism, that is far from real. The intifada raised the consciousness of many women with regards to the gender agenda, as demonstrated in women's publications during the intifada, but this translated in very little power once Oslo was institutionalized. Ashrawi's claim, however, that

> the grassroots work and organizational significance of the women's committees in the social and economic transformation of society . . . has bestowed on the women's movement credibility and legitimacy which have made the articulation of feminist theory not only acceptable, but also desirable[86]

was much exaggerated. Whereas she is correct in claiming that the women's contributions to the intifada facilitated and led to the articulation of feminist issues by many Palestinian women, her claim that this contribution made the articulation of feminist theory "desirable," ostensibly by the nationalist movement and/or Palestinian society, was not persuasive before Oslo and is belied by the actual record of the Palestinian Authority's (PA) performance.[87]

The intifada had indeed increased women's awareness of their position within nationalist thought and the nationalist movement. Ashrawi, for example, responded to the male nationalist rhetoric that conceived of women as "hatcheries" by stating that the "male definition of self-value is based on their own progeny—ego about 'the male line'. . . . keeping a woman pregnant and at home keeps her in a position of subservience, in a role which is biologically determined, according to men."[88] Nevertheless, as Ashrawi herself asserted, in the context of the intifada, where Palestinian men were interested in increasing the Palestinian population, and the Israeli occupiers were interested in limiting it, women's bodies became the site of the battle with little control left to them over their own bodies. It was in this context of the Israeli tear- and poison-gas-induced miscarriages that Palestinian women fought, and still fight, to sustain a pregnancy, a right which the male leadership is supporting based on its own agenda.

In contrast to earlier conceptions of enemy-raped Palestinian women, the intifada brought about some conceptual changes with regards to Palestinian women who are raped by Israeli Jews. Ashrawi noted that

> [w]omen who were in prison before [the intifada] were not "marriageable commodities" because they're "damaged goods." With the intifada there was a sudden change: released women prisoners became desirable because this was a source of honor—that you went to jail, that you had struggled—and the mythological questions of virginity or damaged goods were no longer questions. This was especially true because of support at the feminist level, from the women's committees, and eventually from the general community.[89]

Sadly, this limited progressive change did not herald more radical changes nor led to the questioning of the masculine basis of Palestinian nationalist agency. In fact, Ashrawi herself noted that this change was accompanied by a backlash: "families started trying to protect their daughters by bringing them back into the family unit through marriage, and sometimes early marriage."[90]

Although the Palestinian women's movement, and women's active participation in the intifada pressured the secular leadership into changing part of its conceptual framework, the masculine still reigns supreme in Palestinian nationalist thought.[91] The Palestinian anti-colonial struggle, since its beginnings, has transformed and continues to transform Palestinian women's lives and perceptions of their societal roles. These transformations, however, have not translated into a substantive change in the way Palestinian nationalist thought conceives (of) Palestinian women. They are still considered subordinate members of the nation. Palestinian nationalist thought has changed its conceptions over the decades regarding women's roles and duties to the nation, but these changes have always been made in response to changes in Palestinian nationalist conception of men's roles in the national struggle, and of the exigencies of the national struggle itself. As such, the gap between men's and women's roles, and women's subordinate status, are maintained despite changes in the specificities of these roles in relation to the national struggle. Here, it should be emphasized that post-1948 notions of Palestinian nationalist masculinity differ markedly from the pre-1948 period, insofar as Palestinian nationalist masculinity then did not include being bourgeois and educated as much as being a landholder and/or a peasant who was unwilling to sell land to the Zionists, and who would fight to expel the colonists from Palestine.[92]

Palestinian women might have had more say in Palestinian politics since Oslo and the beginning of PA rule in 1994, but given their discursive construction in nationalist thought, they were able to do so not as *Palestinian women* struggling for Palestinian women's rights, but as *Palestinian* women struggling for discursively constituted Palestinian rights, where Palestinian is always already conceived in the masculine. The recent performance of the PA demonstrates the Palestinian leadership's commitment to the same masculine-supremacist path.[93] In the language of national liberation, one might add that no nation is free with half of its members being secondary and subservient. That this might be considered a specious argument is itself part of the symptom. If the Palestinian struggle does not develop this persistent auto-critique at its most embattled hour, the neglected lessons of history will make a possible victory pyrrhic.

3 Zionism's internal others*

Israel and the Mizrahim

The creation of the State of Israel by European Jews was predicated upon reconfiguring Jewish identities. European Zionist leaders asserted that the creation of a state for European Jews would normalize the abnormal situation of European Jewry insofar as European Jews, like Christian Europeans, would now have a state to call their own, thus becoming a nation. In addition to defending European Jews against anti-Semitic attacks, Zionism was also going to make available to them a whole range of economic activity denied it in Europe, especially in agriculture and soldiery. Hence, the objective of the Zionist movement was not simply to transplant European Jews into a new geographical area, but also to transform the very nature of European Jewish society and identity as it had existed in the diaspora until then—a transformation that was to go beyond the notion of *'Am Yisrael* becoming *Medinat Yisrael*.[1]

The type of Jewish culture that Zionism wanted to create in its state-to-be was one that had nothing to do with diaspora culture—the latter having been a manifestation of oppressed Jewishness, rather than a free independent one. The model for such culture was the European Enlightenment. European Jews, Zionism postulated, will create a European society by Europeans who simply happened to be Jewish. This assimilationist dimension of Zionist ideology was borrowed from the ideas of the Jewish Enlightenment, or Haskala, of the nineteenth century. Zionist ideology, consequently, denigrates diaspora Jews and their culture. Yiddish was and is actively discouraged in Israeli society in favor of Hebrew, due to the stigma attached to Yiddish as a product of diaspora European Jewish culture. The rejection of Yiddish extended beyond its use in the Yishuv to an attack on any Yiddish cultural production, including theater and cinema. When Abraham Goldfaden's operetta *Shulamith* was performed in Yiddish during the British Mandate years, "Hebrew-language fanatics threw stink bombs." When the Yiddish film *My Jewish Mother* (1930) was shown, ink and stink bombs were thrown at the screen. Demonstrations ensued leading to the film's removal from the screen until a compromise was reached—the film was shown without sound.[2] It is important to stress, however, that whereas the Zionists rejected Yiddish as the language of the

* This essay was first published in 1996.

Jewish State, having a Yiddish background commanded, among them, high respect and privilege.

European Zionists were not only uninterested in safeguarding European diaspora Jewish culture or languages, but also Jewish cultures and languages (including Ladino and Arabic) that developed outside Europe, in the rest of the diaspora. Whereas it was Ashkenazi Jews who decided to replace the diasporic Yiddish with the "authentically Jewish" Hebrew, or at least the Ashkenazi version of it,[3] it was also Ashkenazi Jews who held the Arabic of Arab Jews in contempt and forced its replacement with Hebrew. Arabic became the detested and contemptible language of the enemy from which Arab Jews (the Ashkenazi leaders insisted) needed to purify themselves in order to reassert their "Jewishness."[4] In sum, Israel created a new Israeli identity and culture alien to diaspora Jews. Israel redefined Jewishness by creating a new Jew who is land-based and who differs physically, psychologically, and linguistically from diaspora Jews. The New Jew, in fact, would share nothing with diaspora Jews except their common pre-Israel history. Zionism's commitment to cosmopolitan European gentile culture as the identitarian basis for the New Jew led Georges Friedmann to assert that Israel in fact "constitutes a new kind of assimilation liable to produce 'generations of Hebrew-speaking Gentiles'."[5]

The creation of Israel, however, was to have far-reaching effects not only on the identity of European Yiddish-speaking Jews but also on Arabic- and Ladino-speaking Jews (among others), and Palestinian Arabs. Whereas non-European Jews from across the world were classified as Sephardim[6] (Spaniards) and later Mizrahim[7] (Easterners) and juxtaposed to the Yiddish-speaking Jews whose Ashkenazi identity preceded Zionism, Palestinian Arabs were divided into three groups: Druze, Bedouin, and (Christian and Muslim) Arabs. Israel, consequently, was based on a complete overhauling of the ethnic identities of all the sectors of the population over whom it was to have jurisdiction. The irony about Mizrahi identity, however, is not only demonstrated in the fact that it was created by the Ashkenazi establishment, but that the group referred to as Mizrahi was to accept and internalize the imposed identity and launch ethnic protests based on it.

This chapter will examine the Zionist movement's relationship with what became later known as Mizrahi Jews. I will examine the place occupied by and assigned to the Mizrahim in Zionist discourse and practice from the beginning of Zionist settlement in Palestine through the British Mandate and the State period until 1977. This chapter will also review a vast but scattered body of literature on the Mizrahim in an attempt to synthesize it and to critique it. With this as background, an examination of the two major events of Mizrahi protest against the Israeli state will be presented. The causes of the protests will also be examined as will Israeli state response to them, as these are parts of the changing discursive axioms which define the Mizrahim and Ashkenazim and the differences between them with regards to Zionist philosophy. Finally, I will examine the reasons for the failure of these protests to mobilize the Mizrahi population in a way that would force the exaction of major concessions from the Israeli state and their commensurate failure to create a discursive crisis that would shake Zionist axioms so hard that it would effect an epistemological break.

First encounters

Since its inception, the Zionist movement, which was created by European Jews, advocated the colonial settlement of Palestine by European Jews for the purpose of establishing a "Jewish State." The movement's European identity was constantly asserted in its classic texts as well as in the policy proclamations and programs of its leaders.[8] As discussed in Chapter 1, Theodor Herzl, the movement's father, stated clearly that his projected "State of the Jews" will serve as "the portion of the rampart of Europe against Asia, an outpost of civilization as opposed to barbarism."[9] When discussing Jewish immigration, Herzl spoke only of European Jews (who for him included Algerian Jews).[10] As Sami Chetrit demonstrates, Herzl's analysis of "the Jewish Question" is in fact an analysis of the European Jewish Question without any mention of "Oriental" Jews. Whereas Herzl's writings were highly influential on Zionist thought at the time, Zionists did not necessarily accept all of his recommendations. In fact, they adopted many things that Herzl had opposed, like the adoption of the Hebrew language, which Herzl had rejected as the language of the future state (he preferred German). However, the basis of the Zionist movement did not change, it remained in theory and in practice a European movement.

The first Zionist effort to recruit non-European Jews was the bringing to Palestine of 2,000 Yemeni immigrants between 1910 and 1914. Their immigration was proposed in 1907 in the debate over the use of Palestinian Arab labor in Ashkenazi settlements. Self-described "socialist" Zionists stressed the principle of exclusive 'Avodah 'Ivrit (Hebrew Labor) as the condition for the economic "normalization" of the Jews as a people. However, the difficulty encountered by many of the early Ashkenazi settlers in working the land led to the employment of cheap Palestinian Arab labor which was seen as corrupting Zionist ideals and goals. It was in the context of this debate that the Ashkenazi Zionist Shmu'el Yavne'eli stated that Yemeni Jewish labor "can take the place of the Arabs," thus satisfying the requirements of 'Avodah 'Ivrit.[11] Moreover, the Ashkenazi Zionist leader Dr Ya'akov Tehon added that "we [Ashkenazi settlers] could also have [Yemeni Jewish] women and adolescent girls work in the households instead of the Arab women who now work at high salaries as servants in almost every family of the colonists."[12] Once the Yemenis arrived, they were put to hard labor where they encountered exploitation as well as maltreatment by their Ashkenazi employers. Yemeni Jews were, in fact, expelled as unsuitable workers from many settlements (like Milhamia and Migdal) and continued to seek work until they were finally allowed to work in some settlements in the south provided they built their dwellings outside the settlements themselves.[13] The presence of Yemeni Jews was so disturbing to the Ashkenazi leadership that even Ahad Ha'Am, the renown Zionist humanist, expressed his worry that "Yemenite immigration affects the *nature* of the Zionist settlement by dint of their different culture and mentality" [emphasis added].[14]

As Ella Shohat has shown,[15] the hegemony of this racialized view of Jews within Zionist discourse was so strong that it spanned all political currents within the movement irrespective of social and political ideology. Vladimir Jabotinsky, for example, the leader of the revisionist Zionist camp, who occupies the opposite end of the political spectrum when contrasted with Ahad Ha' Am, was also wary of any connection between European Jews and the Orient. In 1926, he stated that the "Jews, thank God, have nothing in common with the East. We must put an end to any trace of the Oriental spirit in the [native] Jews of Palestine."[16] In an earlier article entitled "Jews of the East," he opposed mixed marriages with non-European Jews and the creation of a single Jewish people. He added that he was opposed to any integration because he did not know whether this would result in "a brilliant people or a dull race. Ashkenazi Jews had to preserve their majority status in Jewish society in Palestine."[17] Jabotinsky's insistence on the Europeanness of European Jews included his recommendation for how modern Hebrew should be pronounced. In his essay "The Hebrew Accent," he states that:

> There are experts who think that we ought to bring our accent closer to the Arabic accent. But this is a mistake. Although Hebrew and Arabic are Semitic languages, it does not mean that our Fathers spoke in [an] "Arabic accent"... We are European and our musical taste is European, the taste of Rubinstein, Mendelssohn, and Bizet.[18]

This commitment to West European Enlightenment culture on the part of Zionism denies the actual geographic origins of most European Jews. The culture of the rural, poor, and squalid shtetls of Eastern Europe is suddenly replaced subtextually in Zionist discourse into the cosmopolitan cultures of Berlin and Paris from where relatively few Jews originated.[19]

The Mizrahi population was to increase slightly in number during the British Mandate. In addition to the Yemeni and the Palestinian Jews, a few thousand Kurdish and Persian Jews were brought in during the British Mandate to work in the quarries and do other menial jobs.[20] By the time the State of Israel was proclaimed in May 1948, Asian and African Jews constituted 20–25 percent of the Jewish population.[21]

The state period

Unlike Haskala thought, which saw cultural assimilation of Jews as an antidote to anti-Semitism, Zionism felt this was not enough. It argued that although Jews should assimilate into European gentile culture, this would not be sufficient to forestall future anti-Semitic attacks. Zionism had another complementary project in mind, that of the creation of a Jewish state through colonial settlement of an area under European imperial rule. In doing so, as we saw in Chapter 1, Zionism could market its colonial endeavor as one of spreading European gentile culture with European Jews as its carriers. It is in assuming this European gentile identity and its commensurate ontology and epistemology that Zionism engaged in a self-othering project that transformed European Jewish identity in ways never thought possible before. The views that used to be attributed to assimilated

German Jews about East European Jews, the Ostjuden, and their "backward" culture, were now to be used against "Europe's others," in general, whether Jewish or gentile. The new European Jew, in gentile garb, has internalized through Zionism the European gentile Weltanschauung through which non-Europeans were seen as inferior. With this as background to the establishment of the state of Israel, non-European Jews had already been prediscursively constituted as an inferior other to European Jews and thus in need of European civilization, which Zionism had made available to European Jews themselves.

It was not until after the Second World War during which 6 million (mostly European) Jews were killed that the Ashkenazi Zionist leadership decided to recruit Jews massively from Asia and Africa in its colonial-settler project. This recruitment intensified after the realization that Soviet and East European Jews were no longer allowed to immigrate to Israel.[22] From 1948 to 1956, Israel's population grew exponentially. A total of 450,000 Jews arrived in Israel from Asia and Africa compared to 360,000 Jews from Europe and America.[23] It was this period that irreversibly created what came to be euphemistically called in Israel the social "gap" between the Ashkenazi and Mizrahi communities.[24]

The first Mizrahi encounter with Israeli state racism dates back to their recruitment by the Ashkenazi Zionists in their home countries and their reception by the Israeli Ashkenazi authorities upon their arrival in Israel. For example, the conditions of the camps in which Algerian and Moroccan Jews were placed before transporting them to Israel were extremely poor.[25] When information of anti-Mizrahi discrimination in Israel became known to North African immigrants in their home countries, immigration declined. A Jewish Agency emissary noted that the "first thing one notices now is the obvious reluctance to go to Israel." According to him, this had become a widespread attitude. He added that "the people virtually have to be taken aboard the ships by force."[26]

It was in 1949 that David Ben-Gurion himself gave his stamp of approval on the already common racist views of the Mizrahim. At a meeting with writers and intellectuals Ben-Gurion stated that "even the immigrant from North Africa, who looks like a savage, who has never read a book in his life, not even a religious one, and doesn't even know how to say his prayers, either wittingly or unwittingly has behind him a spiritual heritage of thousands of years."[27] In an article that he wrote the same year for the Israeli Year Book, Ben-Gurion added that Zionism was largely a movement of Western Jews, specifically those of Europe and America.[28] The Jews of Europe, he claimed, were "the leading candidates for citizenship in the State of Israel."[29] He proceeded to explain the meaning of the holocaust:

> The Jewish people to come, according to Herzl (upon whose existence he built his philosophy and Zionist activity), was in fact the Jewish People in Europe who could not and did not wish to remain there; the people who carried the Zionist movement on their shoulders and were ready for its fulfillment—by the will of aliyah. That people is destroyed and uprooted. The destruction that Hitler had brought down on the people of Israel in Europe was a destruction that no other enemy of Israel before him had dared

> to execute and succeeded. But more than Hitler hurt the Jewish people, whom he knew and hated, he injured the Jewish State which he never anticipated. He had annihilated the carrier and the main and central constructive power of the Jewish State. The state was established and the people who longed for it were not there.[30]

In the absence of that (European) "nation," the State of Israel had to bring the Jews from Arab countries. Ben-Gurion compared them with the Africans who were brought as slaves to America.[31] Other Zionist leaders like Yaakov Zrubavel, head of the Middle East Department of the Jewish Agency, stated that "perhaps these are not the Jews we would like to see coming here, but we can hardly tell them not to come..."[32] Such views were not circulated only in Israel, but also conveyed to European dignitaries. Moshe Sharett, Israel's foreign minister, in speaking to the Soviet Deputy Foreign Minister Vishinsky stated that:

> There are countries—and I was referring to North Africa—from which not all the Jews need to emigrate. It is not a question of quantity as of quality.... We are very anxious to bring the Jews of Morocco over... but we cannot count on the Jews of Morocco to build the country, because they have not been educated for this.... So we need people who will remain steadfast in any hardship and who have a high degree of resistance. For the purpose of building up our country, I would say that *the Jews of Eastern Europe are the salt of the earth*... [emphasis added].[33]

The statements by Ben-Gurion and others demonstrate the self-declared missionary tasks of European Zionists insofar as they project their own European experience onto non-European Jews. The "primitiveness" of African and Asian Jews is a result of their diasporic condition, which must be characterized by oppression. The task of European Jewish Zionists, therefore, was not only to "save" these Jews from what Zionism considered to be their "unfortunate" situation, but just as importantly to place them back on the right track to European Jewish civilization as the latter had recently been transformed by Zionism.

Upon arrival in Israel, Mizrahi immigrants were sprayed with DDT (Dichloro-Diphenyl-Trichloroethane) to "disinfect" them and "delouse" them.[34] One of the more cruel chapters of that period involved the kidnapping of hundreds of children of Yemeni immigrants from the transit camps in Israel.[35] The children were given to childless Ashkenazi couples for adoption in and outside Israel. Yemeni parents whose children were sick were taken from them to hospitals where the parents were prevented from going. The parents were later told that their children had died and were buried. Petitions were sent to the police inquiring about the missing children. The Minister of Police did not reply. Ironically, twenty years later, in 1968, the Ministry of Defense sent military draft notices to the addresses of the parents of these children. An investigation was launched by the Knesset in March 1968, but no satisfactory answers were found. The conspiracy was, in fact, sophisticated enough to produce fraudulent death certificates for some of the kidnapped children and to obfuscate all attempts by the children's parents to investigate this crime for decades. On their part, government bureaus hid and manipulated information about the crimes.[36] In 1986, a massive public rally was held by The Public Committee for the Discovery of the Missing Yemeni Children. According to Ella Shohat, the rally was virtually ignored by the Israeli media. Several months later, however, Israeli television broadcast a documentary on the subject blaming the bureaucratic chaos at the time for unfortunate "rumors," and perpetuating the myth that Mizrahi parents are careless and irresponsible breeders.[37]

The important task for European Zionism as it was discursively determined then was twofold: to "civilize" and "raise" the cultural levels of non-European Jews to European standards, without being "brought down" to their "primitive" levels of culture. Ben-Gurion was quite clear on this when he stated that

> those [Jews] from Morocco had no education. Their customs are those of Arabs . . . The Moroccan Jew took a lot from the Moroccan Arabs. The culture of Morocco I would not like to have here. And I don't see what contribution present [Jewish] Persians have to make . . . We do not want Israelis to become Arabs. We are in duty bound to fight against the spirit of the Levant, which corrupts individuals and societies, and preserve the authentic Jewish values as they crystallized in the [European] Diaspora.[38]

Zionism's contradictory valorization of European diaspora culture and its simultaneous denigration of it is clarified by Ben-Gurion's statements. Whereas, according to Zionism's dictates, all Jewish diaspora cultures and languages are to be replaced by the new gentile Israeli culture which uses for its language a new and modern Hebrew, European-assimilated Jewish culture brought from the European diaspora would constitute that new Israeli culture.

In 1949, with the continuing massive Mizrahi immigration to Israel, the Ashkenazi journalist Arye Gelblum echoed these sentiments when he wrote in Israel's liberal and respected newspaper *Ha'Aretz* that:

> This is an immigration of a race we have not yet known in the country . . . We are dealing with people whose primitivism is at a peak, whose level of knowledge is one of virtually absolute ignorance, and worse who have little talent for understanding anything intellectual. Generally, they are only slightly better than the general level of the Arabs, Negroes and Berbers in the same regions. In any case, they are at an even lower level than what we knew with regard to the former Arabs of Eretz Yisrael [i.e. the Palestinians] . . . *These Jews also lack roots in Judaism, as they are totally subordinated to the play of savage and primitive instincts* . . . [emphasis added].[39]

Arrival and discrimination

Upon their arrival in Israel, Mizrahi Jews were crammed in Ma'abarot or transit camps under very poor conditions, while Ashkenazi immigrants were given the homes of the displaced Palestinian population. Many demonstrations took place in the camps protesting, inter alia, discrimination, food shortages, and lack of medical care.[40] The transit camps were erected next to Ashkenazi settlements and large cities in order to provide them with cheap labor. This was induced by the government who after the initial provision of meager rations and social services informed the camp residents that they needed to provide for themselves through work in the Ashkenazi settlements. Due to the high level of unemployment, many Mizrahim, regardless of level of education or skills, had to take up menial unskilled jobs which were the only ones offered them.[41]

Many demonstrations erupted throughout the country in 1949 protesting this situation. In Ashkelon (formerly Majdal), thousands of Mizrahim marched against ethnic discrimination. Similarly, 300 Mizrahi residents from Ramleh staged a "noisy" demonstration in Allenby Street demanding "bread and work" and tried to storm the old Knesset building until they were held back by the Israeli police.[42] Two weeks later, Mizrahim stormed the Jewish Agency building in Haifa and went on a rampage inside the Department of Absorption. They demanded "work and housing." This time the police only managed to overpower them by bringing in reinforcements. Some demonstrators were injured and others were arrested.[43] In July of the same year, Mizrahi demonstrators from Jaffa attacked the former parliament building in Tel Aviv.[44]

In 1952, the Israeli government decided to send the Mizrahi immigrants, particularly, the Moroccans, to Development Towns (Ayarot Pituah) which were largely in rural and frontier areas and which predictably became the target of Arab military attacks. The government's declared policy was to "strengthen the borders" not only against military attacks but also against Palestinian refugees, "infiltrators," trying to return to their homes. Mizrahi immigrants were taken immediately upon arrival to remote areas in the Negev, the Lebanese border and other remote areas.[45] Between 1952 and 1956, 42 percent of the immigrants were taken to the Negev, 42 percent to the Galilee, 8 percent to the Jerusalem area, and 8 percent to the coastal areas.[46] The Development Towns as their name indicates were intended to "develop" the Mizrahim. This modernization schema did not apply to European Jews as their development had already taken place, according to Zionist discourse, during their residence in Europe.

Most of these Development Towns depend on a single factory that is either owned by the state, the Histadrut or Ashkenazi businesses. Over 85 percent of the factory managers are Ashkenazi (who do not live in the towns).[47] Wages in the Development Towns are much lower than the rest of the country. This is the case even within the same industry. In fact, according to the Israeli social scientist, Shlomo Swirski, the wages are not only low, they keep getting lower and lower.[48] The towns are ironically highly "undeveloped," with high levels of unemployment, poor health and educational services.[49]

Those Mizrahim who were not settled in Development Towns were settled in Moshavim or Cooperative Villages which were also located in border and remote areas in the country.[50] These Moshavim are to be distinguished from the old Ashkenazi Moshavim set up before Israel's creation. The Ashkenazi Moshavim (which today form 65 out of the total of 402 Moshavim) are rich settlements with good land, machinery and livestock. The Mizrahi Moshavim were given some of the worst land in the country in comparison with the Ashkenazi Kibbutzim and Moshavim which received the best land. Of all funds invested in agriculture 54 percent went to the Kibbutzim and 37 percent to the Moshavim, in spite of the fact that the Kibbutzim constitute 12 percent of all agricultural settlement in the country and the Moshavim constitute 66 percent.[51] As Gideon Giladi explained, the Ashkenazi settlements were built in the center of the country, which facilitates marketing and maximizes profits, the opposite of the post-1948 Moshavim.

The Mizrahim who ended up in the cities did not fare much better than their Development Towns and Moshavim counterparts, as they live in slums in the big cities of Tel Aviv, Jerusalem, Haifa, and Birsheba. It is in these urban slums that future Mizrahi resistance to racism and economic deprivation would arise. According to Gideon Giladi, the

> only basic economic difference between the development towns and the slum areas is geographic. The development towns lie in the country and supply the Ashkenazi settlements with cheap labour whereas the slum areas form a belt around the large towns and supply Ashkenazi capital [including Ashkenazi Kibbutzim and Moshavim] with cheap labour. They also provide servants for Ashkenazi women.[52]

The situation in the slums is characterized by overcrowding due to lack of housing, low quality educational services, and high unemployment. A majority of the women and girls in these slums have been transformed into a cheap army of domestic laborers. As a result of the extreme poverty in the slums, many women turned to prostitution as a means of survival. According to the Israeli Ministry of Labor and Social Affairs, 97 percent of prostitutes in the country in 1981 were of Mizrahi origin, a profession virtually unknown among the Mizrahi communities before coming to Israel.[53]

Political recruitment Ashkenazi-style

Since the massive arrival of the Mizrahi population in the years 1948–1951, Israel's Ashkenazi parties rushed to the scene to recruit supporters from among the immigrants. This was easily done due to the fact that these parties controlled the allocation of resources to the immigrants. The ruling party Mapai enjoyed wide control over the political and economic system.[54] As the ruling party, Mapai also controlled the Labor Exchange, the Sick Fund and housing companies rendering membership in it highly beneficial. Mapai's practice of favoritism in delivering services to its members was a widespread phenomenon.[55] This patronage system pervaded every aspect of Israeli state–society relations.[56] Much of what the parties promised the immigrants was generally beyond the party's capacity or wishes to deliver. In 1951, G. Yosephtal, the chairman of the Absorption Department of the Jewish Agency and a central figure in Mapai, wrote in his diary that "in the period of the elections we created havoc in the cooperative immigrant villages and in the transit camps by meaningless promises and by the base system of vote buying."[57] From the outset, most of the Mizrahi immigrants (those living in the Ma'abarot) could not elect their leaders due to their classification as "temporary residents." Even when they did elect leaders contravening the authorities, the Ministry of Interior rejected them stating that the local state-appointed authorities were the only recognized authorities. In the new immigrant towns that had their own elected local government, special regulations were passed restricting their authority, a practice unprecedented in any of the Ashkenazi towns. In fact, the first local council in a new settlement was nominated by the Minister of Interior rather than elected. When such councils were elected, the Ministry curtailed their powers whereby the approval of the Minister was required for all important appointments.[58] In general, the Mapai-controlled government bypassed the locally elected Mizrahi leadership recruiting their own Mizrahi agents in the camps as well as in the towns.

The foregoing discussion illuminates some of the central contradictions of Zionist thinking in relation to its secondary clients, the Mizrahim. Having lost what it considered to be the main beneficiaries of its state-building project as a result of the holocaust, Zionism had to devise new ways of reconceptualizing its project. Its commitment to a European-like assimilated Jewish culture manifested itself in the movement's very axioms from the beginning. Transforming Jews into gentile Europeans while continuing to identify them as Jews was always already the cornerstone of its success in the recruitment of support from the anti-Semitic European empires of the time, and its recruitment of the Westernized East-European Jewish intelligentsia. Ultimately, however, whereas theoretical Zionism might have been idealistic, practical Zionism could not afford such chimeras. For European Jews to continue to run Zionism and Israel according to their own ideals and goals, it became necessary for them to devise a thorough program of Europeanization of Zionism's non-European Jewish clients. This discourse, which assigns Europeans the position of adults who have endured a backward childhood on the way to development, portrays them now as being in a position to "help" Third World children to experience growing pains with the goal of European-style civilization as the set telos of this maturation process. Israeli state policies toward the Mizrahim are underlaid by this very evolutionary philosophy from which all such policies derive their legitimacy.

Resisting discrimination—the Wadi al-Salib uprising[59]

It was in the summer of 1959 in Wadi al-Salib where Mizrahi resistance to Ashkenazi discrimination first erupted on a large scale. Before the protest took place, however, Wadi al-Salib referred to a large part of downtown Haifa which used to be inhabited by the large Palestinian population of Haifa and from which that population had been expelled by advancing Zionist troops in 1948.[60] The empty houses were quickly given to new immigrants and soon became overpopulated. By the end of the fifties, the slum/neighborhood was inhabited by a majority Mizrahi population (mostly Moroccan) living in very poor conditions.[61]

A few months before the protest, a small group of residents had set up a group under the leadership of David Ben-Haroush called "The Union of North African Immigrants." The main goal of the group was to deal with the problems confronted by North African immigrants in their neighborhood. The first thing the group did was stop all political parties (which are invariably Ashkenazi-dominated) from entering the neighborhood so as to avoid manipulation of the immigrants by the parties—a common occurrence since 1948—and to weaken the influence of the party agents (who were recruited from among the immigrants themselves) over the rest of the neighborhood. The immediate cause of the uprising was the granting of comfortable housing to new Ashkenazi immigrants from Poland when thousands of Mizrahim were still living in extremely poor housing conditions. Moreover, the Israeli government bought additional apartments from private companies for the Ashkenazi immigrants, and at the last minute gave apartments that were built to house Mizrahim to the Polish immigrants. The spark for the outbreak of the protest took place on July 8, when the police shot a Moroccan man in the street who, the police claimed, was drunk. The man was injured badly and rumors of his death circulated in the neighborhood. The next morning, the Union of North African Immigrants led demonstrations from the neighborhood to the police headquarters carrying black flags and chanting slogans against the police. According to Deborah Bernstein's account of the affair, the police met with a delegation from the demonstrators, promised to look into the affair and peacefully dispersed the crowd. Despite this, rioting began in the neighborhood. Residents threw stones at police cars that patrolled the area and at police forces, which led to injuries and arrests. Three weeks later, events reached a crisis when the Mapai party decided to hold an election rally on the outskirts of the neighborhood with loudspeakers directed at the neighborhood. All movement into Haifa from concentrations of Moroccan immigrants were stopped the morning of the rally. Large reinforcements of police forces were brought in, including the border guard. During the rally shouting began and soon led to violent clashes between the police and the demonstrators that lasted into the night. The police intervened behaving "as if they were putting down an incipient revolution, causing serious causalities amongst women and old men."[62] Eventually they were able to corner the leaders of the uprising, including Ben-Haroush, who opened fire on them as they moved in. Ben-Haroush was finally arrested along with the other leaders of the Union of North African Immigrants. Some of the arrested leaders were beaten up, tried, and sentenced.

Wadi al-Salib's uprising spread to other parts of the country, especially the Mizrahi camps. Spontaneous demonstrations took place with the demonstrators committing acts of sabotage and arson against government buildings causing millions of dollars worth of damage. Branches of the Union were established in various regions of the country though there was no organizational contact with the Haifa leaders. An attempt was made to establish a political party headed by Ben-Haroush (who was still in prison) to run for the upcoming elections. The party's platform called for equal treatment to all and called for an end to Ashkenazi discrimination against the Mizrahim. The party also called for all Mizrahim to leave the Ashkenazi parties and their "Oriental lackeys" and turn to the new party which represented their "real interests."[63] The party, according to Deborah Bernstein, was a failure, even in Wadi al-Salib where Mapai gained more votes than the neighborhood list.

State response

The Israeli state responded to the uprising in a number of ways. The swiftest response was coercion. Many people were detained including four Union leaders who were sentenced to six months imprisonment. This was coupled with ideological delegitimation, whereby the government strongly denounced the demonstrators with ideological rhetoric. For example, three days after the first outbreak of protest, the Minister of Labor, Namir said:

> Only a confirmed enemy of the Jewish People could have invented this treacherous and corrupting deed of inflaming group against group. But we must beware of identifying the entire North African community who fulfill all their social, economic and military obligations, with a limited number of rioters and hooligans. Let us hope that the utmost wisdom and responsibility guide us in our efforts to overcome this dangerous barrier in our way to complete full integration, and may the God of Jewish fraternity be with us.[64]

The government's response included the personal stigmatization of leaders of protests as a means to divide the community. As the Union's leaders lay in prison, rumors were spread that the leaders were bought off and that they had been seen in Ramat Gan. According to Bernstein, the frequent cases in which people had been coopted before made such rumors easy to believe.

The government's strategy, however, was of the carrot and stick variety. While using its coercive apparatus to quell the rebellion, it also extended its recognition of some of the issues leading to the rebellion, thus legitimizing them. David Ben-Gurion's government formed an investigative committee headed by a member of the Israeli High Court to look into the matter, that is, the police shooting which led to the uprising. Whereas the published report gave an accurate account of the course of events, at the same time, it served to legitimate public policy and to denounce the protest. The report stressed that "we don't have the least shade of a doubt that no conscious discrimination exists on the part of the state institutions."[65] The leaders of the uprising were presented implicitly and explicitly as agitators and as threats to Jewish solidarity. The report also insisted that the immigrants themselves were the source of their "feelings of discrimination and deprivation."

The report's authors proceeded to state that:

> The uprooting of the community from an established pattern of life brought with it, for some sections of this ethnic group, a deterioration of values and social frameworks. The transition period [ostensibly to Ashkenazi levels of modernity and civilization], until the formulation and consolidation of new patterns, contains inevitably, grave dangers... An additional factor which enhanced the difficulty of integration of these immigrants was the large size of the families which increased problems of integration, housing and income... Various public organizations and associations from within the ethnic group and outside it reinforced the feeling of separation and discrimination. They built their future, not on constructive work for the improvement of the social, economic and cultural standards of the community, but on the cultivation of the feeling of deprivation.[66]

In addition, attempts at cooptation formed part of the carrot response. In fact, this proved a successful strategy, as some of the leaders were to be later coopted by the government, including Ben-Haroush himself who was subsequently given a new flat and a job.[67]

In the long run, the state took two steps. Rather than renovate and rehabilitate the neighborhood as many of its residents wanted, the residents were dispersed with many of them forcefully compelled to move out to housing estates as the only way out to improve their conditions. The area became deserted. In 1984, the Israeli government built the neighborhood up again as part of Haifa's Commercial and Business District.[68] The second step was to increase the number of Mizrahim among Mapai's Knesset members in the 1959 elections, which took place after the uprising. Other parties followed suit, but to a much lesser extent. This, however, hardly increased Mizrahi representation, since the new Mizrahi Knesset members were those Ashkenazi-appointed functionaries of the parties among the immigrants. This strengthened the position of these individuals who were (and were viewed by the Mizrahi community as) coopted by the Ashkenazi parties "reinforcing the myth that no true leadership has any chance."[69] Four years later, in 1963, the secret "Front for National Equality" was founded by a number of Mizrahim and was immediately eliminated by Shabak, Israel's secret police. For "security reasons," there was a complete media blackout on the event.[70]

The Black Panthers

Israeli government and academic officials viewed the problems encountered by Mizrahi Jews as stemming from their "primitive" backgrounds, which through the process of Ashkenazi-induced modernization would soon disappear. The infamous "gap" according to these officials and academics would close with time. Many sociological works "analyzed" the "modernization" process required to advance the Mizrahi population. This, they asserted, would involve educational and cultural formulae to be applied to the Mizrahim. One of the earliest "scholarly" works on the topic was written in 1949 by the prominent Israeli Ashkenazi sociologist Shmuel Noah Eisenstadt.[71] As Ella Shohat points out, Eisenstadt was heavily influenced by the American structural–functionalist school prevalent at the time. Like his American counterparts, Eisenstadt analyzed the Mizrahi situation as characterized by "social gaps" and not as resulting from class and ethnic stratification resulting from both intentional and unintentional policies carried out by the Israeli government, and the socioeconomic situation from which the different immigrant groups came and in which they were absorbed.[72] Eisenstadt proposed that the Mizrahim had to be desocialized from their "traditional" cultures and resocialized into Israeli (read Ashkenazi) modern culture for modernization to yield results. The endemic ethnocentrism within the Israeli government and more importantly within the Ashkenazi-dominated Israeli academe was so pervasive that books titled The *Rehabilitation of Impaired Intelligence* or *They Think Again*[73] were still characteristic of the type of "scholarship" produced by the various social science disciplines in the country well into the seventies and beyond. This academic consensus provided the ideological framework for government policies toward and views of the Mizrahim with scientific respectability. Such pseudo-scientific analyses led to (among other policies) the establishment of schools for the "culturally deprived" Mizrahi children.[74]

By 1970, the socioeconomic, cultural and political relations between the Ashkenazi and Mizrahi communities were basically unchanged.[75] As mentioned above, it was in the late sixties that the tragedy of the abduction of Yemeni children, which had taken place two decades earlier, resurfaced. It was also around the same time that stories broke out about the Israeli government's involvement in the bombings of Iraqi synagogues and Iraqi Jewish businesses in the early 1950s, and its collaboration with the then Iraqi government of Nuri al-Sa'id which resulted in the mass exodus of Iraqi Jewry.[76] Moreover, during the 1969–1970 period, tension increased substantially in Israeli society mainly on the issue of the new Soviet immigrants and the benefits they were receiving. In the mid-sixties, the Israeli government had offered special material benefits to new immigrants (mainly Ashkenazi) primarily to encourage immigration from affluent Western countries. The Soviet immigrants were the first group of these immigrants to enjoy these benefits. Furthermore, the media and government officials gave the Soviet immigrants an especially warm reception, with Golda Meir appearing at the airport day after day with tearful eyes receiving Israel's most recent "ascenders."[77] Meir welcomed the Ashkenazi '*olim* proclaiming

> you are the real Jews. We have been waiting for you for 25 years. You speak Yiddish!...Every loyal Jew must speak Yiddish, for he who does not know Yiddish is not a Jew. You are a superior breed—you will provide us with heroes.[78]

Meir's statements reflect the double valence that Yiddish holds in Zionist discourse: European Jews who spoke Yiddish in the diaspora are valorized as Zionism's clients and as Israeli citizens, while their diasporic Jewish culture is refused in favor of an assimilated cosmopolitan gentile-based culture in Israel. Meir's warm reception and warmer statements increased the resentment of Israeli Mizrahim who contrasted the lavish reception accorded the Ashkenazim with the DDT reception which awaited them upon their arrival twenty years earlier. They "regarded this as proof of discrimination by the government and of expressed preference of 'Russians' to other groups."[79] The situation was further exacerbated by the racism of the new immigrants toward the Mizrahim. For example, Russian immigrants sent petitions to the Tel Aviv Town Hall to express their indignation at having to live next to "Black" Jews whom they termed "Levantine and uncivilized." The Russians threatened to leave the country unless the government satisfied their demands.[80] The Israeli government responded by removing Mizrahi children from the Ashkenazi schools and the youth clubs in the area and, in some places, kept them out of local swimming pools, as it did in Neveh Sharet. These measures led to more anger whereby some Mizrahi slum residents stoned new Russian immigrants, many of whom left to the United States in search of a higher standard of living.[81]

This situation occurred amidst the unprecedented economic boom experienced by Israel in the wake of the 1967 Arab/Israeli war. This boom exacerbated ethnic grievances due to the increase in the economic "gap" between the Ashkenazim and Mizrahim by rendering more visible the accruing economic benefits to the Ashkenazim, with no parallel development for the majority of the Mizrahim. Also, the context of these events was the post-1967 Arab/Israeli War in which Mizrahim had fought. The Mizrahi participation in the War helped to legitimate their Israeli identity which had always been put in doubt by prevalent Ashkenazi attitudes, which stressed that it was the Ashkenazim who had founded the State and had fought in the "War of Independence," in 1948, and that it was the Ashkenazim, as the Mizrahim's benefactors, who had brought the Mizrahim to an already established Israel. In addition, the 1970 signing of a cease-fire agreement with Egypt ending the "War of Attrition," removed the external threat factor which had until then kept the lid on internal problems. It was with this as background that the "Panterim Sh'horim," or Black Panthers, were formed at the end of 1970.[82]

Another factor affecting the rise of the Black Panthers was plans to gentrify the Musrara slum from which the panthers emerged. After the 1967 occupation of Palestinian East Jerusalem, Musrara acquired sudden strategic economic importance located as it was between the two halves of the city. The Israeli government wanted to raze the old Palestinian houses and build new luxury housing for the arriving Ashkenazi immigrants. This implied the expulsion of the Mizrahi residents which inflamed Mizrahi anger.[83]

The name "Black Panthers" was borrowed from the American Black Panthers, due to the important resonances it would have in Israeli society. Aside from the alleged anti-Semitism of which the American group was accused by Israel and the American Jewish establishment, the projection of the image of Israeli Jews as an ethnically divided society at war with itself jolted an image-conscious Israel. The term "Black," moreover, was one that Mizrahim found suitable due to the similarity of their conditions to that of black Americans and the fact that they were (and still are) often referred to as "Black" by Ashkenazi racists.[84]

The Black Panthers emerged at the end of 1970 and the beginning of 1971 in response to these conflicts and tensions. They began as a slum youth movement from Musrara. For years they protested state discrimination and maltreatment, calling for equality. Whereas the Panthers never achieved a broad grassroots organization, their impact was far reaching, affecting many aspects of the future of Mizrahi life in Israel.

The first massive demonstration led by the Black Panthers took place on March 3, 1971, before the Jerusalem City Hall.[85] Many more demonstrations followed through August of the same year, sometimes drawing between five and ten thousand people.[86] Some of the demonstrators shouted "Golda, teach us Yiddish."[87] The Black Panthers asserted that the Ashkenazi system blocked their chances for advance and denied them the very means of altering their conditions. Moreover, the Mizrahim, the Panthers believed, "had been oppressed and cheated by the Ashkenazi-dominated establishment or even used for its ulterior purposes."[88]

The March demonstration popularized the Black Panthers among Mizrahi slum youth who were to join the demonstrations. Demonstrations were also to take place in other slum areas especially in Hatikvah, in Tel Aviv, where the government used the border guards to crush a June demonstration. A later demonstration in the Hatikvah neighborhood was put down by Herut members (Menachem Begin's party).[89] In May 1971, at one of their largest demonstrations, 260 Black Panthers' supporters were arrested by the police who intervened to break up the demonstration. The chief of police at the time, Shlomo Hillel, who is of Iraqi origin, was termed by the demonstrators "the black collaborator."[90] More demonstrations followed in January and May 1972 in which more police clashes led to shootings. The May 1972 shooting of Ovadia Harari, a demonstrator, sparked off more demonstrations.

After the first demonstrations, the Panthers were approached by several members of the Knesset representing different parties. The Panthers met with senior ministers and the prime minister herself. They also met with members of the Histadrut and the Jewish Agency. Such establishment interest in the movement, however, was to decline significantly after the Panthers increasing inability and failure to mobilize the population against the Israeli government after 1972. The meetings with government leaders, however, were designed by the government to appease or coopt the Panthers' leadership. Most, however, were insulted by the government's and especially Meir's "paternalistic" attitude toward them. The Prime Minister had stated that the Panthers "were good boys, and I hope that they are some among them who will be good boys; but there are a few, I am afraid, who will not change any more."[91] The Panthers' goals included the elimination of slums, free education for those in need, free housing for those in need, the elimination of juvenile delinquency institutions (which housed many Mizrahi youth and in which Panthers' leaders had spent time), increased wages for those supporting large families, and full representation of Mizrahim in all institutions.[92]

State response

As in the aftermath of the Wadi al-Salib uprising, the Israeli state responded to the demonstrations in similar ways. It began by using coercion to put down the demonstrations. Aside from police brutality used in quelling the force of the demonstrations, the government used detention, trials, fines, and suspended sentences in its dealing with the Black Panthers Movement and its supporters. This was coupled with ideological delegitimation of the Panthers and their cause. The government and the Ashkenazi-dominated media emphasized the Panthers' connections to the anti-Zionist Left[93] "which in Israel is enough to put a group beyond the pale of legitimate political action."[94] Delegitimation was also achieved by government repudiation of the Panthers' "violent means" when, in fact, their peaceful demonstrations had outnumbered the violent ones.[95] The government's strategy was supplemented by the personal stigmatization of the leaders of the protests as a means to divide the community. This was done by constant references to the delinquent past of many of the Panthers' leaders and to their being "hardened criminals." This amounted to character assassination of these leaders to ensure that the Mizrahi population would find them objectionable as representatives of Mizrahi ethnic concerns.

Like its previous carrot and stick strategy used to end the Wadi al-Salib uprising, the Israeli government recognized the legitimacy of some of the protesters' concerns. The government tried to depoliticize the Panthers by individualizing their claims, which the government claimed could easily be solved on a personal basis.[96] Following the demonstrations, the government set up the Horovitz Committee to enquire into the "problems." The task of the Committee was to look into the government's official position that the "lower educational level of the Sephardim has caused them to be discriminated against." The Committee's report however reached the opposite conclusion asserting that "as the educational level of the Sephardim is raised, they meet more discrimination." The Committee added that the Mizrahi standard of living had actually declined between 1959 and 1969.[97] Finally, the government launched a cooptation campaign of the Panthers' leadership on an individualist basis. However, many in the Panthers' leadership resisted such attempts.

The decline in support for the Black Panthers evidenced by the dwindling number of participants at their demonstrations pressed the movement's leaders to find a way out of the impasse. Consequently, the Panthers decided to establish themselves as a political party and run for the 1973 elections. They joined up with the Mizrahi MK (member of Knesset) Shalom Cohen's party, the Israeli Democrats, calling the new party the Black Panthers-Israeli Democrats, although the party soon became known as simply the Black Panthers. The party won 1.6 percent at the Histadrut's convention placing three of their members on the Histadrut's Executive Committee. Soon after the elections, the 1973 Arab/Israeli war broke out shifting popular attention back to issues of national security. After the war, the Panthers ran in the 1973 December elections failing to get one candidate in the Knesset or in any of the twenty-six local councils for which they ran.[98] As a result of their electoral failure, the Panthers splintered into Zionist and anti-Zionist factions.[99]

Failure and success

The failure of the Black Panthers movement to become a mass movement with the ability to mobilize large sectors of the Mizrahi community and exact major concessions from the Israeli state can be attributed to a variety of reasons. Foremost among them is the hegemony of Zionist discourse throughout all aspects of every day Israeli life. Unlike Palestinian Arab citizens of the state of Israel, who are not considered clients of Zionist Ideology and against whom the Israeli state has always used coercion as the preferable (but not only) method of control and repression, Mizrahim are specifically targeted as clients by Zionism. The hegemony of Zionist discourse through educational institutions, cultural production, the media, and official government policy contribute to the delegitimation of any Jewish claimant whose grievances question the central tenets of Zionism, including the "unity" of the Jewish people in their building a post-diasporic community and state, and in fighting gentile enemies. This hegemony, however, can be coupled with coercive measures on an ad hoc basis, as the events at Wadi al-Salib or the reaction to the Panthers show. In fact, fear of government repression, arrests and torture was one such reason discouraging many Panthers' supporters from joining the movement or even to show public solidarity with it. This was evidenced by the small number of demonstrators following major government crack downs on Panthers' leaders and supporters. Fear of government and establishment repression included fear of losing one's job and livelihood. Another dimension of the Israeli state's ideological and structural hegemony was manifested in the continued effectiveness of the Israeli government's cooptation efforts of the Panthers. Whereas the government failed to coopt the majority of the Panthers' leaders, it was able to coopt some members with jobs and better housing.

As Gideon Giladi argued, the Panthers' lack of an economic base on which to rely was an important structural factor contributing to their failure. Unlike most parties in Israel which have an economic base (Mapai's economic base is the Histadrut and Histadrut-owned corporations, Mapam's is in the Kibbutzim, Herut, private capital, etc.), the Panthers have no such base for their membership, and their supporters were mostly from the impoverished slums or students. In addition, the majority of Mizrahim live outside the sphere in which the Panthers operated. Whereas the Panthers' major support came from the poor slums, the majority of Mizrahim live in the development towns and the Moshavim (where there was unorganized support for the Panthers). Also, the Panthers' leadership itself came from the margins of Israeli society. They had little education, a situation which prevented the establishment of connections with the trade unions, professionals, and the small Mizrahi business class—some of whose members did in fact support the Panthers' cause. Although it should be stressed that unlike other countries where trade unions and left parties ordinarily support the poorest sectors of society and oppressed ethnic minorities, Israeli trade unions and left parties (including Rakah), which are Ashkenazi dominated, are only willing to support the Mizrahim as workers, and not as an oppressed ethnic group. The Israeli government policy of delegitimation was successful in presenting the

Panthers leaders as "riffraff," thus alienating many including Mizrahi university students (who supported the movement from afar) from joining the movement.[100] This was coupled by the stigmatization of anyone in the community who would voice open support for the Panthers as traitors to the Jewish people and the state of Israel.

Furthermore, lack of organizational experience on the part of the Panthers' leaders led to many internal disagreements which, in turn, led to the splintering of the movement and its cooptation by left establishment and/or Ashkenazi-dominated parties. Some of the reasons for the split were over the issue of solidarity with the Palestinians. This coupled with the issue of national security, which the break out of the 1973 War brought about, was effectively used by the Israeli government, which was able to defuse much of the tension that the Panthers had brought to the fore through invoking the need for unity in the face of external danger.

The Panthers continued to launch and participate in demonstrations against the Israeli government's domestic and foreign policies. A major demonstration followed the Israeli police shooting and murdering of a Yemeni, Shimon Yehoshua, on December 22, 1982. The murder took place in the context of the arrival of the police at Yehoshua's house in Kfar Shalem in Tel Aviv intent on destroying an extra room Yehoshua had added to his house without a government license. Yehoshua was shot while resisting police attempts at demolishing the room (a common practice against Palestinians but not Ashkenazim).[101] Many youths organized demonstrations, burnt tires in the streets and splashed graffiti on the walls such as "Ashke-Nazis,"[102] a, by now, common epithet leveled against the Ashkenazim by Mizrahi demonstrators. Massive demonstrations broke out a few days after the murder prompting the Knesset to delay the burial of Yehoshua until nightfall to prevent disturbances.[103] Following the demolition of more than 100 buildings in Kfar Shalem which took place in 1984, two years after the murder of Yehoshua, more bloody clashes occurred. Demonstrators set fire to a warehouse, blocked the main streets shouting "Ashke-Nazis" at the police.[104]

With the realization on the part of many Mizrahim that extra-systemic movements like the Black Panthers were doomed to fail due to government repression, inter alia, systemic routes, being the only alternative left, became more valued. This led to the biggest mass protest vote in Israeli history on the part of a majority of Mizrahim whose vote helped to bring the Likud Coalition to power in 1977, ending, for the first time since Israel's creation, the one-party monopoly of the State by Mapai/Ma'rakh.[105] Consequently, while the Israeli state's ideological hegemony along with its coercive apparatus contributed to the failure of the Black Panthers and the Union of North African Immigrants before them to bring about substantial material gain to the Mizrahim, the Mizrahi sense of oppression was rechanneled into a successful protest vote in support of the most viable opposition to the governing party (perceived as the Ashkenazi party par excellence), the Likud—that party's ideological and political record on the Mizrahim notwithstanding.[106]

Whereas the Black Panthers' emergence on the Israeli political scene was short-lived, their impact was far-reaching. Unlike the North African-based uprising in Wadi al-Salib, the Panthers' struggle was organized around an identity encompassing all those that Zionism identified as Sephardim and later as Mizrahim. It was after the rise of the movement that Mizrahim began openly demanding cultural rights that had remained repressed until then.

Encouraged by the Panthers' example, an important group emerged in the mid and late seventies. Between 1975 and 1978, the Ma'atz Organization launched many arson and sabotage operations against Israeli state and economic institutions including, according to the Israeli police,[107] plans to blow up the police headquarters of Tel Aviv and the kidnapping of Israeli Minister of Justice, Shmuel Tamir.[108]

One of the Panthers' successes was the momentum they created leading to the 1980's rise of many more groups and organizations representing diverse Mizrahi interests: Ohalim (tents), Oded, the Black Belt Movement, East for Peace, Ma'avak '85 (Struggle 85), etc.[109] extending from advocacy for better housing, increased employment and cultural rights to demands for political representation and solidarity with Palestinian Israelis and Palestinians in the Occupied Territories.

The 1980s and 1990s continued to witness more demonstrations and strikes against the various discriminatory policies of the Israeli state, the latest of which was in Ofakim at the end of 1995. The matter of the kidnapped Yemeni children also continues to mobilize the Mizrahim against the racism of the Ashkenazi state. In 1994, a force of 800 Israeli police officers laid a five-week siege to the home of the Yemeni-born Rabbi Uzi Meshulem and a few dozens of his Mizrahi followers in Yehud (near Petah Tikva) who were demanding information about the kidnapped children. The gathering was dubbed by the Israeli police and the Ashkenazi-dominated media as a cult-like sect à la US Branch Davidians. It was reported that Meshulem's followers were "heavily armed." The Israeli police killed one person and arrested eighteen others. Rabbi Meshulem was lured out of the house and arrested. Following this confrontation, a new government committee was set up to look into the matter, the last having been set up in 1988.[110]

In the 1980s, some Mizrahim continued to call for armed struggle against the Israeli state as the only way to end racial discrimination.[111] At the same time, many Mizrahim were actively pursuing meetings with Palestinians, inside and outside Israel, including the PLO, as well as harassing the mostly Ashkenazi colonial-settlers on the West Bank and Gaza (Mizrahim constitute less than 8 percent of the settlers in the Occupied Territories). Solidarity with the Palestinians spanned the Mizrahi social spectrum: from the slums to the city intellectuals, many Mizrahim were linking the discrimination practiced against them with that used against the Palestinians.[112]

In 1986, the Committee for Israeli–Palestinian Dialogue was formed. Its founders supported the Palestinians' right to self-determination and the struggle for peace and democracy. Its leaders included, among others, the Morrocan Shlomo al-Baz and the Iraqis Sasson Somekh and Latif Dori (from the Labor party). As a result of the groups' meeting with Palestinian Israelis and Palestinians from the Occupied Territories as well as having PLO contacts, the Israeli government issued its

"Counter-Terrorism Act" in August 1986 forbidding any Israeli to meet with the PLO. In defiance of the Act, the group, which also included Ashkenazim, met with PLO officials in November 1986 in Romania. This meeting was followed by another one in Budapest in June 1987. A number of Mizrahim, including former Panther Moni Yakim and Ella Shohat, refused to participate in a joint delegation under the rubric of Israeli–Palestinian dialogue and insisted on a specifically Mizrahi–Palestinian dialogue. Such efforts combined with the support of the Paris-based Perspectives Judeo-Arabes culminated in the historic meeting which took place in July 1989 in Toledo, Spain, in which thirty-eight Mizrahi intellectuals from Israel and others from abroad attended. Among the Palestinians attending was Mahmud Abbas (Abu Mazen) and the Palestinian poet Mahmud Darwish. Many of the Mizrahi delegates addressed the meeting in their native tongue, Arabic.[113]

Despite the intensity of many of these protests and the emergence of a strong Mizrahi cultural identity, the majority of Mizrahim remained within the fold of (Ashkenazi) Israeli society—which attests to the strength and resilience of the Israeli state's hegemonic Zionist ideology. Still, many among them continued to struggle against their situation. Such examples include the Morrocan Mordechai Vanunu who in 1986 blasted the Israeli nuclear program in an interview with *The Sunday Times* of London, an act that resulted in his kidnapping in Europe by the Mossad, landing him in jail with no outside contact for a decade and a half. Others like former Black Panthers Kochavi Shemesh and Sa'adya Marciano, who had launched their Eastern (Mizrahi) Front in support of the Palestinians in 1986, were in the forefront of Israeli groups protesting Israeli repression during the first intifada.[114] Other organizations include the World Organization of Jews from Islamic Countries, which is a New York-based United Nations NGO on the Question of Palestine.

Other groups concerned with issues like educational discrimination against the Sephardim and the Palestinians became active. Such groups, like HILA or the Israel Committee on Education in Oriental Neighborhoods and Development Towns, established in 1987, fights for Mizrahi educational rights,[115] as does the group Kedma which was successful in setting up two alternative schools for Mizrahi children to escape Ashkenazi racism in schools (due to budgetary reasons and government harassment, one of the schools was forced to close down).[116] The two schools are located in Tel Aviv and Jerusalem, and are headed by the activist educators Sami Chetrit (Moroccan) and Clara Yona (Yemeni). Other more recent organizations include the Mizrahi Women Forum (Forum HaNashim HaMizrahiot), which was founded in 1994 and held its first conference in May 1996 in Natanya.[117]

The most important Mizrahi personality to emerge within the Israeli mainstream establishment in the 1990s was the Morrocan-born David Levy. Levy, an ideologically flexible figure, had broken away from Likud in June 1995 giving hope to some Mizrahi intellectuals and activists of establishing a Mizrahi party.[118] Some, like Sami Chetrit, helped him to write his platform, while others did not trust his political history and continued links to the Ashkenazi establishment.

Such hopes, however, were recently shattered when Levy was coopted back into Likud's fold by his former enemy Benjamin Netanyahu by promises for a senior post in the future cabinet.[119]

Five and a half decades after the Mizrahim came face to face with Ashkenazi racism in the context of Israel, their resistance continues unabated. Although, the Ashkenazi establishment has succeeded in assimilating most Mizrahim into Israeli identity and nationality, it has also deepened their sense of subjugation to Ashkenazi discrimination. Over the years, Mizrahi resistance took many forms, ranging from outright revolt and armed struggle to peaceful demonstrations and political organization. In this era of PLO-Israeli (read Ashkenazi) "peace," the place of the Mizrahim remains unclear. What is certain, however, is that until the arrival of one million Russian Jews in the 1990s, half of whom at least turned out to be Christian, Israel remained a country ruled by European Jews who constituted one-fifth of the population and who ruled over and discriminated against, mutatis mutandis, an Asian and African population of Jews, Muslims and Christians, who constituted four-fifths of the country's population. The arrival of Russian Jews increased the European population to about 40 percent, the Russians among whom are facing their own set of economic and cultural discrimination by the Ashkenazi establishment. This is the demographic distribution inside Israel today, excluding the 4 million Palestinians living in the Occupied Territories, and over whom the Ashkenazi establishment continues to rule by denying them all political rights. It is in this analytic context that the South African apartheid analogy, made by many, can be applied to Israel appropriately.[120]

Part II

Origins of the "Peace Process"

Transformation of the Palestinian political field

4 Palestinians and the limits of racialized discourse*

The discursive status of Palestinians in the West has changed in recent years. A new dynamism has infiltrated the static notions that ordinarily characterize Palestinians in Western discourse. Commentators and policy-makers from across the Western political spectrum have expressed views of Palestinians never voiced before. Clearly, the perception of Palestinians is undergoing a modest transformation whose outcome remains uncertain. This chapter is an attempt to describe the framework or landscape of this change in the racialized hegemonic discourse that posits its self-authorized subjects as "white," based on their genetic, religious, and geographical origins, which are in turn discursively determined, and to locate the changing place of Palestinians within it. To do so, I will examine two journalistic documents, which at first glance seem marginal, but which, as I will demonstrate, contain within them the central axioms of this discourse. As this chapter was written in 1992 and published in 1993, it analyzes developments until 1991. I explore developments after 1991 in subsequent chapters.

If we were to use a metaphor in order to describe the hegemonic Western discourse *vis-à-vis* Palestinians, we would see it as a discursive space that places Palestinians on its border, faced with checkpoints that mainly keep us out but do allow some entry. This has frustrated and excited many Palestinian intellectuals who feel that entering the dominant discourse and attempting in some ways to make it overlap with the discourse of Palestinian struggle will help to advance the Palestinian position in the Palestinian/Israeli conflict. This, I will argue, is a mistaken presumption. For the underlying axioms governing where Palestinians fit in this discourse are derived not from what Palestinians do or do not do, but from our discursive relation to European Jews. As I will also suggest, changes in the characterization of Palestinians in this discourse, which were brought about not by means of discursive strategies but by extra-discursive events—mainly Palestinian guerrilla attacks, Israel's 1982 invasion of Lebanon, and more recently the intifada, are pushing the axioms of the dominant discourse to the brink of a crisis that may or may not be reversible. These changes have resulted in a discursive dilemma whose resolution is yet to be determined. My aim here is to uncover and discuss the axioms which govern and disseminate them.

* This essay was first published in 1993.

When dealing with Palestinians, US political commentators range in views from the critical and "hostile" to the critical and "friendly." The different levels of hostility and friendliness expressed by different commentators appear (on the surface) to reflect fundamental differences of discursive positions. Hostile critics, like political commentator George Will, for example, oppose Palestinian nationhood and self-determination and vehemently defend what they consider to be Israeli interests. Nevertheless, Will was able to muster some words of sympathy for the Palestinians after the Sabra and Shatila massacres in 1982. He asserted "Palestinians have now had their Babi Yar, their Lidice. The Beirut massacre has altered the moral algebra of the Middle East producing a new symmetry of suffering."[1] Anthony Lewis, the *New York Times* columnist, occupies the other end of the spectrum, providing qualified support for Palestinian rights. Do such ostensibly divergent views reflect similar or different discursive frameworks?

In attempting to answer this question, I have chosen to look at two commentaries by Anthony Lewis.[2] The importance of the first commentary stems from the fact that it was written after the suspension of the US–PLO "dialogue" in 1990, which further marginalized the PLO. The suspension of the "dialogue," along with subsequent events, not the least of which was the US punishment of the PLO—after it distorted the PLO's stand on the Iraqi invasion of Kuwait—led to the Arab–Israeli "peace" conference in Madrid in 1991. The importance of the second commentary stems from its polemic against Israel's apologists and from its support of Palestinian rights. Although these two opinion pieces are marginal documents, they reflect the central axioms governing dominant views of the Palestinians.

In the commentary of June 5, 1990, Anthony Lewis calls on Chairman Arafat to condemn the then recent guerrilla attack by the Palestine Liberation Front on Israel's shores near Tel Aviv. Arafat's refusal to heed such calls resulted in the US suspension of the "dialogue." Reading Lewis's article, one is faced with a discursive arrangement which holds the victims more accountable than the oppressors. For example, Lewis recommends that Chairman Arafat condemn the attack on Israel, but makes no such recommendations to then prime minister Shamir or President Bush Sr in the wake of the Rishon Le Zion massacre committed a few days earlier by an Israeli gunman and the ensuing killings committed by the Israeli army. In the wake of the massacre at Rishon Le Zion, the US government stated that it was "distressed by the high number of Palestinians killed and wounded by Israeli troops in the violent aftermath of the killing of seven Arabs by the Israeli gunman."[3] The State Department added that the US government was "disturbed" by the number of casualties. The US government did not condemn the former Israeli soldier's slaughter of seven Palestinian workers; it was only "distressed" by the ensuing army killings. This reaction stands out in light of the entirely different US reaction to the failed Palestinian guerrilla attack on Israel, in which there were no Israeli casualties. The US government asserted that it was "horrified at this terrorist attack" and suspended its almost non-existent relations with the PLO.[4] Lewis does not mention this incongruence in the US position, let alone condemn it.

Lewis states that the Palestinian hunger strikers responding to the massacre at Rishon Le Zion "went on a hunger strike in Jerusalem after a deranged [*sic*]

Israeli killed seven Palestinians… Then came the raid. The leaders ended their hunger strike." The suggestion is that the strike was broken due to the raid. This, in fact, is far from what happened. The hunger strikers ended their thirteen-day protest on June 1, when they declared that they were breaking off official contacts with all US envoys and the US consulate-general in Jerusalem. This was in response to what they perceived as the Bush administration's responsibility for "aborting the international consensus" on the need to protect the unarmed Palestinians living under Israel's occupation. Their communiqué was issued after the US had vetoed the UN Security Council resolution, which called for sending a permanent UN team to the Occupied Territories.

Lewis accepts the Israeli government's claim that the Israeli gunman who massacred the Palestinians is "deranged." This is consistent with the then recent trend in Israel of labeling Israeli Jews committing acts embarrassing to the Israeli state as "deranged." First, on May 14, 1990, we learn that an Israeli Jew who defaced a Jewish cemetery in Haifa is "deranged," as declared by the police, although he stated that his (political) motive was to "unite Jews in their hatred of Arabs." Another Israeli Jew who confessed to defiling a Jewish cemetery in Lydda on May 17, 1990 was also considered "deranged." It is in this context that Ami Popper massacres seven Palestinians and is immediately considered "deranged." Lewis participates in this discursive framework by accepting the Israeli government's "explanation." It would be interesting to know how many psychiatric/psychological tests have been carried out on the surviving Palestinian guerrillas, who were captured by Israel, and whether they would qualify for the term "deranged."

"Deranged" is a relative judgment. When passing this judgment, one is implicitly contrasting such behavior with acceptable societal norms. In the case of Israel, as Alexander Cockburn has argued, the action of Ami Popper is no more deranged than the Israeli government's overall anti-Palestinian policy.[5] It is this policy which fosters an environment conducive to acts like Popper's. In fact, when Ami Popper was brought to trial for manslaughter (not for murder), the court asked five psychiatrists to evaluate him. They all concurred that he was sane and suitable to stand trial. The defense lawyer, unable to find any psychiatrist who would offer a contrary opinion, asked permission to drop the plea that Popper was "deranged."[6]

Going back to Lewis, it is clear that he does not question the Israeli account of the guerrilla attack itself. The *Washington Post* reported on May 31, 1991 that one of the guerrilla boats was within two hundred yards of a popular beach club which was packed for the holidays. "The bathers said the Palestinian fighters could have shot Israelis crowding the beach but did not fire." Lewis does not even consider such evidence contradicting the Israeli government's account.

The above distortions are not exceptional; indeed, they are characteristic of Lewis's commentaries on the Palestine Question. Yet Lewis is paraded by many as a voice sympathetic to Palestinians. This, of course, does not mean that there are no differences on the Palestine Question between Israel's apologists and Anthony Lewis. Such differences demonstrably exist. Nor does this argument imply that Anthony Lewis's support for the Palestinians is not genuine. It does imply, however, that the similarities Lewis and Israel's apologists share are a consequence of an all-pervasive discourse in which they have been produced and which Lewis has failed to question.[7]

The only discernible difference between the views of Lewis and Israel's supporters is on the unavoidable issue of real Palestinian physical victimization—deaths, injuries, deportation, detention, torture. Here Lewis supports Palestinians insofar as Palestinians are physical victims, that is *objects* of Israeli violence. But his support does not surpass that limit by much. When Palestinians assume a subject role (in this case our refusal to accept US dictates), condemnation ensues, as if in outrage that objects have presumptuously assumed the role of subjects. Once Palestinians exercise agency, we are considered uncritically to be "irrational" and are consequently dismissed.

Relating European Jews to Palestinian Arabs

It is the discursive status of European Jews that governs how they are viewed in the West in relation to Palestine, and how they are viewed in the Arab World, especially by Palestinians. Whereas, in the West, European Jews are refugees fleeing the Nazis and the subsequent horrors of post-holocaust Europe, survivors of a war of annihilation and victims of British commitments to the Arabs,[8] Palestinians view European Jews from our own direct experiences. For Palestinians, European Jews did not arrive as refugees but as invaders, whose sole purpose was to appropriate Palestine by any possible means in order to realize Zionist aspirations, which began before the rise of Hitler to power. Consequently, Palestinians view European Jews not as helpless refugees, but as armed *colons* committing massacres.[9]

This "transformation" in the status of European Jews which took place *en route* (from the shores of Europe to the shores of Palestine) is absent from the history provided by a racialized "white" discourse. At the outset, one must emphasize that the European Jewish colonial experience is not in itself unique, although the Jews' experience as holocaust-surviving refugees certainly is. Other Europeans had a similar colonial status when they embarked on colonial settlement of the "New World." Despite major historical differences, the Boers are also viewed as refugee/colonists. This, however, is not the case of the English settlers of Rhodesia, South Africa, Kenya, Australia, and New Zealand, nor was this the experience of the French *pieds noirs* in North Africa, or the Spanish and Portuguese *conquistadores* in the Americas. Certainly, most of the later Europeans who settled North America were not "refugees" either, excepting the early pilgrims who were fleeing different types of persecution.

Aside from the crucial difference in the holocaust experience, one of the other major differences between European Jewish emigrant/colonists and their gentile counterparts is the persistence of the refugee status accorded Jews, although that status is no longer applicable to either the Boers or the European settlers of North America. Surely the continued emigration of Jews from their respective homelands is a constant reminder of the "refugee" status the dominant discourse has accorded them, although this status is not accorded to the later gentile "immigrants" into North America, except immigrants from socialist countries. Although this racialized discourse accords these émigrés the status of "refugees" (while denying that status to Central American "brown" refugees), their status is not used as the primary justification for the continued subjugation of the Native American people.[10]

While it is a trivializing reductionism to say that a resolution to the Palestinian/Israeli "conflict" could be reached if Palestinians and the West (Israel being part of the West)[11] were to agree on the status of European Jewish emigrants, it is the difference between these views which *explains* all subsequent actions taken by both Palestinian Arabs and European Jews. A racialized discourse needs to "explain" these actions because they are being committed by discursively non-white, non-Christian peoples. While much of Israel's violence is "explained" by the pre-Israel status of European Jews, Palestinian violence is also viewed hermeneutically through the same status of those same Jews, the status of the Palestinians as products of our own separate history being deemed irrelevant. After all, "[t]he only history is white."[12] Israel's actions, however, are believed to stem from the status of those Jews who arrived on the shores of Palestine after fleeing the Nazi regime and the holocaust, only to be confronted by another violent anti-Semitic campaign, this time by Palestinian Arabs and Arabs from neighboring countries intent on expelling them from their last and only haven.[13] Thus, Israel's violence, regrettable as it may be, is in effect viewed as self-defensive in nature. In the same vein, Palestinian violence, which was/is in self-defense against foreign invaders, is also "explained" out of context as part of this anti-Semitic campaign against Jewish refugees. All discourse involving Palestinians and Israel has been and continues to be situated within the bounds of these hermeneutical axioms—whereby, among other qualities, Jews are *always* refugees fleeing the holocaust and are never viewed in the context of two separate histories and discourses. Much scholarship has been done on the systemic methods and cultural factors which institutionalized this view in the West.[14] What I would like to demonstrate is that such a view is, in effect, a translation of the experiences of European Jews and Palestinians.

Transforming Palestinians and Jews

Many Palestinian intellectuals are of the opinion that Palestinians need to learn the "right lingo" in order to do effective political work within the American system,[15] to gain the support of the US public to the Palestinian side. In a recent study of Palestinians and the "peace process" (based on a survey conducted by three Palestinian social scientists who interviewed forty "leading" Palestinians in the West Bank and Gaza Strip),[16] Palestinian scholars Elia Zureik *et al.* contrast the new generation of Palestinian intellectuals and leaders with the old one of more than twenty years ago.[17] Their conclusion is that there is "a significant generational difference that makes the new Palestinians what Karl Mannheim called a 'generation in itself,' able to learn from history and to imprint *its own style* on the present" (emphasis added).[18] In the next sentence, they inform us that the "new brand of activists is highly educated (*usually in the West*) and better able to articulate ideas *more understandable to the West and more consistent with modern values*" (emphasis added). Aside from the equation of modern with Western, how could these scholars refer to the new Palestinian leaders "*own style*" when they are clearly aware that it is a Western *style* adopted by these leaders to make themselves "more understandable to the West?" Certainly, one does not have to adopt a Western style to be "understandable" to the West. However, the fact that the US rejects Palestinians who refuse to accept the US definition of Palestinian identity and US diktat in setting the Palestinian political agenda does not result from an inability on the part of these Palestinians to "articulate ideas [that are] more understandable to the West," but from the unwillingness of the US to allow Palestinians (mere objects) to define ourselves and to set our own agenda. Zureik *et al.* proceed to state that the new leaders

> tend to be less ideological than the earlier generation of activists, more pragmatic, and more willing to accommodate themselves to new realities. Their language is devoid of rhetoric and clichés. None of the interviews revealed any use of *the old rhetoric generally associated with the literature of resistance*.[19]

Zureik *et al.* do not clarify what they mean by ideological except to imply that ideological thinking is that of resistance. For example, it is never clarified whether the new leaders are considered less ideological and more pragmatic by the Palestinian people or by the "West." It is also never made clear if what the authors consider "rhetoric and clichés" are considered as such by the Palestinian people or by the West. The use of US and Israeli terms to characterize the "older" generation of Palestinian leaders is presented as "objective" truth to which everyone adheres. The subtextual commitment to the Western discourse informing the judgments these scholars make is never revealed textually. Such a revelation would surely undermine their arguments and their authorial position as Western-educated Palestinian scholars *vis-à-vis* the Palestinian people. Finally, in showing that the new leading Palestinian intellectuals have adapted to "new" realities, the authors present this development as a progressive one benefiting the Palestinian people.

It must be stressed, in fact, that the lack of effective work on the part of Palestinians, old or young, in the US or outside it, does not necessarily stem from not learning the right (Western) lingo but from a discursive axiom which defines the location of Palestinians within (and in relation to) the dominant racialized discourse. Entering US political and cultural discourse cannot be attained by simply knowing the right lingo. As Frantz Fanon wrote four decades ago in his *Black Skin, White Masks*, for an African to speak "correct" *francais parisien* or "nigger" French has no effect on whether s/he is listened to or not. By its very own axioms, "white" discourse has to have a white subject for it to remain what it is, a racialized discourse. It can very easily escape attempts at subversion on our part as Palestinians or Africans by excluding us as discursive non-whites, hence as non-subjects. Thus, although the discourse can be subverted to an extent by "learning the right lingo," this will not make things easier for Palestinians—if that were the case, many Palestinians (myself included) who have learned the "right lingo" would not face the difficulties which we constantly do.

Among the many concessions and compromises that the Palestinian leadership made in order to enter the recent US-sponsored "peace" conference, one clearly stands out as the result of a commitment to the "right lingo": accepting the US formula of "land for peace." This formula prejudices the entire process by presupposing that Israel has "land" which it would be willing to give to the "Arabs," and that the "Arabs"—seen as responsible for the state of war with Israel—can grant Israel the peace for which it has longed for decades. Placing the responsibility of the Arab/Israeli wars on the "Arabs" is a standard view that is never questioned in the West. Learning the right lingo (which, in effect, means donning Western spectacles when viewing ourselves) has finally ensured that Palestinians and other Arabs will not question it either. Though it looks like a political compromise, this formula in fact reflects the racial views characterizing (European Jewish) Israelis and Palestinian and other Arabs. Whereas the Israelis are asked (and are presented as willing) to negotiate about property, the (Western) bourgeois right par excellence, Palestinians and other Arabs are asked to give up violence—or more precisely "their" violent means—which is an illegitimate right attributable only to uncivilized barbarians. The fact that Palestinians have already given up our rightful claim to 77 percent of Palestine and are negotiating about our future sovereignty over a mere 23 percent of our homeland does not qualify for a formula of "land for land" on which to base the "peace process." In fact, the proper formula from a Palestinian perspective would be a "land for peace" formula, for it is *we Palestinians who are giving up our rights to our historic homeland in exchange for an end to Israeli oppression of and violence against our people.* Such a formula, however, cannot be adopted or even considered by a racialized discourse premised on white supremacy. Consequently, it is the Western formula of "land for peace" with all its political and racial implications that the current Palestinian negotiators were forced to accept as the basis for negotiations.

In order to locate where Palestinians fit in the dominant discourse in relation to discursive subjects ("white people"), we have to locate the position of European Jews in the same discourse in relation to both the Palestinians and "white people." When we consider the status of European Jews as a pretextual axiom governing discourse on the Palestine/Israel question, it is important to note that both Jews and Palestinians are viewed as objects in relation to "white" gentile European subjects. To white Europeans, European Jews (as Edward Said has shown) represented the Orient inside Europe, with the Arab later becoming their "fearsome shadow."[20] But this objective status that Jews and Palestinians share conceals other discursive relations. Despite the fact that European Jews are seen as holocaust survivors and as helpless refugees (objects of white sympathy and support), this racialized discourse bestows on them an honorary white status *vis-à-vis* the (until now) non-white Palestinians, it is this status as honorary whites which privileges European Jews over the Palestinian Arabs. On the textual level, European Jews are not treated in the same objectifying way as the Palestinians. Israel and European Jews are treated as objects only *vis-à-vis* "authentic" gentile whites. This is why Lewis cannot bring himself to view Palestinians as more than victimized objects *vis-à-vis* European Jews. If he were to do so, he would have to question not only the honorary white status granted to European Jews, but also his authorial status—being a self-authorizing honorary white subject—as a commentator on our affairs.

At this juncture, it is important to point out the symbolic nature of Israel to diaspora Jews and, by extension, to the dominant racialized discourse. In this discourse Israel is believed to represent two important attributes: it is a haven for Jews from gentile persecution and insurance for the preservation of Jewish culture against the onslaught of both anti-Semitism and assimilation.[21] Insofar as Israel represents the realization of these two important goals, Zionism, the movement that brought about its creation, will continue to command majority support among diaspora Jews. In Palestinian discourse, however, Israel represents a colonial settlement by foreigners on Palestinian Arab land. Israel, ipso facto, is non-Palestine—it stands for the erasure of Palestinian national identity. Israel is seen as a result of both imperialist gentile and Zionist Jewish control of Palestine. Israel's Jewish character is ever present in Palestinian discourse. Yet, although Jews are an inherent part of the definition of Israel in Palestinian discourse and in the racialized discourse. Palestinians are never part of the definition of Israel in "white" and honorary white discourse. Insofar as Palestinians have any history at all in such accounts, "it is part of the history given [us] (or taken from [us]: the difference is slight) by the Orientalist tradition, and later, the Zionist tradition."[22]

In the European Jewish Zionist tradition, Palestinians are presented as the Oriental Other (and dismissed as savages accordingly), a view articulated by the "inventor" of modern Zionism, Theodor Herzl himself.[23] For example, Herzl speaks in his romantic novel *Altneuland* (Old–New Land) of "dirty Arabs"[24] and of "blackened Arab villages [in Palestine] whose inhabitants looked like brigands."[25] Consequently, in order for Palestine to be "restored" to its old glory, it would need European Jews.[26] Herzl's Arab Palestinian character expresses gratitude for the civilizing efforts of European Jewry, from whom the Palestinian Arabs have allegedly benefited immensely.[27] As we saw in an earlier chapter, this view of European Jews as embarking on a *mission civilisatrice* in a hostile Arab environment was also articulated by Chaim Weizmann, Israel's first president, who condemned the Palestinians during the Palestinian Revolt of 1936–1939 as "the forces of destruction, the forces of the desert," who were fighting the Jews, whom he identified as the "forces of civilization and building."[28] Other examples abound.

Examining the two beliefs holding Israel to be a safe Jewish refuge from anti-Semitism and a guarantor of Jewish culture against assimilation which form the cornerstone of diaspora Jewish support for Israel (neither belief involves Palestinians), one is struck by their fluidity. Israel, for example, is far from being a safe place for Jews. In fact, it is one of the most dangerous places for Jews to live in the world. Even when the proportion of Israel's Jewish population is taken into account, Israel remains far more dangerous for Jews than the US or the former USSR (both places with a comparable number of Jews) in both the pre-Gorbachev and post-Gorbachev eras. Roberta Strauss Feuerlicht argued that Israel "has built a ghetto in the Middle East where three million Jews are exposed to the next holocaust. [Jewish] Israelis do not sleep better at night [than diaspora Jews]: some sleep with a rifle at their side."[29]

Moreover, instead of helping Jews in facing anti-Semitic attacks, Israel has allied itself with anti-Semitic governments like that of 1982 Argentina under the generals. Israeli officials, who regularly visited Argentina on business, used the offices of the Israel lobby in the US to project a more favorable image of the Argentine generals to the US congress, urging a resumption of aid to that country. Meanwhile, these same generals had just massacred a thousand Argentine Jews and were torturing more in Argentine prisons.[30] Israel did not use its good offices with the generals to end such anti-Semitism since that did not converge with Israeli state interests. On the contrary, Jacobo Timerman states that "I saw with my own eyes how Argentine jailers tortured Jews in prison while the Israeli government requested the Jewish community there to remain silent."[31]

The Zionist movement, in fact, has a clear record of compromising the welfare of Jews in favor of achieving Zionist goals. In the Nazi period, Zionist leaders, for example, protested strongly against granting European Jews refuge in any country other than Palestine. David Ben-Gurion responded to a British offer, in the aftermath of *Kristallnacht*, to take thousands of children directly to Britain by saying: "If I knew it would be possible to save all the children in Germany by bringing them to England, and only half of them by transporting them to Eretz Yisrael (the land of Israel), then I would opt for the second alternative, for we must weigh not only the life of these children but also the history of the people of Israel."[32] Such actions were certainly the norm, not the exception. The Zionist sell-out of Hungarian Jewry (numbering 450,000) was perhaps the worst of all. Rezco Kastner, the head of the World Zionist Organization's Rescue Committee in Budapest, knew that Adolf Eichmann planned to ship Hungary's Jews to Auschwitz but did not warn them in return for a special exemption for a trainload of Jews whom he could select for escape to Switzerland and later to Palestine. When Kastner was brought to trial in Israel in 1953, he was found innocent of collaboration with the Nazis by the Israeli Supreme Court.[33]

Not only was Israel oblivious to the interests of Jews when they interfered with Zionist interests, it in fact deliberately caused misery and hardships for tens of thousands of Jews in order to achieve Zionist goals. Israeli agents, to take another example, bombed Jewish businesses and meeting places, including a synagogue in Baghdad in the early fifties with the express goal of terrorizing Iraqi Jews into thinking that they were the targets of anti-Jewish Iraqi attacks. These bombings, coupled with a secret agreement with the corrupt and anti-Jewish Iraqi royalist government of Nuri al-Sa'id, whereby the emigrating Iraqi Jews were stripped of their Iraqi citizenship and had their property confiscated, were instrumental in causing the exodus of Iraqi Jewry to Israel. Similar agreements were worked out between Israel and the reactionary Yemeni Imam in bringing about the exodus of Yemeni Jews.[34]

Did Israel constitute an insurance policy for the preservation of Jewish culture against the onslaught of anti-Semitism and assimilation? This belief proves to be just as fluid and flexible as the first one. It is a well-known fact that Israeli ideology denigrates diaspora Jews and their culture. In fact, Yiddish was and is actively discouraged in Israeli society in favor of Hebrew, due to the stigma attached to Yiddish as a product of diaspora Jewish culture. As mentioned in an earlier chapter, the rejection of Yiddish extended beyond its use in the Yishuv to an attack on any Yiddish cultural production, including theater and cinema.[35]

Israel never safeguarded diaspora Jewish culture or languages, including Ladino and Arabic. As discussed in the last chapter, it was Ashkenazi Jews who decided to replace the diasporic Yiddish with the "authentically Jewish" Hebrew, or at least the Ashkenazi version of it,[36] and it was also Ashkenazi Jews who held the Arabic of Arab Jews in contempt and forced its replacement with Hebrew.[37] In sum, Israel created a new Israeli culture alien to diaspora Jews. It created a culture based on nationalism, militarism, and racism unknown in pre-Israel Jewish culture. Despite the fact that neither of the beliefs on which diaspora Jewish support for Israel rests is justified by historical record or present reality, the dominant racialized discourse persists in taking each as axiomatic. Although these beliefs may not always be invoked explicitly in this dominant discourse about Israel, *they form the subtext for such discourse.*

Racialization and objectification

In his commentary of July 31, 1990, Anthony Lewis argues against American supporters of Israel who deny Israel's human rights violations. Lewis begins his commentary with an apt declaration asserting his conviction of Israel's "legitimate" birthright. He states that "Israel was created in response to savage inhumanity, and more than most countries it avows humane ideals." Lewis ignores the fact that Israel's "humane" ideals are by design not universal but particular in their applicability, namely to European Jews.[38] Beginning with Israel's self-identification as a Jewish state (and the denial that it is built on Palestinian Arab land), its "Law of Return," its labor and property laws, etc., Israel made no secret of the fact that the Jewish state is a state for the Jews only. From its socialist to its fascist variants, Zionism was always a colonial-settler movement whose aims were attainable at the expense of the Palestinian people. Had Israel included the Palestinians as part of the people to whom its "humane" ideals were to be applied, then Lewis's protests based on an inconsistency between Israeli principles and practice would have been justified? This, however, is not the case.

That Israel "avows humane ideals" is an oft-repeated truism presented with no supporting evidence. For example, how could Lewis make such an assertion when he endorses books that expose the inhumanity of Israel's ideals as well as its policies? These books (like Edward Said's *The Question of Palestine* which he endorsed) reveal that Jews have the right to complete access to over 90 percent of

Israel's land to the exclusion of Israel's Palestinian (Arab) citizens. This is the case despite (or more accurately as a result of) the confiscation by the Israeli government of all that land from the Palestinian Arabs except for less than 7 percent.[39] The minuscule budgets which Palestinian Israeli towns receive in comparison with their Jewish Israeli counterparts do not reflect universal humane ideals. Lewis ignores, in addition, the Israeli government's policy of leaving an empty space next to the item citizenship in the birth certificates of Palestinian Israelis.[40]

Certainly, these do not reflect universal "humane ideals." The subjugation of Israel's Palestinian population under the Emergency laws[41] until 1966 was not humane, nor was the destruction of 418 Palestinian villages. Israel's racist character was in evidence everywhere, from the state's laws all the way to the *Histadrut*. For example, Palestinian Israeli workers were not accepted in the *Histadrut*, Israel's trade union federation, until 1960, following the *Histadrut's* ninth convention. In 1966, following the tenth convention, the *Histadrut*, or the General Federation of *Hebrew Workers* in the Land of Israel (Eretz Yisrael), changed its name to the General Federation of *Workers* in the Land of Israel. Aside from this change, the *Histadrut*'s constitution remained unaltered, including its commitments to "the imparting of the values of the labor movement, the instruction of the Hebrew language."[42]

After asserting Israel's legitimate "birthright," Lewis's opening sentence concludes that "[p]erhaps understandably, then, any criticism of Israel for violating human rights touches sensitive feelings." If one were to accept the opening sentence, one would find this conclusion appropriate. If not, then this conclusion crumbles. What is understandable, then, is not that the "sensitive feelings" of discursive white folks and honorary white Jews are touched because Israel "avows humane ideals," but that it avows such ideals for the exclusive use of Jews, yet it is being judged for its actions against the discursively non-white Palestinians. Here, a comment by Edward Said should be noted:

> [w]hereas in the past it was European Christian Orientalists who supplied European culture with arguments for colonizing and suppressing Islam, as well as for despising Jews, it is now the Jewish national movement that produces a cadre of colonial officials whose ideological theses about the Islamic or Arab mind are implemented in the administration of the Palestinian Arabs, an oppressed minority within the white-European-democracy that is Israel.[43]

Seen in this light, Lewis's response is nothing but a disguised attempt at passing Palestinians off as another group of honorary white objects worthy of both white and honorary white Jewish sympathy (both groups being considered subjects *vis-à-vis* Palestinians). This, he hopes, will circumvent the discursive police guarding the checkpoints into the racialized discourse, thus allowing Palestinians unobstructed entry—unobstructed, that is, except by our new tenuous status as merely honorary white objects. And all this is asserted while Lewis defends Palestinians against Israel's human rights violations and maintains our status as objects of Israel's deportations and killings.

The subjective identity of Jews *vis-à-vis* Palestinians is made clear in Lewis's assertion of the "legitimacy" of Israel's birthright. Once the issue becomes the status of European Jews as the paramount factor that legitimizes the creation of the Jewish state, Palestinians need no longer appear anywhere in the picture. Our national rights are not only irrelevant to Lewis and the dominant discourse at that point; these rights do not even exist. Any acknowledgment of such rights will have to be followed by questioning the refugee status of European Jews, with the obvious implication that their new status might be colons. If this were accepted, however, the racialized discourse would be faced with an irreversible crisis. This is why the fortifications of the discursive police are insurmountable at this checkpoint.

Another point Lewis raises is the issue of deporting dozens of Palestinians from the West Bank and Gaza. Israel's apologists, whom Lewis is criticizing, assert that Arab countries deport Palestinians in large numbers. "That is true and deplorable," comments Lewis. "But there is a deep difference. When Israeli soldiers take a Palestinian from the West Bank and Gaza and drop *him* [*sic*] in Lebanon, they are deporting him *from his own country*" (emphasis added). Aside from the fact that a large number of deportees are women and children, it is important to point out that the documentation Lewis uses to substantiate this conclusion (with which I agree) is all derived from American sources. Palestinian sources documenting Israel's atrocities are not once mentioned. The sources produced by the objects of a racialized discourse cannot be considered as sources at all. Only those sources produced by "white" subjects of the racialized discourse are admissible.[44] The discursive axioms which inform Lewis's choices and those of others who share similar views hold that Palestinian sources are biased due to self-interest, with the implication that discursive white sources are not biased or self-interested but seek "objective" truth.

Lewis elaborates on the double standard which he accuses Israel's apologists of having by stating that they "would surely be outraged if an American citizen were picked up in New York or Chicago and expelled from the United States." He adds with horror: "How can they not understand when Palestinians are the victims? It must be because they think of Palestinians as less entitled to human rights—or less entitled to think of a place where they have lived for hundreds of years as home." Lewis seems to grasp the status of Palestinians at selective points in his argument. This is a clear manifestation of the dilemma he faces concerning the changing discursive position of Palestinians. But if Palestinians are not "white" according to prevailing discursive norms, and are therefore undeserving of equal status with discursive whites, then how can he expect Israel's apologists to compare us with white Americans? Certainly, a more appropriate comparison, as far as the Palestinians' status is concerned, would be, mutatis mutandis, with the thousands of Mexican and Central American refugees who are constantly being deported from the United States. Israel's apologists are not outraged at all at these deportations. After all, Mexicans, Central Americans, and Palestinians are all discursive non-whites.

By way of further explaining his judgment of Israel to its apologists, Lewis states that the "point of all this is not to suggest that Israel live up to some impossibly angelic standard of human rights. It is that Israel live up to its own standards." Lewis is deliberately ignoring that Israel *is* living up to its own standards by not treating Palestinians as equal to Jews. Pretending that Israel has other standards is nothing but distortion.

How white are Palestinians?

This brings us back to European Jews as refugees and (not "or") *colons*. Since the US (and hence the racialized discourse) is committed to Israel, but not necessarily to a Greater Israel, Jewish *colons* in the West Bank and Gaza are referred to as "settlers," not as "colonial settlers." This is an ambiguous term whose interpretation can differ depending on US interests. In a post-colonial world, including the word "colonial" evokes an unambiguous negative connotation. On the other hand, the word settler can be invoked to show similarity with white settlers in the "New World," and it can also be preceded by the word "illegal" when US policy dictates, thus producing the desired negative effect. The question of how to name Jewish colonial settlers in the Occupied Territories is also noteworthy in Israeli political discourse. Whereas early Zionist settlers in Palestine are called *mityashvim*, or settlers, Israeli settlers in the territories are called *mitnachalim*, or "settler inheritors," from *nachalat avot*, or "land of the fathers" where Abraham settled. *Mitnachalim*, in fact, comes from *nachala*, which means inheritance.[45]

The intifada has created what Thomas Kuhn would call a "precrisis" in the dominant discourse. Some subjects of this racialized discourse are able to experience a gestalt switch and thus view European Jews through Palestinian spectacles as colons, and perhaps as refugees and then colons in sequence—but not as refugees and colons at the same time. Certainly, this racialized discourse does not posit that its subjects are armed settlers of North America. In fact, its discursive axioms support the notion of self-determination for most nationalities in the world, except for Native Americans. Many Palestinians (including myself) have marveled at the fact that the American white Left would support all major struggles in the "Third World" except that of the Palestinians. Explanations have vacillated from the so-called invincible power of AIPAC (American Israel Public Affairs Committee) to the racism of Americans (read "white" people)[46] toward Palestinians. Although these are certainly factors, the decisive factor seems to be the discursive heritage that informs the experiences of white European settlers of North America and that they share with their Israeli European Jewish counterparts. The white Left's stance on South Africa, on the other hand, is inspired by the discursive mythology of America's Civil War. Native Americans (the Palestinian equivalent in the Americas) have never received similar redress. The history of the United States, like that of Israel, begins with the advent of European settlement. Native Americans and Palestinians are accounted for in these histories only within the confines of our encounter with European settlers. In the case of Israel, "Israeli" ancient history ends with the expulsion of Palestinian Jews in the first and second centuries AD and begins again with nineteenth-century European Jewish settlement. The only history that exists in the intervening centuries is that of European Jews in Europe.

The intifada is continuing a process begun when Israel invaded Lebanon in 1982. It was then that Palestinians, for the first time, were represented as victims who deserved white sympathy. This process is responsible for the emergence of a number of Palestinians as spokespeople who dress, speak, and act like "white" people. These Palestinians (the Westernized middle class and intelligentsia), in the diaspora or in our homeland, have been increasingly invited by the discursively constituted white world to make the case for the Palestinian people. It is only through this discursive checkpoint (through which Palestinians become honorary white objects) that Palestinians can enter this racialized discourse, constrained by what we have been forced to abandon at the checkpoint: the independence of our Palestinian national identity (itself a reaction to a racialized colonial discourse[47]) from the dominant discourse's axioms. Through this checkpoint Palestinians become ambivalently, in Homi Bhabha's terms. " 'not quite/not white,' on the margins of metropolitan [white] desire,"[48] or, perhaps more appropriately in this case, our new discursive status becomes *white but not quite*.

When Palestinian leaders present the Palestinian cause to the "U.S. public," they present it as a cause of "whites"—that is, a people adhering inter alia to Western values and ideals and aspiring to achieve a modern (Western) society—who are victimized by other "whites" and thus deserving of white sympathy. The extent to which Palestinians are viewed as "honorary whites" by Lewis and by "authentic" whites is the extent to which we enter the dominant discourse at all, albeit as objects. It is this point which many attempt to gloss over. Ascertaining the "whiteness" of Arabs is not, in fact, as subtextual as one would think. In US legal discourse, the "whiteness" of a people has always had major legal ramifications.

In assessing the petition of Ahmed Hassan, a Yemeni Arab, who applied for US citizenship in 1942, a Michigan District Court asserted that "Arabs are not 'white persons' within meaning of statute enumerating classes of people eligible for United States citizenship."[49] Some of the arguments used to deny Mr Hassan's petition and appeal were as follows:

> Apart from the dark skin of the Arabs, it is well known that they are a part of the Mohammedan world and that a wide gulf separates their culture from that of the predominately Christian peoples of Europe. It cannot be expected that as a class they would readily intermarry with our population and be assimilated into our civilization.[50]

Armenians, it was asserted, were considered "white" because they were Christian and lived close to the border with Europe. In addition they intermarried with Europeans, as evidenced by the record of Armenian immigrants in the United States. The court ruled that, consequently, the "petitioner is an Arab and that Arabs are not white persons within the meaning of the act."[51]

Less than two years later, Mohamed Mohriez, "an Arab born in Sanhy, Badan, Arabia," petitioned for US citizenship. To establish whether Mr Mohriez was a "white" person or not, new arguments were presented that were not considered in Mr Hassan's case. The judge argued, inter alia, that in

> the understanding of the common man the Arab people belong to that division of the white race speaking the Semitic languages . . . Both the learned and the unlearned would *compare the Arabs with the Jews* toward whose naturalization every American Congress since the first has been avowedly sympathetic.[52]

Moreover, it was asserted that

> the Arabs have at various times inhabited parts of Europe and lived along the Mediterranean, been contiguous to European nations and been assimilated culturally and otherwise, by them. . . . Indeed, to earlier centuries as to the twentieth century, the Arab people stands as one of the chief channels by which the traditions of white Europe, especially the ancient Greek traditions, have been carried into the present . . . It follows that . . . the Arab passes muster as a white person.[53]

The petition was granted. Here, it must be added that according to Justice Cardoso in the context of another case, " 'White persons' within the meaning of the statute, are members of the Caucasian race, as Caucasian is defined in the understanding of the mass of men," that is, "white" men.[54]

"How white are Palestinians?" is the question currently underlying this discursive dilemma. In fact, proving the whiteness of Palestinians has been the underlying (sometimes unconscious) premise of the PLO's approach since the beginning of its outreach efforts to the West. Part of the agenda of Hamas and other fundamentalists is to counter these attempts to present us as "white"—or "Western" in fundamentalist lingo—with a mythological view of Islamic tradition.[55] This PLO premise is quite similar to how many other groups, including African Americans, try to present themselves *vis-à-vis* the discursively constituted white world. As Abdul R. JanMohamed explains, Third World peoples and metropolitan minorities are caught between two positions:

> on the one hand, there is a desire to define one's ethnic and cultural uniqueness against the pressures of the majority culture and on the other hand an equally strong, if not stronger, urge to abandon that uniqueness in order to conform to the hegemonic pressures of the [white] liberal humanistic culture.[56]

He adds that

> [h]istorically, this anxiety to be included is far stronger than the need to stress the difference. The traditional narcissism of a dominant white culture—that is, the culture's ability only to recognize man in its own image and its refusal

> to recognize the substantial validity of any alterity—puts enormous pressure on Blacks and other minorities to recreate themselves and their culture as approximate versions of the Western humanist tradition, as images that [white] "humanism" will recognize and understand.[57]

We are far from displacing the axioms of this racialized discourse. Despite the intifada's success in creating a discursive precrisis, this success can be easily reversed, as the reaction to the guerrilla attack has amply shown. The increasing anti-Semitism in the former Soviet Union, coupled with the increasing number of Russian Jewish emigrants, has led to the redeployment of the pretextual axioms of the late forties, which asserted that the refugee status of European Jews was the sole factor considered in creating the Jewish state. These assertions were made again in order to reverse the intifada's gains. The attacks on the PLO for its perceived stance on US intervention in Iraq in and Kuwait in 1991 ended up dealing the *coup de grace* to this discursive precrisis.

In examining the three events that have changed the Palestinians' discursive status, it is crucial to note how the dominant discourse has appropriated them. The emergence of the Palestinian guerrilla movement and the eruption of the intifada were two events in which Palestinians acted as subjects of our own historical change, whereas the massacres suffered by the Palestinians and the Lebanese during the Israeli invasion of Lebanon were events in which Palestinians, and of course the Lebanese, were objects. As the three events are incorporated into this discourse, Palestinians are rendered as discursive objects of "white" antipathy (in reaction to the guerrilla movements), objects of sympathy (the massacres in Lebanon), and objects of both sympathy and ambivalence—with no clear-cut hostility—intermittently (the intifada). The Manichean objectification of Palestinians has been consistent. Certainly, the erasure of Palestinian history except as it relates to our encounter with Zionism and imperialism is not unique to Palestinians. Western liberals and Marxists alike have erased the histories of most discursively non-white peoples, in providing a view of history other than the thesis that history begins and ends with class struggle. Amilcar Cabral stated that such a thesis would force us to

> consider—and this we refuse to accept—that various human groups in Africa, Asia, and Latin America were living without history or outside history at the moment when they were subjected to the yoke of imperialism. It would be to consider that the populations of our countries . . . are still living today—if we abstract the very slight influence of colonialism to which they have been subjected—outside history, or that they have no history.[58]

It must be stressed, nonetheless, that the Palestinians' relationship to this racialized discourse is a dynamic one. From being fully excluded from this discourse in any capacity or form to being included in it as objects of antipathy and/or sympathy, the position assigned to Palestinians within this racialized discourse continues to change as a result of extra-discursive events. In locating points of entry, we are able to uncover the dilemma facing the discourse at this stage of its hegemony. This, however, is not to suggest a teleological trend marking the position of Palestinians in this discourse—which, after having allowed the Palestinians entry, will ultimately render us honorary white subjects. As an effect of other discursive and extra-discursive factors outlined above, the position of Palestinians may become static or remain dynamic (in all directions). As Tzvetan Todorov once said, "discourse is not determined by the object it describes, nor by conformity to a tradition, but is constituted solely as a function of the goal it seeks to achieve."[59]

The emergence of postcolonial counter-discourses is helping to create a new discursive space for Palestinians, and for other peoples in a similar position, enabling us to resist the dominant discourse's hegemony. This resistance aims at constituting us as subjects of our own different discourses and histories—the problematic nature of this position notwithstanding.[60] It is the counter-hegemonic force of these discourses that is "bringing hegemonic historiography to a crisis."[61] The subaltern may not be able to speak,[62] but counter-hegemonic discourses are at least helping to open a discursive space where the subaltern subject is rendered visible.[63] The intifada, as the major factor precipitating the discursive precrisis, will continue to subvert the dominant discourse's axioms unless it, too, can somehow be assimilated. A "right lingo" interpretation of the intifada by some leading Palestinians (like the current Palestinian negotiating team) who adopt this formula as a strategy for (in)action, makes such assimilation more likely. If a two-state solution is the most viable political solution to the Palestine Question, it is the language in which negotiations are conducted which will determine the final political outcome. Discourse, as Foucault put it, "can be both an instrument and an effect of power, but also a hindrance, a stumbling block, *a point of resistance and a starting point for an opposing strategy*."[64] Unless subverted, the language or the discursive formulae of the negotiations will only mire the Palestinians in a labyrinth of concessions that will ultimately lead to the final liquidation of the Palestinian struggle for national liberation and independence.

5 Repentant terrorists or settler-colonialism revisited*

The PLO–Israeli agreement in perspective

Since the beginning of the so-called peace process inaugurated in Madrid in 1991, the PLO, through its unofficial negotiators, have conceded Palestinian rights one by one, in a gradual process culminating in the official PLO signing of the Declaration of Principles in Washington on September 13, 1993, otherwise known among many Palestinians, as the final sellout of the Palestinian cause.

The "land for peace" formula which the "peace" talks adopted as a point of departure was, in fact, the first major concession of the PLO. As I argued in the last chapter, this formula alone prejudices the entire process by presupposing that Israel has "land" which it would be willing to give to the "Arabs," and that the "Arabs," seen as responsible for the state of war with Israel, can grant Israel the peace for which it has longed for decades. Placing the responsibility of the Arab/Israeli wars on the "Arabs" is a standard view that is never questioned in the West. The PLO concession, however, has finally ensured that Palestinians and other Arabs too will not question it. Despite its surface appearance as a political compromise, this formula is in fact a reflection of the racial views characterizing (European Jewish) Israelis and Palestinian and other Arabs. Whereas the Israelis are being asked and are ostensibly (presented as) willing to negotiate about property, the recognized (Western) bourgeois right par excellence, Palestinians and other Arabs are being asked to give up violence—or more precisely "their" violent means—which is an illegitimate unrecognized right attributable only to uncivilized barbarians. The fact that Palestinians have already given up our rightful claim to 77 percent of Palestine and are negotiating about our future sovereignty over a mere 23 percent of our homeland does not qualify for a formula of "land for land" on which to base the "peace process." In fact, the proper formula from a Palestinian perspective would be a "land for peace" formula whereby it is Palestinians who are giving up our rights to our historic homeland in exchange for an end to Israeli oppression of and violence against our people.

The PLO, Israel, and the Western media have hailed the September 13 agreement between Yasser Arafat and Yitzhak Rabin as "mutual recognition." This, however, flies in the face of the actual words uttered by both parties, and the projected

* This essay was first published in 1994.

actions based on these words. Whereas the PLO (who wrote the first letter) recognized "the right of the state of Israel to exist in peace and security,"[1] the Israeli government, "in response" to Arafat's letter, "has decided to recognize the PLO as the representative of the Palestinian people and commence negotiations with the PLO within the Middle East peace process." This is hardly mutual recognition. For this to be mutual recognition, either the Israelis would have to recognize the Palestinian people's right to exist in a state of their own in peace and security, or the PLO would have only to recognize the Rabin government as the representative of the Israeli people, without necessarily granting any "right" to the Israeli state to exist in peace and security, or in any other way. The actual agreement, therefore, did not amount to a mutual recognition, rather, it amounted to the final legitimation of the Jewish state as having the "right" to be a racist apartheid state by the very people against whom its racist policies have been/are practiced, with the Israelis committing to nothing substantively new. Giving the PLO the recognition as the representative of the Palestinians, something the majority of the world (except the United States) has recognized since the mid-1970s, commits Israel to no concessions to the Palestinian people. It commits it only to a scenario whereby since the Israeli government is inclined to speak to "representatives" of the Palestinians, it would talk to the PLO, as it now recognizes that party as their representative, whereas before it did not.

To put things a bit more in perspective, one could contrast the PLO recognition with recent ANC (African National Congress) concessions and dealings with the South African Apartheid State. Whereas the ANC has been negotiating with the apartheid state for the express purpose of abolishing formal apartheid, the PLO has, in effect, recognized Israel's right to be an apartheid state, a "right" that no state should have, and surely, one that should not be conferred upon such a state by its own victims. Yet, as Edward Said has recently remarked, the words Arafat pronounced at the signing of the "Declaration of Principles" in Washington had the "flair of a rental agreement. Far from being seen as the victims of Zionism, the Palestinians were characterized before the world as its now *repentant assailants* [emphasis added]."[2] The South African analogy is, in fact, more instructive in this regard. What the Israelis agreed to embark upon is a Bantustan agreement, whereby, the Palestinians could exercise municipal authority, called in Zionist-speak "self-rule," with the additional central function of having a Palestinian police force which would carry out the dirty work that Israeli Jewish soldiers have had to do until now. This is parallel to the South African Apartheid State's use of black police to suppress black resistance, thus reducing the danger to the lives of white policemen. This development, in fact, is a welcome change for Israeli Jewish society. In this scenario, Israel will continue to control the land, the waters, the borders, the economy, Jewish settlements, in short, everything it has sought to control, without Palestinian resistance and its necessary suppression, which would cause the possible death of Jewish boys in the process. The PLO has pledged that no such resistance will be allowed. Now, Palestinian boys (and, it is rumored, also girls)[3] would kill Palestinian boys and girls whom Israeli Jewish boys would have had to kill, endangering themselves in the process. Meanwhile, the Israelis will be reminding the world that their previous murderous campaigns against the Palestinians must have been justified, as it is now the Palestinians themselves who recognize the necessity of controlling a savage and recalcitrant population. Prime Minister Rabin is explicit on this matter: "I'd rather the Palestinians coped with the problem of enforcing order in Gaza. The Palestinians will be better at it than we were, because they will allow no appeals to the Supreme Court and will prevent the [Israeli] Association for Civil Rights from criticizing conditions there by denying it access to the area. They will rule there by their own methods, *freeing, and this is most important, the Israeli army from having to do what they will do* [emphasis added]."[4] Those who in their liberal naiveté may have previously been made to feel uncomfortable with Israel's atrocities against Palestinians should now put their minds at ease. Israel's moral character, as its apologists have always maintained, was never compromised in the process. Thus, Israel gets its cake and eats it too. And, all this can be packaged as major Israeli concessions for the consumption of the Western media and the Westernized, and obviously credulous Palestinian intelligentsia and the Palestinian comprador bourgeoisie—the major clients of Arafat's recent sellout.

In fact, the repressive function of the projected Palestinian police is already being demonstrated. Three self-appointed traffic cops from the armed Fatah Hawks, which belongs to the Arafat wing of the PLO, reportedly ordered a motorist in Gaza to move his car. When he refused, they shot him in both legs. Clyde Haberman, the *New York Times* Israel correspondent, concerned that the Palestinian police will, when it assumes authority, only exercise such mild penalties, asserts that "when that force comes into being in December, it will have to prove its mettle. Certainly, it must show it can do better than [the] three self-appointed traffic cops."[5]

The Israeli recognition of the PLO as the representative of the Palestinian people, I would argue, took place at the exact moment that the PLO ceased to represent the national will of the majority of Palestinians. This is precisely why the Israelis bestowed upon the organization their precious recognition. As Israeli Foreign Minister Peres himself asserted correctly, "We haven't changed—it [the PLO] changed."[6] This is an accurate picture that the PLO would like to erase, since it is interested in convincing the Palestinian people that it was able to extract actual concessions from the Israeli government. The most prominent of such alleged concessions is the Israeli recognition of the PLO. However, if the PLO stood for Palestinian national aspirations (which included the uncompromising demand for national self-determination through the establishment of a Palestinian State, the repatriation and/or monetary compensation of diaspora Palestinians, and an end to Israeli apartheid under whose yoke Palestinian Israelis live), and as such was recognized by the Israeli government, such a recognition would surely have been a veritable concession by the intransigent Israelis. This, however, is far from what happened. The PLO agreement has no place for diaspora Palestinians (except, according to Rabin, for a few thousand people[7]), or for Palestinian Israelis, and, as mentioned earlier, has no provisions for Palestinian national self-determination, or the establishment of a Palestinian state. What then does the PLO still stand for that can be construed in any way as a possible representation of the desires and will of the Palestinian people? Since all the major national aspirations that the PLO embodied have been abandoned by the Arafat leadership, then the Israeli recognition of the organization was not a concession at all; rather, it was a triumph for the Israeli agenda which has always sought to negotiate with people and (Arab) governments that did not actually represent the Palestinian people. The Israeli recognition of the PLO, therefore, did not depart from the Israeli strategy, which successive Israeli governments have followed diligently, of liquidating the Palestinian national cause.

The establishment of the Israeli settler-colony has resulted in the usurpation of all of historic Palestine and, in the process of the last four and a half decades, the physical separation of the Palestinian people into three major segments in relation to Palestine—Palestinians in Israel proper (otherwise known as "Israeli Arabs"), Palestinians in the Occupied Territories, in the West Bank, and the Gaza Strip, and Palestinians in the diaspora. The PLO–Israeli agreement is engineered by definition not to redress the injustices incurred on the Palestinian people as such, rather, of transforming the Israeli occupation over parts of the Occupied Territories into something with which both the PLO leadership and the Israelis, more generally, can live. What this means is that the segment of the Palestinian people who live in the Occupied Territories are being further subdivided into more separate parts. Whereas, since the Israeli occupation and subsequent annexation of the Palestinian city of East Jerusalem, Palestinians living in that city were accorded a different legal and political status by the Israelis, the recent agreement separates those Palestinians who live in Gaza and the town of Jericho (however it may be defined geographically) from Palestinians who live in the remainder of the West Bank. This further subdivision of the Palestinian people aside, even those Palestinians, who number a million people or so (one-sixth of the entire Palestinian people), who are included in this agreement do not receive their minimal national aspirations. The agreement categorically denies the possibility of the establishment of a Palestinian state in those territories within and around which the Israeli military is scheduled to redeploy itself. The Israeli government and its US sponsor have both made declarations that they will not permit such a development at all.

In a nutshell, what this so-called historic agreement (and it certainly is historic) provides for is a South African Bantustan "homeland" solution for 1 million Palestinians with the possibility that another million (those who live in the remainder of the West Bank excluding Jerusalem), with good behavior, may be included in the future. After close to a century of Palestinian anti-colonial resistance to the Zionist project, the PLO has accepted a solution which the South African government had been using as part of the efficient functioning of apartheid rule. According to Uzi Benziman, the chief political correspondent of the prestigious Israeli newspaper *Ha'Aretz*, "Israel intends that the Palestinian entity will have much less power and dignity than a Bantustan."[8] Indeed, in a Bantustan, the police can arrest white South Africans, as opposed to the Palestinian police, which will have no authority, whatsoever, over Jewish settlers. A Bantustan homeland solution which the whole world, much less South African blacks, have condemned as an instrument of oppressive apartheid rule, is considered in the Palestinian case as "liberation" for one-third of the Palestinian people, who are anyway, the only Palestinians that Israel is willing to consider as part of any current or future agreement. Palestinians in the diaspora have received no redress and, according to the provisions of the Declaration of Principles, are owed nothing by a predatory Zionist colonial project, and its proud offspring, the Israeli State. As for the third segment of the Palestinian people, those who are third-class Israeli citizens, the legitimation of their status has been accorded to the Jewish state by recognizing its "right to exist" as a Jewish- (and of course, Ashkenazi-) ruled apartheid state.

The recent agreement has freed some of the American liberal Left from the embarrassment it has suffered for its pro-Zionist sympathies since the Israeli invasion of Lebanon in 1982. The editors of the US magazine *The Nation* could hardly wait for the ink to dry to show their Zionist commitments, which they had attempted to hide (unsuccessfully, I would argue) during the past decade. In *The Nation*'s September 27 issue, the editors declared the PLO–Israeli agreement as having addressed for "the first time since the establishment of the Israeli state in 1948 the 'core' of the conflict [emphasis added]."[9] It is not clear to which core the editors are referring. Since the core of the Palestinian cause has been the establishment of the Jewish settler-colony on Palestinian land, resulting in the expulsion of hundreds of thousands of Palestinians and the subjugation of millions more to Israeli apartheid and/or Israeli military occupation, this core is yet to be addressed. On the other hand, the core of the Zionist project has always been seeking legitimation of its settler-colony by the very people that the settler-colony has victimized and continues to oppress and victimize, thereby, allowing the settler-colony to proceed with the important function for which the various Empires of the North have historically supported it (Britain, France, and the United States in chronological order), namely, the economic domination of the whole region and the safeguarding of its resources for imperial use. This core has surely been addressed by the agreement and by the PLO recognition of the settler-colony's "right to exist in peace and security." It is, of course, this core that *The Nation's* editors are concerned with, since soon after the above sentence, they add optimistically that the PLO–Israeli agreement "begins a diplomatic process that could also quickly produce additional agreements between Israel and Syria, Lebanon and Jordan, as well as a framework for *regional economic cooperation* [emphasis added]"—the last three words being the code words for Israeli economic domination of the area. This of course has been underway since the signing of the agreement, as Israel is concluding different deals with Arab countries.[10] Such agreements are said to have been signed by Qatar,[11] Morocco,[12] and Jordan[13] already. In the meantime, the United States' government is applying increasing pressure on the Arab world to end its economic boycott of Israel.[14]

The Nation's editors are still sober enough after the party to warn their readers that "it is premature to celebrate" (p. 304). They warn of "extremists" on both sides who oppose the agreement. They also recommend that Israel deal with the additional issues of "Palestinian refugees, the eventual disposition of Israeli settlements, the transition from autonomy to sovereignty for the Palestinians and the partial internationalization of Jerusalem." Note that the character of Israel as an apartheid state holding (Ashkenazi) Jewish supremacy as its guiding raison d'être is never questioned by the editors. Therefore, the core of the issue for

Palestinians, which is the continued existence of a Jewish supremacist and racist settler-colony, is not addressed by the Zionist editors, whose Zionism is not compromised by their support for a two-state solution, as long as the integrity of a Jewish supremacist Israel remains intact. The editors proceed to warn the Israelis that if they did not address the above-identified issues, "the Palestinians will likely feel cheated and humiliated and resume armed struggle, probably under far more militant leadership than Yasir Arafat's." Who might this "more militant leadership" be? *The Nation*'s editors do not keep us in suspense much. In the next paragraph, they inform us that

> we should recall how the harsh Versailles settlement imposed on Germany after World War I paved the way for Nazi ultranationalism, racist perversions and militarism. The bitter ironies of such a comparison should encourage Israel and its friends, especially the United States, to satisfy Palestinian aspirations for real independence and sovereign rights.

Any doubt that the reader might have had as to the object of *The Nation*'s editors' sympathies has by now disappeared. It is beloved Israel who may fall victim to the new Nazis who would destroy it and its Jewish citizens. The fact that a racist predatory apartheid state like the Jewish settler-colony becomes, for *The Nation*'s editors, the object of worry from a possible attack by its defenseless victims, who, perhaps, like a Phoenix, may rise from the ashes of their defeat and humiliation to become Nazis and conquer it, shows how deep the Zionism of *The Nation*'s editors actually is. In the Versailles narrative, the Palestinian people, who have been the victims of Zionist massacres, expulsions, land confiscation, imprisonment, torture, etc., are portrayed as a people who have been an equal party to a war in which they were defeated and duly punished by a humiliating agreement. This view is fully consonant with the Rabin performance at the White House in which Palestinians were presented as the murderers of innocent Jews. Due to the sincere Israeli Jewish desire for peace, we are told, not only are Israeli Jews going to forgive the murderous and terrorist Palestinians, but also as Rabin asserts, "we have no desire for revenge."[15] This gesture of magnanimity, whereby the leader of a murderous colonial settlement is asserting that his country's colonial-settler citizens and their offspring do not seek revenge against the Palestinians for having resisted their conquest of their lands and lives and their noble *mission civilisatrice*, is truly worthy of Orwell's *1984*. Unfortunately, the Versailles analogy was recently made, perhaps inadvertently, by Edward Said, to characterize the recent PLO–Israeli agreement, which he, as I, consider as an "instrument of Palestinian surrender."[16] Although, of course, Said's motive (as one of the most courageous Palestinians who are speaking out against this sellout), in making the analogy, was to illustrate the scope of the sense of humiliation and defeat felt by most Palestinians.

A better analogy could have been made with the French colonial conquest of Tunisia a century ago. Like the PLO who has been facing bankruptcy since the cutoff of aid by its Persian Gulf benefactors two years ago, the corrupt

Tunisian Bey, with mounting international debts, had declared bankruptcy in 1869. The French invaded in 1881 "forcing" the Bey to sign a treaty establishing French military occupation. Like the pledge of the Israeli secret service, Mossad, to protect the life of Arafat, which has been in effect since the signing of the agreement, the French undertook to "lend constant support to His Highness the Bey of Tunis against any danger threatening the person or the dynasty of his Highness or compromising the security of his realm."[17] The Bey, similar to Arafat's renouncing of "terrorism and other acts of violence," gave instructions to local leaders that they "should discourage resistance: the French had come as friends."[18] Certainly, a century has passed since the conquest of Tunisia. Since then, instruments of (neo)colonial control have been modified. Unlike the Tunisian Bey who was forced to sign an agreement ratifying French occupation, Arafat *chose* to sign his agreement. Moreover, unlike the Tunisian case, the agreement ratifies the continued military and colonial-settler occupation of those areas in the West Bank and Gaza deemed crucial to Israeli security and settler concerns. Also, Arafat did not have to pledge that a national bourgeoisie would not use protective measures against the incursion of international, including Israeli, capital. On the contrary, in the context of the New World Order, Arafat is pleading, with the Palestinian comprador bourgeoisie (better known as the export–import sector) behind him, for international "investment" in his Municipality to be.

The Palestine Liberation Organization will come down in history as the only Third World liberation movement who has sought liberation through selling the resources it expects to "liberate" to international capital before it even "liberates" them. Western countries and their global instruments of economic domination, the World Bank[19] and the IMF (International Monetary Fund), are already devising different types of plans for investment in the Municipality of Gaza and Jericho once their projected mayor, Yasser Arafat, takes office. The excitement about international investment is gripping a wide sector of the Westernized Palestinian intelligentsia, many of whom have been visiting Washington in the past few months on AID (Agency for International Development)-sponsored training missions. Sari Nusaybah, one of the more visible of West Bank intellectuals, while calling for "sell[ing] the agreement and the development plans [to the Palestinian people]," asserted to the New York Times, that "we want to make a quantifiable leap, not just develop into 'another' third world country [emphasis added]."[20] Ironically, such arrogance and contempt for the Third World is more reminiscent of the Zionists not the Palestinians.[21] In addition, some Palestinians are going so far as to want to emulate the examples of Singapore and Taiwan, as models for Palestinian "development"![22]

It is unclear, however, how Palestinians are to rebuild the economies of the West Bank and Gaza under current conditions. The most important element of the Palestinian economy has always been agriculture. Yet, this area has been so circumscribed by Israeli government theft of Palestinian land and water, that Palestinian agriculture has been almost decimated. Already, 60 percent of the land and all the water resources in the Occupied Territories have been confiscated by the Israeli military for "security reasons" and for colonial settlements. Since the agreement states that the Israeli military will only withdraw from population centers while maintaining its deployment in "security" areas, and stipulates the survival of the colonial settlements, it is unclear what kind of a future Palestinian agriculture would have without more than one-half the land. The agreement, also, does not mention a transfer of control over West Bank and Gaza waters to the PLO. On the contrary, it foresees continued Israeli control. In fact, the agreement only stipulates the return of 2 percent of historic Palestine to Palestinian municipal rule. Given the realities of the Palestinian economy and its continued subjugation to the Israeli economy[23] coupled with the projected plans for international investment, little change (aside from some immediate cosmetic changes in Gaza) will occur in the lives of those Palestinians living in the Occupied Territories, much less those living in Israel or in the diaspora. In the long run, nothing would have changed in the economic and political realties of the Palestinians. This agreement has simply formalized what is. The status of the Palestinian people as a cheap labor force for Ashkenazi Israel has been ratified, through the agreement, by the Palestinian comprador bourgeoisie, who will be the ultimate beneficiary of this arrangement. Furthermore, since the decision concerning the future destiny of 6 million people was made by Yasser Arafat and a handful of his colleagues on the PLO Executive Committee,[24] a future democratically ruled Municipality seems far-fetched. With this as precedent, and with Arafat and colleagues labeling all opponents of the agreement as extremists (read fundamentalists)[25]—whom, PLO ambassador to Tunisia and close Arafat advisor, Hakam Balawi has promised on Israeli television to "crush"[26]—and with his projected police force (said to be recruited in its majority from the diaspora) about to be deployed to insure "order" until the Palestinian elections are held, the possibility of free elections seems remote.[27] Consequently, the agreement will bring no tangible change in the lives of the majority of the Palestinian people, politically or economically. The PLO–Israeli agreement is, in fact, taking the Palestinian people with the speed of a rocket from point A, where they are now, to point B where everything is just the same.[28]

The rewriting of the history of the Palestinian anti-colonial struggle is quickly being undertaken as a result of the agreement. As Arafat has acknowledged to the Israelis that acts of Palestinian resistance to the Zionist colonial conquest were/are, in fact, "terrorism and other acts of violence"[29] which he pledged to "renounce," the PLO/Israeli agreement has finally hailed the triumph of settler-colonialism as a just civilizing project. In this regard, the Israelis and their US sponsor are already undertaking the repeal of UN resolutions, which in the previous forty years have condemned Israeli colonial conquests. Once this is finalized, the Zionist settler-colonial project will have, at last, been redeemed.

6 Political realists or comprador intelligentsia*,[1]

Palestinian intellectuals and the national struggle

> We [should] make the European feel that we see things the way he does... We must learn the way a European learns, feel as a European feels, judge as a European judges, and do as a European does...
>
> Taha Husayn[2]

"The current situation requires us to deal with it in the spirit of political responsibility and national realism."[3] This is how the Palestine National Council (PNC) announced its support for the US-led peace process inaugurated in Madrid in the fall of 1991. After the signing of the Declaration of Principles (DoP) in September 1993 (known as Oslo I), the question of realism stressed by the PNC, was raised to the status of ideology.[4] Those who support Oslo are considered "realists" or "pragmatists" while those who don't are described as anachronisms relegated to the dustbin of history.[5] What is the meaning of realism and of pragmatism in this context? To what are these notions being opposed? What accounts for the rise of this new discourse of pragmatism? This chapter will identify where the notion of "realism" is being deployed in the Palestinian political, economic, and cultural spheres as well as explain the background from which this discourse of pragmatism emerged within the history of Arab intellectual production, recent Arab and Palestinian history and politics, and international developments since the end of the cold war. Moreover, this chapter will demonstrate that these recent developments have transformed many Palestinian intellectuals, who until recently were critical of American, Israeli, and Arab (including Palestinian) solutions, dubbed "realist," into comprador intellectuals allied with the Palestinian comprador bourgeoisie. The arena in which these intellectuals are now active is no longer the one where the Palestinian people are defended against the unceasing onslaughts of their enemies, but rather, as I will show, the import/export sector where intellectuals can receive more benefits as participants in the New World Order's international economy.

I would like to begin by situating the new discourse of realism within the larger sphere of Arab intellectual production. For the past century, the two major currents in modern and contemporary Arab thought have been *al-salafiyyah*

* This essay was first published in 1997.

(traditionalism) and *al-nahdawiyyah* (renaissance thinking). Central to both currents are the notions of the authentic (*al-asalah*) and the contemporary (*al-mu'asarah*). As Muhammad 'Abid al-Jabiri has shown, both currents are part of the same modernist discourse whose model of future Arab society has as its paradigms the Arab–Islamic past, the post-Enlightenment European present, or a combination of the two.[6] Although the nineteenth-century renaissance thinkers gave way to the emergence of the thinkers of revolution (both nationalist and Marxist) in the post-Second World War era, the problematic of the authentic and the contemporary remained the fulcrum around which Arab thought continued to revolve, with no resolution in sight. The questions of what to preserve from the Arab–Islamic past and what to adopt from the modern European present continued to pose themselves insistently, without any acknowledgment of the existing reality of what actually has been preserved from the Arab past and what actually has been adopted from the European present.

The Arab defeat in the 1967 War announced the retreat of the period of secular revolutionary thinking, with the Camp David accords dealing it a final coup de grâce, giving way to a new crop of thinkers: Islamists and realist-pragmatists. Whereas the Islamists continue the quest of combining their modern reading of an Islamic past with the Western technological present, the realist-pragmatists on the rise in the 1980s and 1990s nominally are calling for an abandonment of the dream that Arab "civilization" will rise again, and are calling for the adoption of the Western formula of modernization wholesale, as a way to join the "modern" world as followers of Europe—a course, they assert, that had been followed by equally great nations like the Japanese, and more recently the South Koreans and Chinese. Any attempt to revolt against the West, they believe, even to resist the West is bound to failure and defeat. Those who advocate such solutions are said to inhabit a utopian revolutionary past whose goals are unachievable, if not entirely démodés. "Utopianism" has failed. To be modern, one must become a realist and a pragmatist.

The new historical situation after 1990 effected the final transition for realist-pragmatist Palestinian intellectuals to a new value system, whose slogans replaced the old slogans prevalent before the 1991 Madrid conference. The new value system stresses "nation-building" as opposed to national liberation, "liberal democracy" as opposed to anti-colonial revolution, "accommodation" as opposed to resistance, "pragmatism" as opposed to utopianism and, finally, "realism" as opposed to nostalgia. The historical background giving rise to this realist-pragmatist camp, in the diaspora as well as in the West Bank and Gaza, began to emerge in the early 1970s. After the "death" of Nasserism, the Palestine Liberation Organization actively sought support from the conservative Arab regimes, which, in alliance with the Palestinian bourgeoisie, began bankrolling its coffers. Also, following the 1973 War, many PLO leaders found common cause with Anwar Sadat's conclusion that the United States holds all the cards, and that the Arabs cannot defeat the United States. This view led them to adopt the new strategy of trying to gain US support for the Arab side. Concurrently, the demise of the pro-Jordanian elite in the West Bank and Gaza gave rise to a new Palestinian nationalist elite that supported the PLO. The Lebanese civil war and the PLO's estrangement from Syria, its last supporter outside the conservative Arab camp, enabled the realist-pragmatist wing of the PLO to dominate the movement, to begin consolidating an alliance with the conservative Arab regimes, and to make overtures to their sponsor, the United States. This situation was compounded further by the expulsion of the PLO from Lebanon following Israel's 1982 invasion of that country. This development eroded any independent power that the PLO still could muster without the support of its conservative allies, forcing it to repair relations with Jordan's King Hussein, with whom it launched a new peace initiative based on a future confederation between Jordan and the West Bank and Gaza. The PLO–Jordan rapprochement led to the strengthening of the conservative pro-Jordan elite in the West Bank who joined the pro-PLO nationalist camp in applauding the new initiative. This situation was short-lived, however, and the rupture of relations with Jordan in 1986, the PLO and its pragmatist supporters in the occupied territories reverted to the two-state solution.

In the meantime, the Likud coalition had become a fact of life in Israeli politics. Its popularity inaugurated in the 1977 elections proved permanent. With the increasing horrors visited upon the Palestinians by the Israeli occupation, and Israel's refusal to recognize the PLO, both the PLO and its local supporters began to waiver on Palestinian demands. The level of desperation was so high that Sari Nusaybah, a West Bank intellectual pragmatist, proposed that Israel annex the territories and grant Palestinians citizenship. Nusseibah's proposal counted on the reproductive capacity of Palestinian women to be coopted for the nationalist agenda, wherein he predicted that within twenty years Palestinians would outnumber Jews and, through the electoral process, transform Israel into a secular democratic state.[7] Palestinian pragmatists continued to speak to the Israeli peace camp as well as meet with US officials in the hope that some minimal Palestinian demands would be met.

The Palestinian intifada, which erupted at the end of 1987, heralded the possibility of an end to Israel's military occupation of Palestine, with the Palestinian Declaration of Independence in 1988 being the first step taken on the road to liberation. However, the 1991 Gulf War resulted in a PLO diplomatic fiasco and seemed to reconfirm to Palestinians the one step forward, two steps back scenario of recent Palestinian history. It was in this context that the PLO revived Sadat's strategy used after the 1973 War, namely, to proclaim defeat a victory, metamorphose weakness into strength, and surrender into bravery.[8]

On the international level, events occurring in the second half of the 1980s brought this new political discourse into full bloom, leading to the realist-pragmatist camp's monopoly of Palestinian politics. With the advent of Glasnost and Perestroika and the final collapse of the Soviet Union, many Western political scientists were heralding the final victory of modernization theory, which others had dared to discredit in the intervening two decades. These theoreticians of modernization and their friendly critics, such as Samuel P. Huntington, concluded that after a necessary period of authoritarianism during which the hard work of industrialization and stabilization of political power is accomplished, democracy will show its long-awaited face, thus following the Western historical model of the rise of liberal democracy.[9] The Soviet period that Russia had endured for seventy years constituted, in this theoretical paradigm, but a transitional phase on the way to achieving the political goal of modernization. This model was in fact being applied to the cases of Taiwan and South Korea, the new and celebrated models of third world development. These bastions of authoritarian industrialization had gone beyond the "take-off" stage identified by modernization theory and were said to be transforming themselves into Western-style democracies. These developments inspired many in the Palestinian camp to argue that Palestine, free from Israeli occupation, could be transformed into the Singapore of the Middle East. The importance of this modernization discourse in the post-Soviet and post-Oslo period is demonstrated in the way its axioms are articulated and in the way it produces a Palestinian politico-intellectual idiom that forms the cornerstone of realist-pragmatist thinking.

In light of these transformations, a study was conducted by Palestinian scholars comparing the new generation of Palestinian intellectuals and leaders with that of the early 1970s.[10] The study, as discussed in a previous chapter, was based on interviews of forty leading Palestinian intellectuals/activists in the West Bank and Gaza Strip. Many of these intellectuals were to participate in the official Palestinian delegation to the Madrid conference, and its advisory and guidance committees, and later in the implementation of the Declaration of Principles—Oslo I.[11] Let us revisit the study's conclusion in the context of this chapter. The authors concluded that there is "a significant generational difference that makes the new Palestinians what Karl Mannheim called a 'generation in itself,' able to learn from history and to imprint *its own style* on the present [emphasis added]."[12] The study asserted that the "new brand of activists is highly educated (usually in the West) and better able to articulate ideas *more understandable* to the West and more consistent with modern values [emphasis added]."[13] The authors proceed to state that the new leaders "tend to be less ideological than the earlier generation of activists, more pragmatic, and more willing to accommodate themselves to new realities. Their language is devoid of rhetoric and clichés. None of the interviews revealed any use of the old rhetoric generally associated with the literature of resistance."[14]

The authors do not define what they mean by "ideological," except to imply that ideological thinking is that of resistance. Who considers the new leaders less ideological and more pragmatic is a question they do not answer. Is it the Palestinian people or Western analysts? The authors conclude by asserting that the new leaders and intellectuals want

> to discard the old rhetoric, to define realizable objectives, and to identify clear and helpful mechanisms to accomplish them. The previous discourse relied upon a logic of daring and confrontation. With few exceptions (such as certain Islamist and extreme leftist groups), the new discourse relies more on the logic of accommodation and caution.[15]

The conclusion of this study is quite accurate in that this realist and pragmatist strategy was applied by these intellectuals when they supported the PLO leadership's new bid for a US-sponsored peace under the formula of "land for peace." As I argued in the last chapter, the "land for peace" formula which the "peace" talks adopted as a point of departure was the first major concession of the PLO.

An important feature of realist-pragmatist thinking is an ambivalent upholding of modernization theory's sacred outcome, liberal democracy. On the one hand, it is argued that the new pragmatism of Palestinians, their new accommodationist policies toward the Israelis, and their adoption of a US-sponsored formula for development are reflections of what must be a liberal–democratic political culture. Palestinians, it is stressed further, even have achieved other prerequisites to modernization. Khalil Shikaki, a Palestinian exporter of opinion polls, claims that although "it is possible to make the transition to democracy without [the] prerequisites [set by modernization theory]," the Palestinian case satisfies these prerequisites. "The Palestinian level of socioeconomic development, urbanization, GNP, and literacy rate, particularly in the West Bank, is not far behind (and may even exceed) that of some of the southern European and Latin American countries that have recently made that transition."[16] On the other hand, other Palestinian intellectual pragmatists are not so sure that these prerequisites are in place, and invoke a Huntingtonian notion of Islamic or Middle Eastern culture that is at odds with democracy, indeed one which considers democracy an "external imposition."[17] That the PNA should be penalized for its undemocratic practices is unacceptable to Ahmad Khalidi, a realist-pragmatist. He states without equivocation that "[t]o expect a full-blown democracy is an ahistorical exercise in wishful thinking and in a peculiar sense is both patronizing and discriminatory."[18] Indeed, for Khalidi, a "Middle Eastern democracy is something of an oxymoron."[19] He insists that the "Palestinians should be given a chance; their putative democracy should be subjected to a real test only in ten or fifteen years."[20]

Following the 1988 declaration of independence, the PLO opted to use the intifada as part of its Sadatist pragmatist strategy. In this frame of reference, the intifada (although a spontaneous revolt by the oppressed under Israeli military occupation) came to play the same role for the PLO that the 1973 October War played in Sadat's pragmatist strategy. Here, of course, it is an intifada coopted as an idea of triumph, an idea of strength, which justifies the PLO's "peace" offensive, the "peace of the brave" as Arafat often calls it. Whereas the intifada continued to shake the Israeli occupation to its foundations, the intifada as a bargaining chip for the PLO leadership and its apologists among Palestinian intellectuals was done away with in Oslo. In fact, the road back to the occupation begins in Oslo and is strengthened by subsequent agreements including the Washington summit in October 1996.

Hasan Asfur, one of those who participated in the secret negotiations in Oslo follows a clear Sadatist strategy. According to his fantastic vision,

> Negotiations were not between a defeated party and a victorious one imposing its conditions on the defeated party, it being known that we were not the strong party, but neither were we the weaker party. This is the philosophy that governed the negotiation equation between the PLO and the Israeli government.[21]

The new concessions are packaged as the route to liberation, even though this new vision of liberation resulting in formal apartheid with Palestinian police acting at the behest of the Israeli occupation, was not part of the pre-Madrid Palestinian idea of liberation. The new illusory goals of the PLO leadership and the way they are experienced on the ground is reminiscent of the Zionist response to anti-Semitism in nineteenth-century Europe. Whereas European Jews wanted to end anti-Semitism and discrimination in order to become equal citizens in secular states, Zionism offered them a solution fully complicit with anti-Semitism, one predicated on their voluntary self-expulsion from Europe and the destruction of diaspora Jewish culture and packaged the entire project as Jewish "liberation." Zionism's cooptation of the history of anti-Semitism to legitimate its project is paralleled by Arafat's cooptation of the intifada and its victims and heroes, not to mention the history of terror visited upon the Palestinians by Israel, in order to legitimate his new vassal regime. There is a difference, of course. The Zionist solution produced European Jews as colonial settlers allied with their former enemies, but the PLO solution is producing Palestinians as for ever subjugated to Israeli apartheid and military occupation while their leadership is allied with their enemy and the sponsor of that enemy in ruling the bantustans being carved out of the occupied territories.

On the economic front, following the signing of Oslo I, the promises of international investment in the Israeli-occupied and PLO-administered bantustans gripped a wide sector of the realist-pragmatist Palestinian intelligentsia, many of whom have visited Washington since 1993 on US Agency for International Development (AID)-sponsored training missions. Nusaybah, one of the more visible of the realist-pragmatist intellectuals, while calling for "sell[ing] the agreement and the development plans [to the Palestinian people]," asserted to the *New York Times*, that "we want to make a quantifiable leap, not just develop into *another* third world country [emphasis added]."[22] Nusaybah's views, however, are part of the fantastic schemes that many Palestinian realist-pragmatist intellectuals and the PLO leadership have for a bantustanized Palestine emulating the examples of Singapore and Hong Kong, as models for Palestinian "development."[23]

Another important function for these intellectuals is self-defense against criticisms leveled against them by other Palestinian intellectuals spanning the political spectrum, both inside and outside Palestine.[24] Special venom is reserved for diaspora critics on account of their not living in Palestine (as if this was a choice), an attitude resembling the contempt Israeli Jews have for diaspora Jewish critics on the same grounds. Saeb Erakat criticizes Edward Said for such geographic distance. He asserts that "it is easy to criticize 6,000–7,000 miles away."[25] Arafat echoes Erakat in his direct dismissal of one of Said's books criticizing the Oslo Accords. He says of Said's book:

> This is too absurd a book for me to respond to. Who made the intifada in Gaza? He, in America, did not make the intifada!... The PLO made the intifada through its people and its children... while he, in America does not feel the suffering of his people... ![26]

It should be stressed here that Said's diasporic condition, as he stresses, is one he shares with the majority of the Palestinian people.

Salim Tamari, another pragmatist, has a more demagogical weapon in his "Marxist" arsenal to delegitimize critics of the DoP:

> The people who are against the agreement are afraid of the challenges and the tasks of becoming an oppositional force in a civil society, which is ruled by their own bourgeoisie, their own state, their own repressive authority... They want to go back to the nostalgia of the liberationist struggle.[27]

For Tamari, the Palestinian state is assumed non-ironically to have been established already, and those who deny his fantastic claim, passing as realism, are essentially cowards.[28] In a more sober state, Tamari identifies the two basic challenges facing Arafat's authority as "legitimacy and control."[29] His failure in both is not attributed to his function as an enforcer of the Israeli occupation, but rather to the fantastic claim that in "the case of Palestine, the transition from a revolutionary situation (1988–1992) to a routinized regime of self-government has occurred far too quickly, and without proper substantial decolonization of the South African variety."[30] Despite the increasing tenor of his criticisms of Arafat, Tamari continues to insist on the fantasy that the Israeli protectorate run by Arafat is actually "self-government."

Ahmad S. Khalidi, in turn, supports Arafat's regime, but not because it is a democratic popular regime—he is as aware of its shortcomings as are Erakat and Tamari. For him, however, the

> unpalatable truth... is that there appears to be no credible alternative to this leadership, not from within the Islamic movement, certainly not from amongst the discredited ranks of the secular factions..., nor from amongst the disaffected independents and intellectuals who feel disillusioned and marginalized by the process.[31]

Khalidi presents those opposing Arafat's deal as imprisoned in a miserable past, unwilling to let go of the pain of past injuries, when, in fact, they are critics of present oppressive Israeli policies and of the PLO deal with the Israelis leading to the maintenance if not intensification of these policies. He concludes that

> in the end, nothing can make up for this loss, but nothing can be gained in futile pursuit of the past either. What is needed from Israel is not self-righteousness in peace but rather a genuine appreciation of how—despite everything—the Palestinians are willing to look forward, not back.[32]

What is at stake for Khalidi, then, is not the defeat and humiliation Palestinians are experiencing, but rather Israel's lack of appreciation for how well Palestinian realist-pragmatists are adjusting to the defeat of their own people.

Hanan Ashrawi implicitly criticizes those who dare to oppose Oslo, not because she is unaware of its shortcomings, but rather in the name of her "realist" illusion that what is at stake is "put[ting] Palestine on the map."[33] She asserts that the time of the signing of the DoP "was not time for recriminations, apprehensions, or internal soul searching and accountability."[34] One wonders, if for Ashrawi and her cohorts, such a time will ever come. As for the non-pragmatist critic Edward Said, he stresses that "little has been more demoralizing to the cause of Palestinian self-determination than intellectuals whose premature compromises on matters of principle have made the word 'peace' synonymous with giving up before getting anything."[35]

The need to be accepted by the West, to present Palestinians, or at least their liberal intellectuals, as Western white people, is a desire that both the PLO leadership and these intellectuals have tried to realize in the last ten years. The intifada continued a process begun when Israel invaded Lebanon in 1982. It was then that Palestinians, for the first time, were being shown as victims who deserved the sympathy of white Americans and Europeans.[36] In fact, this process is responsible for the emergence of a number of Palestinians, as spokespeople, who dress, speak and act like "white" people. Proving the "whiteness" of Palestinians has been the underlying premise of the PLO's approach since the beginning of its outreach efforts to the West. Part of the agenda of Hamas and other Islamists is to counter these attempts at presenting Palestinians as "white"—or "Western" in Islamist lingo. Recognizing this trend, Said states that

> all they wanted was acceptance. They weren't interested in fighting, in being equal, they just wanted the white man to say they were Okay. That's all... This leadership is what Frantz Fanon used to call "Black Skin, white Masks." They're desperate to be white.[37]

He describes this trend further by explaining that

> most Palestinian intellectuals have been too anxious to bolster their own case, following Arafat and his lieutenants in the abandonment of their principles and history just to be recognized by the West, to be invited to the Brookings Institution, and to appear on U.S. television.[38]

This transformation wherein Palestinian intellectuals who previously opposed the occupation, PLO concessions, and US hegemony, but now support, wittingly or unwittingly, all three, is not a unique transformation. It would seem that like their Soviet counterparts who rushed to trade in their communism for realist-pragmatism upon the fall of the Soviet state, or their Latin American counterparts who, like Fernando Henrique Cardoso, traded in their dependency theory approach for positions of power (in the case of Cardoso, the position of president of Brazil), Palestinian intellectuals, attuned to the exigencies of political power and the benefits that could accrue to them from it, traded in their national liberation goals for a pro-Western pragmatism. Many among them, like Erakat and Ashrawi, who before Oslo threatened to resign their positions in protest against PLO concessions, were to later hold ministerial positions in the

Palestine National Authority (PNA).[39] Ashrawi, like many in the intellectual pragmatist camp, continued, until recently, to criticize mildly Arafat and his agreements with the Israelis. She even pledged publicly that, despite Arafat's insistent invitations, "I will not be part of any political structure, nor will I accept any official post."[40] She insisted then, on what she called, "a graceful exit,"[41] one which sadly never materialized. When she did leave her official post temporarily while remaining within Arafat's fold, she stated that:

> I was convinced that my place lay outside the political domain. Mine was the difficult choice, and I was aware that in all probability it would be a lonely and painful task. But it had to be done, and I was determined to proceed.[42]

Disclaiming any interest in holding a position of power, she quotes herself telling Arafat: "I personally do not aspire to a position and I did not get into this for power or benefits. I want nothing . . . I don't want any official post."[43] This refusal, she insisted, was "a question of conscience and conviction, as well as a pledge to a future of nation building."[44] Her subsequent acceptance of a ministerial position, however, demonstrates the changing trends that her conscience and conviction undergo continually.

The loss of the aura of the PLO as a liberation movement is described by Ashrawi as a fateful development:

> [w]ith a global embrace, the PLO, our exiled revolutionary leadership, lost its immunity from internal criticism and accountability. The transition from the glamour of a national liberation movement to the mundane tasks of building and running a state had begun.[45]

On another occasion, she claims that part of the difficulty with the PLO in this transitional period is the persistence in it of "a 'liberation movement' mindset as opposed to a state-building mindset."[46] Ashrawi's fantastic "state-building" claims, like Tamari's, are engineered to uphold the fantasy propagated by the PNA. Any questioning of the existence of this phantasmatic Palestinian state renders the critic an extremist non-pragmatist who rejects reality. The fact that more Palestinians have been killed and injured since the PNA assumed "authority" by both the Israelis and the Palestinian police, that land confiscations continue unabated, that the economy has worsened with skyrocketing unemployment, and that the freedom of movement within the West Bank and Gaza has become much more restricted than before, all are glossed over as the whinings of non-pragmatists who refuse the pragmatist position of waiting for the consistently deferred hope of independence, that the pragmatists claim as their strategic goal.

Ashrawi's new ministerial position has not prevented her from leveling mild criticisms against the PNA as a way to legitimize herself as a critical intellectual. However, in doing so, Ashrawi is not alone; even Arafat himself has criticized some of the failings of the PNA. One of her more recent apologies for the Arafatist authority concerns the banning of Edward Said's books in the Palestinian bantustans.

She told *The Chronicle of Higher Education* that she "personally had investigated the confiscations and had concluded that no official Palestinian body had issued any order banning the books."[47] The fact that the books remain banned, however, would not deter a committed "realist" like Ashrawi. Edward Said responded to Ashrawi's "investigations" by lamenting her previous role as a critical intellectual: "It is a tragic pity that so gifted a person as Dr. Ashrawi, who is now a member of Arafat's discredited and impotent 'government,' should find it necessary to engage in disinformation of the kind she once condemned."[48]

These Palestinian apologist intellectuals are not realists at all. Their fantastic schemes demonstrate that "realism" is an effect of a Western liberal discourse that they fail to question. As Said put it: "It is simply not enough to say that we live in the New World Order, which requires 'pragmatism' and 'realism,' and that we must shed the old ideas of nationalism and liberation. That is pure nonsense. No outside power like Israel or the United States can unilaterally decree what reality is . . . ".[49] These realist intellectuals are ultimately reduced to the function of the Palestinian comprador bourgeoisie whom they serve. The new Palestinian intellectuals are comprador intellectuals whose business is the import–export sector. They export opinion polls, sociological data, official apologies, and personal memoirs, in addition to their own voices and images, which are featured in the *New York Times*, on CNN, and on speaking tours in the United States. They import IMF ideas, World Bank plans, international invitations, USAID-sponsored training, Western funding for their local institutions, and Western public and media accolades. They oppose any critical intellectual production at home or in the diaspora, and are linked like the class with which they are allied to imperial interests and policies of which they are the main local beneficiaries. These are indeed organic intellectuals in the Gramscian sense whose class interests are clear. But they are also religious intellectuals. As Edward Said has said: their "new god . . . is the West."[50] They are the kind of intellectuals who choose to "passively allow . . . a patron or an authority to direct [them]" rather than "represent . . . the truth to the best of [their] ability."[51] Unlike secular intellectuals for whom such gods always fail, the god of these religious intellectuals is omnipotent. As for those who don't believe in this god, they are nothing but heretics whose books are to be banned and whose voices must be silenced.

7 Return or permanent exile?*

Palestinian refugees and the ends of Oslo

Before the "peace process" that began in Madrid in 1991 and continued with the inauguration of the Oslo process in 1993, all representatives of the Palestinians inside and outside the Palestine Liberation Organization agreed that the varied interests of the Palestinian people were inherently compatible. The "peace process," however, has altered this equation radically. Following the various agreements signed with Israel by the PLO and subsequently by the Palestinian Authority (PA), the interests of the different sections of the Palestinian people effectively were separated and made incompatible if not outright contradictory. Palestinian Israelis, through their elected leadership, are challenging Israel to shed its Jewish character and become a state of *all* its citizens, while West Bank and Gaza Palestinians, through their elected leadership, seem to be preparing for the fantasy of a sovereign independent Palestinian state. To realize this fantasy, the leadership of the West Bank and Gaza Palestinians is heeding "pragmatic" and "realist" advice on the necessity to concede the rights of refugee and diaspora Palestinians to return and/or be compensated. In turn, diaspora and refugee Palestinians, since the Oslo process began, have been bereft of leadership and with no identifiable goals. Such a development makes it essential to chart briefly the course that led to this outcome and assess the recent positions and proposals advanced by official and non-official Palestinians and Israelis on how to resolve the refugee question.

The road to Oslo

The prerequisite to this situation was the 1988 Declaration of Independence proclaimed by the Palestine National Council at a meeting in Algiers. Until that time, the PLO, at least officially, had sought to create a secular, democratic Palestinian state in all of pre-1948 Palestine, a state wherein all Palestinian refugees would be repatriated, the Israeli occupation of the West Bank and Gaza would end, and the situation of Israeli apartheid, under whose yoke Palestinian Israelis live, would be terminated. Unofficially, however, the change occurred much earlier. Whereas between 1964 and 1974, the PLO had tilted more toward the diaspora in its program for liberation, beginning in the mid-1970s, pressure from the emerging

* This essay was first published in 1998.

pro-PLO Palestinian élite in the West Bank and Gaza to accept a two-state solution was bearing fruit (the PLO has always ignored Palestinians living in Israel). The two-state solution, which became more acceptable as early as 1974, was officially understood to be a prelude to the ultimate unification of Palestine, and that the establishment of a West Bank and Gaza mini-state would not be at the expense of the diaspora and the refugees. Although most groups within the PLO, including leftist groups, had informally accepted that repatriation would be impossible in the context of a two-state solution, officially they all stuck to the position that achieving one did not preclude the achievement of the other.

In those years, the Palestinian leadership rested with the diaspora, which built, nourished, and sustained it. The 1982 defeat of the diaspora leadership in Beirut and its exile to Tunis not only weakened the PLO but also diaspora Palestinians who had sustained the hope that the PLO would be able to realize their dreams. The West Bank and Gaza intifada, which erupted in December 1987, jolted the Palestinian people everywhere. Terrified of an independent Palestinian leadership in the Occupied Territories, the increasingly corrupt PLO sought to undermine it by hijacking the intifada financially and organizationally. But the intifada strengthened the West Bank and Gaza Palestinians' push for an official unequivocal acceptance of the two-state solution. In that context, the Palestine National Council declared an independent Palestinian state in 1988 in the West Bank and Gaza Strip as an expression of the will of the Palestinian people's revolt against their Israeli oppressors. The declaration itself finally constituted the PLO's official stamp on the two-state solution, with no mention of the rights of the diaspora or Palestinian Israelis except in the statement that the independent state shall be the "state of Palestinians wherever they may be."[1]

Until that moment, the PLO did not refer to the 1948 United Nations General Assembly Resolution 194, which affirmed that Palestinian refugees

> wishing to return to their homes and live at peace with their neighbors should be permitted to do so at the earliest practicable date, and that compensation should be paid for the property of those choosing not to return and for loss of or damage to property, which, under principles of international law or in equity, should be made good by the Governments or authorities responsible.[2]

The 1988 declaration marked the first time in its history that the PNC reaffirmed the Palestinian people's right of return based on UN resolutions; previously, that right was always affirmed with no reference to such resolutions.[3] As Rashid Khalidi explains:

> in explicitly accepting the terms of resolution 194 of 1948, the PLO has accepted certain crucial limitations on a putative absolute right of return. The first is that Palestinians who were made refugees in 1948 are offered an option whereby those "choosing not to return" become eligible for compensation for their property... Acceptance of the fait accompli of Israel's creation in 1948 at the expense of the Palestinians has now in effect

> been legitimized by the PLO ... the politically impossible demand that all Palestinians made refugees in 1948 be allowed to return is dropped, without dropping the principle that such people have certain rights in the context of a negotiated settlement, and without abandoning the reading of history which is the basis of this principle. This also makes the demand of implementation of the right of return a slightly more realistic one, without the PLO appearing to make a concession.[4]

Moreover, although neither the PLO nor the PA has specified officially the destinations of returning refugees, individuals associated with both have done so. As early as 1989, Nabil Sha'th and Faysal Husayni made statements to the effect that such destinations would be primarily confined to the Palestinian state-to-be.[5] The subsequent peregrinations of Yasser Arafat to satisfy US conditions for speaking to the PLO were exemplified by his pathetic renunciation of armed resistance, coded "terrorism" in Zionist-speak, and his declaration that the now infamous PLO charter was "caduc."[6] Even these humiliating concessions only achieved a short-term dialogue soon to be terminated by the Americans.

Following the Gulf War, and the American plan to convene an international conference in Madrid, the Palestinians were not even allowed to participate in an independent delegation. Upon Israeli insistence, only West Bank (but not East Jerusalem) and Gaza Palestinians were allowed to participate as part of the Jordanian delegation. As for the PLO, for fear of a competing leadership, it sought to undermine the Palestinians negotiating within the Madrid process by conducting its own secret talks with the Israelis. Its subsequent signing of the Declaration of Principles (DoP) was premised on its transformation from a diaspora leadership to a West Bank and Gaza leadership who would be willing to forsake the rights of the diaspora and the refugees altogether. It was within the confines of the DoP that the PLO leadership was transformed into the Palestinian Authority and the Palestinian refugees were relegated to one of the many issues to be discussed during the "final status talks" whenever they materialize.

By separating the interests of the inside (native West Bank and Gaza Palestinians) and the outside (diaspora and refugee Palestinians) and forcing the PLO to accept that separation officially, Israel effectively laid down the groundwork for the Oslo Process. It was in Madrid that the issue of refugees was separated from the bilateral tracks and relegated to what was called the "multilateral track" which set up a "Refugee Working Group" (RWG) chaired by Canada. The purpose of the RWG is not to negotiate over the status of the refugees, but rather to improve the living conditions of the Palestinian refugees, particularly those outside the West Bank and Gaza. The only political issue that was discussed at the RWG besides Palestinian representation was the question of family reunification wherein the Israelis agreed to increase the pre-existing annual quota of 1,000–2,000, it being understood that Israel had never fulfilled the earlier or later quota anyway.[7]

As for the DoP, its declared aim was to reach a "permanent settlement based on Security Council Resolution 242 and 338."[8] Resolution 242, as is commonly known, calls, as an aside, for a "just settlement of the refugee problem."[9] The DoP asserts that only in the permanent status negotiations between representatives of the Palestinian people and the Israeli government will the remaining issues, including that of the "refugees," be covered.[10] Moreover the DoP called for inviting the governments of Jordan and Egypt to participate in establishing "cooperation arrangements," which will include the "constitution of a Continuing Committee that will decide by agreement on the modalities of admission of persons displaced from the West Bank and Gaza Strip in 1967" (Article XII). As of yet, neither committee has produced anything that is remotely connected to resolving the status of Palestinian refugees. Moreover, the so-called peace process remains frozen on issues pertinent to non-refugee issues which themselves are being compromised.

Protecting Israeli interests as pragmatism

In anticipation of the final status negotiations, much literature has appeared on the question of the refugees. Those proposals that express semi-official positions most likely will be used as a reference for the negotiations—should these ever take place—and thus merit careful scrutiny. Before proceeding to review these different proposals, a presentation of the human dimension of this question is in order, namely the numbers of refugees from 1948 and 1967. In 1995, according to the figures of the United Nations Relief and Works Agency (UNRWA), the 1948 refugees (and their descendants) living in the West Bank, Gaza, Jordan, Lebanon, and Syria numbered 3,093,174 people. As for 1948 refugees who remained in Israel proper (and are referred to by the Israeli government as "present absentees"), they number between 120,000 and 150,000.[11] In 1994, the number of 1967 refugees (termed displaced persons), numbered 1,132,326 people, half of whom also were 1948 refugees, that is, those who had been displaced for the second time.[12] These numbers do not include Palestinian refugees in Egypt, Iraq, North Africa and the Gulf Arab countries, nor do they include Palestinian Bedouins who were no longer allowed to return to their grazing lands within Israel, nor the middle class Palestinian refugees who did not register with UNRWA, nor the children of Palestinian women who married non-refugee Palestinians or non-Palestinians, as UNRWA no longer considers these as refugees. Those belonging to these four categories number around 300,000 people.[13]

What is striking about most of the proposals advancing solutions to the refugee question is the discourse of "pragmatism" and "realism" which they deploy. The definition of pragmatism in this discourse is one wherein everything Israel rejects is "not pragmatic," while everything it accepts is "pragmatic." What this means is that the Palestinians are the only party being asked to be "pragmatic," as Israeli positions function as base referents and are therefore deployed as "pragmatic" a priori. Examples of the deployment of this discourse are found in the two most recent projects that have been advanced to resolve the refugee problem: Donna Arzt's *Refugees Into Citizens, Palestinians and the End of the Arab-Israeli Conflict*,[14] and the proposal advanced by Harvard University's Program on International Conflict Analysis and Resolution, which was debated by a group of Palestinians and Israelis and written by Khalil Shikaki and Joseph Alpher (in addition to Shikaki, the Palestinian group included other Palestinian pragmatists, namely Ghassan Khatib, Ibrahim Dakkak, Yezid Sayigh, Nadim Rouhana, and Nabeel Kassis).[15] Both are important as they are being touted as starting points for the most likely scenario for refugee negotiations.

Arzt's proposal, considered "objective" by mainstream Western, Israeli, and some PA-supported circles, foresees the settlement of Palestinian refugees mostly in neighboring Arab countries and in the West Bank with the multi-conditioned possibility of returning a mere 75,000 refugees to Israel. The premise of the book is that no one can establish who was responsible for the Palestinian exodus in 1948 and therefore everyone must share in the responsibility of resolving the plight of the refugees—not only in terms of resettlement but also in terms of compensation. Some of the possible explanations for the exodus that Arzt lists include Israeli expulsion as well as the now discredited Israeli propagandistic claim that Arab leaders called on the Palestinians to leave in order to clear the way for the advancing Arab armies. Even if one were to accept Arzt's claim that it is impossible to establish who was responsible for the exodus of *every* Palestinian in 1948 and 1967, one, nevertheless, can easily prove with extant *Israeli* evidence that Palestinians living in Lydda and Ramla, to take one salient example, were expelled by Israeli army units led by none other than Yitzhak Rabin, that thousands more were expelled from the Galilee area, and that 12,500 Palestinians were deported individually by the Israeli government between 1967 and 1994.[16] Evidence abounds for other expulsions from different cities and towns. Despite Arzt's interest in verifying responsibility, she never investigates from within her conceptual framework whether those whose expulsion is supported by Israeli government records should be allowed to return to Israel and be compensated by it while the rest be the responsibility of multiple parties, including Israel. Moreover, even if one agreed with Arzt's and the Israeli government's propaganda that Israel should not compensate the refugees because it did not expel them, then should not the compensation for stolen property be the responsibility of those who expropriated it? It is an uncontested fact that Israeli Jews and the Israeli government are the parties that took over the abandoned property of Palestinians in 1948 and refuse to return it to its rightful owners. However, Arzt is only concerned that Israel be spared the financial responsibilities, not to mention the demographic "threat" that Palestinians are said to constitute to its existence. She soberly states that the Palestinian refugee question should be resolved with minimal Israeli pay-backs in order to calm "Israelis who will need assurance that a Palestinian will not someday show up on their children's doorstep demanding title to the property and/or with a multi-million dollar compensation claim."[17] Arzt suggests that Israel's "contribution to the compensation pool could, appropriately, come from the 'rents' it collected in the 1940s and early 1950s from the Jewish users of 'absentee' Arab property."[18] As for returning refugees, Israel could take 75,000 refugees whom it should have the right to carefully screen for a variety of sins and crimes. Arzt is careful to add that such a returning group will most likely be restricted to non-reproductive Palestinians: "A population subgroup very likely to seek return... would be... the oldest living generation of Palestinians, the ones who retain personal memories of life before 1948."[19]

The implicit concern here seems to be that a young population of 75,000 refugees might reproduce in ways detrimental to maintaining Jewish demographic supremacy in Israel!

The Harvard group study proposes four solutions, two "traditional" Palestinian and Israeli solutions and two "compromise" solutions, one Palestinian and one Israeli. A conclusion includes commonalities between the Palestinian and the Israeli compromise solutions. Whereas Arzt's solution is legitimated by a "Foreword" written for her by a Palestinian Jordanian, Rami Khouri, the Harvard paper expresses the views of a committee of Palestinians and Israelis. The Palestinian compromise position "seeks to provide an acceptable, honorable—though not necessarily just—resolution of the refugee issue while accommodating the realities on the ground and Israeli security concerns."[20] Whereas this solution calls on Israel to "fully acknowledge" the "individual moral right of Palestinian refugees to return to their homes and property in Palestine," the proposal writers insist that "[n]o return *en masse* of the Palestinian refugees is envisaged... [rather] a return of only a limited number is seen as feasible."[21] The writers assert that most refugees will opt for compensation and concede to Israel the right "to have a say to the number of refugees allowed to return."[22] However, they do assert that Palestinians who want to return should have the right to return to a Palestinian state-to-be with Israel having no say in that matter. The compromise is stated succinctly by the authors: "In this final settlement, the Palestinians make a strategic trade-off. They demand a return to the 1967 border, in order to absorb the largest possible number of refugees, in return for foregoing the full exercise of the right of return."[23] The remaining refugees should be settled in host countries. Israel should be responsible to find the funds and to pay both individual compensation as well as collective compensation, the latter to be paid to the Palestinian state-to-be. This solution, the authors tell us, "provides *realistic* and *reasonable* justice by granting a moral/political right while acknowledging realities on the ground [emphases added]."[24]

Whereas the Israeli government has officially refused to make the 1948 refugees part of the negotiation agenda and consistently makes statements that only few of the 1967 refugees will be allowed to return, some Israelis are advancing informed proposals about what the Israeli government might be agreeable to in the future. While, on the one hand, Yitzhak Rabin insisted after the DoP that Israel would not allow more than a few thousand 1967 refugees to return, adding that if the PLO "expect[s] tens of thousands [of refugees to return,] they live in a dream, an illusion,"[25] on the other hand, the Israeli compromise position, as the Harvard group of Israeli politicians and pundits see it, insists that Israel can share "practical (but not moral) responsibility, together with the other parties to the process that culminated in the 1948 war, for the plight [but not the flight] and suffering of the refugees."[26] Furthermore, the fact that half of the 1948 Palestinian refugees "left" Palestine before May 14, 1948, is not relevant to the exegetical eye of these authors. These Israelis assert that in their compromise "Israel also accepts the right of return to the Palestinian State, but not to Israel proper. Israel also may accept repatriation of 'tens of thousands' of Palestinian refugees as part of its family reunification program."[27] On the question of compensation, Israel would compensate Palestinians on a "collective basis" in tandem with the "relevant Arab countries creat[ing] a similar mechanism for Arab collective compensation of Jewish refugees"[28]—a reference to Arab Jews who immigrated to Israel between 1949 and 1953. Also the Palestinian state must limit the number of returning Palestinians to its own territory, otherwise the Israelis will curtail their obligations of compensation.[29] The combined authors believe that the ultimate solution would be somewhere in between their two compromise solutions, it being understood that these solutions will not apply to Palestinian Israeli internal refugees.[30] Israel's possible payment of compensation to refugees

> might generate parallel demands by Israeli Arabs who also abandoned lands or were removed from them, even though they remained in Israel. This could have far-reaching implications for Jewish–Arab relations with Israel. Hence the Israeli–Palestinian agreement on refugees must, from the Israeli standpoint, clearly define the PLO role as representing only Palestinians outside of Israel, while the government of Israel is responsible for all Israeli citizens, including Arabs.[31]

Actually, the compromise position presented by the Harvard group of Israelis does not differ much from a proposal presented in 1994 by Shlomo Gazit, a retired Israeli army general with military intelligence background and a close friend of Yitzhak Rabin. Gazit also became an advisor to the Israeli multilateral negotiating teams, with special reference to refugee issues.[32] Gazit, like the Harvard group of Israelis, is clear that "the option of 'return' should never be given to the Palestinians."[33] If Israel does decide to return some refugees on a humanitarian basis, and second only to its security and national concerns, the Palestinians should have no say in the number of those returning.[34]

In addition to these proposals, a number of semi-official Palestinian proposals and positions also have been circulating.[35] One such position is articulated by Salim Tamari, who is a member of the Refugee Working Group created by the Madrid Process. Tamari begins by situating the refugee question in the "peace process." He states that "solving the refugee problem is fast becoming part of the new dichotomy within Palestinian politics between the contingencies of state-building on the one hand and the demands of the diaspora for representation and repatriation on the other."[36]

It was upon Palestinian insistence on including refugees as a final status element that the RWG was born in the first place. This move was engineered to

> send a signal to Palestinian refugees in Jordan, Syria and Lebanon that they had not been forgotten in the protracted interim negotiations. This in turn would lend much-needed legitimacy to the impending signing of an Israeli–Palestinian accord, which was bound to be seen as too conciliatory by diaspora Palestinians without a refugee component.[37]

However, as already mentioned, the RWG was not designed to *resolve* the refugee problem, but rather to *dissolve* it through resettlement and amelioration of standards of living.[38] Tamari concludes by asserting that:

> As final status negotiations loom on the horizon, immense diplomatic pressure will start building on the Palestinians to abandon their insistence on the right of return. The Israelis have made it clear that they will not support any categorical "right of return" for the Palestinians—either to Israel itself or to the West Bank and Gaza.[39]

Whereas it took the Palestinians four decades to finally accept the concessions enshrined in Resolution 194, Tamari surmises that Palestinians will have to forget that resolution altogether. He firmly states that "repeated reference to UN resolutions on Palestinian refugees, particularly General Assembly Resolution 194 (1948) and Security Council Resolution 237 (1967), is futile even though they do constitute the proper international legal framework in which these issues should be addressed."[40] He asserts that "Palestinian negotiators . . . operate under constraints that dictate that issues of principle and ideological predisposition be tempered by what is *realizable* and *obtainable* [emphases added]."[41] Tamari also recommends that in

> return for Arab and Palestinian acceptance to absorb the bulk of Palestinian refugees in the West Bank, Gaza and Arab host countries, Israel should absorb a limited number of refugees. Proper compensation should be paid to all refugees who choose to return as well as to those who choose to be naturalized in their host countries.[42]

Tamari is not alone in his recommendations. For example, Sari Nusaybah (along with the Israeli Mark Heller), in a proposal to deal with the refugee question in the context of a two-state solution, does not require Israel to repatriate the refugees. All he requires is that "Israel should be prepared to entertain applications on a case-by-case basis on humanitarian grounds."[43] Indeed, the pragmatism of these proposals revolves around finding a face-saving formula with minimal costs for Israel, not the Palestinians. Israel is not expected to repatriate the Palestinians it expelled, but were it to ever consider to repatriate a few, this would be considered a "humanitarian" act on its part.

Pragmatism and refugee interests

This discourse of pragmatism is not only prevalent among the group of Palestinian comprador intellectuals associated with the Palestinian Authority, it has also influenced many Palestinian intellectuals who are committed to their people's struggle for justice but who see no way out for the refugees in the face of continued Israeli intransigence and US support of it. In a tentative proposal, Rashid Khalidi wants to offer a solution that he calls "attainable justice, or justice within the realm of the possible."[44] Khalidi, one of the few Palestinians involved in the Madrid process who opted out soon after the PLO's deal at Oslo, asserts that

> the refugee issue cannot be addressed as many other issues have been dealt with in the Israeli–Palestinian negotiations to date . . . [wherein] history has been tossed out the window . . . as if there were no past which had to be accounted for and dealt with.[45]

He says that

> [o]n the refugee issue, there can be no such cavalier treatment of history . . . it is because this issue is so central to the national narrative and the self-view of the Palestinian people that any approach which tries to sweep history under the rug will fail utterly. The Palestinians might put up with humiliating and unequal agreements based on ignoring history in the economic sphere, in the area of security, and in other domains. But it is hard to visualize them standing for an attempt to pretend that the refugee issue does not have specific historic roots, and can be resolved accordingly.[46]

Khalidi's call is a genuine one for a realizable solution. In the light of current and projected Israeli intransigence, he affirms that "to argue seriously for Israeli acceptance of unlimited liability . . . means to argue against the possibility of any real solution to this issue."[47] Whereas Khalidi's pessimism is understandable, arguing seriously for unlimited Israeli liability does not mean that this is the only thing Palestinians would accept; it simply means that this should be the Palestinian opening position in any negotiations, as it is based on historical facts and on historical and national rights. Giving up these UN-sanctioned rights before the negotiations begin will surely snowball into numerous concessions. Khalidi's conclusion that "it is inconceivable that most refugees will be allowed to exercise their right of return to their original homes in what is now Israel for the foreseeable future, or perhaps ever," unfortunately has been taken up by pro-Israeli US academics (such as the Harvard Group led by Leonard Hausman) who quote Khalidi to add legitimacy to their recommendations, which amount to liquidating the refugee issue.[48]

Khalidi asserts the legal right of Palestinians to return in principle. He likens their situation to "people forced to flee their homes by a flood which has permanently inundated their original communities, and who have a right to return which they simply cannot exercise by reason of *force majeure*."[49] The only difference, he hastens to add, is that "unlike the flood, the state of Israel is not a state of nature—although it sometimes may have seemed like one to those unfortunate enough to find themselves in its path. And because it is not a force of nature, it can and must be held responsible for its actions."[50] Khalidi calls on the Israeli government to pay reparations rather than compensation, wherein the former designates its responsibility.

Khalidi's solution includes Israeli recognition of the hurt it inflicted on the Palestinian people, an acceptance that all Palestinian refugees and their descendants have a right to return to their homes in principle, although most won't be able to exercise that right as a result of Israel's refusal and/or because their homes and villages no longer exist. He suggests that "a few thousand or tens of thousands of people" whose villages still exist or who have family in Israel should be allowed to return.[51] A third element of Khalidi's solution is the payment of reparations for all those not allowed to return and compensation for those who lost property in 1948. These sums for property losses alone (not to mention reparations) range from $92 billion to $147 billion at 1984 prices. In addition to the compensation, Khalidi comes up with a reparation figure of $20,000 per person for an arbitrarily chosen figure of 2 million refugees totaling $40 billion, which amounts to little more than a decade worth of US aid to Israel (Atif Kubursi's calculations in 1994 prices reach the figure of $253 billion in reparations and compensation).[52] It is important to note that Israeli colonial settlers who had to vacate illegal Israeli colonies set up on stolen land in the Sinai before it was returned to Egypt were paid $250,000 per household.[53] The fourth element of Khalidi's solution is the right of Palestinian refugees to live in the state of Palestine-to-be, which will only be circumscribed by its absorptive capacity, and finally a resolution to Palestinian refugees in Lebanon and Jordan.[54]

Is return pragmatic?

Salman Abu Sitta is the only Palestinian intellectual to date who is not awed by what is "realistic," "pragmatic," or "reasonable" within the confines of the Madrid and Oslo process. Unlike most proposals dealing with refugees, which look at what is practical from the viewpoint of Israeli leaders and which aim to resolve the Israeli part of this problem at the expense of Palestinians, Abu Sitta proposes what he simply calls "The Feasibility of the Right of Return." He begins by affirming that:

> One of the persistent myths is the "impracticality" of the return of the refugees, on the assumption that the country is full of immigrants, the villages are destroyed and it is impossible to find old property boundaries. This view is advanced by the Israelis and by well-meaning people who agree that the Right of Return is perfectly legal but cannot be implemented on physical grounds.[55]

Abu Sitta counters these claims by demonstrating that the "return of the refugees is practically feasible, and even desirable for permanent peace to prevail."[56] The elements of Abu Sitta's proposal are as follows: The majority of refugees whether they live inside or outside Palestine are within a 100 mile radius of their former homes. Although most of their houses are destroyed,

> a return would be to the same land, most frequently the same site, with reconstruction of villages and repairing long-neglected Palestinian cities. With the exception of the Central District, relatively few village sites are occupied by modern construction. Most Kibbutz and prefab units are installed away from old village remains.[57]

Also,

> it is claimed that boundaries have disappeared and are impossible to determine. Available Palestine and Israel maps, assisted by modern technology, now used by Israel to lease refugee's land, are sufficient to determine old and new boundaries. It can be demonstrated that all boundaries and ownerships are well recorded. Not only the villages are kept [*sic*] in the memory of the refugees and their children, but their images are kept for posterity through the British aerial survey of 1945–46.[58]

To the ostensible horror of Israelis, Abu Sitta dares to divide Israel into Areas A, B, and C. Area A includes 8 percent of the land in Israel and is occupied by 68 percent of the Israeli Jewish population. Area B encompasses 7 percent of the land and is inhabited by 10 percent of the Jewish population. Thus 78 percent of Jews in Israel live on 15 percent of the land. Area C encompassing 85 percent of the land area in Israel "is remarkably similar, but not exactly identical, to the Palestinian land from which they were driven." The inhabitants of Area C include 800,000 urban Jews living in urban centers, 154,000 rural Jews and 465,000 Palestinian Israelis. "Thus 154,000 Jews cultivate the land of 4,476,000 refugees who are prevented from returning to it."[59] Since most of the rural Jews are leasing the land, once the lease is up, the land can be given back to the Palestinians. Even with the return of the refugees, overall population density in Israel would be 482 persons/sq. km., instead of the present 261. "The new overall density of 482 p/sq. km., is a far cry from the congested miserable conditions which the refugees have to endure while their land is the playground of the privileged Kibbutz."

If his plan is implemented, Abu Sitta states that Area A will remain largely Jewish (76 percent), Area B will be mixed, and Area C will be largely Palestinian (81 percent). Since area A would be congested, Palestinians from that area (numbering 900,000) can relocate to Areas B and C, while the rural Jews of Area C (numbering 154,000) can relocate to Area A should they not want to live with Palestinians.[60] Abu Sitta concludes by asserting that his "proposed plan represents the most congested (worst) case, i.e. all refugees return and all Jews stay."[61] Since many refugees might not take that option, reality would be even less congested than this maximalist proposal. Abu Sitta adds that

> even in the most congested case, only 154,000 Jews may choose to relocate elsewhere in Israel to allow 4,476,000 refugees to return to their homes and end half a century of destitution and suffering. This is a very cheap price[that] Israel should pay for what it inflicted upon the Palestinians and still cheaper price to pay for a secure future for both peoples.[62]

Abu Sitta states that

> the Palestinians have no obligation, moral or legal, to accommodate the Israelis at their expense. By any standards, the Israelis have such an

> obligation—to correct a monumental injustice they have committed. Nevertheless, the refugees' return has nothing to do with Israel's sovereignty. It has nothing to do with whether [the] Oslo agreements succeed or fail. It has nothing to do with settlements, boundaries, or even Jerusalem. Let all these issues take their natural course.[63]

What Abu Sitta's proposal offers is a challenge to the pervasive discourse of pragmatism and realism. Proposing a feasible solution, he challenges the capitulationist stance of the PA and its apologist intellectuals. In fact, in their overzeal for pragmatism, these comprador intellectuals are going beyond what even the PA and the PLO think is acceptable. As'ad 'Abd al-Rahman, a member of the PLO executive committee and the PLO appointee responsible for the refugee portfolio, implored these intellectuals to "save us from your harmful interest." He added that the involvement of Palestinian intellectuals in discussions with Israelis on how to resolve the refugee issue would have been fine had they had the "national interest" as a priority and had they "pursued the realization" of the national interest. 'Abd al-Rahman affirmed that any scenario or proposal that veers off international legality with regards to the refugees' right of return constitutes a "free concession" even if it were presented in an unofficial capacity. He concluded by asserting the refugees' right to return and by affirming that it is not the

> mission of Arab intellectuals, especially the Palestinians among them, to give up a basic human right, that of living in one's home, nor should their goal be to find solutions to Israeli problems by intensifying problems for the Palestinians, nor to present free concessions before even reaching the stage of refugee negotiations.[64]

Elia Zureik, a member of the RWG, provides an accurate summary of the official Palestinian position in the context of the Madrid process:

> In succumbing to the dictates of the Madrid Conference, Palestinians have been framing the debate, implicitly if not explicitly, over the issue of the right of return *not* as one of whether the refugees should return to their 1948 homes, but rather as a debate over (1) whether there should be unhampered right of return for all refugees and displaced Palestinians to an independent state in the West Bank and Gaza; (2) how to compensate the refugees and normalize the civil and human rights of nonreturnees in neighboring countries; (3) whether to grant Palestinian passports to all refugees remaining in their places of refuge; and (4) how to get Israel to allow a symbolic return of some refugees from the 1948 war to Israel proper and to recognize that a historical injustice was done to the Palestinian people."[65]

Indeed, rumors circulating since 1996 and reported by the Israeli newspaper *Ha'Aretz*, claim that secret talks between the PA and Shimon Peres resulted in an agreement, wherein the Israeli government would help resettle the refugees outside its borders, in neighboring countries.[66]

Separating Palestinian political interests

Native West Bank and Gaza Palestinians are reaping the benefits of a phantasmatic state-to-be by forsaking refugee rights, just as Zionists who never included the rescue of European Jews as a priority in their political program, received the financial and political benefits for the murder of these Jews by Nazi Germany.[67] The premise that diaspora and refugee Palestinians are part of the final settlement of the "peace process" presupposes that they are one with native West Bank and Gaza Palestinians. Yet all proposed resolutions by PA elements and its coterie of comprador intellectuals sacrifice most of their rights in favor of separating them from native West Bank and Gaza Palestinians who are the ultimate beneficiaries of whatever Israeli largesse the PA and its cronies are able to extract. Palestinian refugees living in the West Bank and Gaza (numbering upwards of 1.2 million people) have been disproportionately impoverished by the dismal economic performance of the PA.[68] They are also increasingly denigrated on the bases of status and class by native West Bankers and Gazans, as the refugees' role as canon fodder during the intifada is no longer needed and has been rendered démodé by the PA–Israeli peace process. Despite their increasingly difficult situation since the PA came to power, West Bank and Gaza refugees have mobilized themselves through convening a number of popular refugee conferences, organized by the refugee camps' Union of Youth Center, as early as December 1995 in Far'a (the site of a former Israeli prison). This was followed by conferences in the Deheishe Refugee camp for the Bethlehem area refugees in 1996, as well as other popular conferences in Gaza.[69] Recommendations were issued, especially at the 1996 conference in Deheishe;[70] however, due to the diversity of opinions among refugees regarding relations with the PA and the PLO, the conference program and recommendations were not implemented; as a result, refugees have not been able to elect their own leadership. Salah Abed Rabbo states that the obstacles facing West Bank and Gaza refugees include: the hostile attitude of the PA and some PLO factions to any independent refugee leadership, which they regard as a threatening alternative leadership to themselves; the PA and other factions' view that the right of return has been rendered "obsolete"; the belief by the Palestinian opposition that a refugee leadership could easily be coopted by the PA; and the fact that refugees in the diaspora (in Jordan, Lebanon and Syria) have not joined the refugee conferences nor held their own.[71] Despite the lack of progress, a number of organizations (like Badil) have emerged in the West Bank and Gaza to defend refugee rights, a situation that is unmatched among diaspora refugees.

But if the Palestinian diaspora, which is composed of a majority of refugees is not the beneficiary of this "peace process," why must it acquiesce in it by conceding all its rights? To ask the diaspora and the refugees to sacrifice their rights, hopes, and dreams, so that some meager political benefits can accrue to native West Bank and Gaza Palestinians is to ask the diaspora and refugees more generally, to commit national suicide. Since those who are now conceding Palestinian diaspora and refugee rights have never been elected to their positions nor have they ever been given a mandate by diaspora and refugee Palestinians to concede their rights, then they perforce have no authority to negotiate on behalf of the diaspora and the refugees. Faced with a similar situation wherein their interests have been ignored by the PA, Palestinian Israelis, who have their own elected leadership, have been pursuing their own goals and interests separate from the peace process—their main goal being the transformation of Israel from an apartheid state of world Jewry to a state of its own Israeli citizens, Jews and Arabs. Moreover, Palestinian Israeli internal refugees, numbering between 120,000 and 150,000 people and constituting one fifth of Palestinian Israelis, are also seeking compensation on their own from the Israeli government. In March 1995, the Committee for the Defense of the Rights of Refugees in Israel convened a conference to register refugee grievances. The conference was attended by 300 delegates from 40 uprooted villages within Israel proper.[72] The Committee was founded in 1992 after the Madrid conference, as according to one its founders "the convening of the Madrid Conference convinced us beyond the shadow of a doubt that the PLO and Arab countries had abandoned the Arabs of '48. Therefore, we decided to take matters into our own hand."[73]

Since Israel only agreed to negotiate with West Bank and Gaza Palestinians in Madrid and with the PLO only insofar as the latter transformed itself into the PA and ceased to represent the diaspora, no official body representing diaspora Palestinians has been a party to the Madrid or Oslo processes. This situation makes it imperative, as many Palestinians have recommended in recent years, that free elections must be held in the diaspora to elect a new representative leadership that can negotiate with Israel and the international community on behalf of diaspora Palestinians. The diaspora and the refugees must extricate themselves completely from the West Bank and Gaza leadership, effectively seceding from it and from a "peace process" that addresses only native West Bank and Gaza Palestinians, as they have nothing to gain from it and everything to lose.[74]

Israel has succeeded in destroying the political unity of the Palestinian people, a goal whose achievement was finally formalized in Madrid and has since then been further solidified by the Oslo process. Diaspora and refugee Palestinians must harbor no illusions about the intentions of the PA, which has separated de facto the interests of the refugees and the diaspora from those of native West Bankers and Gazans (and this is aside from the actual and *real* separation between West Bankers and Gazans themselves to the detriment of the latter). Diaspora and refugee Palestinians must seek to separate their interests *de jure* from native West Bank and Gaza Palestinians and pull the rug from under the PA. The refugees' and the diaspora's conflict with Israel is different from that of the PA and its supporters. Although the Palestinian people remain one spiritually, their material interests are different. The "peace process" from Madrid to the present has not only deepened the differences between these material interests, it also rendered them contradictory in an Israeli-dictated and PA-accepted zero-sum game, wherein so-called gains for native West Bank and Gaza Palestinians must be attained at the expense of real losses on the part of the refugees and the diaspora.

8 Palestinians and Jewish history*

Recognition or submission?

Ever since Zionism embarked on its colonial-settler project in Palestine, Zionist history and Jewish history have become one. Zionism was not seen as a break with Jewish history but rather its legitimate continuation. The diasporic condition had derailed Jewish history from its proper path, and Zionism was going to redirect it toward its intended telos of statehood. Attempts to delink Jewish history and Zionist history were made until mid-century, but ultimately failed after the political success of Zionism. Thereafter, Jewish history was rewritten by Zionism; one could say, it has been Zionized. Jewish history now became the triumphant history of the ancient Hebrews, interrupted by an ignominious European Jewish history of pogroms and oppression culminating in the Jewish holocaust, and then continuing with the triumphant history of Zionism.

A second consequence of the triumph of the Zionist project was that Palestinian Arab history and Zionist Jewish history have become inextricably linked. Events in Jewish history that Zionism appropriated became perforce connected to Palestinian history. Paramount among such events is the Jewish holocaust during the Second World War, which Zionists used for propagandistic purposes to assert their "right" to Palestine to which they had laid their suspect colonial claim half a century earlier. In appropriating the holocaust and its victims, Zionism and Israel asserted that any acknowledgment of the holocaust is an acknowledgment of Israel's "right to exist," and conversely that any attempt to deny Israel its alleged right to exist was perforce a denial of the holocaust. Indeed, the coupling of the holocaust with the creation of Israel was enshrined in the Declaration of the Establishment of the State of Israel:

> The Holocaust committed against the People of Israel in recent times, during which millions of Jews were slaughtered in Europe, again proved manifestly the necessity of a solution to the problem of the Jewish people, who lack a homeland and independence. The solution is the renewal of the Jewish state in Israel, which will open wide the gates of the homeland to every Jew and which will grant every Jew the status of a people with equal rights among the family of nations.

* This essay was first published in 2000.

In this same vein, Moshe Sharett stated that

> the Zionists do not mean to exploit the horrible tragedy of the Jews of Europe... but they cannot refrain from emphasizing the fact that events have totally proven the Zionist position on the solution of the Jewish problem. Zionism predicted the Holocaust decades ago.[1]

The Jewish holocaust, therefore, could be apprehended only through the mediation of Zionism and Israel. Israel insisted on freezing the moment at which the holocaust survivors became such. The fact the Palestinians encountered them as colonial settlers is immaterial to Zionist discourse. As public discourse on the Jewish holocaust, which lay dormant for two decades, was resurrected in the 1960s, and increasingly as of the 1970s, by Israel and by American Jews as an argument to be deployed in the ideological defense of Israel and its violence against the Palestinian people and other neighboring Arab states, Palestinians and other Arabs were called upon to accept the Jewish holocaust and Israel's "right to exist" as a package deal. Ben-Gurion unequivocally asserted after the holocaust that "The Jewish State is the heir of the six-million... the only heir... If they had lived, the great majority of them would have come to Israel."[2] In late 1942, after news of the Jewish holocaust began to reach the world, Ben-Gurion expressed Zionism's appropriative strategy:

> Tragedy is power, if channeled in a productive direction. The essence of Zionist strategy is that it knows how to transform our catastrophe not into a source of despair and paralysis, as did the Diaspora, but into a spring of creativity and spiritedness.[3]

The response of Palestinians and Arabs to Israel's linkage has varied. Some, falling into the Zionist ideological trap, reasoned that if accepting the Jewish holocaust meant accepting Israel's right to be a colonial-settler racist state, then the holocaust must be denied or at least questioned. The Palestine Liberation Organization, on the other hand, along with many Arab intellectuals and journalists, actively sought, in word and deed, to delink the two events and to view the Jewish holocaust outside Zionism's mediation. These attempts at delinkage were and are still condemned by Zionism and its supporters, as is the Palestinian insistence that the holocaust survivors left the shores of Europe as refugees but arrived on the shores of Palestine as armed colonial-settlers.

Survivors' gain, Palestinians' loss

While insisting that Palestinians and Arabs link the holocaust with Israel's right to exist, the Zionist movement and the Israeli state have until today consistently refused to acknowledge the organic link between Zionism's successful history and the catastrophic history its success visited on the Palestinian people. Not only is much of modern Palestinian history not seen as having been set in motion by

Zionism's colonial claims to Palestine, more importantly, Palestinian history, to the extent that it forced itself on Zionism, was coded by Zionism as a continuation of European anti-Semitism, indeed a continuation of Hitlerism. Ben-Gurion was clear on this. In addressing a group of holocaust survivors, he asserted that "We don't want to reach again the situation that you were in. We do not want the Arab Nazis to come and slaughter us."[4] Palestinians, for their part, have argued that the holocaust was a European crime for which the Palestinian people have been forced to atone.[5] But, while Palestinians are a lone voice demanding that Israel acknowledge the crimes it committed and commits against the Palestinian people, Israel is joined by a large international chorus in demanding that the Palestinians accept Zionism's ideological deployment of the Jewish holocaust to justify its crimes against the Palestinians.

To the extent that Zionism saw any role for the Palestinians in its project, it was in having them internalize Zionism's version of their history and appreciate its *mission civilisatrice*. Indeed, the demand that Palestinians view their own history as well as that of Zionism from a Zionist standpoint is as old as Zionism itself. In his celebrated novel *Altneuland*, Theodor Herzl included a Palestinian character called Reschid Bey who extols Zionist achievement. He insists that Zionism "was a great blessing for all of us."[6] When pressed by a European gentile as to why Palestinian Arabs did not hate the Jewish colonial-settlers as "intruders," Herzl's Reschid Bey angrily responds: "Would you call a man a robber who takes nothing from you, but brings you something instead? The Jews have enriched us. Why should we be angry with them?"[7] Indeed Reschid Bey goes on to explain that

> nothing was more wretched than an Arab village at the end of the nineteenth century. The peasants' clay hovels were unfit for stables. The children lay naked and neglected in the streets and grew up like dumb beasts. Now everything is different. They benefited from the progressive measures of the New Society.[8]

As most Palestinians came to disappoint Herzl's expectations of them, Zionism had to cast them in a new light. Palestinians in Zionist and Israeli propaganda became anti-Semites whose sole grievance against Israel was its Jewishness, and were presented as the real colonizers of this ancient Jewish land.

How did Palestinians encounter holocaust survivors? The fact that around 22,000 soldiers, or a third of the Haganah during the 1948 war, were holocaust survivors is important in this regard,[9] as they participated in the expulsion of the Palestinians and in the many massacres of the 1948 war. In a rare commentary on such occurrence in the Israeli press, *HaOlam Hazeh* ran a photograph of Israeli soldiers expelling Palestinians in 1950 with the caption: "Note the number tattooed on the guarding soldier's arm. Many of the immigrants who have been through the hell of the European concentration camps lack the proper attitude toward the Arab captives of the State."[10]

The holocaust survivors complained of being used as "cannon fodder" by the Zionist leadership as they were mostly sent to the frontline and were never given administrative duties because of their ignorance of Hebrew.[11] According to a Haganah report, "the recruits were being sent from the ships on which they arrived directly to the reception centers for conscripts, and from there to their brigades or services."[12] Due to the death of many of them in battle, the Haganah report recommended that "instructions must be issued to all units that these enlisted men are to be admitted to combat operations as soon as [but not before] they have received appropriate training."[13] After the massacre of 200 Palestinians at the village of Tantura by the Haganah's Alexandroni Brigade,[14] the new Kibbutz Nasholim was erected by holocaust survivors on the ruins of the village.[15] Kibbutz Lohamei Hagetaot, which houses the Ghetto Fighters Museum, was built by Warsaw Ghetto survivors on top of the destroyed Palestinian village of al-Sumayriyya, whose inhabitants had been deported during the 1948 war.[16] In his seminal book, *The Seventh Million: The Israelis and the Holocaust*, Tom Segev writes in reference to Kibbutz Lohamei Hagetaot that there "is no settlement in Israel that better illustrates the link between the Holocaust and the Palestinian tragedy."[17]

Many holocaust survivors were to partake of the loot and pillage of abandoned Palestinian property. According to Segev:

> Hundreds of thousands of Arabs fled, and were expelled from their homes. Entire cities and hundreds of villages left empty were repopulated in a short order with new immigrants. In April 1949, they numbered 100,000, most of them Holocaust survivors. The moment was a dramatic one in the war for Israel, and a frightfully banal one, too, focused as it was on the struggle over houses and furniture. Free people—Arabs—had gone into exile and become destitute refugees; destitute refugees—Jews—took the exiles' places as a first step in their new lives as free people. One group lost all they had, while the other found everything they needed—tables, chairs, closets, pots, pans, plates, sometimes clothes, family albums, books, radios, and pets.... For a few months the country was caught up in a frenzy of take-what-you-can, first-come, first-served.... Immigrants also took possession of Arab stores and workshops, and some Arab neighborhoods soon looked like Jewish towns in pre-war Europe.[18]

In defense of Zionism, Isaac Deutscher, a pained but ambivalent Zionist (whom we encountered in an earlier chapter), soberly asserted that what happened to the Palestinian people as a result of Zionist colonialism cannot "in fairness" be blamed on the Jews: "People pursued by a monster and running to save their lives cannot help injuring those who are in the way and cannot help trampling over their property."[19] Deutscher, it would seem, never stopped to consider that European Jews could have still fled as refugees without becoming colonists. He never investigated the transformation of European Jews from refugees into colonial soldiers.[20]

The Nazi analogy

It was the Mufti of Jerusalem, Haj Amin al-Husayni, who provided the Israelis with their best propaganda linking the Palestinians with the Nazis and European anti-Semitism. Fleeing British persecution, the Mufti ended up in Germany during the war years and attempted to obtain promises from the Germans that they would not support the establishment of a Jewish National Home in Palestine. Documents that the Jewish Agency produced in 1946 purporting to show that the Mufti had a role in the extermination of Jews did no such thing; the only thing these unsigned letters by the Mufti showed was his opposition to Nazi Germany's and Romania's allowing Jews to emigrate to Palestine.[21] Yet the Mufti continues to be represented by Israeli propagandists as having participated in the extermination of European Jews. Peter Novick notes that in the four-volume Yad Vashem-sponsored *Encyclopedia of the Holocaust*, the article on the Mufti is twice as long as the articles on Goebbels and Göring and longer than the articles on Himmler and Heydrich combined. Of the biographical entries, its length is exceeded, and then just slightly, only by the article on Hitler.[22] The writer of the encyclopedia entry, Irit Abramski-Bligh, alleges without any substantiation that the Mufti "tried to persuade the Axis powers to extend the extermination program to include the Jews of Palestine, the Middle East, and North Africa."[23] At Yad Vashem, an entire wall is devoted to the connections tying al-Husayni to Nazi officials. Tom Segev comments that "[t]he visitor is left to conclude that there is much in common between the Nazis' plan to destroy the Jews and the Arabs [*sic*] enmity to Israel."[24] It is never remarked for example that the Mufti's contacts with the Nazis were themselves in response to the much more extensive contacts between the Zionist movement (both the labor and revisionist branches) and the Nazis.

Gamal 'Abd al-Nasir and later Yasser Arafat were subjected to similar slander simply because, like al-Husayni, they opposed Zionist colonialism. Israel as well as its American supporters were to engage in such rhetoric. The *New York Times* referred to Nasir as "Hitler on the Nile."[25] Ben-Gurion called Nasir a "fascist dictator," while Menachem Begin insisted that he was surrounded by Nazi emissaries. The Egyptians, in fact, had been accused by the Israelis of Nazi-style persecution of Jews since 1948.[26] The Israeli newspaper *Maariv* justified the 1956 invasion of Egypt by claiming that it prevented Nasir from turning into "Hitler of the East." Eliezer Wiesel, later to become a Nobel Peace Laureate, alleged at the time in an article that did not provide a shred of evidence that the departure of most Egyptian Jews from Egypt after the 1956 invasion was planned by an SS (Schutzstaffel) man.[27] Indeed, Ben-Gurion himself, in a speech to the Knesset, spread the outright lie that Egyptian tanks had swastikas painted on them.[28] In correspondence with foreign leaders, the Israelis insisted that their invasion was in self-defense and invoked the memory of the holocaust as a time when no one defended the Jews.[29]

Not only for Israeli Jews but also for American Jews, the holocaust was becoming increasingly identified with Israeli politics. After Israel's victory in the 1967 War, Rabbi Irving Greenberg, later director of the President's Commission on the Holocaust, asserted that "In Europe [God] had failed to do His task. … the failure to come through in June would have been an even more decisive destruction of the covenant."[30] Before the outbreak of the 1967 War, *Ha'Aretz* printed a catalog of allegedly "comparable" statements by Nasir and Hitler, such as Nasir's 1967 statement that "If Israel wants war—fine: Israel will be destroyed!"; and Hitler's 1939 statement that "If the Jews drag the world into a war, world Jewry will be destroyed."[31] Israel's insistence on its vulnerability reflected a conscious strategy. General Matitiahu Peled, one of the architects of the 1967 Israeli invasion, revealed a few years after the war:

> There is no reason to hide the fact that since 1949 no one dared, or more precisely, no one was able, to threaten the very existence of Israel. In spite of that, we have continued to foster a sense of our own inferiority, as if we were a weak and insignificant people, which, in the midst of an anguished struggle for its existence, could be exterminated at any moment.[32]

During the 1973 War, Elie Wiesel wrote of being for the first time in his adult life "afraid that the nightmare may start all over again." For Jews, he said, "the world has remained unchanged . . . indifferent to our fate."[33] At the time of his 1982 invasion of Lebanon, Begin justified the massive destruction of Beirut by referring to 1945: the destruction of Arafat's headquarters there "had given him the feeling that he had sent the Israeli army into Berlin to destroy Hitler in his bunker."[34] Earlier, Begin had described the PLO as a "neo-Nazi organization."[35]

Palestinians and Arabs were not the only ones cast as "Nazis." Israel was also accused—by Israelis as well as by Palestinians—of Nazi-style crimes. In the context of Israeli massacres of Palestinians in 1948, a number of Israeli ministers referred to the actions of Israeli soldiers as "Nazi actions," prompting Benny Marshak, the education officer of the Palmach, to ask them to stop using the term. Indeed, after the massacre at Al-Dawayimah, Agriculture Minister Aharon Zisling asserted in a cabinet meeting that he "couldn't sleep all night . . . Jews too have committed Nazi acts."[36] Similar language was used after the Israeli army gunned down forty-seven Palestinian Israeli men, women, and children at Kafr Qasim in 1956. While most Israeli newspapers at the time played down the massacre, a rabbi wrote that "we must demand of the entire nation a sense of shame and humiliation . . . that soon we will be like Nazis and the perpetrators of pogroms."[37]

The Palestinians were soon to level the same accusation against the Israelis. Such accusations increased during the intifada. One of the communiqués issued by the Unified National Leadership of the Uprising defined the intifada as consisting of "the children and young men of the stones and Molotov cocktails, the thousands of women who miscarried as a result of poison gas and tear gas grenades, and those women whose sons and husbands were thrown in the Nazi prisons."[38] The Israelis were always outraged by such accusations, even when the similarities were stark. When the board of Yad Vashem, for example, was asked to condemn the act of an Israeli army officer who instructed his soldiers to inscribe numbers on the arms of Palestinians, board chairman Gideon Hausner "squelched the initiative, ruling that it had no relevance to the Holocaust."[39]

Palestinians and the Jewish holocaust

Since its emergence on the international scene, the PLO has always distinguished between Zionists and Jews. In this it differs sharply from Israel and all the major Jewish and Zionist organizations worldwide, which identify Zionism and Israel as Jewish and make their claim to Palestine on the basis of that Jewishness. The PLO has always rejected this coupling, referring to Israel not as the "Jewish State" but as the "Zionist Entity." In contrast to the PLO and Palestinian intellectuals, however, most Palestinians call their oppressors "Jews," a name their oppressors chose for themselves and on whose basis they justify their oppression of the Palestinians. But Israel and Zionism are horrified by such a reference and judge it as a sign of Palestinian anti-Semitism. Not only, then, should Palestinians be oppressed by enemies who call themselves Jews and base their oppressive policies on their Jewishness, but Palestinians are condemned for calling their enemies by their chosen name and are called upon to exercise vigilance by making distinctions between Zionists and Jews that their enemies often fail to make.

The PLO has accepted this burden of vigilance. It has also always made a point of demonstrating its sympathy with the Jewish victims of the holocaust and in condemning the Nazi regime. When Arafat addressed the UN General Assembly in New York in 1974, he "vociferously condemn[ed] the massacres of Jews under Nazi rule."[40] He stated that the Palestinians would have welcomed the survivors of the holocaust, as they had earlier welcomed Circassian and Armenian refugees, had the objective of the Jewish immigration been "to live side by side with us, enjoying the same rights and assuming the same duties." But as the goal had been "to usurp our homeland, disperse our people, and turn us into second-class citizens—this is what no one can conceivably demand that we acquiesce in or submit to." He emphasized that the PLO's struggle was not against Jews but against "racist Zionism," not only against Palestinians but also against "Oriental Jews." In this sense, he concluded, "ours is also a revolution for the Jew, as a human being... We are struggling so that Jews, Christains, and Muslims may live in equality... free from racial or religious discrimination."[41]

In arguing against Zionism's designation of the Palestinian revolution as "terrorism," Arafat likened the Palestinian resistance to the American Revolution, the European anti-Nazi resistance, and the anti-colonial struggles in Asia, Africa, and Latin America.[42] After reviewing the British and Zionist outrages against the Palestinian people, Arafat emphasized that

> all this has made our people neither vindictive nor vengeful. Nor has it caused us to resort to the racism of our enemies.... For we deplore all those crimes committed against the Jews, we also deplore all the real discrimination suffered by them because of their faith.[43]

Arafat concluded by calling on Jews to oppose racism and desist from supporting the racist Israeli state, enjoining them to live as equals with Palestinians in a democratic Palestine.[44]

The PLO stance *vis-à-vis* the Jewish holocaust was followed with action in the next decade. On the fortieth anniversary of the Warsaw Ghetto Uprising, the PLO announced its plans to place a memorial wreath at the Warsaw Ghetto monument to honor "the hero Jews." Fuad Yassin, PLO representative in Poland, said that the Jews who died fighting to repel the German occupation troops are "our comrades and brothers... we consider these the hero Jews."[45] The PLO plan immediately drew protests from leaders of the Simon Wiesenthal Center, a US group participating in the commemoration efforts.[46] Rabbi Alexander Schindler, the leader of the US delegation, expressed outrage: "The participation of those who murder Jewish women and children and who celebrate the slaughter of innocents would make a hideous mockery of everything for which this commemoration stands."[47] Yassin expressed surprise; for him, Palestinians wanted to honor Ghetto heroes because "we are still facing that kind of fascism against our people."[48] At the ceremony itself, Yassin, accompanied by other PLO delegates, laid a wreath at the monument and asserted that "I have placed a wreath because the Jewish people were victims of Nazism and the Palestinian people are the victims of the new Nazis... the Zionists and Israel."[49] Israel asked its delegates to return home in protest, with other Jewish delegates, including Americans, expressing outrage.[50] A few days before the commemoration, the PLO appointed Ilan Halevi, an Israeli Mizrahi Jew, as the PLO's representative at the Socialist International to replace the slain 'Isam Sartawi.[51]

As a reward for Oslo in 1993, Arafat, along with Yitzhak Rabin and Shimon Peres, was nominated for the Nobel Peace Prize. Upon hearing the news, Elie Wiesel whose career was built on his holocaust experience, declared in outrage:

> At least he should apologize... The past cannot be erased. At least let him come forward and say "I apologize for having given the order to kill Jewish children at Ma'alot, and Jewish civilians in the street, and all the other innocent people."

What particularly galled Wiesel was that:

> All of a sudden I'm in the same group as he is. Imagine! We both have memberships, he and I... It is hard to swallow.... And this man, at least, for 25 years, has been the leader of a terrorist organization that was created to kill Jews. The man has done so much harm, has shed so much blood.... and all of a sudden he becomes a *tzaddik*.[52]

Not surprisingly, Wiesel did not mind the blood of thousands of Palestinians on the hands of Rabin and Peres.

Indeed, Oslo in no way dampened attempts by Israelis and their supporters to liken the Palestinians to the Nazis. When Lech Walesa planned to invite Nobel Peace Prize winners, including Arafat, to the fiftieth anniversary of the liberation of Auschwitz in January 1995, holocaust survivors, including Yad Vashem officials, and Jewish groups around the world were up in arms. Menashe Lorency, head of the Mengele Twins Organization, stated that "Arafat doesn't have to be in Auschwitz... He was a continuation of what they did [there]."[53] But one member of the organization, Vera Kriegel, who believed that Arafat should go so that he could learn the lessons of the holocaust, told Israel Radio: "I would take him by the hand and show him everywhere the horror took place." "If you do that," retorted deputy Knesset speaker Dov Shilansky, "you will never hold my hand again." Poland's chief Rabbi Pinhas Menahem Yoskowitz approved of Arafat's coming as this might "prevent killing or war,... achieve security for the Jewish people... if the politicians think that by Arafat's visit to Auschwitz these things can be achieved—I am for it... Sometimes you have to do unpleasant things."[54] The European Jewish Congress called for a boycott of the event because Arafat "represents a great suffering for the Jewish people."[55] With the mounting pressure against the Polish Government, Walesa sidestepped the issue by not inviting the Nobel Laureates.[56] Yossi Beilin, Israel's Deputy Foreign Minister at the time, regretted the decision. Since, in his view, the refusal of Arab governments to screen *Schindler's List* constituted denial of the holocaust, Arafat's attendance would constitute acknowledgment of the holocaust, and "recognition of the fact of the Holocaust would be an indirect admission of Israel's right to exist."[57] Dov Shilansky, a holocaust survivor who during the 1948 War commanded a platoon and who subsequently served a twenty-one-month term in Israeli jails for terrorism,[58] thought otherwise: "Arafat will go to Auschwitz to learn from his teacher, Hitler, how to destroy us."[59]

Recognition or submission?

Despite the earlier rebuffs, in the context of continued capitulation to the Israelis and the United States, Arafat was persuaded in 1998 by the Clinton administration to pay a visit to the US Holocaust Memorial Museum in Washington DC. The visit had been conceived by US deputy special Mideast envoy Aaron Miller and State Department official Dennis Ross (both are American Jews) as a "gesture of reconciliation." The museum, however, rejected Arafat's overture. Museum sources told the *Washington Post* that members of the American Jewish community warned museum director Walter Reich that "this [Arafat] is Hitler incarnate." When museum officials informed Arafat that he could visit the museum only as an individual without the security and protocol routinely accorded to world leaders, he cancelled the visit. Embarrassed by the episode, Arafat operative Nabil Abu Rdeneh lamented how the Palestinian Authority had been "extending our hands since the days of Rabin, and our hands are still slapped. Somebody is still living in the past."[60] Many Israeli officials applauded the rebuff, but there was a public outcry in Washington. Faced with a rebellion by the museum's governing board, Miles Lerman, chairman of the Holocaust Memorial Council, reversed his earlier support for museum director Reich's decision and extended an invitation to Arafat, who said that he was "keen to visit the museum." An Israeli embassy official, Lenny Ben David, explained that if Arafat "is going to learn about the Holocaust, and if he's not going to deny it, then all the better."[61] Avner Shalev, chairman of the Yad Vashem directorate, added "Maybe Arafat will be more reluctant to deny [the holocaust]."[62] The fact that neither Arafat nor the PLO had ever denied the Jewish holocaust and had always expressed solidarity with its victims was immaterial to such propaganda. Arafat finally opted not to go.[63] The fracas cost museum director Reich his job.[64]

What has caused the Zionist and Israeli consensus on Arafat and the holocaust to break? Since condemnation of Arafat, the PLO, and any Palestinian attempt to show solidarity with the holocaust continued as late as 1994, what accounts for this sudden vacillation? The answer is simple. Arafat's prospective visit to the Holocaust Museum was no longer to be staged by the Palestinian leader as one of solidarity between a people who *are* victims of oppression and another people who *were* victims of a greater oppression, but rather as an affirmation on his part that he understands and sympathizes with Israel, his erstwhile enemy, whose crimes he forgave and has continued to forgive since he signed the Oslo Accords. His visit to the museum was to ratify Palestinian acquiescence in viewing the Jewish holocaust through Israeli mediation. His recognition of the links that, Zionism insisted, connected the Jewish holocaust with Israel's raison d'être constitutes his final submission to the Zionization of Palestinian and Jewish histories. In an ambivalent celebration of this achievement, the *Jerusalem Post* ran an article titled "Learning to see 'the enemy' as victims."[65] Indeed, the PLO's submission to Israel's rewriting of the conflict had begun even before Oslo: part of the price for the Madrid Conference was the repeal, in December 1991, of the 1975 UN General Assembly Resolution no. 3379 (XXX) characterizing Zionism as "a form of racism and racial discrimination."[66] When the resolution was passed in 1975, Israel's UN ambassador, Haim Herzog, had told the General Assembly delegates that Hitler would have felt at home among them.[67]

Arafat's prospective visit to the museum recalls Anwar Sadat's visit to Yad Vashem in 1977 in the company of Menachem Begin. Sadat's visit was also a symbolic submission to the Zionization of the holocaust and to its appropriation by Israeli propagandists for their own purposes. During Sadat's visit, Begin declared:

> No one came to save us—neither from the East nor from the West. For this reason, we have sworn a vow, we, the generation of extermination and rebirth: Never again will we put our nation in danger, never again will we put our women and children and those whom we have a duty to defend... in range of the enemy's deadly fire.[68]

Unlike Arafat or Nasir, Sadat had been an avid admirer of Hitler. Upon hearing a rumor in 1953 that Hitler was still alive in Brazil, the Egyptian weekly *al-Musawwar* asked seven public figures what, supposing the rumor were true, they would say to Hitler. Five condemned the Nazi dictator while two exalted him. The more prominent of the two was Anwar Sadat, who was still motivated by his anti-British stance dating from colonial days. His message to Hitler was as follows:

> I congratulate you with all my heart, because, though you appear to have been defeated, you were the real victor, you were able to sow dissension

> between Churchill, the "old man," and his allies on the one hand and their ally, the devil, on the other... There will be no peace until Germany is restored to what it was... That you have became immortal in Germany is reason enough for pride. And we should not be surprised to see you again in Germany, or a new Hitler in your place.[69]

In assessing Sadat's enthusiasm for Hitler, however, it should be noted that unlike the many Zionist leaders (of both the Labor and Revisionist camps) who collaborated with the Nazis, some up to 1941 but others as late as 1944, Sadat only supported them from afar.[70]

More recently and in an important article in *al-Hayat* which generated a long debate among Arab intellectuals, Edward Said argued against the "retrospective attempts made by Israelis or Palestinians to use the Holocaust."[71] Said asserted that

> there is a link between what happened to Jews in World War II and the catastrophe of the Palestinian people, but it cannot only be made *rhetorically*, or as an argument to demolish or diminish the true content both of the Holocaust and of 1948. Neither is equal to the other; similarly neither one nor the other excuses present violence; and finally, neither one nor the other must be minimized [emphasis added].

What Said seems to invoke in his article is the understanding that the Jewish holocaust generated support for the establishment of a Jewish state and that the suffering of the Jews at the hands of the Nazis led to the suffering of the Palestinians at the hands of the Zionists. Said is clear that

> unless the connection is made by which the Jewish tragedy is seen to have led directly to the Palestinian catastrophe by, let us call it "necessity" (rather than pure will), we cannot co-exist as two communities of detached and uncommunicatingly separate suffering.

But in fact the Jewish tragedy did not create the Palestinian catastrophe. Zionism had sought to dispossess the Palestinians and establish its state long before the Jewish holocaust. Also, the majority of holocaust survivors who ended up in Palestine did so mostly because they could not go to the United States. Furthermore, the claim made by some Zionists and Palestinians that the international support for the establishment of Israel resulted from the world community's sense of guilt for failing to rescue Jews from the Nazis is unsubstantiated. Peter Novick convincingly argues that this was not the case at all. He explains that:

> Of the countries that supported the establishment of the state of Israel—for practical purposes, those which voted for the United Nations partition resolution of November 1947—there is no evidence that any of them were moved by "guilt" for the Holocaust. Not the crucial Soviet bloc, which hoped to

> weaken British power and get a foothold in the Middle East; not the countries of Latin America, which contributed the lion's share of the votes; not those other countries that supplied the needed two-thirds majority. The Allied nation against which charges of guilty complicity have most often been brought, Great Britain, which had closed down immigration to Palestine before the war, did not support partition.[72]

According to the Israeli historian Evyatar Friesel, who examined the UN proceedings, only South Africa was whole-heartedly pro-Zionist from the beginning, with other countries equivocating until the partition vote took place.[73] He concludes that there is "little indication in the opinions expressed by the different nations to show that the Holocaust had influenced their positions."[74] In fact, "the Zionist representatives who appeared before the [UN Special Committee on Palestine] barely alluded to the subject."[75] As for the United States, Novick explains that "There is no evidence that guilt for inaction during the Holocaust played any role in the American government's (halting and ambivalent) support for Israeli statehood."[76]

It is unclear, then, how a linkage between the Jewish holocaust and the Palestinian *Nakba* can be made *except* rhetorically. It is Israeli and Zionist propagandists who make the link rhetorically, and many Palestinians and Arabs accept the link at face value and blame the international community for forcing the Palestinians to pay for European crimes against the Jews. But clearly this is not what happened. The European powers, like the Zionists, simply treated the Palestinians the same way they treated all other non-white peoples. Palestinian desires and needs did not count for the West, and these desires and needs certainly did not constitute rights! Western and Soviet support for the establishment of Israel was an issue of neo-colonial strategies and/or cold-war alliances in which the Palestinian natives did not figure much.

While support for the Partition Plan was not based on guilt about the holocaust, support for refugee settlement in many cases was. The report issued on November 11, 1947 (eighteen days before the Partition resolution was passed) by one of the two subcommittees set up by the UN General Assembly to study the proposals of UNSCOP asserted that the

> question of the relief of Jewish refugees and displaced persons is not strictly relevant to the Palestine problem, but the Sub-Committee has found it desirable to refer to it in view of the misconceptions which are entertained in certain quarters about this matter, and also in view of the fact that it has unnecessarily complicated the Palestine issue and rendered more difficult the reaching of a just and satisfactory settlement.... The recommendations of the majority of the Special Committee envisage the admission into the country of 150,000 Jewish refugees. In the course of the general debate in the Ad Hoc Committee, certain delegations based their support for those recommendations on the persecution which the Jews had undergone in Europe and on the presence of European displaced persons centers of a large number of Jews.[77]

The report emphasized "that a programme of international action for the relief of Jewish displaced persons is 'a vital prerequisite to the settlement of the difficult conditions in Palestine.' "[78] It went on to insist that the "specific problem of Jewish refugees and displaced persons is an international responsibility, Palestine cannot provide the solution for it."[79] The report enumerated the political, legal, and economic grounds on which it based its conclusion:

> The main political ground is that Jewish immigration into Palestine is opposed by the large majority of the population. There can be no justification for recommending any immigration into any country against the wishes of the majority of its inhabitants.[80]

The Arab countries, understanding that the arrival of holocaust survivors in Palestine would increase the Zionists' numbers and manpower, introduced a UN resolution calling for Western countries to take in the holocaust refugees. All the countries that supported the Partition Plan resolution voted against or abstained on the refugee resolution.[81]

If a direct and non-rhetorical argument is to be made linking the Jewish holocaust and the dispossession of the Palestinians, it would center on the extent to which the 22,000 soldiers who were holocaust survivors—one third of the Zionist army—were central to the triumph of the Yishuv in 1948. To my knowledge, there is no logistical study of the Israeli army and its performance in 1948 that has argued this point. If anything, the lack of training of many among them might have been a hindrance to the war effort. Given the general weakness of the Arab armies, it is likely that even without the holocaust-survivors-turned-colonial-soldiers the Haganah would still have won the war, albeit with less conquest of land.

Said concludes his article by asserting that "we must accept the Jewish experience in all that it entails of horror and fear, but we must require that our experience be given no less attention or perhaps another plane of historical actuality." Indeed, Said is careful to stress that "at a time when Palestinian land is still being taken, when our houses are demolished, when our daily existence is still subject to the humiliations and captivity imposed on us by Israel and its many supporters in Europe and especially in the United States, I know that to speak of prior Jewish agonies will seem like a kind of impertinence." Said's call is a careful one which attempts to navigate the ideological waters between Zionism's insistence on linking the Jewish holocaust with the establishment of the Jewish state and Palestinian and Arab popular insistence on rejecting that coupling, if not rejecting the reality of the holocaust altogether. What is important to stress, however, is that it is Israel's package deal of linking the holocaust with Zionism's colonial claims that produces the denial. Arabs and Palestinians who deny or question the Jewish holocaust do so because they have bought into Israel's package deal, which leaves them with one option for opposing Israeli colonialism—denial. Israel, of course, rejects this position, but it also rejects the insistent refusal of its linkage by the PLO and many Palestinian and Arab intellectuals.

The only position Israel and Zionism accept is the more recent Arafatist position, that of accepting Zionism's linkage and its rewriting of Jewish and Palestinian histories. The attempt to engage Palestinians with Jewish history, including the history of the holocaust, is an attempt to deflect Palestinian engagement from the Jewish and Israeli present and an attempt to justify this present that is characterized by the oppression of the Palestinian people. The holocaust tragedy has been abducted by Israeli strategists, with few Jewish protests, for Israel's ideological acrobatics. As Palestinian recent history has shown, no Palestinian engagement with the holocaust will be satisfactory to Israel and its supporters. Israeli demands that Palestinians recognize the holocaust are not about the holocaust at all, but rather about the other part of the package, namely recognizing and submitting to Israel's "right to exist" as a colonial settler racist state. The Palestinian Authority has given up, but the Palestinian people should continue to resist this Zionist package deal. Their resistance is the only remaining obstacle to a complete Zionist victory, one that seeks to be sealed by Zionism's rewriting of both Palestinian *and* Jewish histories.

9 The ends of Zionism*

Racism and the Palestinian struggle

Zionism as a colonial movement is constituted in ideology and practice by a religio-racial epistemology through which it apprehends itself and the world around it. This religio-racial grid informs and is informed by its colonial-settler venture. The colonial model remains the best model through which Zionism should be analyzed, but it is important to also analyze the racial dimension of Zionism in its current manifestation, which is often elided. While Zionism in its early history presented itself unashamedly as a colonial-settler movement, it later insisted that it was nothing less than a Jewish national liberation movement which could even be viewed as "anti-colonial." What Zionism remained unashamed about throughout its history, however, was its commitment to building a demographically exclusive Jewish state modeled after Christian Europe, a notion pervaded, as the following will illustrate, by a religio-racial epistemology of supremacy over the Palestinian Arabs, not unlike that used by European colonialism with its ideology of white supremacy over the natives. More recent debates about a solution to the Palestinian–Israeli "conflict" rarely if ever discuss the question of racial supremacy. As I have discussed Zionism's colonial pedigree in the first chapter, in this chapter, I will focus on this supremacist grid, an analysis of which, I believe, is a prerequisite to the victory of the Palestinian struggle.

It is no longer contested, even among many Israelis, that the impact of Zionism on the Palestinian people in the last one hundred years includes: the expulsion of a majority of Palestinians from their lands and homes, the prevention of their return, and the subsequent confiscation of their property for the exclusive use of Jews; imposing a military apartheid system on those Palestinians who remained in Israel from 1948 until 1966, which since then has been relaxed to a civilian Jewish supremacist system of discrimination; and the military occupation and apartheid system imposed on the West Bank and the Gaza Strip and their population for the last thirty-five years as well as continued colonization of these occupied territories. Can there be a solution to the conflict that Zionism brought from Europe and imposed on a mostly peasant population?

* This essay was first published in 2003.

Ever since the Oslo "peace process" began in 1993, most debates among official Israelis, Americans, and Palestinians about how to "end" the conflict between Zionism and the Palestinians stress the question of pragmatism as opposed to idealism. As I explained earlier in the book, the logic runs as follows: it is not pragmatic to give the refugees the right of return; it is not pragmatic to give them back their property, it is not pragmatic to dismantle the colonial settlements in the occupied territories; it is not pragmatic to return all the territories to Palestinian control; it is not pragmatic to end all aspects of the occupation. Moreover, although Israel's Jewish character was never part of the negotiations, it has always been made explicit that transforming Israel into a non-Jewish (read non-racist) state is not pragmatic.

On the pragmatic side, the arguments run as follows: it is pragmatic for Palestinians to give up the right of return; it is pragmatic for Palestinians to accept to live in a Jewish supremacist state as third class citizens; it is pragmatic for Palestinians to live in Israeli-controlled and besieged bantustans rather than opt for independence; and it is pragmatic for Israel to remain a Jewish supremacist state. Identifying the criteria by which these solutions are judged as pragmatic or non-pragmatic is then the question that poses itself insistently.

Pragmatism or racialism?

Is the return of the Palestinian refugees not pragmatic because Israel is too small geographically? This does not seem to be the case as Israel continues to market itself as a final destination for millions of diaspora Jews in the Americas and in Russia whose interest in moving there, despite valiant Zionist efforts, is less than enthusiastic (those who moved from Russia between 1990 and 2000—many of whom turned out to be not Jewish at all—are excepted). In November 2001, as Israel's military continued to kill, strafe, and assassinate the resisting Palestinians of the Occupied Territories, Prime Minister Ariel Sharon had vowed to bring one million more Jews to Israel. Since the Russian Jewish well has almost dried up, it is said that Sharon may opt to encourage the half-million Argentine Jews to come and colonially settle in the Jewish State.[1] American Jews have overwhelmingly opted not to be "redeemed," making it up to Israeli Jews through the financial and political support that they give to the Jewish supremacist state while remaining in their American "exile."

Surely, if Israel can accommodate more millions of Jews in its small territory, it could conceivably do the same for the Palestinian refugees whom it expelled and whose land it invites these Jews to colonize. Yet all solutions that have been advanced by official and non-official Palestinians and Israeli Jews to resolve the refugee "problem," seem to agree on the non-pragmatism of the return of the refugees to their lands. Recent examples of such proposals include Donna Arzt's book *Refugees Into Citizens*,[2] and the proposal advanced by Harvard University's Program on International Conflict Analysis and Resolution, which were discussed in an earlier chapter.[3] What is at stake for the authors of these proposals and of many others is Israel's maintenance of its Jewish-supremacist character (dubbed its "Jewish character"). Indeed, in November 2001, Yasser Arafat, in his continued attempts to maintain power at the expense of his peoples' lives and rights delegated one of his lieutenants, Sari Nusaybah, who is the Palestinian Authority representative in East Jerusalem, to concede the Palestinian refugees' right of return. Nusaybah also asserted to a group of Knesset members, representing the leftist Meretz party, that "if Palestinians want a solution, we must take Israel's refusal [of allowing the Palestinians to return] into consideration"—a concession immediately welcomed by the Knesset members who thought it worthy of "study."[4] Indeed the liberal Israeli newspaper *Ha'Aretz* welcomed the concession immediately as did one of its leading journalists, Danny Rubinstein (usually seen as sympathetic to the Palestinians), who praised Nusaybah's concession but lamented that the latter did not represent the majority opinion among Palestinians.[5] Nothing came of this, however, at the official level. Concerned that Israel may not take Nusaybah's concession seriously, Arafat himself frankly expressed his "understanding" and "respect" of the Israeli need to maintain Jewish supremacy in an editorial he published in the *New York Times*. He shamelessly asserted that:

> We understand Israel's demographic concerns and understand that the right of return of Palestinian refugees, a right guaranteed under international law and United Nations Resolution 194, must be implemented in a way that takes into account such concerns.[6]

He proceeded to state that he is looking to negotiate with Israel on "creative solutions to the plight of the refugees while respecting Israel's demographic concerns," that is, "respecting" its Jewish supremacist concerns. However, what makes the return of Palestinian refugees whom Israel expelled and whose land it stole and steals non-pragmatic is not some geographic or "demographic" consideration, not some environmental or logistical obstacle; what makes their return not pragmatic is that they are *not Jews*.

It is further argued that Israel would no longer remain a *Jewish* state but would become an Israeli state of all its citizens. Indeed, racist talk about the demographic "threat" that the Palestinians constitute for a Jewish supremacist Israel is not confined to Ariel Sharon and the Israeli Jewish rightwing (which is anyway a majority in Jewish Israel), but are also voiced by liberal and leftist Israeli Jews. In December 2000, The Institute of Policy and Strategy at the Herzlia Interdisciplinary Center in Israel held its first of a projected series of annual conferences dealing with the strength and security of Israel, especially with regards to maintaining its Jewish supremacist character. One of the "Main Points" identified in the fifty-two-page conference report is the concern over the numbers needed to maintain the Jewish supremacy of Israel:

> The high birthrate [of "Israeli Arabs"] brings into question the future of Israel as a Jewish state . . . The present demographic trends, should they continue, challenge the future of Israel as a Jewish state. Israel has two alternative strategies: adaptation or containment. The latter requires a long-term energetic Zionist demographic policy whose political, economic, and educational effects would guarantee the Jewish character of Israel.[7]

The report adds affirmatively that "those who support the preservation of Israel's character as . . . a Jewish state for the Jewish nation . . . constitute a majority among the Jewish population in Israel." The conference was not a lonely effort. None other than Israel's President Moshe Katsav welcomed the attendees. Reflecting the predominant Jewish supremacist views among Israeli and American Jews, the conference was cosponsored by the American Jewish Committee, the Israel Center for Social and Economic Progress, the Israeli defense Ministry, the Jewish Agency, the World Zionist Organization, the National Security Center at Haifa University, and the Israeli National Security Council of the Prime Minister's Office. The conference featured fifty speakers: senior government and military officials—including ex- and future prime ministers—university professors, business and media personalities, as well as American Jewish academics and operatives of the US Zionist lobby.

The conference's findings and commitments are hardly a new phenomenon in Zionist thought. Jewish demographic supremacy, which has always been the ideological cornerstone for imposing ethno-racial Jewish supremacy in Palestine (however the Jewish "race" or Jewish "ethnicity" may be defined), is as old as the Zionist movement itself. It was the founder of the movement, Theodor Herzl, who, in his Zionist musings, understood that European Jews would have to establish their ethno-racial supremacy through demographic supremacy. He soberly states that:

> An infiltration [of Jews] is bound to end badly. It continues till the inevitable moment when the native population feels itself threatened, and forces the government to stop further influx of Jews. Immigration is consequently futile unless we have the sovereign right to continue such immigration.[8]

To achieve this, the Jewish settlers would "gently" expropriate the natives' property and

> try to spirit the penniless population across the border by procuring employment for it in the transit countries, while denying it any employment in our own country . . . The property-owners will come over to our side. Both the process of expropriation and the removal of the poor must be carried out discreetly and circumspectly . . . Let the owners of immovable property believe that they are cheating us, selling us things for more than they are worth. But we are not going to sell them anything back.[9]

Before the natives are removed, however, they will be needed for some important tasks:

> If we move into a region where there are wild animals to which the Jews are not accustomed—big snakes, etc.—I shall use the natives, prior to giving them employment in the transit countries, for the extermination of these animals. High premiums for snake skins, etc, as well as their spawn [will be offered by the Jews].[10]

The Jewish supremacist plan that the Zionists had in mind for their state-to-be was not carried out as discreetly and circumspectly as Herzl had hoped. Indeed, part of their "conquest of labor," wherein only Jews were supposed to work "Jewish" land, manifested in a celebrated incident. When in 1908, Zionist colonists found out that the saplings of a forest that was founded in Ben Shemen near Lydda in memory of Theodor Herzl had been planted by Arabs, they uprooted and replanted them.[11]

The concern about maintaining Jewish supremacy in Israel is so widespread that in January 2002 the leading Israeli–Russian daily *Novosti* published an article by one of its leading journalists, Marian Belenki, called "How To Force Them To Leave," suggesting that the Israeli government use the threat of castration to encourage the Arabs to leave the country. The author, according to the Israeli newspaper *Ha'Aretz*, also proposed

> that the Chinese method for lowering birth rates be implemented in Israel for the Arab population in order to lower their birth rates. According to this method, people who have more than one child are deprived of various benefits, lose their jobs, and are under threat of exile. Cash prizes for young men who voluntarily agree to the castration will also be provided, according to the proposed method.

The newspaper editor subsequently said that publishing the article was "a grave mistake" and suspended the editor responsible for its publication for three months. However, *Ha'Aretz*, found it surprising that the newspaper "did not receive any responses from readers or public representatives of the Russian community."[12] Indeed, what is surprising is that *Ha'Aretz* was surprised at all. On February 1, 2002, Tourism Minister Benny Elon (of the Moledet Party), who had recently replaced the assassinated Israeli minister Rehbeam Ze'evi, like his predecessor, proposed that the entire Arab population of Israel be expelled altogether.[13]

In addition to the Palestinian population who understood Zionism for what it was and resisted it from its inception in the late nineteenth century,[14] also many of the Jewish detractors of Zionism opposed the movement, not only because they disagreed with its plans for Jews, but also because of its plans for Palestinians. As early as 1919, Julius Kahn, a Jewish Congressman from San Francisco delivered a statement endorsed by 299 Jews, both rabbis and laymen, to President Wilson. The document, which denounced the Zionists for attempting to segregate Jews and to reverse the historical trend toward emancipation, objected to the creation of a distinctly Jewish state in Palestine as contrary "to the principles of democracy."[15] Indeed, many prominent American Jews continued to be horrified by the Zionist plan through the 1940s. James N. Rosenberg of the American Jewish Committee denounced the Zionist plans to set up an exclusively Jewish state as undemocratic. In a major article that later appeared in the American press rebutting Zionist arguments, he objected to the cancellation of the rights of non-Jews as a result of the establishment of a Jewish supremacist state.[16] Due to Zionist tactics of silencing any Jewish criticisms within US Jewish organizations, and their threats to their opponents at the convention of the Central Conference of American Rabbis in June 1943, Reform Rabbi Louis Wolsey, a fierce anti-Zionist, feared that the prominent American Zionist Rabbi Stephen Wise had "revealed by his tyranny over the non-conformist what the Zionists would do to the Arabs."[17] American Jewish anti-Zionists, continued to oppose Zionism's Jewish supremacist plans until 1948 when most of the support they had received over the decades dwindled against the reality of the holocaust and the establishment of the Jewish supremacist state.

Israeli Jewish society in Israel as well as the Israeli Jewish leadership continue to uphold Jewish supremacy as sacrosanct and non-negotiable. This manifests in their continued commitment to the laws that safeguard Jewish supremacy in Israel, including the Law of Return (1950), the Law of Absentee Property (1950), the Law of the State's Property (1951), the Law of Citizenship (1952), the Status Law (1952), the Israel Lands Administration Law (1960), the Construction and Building Law (1965), and a myriad others. Such commitment extends to the maintenance of the exclusive Jewish symbolism that Israel deploys, ranging from its Jewish flag and national anthem (which only speaks of Jews) to its ceremonial national days and the practices of institutionalized discrimination against its Arab non-Jewish citizens in every facet of life.[18] Shimon Peres, the dove of official Israel, worried recently about the Palestinian demographic "danger," as the Green Line, which separates Israel from the West Bank, is beginning to "disappear… which may lead to the linking of the futures of West Bank Palestinians with Israeli Arabs." He hoped that the arrival of 100,000 Jews in Israel would postpone this demographic "danger" for ten more years, as ultimately, he stressed "demography will defeat geography."[19] Indeed, there is very little to distinguish between the attitudes of Peres and Sharon on Jewish supremacy from the attitude of Golda Meir who could not sleep in the early 1970s horrified at the number of Palestinians born and conceived every night.[20]

It is further argued that Israel cannot end its occupation of the West Bank and Gaza because it needs to protect Jewish colonial settlers there, to maintain complete control of Palestinian water for Jewish use, and guarantee the security of Israel from threats to it as a *Jewish* state that might arise from an independent West Bank and Gaza state. This rhetoric was foundational to the Madrid-launched "peace process" in 1991 that culminated in the Oslo Process in 1993—the oppressive results of which the Palestinians have been encountering for the last ten years of "peace" negotiations, and particularly in the last two years during which they have been subjected to systematic massacres by the Israeli occupation army.

Zionism and anti-Semitism

Since its inception, Zionism's Jewish supremacy borrowed much from anti-Semitic rhetoric. Not only did Herzl agree with anti-Semites that it was Jews who "caused" anti-Semitism—"Where [anti-Semitism] does not exist, it is carried by Jews in the course of their migrations… The unfortunate Jews are now carrying the seeds of Anti-Semitism into England, they have already introduced it into America"[21]—but also with the anti-Semitic conclusion that the end of anti-Semitism could only be brought about by the removal of Jews from gentile societies. Hence, Herzl's expectation that anti-Semites would immediately rally to the support of the Zionists proved correct, as many among them, including the Nazis, did.[22] Like European anti-Semites, Zionism believes that European Jews, unlike European Christians, are not Europeans but foreigners who need to leave Europe to its "real" people and be "repatriated" to their own state in Palestine. Today's Israeli Jewish supremacists are reviving anti-Semitic ideas of the turn of the century that had accused Jews of seeking to control the world. From the infamous czarist *Protocols of the Elders of Zion* to genocidal Nazi propaganda, Jews as a "power-hungry" people was a notion that was part and parcel of the anti-Semitic lexicon. Today's Israeli Jewish supremacists seem to agree with the anti-Semites that if Jews do not control the world, they at least control America. In September 1994, during the Clinton administration, the Israeli tabloid *Ma'ariv* published an exposé on "The Jews who Run Clinton's Cabinet." The newspaper noted the increasing "Jewish power" in the US government since the Reagan years. While the newspaper asserted that American Jews had had key positions regarding US policy on the Middle East before Clinton, under his administration, "Jewish power" expanded measurably. Aside from Deputy National Security Advisor Samuel Berger and National Security Advisor to the Vice President Leon Perth, "In the National Security Council, 7 out of 11 top staffers are Jews. Clinton had especially placed them in the most sensitive junctions in the US security and foreign administrations." The article proudly proclaims how American Jews staff top positions in charge of US policy not only on the Middle East but also on Africa, South Asia, Western Europe, and Latin America. Indeed, the newspaper article provided its readers with the biographies of many of these so-called warm Jews—"warm" meaning Jews who identify with Jewish interests defined as Israeli interests. Lest we think that this alleged "Jewish power" is limited to the Democratic Party, the article explains that "there are also many warm Jews heading for the top positions in the Republican Party." The article quoted a Washington DC-based rabbi asserting that

> for the first time in American history ... we no longer feel that we live in the diaspora. The US no longer has a government of Goyim, but an administration in which the Jews are full partners in the decision-making at all levels ...[23]

The Israeli Jewish journalist was particularly impressed with how "Jewish" the American government had become when he phoned the State Department with regards to the then Haiti crisis requesting a briefing from the person in charge of that area:

> They referred me to Yehuda Mirsky. I introduced myself to his secretary. Suddenly someone picked up the receiver and then I heard a voice saying in perfect Israeli Hebrew: "Good morning, how can I help you?" For a moment I thought that I had mistakenly dialed the Israeli Foreign Ministry.[24]

This major ideological convergence between anti-Semites and Jewish supremacists in Israel is hardly surprising if one understands Zionism's project as nothing short of turning the Jew into the anti-Semite.[25] Certainly, no American Jewish leader and no respectable American newspaper, Jewish or gentile, would have published an anti-Semitic article of the caliber published by *Ma'ariv*. The only exception would be anti-Semitic rags. This is not to say, however, that the leaders of the US pro-Israel lobby do not regularly brag about their crucial influence on US policy in Congress and in the White House. That they have done regularly since the late 1970s.[26] What these anti-Semitic notions miss, however, is that the "Jewish lobby" is only powerful in the United States because its major claims are about advancing US interests and that their support for Israel is contextualized in their support for the overall US strategy in the Middle East. As such, the "Jewish lobby" plays the same role that the China lobby played in the 1950s and the Cuba lobby still plays to this day. The fact that it is more powerful than any other lobby on Capitol Hill testifies to the importance of Israel in US strategy and not to some alleged Jewish "power" independent of and extraneous to the US "national interest."

By accepting the preposterous anti-Semitic characterizations of Jews as "in control of America," Israel's Jewish supremacists fail to see that the extent to which American Jews are represented in the US government is the extent to which they have become assimilated into a generic American whiteness, and how much their Jewishness, warm or cold, has been integrated into Americanness.[27] American Jews who serve in government are no more pro-Israel than their Christian counterparts, and when they happen to be more pro-Israel, this is more a function of believing that support for Israel is in America's best interests (as well as in the best interests of American Jews whose interests are seen as the same as general American interests). The real danger of these anti-Semitic/Jewish supremacist views is the effect they would have on the lives and livelihoods of American Jews (whether supremacists or not) if taken up by American anti-Semites and their friends. According to this Jewish supremacist Weltanschauung, and in line with anti-Semitic rhetoric, not only will Jews be supremacists over the native Palestinians whom they conquered and must continue to conquer; they are also said to be supreme on a global scale. The complicity between Zionism and anti-Semitism has become complete.

As for the Zionist project of turning Jews into anti-Semites, it was in evidence early on when Jewish *Haskala* thinkers, or *Maskilim* (like Smolenskin, among others), who had much influence on Zionist thinkers, accepted anti-Semitic characterizations of Jews as "dirty," "medieval," "superstitious," and "effeminate." Herzl himself described French Jews in his diaries in the following way: "I took a look at the Paris Jews and saw a family likeness in their faces: bold, misshapen noses; furtive and cunning eyes" (Herzl 1960, 11). To transform Jews from the "effeminate schlemiels" that anti-Semitism and Zionism thought they were into manly men modeled after anti-Semites, turn-of-the-century Zionist ideologue Max Nordau set up gymnastic clubs for Jewish men.[28] Nordau's "Bar Kochba clubs," as we discussed in the first chapter, were engineered to "restore" male

Jews physically to the condition of their alleged Hebrew forefathers who were athletic fighters like the Greeks, as he believed his contemporary male Jews to be as "effeminate" as anti-Semitic claims had made them out to be (more on this in the last chapter).

As for Jewish racial supremacy over the Palestinians, it has become part and parcel of an international discourse on Jewish racialism that has even infiltrated academia. It is in this context that a recent keynote research paper showing that Jews and Palestinians are genetically almost identical was pulled from a leading scientific journal, *Human Immunology*. The paper titled "The Origin of Palestinians and their Genetic Relatedness with other Mediterranean Populations," involved studying genetic variations in immune system genes among people in the Middle East. According to the London *Observer*:

> In common with earlier studies, the team found no data to support the idea that Jewish people were genetically distinct from other people in the region. In doing so, the team's research challenges claims that Jews are a special, chosen people and that Judaism can only be inherited.

Due to major protests, and the threat of mass resignations from the editorial board, the journal's editor responded swiftly: "Academics who had already received copies of *Human Immunology* have been urged to rip out the offending pages and throw them away." The article's lead author, Spanish geneticist Professor Antonio Arnaiz-Villena was "stunned." The *Observer* adds:

> The journal's editor, Nicole Sucio-Foca, of Columbia University, New York, claims the article provoked such a welter of complaints over its extreme political writing that she was forced to repudiate it. The article has been removed from *Human Immunology's* website, while letters have been written to libraries and universities throughout the world asking them to ignore or "preferably to physically remove the relevant pages." Arnaiz-Villena has been sacked from the journal's editorial board. Dolly Tyan, president of the American Society of Histocompatibility and Immunogenetics, which runs the journal, told subscribers that the society is "offended and embarrassed."[29]

Practical solutions?

Israel's continued refusal to change its Jewish supremacist character or its racist policies toward the Palestinian people is portrayed in the international press and by official Israeli rhetoric as a defense of its "democratic" principles and in defense of a Jewish people whose historic persecution came to a halt only because of Zionism's intervention. However, the only way these arguments acquire any purchase is in the context of an international (read Western) commitment to Jewish supremacy, wherein Jews are seen as white Europeans defending white European values and civilization against the primitive Arab hordes. The cornerstone of Jewish supremacist thought is the commitment to establishing a Jewish

State, where Jews (whether as a "chosen people," as Europeans with *a mission civilisatrice*, or as a historically persecuted group who must be liberated at whatever cost), would have rights *qua* Jews over non-Jews and all the accoutrements that follow from such a racially supremacist system. It is Jewish supremacy that makes the question of Israel as a Jewish, rather than an Israeli, State sacrosanct, whose change would be *non-pragmatic*. It is a commitment to Jewish supremacy that makes the return of Palestinian refugees a "demographic threat" to the Jewish majority of Israel (which became a fact precisely because the Palestinians now seeking to return to their lands and homes were expelled from them in the first place), that continues to legitimize the treatment of Israeli Palestinian citizens as third-class citizens, and that legitimizes the continuation of the occupation as a safeguard against threats to a Jewish-supremacist Israel.

If we subtract the commitment to Jewish supremacy, then a solution to the Zionist-imposed conflict on the Palestinians would be more easily found. Let us imagine a world where the majority of Israeli and diaspora Jews and their gentile supporters are no longer committed to Jewish supremacy. Israel will become an Israeli state that treats all its citizens equally and will not hold that Jews should have a supremacist status. Israel will allow the Palestinian refugees to return to it, as they will not constitute a demographic threat to Jewish racial supremacy. Israel will no longer have to occupy the Palestinian West Bank and Gaza Strip because it will no longer be committed to Jewish colonization of Palestinian land or to the theft of their water or to the military occupation of the territories as it will no longer fear for its security. The basis on which Palestinians constitute a threat to Israeli security—namely, Israel's maintenance of Jewish supremacy, which translates into the oppression of the Palestinians—will no longer exist and neither will the "threat." The Palestinians can then either have a Palestinian state in the West Bank and Gaza or, along with the Israelis, opt for a binational state in all of Mandatory Palestine.

How can this be brought about? Institutionalized white supremacy in the United States and South Africa ended when the costs of maintaining it became too high to bear by white supremacists in both countries. It was only after the costs became high that people and rulers in both countries opted to end the institutionalized basis of white supremacy. Today, one would find only a small minority of people in the United States or South Africa who would comfortably avow publicly that they ever supported white supremacy, when they had done so very comfortably a few years ago. The Jewish supremacists in Israel, both rulers and population, have not paid much for the maintenance of Jewish supremacy. They have not only maintained the land they conquered but constantly expanded it. They have not only been able to eke out a living but also prospered economically, socially, and culturally.

It is the Palestinians who have had to pay the price for the maintenance of Jewish supremacy until now. It is only by making the costs of Jewish supremacy too high that Israeli Jews will give it up. This can be done by the continuing resistance of Palestinians in Israel and the occupied territories to all the civil and military institutions that uphold Jewish supremacy. It can also be done by applying international pressure including divestment from Israel, imposing an international economic blockade on the country, cultural and tourism boycotts, and instituting an international diplomatic isolation of the country. This will hit Israeli Jewish supremacists economically, in the comfort of their daily lives. It is then and only then that the majority of Israeli Jews will be convinced that the costs of Jewish supremacy are too high to bear and will become much more comfortable in publicly disavowing Jewish supremacy and in claiming, like many of their white counterparts in South Africa and the United States, that they had never supported it in the first place. While this solution may seem non-pragmatic in the contemporary international political context, it is no less pragmatic than the faltering "peace process" that continues to be sold to the world and to the Palestinian people as pragmatic. All solutions that ignore the maintenance of Jewish supremacy in Israel will fail. Unless the elimination of Jewish supremacy becomes the major goal of a real "peace process," all other solutions will simply perpetuate the oppression of the Palestinian people.

10 History on the line*

Joseph Massad and Benny Morris discuss the Middle East

Introduction

If there has been little purposeful dialogue in recent years between Israeli and Palestinian political leaders, the extent of intellectual exchange across one of the world's most pronounced diplomatic fault lines has also been conspicuously modest. The two traditions are not on talking terms. "The most demoralising aspect of the Zionist–Palestinian conflict," according to the Palestinian academic and writer, Edward Said, "is the almost total opposition between mainstream Israeli and Palestinian points of view. ... There is simply no common ground, no common narrative, no possible area for genuine reconciliation."

In that same article in the *London Review of Books* (December 14, 2000), Edward Said suggested that respected Palestinian and Israeli historians and intellectuals should hold a series of meetings "to try to agree a modicum of truth about this conflict...which in turn might reveal a way out of the present impasse." Not a Truth and Reconciliation Commission, at least not yet, but perhaps something along the lines of a "Historical Truth and Political Justice Committee."

The obvious way of examining the potential of Edward Said's proposal is to engage prominent Palestinian and Israeli academics in discussion. That's what *History Workshop Journal* has done. Joseph Massad is a colleague of Edward Said at Columbia University in New York, where he is Assistant Professor of Modern Arab Politics and Intellectual History. His most recent publication is *Colonial Effects: The Making of National Identity in Jordan* (New York, 2001). He was in Amman at the time this discussion was recorded in July 2001. Benny Morris is, with Avi Shlaim, perhaps the most prominent practitioner of what has been called the "new" or "revisionist" school of Israeli history, and is the author of *Righteous Victims: A History of the Zionist–Arab Conflict, 1881–1999* (London, 2000). He is Professor of History at Ben-Gurion University in Israel. He took part in the discussion from Dartmouth College in New England, where he was a visiting professor. Professor Massad and Professor Morris had never met prior to this conversation. Both participants have had the opportunity to revise and correct their contributions. I moderated the discussion from London on a conference phone call.

Andrew Whitehead

* This debate was first published in 2002.

AW: Professor Morris—you are a leading practitioner of the "new" history, revisionist history, in Israel. What is new and revisionist about it and what is its political impulse?

BENNY MORRIS: To begin with what you call the political impulse behind the new historiography—I think it depends on who you are talking to. I think some new historians were driven, are driven, by political motivation in their historical writing. For myself, I like to believe that I'm not—that I write history unconnected to my political beliefs. The only impulse behind the writing of history, in my view, should be to get at the truth, the historical truth—to find out what actually happened, to describe what happened, and to analyze and explain what happened, current politics aside.

The new historiography itself arose in Israel in the 1980s, when a batch of not-coordinated, relatively young historians—in their thirties and forties at the time—were given access to Israeli archives. These had begun to open their papers in the 1980s, in accordance with the thirty year rule, as exists in most democracies, about what happened in and around 1948 [when the state of Israel was created]. And this opening of the papers, coupled with their viewing by historians who were relatively young and not as committed as previous Israeli historians had been to Zionist ideology and the Zionist vision, led to the writing of a new historiography about what had happened in 1948, and by extension about the Israeli–Arab conflict in general. In short, this new historiography, being a new look at the history of the state of Israel and the Zionist movement that preceded it, and in later years also looking afresh at what happened in the 1950s and 1960s, led basically to the undermining of the official Zionist historiography which had reigned supreme in Israel, at universities and newspapers and so on, during the 1950s, 1960s, and 1970s. And also, it in my view undermined the tenets of traditional, and always official, Arab historiography regarding what happened in 1948.

AW: Dr Massad, how do you view the new Israeli historiography, and do you think it offers the possibility of bringing together two traditions of historiography, the Arab and the Israeli?

JOSEPH MASSAD: I do believe that the new historians or the revisionist historians in Israel have come much closer to the Palestinian and some of the Arab versions of the historical events that transpired since the inception of the Zionist movement, and more importantly since 1948 onwards. And much of what came to light from the archives of the state of Israel, the archives that many of these historians have relied on, confirmed, in many ways, many of the claims and contentions made by Arab and Palestinian historians since the 1950s, claims which had been constantly assailed by the Israeli academy as nothing but pure propaganda.

Clearly there are many differences that remain between basically the predominant Palestinian version of history and some Israeli historians. But I believe there is a political impulse, and a political effect, that is attendant to the writings of these Israeli historians. I do believe that one's politics governs one's choice of research, governs one's interpretative view of the evidence and how one selects evidence. So although I take Mr Morris at his word that consciously he tries to avoid placing his political views in the way of his writing history, I do believe that unconsciously, many of the political givens that one holds do enter in one's choice of writing history.

AW: Professor Morris, your writings, and Avi Shlaim's writings, particularly about 1948, acknowledge a historical injustice. But is it simply an acknowledgement, or an acknowledgement that should lead to a redress of that injustice?

BENNY MORRIS: I don't use the word "injustice" and I actually wouldn't use the word "injustice" in relation to what happened in 1948. You might well say that there was injustice in the attack by the Arab states on May 15th, May 16th, on the new-born state of Israel in violation of the United Nations partition resolution of November 29, 1947. That could also be termed an injustice. Why did Arab states suddenly attack a new state which had been given the warrant for existence by the world community?

You're talking of course about the injustice done to the Palestinians who became, many of them, refugees in 1948. But you could also turn that around and say they began the war, they started shooting, they rejected the United Nations resolution, and therefore a Palestinian refugee problem arose out of that war. So I don't use the word "injustice." I try to look at history objectively, and try to sort out what happened, why it happened, how people acted, and so on.

I wanted just to add one comment to something Dr Massad said—I agree with him only about the choice of subject of historians as a function of their politics, their ideology, their upbringing and so on. In other words, probably a right-wing historian in Israel wouldn't have come upon, or chosen, in the 1980s to write about the Palestinian refugee problem, whereas I did, being more to the centre or left of the political spectrum. The choice of subject, I think, does come into play here. But the actual practice of the writing—there may be subconscious elements, but consciously I try to stay away from my political beliefs. And I do believe that there is such a thing as historical truth, not just various narratives. Some of them are closer to the truth and some are less close to the truth, some are better written and some are worse written, some are good history and some are bad history—that's how I view it, and not that everything is one big hodgepodge of equal value and therefore of equal non-value.

JOSEPH MASSAD: I think Professor Morris's assertion—that the injustice could be seen as one that was perpetrated by the Palestinian rejection of the 1947 partition plan—illustrates the point I was trying to make earlier. That plan itself was an imposition of an international unjust action on the Palestinian people. His statement tells me that he does hold on to certain political positions that direct his selection of facts and interpretation. In fact, much of what he said is part and parcel of the hegemonic ideology, and the official defence that the state of Israel and its media have used consistently right since 1948. This is the myth, that some historians in Israel had debunked, that the Palestinians were the ones who rejected the 1947 partition plan alone, as if the Zionist movement was going to be so excited about peace and the two-state solution. We know that was not the result. We know that the Arab states, for example, who did attack the new state of Israel in 1948, did so after six to seven months of systematic expulsion of the Palestinian population by the Zionist forces. So there was indeed a casus belli as far as the Arab states were concerned.

And we should also be more careful in the details, because some Arab states actually did not attack the state of Israel but attacked, or tried to defend, the area of Palestine that the partition plan had safeguarded for the Palestinian state. For example the Jordanian army in 1948 did not attack except for East Jerusalem (which according to the Partition Plan was supposed to be a *corpus separatum* under UN jurisdiction). Basically, for the bulk of the war it simply tried to hold positions within territory which was allocated to the Palestinians. So there are all these myths that are hegemonic on the Israeli scene, both official and academic, that seem to be reproduced in the response Professor Morris just gave. And I think it illustrates that one's politics, in many ways, do influence one's selection of facts.

What is the point of departure for what justice and lack of injustice may be? Is it, for example, the Zionist colonial venture in Palestine from the late nineteenth century onwards, that culminated in 1948 in the establishment of the state? Or should we look at international action in 1947, meaning the Partition Plan, as being indeed a legitimate action, so that the Palestinians by rejecting it suddenly brought about an injustice onto themselves?

BENNY MORRIS: Look, there are facts apart from myths. You may believe that Zionist hegemonic thinking has completely occupied my brain. I may believe that the official Palestinian line has completely occupied yours to the detriment of good history. But there are facts that have to be established. One is very simple, that on November 29, 1947, the Palestinian authorities—that is the Arab Higher Committee and the Palestinian leadership under Amin al-Husseini—rejected the UN partition resolution, rejected what the United Nations thought was a fair deal for Palestine. And then they started shooting at Israelis, killing Israelis. They began the violence that snowballed into a civil war. The fact that in the end the Zionists won and in some ways drove out the Palestinians, that is also true. Nobody is rejecting that. But the origin of the war—you must admit, the Jews accepted the partition resolution, while the Palestinian Arabs and subsequently the Arab states (whatever their self-justifications in invading Palestine–Israel were) rejected that resolution, and violated it quite brutally. Those are facts. After that, you can discuss all sorts of interpretations, and I'm sure there's various differences between us about how we interpret various things, but certain facts must be established correctly.

AW: But those facts are often in contention.

BENNY MORRIS: These facts are not in contention. The fact that the Israeli side accepted, and the Zionist leadership accepted formally, the United Nations partition resolution, and the Palestinian leadership rejected it and then began shooting—acting against this resolution—those are not disputable facts. The fact that the Arab states invaded the area of Palestine, some of them attacking Israel and some of them just to occupy Palestinian territory (which Dr Massad says was to defend the Palestinians, I don't think actually he even buys that, the Jordanians basically took the West Bank in order to annex a piece of territory) is a fact. Israel didn't invade the Arab states.

AW: Let me put to both of you something that Edward Said wrote a few months ago. He said of the two historical traditions: "There is simply no common ground. No common narrative. No possible area for genuine reconciliation." He proposed what he called something like a Historical Truth and Justice Committee to try to establish the bare bones of what has happened in the recent history of the Middle East. Dr Massad, does that suggestion have value to you?

JOSEPH MASSAD: I think it does have value, but I'm not sure if it's realizable in the near future. As you can see, we already have a dispute on key events that took place in 1947 and 1948. If I can just go back—my position on the Jordanian intervention was not that it did so to defend the Palestinians, but that it did not invade Israel. And the claim that all these armies invaded Israel is not true.

BENNY MORRIS: I never made that claim.

JOSEPH MASSAD: What I did say is that the Arab states used the expulsion of the Palestinians, that went on from November 29, 1947 until May 15, 1948, as a casus belli. Now, whether they did so in order to defend the Palestinians really, or simply used it as a casus belli, is a different story, and we can discuss that.

What I do think is important is precisely the significance of these historical events. Take the 1947 Partition Plan. The standard Zionist line has always been: "we are a peace loving movement, we have tried to make peace with these people, and we have accepted what a so-called objective and neutral party, meaning the United Nations, had done in 1947." What of course goes unmentioned is that the Jewish population of Palestine at the time of the resolution was a third of the total population—the remaining two-thirds were Palestinian Arabs. According to Jewish sources, Jews owned a mere 6.5 or 6.6 percent of the total amount of the land, yet they were given a majority of the land, almost 55 percent of the land of Palestine, by the Partition Plan. This to the Palestinians, of course, seemed utterly unjust and unfair.

Professor Morris knows quite well that the United Nations decision in 1947 was not an easy or done deal. There was all kinds of superpower politics taking place behind closed doors, much arm twisting by the United States. And the United Nations, after the war, really did not have the legitimacy it subsequently carried in the 1960s and 1970s on account of its limited membership at the time.

AW: Can I urge you to address Edward Said's idea of a Historical Truth and Justice Committee. You seem to be saying—nice idea, but it's not going to work.

JOSEPH MASSAD: I think it's not going to work, because there are ideological differences. There are a few Israeli historians—one that I can think of off hand, someone like Ilan Pappe [author of *The Making of the Arab–Israeli Conflict, 1947–1951*, London, 1988], who is much more forthcoming on these questions, and in rejecting many of the ruling ideas in Israel. Basically, historians and academics will have to rid themselves of a lot of this ideological baggage.

AW: On both sides? Or are you simply saying that the Israeli tradition has got to change?

JOSEPH MASSAD: Well, on both sides. The Israeli tradition will have to change a lot more, after all, because it is the ruling tradition. The Palestinians lost the war, the Palestinians have been telling their story for decades and no one—and by that I mean no one in Western, pro-Israel countries—has ever listened to them.

BENNY MORRIS: And the Palestinian story is correct?

JOSEPH MASSAD: What I am saying is, yes, it has many, many elements of truth, and many of those elements of truth have been confirmed by many historians.

BENNY MORRIS: So essentially, the Israeli side should change its thinking?

JOSEPH MASSAD: I think the Palestinian side has to change its thinking also about the role of its politicians and of its leadership. And I think there have been many attempts already about rethinking what Palestinian politicians have done in the 1920s, 1930s, and 1940s. What I'm speaking about is not whether Palestinians should rethink the role of their own politicians—this is, of course, true, and I think Palestinians have been doing this ever since the 1950s. What I'm saying is that Palestinians need not change their mind about the very injustice of their situation, the injustice that was visited upon them by the Zionist movement and the Israeli state. In addition, what they should rethink is also the injustices visited upon them by Arab regimes, and by their own leadership. That, of course, needs to be rethought by the Palestinians more and more. There's an immense amount of literature already by Palestinian historians which uncovers the role of Arab regimes, which uncovers and critiques the role of the Palestinian leadership.

What Israelis want Palestinians to do is to rethink what they, the Palestinians, believe, and what I believe is an objective truth, which is the utter injustice visited upon them by the Zionist movement and the Israeli state, and which continues to be visited upon them. This I don't believe the Palestinians should ever rethink.

AW: Professor Morris, can I ask you what you think is the possible scope of Edward Said's idea of a Historical Truth and Political Justice Committee?

BENNY MORRIS: I do think it's problematic. I think the basic difference lies in 1881 [the start of the Zionist Jewish migration]. It doesn't have anything to do with 1948, or only marginally to do with what happened later. The basic difference is to do with the view of Zionism and the Zionist influx into Palestine as something which had a moral legitimacy. I'm not saying the absolute moral legitimacy, but moral legitimacy—alongside later Palestinian nationalism, which also had legitimate claims and aspirations to sovereignty and self-determination. This is the basic problem.

The basic problem here is from the start, for both sides to recognize the legitimacy of the claims of the other side, and therefore leading in the end to some form of partition of Palestine, with both sides having a stake inside Palestine. The problem is that, at least until not long ago, Zionists basically disclaimed the legitimacy of the Palestinians, basically fearing that admission of such claims would be at the expense of Zionism itself. And on the other side is the Palestinian total negation of the very legitimacy of Zionism. The problem is for Palestinians to admit, and then historically follow through with this, the legitimacy of Zionism, of the need of the Jewish people for a homeland, of their connection to Palestine. Yasser Arafat, for example, continues to reject this by saying "there was never any Jewish temple on the Temple Mount [in Jerusalem], it's all one big myth, only the Muslims have any stake in that piece of territory." That line of reasoning says basically that Zionism has no legitimacy, that we may in the end have to bow to it in some way and recognise that there is a state of Israel because of Zionist power and international support for the Zionist state, but it will never be legitimate, it will never be just, and therefore we will never recognise it. This is really the basis of the problem. Everything else follows through from it.

It's nice for Palestinians today to say, well, their leaders made mistakes in the past, as if this is a great admission on their part. But it isn't. What they are basically saying is that their leaders in the 1940s were incompetent because they were not able to stop the Zionists, not because they didn't agree to a mutual, legitimate claim by both sides. It's obvious that they were incompetent and ended up leading the Palestinians to disaster. You don't need any great historian to discover that. You do need a certain amount of, I suppose, a will to truth to admit it, but it's as clear as daylight.

One of the problems of reaching some form of agreement, or even moving towards a mutual understanding of what happened in Palestine from 1881 until the present day, is the availability on only one side of historical records. On the Israeli side. Israel acts like a democracy and opens its records, even its military records during the past decade, regarding the conflict. On the other side, there are no actual records. Dr Massad was speaking of Palestinian historiography. I don't read Arabic fluently, unfortunately, but I don't really know of any serious Palestinian work based on Palestinian records—except perhaps Yezid Sayigh's work [notably *Armed Struggle and the Search for State, the Palestinian National Movement, 1949–1993*, Oxford, 1997] which is of much later vintage and talks about the 1960s, 1970s, and 1980s—because there are no Arab records available. If the Arab states opened their records, then perhaps we would be able to start moving towards a full understanding of how the Arab states operated, why they went to war in 1948, what they were doing in the 1950s and 1960s. So long as these records are closed, no real historiography about the Arab side can be written. Whatever anybody calls the writing that emerges without historical records, it's not real history.

JOSEPH MASSAD: I have a problem with the adversary which Professor Morris chooses for Israel. Is it the Palestinians or the Arab states? The Palestinians have never had any state or political apparatus or national archives to open or close. All the archives that they had were in Lebanon and—I'm sure as Professor Morris recalls—they were fully abducted to Israel during the Israeli invasion of Lebanon in 1982, and subsequently returned to the PLO during a prisoner exchange deal conducted later. Those archives that the PLO has are open, all or most of them are open. As far as other Arab states are concerned, Palestinians are not responsible for the Arab states. They have no political power or authority over them.

There is a kind of liberal premise that asserts that a Jewish colonial movement that defines itself as a national liberation movement, from Europe, coming in and being able to colonize and take over somebody else's land, as a colonizer with immense power (which has been demonstrated from 1881 through 1948 and after), can be equated with their victims—victims who don't have the same privileges, don't have the same power. It does not need a great historian to uncover, as Professor Morris said, that in 1948 the incompetence of the Palestinian leadership was clear to everyone. Also, for most Palestinian refugees, they did not need any Israeli historian, or Professor Morris for that matter, to uncover the 1948 expulsion for them. What Professor Morris did, which is extremely valuable, is to document much of this, not all of it, much of this, from Israeli archives. And given race relations in the West, and who is believable and who is not, Professor Morris's version of events had much more credibility to Western audiences. Although it is also, of course, held suspect by some of them on an ideological basis.

AW: Are you saying that Arab historical writing is not as easily accepted by the West—because it is seen as Arab, or Islamic, or non-European?

JOSEPH MASSAD: Absolutely. All of the above—due to political biases in the west, as well as racial biases. What is really important to talk about—and I agree with Professor Morris—is the nature of Zionism itself, and whether it has any legitimacy or not. Not for its own clientele—meaning European Jews and subsequently other Jews—but also (and this is what Mr Morris and many other Israelis would like it to have) legitimacy for the Palestinians. So the victims of Zionism need to legitimize, need to accept, Zionism's legitimacy as a starting point. This is, of course, what the Israelis and the PLO officials were able to do at Oslo [with the signing of the Oslo accords which envisaged a final settlement of the Israel–Palestine dispute], where finally the Palestinian leadership in 1993 accepted, in many ways, the Zionist version, both of Jewish and Palestinian histories, and succumbed to it. What Professor Morris would like is for the rest of the Palestinians to follow suit.

From the Palestinian perspective, the nature of Zionism has always been clear, and I think this is exactly where the problem arises. At the time of the rise of Zionism, Zionism itself was not viewed as a Jewish liberation movement but as a movement for the colonization of Palestine by Jews. Indeed it was opposed by the majority of Jews, secular and religious, until well into the 1930s. And it is also important to remember that the majority of Jews who reside in Israel today, or at least who emigrated to Israel in the 1930s and 1940s and 1950s, did not come to Israel because of Zionist reasons. We have to remember that the larger segment of the Israeli Jewish population came to Israel as refugees after the war, and after 1948, from both Europe and the Arab countries, not because of the success of Zionism, but because they were refugees and had no other place to go.This is actually a failing of Zionism that goes unmentioned. And of course many Arabs also fall victim to the Zionist mythology that all Jews who came to Palestine and to Israel were actually active Zionists who simply fell in love with Zionism and believed in it and were strong adherents to it. This is simply not the case.

BENNY MORRIS: You were asking about a Truth and Reconciliation Commission which might in some way align the histories, or bring closer together the historiographies of the two sides. And the problem here still—and I can hear it from Professor Massad—is that one side, it took a long time, but eventually came to accept the legitimacy of the other. And that is the Jewish side *vis-à-vis* the Arab side, the Palestinian side. (I'm not talking here about Arab states. Their rejection of Israel is very little to do with the essential claim—it's a xenopobic, Muslim rejection of the other which has existed throughout Muslim history.) The problem is that on the other side of the Israeli–Palestinian divide, the Palestinian side cannot grant legitimacy to the Zionist claim from the beginning, and therefore can't look at its history in any objective way, in any accepting way. They don't say, well, there is this side and there is that side. For them, there is only one side which is credible, because there justice lies.

JOSEPH MASSAD: From 1881 onwards, the expulsion of Palestinians had begun, not militarily, but through the purchase of land and the colonization of land that many of the Palestinian peasants had been leasing and working on for generations. When the Zionist movement began to colonize this land through purchasing it, through the power of money, it was able to evict Palestinian peasants off their land. The expulsion in different ways—financially, and later militarily—had begun in the 1880s. To request or require that the Palestinians give legitimacy to a movement predicated on destroying their society and pushing them off their land is I think a bit preposterous. It's one thing to say that today a majority of Israelis, or a large section of the Israeli population, have been born there, they have no other place to go, this is also their country. That, of course, is readily acceptable. What of course is preposterous to claim is that the Jewish side has accepted the Palestinian claims. This is utterly untrue. The so-called Jewish side, whatever that may be, has not accepted anything.

The Jewish side, and by that I mean both Israeli Jewish society and the Israeli government, are still as Zionist as they have always been, and committed to Jewish supremacy. Jewish supremacy is the basis of the Israeli state. This is exactly the crux of the matter. As soon as the Jewish population and the Jewish state in Israel—like white South Africans before them—accept that they cannot have supremacist rights, that they cannot have supremacist privileges, only then will there be a political solution.

BENNY MORRIS: The word supremacist is ridiculous of course. Israelis, Zionists, throughout the history of Zionism would have much preferred Palestine to be empty of Arabs with therefore no need for Jews to be supreme over anybody. They simply wanted a Jewish state. They in fact abhorred the idea of a supremacist apartheid-like state. And that may have been in fact one of the driving reasons for trying to buy out and clear out Arabs along the way. They didn't want to rule over anybody else. It's a ridiculous use of the word "supremacist."

JOSEPH MASSAD: But they did rule over somebody else in a supremacist way. They still do.

BENNY MORRIS: What I'm saying is you can start history at different points in time. And what Palestinians have done, unfortunately, is to start history from 1881, 1882, and say, well look, the land was full of Arabs, the Zionists were moving in, and therefore they were colonizers, imperialists, whatever you want to call it. It could also equally be legitimately claimed that if you start history much earlier, say at the year zero, around the time of Christ, the land was populated only by Jews, there was no such thing as Arabs, and what the Arabs who came later did in the seventh century and subsequently, they were usurpers who stole the land from its legitimate owners who were the Jews. It depends at what point in time you begin this historical reckoning. From the Zionist perspective, the historical reckoning begins with Abraham and the Jewish arrival and occupation of the land of Palestine—though Palestine is a much later word.And to start talking about the land only from the point at which there were Arabs who had taken over the land from previous owners doesn't make any sense. Therefore the whole idea of only one justice, only the Palestinians have the true history of the land and a claim to it, is ridiculous.

JOSEPH MASSAD. The claim made by the Zionists, and by Professor Morris, that late nineteenth-century European Jews are direct descendants of ancient Palestinian Hebrews is what is preposterous here. This kind of anti-Semitic claim that European Jews were not European that was propagated by the racist and biological discourses of the nineteenth century, that they somehow descend from first century Hebrews, despite the fact that they look like other Europeans, that they speak European languages, is what is absurd. Basically by this kind of analogy, the Germans of today should claim northern India as the place of the birth of their nation and go back there.

BENNY MORRIS: You're saying that Jews are not Jews. That's what you're saying.

JOSEPH MASSAD: Many can claim easily that the Palestinians of today are the descendants of the ancient Hebrews, and this is the bigger irony.

AW: When we had a similar discussion involving writers concerned with the history of India and Pakistan, there was a clear determination on both sides to supercede the past and move on and to establish an intellectual dialogue between the two traditions. The rather depressing impression I get from this discussion is that in the Middle East, we are not at that stage.

BENNY MORRIS: I fear so, yes. There's no meeting of minds about the history, or the basic claims which underlie the history, of each side. That's right.

JOSEPH MASSAD: I believe that what happened in 1881, and through the entire twentieth century, continues to take place today. So basically there's no reconciliation because Palestinians still live under different forms of Israeli rule—whether it's occupation direct or indirect in the West Bank and Gaza, or under an apartheid Jewish supremacist state in Israel itself, or whether they are languishing in refugee camps around their homeland and are prevented from going there by Jewish supremacist rules within Israel itself. How can you reconcile with an enemy who is still oppressing you? The story of the oppression of the Palestinians by the Zionist movement and Israel continues as we speak. It has not ended. For there to be a reconciliation, there has to be an end to this oppression. There has to be an abandonment of Jewish supremacy, not only by the Israeli state, not only by the Israeli media, but also by academics and the population. Many Israeli liberals are on record as making statements rejecting the right of the Palestinian people to return to their homeland after being expelled for fifty years, yet they support—as Mr Morris does—the return of European Jews of the nineteenth century with problematic descent from the ancient Hebrews to their so-called homeland after nineteen centuries.

BENNY MORRIS: I'm a bit surprised by Dr Massad's racism. There is a clear line of descent of Jews—that's one of the unusual things about the Jews, which is accepted by historians the world over, that they are one of the few people from ancient times who have managed to more-or-less survive and endure into the twenty-first century. You are of course right that they intermarried and intermingled and so on, but there is a clear, direct line of descent. I'm sure it's genetic as well, but it's certainly religious, and in terms of historical tradition and culture and memory and so on, and the Hebrew language is a living proof of that. It's ridiculous to disclaim any connection between the Jews of today and the Jews of yesteryear. It makes sense in terms of Palestinian propaganda, because they want to disclaim any connection between Jews and Zionists of today and the ancient land of Israel.

JOSEPH MASSAD: I resent your accusation of racism and I think you need to defend it.

BENNY MORRIS: I think you are one of the few people I've ever heard who said that there's no connection between the Jews of today and the Jews who lived in the land of Israel 2,000 years ago.

JOSEPH MASSAD: Yes, it's a very problematic connection.

BENNY MORRIS: There's language and religion, and in fact some genetic truths which tie this in, which prove this.

JOSEPH MASSAD: I'm not a believer in eugenics or in these kinds of genetic theories. But as far as generalizations of racism, Professor Morris it is you who seconds ago told us about the alleged Muslim tradition of xenophobia.

BENNY MORRIS: It's not racist. It's a cultural tradition which denies the stranger legitimacy.

JOSEPH MASSAD: These are Orientalist and racist claims.

BENNY MORRIS: Christians and Jews in the Islamic empire were always considered second-class citizens and the rest of the world was considered infidel, unbelievers, and given to the sword. And you know that.

JOSEPH MASSAD: This is just a rehearsing of tired old Orientalist claims.

BENN MORRIS: This is Koranic tradition.

JOSEPH MASSAD: Perhaps from the Zionist and the racist Orientalist perspective, this is indeed the Muslim tradition as viewed by them, but not in reality.

11 The persistence of the Palestinian Question*

Predictions that the Palestinian Question would be resolved have foundered in the last 100 years. Some, like Theodor Herzl, thought that the Palestinians would welcome the civilizing efforts of colonizing Jews and thus the Palestinians would not even become a Question.[1] Others later thought that, had the Palestinians accepted the Zionist colonial conquest of much of their country, legitimated by the 1947 UN Partition Plan, and set up a small state on the remaining land, their Question would have been resolved. Still later, others thought that, had the Arab states absorbed the Palestinian refugee population after 1948, the Question would surely have been resolved then. An impatient and exasperated world breathed a sigh of relief when Yasser Arafat and the Israeli government signed the Oslo agreement in 1993 that transformed Arafat from a Nelson Mandela into a Mangosuthu Gatsha Buthelezi, but the Question was still not resolved.[2] Finally, some thought that, if the Arab states would only accept Israel's right to be a Jewish state, that is, a state that has the right to discriminate racially and religiously against its non-Jewish citizens by law and practice (which they did at their Beirut Summit in March 2002), the Palestinian Question would have been resolved. But the Palestinian Question persisted and still persists. A decade after Oslo, it is as intransigent as it was in 1917, when the Balfour Declaration was issued. What, then, makes the Palestinian Question persist in the face of so many expectations and desires that it be resolved?

Anti-Semitism

In the last century and a half, many have tried to explain the persistence of the Jewish question, which has always been entangled with the persistence of anti-Jewish sentiment across Western history.[3] This sentiment, whether based on religious, social, ethnic (geographic and linguistic origins), or racial grounds, clustered together in the nineteenth century in a full-fledged othering ideological edifice that came to be known as anti-Semitism. In the nineteenth century, Karl Marx postulated that the Jewish Question would be resolved alongside human emancipation, which required the ending of the division between humans as

* This essay was first published in 2005.

"egotistical" beings inhabiting civil society and humans as "abstract" citizens in the realm of the state.[4] As such emancipation failed to materialize, twentieth-century authors, with as widely differing views as Sigmund Freud, Hannah Arendt, Theodor Adorno, Max Horkheimer, Isaac Deutscher, Abram Leon, and Jean-Paul Sartre, attempted to analyze the basis of this anti-Jewish sentiment across the ages, with most concentrating on the new ideology of anti-Semitism that emerged within the belly of Romantic modernity.[5] Their answers ranged from psychosexual explanations to socioeconomic ones. Adorno and Horkheimer argued, in the *Dialectic of Enlightenment*, that Enlightenment had done away with the dialectic and posited itself as the end of history and then sought to control everything totalistically. In so doing, Jews were posited and projected by anti-Semites as a "negative principle." Thus Enlightenment transformed itself into the nightmare of Nazism and a mediocritizing capitalism.[6] Leon turned to Marxian economics and posited historical Jews as a people-class made necessary by Christian European economics.[7] Freud, among other things, identified the horror felt by Christian boys when they hear of the circumcision of Jewish boys, which they interpret as castration, as one of the reasons for the contempt they feel for Jewish men.[8] Others saw the very basis of gentile identity as necessitating the hatred of the Jew, wherein Sartre's thesis that "if the Jew did not exist the anti-Semite would invent him" tops the list.[9] Notwithstanding Sartre's reduction of the Jew to an object of gentile hatred lacking agency, his important thesis linked the persistence of the Jewish Question to the persistence of anti-Semitism.

The European Renaissance had been predicated on a rejection of the recent European barbarism. This negative assessment of what came to be known later as the Middle Ages motivated Renaissance and, later, Enlightenment thinkers to attempt to invent a heroic, glorious past by appropriating Greek civilization and incorporating it into the recently invented Europe.[10] This process was parallel to Protestantism's appropriation of the Hebrew Bible in ways that the Catholic Church had previously shunned. European colonialism, having learned the lessons of the Renaissance and the Enlightenment, was going to impart to all the colonized a similar cultural self-hatred, calling for the adoption of enlightened European Christian culture as model. While colonialism began to rule over peoples and cultures it had othered a priori, Jews living in Europe had experienced this othering for a much longer time, albeit intermittently. The Jewish *Haskala* emerged within this European history of self-rejection and reinvention as an assimilationist project seeking to transform Jewish culture from something identified by post-Enlightened Europe as non-European, if not un-European, into something more in line with the newly invented image of Europe and its Enlightenment. Indeed, Moses Mendelssohn's *Jerusalem* was seen by many as an attempt to transform Judaism into a form of Enlightened Christianity, leading many of his critics to call upon him to take the extra step and convert. He did not, but his children did.[11] Reform Judaism, a German innovation, would pick up the mantle of Christianizing Judaism in the middle of the nineteenth century.[12] The rejection of things Jewish in favor of things European were to define much of the *Haskala* project, which saw in assimilation the final integration of an othered

Jewry into the new European self.[13] While the project seemed successful in a number of ways, especially in Germany and France and less so in "unenlightened" Eastern Europe, it ultimately led to official Christianization through formal conversions. Indeed, Herzl himself, a mere three years before launching the Zionist project, which was to serve as a mild corrective to the *Haskala*, had proposed the mass baptism of European Jews to Catholicism in a now famous proposal to the Pope.[14]

Zionism, like the *Haskala*, adopted European, especially German, Enlightenment thought as its evaluative mode of assessing Jewishness and Judaism and sought their transformation into European enlightenment. It was not that the anti-Semites were wrong that Jews had "bold, misshapen noses; furtive and cunning eyes" as Herzl described French Jews, for example,[15] or that they spoke a debased German that was nothing less than "the stealthy tongues of prisoners" as Herzl described in *Der Judenstaat*,[16] but rather that the anti-Semites did not offer a solution to this despicable Jewish condition. Zionism, which espoused these views of Jews while conscious of their anti-Semitic pedigree, simply wanted to rid Jews of such traits and teach them how to be Europeans. While Zionism espoused the goals of the *maskilim* and other Jewish assimilationists in its understanding that the mark of Jewish otherness had to be removed, it differed from both in affirming that the attempt by Jews to prove that they could become Europeans inside Europe would not be allowed by European Christians. The solution seemed self-evident: Zionism, in Herzl's words, would set up a state for the Jews that would constitute "the portion of the rampart of Europe against Asia, an outpost of civilization as opposed to barbarism."[17] This state, as Herzl's novel *Altneuland* uncovered, would outdo the Europeans at their own game of civilization. The settler colony was going to be the space of Jewish transformation. To become European, Jews must exit Europe. They could return to it and become part of it by emulating its culture at a geographical remove. If Jews were Asians in Europe, in Asia, they will become Europeans.[18] Herzl affirms that it is not a question of taking Jews away "from civilized regions into the desert," but rather that the transformation "will be carried out in the midst of civilization. We shall not revert to a lower stage, we shall rise to a higher one."[19] In the new settler colony, Jews would no longer be "dirty," "cunning," "parasitical," "lazy," "superstitious," "weak," "effeminate," as anti-Semitism and Zionism posited them, but would become hardworking, scientifically minded, strong, rational, clean, and civilized—in short, European.[20]

Upon encountering the Palestinian Arabs, Zionism's transformative project expanded. While it sought to metamorphose Jews into Europeans, it set in motion a historical process by which it was to metamorphose Palestinian Arabs into Jews in a displaced geography of anti-Semitism. We will see how the persistence of this anti-Semitic impulse in European Christian thought in the nineteenth century, transmitted to and internalized by Jewish Zionism, will organize much of Zionism's cultural outlook and the political projects attendant to it in the next century.[21] The ultimate project of cultural transformation that Zionism embarked upon, then, was the metamorphosis of the Jew into the anti-Semite, which Zionism understood correctly to be the ultimate proof of its Europeanness.

The Jewish holocaust only served to strengthen this belief by Zionism, which insisted that only those Jews who answered its transformative call in its settler colony escaped the fate that befell Jews who insisted on their diaspora/Jewish condition. Herein lies Zionism's contempt for the diaspora and holocaust victims.[22] But Zionism's project proved to be twofold: in transforming the Jew into the anti-Semite (or into the "anti-Jew," as Israeli clinical psychologist Benjamin Beit-Hallahmi posited),[23] it became necessary to transform the Palestinian Arab into the disappearing European Jew.

Settler-colonialism

In order to transform Jews into Europeans in Asia, Zionism sought to make available to them a battery of professions intermittently denied them during their residence in Europe, namely in the fields of agriculture and soldiery, thus making them productive laborers and manly conquering "sabras" in one sweep.[24] What would afford them these opportunities was an Asiatic land "reclaimed" by Zionism as the inheritance of modern Jews from what it posited as their "Hebrew forefathers." Excavating the Hebrew past in order to serve as the basis for the Jews' future would become a central task of the Zionist project.[25] Zionism understood well that, for Jews to become European, they could not remain identified in tribal or religious terms, but rather in terms of race and nationhood. It is in this context that the religious origins of Judaism are transformed into national and racial origins, and ancient Hebrew kings become the progenitors of modern Jews. This was carried out at the beginning of the century through Zionist investment in the new science of statistics, which it insisted on incorporating within what was previously known as *Wissenschaft des Judentums*, transforming it into a *jüdische Wissenschaft*. Arthur Ruppin directed the Bureau for Jewish Statistics, set up in Berlin in 1904 to demonstrate scientifically how Jews were a *Volk* and a race.[26] Ruppin was most interested in eugenics and had won a "major prize" for a study on genetics.[27] He would be appointed a decade later as the Zionist Executive's representative in Palestine.[28] According to a recent study by Israeli scholar Sachlav Stoler-Liss, throughout the 1930s, prominent members of the Zionist medical establishment in Palestine advocated "castrating the mentally ill, encouraging reproduction among families 'numbered among the intelligentsia,' limiting the size of 'families of Eastern [Mizrahi] origin,' and 'preventing . . . lives that are lacking in purpose.' "[29] The Israeli newspaper *Ha'Aretz* marveled that "these proposals are not from some program of the Third Reich but rather were brought up by key figures in the Zionist establishment of the Land of Israel during the period of the British Mandate."[30] These ideas would continue to guide the Zionist movement all the way to the present, manifesting most clearly in its desperate contemporary search for Jewish "genetic markers."[31]

The European nationalist principles of *blut und boden* would guide Zionism's invention of Jews as a nation with its own land. To bring this about, the first item on their agenda was to colonize and settle such land. This "nahalat avot," or the land of the forefathers, the Jewish settlers were going to transform from a "desolate" and "neglected" Asiatic desert into a blooming, green European terrain full of forests and trees—a persistent point of pride for Israeli Jews. Not only did Herzl's futurist novel *Altneuland* serve as a fantastical blueprint for this effort, but also the very image of the Jew as carrier of European gentile civilization to a barbaric geography was definitional of Zionist political argumentation. Thus in 1930, Chaim Weizmann articulated the project thus: "We wish to spare the Arabs as much as we can of the sufferings which every backward race has gone through on the coming of another, more advanced nation."[32] As the Palestinians decided to resist this *mission civilisatrice*, Weizmann, who was to become Israel's first president, characterized the tasks before Zionism in quashing such resistance as follows: "On one side, the forces of destruction, the forces of the desert, have arisen, and on the other side stand firm the forces of civilization and building. It is the old war of the desert against civilization, but we will not be stopped."[33] Indeed they were not. They went on to destroy much of Palestinian society and expel the majority of its population. Much anxiety, however, remained constitutive of Zionism regarding the remaining signifying traces of the Palestinians and the purported traces of the Hebrews that Zionism insisted could be excavated. Thus Moshe Dayan's now famous words about what befell Palestinian towns tell us not only about the destruction of the non-Jewish past of Palestine, but also about the production of a Jewish past that Zionism collapsed into Hebrewness. His words bear repeating:

> Jewish villages were built in the place of Arab villages. You don't even know the names of these Arab villages, and I don't blame you, because these geography books no longer exist. Not only do the books not exist, the Arab villages are not there either. Nahalal arose in the place of Mahlul, Gvat in the place of Jibta, Sarid in the place of Haneifa, and Kfar-Yehoshua in the place of Tel-Shaman. There is not one single place built in this country that did not have a former Arab population.[34]

This palimpsestic operation was not at all arbitrary, but rather was well planned from the beginning of colonization with the establishment of the Jewish National Fund's "Place-Names Committee," which was itself renamed, after 1948, the "Israel Place-Names Committee."[35] Zionist renaming continued unabated upon Israel's occupation of the West Bank and the Gaza Strip.[36] The new names persisted after the Oslo agreement. Thus, the West Bank still carries its excavated Zionist names, Judea and Samaria, names that are used in government and journalistic parlance, by Likud and by Labor leaders and followers alike.

Not only have the new excavated names persisted, but also the very colonial project that was the originary driving force of Zionism has not abated either. Since 1948, Zionist colonial settlement has transformed Palestine's terrain by erecting new towns and cities on the ruins and traces of Palestinian lives. European Jewish colonists inhabited those Palestinian spaces that they did not destroy by converting them into European Jewish locales. As cited earlier, in his discussion of the early colonization efforts of holocaust survivors upon arriving in Palestine, Israeli historian Tom Segev's words also bear repeating:

> The War of Independence broke out, and tens of thousands of homes were suddenly available... Hundreds of thousands of Arabs fled, and were expelled from their homes. Entire cities and hundreds of villages left empty were repopulated in a short order with new immigrants. In April 1949, they numbered 100,000, most of them Holocaust survivors. The moment was a dramatic one in the war for Israel, and a frightfully banal one, too, focused as it was on the struggle over houses and furniture. Free people—Arabs—had gone into exile and become destitute refugees; destitute refugees—Jews—took the exiles' places as a first step in their new lives as free people. One group lost all they had, while the other found everything they needed—tables, chairs, closets, pots, pans, plates, sometimes clothes, family albums, books, radios, and pets. Most of the immigrants broke into the abandoned Arab houses without direction, without order, without permission. For a few months the country was caught up in a frenzy of take-what-you-can, first-come, first-served. Afterwards the authorities tried to halt the looting and take control of the allocation of houses, but in general they came too late. Immigrants also took possession of Arab stores and workshops, and some Arab neighborhoods soon looked like Jewish towns in pre-war Europe, with tailors, shoemakers, dry-goods merchants—all the traditional Jewish occupations.[37]

Zionism would further transform these towns into purely European locales with a Hebrew flavor, which it conflated with the new Jewish identity. Not only did Zionism reappropriate the secular and religious history of the Hebrews from a European Protestantism intent on appropriating the Hebrews' religious philosophy, it also adopted as its own, Europe's suspect Greek heritage, on account of its European civilizational commitments. In this spirit, the schismatic divide between Jewish and Christian ethics was unified after the Second World War as the so-called Judeo-Christian ethical legacy common to all the civilized.[38] The Palestinian Question persisted throughout Zionism's pre-State history as the national question, as well as the land question. Israel's establishment in 1948 set in motion an uninterrupted process of colonization, with its 1967 conquest of the West Bank and the Gaza Strip marking an intensified effort that was given an even stronger push since the Oslo agreement was signed, as the number of Jewish colonial settlers in the still-occupied territories have doubled since 1993. But as Zionism's colonization continues, so does Palestinian resistance. The Palestinian Question, therefore, persists as long as Zionism's colonial venture persists.

Racism

As Zionism was metamorphosing Palestine into the land of the ancient Hebrews, which would then be repackaged as the land of modern and future Jews, Zionism also set its cultural production in motion. Zionism's objective was to ensure Israel's Europeanness and its non-Asianness, or, in Zionist parlance, its non-"levantineness." The possible levantinization of Zionism's new Asian-turned-European geography was blamed not solely on the persistence of Palestinian traces and bodies within the newly declared Euro-Jewish space, but more terrifyingly on Zionism's abduction of Arab Jews into the heart of its project. The anxiety that the Arab Jews caused, as Ella Shohat has demonstrated,[39] was as great as that caused by the Palestinians, added to which were the "hordes" of Arabs surrounding this new oasis of European culture—what Israeli Jews call today their "tough neighborhood."[40] This, however, never stopped Zionism from appropriating the fruit of the land that Palestine's peasants produced. It is in this vein that Zionism appropriated Palestinian and pan-Syrian food like hummus, falafil, tabbulah, *maftul* (increasingly known in the United States and Europe as "Israeli couscous"), and finely diced Palestinian rural salad (now known in New York delis as "Israeli salad") as its own national dishes.

Palestinians have figured in different, albeit related, ways to the chain of Zionist ideologues from Herzl to Menachem Begin and Ariel Sharon. While Herzl saw them as a "dirty" people who looked like "brigands,"[41] Menachem Begin was to see them as "two-legged beasts."[42] Note the complete congruence between anti-Semitic adjectives used against European Jews and their adoption by Zionism to describe the Palestinians. While Herzl sought to "transfer the penniless population" to the surrounding countries, Ben-Gurion and the Zionist leadership carried out that task successfully in 1948 when they expelled the majority of the Palestinian population, and less successfully in 1967 when they expelled only a few hundred thousands. The tolerance of Israeli Jews of "dirty foreigners" among them has its limits. According to the Israel Institute for Democracy, in a report it released in February 2004:

> As of 2003, more than half (53%) of the Jews in Israel state out loud that they are against full equality for the Arabs; 77% say there should be a Jewish majority on crucial political decisions . . . and the majority (57%) think that the Arabs should be encouraged to emigrate,

a veiled reference to expulsion or "transfer."[43] This is a key practice in Zionism's program of transforming the Palestinian into the Jew. Through the mechanism of expulsion, the land-based Palestinian is metamorphosed overnight into the landless wandering diaspora Jew for whom Zionism has only contempt. While the adoption of anti-Semitic epistemology in viewing the Palestinians organized Zionism's overall encounter with this mostly peasant population, physical expulsion became the principal instrument at the disposal of Zionism and Israel to effect this metamorphosis.

But despite Zionism's efforts, it was unable to expel all Palestinians. It transformed those who remained inside Israel into foreigners in their own land and, from 1948 until 1966, subjected them to life under a military, racialist system of rule that was reminiscent of the life of European Jews under the worst types of anti-Semitic rule[44]—here the 1956 massacre of Kafr Qasim, in which forty-seven Palestinian Israeli citizens (all of them unarmed civilians) were gunned down by Israeli soldiers is not unlike many of the pogroms to which European Jews fell victim.[45] Since 1966, this population has lived under a civilian, racialist system of rule reminiscent of the less extreme experiences of European Jews living under anti-Semitic discriminatory laws.[46] As for the Palestinian population of the West Bank and Gaza, whom Israel captured in 1967, it transformed their lands and homes into besieged ghettoes, walled in and surrounded by mobs of Jewish colonial settlers and the Israeli army. If anti-Semitic Jews could make the Palestinian "desert" bloom, evidence of Palestinian agriculture had to be erased. To this end Jewish Israel has undertaken the desertification of Palestinian lands. The Israeli military's and Jewish settlers' uprooting of hundreds of thousands of Palestinian olive trees in the West Bank and Gaza Strip as well as the Israeli military's recent razing of four million square meters of cultivated land are engineered, among other things, to prove that Palestinians would only be allowed to live in a desert.[47] Only anti-Semitic Jews can live in a European simulacrum of green hills and meadows. The Judaized Palestinian will live in the desert, if allowed to live at all.

Israel was able to replicate the different conditions under which European Jews suffered under extreme anti-Semitic conditions by imposing similar conditions on the different sectors of the Palestinian people, with one important twist: Jews are now the anti-Semitic enforcers of oppression against a recently Judaized population. Indeed, the expelled Palestinians have experienced a life uncannily similar to that of Jews in Europe of the nineteenth and part of the twentieth century. In those countries where Palestinians are granted equal legal rights, as in Jordan, they face unofficial discrimination at every level of government, with political campaigns by extremists calling for their expulsion or "repatriation"—a term not lost on those who know the history of anti-Semitic campaigns to expel Jews from Europe.[48] In those countries that refused to grant them equal rights, such as Lebanon, they have been languishing in refugee camps for fifty-seven years with no rights and constant police harassment and militarized campaigns to massacre them and "repatriate" them.[49] Even those diaspora Palestinians seeking assimilation in their new homes are prevented from doing so on a regular basis in much of the diaspora. The transformation of Palestinians into Jews is located precisely in these parallels. The fact that the anti-Semitic epithet "dirty Jew" has metamorphosed into the favorite Israeli Jewish insult against Palestinians, namely "dirty Arabs" or " 'Aravim milukhlakhim," encapsulates this process perfectly.

But turning Palestinians into Jews does not mean that they can have access to their own Palestinian Hebrew ancestors. On the contrary, it is precisely through Zionism's appropriation of the history of the Palestinian Hebrews as the ancestors of the European-Jews-turned-anti-Semites that the Palestinian Arabs lose any connection to their Hebrew ancestry. While neighboring Egyptians, Jordanians, Lebanese, and Iraqis can narrate a national history that extends to the Pharaohs, the Nabateans, the Phoenicians, and the Babylonians, Palestinians cannot lay any national claims to Palestine's past. As recent converts to landless Jewishness, they cannot access the past of a land colonized by anti-Semitic Hebraic Jews, nor can they claim ancestors uncovered by Zionism to be the Jews' own exclusive progenitors. This is not so unlike the process through which the Hebrew prophets were abducted from the Jewish tradition into Christianity. It is, however, ironic, and particularly scandalous for Zionism, in this regard to find that a young David Ben-Gurion had postulated in 1918 that it was indeed the Palestinian peasants who were the descendants of the Jews who had remained in Palestine, and that, despite the Islamic conquest, these peasants had held on to their Hebrew ancestors' traditions, most obviously through maintaining the same names for their villages.[50] Ben-Gurion went so far as to assert that

> in spite of much intermixing, the majority of the [Palestinian] fellahin in Western Palestine are unified in their external appearance and in their origin, and in their veins, without a doubt, flows much Jewish blood—from the Jewish peasants who in the days of the persecutions and terrible oppression had renounced their tradition and their people in order to maintain their attachment and loyalty to the land of the Jews.[51]

Ben-Gurion's early and now forgotten opinion notwithstanding, the constants of Zionist thought persist uninterrupted, from Herzl's *Der Judenstaat* (State of the Jews) to a living and prospering *Medinat Yisrael* (the State of Israel) that hopes to become once and for all *Palästinenser-rein*. Evidently, this Zionist desire for national, racial, and religious purity uncontaminated by an *other* hardly deviates from European anti-Semitic nationalist precedents.

The Europeanness of the state was a clear goal at the outset. Herzl saw the state as adopting German for its language, as well as for the name of its cities. In his novel, he proposed "Neudorf" as one such city name. He rejected Yiddish as the language of the settler colony owing to its being a "ghetto" language and a "miserable stunted jargon."[52] The East European Zionist Hebraists showed a better understanding of Europeanness than the West European Herzl, who sought blind emulation, for they insisted on an ancient language in an ancient land, echoing the European nationalist principles of *Blut und Boden*. While the Hebraists insisted that a new secular Hebrew could better serve as the language of the new redeemed Jews, thus further conflating the ancient Hebrews with modern Jews, they worried about Hebrew pronunciation. In this vein, as we saw earlier, Vladimir Jabotinsky, the founder of revisionist Zionism, insisted in his 1930 essay "The Hebrew accent" that

> there are experts who think that we ought to bring our accent closer to the Arabic accent. But this is a mistake. Although Hebrew and Arabic are Semitic languages, it does not mean that our Fathers spoke in [an] 'Arabic accent.' … We are European and our musical taste is European, the taste of Rubinstein, Mendelssohn, and Bizet."[53]

Expressing his anxiety about Moroccan Jews weakening the cultural metamorphosis of Ashkenazi Jews into Europeans, David Ben-Gurion stated: "We do not want Israelis to become Arabs. We are in duty bound to fight against the spirit of the Levant, which corrupts individuals and societies, and preserve the authentic Jewish values as they crystallized in the [European] Diaspora."[54] The newspaper *Ha'Aretz* worried in 1949 that some of the Arab Jews were "at an even lower level than what we knew with regard to the former Arabs of Eretz Yisrael."[55] A whole cultural operation of civilizing non-European Jews was devised, however unsuccessfully, to "develop" them.[56]

As Michael Selzer has shown in his classic book *The Aryanization of the Jewish State*, German anti-Semitism started a domino effect that began in Germany and ended in Palestine. If German anti-Semitism saw German Jews as dirty and cunning, medieval, and effeminate, German Jews would project such images on the *Ostjuden*—East European Jews—in much of their descriptions. Now it was the turn of the *Ostjuden* to use such adjectives to describe Arab Jews.[57] While Selzer did not carry his argument further to include the Palestinians, they were to become the ultimate object of such displacement. Within the settler colony, the Jewish population, regardless of ethnic origins, has internalized this anti-Semitic epistemology in describing the Palestinians.

This is not simply a superstructural neurosis that has afflicted Zionism; it is rather the epistemological foundation on which it rests. If Zionism proceeded from a rejection of all things Jewish in favor of European culture, then its pedagogical mission was to transform all Jews into that model. To justify its colonization efforts of Palestine to a gentile European world, Zionism would present Jews as carriers of European civilization to a land burdened by a barbaric, "parasitical" population who neglected it and transformed it into a desert. Much of what anti-Semitism projected onto European Jews would now be displaced onto Palestinian Arabs, who were seen to embody the attributes that both Zionism and anti-Semitism insisted had been previously embodied by diaspora Jewry. The question of Palestinian "neglect" of the land of Palestine on which they were living "parasitically" is hardly foreign to the anti-Semitic notion that described European Jews as unproductive usurers living "parasitically" off European Christian society.

Even when the parallels between anti-Semitic and Zionist practices would correspond fully to each other, Zionism and Israel showed, and still show, no embarrassment. If anything, as the following will demonstrate, Israeli Jewish soldiers today are willing disciples of anti-Semites. This is not a new development, but harks back to the primal scene of Jewish Zionism's marriage to anti-Semitism. This is clearest in the thought of Herzl, who wrote in his diaries in 1895 that anti-Semitism was "more than understandable," and that it was "salutary" and "useful to the Jewish character." He went further to explain that anti-Semitism constituted an "education of a group by the masses." He would predict that with "hard knocks," "a Darwinian mimicry will set in."[58] Herzl later went to foster alliances with the anti-Semites of his day. His rationale would persist to the present. Israeli soldiers, engaged in putting down the second Palestinian uprising against Israeli military occupation, found pedagogical inspiration in an anti-Semitic precedent. According to the Israeli newspaper *Ha'Aretz*:

> In order to prepare properly for the next campaign, one of the Israeli officers in the territories said not long ago, "it's justified and in fact essential to learn from every possible source. If the mission will be to seize a densely populated refugee camp, or take over the casbah in Nablus, and if the commander's obligation is to try to execute the mission without casualties on either side, then he must first analyze and internalize the lessons of earlier battles—even, however shocking it may sound, even how the German army fought in the Warsaw ghetto." The officer indeed succeeded in shocking others, not least because he is not alone in taking this approach. Many of his comrades agree that in order to save Israelis now, it is right to make use of knowledge that originated in that terrible war, whose victims were their kin.[59]

The more recent practice of writing numbers on the arms of the thousands of Palestinians that have been crammed into Israeli detention camps since February 2002 further demonstrates that the Nazi precedent acts, not as a deterrent, but rather as a pedagogical model for the Israeli army.[60]

The racism of Zionism clearly derives from a prior anti-Semitism whose object has simply been exchanged. The persistence of the Palestinian Question, therefore, is organically linked to the persistence of the Jewish Question, whose Zionist resolution was accomplished through displacement. Zionism was not entirely convinced that its colonial settler project would be sufficient to transform Jews into Europeans. Its higher objective was that Jews would be normalized only when they have become European anti-Semites, when they began to view diaspora Jewishness through the eyes of anti-Semitism. Examples of this abound. As discussed earlier, in line with Zionism's contempt for the Jewish diaspora, as well as for Jewish victims of the holocaust as passive weaklings, is the popular modern Hebrew term for "sissy": the word "sabon" or soap. The term appeared in the wake of the Second World War when stories circulated about Jews being turned into soap by the Nazis.[61] Even holocaust survivors were seen through the spectacles of anti-Semitism. Ben-Gurion himself spoke of survivors as a "people who would not have survived if they had not been what they were—hard, evil, and selfish people, and what they underwent there served to destroy what good qualities they had left."[62] In this context, Zionism's achievement was precisely this metamorphosis of the Jew into the anti-Semite. The persistence of anti-Semitism within Zionism as a guiding epistemology accounts, then, for much of the persistence of the Palestinian Question.

Nationalism

Zionism is first and foremost a nationalist ideology in the European Romantic tradition, albeit a latecomer to that tradition. The influence of German Romanticism (including philosophers like Herder and Fichte, inter alia), the German youth movement (which Zionism emulated), as well as fin-de-siècle evolutionist thought and theories of race and degeneration inform much of its ideological makeup. Max Nordau, the theorist of degeneration par excellence, was one of Zionism's philosophical fathers, calling for the regeneration of the degenerated Jews.[63] Nordau was careful to emphasize that "We shall not become Asians there [in Palestine], as far as anthropological and cultural inferiority are concerned, any more than the Anglo-Saxons became Indians in North America, Hottentots in South Africa, or members of the Papua tribes in Australia."[64]

Like all nationalisms, Zionism is founded on a binary of self and other for its identitarian project. What is noteworthy in this regard is how it is the anti-Semite, not the Jew, who constitutes the self for Zionism, with the Jew being the other against whom the new self must be based. In internalizing anti-Semitic subjectivity, Zionism adopts its epistemology lock, stock, and barrel, thus seeing the Jew as everything the new Zionist identity is not. In Zionist lingo, this is translated into a forsaking of the diaspora Jew for the benefit of the new land-based Israeli Jew, who is modeled after the anti-Semite in opposing the very existence of the diaspora Jew. If the anti-Semite seeks the physical expulsion and annihilation of the diaspora Jew, the Israeli Jew is committed to a similar project. The assistance rendered by Zionism to anti-Jewish regimes in expelling their Jews to Israel is now the stuff of history,[65] but equally important is Zionism's commitment to the annihilation of the diaspora Jew ontologically, if not physically. The new Zionist Jew is then ontologically constituted in opposition to all things diasporically Jewish (and that was, for the most part, much of Jewish existence when Zionism emerged), which are viewed through the spectacles of anti-Semitism. By attempting to repress the diaspora Jew within its new subjectivity, Zionism, as Shohat has explained, is always ill at ease and fears the return of the repressed.[66] By externalizing its anxiety onto the Palestinians as the new diaspora Jews, it ensures the continued stability of its new subjectivity by repressing them. Thus, the persistence of Zionism's oppression of the Palestinians is necessary for Zionism's ability to maintain the ontological structure of its new identity, without which, it fears, the diaspora Jew within might return to haunt it. Here we are reminded of the Sartrean formula of the necessity of the Jew for the ontological existence of the anti-Semite.

Zionism is also a colonial movement made possible by a European colonizing world, which Zionism hoped it could both assist and extend. The end of formal colonialism, which culminated in the liberation of Algeria in 1962 and the independence of Portugal's African colonies (including Angola and Mozambique) in 1975, left Israel battling alongside Rhodesia and South Africa as the only remaining settler-colonies in Asia and Africa. Being the last settler-colony since 1994 has not been a reassuring status for Israel. The jingoistic nationalism of Israeli society, its high militarization, and its racially supremacist ideology mask an increasing anxiety about its place in the world.[67] Zionism's transformation of the Jew into the European anti-Semite, however, is the reassuring element in its persistent strategy of garnering continued support.

Israel's packaging itself as an extension of Europe is what accounts for much of the support the settler-colony has received from Europe and America over the past century. Herzl understood this only too well when he predicted that the anti-Semites would be Zionism's best supporters: "the Governments of all countries scourged by Anti-Semitism will be keenly interested in assisting us to obtain [the] sovereignty we want."[68] Indeed, "not only poor Jews" would contribute to an immigration fund for European Jews, "but also Christians who wanted to get rid of them."[69] Furthermore, "honest Anti-Semites . . . will combine with our officials in controlling the transfer of our estates."[70] His understanding of the role of anti-Semites in Zionist efforts could not be clearer. He unapologetically affirmed: "The anti-Semites will become our most dependable friends, the anti-Semitic countries our allies."[71]

The persistence of anti-Semitism in Euro-American thought today, together with its continued hatred of the figure of the Jew, is precisely what informs European and American support for the anti-Semitic Jews inhabiting Israel. It is hardly a coincidence in this regard that anti-Semitic Christian fundamentalists are Israel's strongest supporters in the United States. Zionism understands this all too well, having based its entire project on this correct assumption and expectation.

The Palestinian people's resistance to the Zionist project and their demand for the end of Israeli racism and colonialism, and for the transformation of Israel into a nonracialist binational state, are registered by Zionism as "anti-Semitic." The irony of an anti-Semitic Zionism depicting the Palestinians as the real anti-Semites is not a simple rhetorical move, but instead is crucial to Zionism's fashioning of Jewish public opinion, both in Israel and on a global scale. If European anti-Semitism, and Zionism with it, targeted the Asiatic Jew of Europe, then Palestinian resistance, dubbed "anti-Semitism" by Zionism, is similarly targeting the Europeanized Jew in Asia. What Palestinian resistance demands is the de-Europeanization of the Jew; it calls for Zionism's abandonment of European anti-Semitism as its inspirational source. What the Palestinians are calling for is the Asianization of Israel's European Jews, with the result that they come to view themselves as not only *in* the Middle East, but *of* it. In doing so, Palestinians are striking at the very heart of the Zionist project, namely the Europeanization of the Jew in an Asian milieu. The insistence of Zionist ideologues on their project is governed by their rejection of the return of the Asiatic in the Jew, which they know would result in loss of European and American support.

Zionism did not struggle for a hundred years to transform the Jew into the anti-Semite and thus become part of Europe, only to be defeated by the "New Jews." Its persistence in oppressing the Palestinians is precisely its persistence in suppressing the Jew within. American and European anti-Semitic commitments to support de-Judaized Jews in Israel lies at the heart of the Palestinian Question. The persistence of the *Palestinian* Question, therefore, *is* the persistence of the *Jewish* Question. Both questions can only be resolved by the negation of anti-Semitism, which still plagues much of Europe and America and which mobilizes Zionism's own hatred of Jewish Jews *and* of the Palestinians.

Notes

Introduction: the opposite of terror

1 On the Special Night Squads, see Leonard Mosley, "Orde Wingate and Moshe Dayan," and David-Ben Gurion, "Our friend: what Wingate did for us," in Walid Khalidi (ed.), *From Haven to Conquest, Readings in Zionism and the Palestine Problem Until 1948* (Washington, DC: The Institute for Palestine Studies, 1987), 375–388.
2 David Ben-Gurion to Va'ad Leumi in Tel Aviv, May 5, 1936; David Ben-Gurion, *Zikhronot* (Memoirs) (Tel Aviv: Am Oved, 1971–1982), Volume III (164), cited in Shabtai Teveth, *Ben-Gurion and the Palestinian Arabs, From Peace to War* (Oxford: Oxford University Press, 1985), 174.
3 See ibid.
4 For a list of these attacks, see Walid Khalidi, "The United States and the Palestinian people," in Walid Khalidi, *Palestine Reborn* (London: I.B. Taurus, 1992), 151–152, 168–170.
5 Hannah Arendt, Albert Einstein, *et al.*, "New Palestine Party: visit of Menachem Begin and aims of political movement discussed," Letter to the Editor, *New York Times*, December 4, 1948.
6 Menachem Begin, *The Revolt, Story of the Irgun* (New York: Henry Schuman, 1951), 59–60.
7 Vladimir Jabotinky, "The Iron Wall, (We and the Arabs)," *Rasswyet*, November 14, 1923, quoted in Lenni Brenner, *The Iron Wall, Zionist Revisionism from Jabotinsky to Shamir* (London: Zed Books, 1984), 74.
8 Ibid., 75.
9 Quoted by Nahum Goldmann, *The Jewish Paradox* (New York: Fred Jordan Books, 1978), 99.
10 *New York Times*, December 13, 1954.
11 *Al Hamishmar*, September 7, 1976.
12 *Ha'aretz*, June 3, 1998.
13 *Reuters*, September 11, 1997.
14 "Takhrib," which literally means subversion and its derivative "mukharrib" subversive are used by the Israelis interchangeably with "irhab" and "irhabi" meaning terrorism.
15 Cited in Edward Said, *After the Last Sky* (New York: Pantheon Books, 1986), 65.
16 Ibid., 113–114.
17 For a discussion of the role of song in the Palestinian struggle, see Joseph Massad, "Liberating songs: Palestine put to music," in Ted Swedenberg and Rebecca Stein (eds), *Popular Palestine: Cultures, Communities, and Transnational Circuits* (Durham, NC: Duke University Press, 2005).
18 St. Augustine, *City of God* (New York: Penguin Books, 1984), 139. See also Noam Chomsky, *Pirates and Emperors, International Terrorism in the Real World* (New York: Claremenot Research and Publications, 1986).

19 Ari Shavit, "Survival of the fittest," an interview with Benny Morris, *Ha'Aretz*, January 9, 2004.
20 See Joseph Massad, "Rome and Jerusalem Revisited," *Al-Ahram Weekly*, February 19–24, 2004.

1 The "post-colonial" colony: time, space, and bodies in Palestine/Israel

1 This essay was originally published in Fawzia Afzal-Khan and Kalpana Seshadri-Crooks (eds), *The Pre-Occupation of Post-Colonial Studies* (Durham, NC: Duke University Press, 2000).
2 On the continuing colonial privileges of white colonial settlers in post-1980 independent Zimbabwe, see Andrew Astrow, *Zimbabwe, A Revolution That Lost Its Way?* (London: Zed Press, 1983).
3 On Israeli academic apologia about the nature of Israel, see the discussion in Elia Zureik, *Palestinians in Israel, A Study in Internal Colonialism* (London: Routledge and Kegan Paul, 1979), 76–82.
4 For an elaboration on the problematic uses of the term "post-colonial," see Ella Shohat "Notes on the 'post-colonial'," *Social Text*, 31–32 (1992), 99–113, and Arif Dirlik, "The post-colonial aura: Third World criticism in the age of global capitalism," *Critical Inquiry*, 20 (Winter 1994), 328–356.
5 See Richard Stevens "Zionism as a phase of Western imperialism," in Ibrahim Abu-Lughod (ed.), *The Transformation of Palestine* (Chicago, IL: Northwestern University Press, 1971).
6 Cited in Regina Sharif, *Non-Jewish Zionism, Its Roots in Western History* (London: Zed Press, 1983), 53.
7 See Nathan Weinstock, *Zionism: False Messiah* (London: Ink Links, 1979), 39. It should be noted that Zionism was to adopt the slogan of a "Jewish State" rather than "a State for the Jews" as its rallying cry.
8 Theodor Herzl, *The Jewish State, An Attempt at a Modern Solution to the Jewish Question* (London: H. Porders, 1972), 30.
9 Moses Hess, *Rome and Jerusalem, A Study in Jewish Nationalism*, translated by Meyer Waxman (New York: Bloch Publishing House, 1918), 149.
10 Palmerston to Ponsonby, Public Record Office Mss, F.O. 78/390 (No. 34) August 11, 1840, cited in Sharif, *Non-Jewish Zionism*, 56.
11 Paul Goodman, *Zionism in England* (London: Zionist Federation of Great Britain and Ireland, 1949), 18–19, cited by Sharif, *Non-Jewish Zionism*, 74.
12 *Protocols of the Fourth Zionist Congress* (London: 1900), 5, cited by Sharif, *Non-Jewish Zionism*, 74.
13 Raphael Patai (ed.), *The Complete Diaries of Theodor Herzl*, translated by Harry Zohn, Volume IV (New York: The Herzl Press Thomas Yoseloff, 1960), 1367.
14 Ibid., 1473.
15 Ibid., 1473.
16 Ibid., 1499.
17 Ibid., 1499.
18 Ibid., 1601.
19 Ibid., 1597.
20 Ibid., 1600, "but it is also the home of others."
21 Ibid., 1600.
22 The Pale of Settlement is the area covering those parts of Russia and Poland where Jews were restricted to live. However, the area also included gentile Russians and Poles.
23 *The Complete Diaries*, 1361.
24 Leo Pinsker, *Auto-Emancipation*, reprinted in Pinsker's *Road to Freedom* (New York: Scopus Publishing, 1975), 104.

25 *Auto-Emancipation*, 105.
26 *The Complete Diaries*, 1474.
27 "The strategic importance of Syria to the British Empire," General Staff, War Office, December 9, 1918, F.O. 371/4178, PRO, cited in the "Introduction" to A. W. Kayyali (ed.), *Zionism, Imperialism and Racism* (London: Croom Helm, 1979), 17.
28 Quoted in A. W. Kayyali, "Introduction," 16.
29 Shimon Shama, *Two Rothchilds and the Land of Israel* (London: Collins, 1978), 63, 68, 79–80, cited by Gideon Shafir, *Land, Labor and the Origins of the Israeli–Palestinian Conflict, 1882–1914* (Cambridge: Cambridge University Press, 1989), 51.
30 Quoted in Simha Flapan, *Zionism and the Palestinians* (London: Croomhelm, 1979), 71.
31 Ber Borochov, "Eretz Israel in our Program and tactics," in Mitchell Cohen (ed.), *Class Struggle and the Jewish Nation, Selected Essays in Marxist Zionism* (New Brunswick, NJ: Transaction Books, 1984), 203.
32 F. H. Kisch, *Palestine Diary* (London: Victor Gollancz, 1938), Entry of May 28, 1931, 420.
33 On the history of Revisionist Zionism, see Lenni Brenner, *The Iron Wall, Zionist Revisionism from Jabotinsky to Shamir* (London: Zed Press, 1984).
34 On the assassination of Bernadotte, see ibid., 202–203.
35 For details on this massacre, see Benny Morris, *The Birth of the Palestinian Refugee Problem, 1947–1949* (Cambridge: Cambridge University Press, 1989), 222–223.
36 For details of Dayr Yasin, see David Hirst, *The Gun and the Olive Branch, The Roots of Conflict in the Middle East* (London: Faber & Faber, 1984), 124–129.
37 It must be noted, however, that the Haganah leadership condemned the Irgun massacre at Dayr Yasin due mainly to its enmity toward the Irgun leaders and its desire to discredit them.
38 See Walid Khalidi (ed.), *All That Remains, The Palestinian Villages Occupied and Depopulated by Israel in 1948*, (Washington, DC: Institute for Palestine Studies, 1992).
39 On this point, see the discussion in Uri Davis and Walter Lehn, "And the Fund still lives, the role of the Jewish National Fund in the determination of Israel's land policies," *Journal of Palestine Studies*, 7: 4 (Summer 1978), 4–7.
40 See the important contribution of Maxime Rodinson on this question in his classic *Israel, A Colonial-Settler State?* (New York: Monad Press, 1973).
41 Ibid., 80–82.
42 Ibid., 88.
43 On the importing of Yemeni Jewish laborers by the Zionists, see Gideon Giladi, *Discord in Zion, Conflict between Ashkenazi and Sephardi Jews in Israel* (London: Scorpion Publishing, 1990), 41–48. Also see Joseph Massad, "Zionism's internal others: Israel and the Oriental Jews," *Journal of Palestine Studies*, 100 (Summer 1996), 53–68.
44 Isaac Deutscher, "Israel's spiritual climate," in Tamara Deutscher (ed.), *The Non-Jewish Jew and Other Essays* (New York: Hill and Wang, 1968), 111–112.
45 Ibid., 112.
46 Ibid., 116.
47 On the refugee–colonist status of European Jews, see Chapter 4.
48 "Israel's tenth birthday," in Deutscher, *The Non-Jewish Jew*, 118.
49 Colonial Office [CO] 733/297/75156/II/Appendix A, extract from Weizmann's speech, April 23, 1936, Great Britain, Peel Commission Report, 96–97, cited in Philip Mattar, *The Mufti of Jerusalem: Al-Hajj Amin-al-Husayni and the Palestinian National Movement* (New York: Columbia University Press, 1988), 73.
50 "The non-Jewish Jew," in Deutscher, *The Non-Jewish Jew*, 40–41.
51 "Israel's spiritual climate," in Deutscher, *The Non-Jewish Jew*, 103.
52 "The Israeli–Arab war, June 1967," in Deutscher, *The Non-Jewish Jew*, 138.

53 Joel S. Migdal, *Strong States and Weak Societies, State–Society Relations and State Capabilities in the Third World* (Princeton, NJ: Princeton University Press, 1988), 45.
54 Ibid., 46.
55 Ibid., 145.
56 On Lipset and Memmi, see Zureik's discussion of their views in Zureik, *Palestinians*, 77–78.
57 Kwame Anthony Appiah, *In My Father's House, Africa in the Philosophy of Culture* (Oxford: Oxford University Press, 1992).
58 Ibid., 17.
59 Ibid., 43.
60 Ibid., 43.
61 Quoted in an interview with Lawrence Grobel in *Conversations with Brando* (New York: Hyperion,1991), 109.
62 Cited in ibid., 119–120. Brando' s support for Begin's right-wing terrorist group was a result of his disappointment with the Haganah and its leader David Ben-Gurion who were not "doing as they should have done."
63 Joan Peters, *From Time Immemorial: The Origins of the Arab–Jewish Conflict Over Palestine* (New York: Harper & Row, 1984).
64 See Edward Said and Christopher Hitchens (eds.), *Blaming the Victims, Spurious Scholarship and the Palestinian Question* (London: Verso, 1988), and the following reviews of the book: Ian Gilmour and David Gilmour, "Pseudo-travellers," *London Review of Books* (February 7, 1985), 8–10, Alexander Cockburn, *Nation* (September 29, 1984 and October 13, 1984)—Cockburn renamed the book "From Lies Immemorial"—and Norman Finkelstein's "Disinformation and the Palestine question: the not-so-strange case of Joan Peter's *From Time Immemorial*," in Said *et al.*, *Blaming*, 33–69.
65 *Conversations with Brando*, 105.
66 Edward Said, *The Question of Palestine* (New York: Vintage, 1980), 87.
67 Benjamin Beit-Hallahmi, *Original Sins, Reflections of the History of Zionism and Israel* (London: Pluto Press, 1992), 82.
68 Max Nordau, "Jewry of muscle," translation of "Muskeljudentum," in *Juedische Turnzeitung* (June 1903), in Paul Mendes-Flohr and Jehuda Reinharz (eds.), *The Jew in the Modern World, A Documentary History* (Oxford: Oxford University Press, 1980), 434–435. For an overview of Nordau's political thought, see George Mosse, *Confronting the Nation, Jewish and Western Nationalism* (Hanover, NH: Brandeis University Press, published by the University Press of New England, 1993), 161–175.
69 "Jewry of muscle," 434–435.
70 Bar Kochba was the leader of the last organized Jewish resistance to the Romans which was defeated at Betar in 135 AD.
71 Paul Breines, *Tough Jews, Political Fantasies and the Moral Dilemma of American Jewry* (New York: Basic Books, 1991).
72 Ibid., 47.
73 See Sander Gilman, *The Jew's Body* (New York: Routledge, 1991).
74 The importance of Masada is related to its Jewish defenders who chose suicide rather than accept capture by the Romans. It should be pointed out that the women and children of Masada were actually killed by the husbands and fathers before the latter committed suicide. On the incorporation of Masada in Zionist national mythology, see Yael Zerubavel, *Recovered Roots, Collective Memory and the Making of an Israeli National Tradition* (Chicago, IL: University of Chicago Press, 1995).
75 See Ella Shohat's discussion of the masculine Israeli colonial explorer in her *Israeli Cinema, East/West and the Politics of Representation* (Austin, TX: University of Texas Press, 1989).
76 See Part II of Breines' book entitled "From Masada to Mossad: a historical sketch of tough Jewish imagery," 75–167.

77 See Simona Sharoni, "Militarized masculinity in context: cultural politics and social constructions of gender in Israel," Paper presented at the Middle East Studies Association conference held in Portland, OR (October 1992).
78 *Europa Europa*, directed by Agnieszka Holland, an Artur Brauner and Margaret Menegoz Production, Orion Pictures (1991). The film became the second-highest grossing German movie in the United States after *Das Boot*. It won the Golden Globe prize and a New York Film Critics Award. See "Holland without a country," in the *New York Times Magazine* (August 8, 1993), 28–32.
79 See Gilman, *The Jew's Body*, 169–193.
80 Nordau, "Jewry of muscle," 435.
81 Quoted in the *New York Times Magazine*, "Holland," 32.
82 Ibid.
83 See Beit-Hallahmi, *Original Sins*, 128–129.
84 Sigmund Freud, "Analysis of a phobia in a five-year-old boy," in *The Standard Edition of the Complete Psychological Works of Sigmund Freud* (London: Hogarth Press, 1953–1974) Vol. X, 36f.
85 Benjamin Beit-Hallahmi, *The Israeli Connection, Who Israel Arms and Why* (New York: Pantheon, 1987), 238–239.
86 Tom Segev, *The Seventh Million: Israelis and the Holocaust* (New York: Hill and Wang, 1993), 421.
87 On Zionism's gendered agency and its relationship to Palestine, see Ella Shohat, "Eurocentrism, exile and Zionist discourse," Paper presented at the Middle East Studies Association Annual Conference, Washington, DC, 1991, and Shohat's "Imaging terra incognita: the disciplinary gaze of Empire," *Public Culture*, 3: 2 (Spring 1991), 41–70.
88 Melanie Klein, "Love, guilt and reparation," in her *Love, Guilt and Reparation and Other Works, 1921–1945* (New York: The Free Press, 1975), 334.
89 On the analogy between Israeli Sabras and the American Adam, see Ella Shohat, "Staging the quincentenary, the Middle East and the Americas," *Third Text*, 21, (Winter 1992–1993), 102.
90 This story is told during a meeting in 1970 between Prime Minister Meir and a group of Israeli writers. Cited in Benjamin Beit-Hallahmi, *Original Sins*, 74.
91 See Simona Sharoni "To be a man in the Jewish State, the sociopolitical context of violence and oppression," *Challenge*, 2: 5 (September/October 1991), 26–28.
92 See Susan Gubar " 'This is my rifle, this is my gun': World War II and the blitz on women," in Margaret Higonnet *et al.* (ed.), *Behind the Lines, Gender and the Two World Wars* (New Haven, CT: Yale University Press, 1987), 252.
93 See Angela Davis, *Women, Race and Class* (New York: Vintage, 1981), 172–201. Of course, other oppressive societies have used and continue to use the penis as a weapon; a prominent example of this is the Cossacks' rape of Jewish women in Czarist Russia.
94 See Arlene Eisen-Bergman, *Women of Vietnam* (San Francisco: People's Press, 1975), Part I, Chapter 4, 60–79.
95 See Cynthia Enloe, *Bananas, Beaches and Bases, Making Feminist Sense of International Politics* (Berkeley, CA: University of California Press, 1990).
96 For detailed descriptions of Israeli soldiers' (some of whom were Holocaust survivors) rape and murder of Palestinian women and children in 1948 especially at Al-Dawayimahh and Dayr Yasin among others, see Benny Morris, *The Birth*, 222–223, and David Hirst, *The Gun*, 124–129.
97 Herzl to Heinrich Kana, June 8, 1882, Herzl–Kana Correspondence, Central Zionist Archives, Jerusalem, cited in Desmond Stewart, *Theodor Herzl* (Garden City, NY: Doubleday & Company, 1974), 71–72. Also see Peter Lowenberg, "Theodor Herzl: a psychoanalytic study in charismatic political leadership," in Benjamin Wolman (ed.),

The Psychoanalytic Interpretation of History (New York: Basic Books, 1971), 152–153. I would like to thank Gadi Gofbarg for referring me to the Herzl story.

98 Lowenberg, "Theodor Herzl" 153.

99 See Nira Yuval-Davis, "National reproduction and 'the demographic race' in Israel," in Nira Yuval-Davis and Floya Anthias (eds), *Woman–Nation–State* (London: Macmillan, 1989), 92–109.

100 See David Hirst, *The Gun*, 242–243. For the reproductivist tendencies of Palestinian nationalism itself, see Joseph Massad, "Conceiving the masculine: gender and Palestinian nationalism," *Middle East Journal*, 49: 3 (Summer 1995), 467–483.

101 *London Sunday Times*, June 15, 1969.

102 Part of a funeral oration, delivered by Moshe Dayan, of a young Jewish settler killed by Palestinians as he was harvesting grain near the Egyptian border, cited by Uri Avneri in *Israel Without Zionists: A Plea for Peace in the Middle East* (New York: Macmillan, 1968), 134. Dayan's speech was broadcast on Israeli radio, *Kol Yisrael*, on the eve of the 1967 Arab/Israel War, which coincided with the anniversary of the settler's death and Dayan's own birthday.

103 *Ha'Aretz*, April 4, 1969, cited in David Hirst, *The Gun*, 221.

104 See Saul Cohen and Nurit Kliot's "Israel's place-names as reflection of continuity and change in nation building," in *Names, Journal of the American Name Society*, 29: 3 (September 1981). The Jewish National Fund was/is the Zionist organization that owns all Jewish-"acquired" lands in Palestine.

105 See Saul Cohen and Nurit Kliot's "Place-names in Israel's ideological struggle over the administered territories," in *Annals of the Association of American Geographers*, 82: 4 (1992).

106 David Hirst, *The Gun*, 240.

107 Sigmund Freud, *Leonardo da Vinci and a Memory of His Childhood*, *The Standard Edition*, Vol. XI, 83–84.

108 Jacques Lacan, "The mirror stage as formative of the function of the I as revealed in psychoanalytic experience," in *Écrits, A Selection* (New York: W. W. Norton, 1977), 2, emphasis in the original.

109 The Arabic words Sabrah, Sabbar, or Sabr derive from the same root as the word patience "Sabr." The Sabra cactus is a desert fruit characterized by its *patient* waiting for rain and water. It is a *patient* plant.

110 Georges Friedmann, *The End of the Jewish People?* (Garden City, NY: Doubleday & Company, 1967), 115.

111 The Sabra was the subject of Gadi Gofbarg's multimedia installation titled "Tough and tender," exhibited at the Alternative Museum of New York from September 29–November 7, 1992. Also see "Tough and tender: an interview with Gadi Gofbarg," in *Afterimage*, 20: 3 (October 1992).

112 Benjamin Beit-Hallahmi, *Original Sins*, 129.

113 I should note here that the standard Zionist response to these accusations is that these foods and dances are also shared by Arab Jews who immigrated to Israel and therefore are not appropriated from the Palestinians. This, however, flies in the face of the facts that there are very few Syrian, Palestinian, or Lebanese Jews in Israel (the majority of Syrian and Lebanese Jews immigrated to the United States and Latin America, especially Mexico, while there are very few Palestinian Arab Jews left anywhere). The vast majority of Arab Jews in Israel come from Morocco, Iraq, and Yemen, countries where Hummus and Falafil are not eaten and where Dabkah line-dancing is not practiced.

114 See Beit-Hallahmi, *Original Sins*, 123–124.

115 Ibid., 124. I should mention that Zionists also chose less violent names connected to nature such as names of trees and birds: Ilana, Tamar, Ella, Alona, Oren, although most of the "peaceful" names, with few exceptions, were women's first names.

116 Yigael Yadin, *Bar Kochba, The Rediscovery of the Legendary Hero of the Second Jewish Revolt Against Rome* (Jerusalem: Weinfeld and Nicholson, 1971), 15. On Yadin and his discoveries, see G. W. Bowersock, "Palestine: ancient history and modern politics," in Edward Said *et al.* (eds), *Blaming the Victims*, 181–191.
117 Yael Zerubavel, quoting Yisrael Eldad, *Recovered Roots*, 58.
118 See Keith Whitlam, *The Invention of Ancient Israel, The Silencing of Palestinian History* (New York: Routledge, 1996).
119 On the destroyed Palestinian villages, see Walid Khalidi (ed.), *All That Remains*.
120 Israel Shahak, "Arab villages destroyed in Israel," Report dated December 2, 1973, in Uri Davis and Norton Mezvinsky (eds), *Documents from Israel 1967–1973* (London: Ithaca Press, 1975), 43–44.
121 See Nur Masalha, *Expulsion of the Palestinians* (Washington, DC: Institute of Palestine Studies, 1992), and Benny Morris, *The Birth*.
122 Yael Zerubavel, *Recovered Roots*, 57. Also see the pioneering work of Nadia Abu El-Haj, *Excavating the Land, Creating the Homeland: Archaeology, the State and the Making of History in Modern Jewish Nationalism*, PhD Dissertation (Durham, NC: Duke University, 1995).
123 Zerubavel, *Recovered Roots*, 57–59.
124 See Sabri Jiryis, *The Arabs in Israel* (New York: Monthly Review Press, 1976).
125 Abraham Granott, *Agrarian Reform and the Record of Israel* (London: Eyre and Spottiswoode, 1956), 28.
126 See G. N. Giladi, *Discord in Zion*, also see Walter Lehn, *The Jewish National Fund* (London: Kegan Paul International, 1988).
127 David Harvey, *The Condition of Post-Modernity, An Inquiry into the Origins of Cultural Change* (Cambridge: Basil Blackwell, 1990).
128 Israeli emigrants are labeled "yordim," or descenders, while Jewish immigrants to Israel are called " 'olim," or ascenders.

2 Conceiving the masculine: gender and Palestinian nationalism

1 An earlier version of this paper was presented at the annual conference of the Middle East Studies Association held in Portland, OR, October 1992.
2 See Partha Chatterjee, *Nationalist Thought and the Colonial World, A Derivative Discourse* (London: Zed Press, 1986).
3 Nationalist agency refers to the abilities and the will to perform a set of acts and practices aimed at achieving nationalist goals as those (the abilities, the acts, the practices, and the goals) are defined by nationalist discourse. The nationalist agent is someone who identifies as, and is identified by nationalist discourse as, part of the nation, *and* one whom nationalist discourse considers to be a possessor of the aforementioned abilities and will based on criteria set by nationalist discourse.
4 Kumari Jayawardena, *Feminism and Nationalism in the Third World* (London: Zed Press, 1986), 15.
5 On traditionalization, see Abdullah Laroui, *The Crisis of the Arab Intellectual, Traditionalism or Historicism?* (Berkeley, CA: University of California Press, 1976).
6 African anti-colonial nationalism had to confront a different European colonial discourse from its Asian counterpart. While Orientalism constructed the idea of an Orient in need of Occidental civilization, colonial discourse constructed Africa in the European imagination as the "dark continent" in need of European colonial Enlightenment.
7 On the history of the PLO, see Alain Gresh, *The PLO: The Struggle Within, Towards an Independent Palestinian State* (London: Zed Press, 1985), and Helena Cobban, *The Palestinian Liberation Organization, People, Power and Politics* (New York: Cambridge University Press, 1984).

8 On Palestinians in Lebanon and on the Intra Bank débâcle, see Tabitha Petran, *The Struggle Over Lebanon* (New York: Monthly Review Press, 1987).
9 On Palestinians in the Gulf, see Laurie Brand, *The Palestinians in the Arab World: Institution Building and the Search for a State* (New York: Columbia University Press, 1988).
10 On the events in Jordan, see David Hirst, *The Gun and the Olive Branch, the Roots of Conflict in the Middle East* (London: Faber and Faber, 1984).
11 On the Palestinian bourgeoisie in the diaspora, see Pamela Ann Smith, *Palestine and the Palestinians, 1876–1983* (London: Croomhelm, 1984).
12 On representations of the Palestinians in the West, see Edward Said's classic, *The Question of Palestine* (New York: Vintage, 1979).
13 Andrew Parker, Mary Russo, Doris Sommer, and Patricia Yaeger (eds), *Nationalisms and Sexualities* (New York: Routledge, 1992), 5.
14 Palestine Liberation Organization, "al-Mithaq al-Qawmi al-Filastini." Reproduced in Faysal Hurani, *al-Fikr al-Siyasi al-Filastini, 1964–1974, Dirasat lil-Mawathiq al-Ra'isiyyah li-Munazzamat al-Tahrir al-Filastiniyyah* (Beirut: Markaz al-Abhath, Munazzamat al-Tahrir al-Filastiniyyah, 1980), 228.
15 Such views are common to most anti-colonial nationalisms. Frantz Fanon, for example, spoke of the "Western penetration of native space," while Aimé Césaire spoke of the "stripping" and "raping" of Africa. Palestinian nationalism articulates itself within the same masculinist discourses. See Frantz Fanon, *A Dying Colonialism* (New York: Grove Weidenfeld, 1965), 42, and Aimé Césaire, "Introduction," in Victor Schoelcher, *Esclavage et Colonisation* (Paris: Presses Universitaires de France, 1948), 7.
16 On the image of a feminine diaspora Jew, see Paul Breines, *Tough Jews, Political Fantasies and the Moral Dilemma of American Jewry* (New York: Basic Books, 1991), and Sander Gilman, *The Jew's Body* (New York: Routledge, 1991).
17 On the importance of the masculinization of diaspora Jewish men upon arrival in Palestine/Israel, see Joseph Massad, "The 'post-colonial' colony: time, space and bodies in Palestine/Israel," in Fawzia Afzal-Khan and Kalpana Seshadri-Crooks (eds), *The Pre-Occupation of Post-Colonial Studies* (Durham, NC: Duke University Press, 2000). On Zionism's gendered agency in/and relation to Palestine, see Ella Shohat, "Eurocentrism, exile and Zionist discourse," Paper presented at the Middle East Studies Association Annual Conference, Washington, DC, 1991, and Shohat's *Israeli Cinema, East/West and the Politics of Representations* (Austin, TX: University of Texas Press, 1989). Also see Simona Sharoni, "Militarized masculinity in context: cultural politics and social constructions of gender in Israel," Paper presented at the Middle East Studies Association Annual Conference, Portland, OR, 1992.
18 Edward Said, "Orientalism reconsidered," *Cultural Critique*, 1 (Fall 1985), 103.
19 Benedict Anderson, *Imagined Communities* (London: Verso, 1991).
20 George Mosse, *Nationalism and Sexuality, Respectability and Abnormal Sexuality in Modern Europe* (New York: Howard Fertig, 1985).
21 Mosse, *Nationalism*, 67.
22 Anderson, *Imagined*, 7.
23 Ibid., 5.
24 Palestine Liberation Organization, "al-Mithaq al-Watani al-Filastini," in Hurani, *al-Fikr*, 236.
25 Ibid., 236. 1947 is the year Palestine was partitioned by the UN—a decision that was made without consulting the Palestinian people. Immediately thereafter (as early as December 1947), Zionist forces began expelling the Palestinian population.
26 In the British case, as Francesca Klug demonstrates, "women were only allowed to reproduce the British nation on behalf of their husbands. They could not pass their nationality to their children in their own right." In fact, British women who married outside the nation lost their British nationality, as did their children. On the other hand, the children of British men and non-British wives would be automatically

British, as would the non-British wives. Some of these laws were changed in 1981 and 1985 whereby British women won the right to transfer their citizenship to their own children born abroad. Francesca Klug, " 'Oh to be in England': the British case study," in Nira Yuval-Davis and Floya Anthias (eds), *Woman-Nation-State* (London: Macmillan, 1989), 21. It is this British model which was transported to the colonies. It should be noted here that all children born inside the British Empire since 1971 are considered British regardless of parentage.

27 Yasser Arafat, "al-Harb Tandali' min Filastin, wa al-Silm Yabda' min Filastin," (Arafat's UN Address to the General Assembly), 8. The original Arabic text is in *Shu'un Filastiniyyah* (December, 1974) 5–19. It should be noted that the word for rape "Ightisab" is more often translated as usurpation. The etymological root of the word is "Ghasaba," meaning to force someone to do something against her/his will. Although "Ightisab" can be used in the context of usurpation as in "Ightisab al-huquq," meaning the usurpation of rights, it always retains its double meaning and its sexual symbolism.

28 Ibid., 12.

29 Palestine Liberation Organization, "Al-Bayan Al-Siyasi," the official Arabic text is published in *Shu'un Filastiniyyah*, 188, November, 1988, 8.

30 Arafat, *al-Harb*, 10.

31 Ibid., 11.

32 Palestine Liberation Organization, "I'lan al-Istiqlal," "The Declaration of Independence," the official Arabic version published in *Shu'un Filastiniyyah*, 188, November, 1988, 5.

33 Unified National Leadership of the Uprising, *al-Intifada min Khilal Bayanat al-Qiyadah al-Wataniyyah al-Muwahhadah* (Tunis: Majallat Al-Hurriyyah, 1989). I will limit myself mostly to examining the first thirty Communiqués which were issued in the first year of the intifada.

34 "Manabit," actually means plant nurseries, like a greenhouse, or a combination of several elements, soil, climate and environment—the proper conditions for plant growth.

35 Communiqué no. 10.

36 On the ideological role assigned to Israeli women in the reproduction of Israeli Sabras and its centrality in Zionist colonial discourse, see Nira Yuval-Davis, "National reproduction and 'the demographic race' in Israel," in Davis *et al.*, *Woman*, 92–109.

37 Communiqué nos 2 and 3, among others.

38 Communiqué nos 12, 14, 21, and 24.

39 Interestingly communiqué no. 5 lists occupational sectors such as students, workers, etc., and vulnerable sectors, children, older people with women being clearly listed among the vulnerable rather than the occupational sector: "Oh our merchants, workers, peasants, students, children, women, older people, relatives, all relatives, Oh all sectors of our heroic people. . . . " In the same communiqué, men, women, young and old people are called upon to resist the occupation. At the end of the same communiqué, women are listed with peasants, students, and workers.

40 Communiqué nos 12, 14, 21, and 24. In Communiqué 12, "men and children of the intifada" are the two categories of people listed as being detained by the Israeli Occupation authorities.

41 Communiqué no. 12.

42 Communiqué nos 8 and 12.

43 Communiqué no. 8.

44 Communiqué no. 10.

45 Communiqué no. 12.

46 Communiqué no. 29.

47 Communiqué no. 30.

48 Communiqué nos 17 and 22.

49 Communiqué no. 21.
50 Communiqué no. 6.
51 Communiqué no. 12.
52 Communiqué nos 9, 12, and 23.
53 On the dilemmas facing Palestinian women's efforts to develop a feminist agenda in the context of national struggle, see Rita Giacaman and Penny Johnson, "Palestinian women: building barricades and breaking barriers," in Zachary Lochman and Joel Beinin (eds), *Intifada, the Palestinian Uprising Against Israeli Occupation* (Boston, MA: South End Press, 1989), 155–169.
54 Islah Abdul-Jawwad, "The evolution of the political role of the Palestinian Women's Movement in the uprising," in Michael Hudson (ed.), *The Palestinians: New Directions* (Washington, DC: Center for Contemporary Arab Studies, 1990), 71.
55 Communiqué no. 35, Joost Hiltermann, *Behind the Intifada, Labor and Women's Movements in the Occupied Territories* (Princeton, NJ: Princeton University Press, 1991), 201.
56 Communiqué no. 53, March 6, 1990, cited by Hiltermann, 201. All references to the communiqués issued in 1989 and 1990 are from Joost Hiltermann, *Behind the Intifada*, 200–201.
57 See Communiqués 21, 23, and 28. Like its English counterpart, the verb "to enter" in Arabic can be used to designate the beginning of periods, such as a storm "has entered its second day," or a revolution "has entered its third year," etc. Its connection to pregnancy in this context, however, is made direct due to the use of the verb "to abort" in reference to the Israeli occupiers' constant attempts to terminate the intifada with military force.
58 Communiqué nos 15, 16, 18, 19, 28.
59 Communiqué no. 29.
60 Communiqué no. 28.
61 Chandra Talpade Mohanty, "Introduction, cartographies of struggle, Third World women and the politics of feminism," in Chandra Talpade Mohanty, Ann Russo, and Lourdes Torres (eds), *Third World Women and the Politics of Feminism* (Bloomington, IN: Indiana University Press, 1991), 1–49.
62 *The Palestinian National Charter*, in Hurani, *al-Fikr*, 236. The rest of the Charter is written in the "universal" language of the individual, see Articles 17 and 30. On the always already gendered "universal" and its use in contract theory, see Carole Pateman, *The Sexual Contract* (Stanford, CA: Stanford University Press, 1988).
63 Arafat, *al-Harb*, 16.
64 Judith Butler, *Gender Trouble, Feminism and the Subversion of Identity* (New York: Routledge, 1990).
65 On interpellation, see Louis Althusser, "Ideology and ideological state apparatuses," in *Lenin and Philosophy and Other Essays*; trans. By Ben Brewster (New York: Monthly Review Press, 1971).
66 Leila Khaled, *My People Shall Live: The Autobiography of a Revolutionary*, edited by George Hajjar, (London: Hodder and Stoughton, 1973), 59.
67 Communiqué no. 4.
68 Communiqué no. 5.
69 Communiqué no. 17.
70 Communiqué no. 24, emphasis added.
71 Communiqué no. 8.
72 Communiqué no. 10.
73 Communiqué no. 22.
74 Communiqué no. 28.
75 It is important to stress, however, that the discursive construction of Palestinian masculinity and its subordinate, femininity, permeates all types of Palestinian literary and

cultural production in the very same way European (and indeed global) nationalist construction of sexuality pervades not only European cultural production but also European policies toward Europe's own population, and by intersecting with the discourses on race and class, the peoples whom Europe colonized. For the experience of Palestinian women inside the Palestinian national movement, see the pioneering auto-critical study by Khadijeh Abu-'Ali, *Muqaddimah Hawl Waqi' al-Mar'a wa Tajribatiha Fi al-Thawrah al-Filastiniyyah* (Beirut: General Union of Palestinian Women, 1975). On the representation of Palestinian women in their traditional roles in poetry, see Ilham Abu-Ghazaleh, "the portrayal of women in intifada poetry," paper presented at the Alif Gallery, Washington, DC 1992. On the representation of women in Palestinian popular literature, see 'Abid 'Ubayd Al-Zuray'i, *Al-Mar'a fil-Adab al-Sha'bi al-Filastini* (Beirut: Manshurat al-Hadaf, 1986) (second and modified edition). On the portrayal of women in the Palestinian press, see 'Urayb Najjar, "al-Taghtiyah al-I'lamiyyah Lilnisa' fi Suhuf al-Diffah al-Gharbiyyah," in *Shu'un al-Mar'a*, No. 3, June 1992, 142–158.

76 On the recent PLO–Israeli agreement, see Joseph Massad, "Repentant terrorists or settler-colonialism revisited: the PLO–Israeli agreement in perspective," *Found Object*, 3, 1994, 81–90. See also Joseph Massad, "Palestinians and the limits of racialized discourse," *Social Text*, 34, 1993, 94–114.

77 Rema Hammami, "Women, the Hijab and the intifada," *Middle East Report*, 164–165, 1990, 24–28.

78 Ann McClintock, "No longer in a future heaven, women and nationalism in South Africa," *Transitions*, 51, 1991, 122.

79 For more information on women and the intifada, see Orayb Nayef Najjar, *Portraits of Palestinian Women* (Salt lake City, UT: University of Utah Press, 1992).

80 Interview with an UPWWC activist, Nablus, December 17, 1989, cited in Hiltermann, 200.

81 Interview with an UPWWC activist, Jerusalem, October 21, 1989, cited in Hiltermann, 203. In the context of the intifada, Rita Giacaman and Penny Johnson argue that Palestinian women "have enlarged or extended their traditional role rather than adopting a completely new role. Many of their forms of political participation are based on aspects of this role, particularly defense of family, nurturing and assisting family members, and mutual aid between kin. These aspects of women's role have become a source of resistance because women have transformed their family responsibilities to encompass the entire community." Giacaman, *et al.*, "Palestinian Women," 161.

82 Palestinian women have been able, however, to force the UNLU to take up some of their issues. After months of struggle, the UNLU agreed to issue Communiqué #45, in which it opposed Hamas's control over the daily lives of Gazan women. See Hammami, "Women."

83 Hanan Mikhail Ashrawi, "The feminist behind the spokeswoman—a candid talk with Hanan Ashrawi," Interview by Rabab Hadi, *Ms.*, March/April 14–17, 1992.

84 Ashrawi, 14.

85 Ibid.

86 Hanan Mikhail Ashrawi, "the politics of cultural revival," in Michael Hudson (ed.), *The Palestinians: New Directions* (Washington, DC: Center for Contemporary Arab Studies, 1990), 81.

87 Despite the above-cited skepticism, the assumption that Palestinian women will legally obtain their rights along with national independence continues to prevail among many a Palestinian woman. As Islah Jad has argued, however, "a study of the Palestinian national movement does little to justify that assumption." She adds that the "absence of social critique in the national movement, especially on the part of Fateh, which is its backbone, adds to the danger facing the women's movement." Islah Jad, "From salons to the popular committees, Palestinian women, 1919–1989,"

in Jamal Nassar and Roger Heacock (eds), *Intifada, Palestine at the Crossroads* (New York: Praeger, 1990), 138.

88 Ashrawi, "The Feminist," 16.

89 Ibid., 15.

90 Ibid.

91 On the lack of any major change in the way the nationalist movement views women, see Suhayr al-Tal's "al-Mas'alah al-Ijtima'iyyah, Intifadah fi al-Intifadah," *Sawt al-Watan* (Cyprus: January 1990), 15–18.

92 On Palestinian male guerrilla fighters' views of gender relations in relation to the national struggle, see Ghazi al-Khalili, *'Al-Mar'ah al-Filastiniyyah wa al-Thawrah* (Beirut: Markaz al-Abhath, Munazzamat al-Tahrir al-Filastiniyyah, 1977).

93 See for example the critiques leveled by Ashrawi herself against the PA's record on women in her recent autobiography, *This Side of Peace, A Personal Account* (New York: Simon and Schuster, 1995), 293–294. See also the papers presented at the Cairo Palestinian Population and Family Planning Conference, April 3, 1994, many (although not all) of which are pro-natalist and conceive of Palestinian women's bodies and their reproductive capacity as part and parcel of the national struggle. See especially Dhiyab 'Ayyush's paper, "Towards a national population policy in Palestine," which argues that the increase or decrease of the Palestinian population should be subject to the exigencies of the national struggle. Ayyush is the PNA's (Palestine National Authority) Deputy Minister of Social Welfare.

3 Zionism's internal others: Israel and the Mizrahim

1 *Am Yisrael*, or the people of Israel is how the Jewish God addressed the Jews and how Jews referred to themselves. *Medinat Yisrael* means the State of Israel, or the State of the Jewish People.

2 Ella Shohat, *Israeli Cinema, East/West and the Politics of Representation* (Austin, TX: University of Texas Press, 1989), 53–56.

3 On the rejection of the Sephardi Arabic pronunciation of Hebrew (with minor exceptions) and the imposition of a Europeanized Hebrew as the model for Israeli *Sabra* culture, see Shohat, *Israeli Cinema*, 54–56, and G. N. Giladi, *Discord in Zion, Conflict between Ashkenazi and Sephardi Jews in Israel* (London: Scorpion Publishing Ltd., 1990), 200–201, also see Sammy Smooha, *Israel, Pluralism and Conflict* (Berkeley, CA: University of California Press, 1978), 185, fn. 2.

4 On Ashkenazi racism and discrimination against Arab Jews and Mizrahi/Sephardi Jews in general, see Ella Shohat, "Sephardim in Israel: Zionism from the standpoint of its Jewish victims," *Social Text*, 19/20 (Fall 1988), 1–35, and Giladi, *Discord*.

5 Georges Friedmann, *The End of the Jewish People?* (New York: Doubleday, 1967), 243–245. On Jewish identity in Israel, see Akiva Orr, *The UnJewish State, The Politics Of Jewish Identity in Israel* (London: Ithaca Press, 1983).

6 Whereas Sephardi (literally Spanish) referred initially to Ladino-speaking Spanish Jews who were exiled from Spain in 1492, it also referred to the specific religious customs of Ladino-speaking as well as some Arabic- and Persian-speaking Jews—whose religious customs differed from Yiddish-speaking Jews and often among themselves. See Harvey Goldberg, "Introduction: culture and ethnicity in the study of Israeli society," *Ethnic Groups*, Vol. 1 (February 1977), 164–165.

7 Although the term Mizrahim came into wide usage only in the 1980s, for the sake of convenience, I will be using it in the text throughout the studied period. Other terms that have historically been used are "Sephardim" or "Jews from Asian and African countries." All such terms are ultimately problematic and ideologically charged, including, of course, the term Mizrahim, except that the latter is the one currently adopted by the Mizrahim themselves as well as the Ashkenazi state.

8 On Zionism's European character, see Raphael Shapiro, "Zionism and its Oriental subjects, the Oriental Jews in Zionism's dialectical contradictions," *Khamsin*, 5, (1978), also see the pioneering book of Michael Selzer, *The Aryanization of the Jewish State* (New York: Blackstar Publishing, 1967). On the European and anti-Mizrahi Ashkenazi Zionist cultural and artistic production, see Shohat, *Israeli Cinema*.

9 Theodor Herzl, *The Jewish State, An Attempt at a Modern Solution to the Jewish Question* (London: H. Porders, 1972), 30.

10 Ibid., 22. On the question of Oriental Jews and Herzl, see Sami Chetrit, "New state, old land, the East and the Easterners in *The Jewish State* of Theodor Herzl" (New York: Columbia University, 1992), unpublished paper. Algerian Jews at the time formed two communities, the Arab Jewish community, and the European French Jews who had immigrated from France along with French Christians as colonial settlers. In 1870, prior to Herzl's writings, all Algerian Jews were granted French citizenship by the French colonial government as part of its policy of *divide et impera*, thus rendering Algerian Jews Europeans as far as Herzl was concerned. See Alistair Horne, *A Savage War of Peace, Algeria 1954–1962* (Hammondworth: Penguin, 1977), 58–59. It must be noted that throughout the period of French colonization, many Algerian Arab Jews were in the forefront of the Algerian struggle for independence. Prominent among them was Yehuda Ben-Drane, a Jew from Oran, who is an Algerian national hero and who was an advisor to the emir Abdel-Kader in the anti-colonial resistance of the 1830s, see Ilan Halevi, *A History of the Jews, Ancient and Modern* (London: Zed Press, 1988), 218. A century later, the French colonial authorities had succeeded in integrating many Algerian Jews into French culture. It was within this context that the FLN (Front pour la Liberation Nationale) leadership asked patriotic Algerian Jews ready to join the anti-colonial struggle to be "the eyes and the ears of the Revolution within the colonialist camp," cited by Frantz Fanon, *A Dying Colonialism* (New York: Monthly Review Press, 1965). Ilan Halevi correctly observes that the FLN requested that Algerian Jews be the eyes and ears "not the arms and the legs" of the revolution, Halevi, *A History*, 218, also see Richard Ayoun, "Les Juifs d'Algérie," in *Le Second Israël*, A special issue of *Les Temps Modernes* (Paris, May 1979), 146–161.

11 Quoted in Meir Yosef, *Beyond the Desert* (Israel: Ministry of Defense Press, 1973), in Hebrew, 48, cited by Chetrit, "New State," 19.

12 Quoted by Meir Yosef, 48, cited in ibid.

13 Yehuda Nini, *Aliyot Yehude Teman le-Eretz Yisrael* (The immigration of the Jews of Yemen to the land of Israel), PhD Dissertation, University of Tel Aviv (1976), and "Ole Teman 1882–1914" (Immigrants from Yemen 1882–1914), cited in *Cathedra* (October 1977).

14 Ahad Ha'Am, *Kol Kitve Ahad Ha'Am* (All the writings of Ahad Ha'Am) (Tel Aviv: Dvir Publication House, 1947), 426 (Hebrew) cited by Giladi, *Discord*, 47.

15 See Shohat, "Sephardim in Israel: Zionism from the standpoint of its Jewish victims," *Social Text*, 19/20 (Fall 1988), 1–35.

16 Vladimir Jabotinsky, "The East," cited by Giladi, *Discord*, 209.

17 Vladimir (Ze'ev) Jabotinsky, "Jews of the East," (1919) quoted in *Ha'Aretz*, July 22, 1983.

18 Vladimir Jabotinsky, *The Hebrew Accent* (Tel Aviv: HaSefer, 1930), 4–9, cited by Shohat, *Israeli Cinema*, 55.

19 During the Mandate, Ashkenazi Zionists enlisted the help of the British in undermining the power of the native Palestinian Jewish leadership. Viewing native Jewish leaders as part of the Ottoman Empire, the British authorities assisted the Ashkenazi Zionists by refusing to include Palestinian Jews in the government which included Ashkenazi colonial settlers. More importantly, the Mandatory authorities weakened the position of the Palestinian chief rabbi by appointing an Ashkenazi chief rabbi as well as a rabbinical committee made up of equal numbers of Ashkenazi and

Palestinian Jews. See Giladi's discussion of Palestinian Jewish resistance to Ashkenazi settlement, *Discord*, Chapters 2 and 3.

20 Ibid., 58.

21 D. Horowitz, and M. Lissak, *The Origins of Israeli Society* (Tel Aviv: Am Oved, 1977), 155 (Hebrew) cited in Deborah Bernstein, "Political participation, new immigrants and veteran parties in Israeli society," *Plural Societies*, Vol. 15(1) (February 1984), 15.

22 It must be noted that from 1948 to 1950, Soviet and East European Jews were allowed to emigrate to Israel under the cover of "reuniting families" which was part of the pro-Israeli Soviet policy of the time. However, only a small number (especially from Eastern Europe, less from the USSR) did. Emigration doors were closed in the USSR in 1950 (but not from Eastern Europe, evidenced by the immigration in the early to mid-fifties of Romanian and Polish Jews) as a result of deteriorating Soviet/Israeli relations (Halevi, *History*, 196–197). Here it must be added that Romanian Jews who were not Zionist came from rural Romania and did not speak Yiddish. This resulted in their being maltreated by the Ashkenazi establishment, albeit not as badly as the Oriental Jews. However, on account of their European origins, they were quickly integrated as part of the Ashkenazi community (Raphael Shapiro, "Zionism," 25, fn. 30).

23 *Statistical Abstract of Israel 1978*, Israel Central Bureau of Statistics, Jerusalem 1979, 137, cited in Shlomo Swirski, "The Oriental Jews in Israel," *Dissent*, 30 (Winter 1984), 79. It should be noted that official Israeli figures assume that all the European immigrants were Ashkenazi, thus conveniently eliding European Sephardim who also immigrated to Palestine with their Ashkenazi co-religionists. European Sephardi communities existed (and in most cases still exist) in Soviet Asia, Bulgaria, Greece, Yugoslavia, Holland, England, Italy, and France.

24 On the integration of Mizrahi immigrants in Israel, see Avraham Shama and Mark Iris, *Immigration Without Integration, Third World Jews in Israel* (Cambridge, MA: Schenkman Publishing Company, 1977).

25 Tom Segev, *1949: The First Israelis* (New York: The Free Press, 1986), 169.

26 *Eli Peleg's Report*, July 24, 1949, Central Zionist Archives, S20/562, cited in ibid., 171.

27 Ben-Gurion's meeting with writers, (October 11, 1949), Divrei Sofrim, State Archives, cited in ibid., 156.

28 Ben-Gurion, *Netsah Yeisrael*, 14, cited in Segev, *1949*, 157.

29 Ben-Gurion, *Nestah Yeisrael*, 34, cited in ibid.

30 David Ben-Gurion, *Netsah Yeisrael, The Israeli Government Year Book*, 17, Hebrew, cited in Sami Chetrit, "New State." Also see Segev, *1949*, 157.

31 Ben-Gurion, *Nestah Yeisrael*, 23, cited by Segev, *1949*, 157.

32 *Zionist Executive*, June 5, 1949, cited in ibid., 156.

33 *Sharett Report*, December 12, 1948, State Archives, Foreign Ministry, 130.11/2502/8, cited in ibid., 173.

34 See Giladi, *Discord*, 103. Also see Segev, *1949*, 119. Segev's account of the DDT affair includes its use against Ashkenazi immigrants who arrived from detention camps.

35 Segev, *1949*, 191–193.

36 Dov Levitan, "The Aliyah of the 'magic carpet' as a historical continuation of the earlier Yemeni Aliyahs," MA Thesis in Political Science, Bar Ilan University (Israel 1983), in Hebrew, cited by Shohat, "Sephardim," 17. Also see Segev, *The First*, 193.

37 See Shohat, "Sephardim," 17–18.

38 Cited in Smooha, *Israel*, 86–88.

39 *Ha'Aretz*, April 22, 1949.

40 *Central Zionist Archives*, S 41/2471—Yosephtal to Locker, June 9, 1949, cited in Giladi, *Discord*, 104.

41 On the conditions of the Ma'abarot, see Giladi, *Discord*, 115–129.

42 *Ha'Aretz*, April 26, 1949.

43 Ibid., May 9, 1949.
44 Knesset Minutes, July 26, 1949, cited in Giladi.
45 See Giladi, *Discord*, 129–136. Giladi refers to the towns as "cheap labour camps." Also, see Shohat, "Sephardim," 18–19, Deborah Bernstein and Shlomo Swirski, "Rapid economic development of Israel and the emergence of the ethnic division of labour," *British Journal of Sociology*, Vol. XXXIII, 1, (March 1982), and Shlomo Swirski, "The development towns of Israel," *Israel, The Oriental Majority* (London: Zed Press, 1990), Chapter 3, 31–43.
46 Giladi, *Discord*, 129.
47 Swirski, *Israel*, 33.
48 Ibid., 34. Swirski provides a comparative table for the years 1960 and 1982 to illustrate his point.
49 Ibid., 34–43.
50 See Giladi's discussion of the Moshavim in *Discord*, 142–148.
51 Moreover, an Ashkenazi Moshav member owned on average 2.3 cows, 300 chickens and 2.5 tractors, whereas a member of a post-1948 Moshav owned 1.5 cows, 50 chickens and 0.7 tractors.
52 Giladi, *Discord*, 149.
53 *Ha'Aretz*, September 18, 1981. It must be noted that these demographics changed in the late eighties and early nineties with the arrival of Soviet immigrants.
54 Asher Arian, *Ideological Change in Israel* (Cleveland, OH: Case Western Reserve University, 1968), 173.
55 Bernstein, "Political," 19. Bernstein researched the Absorption Department files of Mapai which contained many letters sent by the Department to party functionaries directing them to give special aid in housing or work to specific individuals because of their party connections.
56 Files of Absorption Department, 1951; 1956, Mapai Archive, cited by Bernstein, "Political," 19.
57 G. Yosephtal, *His Life and Works* (Tel Aviv: Mapai Publication, 1963), 148, Hebrew, cited in ibid.
58 D. Rosen, *Municipal Survey: Municipalities and Local Authorities* (Jerusalem: Ministry of Interior, 1973), 519, Hebrew.
59 Although the Arabic name of the neighborhood, after which the uprising is named, is "Wadi *al*-Salib," it has been adapted to "Wadi Salib," dropping the "al," in modern Hebrew usage, and is used thus in reference to the uprising.
60 On the expulsion of Palestinians, see Benny Morris, *The Birth of the Palestinian Refugee Problem, 1947–1949* (Cambridge: Cambridge University Press, 1987), also on the specific expulsion of Palestinians from Haifa see the debate between Norman Finkelstein and Nur Masalha on one side, "Myths, old and new," and Benny Morris on the other, "Response to Finkelstein and Masalha," in the *Journal of Palestine Studies*, Vol. XXI, 81 (Autumn 1991), 68–89 and 98–114 respectively, see also Finkelstein's "Rejoinder to Benny Morris," in ibid., Vol. XXI, 82 (Winter 1992), 61–71. See also Nur Masalha, *Expulsion of the* Palestinians (Washington, DC: Institute of Palestine Studies 1992).
61 Bernstein, "Political," 28. The following account of events is based on Bernstein, ibid., 28–31, and Giladi, *Discord*, 253–254. Also on the North African community in Israel, see Dima Abdul-Rahim, "Yahud al-Maghrib al-Arabi fi Isra'il," *Shu'un Filastiniyya*, No. 120, November 1981, 62–73.
62 Giladi, *Discord*, 254.
63 Bernstein, "Political," 30.
64 *Davar*, July 12, 1959.
65 *Report of the Wadi Salib Inquiry Committee*, Jerusalem, 1959.
66 Report, 16, 17, and 19, respectively.
67 Giladi, *Discord*, 254.

68 Bernstein, "Political," 31.
69 Ibid.
70 Giladi, *Discord*, 254.
71 S.N. Eisenstadt, *The Absorption of Immigrants* (Glencoe, IL: Free Press of Glencoe, 1955), this was the translation of the 1949 Hebrew original. On Eisenstadt and other Israeli academic representations of the Mizrahim, see Shohat, "Sephardim."
72 Examples of analyses incorporating the intersection of class and ethnicity are found in, among others, Pierre Trigano, "Sépharades, Prolétariat, Sionisme," in *Le Second Israël*, 268–302, also see Shmuel Trigano "Economie Générale du Rôle Sépharade," in *Le Second Israël*, 349–366, Emmanuel Farjoun, "Class divisions in Israeli society," *Khamsin*, 10, 1983. See also the important work of Uri Davis, *Israel: Utopia Incorporated* (London: Zed Press, 1977), Chapter 2, 33–44. For an example of a radical leftist critique of Israeli society employing class analysis but ignoring the Mizrahim and the ethnic factor altogether, see Arie Bober (ed.), *The Other Israel, The Radical Case Against Zionism* (New York: Anchor Books, 1972). An example of a Zionist Sephardi analysis claiming that the Sephardim have also brought Western culture to Israel, see Daniel Elazar, "Israel's Sephardim: the myth of the two cultures," *The American Sephardi*, Vol. 11(2) (June 1967), and Elazar's *The Other Jews, The Sephardim Today* (New York: Basic Books, 1989).
73 Carl Frankenstein, *The Rehabilitation of Impaired Intelligence* (Jerusalem: The School of Education at the Hebrew University, 1970), and *They Think Again* (Jerusalem: The School of Education of the Hebrew University, 1972).
74 Swirski, *Israel*, 27.
75 Bernstein, Deborah, "Conflict and protest in Israeli society, the case of the Black Panthers of Israel," *Youth and Society*, Vol. 16(2) (December 1984), 132. For an account of ethnic relations in Israel until the late sixties which dismisses the potential for ethnic conflict (the article was written a few months before the rise of the Black Panthers), see Yochanan Peres, "Ethnic relations in Israel," *American Journal of Sociology*, Vol. 76(6) (1971).
76 On Israeli bombings of Jewish institutions in Iraq, see "The Iraqi Jews and their coming to Israel," *The Black Panther* (November 9, 1972), reproduced in English in Uri Davis and Norton Mezvinsky (eds), *Documents from Israel, 1967–73, Readings for a Critique of Zionism* (London: Ithaca Press, 1975), 126–133, Gideon N. Giladi, *Discord*, 67–102, Abbas Shiblak, *The Lure of Zion, The Case of the Iraqi Jews* (London: Al Saqi Books, 1986), Marion Woolfson, *Prophets in Babylon, Jews in the Arab World* (London: Faber & Faber, 1980), 155–163, and David Hirst, *The Gun and the Olive Branch* (London: Faber & Faber, 1984), 155–164. Also see Joseph Massad, "The partial truth about Saddam's Rule," reviewing Samir al-Khalil's *Republic of Rear* in *Against The Current*, 31, March–April 1991, and the debate it generated over the question of Iraqi Jewry between Israel Shahak in his "The fate of Iraq's Jews," and Joseph Massad in "A response to Israel Shahak," in *Against The Current*, 33, July–August 1991, 38–40.
77 "'Olim" means literally, "ascenders," with the implication that immigrating to Palestine was an ascent (aliya) toward Heaven. By the same logic, emigrating from Israel is called "Yeridah" or descent with the implication that those leaving Israel are descending toward Hell. Emigrants are called "yordim" or descenders.
78 Giladi, *Discord*, 255. For similar quotes, see Woolfson, *Prophets*, 267–268.
79 Bernstein, "Conflict," 132. For a detailed list of all the benefits received by Russian immigrants, see Giladi, *Discord*, 255, see also Erik Cohen, "The Black Panthers and Israeli society," *Jewish Journal of Sociology*, 14 (1972), 99.
80 *Ha'Aretz*, March 22, 1971. The Russian petition published in *Ha'Aretz* is partly reproduced in Woolfson, *Prophets*, 268.
81 *ISRACA* No. 17 and 18, and Woolfson, *Prophets*, 268. On Russian Jewish racism, see Charlie Biton, "The ugly Russian," *The Black Panther*, November 11, 1972, reproduced in English in Davis *et al.* (eds), *Documents*.

82 On the history and development of the Black Panthers, see Bernstein, "Conflict," Giladi, *Discord*, 254–268, Shalom Cohen and Kokhavi Shemesh, "The origin and development of the Israeli Black Panther movement," *MERIP*, 49 (July 1976), 19–22, Shlomo Malka, "Les Panthères Noires, Historique d'une Revolte," in *Le Second Israël*, 315–326, "Entre La Revolte et L'Autisme (Entretien avec les Panthères Noires d'Israël)," in *Le Second Israël*, 327–342, Erik Cohen, "The Black," 93–109, Moshe Ater, "The Black Panthers and the economy," *The Jerusalem Post*, May 27, 1971, Sammy Smooha, "Israel and its Third World Jews, Black Panthers: the ethnic dilemma," *Society* (May 1972), Vol. 9(7) 31–36, Mark Iris and Avraham Shama, "Black Panthers: the movement," *Society* (May 1972), Vol. 9(7) 37–39, Micah Bar-Am and Sammy Smooha, "Black Panthers of Israel," *Society* (May 1972), Vol. 9(7) 40–44.

83 Giladi, *Discord*, 256.

84 A common Ashkenazi racist epithet against Mizrahim is "Shwartze Chayis" or "Black animal," see Shohat, "Sephardim," 6.

85 Bernstein, "Conflict," 134, Giladi, *Discord*, 259.

86 Bernstein, "Conflict," 136, also see Shalom Cohen *et al.*, "The Origin," 19. Cohen gives the numbers of the demonstrators to be between ten and fifteen thousand.

87 Erik Cohen, "The Black," 100.

88 Ibid.

89 *Ma'ariv*, June 8, 1971.

90 Giladi, *Discord*, 260.

91 Quoted in Erik Cohen, "The Black," 101. The Hebrew word "yeladim" translated by Erik Cohen as "boys" also means "children" or "kids."

92 Bernstein, "Conflict," 140. On the general political views of the Black Panthers, also see Giladi, *Discord*, 261–266, and Erik Cohen, "The Black." See also "Entre La Revolte et L'Autisme," in *Le Second Israël*, 327–342, and Sammy Smooha, "Israel and its Third World Jews."

93 Whereas the Israeli Left (both Zionist and anti-Zionist) and Right (especially Herut) tried to coopt the Panthers, the Panthers accepted some of their help without being coopted into their organizations, see Bernstein, "Conflict," Giladi, *Discord*, and Erik Cohen "The Black," on these connections.

94 Bernstein, "Conflict," 146.

95 Examples of participation by Ashkenazi academics in such delegitimation includes Gerald Cromer, "The Israeli Black Panthers: fighting for credibility and a cause," *Victimology*, Vol. 1(3) (Fall 1976). Cromer presents the Black Panthers as juvenile delinquents who are too psychologically impaired to blame themselves for their personal failures and as such shift the blame onto the innocent Israeli state. See also Gideon Kressel, "Arabism (Urubah): a 'concealed' cultural factor in the ethnic 'gap' in Israel," *Israeli Social Science Research*, Vol. 2(1) (1984). Kressel argues that it is Arab culture which the Mizrahim have that can explain the "cultural gap" in Israel asserting that there is academic dishonesty by Israeli scholars who, for ideological reasons, fear identifying Mizrahim with Arabs. More recent studies on the ethnic situation in Israel by Israeli scholars include Eliezer Ben-Raphael (ed.), *The Emergence of Ethnicity, Cultural Groups and Social Conflict in Israel* (Westport, CT: Greenwood Press, 1982), and Alex Weingrod (ed.), *Studies in Israeli Ethnicity, After the Ingathering* (New York: Gordon and Breach Science Publishers, 1985), see also the important summary of the different theoretical approaches that are used to explain the Mizrahi situation in Israel provided by Sammy Smooha, "Three approaches to the sociology of ethnic relations in Israel," in *The Jerusalem Quarterly*, 40 (1986).

96 Bernstein, "Conflict," 146.

97 Raphael Shapiro, *Khamsin*, 5(24) and *Israleft*, November 20, 1972.

98 Bernstein, "Conflict," 147.

99 Ibid., 149.

100 Bernstein, "Conflict," and Giladi, *Discord*, 267.
101 Israeli newspapers reporting the incidents stated that while the government had issued demolition orders against Ashkenazi illegal buildings in the Dizengoff Center and the Plaza Hotel, the demolitions were never carried out. See Giladi, *Discord*, 290. It should be noted, however, that most Ashkenazim are economically prosperous and do not need to resort to illegal construction, which the Mizrahim, thanks to the systematic and institutionalized discrimination they face, sometimes need to. I'd like to thank Ella Shohat for this point.
102 "Ashkenazi," in Hebrew means literally "German."
103 *International Herald Tribune*, December 31, 1982 and *Zu Haderekh*, December 29, 1982.
104 *Ha'Aretz*, December 28, 1984.
105 For an analysis of Mizrahi voting behavior, see Emmanuel Farjoun, "Class divisions in Israeli society," *Khamsin*, No. 10 (1983), Avishai Ehlrich, "The Oriental support for Begin—a critique of Farjoun," *Khamsin*, No. 10 (1983), A. Hoder, "Oriental Jews in Israel—Collective schizophrenia," *Khamsin*, No. 10, (1983), Israel Shahak, "The Oriental Jews in Israeli politics," *Middle East International* (June 15, 1984), Giora Goldberg and Efraim Ben Zadok, "Voting patterns of Oriental Jews in development towns," *The Jerusalem Quarterly*, 32 (Summer 1984), Maurice Roumani, "The Sephardi factor in Israeli politics," *Middle East Journal*, Vol. 42(3) (Summer 1989), Shlomo Swirski, "The Oriental Jews in Israel, why many tilted toward Begin," *Dissent*, 30 (Winter 1984), Sammy Smooha, "Internal divisions in Israel at forty," *Middle East Review*, Vol. XX (4) (Summer 1988). For conservative Ashkenazi-centric analyses of the Mizrahi vote, see Yael Yishai, "Hawkish Proletariat: the case of Israel," *Journal of Political And Military Sociology*, Vol. 13(1) (Spring 1985), Ken Shachter, "The ethnic factor," *Jerusalem Post* (June 17, 1988), 6, and Ofira Seliktar, "Ethnic stratification and foreign policy in Israel: the attitudes of Oriental Jews towards the Arabs and the Arab–Israeli conflict," *Middle East Journal*, Vol. 28(1) (Winter 1984), 34–50.
106 On the lack of pluralism in Israel, see Muhammad Arafah, "al-Ta'addudiyyah fil Mujtama'al-Isra'ili," *Al-Mustaqbal al-Arabi*, No. 82, December 1985, 48–73.
107 *Ha'Aretz*, October 13, 1978.
108 Shalom Cohen, "L'Exil Dans le Retour," in *Le Second Israël*, 197.
109 On "Ma'avak '85," see "Dissent, Ma'avak '85 (Struggle '85)," *New Outlook* (February–March 1985), on "East for peace," see "The Oriental Jewish peace movements—a ray of hope," *The Other Israel*, Newsletter of the Israeli Council for Israeli–Palestinian Peace, 26 (June 1987), 7–9, on "Ohalim," see Shlomo Hassan, "The emergence of an urban social movement in Israeli society—an integrated approach," *International Journal of Urban and Regional Research*, Vol. 7(2) (1983), 157–174, also on "Ohalim" and "Oded," see Giladi, *Discord*, 282–295.
110 "Israeli cops trade fire with Rabbi's followers," *Chicago Tribune*, May 11, 1994.
111 See Giladi, *Discord*, 293–294.
112 *Ha'Aretz* reported on August 23, 1985, that slum activists had declared that "those who harm the Palestinians, harm the Sephardim..." cited by Giladi, *Discord*, 313. On Mizrahi relations with Palestinians, also see Maurice Roumani, "The Sephardi factor in Israeli politics," *Middle East Journal*, Vol. 43(3) (Summer 1988), 432–434.
113 For more information about these meetings, see Giladi, *Discord*, 316–326. I would also like to thank Ella Shohat, one of the Sephardi delegates in Toledo, for sharing her observations with me.
114 See their interview in *Filastin al-Thawra* on 11 October, 1986.
115 See *The Israel Equality Monitor*, 1 (September 1991) for more information. On HILA and Kedma, I would like to thank Sami Chitrit for the information he provided me.
116 Personal communication with Sami Chitrit.

117 On the Mizrahi feminist movement and its organization, see Ella Shohat, "Mizrahi feminism: the politics of gender, race, and multiculturalism," forthcoming in *News From Within*, May 1996. *News From Within* is published by the Alternative Information Center in Jerusalem and Bethlehem.
118 See *Middle East International*, June 9, 1995.
119 See ibid., March 29, 1996.
120 Ella Shohat argues that the US analogy is also appropriate to Israel wherein Palestinians are similar to Native Americans and the Mizrahim to African Americans (the former being native and the latter imported). See Shohat's "Staging the Quincentenary: the Middle East and the Americas," in *Third Text*, 21 (Winter 1992–1993) 102.

4 Palestinians and the limits of racialized discourse

1 *Washington Post*, September 23, 1982, cited in Amnon Kapeliouk, *Sabra and Chatila: An Inquiry into a Massacre*, trans. and ed. by Khalil Jahshan (Belmont, MA: Association of Arab–American University Graduates, 1984), 69.
2 The first commentary was published in the *New York Times* on June 5, 1990, while the second was published in the *New York Times* on July 31, 1990.
3 Ibid., May 22, 1990.
4 Ibid., May 31, 1990.
5 Wall Street Journal, May 24, 1990, A15.
6 *Ha'Aretz*, July 10, 1990, translated in *Israel Mirror*, No. 800 (July 28, 1990). I would like to thank Noam Chomsky for bringing this source to my attention.
7 The differences and similarities between Lewis and Israel's apologists are not all too different from the similarities and differences that Abdul R. JanMohamed describes as existing between the "New Humanists" and "Liberal Humanists" in his article "Humanism and minority literature: toward a definition of counter-hegemonic discourse," *Boundary 2* 12, No. 3; 13, No. 1 (Fall 1984), 288.
8 In fact, a number of Jews decided to return to their homes in Eastern Europe after the war instead of emigrating to Palestine. However, they were met with blatant anti-Semitism and in some cases, like in Kielce, Poland, outright pogroms which only the intervention of the Red Army halted. As for the unfulfilled British commitments, this is in reference to the camps in which European Jews were detained in Cyprus by the British while heading to Palestine.
9 See Edward Said, The *Question of Palestine* (New York: Random House, 1979), especially his second chapter. "Zionism from the Standpoint of its Victims," 56–114.
10 Other "justifications," whose nature cannot be discussed in this paper due to reasons of space, predominate.
11 The European (Western) Jewish identity of Israel is Israel's only recognized identity in this racialized discourse, to the exclusion of Israeli Palestinian Arabs. The majority Sephardi/Mizrahi Israeli Jews are recognized insofar as their identity has been assimilated into Israel's Western culture and insofar as their "former" Eastern cultures are viewed through the lens of Ashkenazi anthropological scholarship.
12 Aimé Césaire, *Discourse on Colonialism* (New York: Monthly Review Press, 1972), 54. Césaire is quoting Gobineau.
13 In this discourse, "anti-Semitic" means exclusively "anti-Jewish" to the exclusion of other "Semitic" peoples, in this case, Arabs.
14 On cultural factors see, for examples, Regina Sharif, *Non-Jewish Zionism: Its Roots in Western History* (London: Zed Press, 1983): on the effect of the Israeli lobby, see Paul Findely, *They Dare to Speak Out: People and Institutions Confront Israel's Lobby* (Westport, CT: Laurence Hill, 1985): and Edward Tivnan, *The Lobby: Jewish Political Power and American Foreign Policy* (New York: Touchstone Books. 1988).

15 Such views were voiced by a number of Palestinian intellectuals at a conference on Palestinian academic freedom under Israeli occupation held in Washington DC in June 1990. Some of those present, although advocating a similar formula as a tactic, did not see it as a panacea to the problems Palestinians face in the West.

16 It must be noted that a number of these intellectuals, including Hanan Mikhail Ashrawi, Zakaria al-Agha, Ghassan al-Khatib, Zahira Kamal, Sari Nusaybah, and Haydar 'Abd Al-Shafi, were to become part of the official Palestinian delegation and its advisory and guidance committees approved by Israel and the US to participate in the "peace" conference in Madrid and later in Washington.

17 Elia Zureik, Fouad Moughrabi, Manuel Hassassian, and Aziz Haidar, "Palestinians and the peace process," *Journal of Palestine Studies* 21 (1) (Autumn 1991), 36–53. A list of the interviewees appears on page 53.

18 Ibid., 43.

19 Ibid., emphasis added.

20 Edward Said, *Orientalism* (New York: Vintage Books, 1979), 286.

21 See Roberta Strauss Feuerlicht's *The Fate of the Jews: A People Torn Between Israeli Power and Jewish Ethics* (New York: Times Books, 1983), 219–288. Feuerlicht states that "[s]ome Americans [Jews] equate their contributions to Israel with premiums on an insurance policy. By paying a certain amount each year, they guarantee themselves a home if they are ever forced to flee America," ibid., 241.

22 Said, Orientalism, 286.

23 Theodor Herzl, *Altneuland*, 3rd ed. (Haifa: Haifa Publishing Company, Ltd., 1964).

24 Ibid., 31.

25 Ibid., 32.

26 Ibid., 33.

27 Ibid., 94–95, 100–101.

28 Colonial Office [CO] 733/297/75156/II/Appendix A, extract from Weizmann's speech, April 23, 1936, Great Britain, Peel Commission Report, 96–97, cited in Philip Mattar. *The Mufti of Jerusalem: Al-Hajj Amin-al-Husayni and the Palestinian National Movement* (New York: Columbia University Press, 1988), 73.

29 Feuerlicht, *The Fate of the Jews, 283.*

30 See Noam Chomsky, *The Fateful Triangle: Israel, the United States, and the Palestinians* (Boston, MA: South End Press, 1983), 110.

31 Jacobo Timerman in an interview with the Israeli newspaper *Ha'Olam HaZe*, December 22, 1982, cited in Chomsky: *The Fateful Triangle*, 110.

32 Yoav Gelber, "Zionist policy and the fate of European Jewry, 1939–42," *Yad vashem Studies* (West Jerusalem) 12 (1974), 199, cited in Lenni Brenner, *Jews in America Today* (Secaucus, NJ: Lyle Stuart Inc., 1986), 167; see also Brenner's *Zionism in the Age of the Dictators: A Reappraisal* (Westport, CT: Laurence Hill & Company, 1983), in which Brenner discusses the general Zionist response to the rescue of Jews, 228–251.

33 Ibid., 252–264.

34 On Israeli collaboration with the Iraqi and Yemeni governments, see Gideon N. Giladi, *Discord in Zion: Conflict Between Ashkenazi and Sephardi Jews in Israel* (London: Scorpion Publishing, 1990), 67–102; Abbas Shiblak, *The Lure of Zion: The Case of the Iraqi Jews* (London: Al Saqi Books, 1986); Marion Woolfson, *Prophets in Babylon: Jews in the Arab World* (London: Faber & Faber, 1980), 155–163; and David Hirst, *The Gun and the Olive Branch* (London: Faber & Faber, 1984), 155–164.

35 This and other references to the rejection of Yiddish cinema and theater is taken from Ella Shohat's pioneering work, *Israeli Cinema: East West and the Politics of Representation* (Austin, TX: University of Texas Press, 1989), 53–56.

36 On the rejection of the Sephardic Arabic pronunciation of Hebrew (with minor exceptions) and the imposition of a Europeanized Hebrew as the model for Israeli Sabra culture, see Shohat, *Israeli Cinema*, 54–56, and Giladi, *Discord in Zion*, 200–201.

37 On Ashkenazi racism and discrimination against Arab Jews and Mizrhi/Sephardi Jews in general, see Ella Shohat, "Sephardim in Israel: Zionism from the standpoint of its Jewish victims," *Social Text* 19/20 (Fall 1988), 1–35, and Giladi, *Discord in Zion*.

38 On the place occupied by Mizrhi Jews in Zionist ideology, see Sami Chetrit, "New state, old land, the East and the Easterners in *The Jewish State* of Theodor Herzl," 1992, unpublished paper.

39 Abraham Granott, *Agrarian Reform and the Record of Israel* (London: Eyre and Spottiswoode, 1956), 28. Granott was the head of the Jewish National Fund.

40 Uri Davis, *Israel: An Apartheid State* (London: Zed Press, 1987), 28–30.

41 Yaacov Shimshon Shapira, who was to become a minister of justice in Israel, had remarked in 1946 after the British had imposed the same Emergency Regulations to combat Zionist terrorism that "[e]ven in Nazi Germany there were no such laws." *Hapraklit*, February 1946, 58–64, cited in Sabri Jiryis, *The Arabs in Israel* (New York: Monthly Review Press, 1976), 12.

42 Constitution of the *Histadrut*, 13, cited by Israel Davis, 51, emphasis added.

43 Edward Said, "Orientalism reconsidered," *Cultural Critique*, No. 1 (Fall 1985), 99.

44 Edward Said had complained about the avoidance of Middle Eastern sources by US commentators who are sympathetic to the Palestinians in an interview in *MERIP: Middle East Report*, No. 150 (January–February 1988), 35.

45 I would like to thank Sami S. Chetrit for explaining the differences between these terms and the words and concepts from which they derive.

46 Following its use in racist US discourse, the term "American" implies white Americans unless the term is otherwise specified.

47 See Partha Chatterjee, *Nationalist Thought and the Colonial World: A Derivative Discourse* (London: Zed Books, 1986).

48 Homi Bhabha, "Of mimicry and man: the ambivalence of colonial discourse," *October* 28 (Spring 1984), 133.

49 *In Re Ahmed Hassan*, 48 Federal Supplement (No. 162148), District Court, E.D. Michigan, S.D., December 15, 1942, 844.

50 Ibid., 845.

51 Ibid., 846.

52 *Ex. parte Mohriez*, 54 Federal Supplement, No. 1500, District Court, D. Massachusetts, April 13, 1944, 942, emphasis added.

53 I would like to thank Beth Kaimowitz for providing me with information about these legal cases.

54 *Morrison et al. v. People of State of California*, 54 Supreme Court, No. 487, argued December 12, 1933, decided January 8, 1934, 283.

55 On traditionalization versus traditionalism, see Abdullah Laroui, *The Crisis of the Arab Intellectual:* Traditionalism or Historicism? (Berkeley, CA: University of California Press, 1976), 33–43.

56 JanMohamed, "Humanism and minority literature," 289.

57 Ibid., 290.

58 Amilcar Cabral, "The weapon of theory: presuppositions and objectives of national liberation in relation to social structure," in *Unity and Struggle: Speeches and Writings, Texts Selected by the PAIGC*, trans. by Michael Wolfers (New York: Monthly Review Press, 1979), 124.

59 Tzvetan Todorov, *The Conquest of America: The Question of the Other* (New York: Harper Torchbooks, 1984), 116.

60 On the problematic nature of rending the subaltern the subjects of their own histories, see Robert Young's discussion of the works of Said, Bhabha, and Gayatri Chakravorty Spivak in *White Mythologies: Writing History and the West* (New York: Routledge, 1990), 157–175.

61 Gayatri Chakravorty Spivak, "Subaltern studies: deconstructing historiography," in Gayatri Chakravorty Spivak (ed.), *In Other Worlds: Essays in Cultural Politics* (New York: Methuen, 1987), 198; see also Bell Hooks, *Yearnings: Race, Gender, and Cultural Politics* (Boston, MA: South End Press, 1990), especially the essay entitled "Choosing the margin as a space of radical openness," 145–153.
62 Gayatri Chakravorty Spivak, "Can the subaltern speak?," in Lawrence Grossberg and Cary Nelson (eds), *Marxism and the Interpretation of Culture* (Urbana, IL: University of Illinois Press, 1988), 271–313.
63 See Robert Young's presentation of Spivak's position in *White Mythologies*. See also Bill Ashcroft, Gareth Griffiths, and Helen Tiffin, *The Empire Writes Back: Theory and Practice in Post-Colonial Literatures* (New York: Routledge, 1989). See also Henry Louis Gates Jr (ed), *"Race," Writing, and* Difference (Chicago, IL: University of Chicago Press, 1985).
64 Michel Foucault, *The History of Sexuality*, *Vol. 1*: *An Introduction*, trans. by Robert Hurley (New York: Vintage Books, 1980), 101, emphasis added.

5 Repentant terrorists or settler-colonialism revisited: the PLO–Israeli agreement in perspective

1 For the texts of the letters of recognition between Israel and the PLO, see the *New York Times*, September 10, 1993, A12.
2 Edward Said, "The morning after," *London Review of Books*, October 21, 1993, 3.
3 See the *New York Times*, September 22, 1993, A16.
4 Quoted by Israel Shahak, "The Oslo Accords: interpreting Israel's intentions," *Middle East International*, October 22, 1993, 17. Shahak's article includes a thorough description of the future functions of the Palestinian police as described by Israeli political analysts that are close to the government.
5 Clyde Haberman, *New York Times*, October 31, 1993, E6.
6 Quoted in the *New York Times*, September 10, 1993, A12.
7 *New York Times*, October 27, 1993, A3, Rabin asserted that if the PLO "expect[s] tens of thousands [of returnees,] they live in a dream, an illusion."
8 *Ha'Aretz*, September 5, 1993, cited by Shahak, 18.
9 *The Nation*, September 27, 1993, 303.
10 See "Courting the Israelis, with barriers down, Arab lands compete to conclude deals with an ancient enemy," *New York Times*, November 10, 1993, A1.
11 Ibid., October 29, 1993, A10.
12 Ibid., December 13, 1993, A7.
13 Ibid., November 8, 1993, A3.
14 Ibid., November 9, 1993, D2.
15 Rabin's speech at the signing of the Declaration of Principles, *New York Times*, September 14, 1993, A12.
16 Edward Said, "The Morning After," *London Review of Books*, October 21, 1993, 3.
17 Quoted in Lisa Anderson, *The State and Social Transformation in Tunisia and Libya, 1830–1980* (Princeton, NJ: Princeton University Press, 1986), 116.
18 Ibid., 117.
19 On the World Bank plans for the West Bank and Gaza, see the *New York Times*, September 12, 1993, 11.
20 Ibid., September 7, 1993, A13.
21 On Israeli relations with and characterizations of the Third World, see Benjamin Beit-Hallahmi, *The Israeli Connection, Who Israel Arms and Why* (New York: Pantheon, 1987).
22 This has been proposed as early as the first years of the intifada prompting some Palestinians to write about the costs of "success" in Taiwan and Singapore, see *Taywan, Singhafurah... Thaman al-Najah!! Mulahazat Naqdiyyah Hawl*

Namudhajay Taywan wa Singhafurah wa Imkaniyyat Tatbiqiha Mahalliyyan, by Majdi al-Malki, Development Studies Committee, Bisan Center for Research and Development, Ramallah, West Bank, October 1990.

23 On the plans of the Israeli bourgeoisie for the Palestinian economy, see Asher Davidi, "Israel's economic strategy for Palestinian independence," *Middle East Report*, September–October 1993, 24–26.

24 See Edward Said, *Nation*, September 20, 1993, 269.

25 See Mouin Rabbani, " 'Gaza-Jericho first!': the Palestinian Debate," in *Middle East International*, September 24, 1993, 16–17.

26 *Middle East International*, October 22, 1993, 6.

27 On the recent complaints against Arafat's undemocratic methods by his own group, *Fath*, see the *New York Times*, December 5, 1993, 19.

28 This analogy is borrowed from Max Horkheimer and Theodor Adorno's *Dialectic of Enlightenment* (New York: Continuum, 1991), 149.

29 See Arafat's letter of recognition, *New York Times*, September 10, 1993, A12.

6 Political realists or comprador intelligentsia: Palestinian intellectuals and the national struggle

1 A shorter version of this chapter was originally presented at the "After Orientalism: a conference on the work of Edward Said," at Columbia University, New York, October 1996. An earlier Arabic version of this paper was published as "Sasah Waqi'iyyun Am Muthaqaffun Kumbraduriyyun: Al- Muthaqaffun Al-Filastiniyyun wa Al-Nidal Al-Watani," in *Kan'an*, No. 85, April 1997.

2 Taha Husayn, *Mustaqbal al-Thaqafah Fi Misr* (Cairo: al-Hay'ah al-Misriyyah al'Ammah Lil-Kitab, 1993), 44.

3 Political Statement of the 20th Palestine National Council, Algiers, September 28, 1991, reproduced in the *Journal of Palestine Studies*, Vol. XXI(2) (Winter 1992), 151, emphasis added.

4 On the Oslo agreement, see Joseph Massad, "Repentant terrorists, or settler-colonialism revisited: the PLO–Israeli agreement in perspective," *Found Object*, No. 3 (Spring 1994) 81–90. I should note here that many reports have confirmed that Yasser Arafat signed the DoP without even reading it. Connie Bruck of *The New Yorker*, in a revealing article, quotes an Israeli participant in the negotiations saying that "Arafat had not read the agreement . . . He'd read the headings—and his people gave him a rosier picture." Connie Bruck, "The wounds of peace," *The New Yorker*, October 14, 1996, 74.

5 On the position of different Palestinian groups in relation to the DoP, see Mouin Rabbani, " 'Gaza-Jericho first': the Palestinian debate," *Middle East International*, September 24, 1993, 16–17.

6 Muhammad 'Abid al-Jabiri, *Al-Khitab al-'Arabi al-Mu'asir, Dirasah Tahiliyyah Naqdiyyah*, (Beirut: Dar al-Tali'ah, 1982).

7 Nusaybah's proposal is cited in Emile Sahliyeh, *In Search of Leadership, West Bank Politics since 1967* (Washington, DC: The Brookings Institution, 1988), 173. For gender and Palestinian nationalism, see Joseph Massad "Conceiving the masculine: gender and Palestinian nationalism," *Middle East Journal*, Vol. 49(3) (Summer 1995), 467–483.

8 On the developments leading to the Oslo Agreement, see Naseer Aruri, *The Obstruction of Peace, The U.S., Israel, and the Palestinians* (Monroe, ME: Common Courage Press, 1995).

9 The only exception for someone like Samuel P. Huntington, was if such countries were "Islamic," in which case they are barred culturally from ever reaching the democratic telos. Huntington has been arguing this point long before his recently celebrated "clash of civilizations" theory. See e.g. his "Will more countries become democratic?," *Political Science Quarterly* 99, No. 2 (Summer 1984), 193–218.

10 Elia Zureik, Fouad Moughrabi, Manuel Hassassian and Aziz Haidar, "Palestinians and the peace process," *Journal of Palestine Studies*, 81, Vol. XXI, No. 1 (Autumn 1991), 36–53. A list of the interviewees appears on page 53.

11 Examples include Hanan Mikhail Ashrawi, Zakaria al-Agha, Ghassan al-Khatib, Zahira Kamal, Sari Nusaybah, and Haydar 'Abd Al-Shafi.

12 Zureik *et al.*, "Palestinians," 43.

13 Ibid.

14 Ibid., emphasis added.

15 Ibid., 43.

16 Khalil Shikaki, "The peace process, national reconstruction, and the transition to democracy in Palestine," *Journal of Palestine Studies*, Vol. XXV, No. 2 (Winter 1996), 11.

17 Ahmad S. Khalidi, "The Palestinians' first excursion into democracy," *Journal of Palestine Studies*, Vol. XXV, No. 4 (Summer 1996), 21.

18 Ibid.

19 Ibid., 20.

20 Ibid., 21.

21 Hasan Asfur, "Ru'yah Li-Itifaq I'lan al-Mabadi'," *Majallat al-Dirasat al-Filastiniyyah*, Beirut, No. 16 (Fall 1993), 21.

22 *New York Times*, September 7, 1993, A13. On Israeli relations with and characterizations of the Third World, see Benjamin Beit-Hallahmi, *The Israeli Connection, Who Israel Arms and Why* (New York: Pantheon, 1987).

23 This has been proposed as early as the first years of the intifada prompting some Palestinians to write about the costs of "success" in Taiwan and Singapore, see *Taywan, Singhafurah... Thaman al-Najah!! Mulahazat Naqdiyyah Hawl Namudhajay Taywan wa Singhafurah wa Imkaniyyat Tatbiqiha Mahalliyyan*, by Majdi al-Malki, Development Studies Committee, Bisan Center for Research and Development, Ramallah, West Bank, October 1990. Edward Said, among others, has characterized such "talk of a 'new Singapore' or that [a bantustanized Palestine] would become a banking center in the area or a tourist center [as] illusions that interest those who repeat them without any foundation," Interview with Edward Said by Abdullah al-Sinnawi, *Al-Arabi*, Cairo, January 30, 1995, translated by Joseph Massad and reproduced in *Peace and Its Discontents, Essays on Palestine in the Middle East Peace Process* (New York: Vintage Books, 1996), 177.

24 On the views of Palestinians supportive of and opposed to the agreement, see "Hiwarat Filastiniyyah Fil Kharij wal Dakhil: Mawqif al-Mu'aradah wa Sighat Madrid," *Majallat al-Dirasat al-Filastiniyyah*, No. 15 (Summer 1993), 108–164. Those who oppose Oslo include Khalid al-Fahum (former president of the PNC), Nayif Hawatmeh (DFLP), Abu 'Ali Mustafa (PFLP), Fadil Shruro (PFLP-GC), Mahir al-Sharif (Sawt al-Watan magazine). Those in support of Oslo include 'Azmi al-Shu'aybi, Nabil Qasis, and Salim Tamari; all three are part of the official team of Arafat-sponsored negotiations with the Israelis. For the views of Palestinian intellectuals in Syria, see Majid Kayyali, "Muthaqafun Filstiniyyun fi Surya Yunaqishun al-Azma al-Filastiniyyah al-Rahinah: Asbabuha, Ishkalatuha, al-Tasa'ulat allati Tatrahuha," *Majallat al-Dirasat al-Filastiniyyah*, No. 25 (Winter 1996), 123–154. On Islamist criticisms of the "peace process," see, e.g. the early book of Hasan Khalil Hasan, *Hiwar Ma 'Hamas Hawl al-Mu'tamar al-Dawli* (Amman: Dustur Publishers, 1992). See also Munir Shafiq, *Ittifaq Uslu wa Tada'iyatahu* (London: Manshurat Filastin al-Muslimah, 1994).

25 Saeb Erakat, "Facing the critics on the long road to self-rule: an interview with Saeb Erakat," *Journal of Palestine Studies*, Vol. XXIV, No. 2 (Winter 1995), 74. Complaining about criticism of Arafat's cronyism in making PNA appointments, Erakat incredulously states: "I wonder why these people should say such things," 75.

26 The Arafat interview was published in the Egyptian magazine *Al-Musawwar*, cited in Said, *Peace and Its Discontents*, 165.

27 An Interview with Salim Tamari, *Middle East Report*, No. 186, January–February 1994, 18. In December 1995, in a talk at Columbia University's Middle East Institute, Tamari continued to apologize for the Arafatist authority, albeit with some criticisms of its inflated bureaucracy (but not its inflated security apparatus) and to attack its critics, with special attention to Edward Said and the author.

28 Yezid Sayigh, one of those pragmatists who negotiated the Oslo agreement with Israel, claims that with the DoP "the prospect of eventual Palestinian statehood became probable, if not virtually inevitable." See Yezid Sayigh, "Redefining the basics: sovereignty and security of the Palestinian State," *Journal of Palestine Studies*, Vol. XXIV, No. 4 (Summer 1995), 5.

29 Salim Tamari, "Fading flags, the crises of Palestinian legitimacy," *Middle East Report*, May–June/July–August 1995, Nos. 194–195.

30 Ibid., 12, emphasis added.

31 Ahmad S. Khalidi, "The Palestinians: current dilemmas, future challenges," *Journal of Palestine Studies*, Vol. XXIV, No. 2 (Winter 1995), 9.

32 Ibid., 13.

33 Hanan Ashrawi, *This Side of Peace, A Personal Account* (New York: Simon & Schuster, 1995), 262.

34 Ibid.

35 Said, *Peace and Its Discontents*, 39.

36 On the racial status of the Palestinians in the West, see Joseph Massad "Palestinians and the limits of racialized discourse," *Social Text*, No. 34 (Spring 1993), 94–114.

37 "Symbols versus substance: a year after the declaration of principles, an interview with Edward Said," *Journal of Palestine Studies*, Vol. XXIV, No. 2 (Winter 1995), 64.

38 Said, *Peace and Its Discontents*,160. On the commercialization of the Palestinian cause by Wetsern do-gooders, see Salim Tamari, "Tourists with Agendas," *Middle East Report*, September–October 1995, No. 196, 24. Tamari cites the danger mediocre Western researchers pose to scholarship on Palestine as well as on low-paid Palestinian scholars in the West Bank and Gaza. Fearing the pressure of their competion, and their successful cooptation, through money, of many Palestinian talents, Tamari states: "Palestinian scholars, like their Arab and Western counterparts, are often ready to sell themselves and their work for the right price," quote in ibid.

39 One of the few principled people who participated in the Madrid peace conference but refused to become part of the Oslo charade is Haydar 'Abd Al-Shafi. On his views, see "Moving beyond Oslo, an interview with Haydar 'Abd Al-Shafi," *Journal of Palestine Studies*, Vol. XXV(1) (Autumn 1995), 76–85, and "Reflections on the peace process, an interview with Haydar 'Abd Al-Shafi," *Journal of Palestine Studies*, Vol. XXII(1) (Autumn 1992), 57–69. Also see "The Oslo Agreement, an interview with Haydar 'Abd Al-Shafi," *Journal of Palestine Studies*, Vol. XXIII(1) (Autumn 1993), 14–19, it is interesting to note that in this interview, 'Abd Al-Shafi refuses to waiver in his opposition to the Oslo Agreement despite the insistent "pragmatist" arguments of one of his interviewers.

40 Ashrawi, *This Side of Peace*, 281.

41 Ibid., 262, 274.

42 Ibid., 297.

43 Ibid., 274.

44 Ibid., 281.

45 Ibid., 279–280.

46 An Interview with Hanan Ashrawi, *Middle East Report*, No. 186, January–February 1994, 21.

47 Haim Watzman, "The Israeli–Palestinian peace process fails to aid universities in the West Bank," *The Chronicle of Higher Education*, September 20, 1996, A50. On the banning, of Said's books, see Serge Schmemann, "Palestinian security agents ban books by a critic of Arafat," *New York Times*, August 25, 1996. On the condemnation of the book banning, see Faysal Darraj, "Idward Sa'id wa Ashbah Mahakim al-Taftish"

(Edward Said and the pseudo-inquisition courts), and Ibrahim Nasrallah, "al-Namudhaj al-Asfa Lil Muthaqqaf Fi Nihayat al-Qarn" (the purer model for the intellectual at the fin de siècle), in *Al-Hayat*, October 7, 1996, 11.

48 Letter to the editor by Edward Said, "Columbia Professor's books banned by the PLO," *The Chronicle of Higher Education*, October 25, 1996, B9.

49 Said, *Peace and its Discontents*, xxxiv. Edward Said also suggets that "Ignorance and laziness are certainly part of the answer. Because Palestinian leaders were concerned mainly about themselves, and because so many Arab and Palestinian intellectuals (especially those who speak loftily of pragmatism, the New World Order, and 'the peace process') have capitulated morally and intellectually, we find ourselves in the middle of peace negotiations that never raise the obvious and fundamental questions." *Peace and Its Discontents*, 130.

50 Edward Said, *Representations of the Intellectual* (New York: Vintage, 1996), 119.

51 Ibid.,121.

7 Return or permanent exile? Palestinian refugees and the ends of Oslo

1 Palestinian Declaration of Independence, November 15, 1988, Algiers, reproduced in the *Journal of Palestine Studies*, No. 70 (Winter 1989), 215.

2 United Nations General Assembly Resolution 194 (III), December 11, 1948, Article 11. Reproduced in George J. Tomeh (ed.), *United Nations Resolutions on Palestine and the Arab-Israeli Conflict, Volume One 1947–1974* (Washington, DC: Institute for Palestine Studies, 1975), 16.

3 See Rashid Khalidi, "Observations on the right of return," *Journal of Palestine Studies*, No. 82 (Winter 1992), 35.

4 Ibid., 36.

5 See "Interview with Faysal Husayni," in the *Journal of Palestine Studies*, No. 72 (Summer 1989), 11–12. Sha'th's and Husayni's views are cited in Khalidi, "Observations," 36.

6 Statement made by Arafat at a press conference on December 14, 1988, Geneva, reproduced in the *Journal of Palestine Studies*, No. 71 (Spring 1989), 181.

7 Salim Tamari, *Palestinian Refugee Negotiations, From Madrid to Oslo II*, A Final Status Issues Paper (Washington DC: Institute for Palestine Studies, 1996), 7, 9–13.

8 *Israeli–PlO Declaration of Principles*, December 13, 1993 (Article I), reproduced in the *Journal of Palestine Studies*, No. 89 (Autumn 1993), 115.

9 United Nations Security Council 242, 1967, Article 2B, reproduced in Tomeh, *United Nations*, 143.

10 *Israeli–PlO Declaration of Principles*, December 13, 1993 (Article V–3), reproduced in the *Journal of Palestine Studies*, No. 89 (Autumn 1993), 117.

11 See Elia Zureik, *Palestinian Refugees and the Peace Process* (Washington DC: Institute for Palestine Studies, 1996), 18–19.

12 Ibid., 23.

13 Ibid., 19.

14 Donna E. Arzt, *Refugees into Citizens, Palestinians and the End of the Arab-Israeli Conflict* (New York: Council on Foreign Relations, 1997).

15 Joseph Alpher and Khalil Shikaki, The Palestinian Refugee Problem and the Right of Return, Working Paper Series, Paper No. 98–7, Weatherhead Center for International Affairs, Harvard University, May 1998. Of the Palestinian group, only Kassis did not partake of the final drafting of the report (see x). Israeli and US Jewish participants included Joseph Alpher, Gabriel Ben-Dor, Yossi Katz, Moshe Ma'oz, Ze'ev Schiff, Shimon Shamir, and Herbert Kelman.

16 On Lydda and Ramla and other expulsions, see Benny Morris, *The Birth of the Palestinian Refugee Problem, 1947–1949* (Cambridge: Cambridge University Press,

1988), on the Galilee expulsions, see also Benny Morris, "Operation Hiram revisited: a correction," in the *Journal of Palestine Studies*, No. 110 (Winter 1999), 68–76.
17 Arzt, *Refugees into Citizens*, 99.
18 Ibid., 98.
19 Ibid., 91.
20 Joseph Alpher and Khalil Shikaki, *The Palestinian Refugee Problem*, 17.
21 Ibid.
22 Ibid., 18.
23 Ibid.
24 Ibid., 18–19.
25 *New York Times*, October 27, 1993, A3.
26 Joseph Alpher and Khalil Shikaki, *The Palestinian Refugee Problem*, 20.
27 Ibid.
28 Ibid.
29 Ibid., 21.
30 Ibid., 23.
31 Ibid., 26.
32 See Zureik, *Palestinian*..., 73. For Gazit's propoal, see Shlomo Gazit, *The Palestinian Refugee Problem* (Tel Aviv: Jaffee Center for Strategic Studies, 1994).
33 Gazit, *The Palestinian*, 12.
34 Ibid., 14.
35 See, e.g., Ziad Abu Zayyad, "The Palestinian right of return: a realistic approach," in *Palestine–Israel Journal of Politics, Economics and Culture*, No. 2 (Sping 1994), 74–78. Abu Zayyad is a member of the Palestinian Legislative Council.
36 Salim Tamari, *Palestinian Refugee Negotiation, From Madrid to Oslo II* (Washington DC: Institute for Palestine Studies, 1996), 2.
37 Ibid., 3.
38 Tamari is clear that "The debate over compensation versus return is a false dichotomy that is often raised in the negotiations. It is clear from a 1961 UNCCP Report that two modes of compensation were being considered: one for returning refugees and one for nonreturning refugees." See ibid., 44.
39 Ibid., 45.
40 Ibid., 51. UNSC Resolution 237 to which Tamari refers "calls upon the Government of Israel...to facilitate the return of those inhabitants who have fled the areas since the outbreak of hostilities," Article 1 of Security Council Resolution No. 237 of June 14, 1967, reproduced in Tomeh, *United Nations*, 142.
41 Ibid.
42 Ibid., 53.
43 See Mark Heller and Sari Nusaybah, *No Trumpets, No Drums, A Two-State Settlement of the Isareli–Palestinian Conflict* (New York: Hill and Wang, 1991), 95.
44 Rashid Khalidi, "Toward a solution," in *Palestinian Refugees: Their Problem and Future*, A Special Report (Washington, DC: Center for Policy Analysis on Palestine, October 1994), 21.
45 Ibid.
46 Ibid., 22.
47 Ibid.
48 See George Borjas, Leonard Hausman, and Dani Rodrik, "The Harvard project on Palestinian refugees," paper presented to the United Nations Department of Political Affairs, International NGO Meeting, European NGO Symposium on the Question of Palestine, Palais des Nations, Geneva, Switzerland on September 2, 1996, 7.
49 Rashid Khalidi, "Toward a solution," 23.
50 Ibid.
51 Ibid., 24.

52 See Atif Kubursi, *Palestinian Losses in 1948: The Quest for Precision*, Information Paper No. 6, (Washington, DC: Center for Policy Analysis on Palestine, August 1996), 5. See also Sami Hadawi and Atif Kubursi, *Palestinian Rights and Losses in 1948, A Comprehensive Study* (London: Saqi Books, 1988).
53 Cited by Zureik, *Palestinians*, 122.
54 Rashid Khalidi, "Toward a solution," 24–25.
55 Salman H. Abu Sitta, "The feasibility of the right of return," ICJ and CIMEL paper (June 1997), 1. The paper is available on the internet at: www.arts.mcgill.ca/mepp/prrn/papers.
56 Ibid.
57 Ibid., 2.
58 Ibid.
59 Ibid., 4.
60 Ibid., 5.
61 Ibid., 6.
62 Ibid.
63 Ibid., 9.
64 Cited in "Tahdhir Filastini min al-Mubadarat al-Fardiyyah Lil-Bahth fi Qadiyyat al-Laji'in ma' al-Isra'iliyyin" (A Palestinian warning against individual initiatives to look into the refugee issue with the Israelis), in *Al-Hayat*, March 3, 1999, 5.
65 Zureik, *Palestinians*, 119.
66 Ze'ev Schiff, *Ha'Aretz*, February 22, 1996, cited by Zurek, *Palestinians*, 117–118.
67 On Zionism's policies towards the rescue of European Jews from the Nazis, see Lenni Brenner, *Zionism in the Age of the Dictators* (Westport, CT: Lawrence Hill, 1983).
68 Sara Roy, "Dedevelopment revisited: Palestinian society and economy since Oslo," *Journal of Palestine Studies*, No. 111 (Spring 1999).
69 For information about the refugee conferences, see "The voice of Palestinian refugees in Palestine," in *Article 74*, Issue 15, April 1996, "First refugee conference—Bethlehem," in *Article 74*, Issue 17, Spetember 1996.
70 See "Recommendations and decisions issued by the First Popular Refugee conference in Deheishe refugee camp/Bethlehem," in *Article 74*, Issue 17, September 1996.
71 See Salah Abed Rabbo, "A unified strategy against all odds: the popular refugee movement," in *Article 74*, Issue 22, December 1997.
72 See Ahmad Ashkar, "Internal refugees: their inalienable right to return," *News From Within*, Vol. XI(8), August 1995, 14–17.
73 Ibid., 17. On internal refugees in Israel, see also Ahmad Ashkar, "1948 Palestinian refugees: 'We'll return to the village alive or dead'," *News From Within*, Vol. XI(9), September 1995, 21–24.
74 Hamid Shaqqura makes the important suggestion that West Bank and Gaza refugees are related to the Palestinian authority not as "citizens" but as refugees from another country. Therefore the PA cannot speak for them or simply treat them as "citizens." See Hamid Shaqqura, "Refugees and the Palestinian Authority," *News From Within*, Vol. XI(8), August 1995, 18–20.

8 Palestinians and Jewish history: recognition or submission?

1 Quoted in Tom Segev, *The Seventh Million, The Israelis and the Holocaust*, trans. by Haim Watzman (New York: Hill and Wang, 1993), 98.
2 Quoted in ibid., 330–331.
3 Central Zionist Archives, S25/293, October 15, 1942, cited by Dina Porat, "Ben-Gurion and the Holocaust," in Ronald W. Zweig (ed), *David Ben-Gurion: Politics and Leadership in Israel* (London: Frank Cass, 1991), 151.
4 Segev, *The Seventh Million*, 369.

5 See, for example, Walid Khalidi, *Before Their Diaspora, A Photographic History of the Palestinians 1876–1948* (Washington, DC: Institute for Palestine Studies, 1984), 305–306.
6 Theodor Herzl, *Old New Land*, trans. by Lotta Levensohn (Princeton, NJ: Markus Wiener Publishers, 1997), 122.
7 Ibid., 124.
8 Ibid., 123.
9 Tom Segev, *The Seventh Million*, 177.
10 *HaOlam Hazeh*, June 22, 1950, cited by Tom Segev, *1949: The First Israelis* (New York: Free Press, 1986), 63.
11 Hannah Torok-Yablonka, "The recruitment of Holocaust survivors during the War of Independence," *Studies in Zionism*, Vol. 13(1), 1992, 53. I would like to thank Walid Khalidi for directing me to this article.
12 Memo from Recruiting Officer Tuviah Kuznitsky to Zadok, May 12, 1948, Israel Defence Forces Archives, 1042/49/21, cited in ibid, 50.
13 Ibid.
14 Reuters report, January 13, 2000. The Tantura massacre was recently uncovered by an Israeli researcher at Haifa University, Teddy Katz, based on information he found in Israeli army archives.
15 Segev, *The Seventh Million*, 156.
16 On al-Sumayriyya, see Walid Khalidi, *All That Remains, The Palestinian Villages Occupied and Depopulated by Israel in 1948* (Washington, DC: Institute for Palestine Studies, 1992), 30–31.
17 Segev, *The Seventh Million*, 451.
18 Ibid., 161–162.
19 Isaac Deutscher, "Israel's spiritual climate," in Tamara Deutscher (ed.), *The Non-Jewish Jew and Other Essays* (New York: Hill and Wang, 1968), 116.
20 On Deutscher's Zionism, see Joseph Massad "The 'post-colonial' colony: time, space, and bodies in Palestine/Israel," in Fawzia Afzal-Khan and Kalpana Seshadri-Crooks (eds), *The Pre-Occupation of Post-Colonial Studies* (Durham, NC: Duke University Press, 2000).
21 See Philip Mattar, *The Mufti of Jerusalem, Al-Hajj Amin Al-Husayni and the Palestinian National Movement* (New York: Columbia University Press, 1988), 105–107.
22 Peter Novick, *The Holocaust in American Life* (New York: Houghton Mifflin, 1999) 158.
23 Israel Gutman (ed.), *Encyclopedia of the Holocaust* (New York: Macmillan Publishing, 1990), Vol. 2, 706.
24 Segev, *The Seventh Million*, 425.
25 Cited by Joel Beinin, *The Dispersion of Egyptian Jewry, Culture, Politics and the Formation of a Modern Diaspora* (Berkeley, CA: University of California Press, 1998), 107
26 Ibid., 91.
27 See Tom Segev, *The Seventh Million*, 297.
28 *New York Times*, November 29, 1967, cited by Beinin, 107.
29 Segev, *The Seventh Million*, 297.
30 American Histadrut Cultural Exchange Institute, *The Impact of Israel on American Jewry: 20 Years Later* (New York, 1969), 12, cited by Novick, *The Holocaust in American Life*, 150.
31 "Between Hitler and Nasir," *Ha'Aretz*, June 5, 1967, cited by Segev, *The Seventh Million*, 391.
32 *Ma'ariv*, March 24, 1972, cited in David Hirst, *The Gun and the Olive Branch: The Roots of Violence in the Middle East* (London: Faber and Faber, 1984), 210–211.
33 Elie Wiesel, "Ominous signs and unspeakable thoughts," *New York Times*, December 28, 1974.

34 Segev, *The Seventh Million*, 400.
35 William E. Farrell, "Israel affirms conditions on West Bank talks," *New York Times*, August 20, 1981, A15. Cited by Novick, 161.
36 Cited in Benny Morris, *The Birth of the Palestinian Refugee Problem, 1947–1949* (New York: Cambridge University Press, 1987), 232–233.
37 Rabbi Benyamin, "Kfar Kasim at the Gates of the Knesset," *Ner*, November–December 1956, 19, cited by Segev, 300.
38 Communiqué no. 12, Unified National Leadership of the Uprising, *al-Intifada min Khilal Bayanat al-Qiyadah al-Wataniyyah al-Muwahhadah* (The intifada through the Communiqués of the Unified National Leadership) (Tunis: Majallat Al-Hurriyyah, 1989).
39 Segev, *The Seventh Million*, 401.
40 Yasser Arafat, speech to the United Nations General Assembly in New York on November 13, 1974, reproduced in Jorgen S. Nielsen (ed.), *International Documents on Palestine 1974* (Beirut: Institute for Palestine Studies, 1977), 134–144, 140.
41 Ibid.
42 Ibid., 140.
43 Ibid., 143.
44 Ibid., 144.
45 "PLO plans to honor Jews who fought Nazis in Warsaw," UPI dispatch, *New York Times*, April 13, 1983.
46 Ibid. See also "Plan of PLO to honor Jews in Warsaw ghetto stirring protests," UPI dispatch, *New York Times*, April 15, 1983.
47 Quoted in John Kifner, "Few flowers at the ghetto," *New York Times*, April 17, 1983.
48 Ibid.
49 "Walesa detained for a third time," *New York Times*, April 20, 1983.
50 Ibid.
51 See E.J. Dionne Jr, "PLO picks Israeli Jew to replace slain aide," *New York Times*, April 13, 1983.
52 Quoted in Jeff Jacoby, "The en-Nobeling of Arafat," Op-ed., *The Boston Globe*, City Edition, October 20, 1994, 19. I should note here that the attack in Ma'alot was committed by guerrillas from Nayif Hawatmah's Popular Democratic Front over whose actions Arafat had little power.
53 Quoted in Batsheva Tsur, "Walesa plans to invite Arafat to Auschwitz," *Jerusalem Post*, November 3, 1994.
54 Ibid.
55 Reported in Julian Borger, "Arafat 'sure to be asked' to Auschwitz," *Guardian*, London, November 5, 1994.
56 *Jerusalem Post*, November 6, 1994.
57 "Beilin: Arafat should be invited to Auschwitz," *Jerusalem Post*, 17 November 1994.
58 See Segev, *The Seventh Million*, 237–238.
59 Ibid.
60 *Washington Post*, January 17, 1998.
61 *Washington Post*, January 20, 1998.
62 Quoted in Elli Wohlgelernter, "Learning to see 'the enemy' as victims," *Jerusalem Post*, January 23, 1998.
63 *Washington Post*, January 23, 1998.
64 *Washington Post*, February 19, 1998.
65 Elli Wohlgelernter, *Jerusalem Post*, January 23, 1998.
66 The text of the resolution is reproduced in Regina Sharif (ed), *The United Nations Resolutions and the Arab–Israeli Conflict, Volume Two, 1975–1981* (Washington, DC: Institute for Palestine Studies, 1988), 7. The text of the 1991 resolution is reproduced in Jody Boudreault (ed), *The United Nations Resolutions and the Arab–Israeli Conflict, Volume Four, 1987–1991* (Washington DC: Institute for Palestine Studies, 1993), 194.
67 Cited by Segev, *The Seventh Million*, 398.

68 Ibid.
69 *Al-Musawwar*, September 18, 1953, cited in David Hirst and Irene Beeson, *Sadat* (London: Faber and Faber, 1981), 88.
70 On Zionist collaboration with the Nazis, see Lenni Brenner's classic, *Zionism in the Age of the Dictators, A Reappraisal* (Westport, CT: Lawrence Hill and Co., 1983), and Tom Segev's *The Seventh Million*. On Revisionist Zionism's collaboration with the Nazis including an offer by the Stern gang to set up a Jewish State in alliance with the Third Reich as late as 1941, see Lenni Brenner, *The Iron Wall, Zionist Revisionism from Jabotinsky to Shamir* (London: Zed Press, 1984), 194–197.
71 Idward Sa'id, "Usus Lil-Ta'ayush" (Bases for coexistence), in *Al-Hayah*, November 5, 1997. For a critique of Said's article by the eminent Bahraini intellectual Muhammad Jabir al-Ansari, see "Muraja'ah Am... Taraju'" (Revision or retreat), *Al-Hayah*, November 11, 1997. For a rebuttal of al-Ansari, see Juzif Mas'ad, "Tashwih Maqsud Aw Su' Fahm li-Afkar Idward Sa'id: Rad 'ala Muhammad Jabir al-Ansari," (Deliberate distortion or a misunderstanding of the ideas of Edward Said: a response to Muhammad Jabir al-Ansari), *Al-Hayah*, November 22, 1997.
72 Novick, 71. For the pressure placed on countries like Haiti, the Philippines, Greece, Ethiopia, and Liberia among others, see General Carolos P. Romulo, "The Philippines changes its vote," and Kermit Roosevelt, "The partition of Palestine: a lesson in pressure politics," in Walid Khalidi (ed.), *From Haven to Conquest, Readings in and the Palestine Problem Until 1948* (Washington, DC: Institute for Palestine Studies, 1971), 723–726 and 727–729 respectively.
73 Evyatar Friesel, "The Holocaust and the birth of Israel," *Wiener Library Bulletin*, Volume XXXII, Nos 49/50 (1979), 55.
74 Ibid.
75 Ibid.
76 Novick, 72.
77 Paragraph 36 of the report. For the text of the report, see Walid Khalidi (ed.), *From Haven*, 645–699.
78 Ibid., Article 40.
79 Ibid., Paragraph 41.
80 Ibid., Article 42.
81 For the draft of the resolution, see Walid Khalidi (ed.), *From Haven*, 692–693. On the votes on the two resolutions, see Regina Sharif, *Non-Jewish Zionism, Its Roots in Western History* (London: Zed Press, 1983), 126.

9 The ends of Zionism: racism and the Palestinian struggle

1 Emma Brockes and Ewen MacAskill, "Sharon wants 1m new Jews for Israel," *The Guardian* (London), November 7, 2001.
2 Donna E. Arzt, *Refugees into Citizens, Palestinians and the End of the Arab–Israeli Conflict* (New York: Council on Foreign Relations, 1997).
3 Joseph Alpher and Khalil Shikaki, *The Palestinian Refugee Problem and the Right of Return*, Working Paper Series, Paper No. 98–7, Weatherhead Center for International Affairs, Harvard University, May 1998. Of the Palestinian group, which, in addition to Shikaki, included other Palestinian pragmatists, namely Ghassan Khatib, Ibrahim Dakkak, Yezid Sayigh, Nadim Rouhana, and Nabeel Kassis, only Kassis did not partake of the final drafting of the report (see x). Israeli and US Jewish participants included Joseph Alpher, Gabriel Ben-Dor, Yossi Katz, Moshe Ma'oz, Ze'ev Schiff, Shimon Shamir, and Herbert Kelman.
4 As'ad Talhami, "Filastiniyun yattahimun al-sultah bi-itlaq balun ikhtibar bi-sha'n qadiyyat al-laji'in wa isra'iliyyun yurahhibun bi- 'al-waqi'iyyah'" (Palestinians accuse the authority of testing the waters regarding the refugee question, and Israelis welcome "pragmatism"), *Al-Hayah*, November 16, 2008, 8.
5 Ibid.

6 Yasser Arafat, "The Palestinian vision of peace," *New York Times*, February 3, 2002.
7 "The Herzlia conference on the balance of national strength and security in Israel," selections reproduced in the *Journal of Palestine Studies*, No. 121, Autumn 2001, 50–61.
8 Theodor Herzl, *The Jewish State* (New York: Dover Publications, 1988), 95.
9 Theodor Herzl, *The Complete Diaries of Theodor Herzl*, edited by Raphael Patai, and translated by Harry Zohn, Vol. I (New York: Herzl Press and Thomas Yoseloff, 1960), 88.
10 Ibid., 98.
11 David Hirst, *The Gun and the Olive Branch, The Roots of Violence in the Middle East* (London: Faber and Faber, 1984), 25.
12 Lily Galili, *Ha'Aretz*, January 28, 2002.
13 No author, "Khalifat Zi'ifi yad'u li-tarhil al-Filastiniyin" (Zeevi's successor calls for the eviction of Palestinians), *al-Hayah*, February 2, 2002.
14 On Palestinian resistance, see Rashid Khalidi, *Palestinian Identity, The Construction of Modern National Consciousness* (New York: Columbia University Press, 1997), and Hirst, *The Gun*.
15 "Protest to Wilson against Zionist State," *New York Times*, March 5, 1919, 7, cited in Thomas Kolsky, *Jews Against Zionism, The American Council For Judaism, 1942–1948* (Philadelphia, PA: Temple University Press, 1990), 31.
16 Ibid., 41.
17 Ibid., 73.
18 On Israel's racist laws and treatment of its Palestinian Arab citizens, see Sabri Jiryis, *The Arabs in Israel* (New York: Monthly Review Press, 1976), and Ian Lustick, *Arabs in the Jewish State, Israel's Control of a National Minority* (Austin, TX: University of Texas Press, 1980).
19 "Biriz yuhadhdhir min 'al-khatar al-dimughrafi' al-filastini wa yashunnu hujuman haddan 'ala al-nuwwab al-'arab fi al-kinisit" (Peres warns of Palestinian 'demographic danger' and launches a sharp attack against Arab members of the Knesset), *Al-Hayah*, August 24, 2001.
20 Hirst, *The Gun*, 242–243.
21 Herzl, *The Jewish State*, 75.
22 Ibid., 93.
23 Avinoam Bar-Yosef, "The Jews who run Clinton's cabinet," *Ma'ariv*, Tel Aviv, September 2, 1994, reproduced in the *Journal of Palestine Studies*, No. 94 (Winter 1995), 148–151.
24 Ibid.
25 On Zionism's complicity with anti-Semitism and its use of anti-Semites as model, see Michael Selzer, *The Aryanization of the Jewish State* (New York: Black Star, 1967).
26 On the pro-Israel lobby in the United States, see Edward Tivnan, *The Lobby: Jewish Political Power and American Foreign Policy* (New York: Touchstone Books, 1988). Paul Findley, *They Dare to Speak Out: People and Institutions Confront Israel's Lobby* (New York: Lawrence Hill and Company, 1985).
27 In this regard, see Karen Brodkin, *How Jews became White folks & What That Says about Race in America* (New Brunswick, NJ: Rutgers University Press, 1998).
28 Max Nordau,"Jewry of muscle," translation of "Muskeljudentum," in *Juedische Turnzeitung* (June 1903), in Paul Mendes-Flohr and Jehuda Reinharz (eds), *The Jew in the Modern World, A Documentary History* (Oxford: Oxford University Press, 1980), 434–435. For an overview of Nordau's political thought, see George Mosse, *Confronting the Nation, Jewish and Western Nationalism* (Hanover, NH: Brandeis University Press, 1993), 161–175, and Paul Breines, *Tough Jews, Political Fantasies and the Moral Dilemma of American Jewry* (New York: Basic Books, 1991).
29 Robin McKie, "Journal axes gene research on Jews and Palestinians," *The Observer*, November 25, 2001.

11 The persistence of the Palestinian Question

1 This view is elucidated by Herzl in his futurist novel *Altneuland*, whose Palestinian character, Rechid Bey, welcomes Jewish colonization. See Theodor Herzl, *Old New Land*, trans. by Lotta Levensohn (Princeton, NJ: Markus Wiener Publishers, 1997), 122–123.
2 On the transformative effects of Oslo on the Palestinian national movement, see Chapter 5.
3 See, for example, Maxime Rodinson's collected essays in his *Cult, Ghetto, and State: The Persistence of the Jewish Question* (London: Al Saqi Books, 1983).
4 Karl Marx, "On the Jewish Question" (1843), in Robert Tucker, *The Marx–Engels Reader* (New York: Norton, 1978), 26–52.
5 The rise of full-fledged anti-Semitism in nineteenth-century Europe was part and parcel of the rising nationalisms following the French Revolution and the elaboration of biological race theories and theories of evolution and degeneration. While some of these ideas already existed in the eighteenth century, especially in the field of philology, they would become fully articulated during the nineteenth.
6 See Max Horkheimer and Theodor Adorno, *Dialectic of Enlightenment* (New York: Continuum, 1972), especially the section "Elements of anti-Semitism, the limits of enlightenment," 168–208.
7 Abram Leon, *The Jewish Question: A Marxist Interpretation* (New York: Pathfinder Press, 1970).
8 Sigmund Freud, "Analysis of a phobia in a five-year-old boy," in *The Standard Edition of the Complete Psychological Works of Sigmund Freud* Vol. 10 (London: Hogarth Press, 1953–1974), 36.
9 Jean-Paul Sartre, *Anti-Semite and Jew* (New York: Schocken, 1965), 13. See also Hannah Arendt's intelligent and provocative analysis of the historiography of anti-Semitism and Jew hatred in her introductory remarks in "Preface to part one: anti-semitism," in her 1951 classic, *The Origins of Totalitarianism* (New York: Harcourt Brace Jovanovich, 1973), xi–xiii. On Deutscher's views, see his *The Non-Jewish Jew and Other Essays* (London: Oxford University Press, 1968). For a critique of Deutscher's view on anti-Semitism and Zionism, see Chapter 1.
10 For a critical assessment of this process, see Martin Bernal's classic, *Black Athena: The Afroasiatic Roots of Classical Civilization, Vol. 1, The Fabrication of Ancient Greece 1785–1985* (New Brunswick, NJ: Rutgers University Press, 1987).
11 Moses Mendelssohn, *Jerusalem, or On Religious Power and Judaism*, trans. by Allan Arkush (Hanover, NH: Brandeis University Press, 1983). Mendelssohn was a good friend of Gotthold Ephraim Lessing who, as a towering figure of the German Enlightenment and a rationalizer of Christianity, bypassed all European medieval thinkers to become a follower of Diderot, whom he thought was Aristotle's only true heir. For Lessing's revival of the classical Greek notion of friendship as a model for the future, see his play Nathan the Wise in *"Nathan the Wise," "Minna von Barnheim," and Other Plays and Writings* (New York: Continuum, 1991).
12 See Michael A. Meyer, *Response to Modernity: A History of the Reform Movement in Judaism* (New York: Oxford University Press, 1988).
13 On the Haskala's relationship to Jewish culture, see Michael Selzer's *The Wineskin and the Wizard* (New York: Macmillan, 1970) and his *Aryanization of the Jewish State* (New York: Blackstar, 1967), 9–50.
14 On Herzl's letter, see Walter Laqueur, *A History of Zionism* (New York: Holt, Rinehart and Winston, 1972), 88–89.
15 Theodor Herzl, *The Complete Diaries of Theodor Herzl*, Vol. II, edited by Raphael Patai, translated by Harry Zohn (New York: Herzl Press and Thomas Yoseloff, 1960), 11.
16 Theodor Herzl, *The Jewish State* (New York: Dover Publications, 1988), 146.
17 Ibid., 96.
18 See Herzl, *Old New Land*.

19 Herzl, *The Jewish State*, 82.
20 On the transformation of Jews into tough masculine men, see Paul Breines, *Tough Jews: Political Fantasies and the Moral Dilemma of American Jewry* (New York: Basic Books, 1991).
21 On the gentile history of Zionism, see Regina Sharif, *Non-Jewish Zionism: Its Roots in Western History* (London: Zed Press, 1983). On the internalization of anti-Semitism by Zionism, see Nathan Weinstock, *Zionism: False Messiah*, trans. and ed. by Alan Adler (London: Ink Links, 1979), 44–45.
22 On Zionism and Israel's relationship to the Jewish holocaust, see Tom Segev, *The Seventh Million: The Israelis and the Holocaust*, trans. by Haim Watzman (New York: Hill and Wang, 1993); Hannah Torok-Yablonka, "The recruitment of holocaust survivors during the war of independence," *Studies in Zionism*, 13(1) (1992); Peter Novick, *The Holocaust in American Life* (New York: Houghton Mifflin, 1999); Lenni Brenner, *Zionism in the Age of the Dictators: A Reappraisal* (Westport, CN: Lawrence Hill, 1983); and Norman Finkelstein, *The Holocaust Industry* (New York: Verso, 2000).
23 Benjamin Beit-Hallahmi, *Original Sins: Reflections of the History of Zionism and Israel* (London: Pluto Press, 1992), 129. In this regard, Georges Friedmann explains that Israel "constitutes a new kind of assimilation liable to produce 'generations of Hebrew-speaking Gentiles.' " See Georges Friedmann, *The End of the Jewish People?* (New York: Doubleday, 1967), 243–245.
24 The term sabra refers to the Palestine-born children of European Jewish colonial settlers. The word means "cactus fruit," which, it is said, resembles the New Jew (invariably male), who is "tough on the outside and tender on the inside." For a history of the term sabra, see Chapter 1.
25 On the ideological basis and the actual practice of Israeli archaeology, see Nadia Abu El-Haj, *Facts on the Ground: Archaeological Practice and Territorial Self-Fashioning in Israeli Society* (Chicago, IL: University of Chicago Press, 2001).
26 See Mitchell B. Hart, *Social Science and the Politics of Modern Jewish Identity* (Stanford, CA: Stanford University Press, 2000), 56–73.
27 See Laqueur, *A History of Zionism*, 152.
28 Ibid.
29 As quoted in Tamara Traubmann, "Do not have children if they won't be healthy," *Ha'Aretz*, June 11, 2004.
30 Ibid.
31 On Zionism's search for Jewish "genetic markers" and its continued investment in the racial separateness of Jews, see the forthcoming work of Nadia Abu Elhaj.
32 Quoted in Simha Flapan, *Zionism and the Palestinians* (London: Croomhelm, 1979), 71.
33 Colonial Office [CO] 733/297/75156/II/Appendix A, extract from Weizmann's speech, April 23, 1936, Great Britain, Peel Commission Report, 96–97, cited in Philip Mattar, *The Mufti of Jerusalem: Al-Hajj Amin-al-Husayni and the Palestinian National Movement* (New York: Columbia University Press, 1988), 73.
34 *Ha'Aretz*, April 4, 1969, cited in David Hirst, *The Gun and the Olive Branch: The Roots of Violence in the Middle East* (New York: Nation Books, 2003), 221.
35 See Saul Cohen and Nurit Kliot's "Israel's place-names as reflection of continuity and change in nation building," *Names: Journal of the American Name Society*, 29(3) (September 1981). The Jewish National Fund was and is the Zionist organization that owns all Jewish-"acquired" lands in Palestine.
36 See Saul Cohen and Nurit Kliot's "Place-names in Israel's ideological struggle over the administered territories," *Annals of the Association of American Geographers*, 82(4) (1992).
37 Tom Segev, *The Seventh Million*, 161–162.
38 On the origins of the neologism "Judeo-Christian tradition," see Novick, *The Holocaust*, 28.

39 See Ella Shohat, *Israeli Cinema: East/West and the Politics of Representation* (Austin, TX: University of Texas Press, 1989) and her "Sephardim in Israel: Zionism from the standpoint of its Jewish victims," *Social Text* 19/20 (Fall 1988): 1–35.
40 The "tough neighborhood" description is a favorite of Israeli former (and possibly future) Prime Minister Benjamin Netanyahu. See, for example, his discussion with US Secretary of State Madeleine Albright on November 14, 1997, in London, where he told her that "we live in a tough neighborhood." The transcript of the meeting is available at the Website of the US embassy in Israel at www.usembassyisrael.org.il/publish/peace/archives/1997/me1114b.html
41 Herzl, *Old New Land*, 42.
42 Menachem Begin, speech to the Knesset, quoted in Amnon Kapeliouk, "Begin and the 'Beasts,'" *New Statesman*, June 25, 1982.
43 See their Website at www.idi.org.il/english. This poll marks an increase in Jewish support for the expulsion of Palestinians. A previous poll, taken on March 22, 2002, by the Israeli Jaffee Center for Strategic Studies, had 46 percent of Israeli Jews supporting expulsion.
44 See Sabri Jiryis, *The Arabs in Israel* (New York: Monthly Review Press, 1976).
45 See Hirst, *The Gun and the Olive Branch*, 312–314.
46 See Uri Davis, *Israel: An Apartheid State* (London: Zed Press, 1987).
47 The Palestinian Ministry of Agriculture cited the number of 374,000 uprooted trees in the first eight months of the intifada that broke out in September 2000. Other sources, like the Palestinian Initiative for the Promotion of Global Dialogue and Democracy, put the number at 227,995 trees, as posted on the Website at www.miftah.org/report.cfm
48 On Palestinians in Jordan, see Joseph Massad, *Colonial Effects: The Making of National Identity in Jordan* (New York: Columbia University Press, 2001), Chapter 5.
49 On Palestinian refugees in Lebanon, see Wadie Said, "The obligation of host countries to refugees under international law: the case of Lebanon," in Naseer Aruri (ed.) *Palestinian Refugees: The Right of Return* (London: Pluto Press, 2001).
50 David Ben-Gurion and Itzhak Ben Zvi, *Eretz Yisrael be'Avar vebeHayyah* (Eretz Israel in the past and the present), translated from the Yiddish by D. Niv (Jerusalem: Yad Yitzhak Ben Zvi Publishing, 1979), 195–206. The book was initially published in Yiddish in 1918 under the title "Palestine in the past and the present."
51 Ibid., 201. I would like to thank Gil Anidjar for his help in translating this quote from Hebrew.
52 Herzl, *Jewish State*, 146.
53 Vladimir Jabotinsky, *The Hebrew Accent* (Tel Aviv: HaSefer, 1930), 4–9, cited in Shohat, *Israeli Cinema*, 55.
54 Sammy Smooha, *Israel: Pluralism and Conflict* (Berkeley and Los Angeles, CA: University of California Press, 1978), 86–88.
55 Aryeh Gelblum, *Ha'Aretz*, April 22, 1949.
56 See Shohat, "Sephardim in Israel." See also Chapter 3.
57 Selzer, *Aryanization*, 86. While German anti-Semites constructed German and East European Jews as merciless capitalists and as rich and covetous of Aryan jobs and wealth, they also characterized them as poor and dirty, sullying Aryan cleanliness, and as subversive communists. The contradictions in German anti-Semitism are internal to its specific ideology of racism and not necessarily the result of any observable differences between East European unassimilated Jews and German assimilated Jews. Assimilated German Jews were identified by stereotypes aimed at uncovering their apparent sameness as intrinsically different, hence the exposure of their "passing" as just that, while unassimilated Jews, German or East European, were identified by stereotypes that affirmed their observable alterity (sartorial, racial, epidermal, nasal, and so on). In certain instances, one can speak of the stereotypes as being of two

varieties, one set targeting German Jews and the other the Ostjuden, but that was not always fixed (as the two groups were often conflated as one) on the one hand, and it was not the case at all historically (when all European Jews were seen as the same). Moreover, stereotypes of the degenerate Jew, the parasitic Jew, the feminine, and profligate Jew, among others, applied to both sets of Jews synchronically in nineteenth- and twentieth-century German anti-Semitism.

58 Herzl, *Complete Diaries*, Vol. I, 10.

59 Amir Oren, "At the gates of Yassergrad," *Ha'Aretz*, January 25, 2002.

60 Gideon Alon and Ori Nir, "Mofaz: IDF will stop writing numbers on prisoners' arms," *Ha'Aretz*, March 13, 2002.

61 See Beit-Hallahmi, *Original Sins*, 128–129.

62 Quoted in Peter Novick, *The Holocaust*, 69.

63 In this regard, see his important essay "Jewry of Muscle," a translation of "Muskeljudentum," originally published in *Juedische Turnzeitung* (June 1903), reprinted in Paul Mendes-Flohr and Jehuda Reinharz (eds), *The Jew in the Modern World: A Documentary History*, 434–435 (Oxford: Oxford University Press, 1980).

64 Yosef Gorny, *The Arab Question and the Jewish Problem* (Tel Aviv: Am Oved, 1985), 39.

65 On Zionist collaboration with Nazism, see Lenni Brenner, *Zionism in the Age of the Dictators: A Reappraisal* (New York: Lawrence Hill, 1983). On their collaboration with the Iraqi and Egyptian regimes to bring about the exodus of Iraqi and Egyptian Jews, see Hirst, *The Gun and the Olive Branch*, 281–297. On their collaboration with the Argentinean generals who pursued anti-Semitic policies targeting Argentine Jews in the late 1970s and early 1980s, see Jacobo Timerman's interview with the Israeli newspaper *Ha'Olam HaZe*, December 22, 1982, cited in Noam Chomsky, *The Fateful Triangle: The United States, Israel, and the Palestinians* (Boston, MA: South End Press, 1983), 110.

66 Shohat, "The Sephardim in Israel."

67 On Jewish supremacy in Israel and its complicity with anti-Semitism, see Chapter 9.

68 Herzl, *Jewish State*, 93.

69 Ibid., 122.

70 Ibid., 112.

71 Herzl, *Complete Diaries*, 1: 94.

Index

CW01626509

Praise for *T*

'Much more than a Christmas story…a stunning and unique debut' – *Rachel Dove, author of The Flower Shop on Foxley Street*

'Beautifully crafted from the first line to last' – *Laurie Ellingham, author of One Endless Summer*

The Manor on the Moors

Happy reading!

Liz Taylor

Liz Taylorson

Manatee Books
First published in 2019.

This book is primarily a work of fiction. Other names, characters, businesses, organisations, places and events are the product of the authors imagination or are used fictitiously. Any resemblance to actual persons, living or dead, events or locales is entirely coincidental.

Published by Manatee Books

Paperback ISBN: 978-1-912347-26-1
Kindle ISBN: 978-1-912347-27-8

Cover design by Aimee Coveney of Bookollective
Images used under licence from Shutterstock.com

To Daniel and Phoebe, who helped me in many ways

Chapter 1

Special Friends.

Caroline could hear voices where there shouldn't be any voices. Alice was meant to be hard at work on her PhD research in the Octagon Library, she was meant to be on her own, she was meant to have her phone turned off and the doors were meant to be locked, so unless Alice had started talking to herself – not impossible, she was an academic, after all, and academics could be a bit like that - then there was somebody else in the West Wing.

Caroline had been forced to chase visitors out of the West Wing far too often since the gardens of Misterley Manor had been open to the public; even though it quite clearly stated "Private, STRICTLY No Admittance" on every one of the doors, still hopeful pensioners thought that they could sneak a quick peek inside. Hopefully *this* time the intruder wasn't eating tuna and sweetcorn sandwiches out of a Tupperware box in Sir Edward Lattimore's antique leather armchair by the library fireplace.

She hauled herself up from her desk, where she had been working since half past six this morning, trying to put together yet another hopeless bid for lottery funding to mend the roof, and she opened the door into the Octagon Library.

There was a man there with Alice, a rather short young man with floppy blonde hair and the cleanest shoes she had ever seen. He carried an enormous bunch of white lilies and he stepped hurriedly backwards as Caroline came into the library, her footsteps echoing on the floor, marking out her territory.

'Who are you and what are you doing in my house?' she snapped. She hadn't always been this snappy but most of the time these days she was too tired to bother with niceties when talking to intruders.

'Oh, I, er… I was…' the young man had an impossibly posh accent to match his impossibly shiny shoes.

'This is Sebastian. My…' Alice had looked up, worry written clearly across her features, when Caroline entered the room. She was such a mousy woman, Caroline found her lack of backbone frankly irritating. But she was young. Perhaps it was something she would grow out of – and she sometimes wished that her own daughter, Emily, who wasn't that much younger than Alice, had slightly LESS backbone. Her daughter was another worry to add to her overflowing inbox of stress.

Alice now seemed to be struggling to describe the young man, who was quite clearly her lover from the enormous bunch of flowers he had brought her. 'This is my special friend,' she finished lamely, looking up at him, blatantly seeking his approval. Caroline tutted.

'Can I ask how your "special friend" got in here? The door should be locked. Daddy doesn't like uninvited visitors,' Caroline said.

Caroline's father, Sir Henry Lattimore, hardly stirred from his suite of rooms on the second floor of the main house these days, since he had started losing his sight – but he heard everything. Every movement, every whisper, every creak of every door, every gossiping old biddy in the garden, every unannounced lover arriving with lilies. He would know there was someone in the West Wing and he would blame her for it. He always blamed her because there was nobody else to blame, and though at the age of fifty-three she was no longer frightened of her father's rages, well, it wasn't pleasant. It wasn't *nice*. It would be better if there were no unannounced strangers with large bunches of lilies in the Octagon Library for her father to object to.

'There was an older lady in the courtyard. A tall lady, short grey hair, parrot earrings and a purple kaftan? She let me in.'

'Ah. I see. Aunty Marjorie.'

Who else could it have been? That woman was a law unto herself. Caroline sighed.

'The lady said that as I had come to see my Ally-Bee she would let me in,' the young man said, turning up the fake public school-boy charm. Caroline had been to a public school herself and she could recognise a comprehensive school boy with delusions of grandeur when she saw one. The real thing never needed to try this hard.

'Ally-Bee?' Caroline raised an eyebrow.

'Alice. I mean Alice,' he said, with a patronising little smirk at his girlfriend, who squirmed in her seat, presumably at his public use of her pet name. Thankfully Caroline had never had a lover who endowed her with such a sickening nickname. She hadn't had a lover at all since she had divorced That Man – maybe the odd pet name would have been a small price to pay for some moral support in the last few, lonely years that she had spent locked away here at Misterley Manor fighting the rising tide of debt, decay and disorder. Disorder to which the pasty-looking young man standing before her was contributing with his enormous bunch of flowers.

'Why have you brought those in here?' she said. 'We can't risk pollen getting on the Fox-Travers letters,' she turned back to Alice, 'I thought you would have known that?'

'I haven't let them bring them anywhere near the letters, I know how precious they are,' Alice said meekly, looking stricken.

Of course she knew that, Caroline reminded herself; she had been so pathetically grateful to be allowed to study those letters when they had finally been removed from the safe of the Lattimore family's solicitor where they had lain, wrapped in brown paper, string and sealing wax, for the last one hundred years. Alice probably valued the

Fox-Travers letters even more highly than Caroline herself did – for Caroline it was all about how much money the discovery of the letters might bring to Misterley – but for Alice, Gilbert Fox-Travers and his art was her life's work. For the three weeks she had been working here on her PhD it was all she could talk about. Fox-Travers did this, Fox-Travers said that, drew this, wrote that, believed the other…

Although Caroline knew only too well what an important artist and architect Gilbert Fox-Travers had been, there *were* other subjects of conversation. Just for once it would be nice to talk to Alice about something other than early twentieth century art.

'Sebastian, why don't you take those lilies outside? Wait for me in the rose garden, I'll be out in a minute,' said Alice quietly, and the young man couldn't disappear fast enough. 'I'm so sorry, Caroline, I didn't know he was coming, otherwise of course I would have told him…'

Caroline suddenly felt sorry for Alice who looked utterly contrite. She had never done anything except try to please since she had been at Misterley. 'It doesn't matter, Alice. Don't worry. Make sure you lock the letters away safely before you go outside. You never know who is going to walk in here next when Marjorie's around to let them in. I want to keep those letters away from prying eyes.'

Alice stood up. It was easy to forget, with her self-effacing manners, that Alice was an imposing six-feet tall. She was nearly a foot taller than the petite, white-haired Caroline but there was no mistaking who was the mistress of Misterley Manor and who was the visiting academic as Alice painstakingly gathered up the letters and locked them safely away in the library cupboard, and Caroline looked on, making sure everything was secure. Because who knew when That Man would turn up and ruin everything?

Alice found Sebastian sitting awkwardly in an arbour, surrounded by trailing pink roses, still clutching his extravagant bunch of lilies and a

Fortnum and Mason carrier bag. She took a deep breath as she walked underneath the arches of the rose walk, breathing in the heather-scented warmth of the late summer afternoon as she moved out of the cold-stone chill of the library. Sebastian often bought her flowers; elegant and showy lilies like these to suit the minimalist design of his apartment.

'She's fierce, isn't she!' he laughed, mimicking Caroline now she was safely out of the way. '*What are you doing in my house?*' He had dropped the stupid posh accent now, she noticed, now there was only her and nobody to impress she could hear his Mancunian vowels.

'Don't, Sebastian. She might hear you, or Sir Henry might.' Although she hadn't yet met Sir Henry she was bizarrely afraid of encountering him; every time Caroline mentioned her father Alice's mental image of him became more sinister still. In her imagination he was a tall, thin man with a hooked nose like Caroline's, his skeletal hands ruling the estate with an iron grip. She turned around to look at the manor house behind her and indeed, she could see a dim figure silhouetted in the window of Sir Henry's rooms. He was too far away to hear them, she was relieved to notice. She let her gaze stray over the ornate stone-carved balconies and battlements of Misterley Manor, the towers, the soaring arches, the windows – no two of them the same – and the stained glass that glowed like jewels; amethyst, garnet, amber, emerald and sapphire. She loved this house.

Sebastian, arms folded around his precious lilies, walked down the rose walk towards her, treading carefully on the dusty gravel so as not to get dirt on his shoes.

'These are for you!' He handed over the enormous bunch of white lilies to her with a flourish.

'Thank you,' Alice said, glancing down at him as she accepted them. He hated it when she looked down at him and she always tried to make sure she was standing on a step below him if she could be, but there were no steps in this part of the garden. She wished she wasn't so very tall – it wasn't that Sebastian was short, he was average height for a man, but she was still an inch or so taller than him.

All through her life people had told her that she "looked just like an *Alice*!" with her thick blonde hair and blue eyes, but the hair and eyes were all that fitted with the picture-book-pretty idea of an *Alice*. Her face was too square, and her jaw was too strong for an *Alice*, her shoulders were too broad, and her teeth were too prominent. *Alices* were neat, pretty and petite with pointed faces and dainty feet. Alice's feet were a size eight, she was six feet tall, dainty was never a word that could be used to define her and now she was in her mid-twenties she was far too old for an *Alice* as well. All her life she had secretly been hoping for a little bottle marked "drink me" that would make her pretty like all the other girls.

'So, Sebastian, it's lovely to see you, but why are you here?'

'I missed you. I wanted to see you!' he said, 'and I've brought you a treat. Bet you can't get *these* in Rawscar! You must be bored of fish and chips by now.'

'I like fish and chips -' she began to explain as from his glossy carrier-bag he pulled out a box of expensive looking macarons, a half bottle of champagne and two plastic glasses. His favourite treat, an extravagant gesture that would have been unthinkable when they had first met as students, living on Bourbon biscuits and cheap lagers from Tesco, but since he had become an asset manager a couple of years ago no gesture was too grand for Sebastian.

'For us!' he announced, waiting for her to tell him how generous and kind he was.

'It's so kind and generous of you!' she said, even though she didn't much like macarons *or* champagne. She had never lost the liking for cheap lager.

There was a pause as he seemed to be waiting for her to say something; she wasn't sure what he was waiting for but she had to say something to fill the suddenly awkward pause.

'From the top of the lawn you can see right down over the cliffs towards Rawscar -' she began but he cut her short.

'I've got something important to ask you.'

Her heart stopped for a moment.

This was it.

This is what the champagne was for, the macarons, the enormous bunch of flowers. He was going to propose. Would he get down on one knee amidst the macarons? Had he already bought her a ring, did he have it in his pocket?

Everything was going to be OK, after all the doubts and worries of the last few months, he *did* love her after all, it wasn't all about money and promotion for Sebastian as she had begun to fear. He had put so much thought into this that she wanted to memorise it; the warmth of the sun on the back of her hands, the smell of the heather and the bleating of the sheep on the moors beyond the garden wall. She wanted to remember every little tiny detail of the moment, even the look of hope and expectation on Sebastian's face, as he turned to her, took a deep breath and said:

'Alice, there's a job going at C.C.T. Asset Management. PA to the MD. I've spoken to him and he's prepared to consider you, even though your CV isn't exactly on point. You've got an interview next Monday, isn't that fantastic?'

'But...' The sounds and scents that she had been trying to immortalise in her mind suddenly faded; all she could see was his expectant face.

'But... *this* is my work, here at Misterley. My PhD!' Her chest tightened as she tried to prevent her unhappiness showing too clearly on her face.

'It's time you grew up, Ally-Bee. You can't be a student all your life.'

She seemed to remember that it was only two years since they had *both* been students and now here he was talking down to her like a child from his lofty position as a very, very junior asset manager. It appears it wasn't enough for Sebastian's life to focus on money and promotion – now he wanted hers to as well.

'I don't want to be a student all my life,' she protested. 'I'm hoping to get a teaching post once I finish my PhD.'

'You've never been out in the real world, have you, like I've had to? Camden College isn't exactly a world beating university either, is it? Don't you think it's time you got a proper job?'

'But...' she said, so taken aback that she didn't know where to begin. 'But... the Fox-Travers letters – nobody has ever studied them before. They've been locked away in the family solicitor's office for a hundred years. I'm so lucky that the Lattimores even agreed to let me in to Misterley Manor; I can't let them down now.'

'Sometimes I think you love Gilbert Fox-Travers more than me,' he said, sulkily.

Sometimes, recently, Alice had begun to wonder if she did too. The long-dead artist and the mystery of his disappearance had been the focus of her academic studies since her undergraduate days and sometimes he felt as real to her as the living, breathing people around her.

'Of course I don't -' she began to protest, but he cut her short again.

'Then come home! Get a real job and come home. I know you can't be happy up here in the back of beyond without me.'

And yet she *was* happy. The three weeks since she had moved here had been peaceful. She had felt the fresh sea air on her face every day and she had room to stretch and breathe away from the city. Camden was a vibrant place to live but even with Sebastian's generosity in letting her live rent-free in his apartment, life there was expensive. Sometimes she felt like she was always on the outside of that world, looking in. It was like when she had met Sebastian back in their Oxford days – but then they had both been on the outside and now Sebastian had found his way inside while she still had her nose pressed up against the window of his world. It seemed to her like a pane of glass separated them and she wasn't brave enough or strong enough to break through to the other side. Now he was offering her the opportunity to join him on his side of the window, she wasn't sure whether she wanted to.

'But Sebastian, I love it here, really, I do. The moors, the sea, this house - my work.'

'But that's the thing, isn't it? It isn't *proper* work, is it? If you had a real job, then we could move to a bigger apartment, get a better car, have those holidays we've always talked about. Japan, Thailand, Indonesia.'

'We've never talked about going to Indonesia. I don't want to go to Indonesia, I've never wanted to go to Indonesia. I'm quite happy with holidays in Cornwall, I like Cornwall!'

'But I want more than that. Come on Alice, we could be so much happier, if you would think about what's best for *us,* not only what's best for *you.* Look, I can't stop for long, I've got to get up to Edinburgh for an important client meeting this evening.' These days Sebastian didn't seem to have a meeting that wasn't "important," unless it was a meeting with her, of course.

'You don't have to decide now, you can think about it. But I'll be back to stay for a couple of nights next weekend and I'll take you back to London with me for the interview, OK?'

No! she wanted to scream, *no it is NOT OK!* but that would upset him, and she hated it when Sebastian was upset with her. So, she smiled, hesitantly, and said:

'Thank you for the flowers.'

Chapter 2

Pride and Strength.

Caroline watched through the open door of her office as Alice trudged back into the Octagon Library. She looked utterly miserable. She must be sad to say goodbye to her "special friend". Caroline had heard his car spinning gravel beneath its wheels as he went up the drive a few minutes ago.

'Caroline? Hi, I'm so sorry to bother you, but could I have the key for the library cupboard, so I can get the Fox-Travers letters out again?'

'It's not a bother,' said Caroline with a weary sigh intended to show that it clearly *was* a bother. 'Has your friend gone?'

'Yes, he had an important client meeting to get to in Edinburgh.'

Caroline knelt beside the old oak cupboard and opened the door for her. Alice was very careful with the letters, Caroline had to give her that, they had been put away very neatly.

'It was nice of him to come and see you,' Caroline said, in an attempt to make conversation with the PhD student. 'You must miss him?' she asked, in what she hoped was a sympathetic way. Alice paused for a moment before kneeling beside Caroline at the cupboard to pick up the letters with a tenderness usually reserved for fragile china or babies.

'It's strange, but I don't. I thought I would, I thought I would be homesick being away from him but - I'm sorry if this sounds callous - but it's quite nice being on my own sometimes.'

Caroline could certainly sympathise with her there. 'That's what I felt like when I finally got rid of That Man.' She stood up, stretching, and handed the pile of letters to Alice who carried them to the huge circular oak table in the middle of the library.

No matter how many times she told other people that she was better off on her own, sometimes the hardest person to convince was herself. It wasn't that she missed her ex-husband exactly, it was just that she sometimes found a large empty space where he had once been.

'And do you know what? I really like being able to eat fish and chips without worrying about the smell in the flat!' Alice said with a grin, 'and I like drinking lager instead of artisan gin. And staying up as late as I like without worrying about him being tired for his breakfast meeting. I mean, his *important* breakfast meeting.'

'Is there any other kind of breakfast meeting?' Caroline asked.

'No. No, there is not!'

It was the first time that Caroline could remember seeing the serious young researcher smile. She had a beautiful smile, it lit up her rather angular face in unexpected ways.

'It'll be a while before you see him again, will it?'

'No, he's coming back again on Friday,' she said, suddenly sounding miserable again.

'Well, that's not long!' Caroline tried to cheer her up. 'No need to get upset!'

'I'm not upset. Well, not about that.' She sat down at the end of the table.

Oh hell, Caroline should have put two and two together. Lilies were such a funerial flower; perhaps he had come to bring her some bad news. She knew that Alice had lost her mother a few years ago – perhaps it was a significant anniversary?

'Is everything OK?' she said awkwardly, hoping that Alice would tell her that everything was fine, but knowing that she should at least offer some attempt at sympathy. 'Nothing's wrong, is it?'

'Everything's fine,' Alice said with a brittleness to her voice which told Caroline that everything wasn't fine. But that would do, she had tried to help, and if Alice didn't want her to help then that wasn't her problem. She had done everything she needed to, and she could go back to work with a clear conscience.

'Well, that's good,' she said, as she headed back towards her office. She turned at the doorway. 'By the way, what did you do with that enormous bunch of flowers? Do you need some water for them?'

'No,' said Alice. 'No, I... I put them on the compost heap.' Her voice quivered.

'You did what?' Caroline came back into the library.

'I don't like lilies. The pollen makes my chest hurt,' she said briefly.

'Oh, I see. Asthma. Well, that's a shame,' Caroline was turning back to the office again.

'I'm sorry, I should have thought; would you have liked them for the house? I can go and get them back again?' she offered politely.

'Good Lord, no! They might poison Marjorie's cats.' Although thinking of the claw marks on the original Fox-Travers curtain fabric where Marjorie's cats had climbed them – yet another thing that she couldn't afford to restore - perhaps poisoning Marjorie's cats would not be an unmixed blessing. 'I hate lilies too,' she added. 'They remind me of my wedding day.'

'Caroline, can I talk to you about something?' Alice said, quietly. 'I need some advice. I don't know what to do.'

Oh hell, she should have made her exit when the going was good – she didn't have time for the woes of a love-stricken twenty-something-year-old right now.

'What's up?' she asked.

'He wants me to go back to London. He's coming to get me on Friday for a job interview at the firm where he works.'

It didn't make sense to Caroline. Alice was halfway through her PhD, she had spent nearly a year trying to persuade Caroline and her father to let her study here. Why would she want to give up now when she had only been here for three weeks of the four months she was meant to be staying?

'What about your PhD? How do you expect to complete your study of the building of Misterley Manor if you're working in an office in London?'

'I don't. I don't want to go to the interview, I don't want the job, I want to finish my PhD... but he thinks I should give it up because he wants me back at home. He wants me to get a proper job and go to... Indonesia...'

The very thought of going to Indonesia seemed to be making the tears brim in Alice's eyes. Caroline had never been to Indonesia herself, but she was sure it couldn't be that bad.

'Indonesia? I'm sure it's not that unpleasant. I think Marjorie went to Indonesia in her youth. But Marjorie's been everywhere.'

'I don't want to go to Indonesia. Oh Caroline, I'm so sorry...'

Oh God, Alice was going to cry. Caroline had been taught from a very early age not to cry under any circumstances; *Superbia et Vires*, *Pride and Strength*, that was the Lattimore motto. Debt, disease, divorce and death had always been faced with a stoical shrug of the shoulders and so she didn't think she could deal with tearful academics sobbing in the Octagon Library.

'Come on, Alice, it's not worth tears. After all the trouble you went through to come here to study – you were on the phone to me nearly every day until I said yes - you can't give it all up just because some man wants you to go to Indonesia.'

'I should have listened – I knew he didn't want me to do the PhD, but I didn't realise he felt *this* strongly.'

'I'd tell him where to shove his job, and if he really loves you, he'll wait for you,' Caroline said bluntly.

'I... I can't...' sobbed Alice. 'When Mum died, he was my rock. He was there for me, he was the one that kept me going. He even gave me a place to live; I couldn't afford to live in London without him. I owe him something.'

Perhaps there was more to this than Alice had said; perhaps there was something wrong with Sebastian.

'Alice, is he ill?'

'No. He's lonely without me, that's all. He doesn't like waking up alone in his flat.'

Was that all? Alice's boyfriend was missing his rumpy pumpy and after three weeks without her he was prepared to ask her to sacrifice her work for his gratification. Perhaps he should try struggling on alone and bearing the burden of a house like this, and Daddy, and Marjorie and Emily and everything alone for years and years and years? Struggling on against a rising tide of financial worries and crumbling stonework, roofs that leak and damp that rises? Sex, or the lack of it, was the least of her problems.

'Oh, that is such utter rubbish! You can't let a man ruin your life just because he's missing his little bit of nookie. You stand your ground and finish your PhD if it's important to you. Don't you ever let any man tell you what to do. If he truly understands how important your work is then he won't make you choose. If he doesn't understand then you should bloody well choose your work.'

Just like Caroline had done fifteen years ago.

Chapter 3

What Exactly is the Lady of Shalott Doing?

Dry sand, blown into all the corners along Quay Street, made Alice think of all the homeward bound holiday makers who had shaken it from their shoes, their buckets and spades or their picnic blankets as they made their way from the beach back up to the car park, saying goodbye to Rawscar as the summer came to an end. Now it waited for the winds and rain of autumn to come and wash it all away, back down to the beach again. Alice hummed under her breath as she climbed the hill out of the little old seaside village. No cars were allowed in Old Rawscar and so every day for Alice started with a brisk climb up the hill from her tiny bedsit above a fish-and-chip shop to the village car park. Sometimes if the weather was nice she would walk along the clifftop path all the way to Misterley Manor.

Today might be one of the last days of high summer, so Alice had decided to walk to work this morning, out along the clifftop path, recently re-opened following a massive cliff fall in the winter which had destroyed several houses. The gate to what had been the old coastguard cottage led to the cliff-edge, and only squares marking the foundations were left of what had once been a terrace of small houses. It gave Alice a strange feeling to see the ruins of what had once been someone's home. The gardens still flourished; rose bushes and lavender growing along the edge of the cliff and she could make out where the doors had been, downstairs toilets, even the fireplaces – this time last year there would have been people living in those houses.

She was always glad to get past the site of the cliff-fall and see Misterley Manor ahead of her at the edge of the moors. She felt her pulse quicken, as it did every day, at the first sight of Fox-Travers's masterpiece of architecture, battlements and arches and soaring gothic pinnacles reaching up towards the blue sky. Since the age of fourteen she had been obsessed with the enigmatic artist Gilbert Fox-Travers and his mysterious disappearance. All through her undergraduate and masters' degrees she had studied his work, and now with her PhD she finally got to devote her entire academic study to him. Nominally she was completing a PhD with the rather dry title: *Re-awakening Camelot: the medieval inspiration for the art and architecture of Gilbert Fox-Travers at Misterley Manor* but actually she was hoping to be the one to solve the mystery – to find out what had happened to Fox-Travers in 1912. It had to be here somewhere, in the correspondence which had passed between Fox-Travers and the family that had been locked away for a hundred years since the death of Sir Edward Lattimore, Caroline's great-grandfather. Popular myth suggested that Fox-Travers had gone down with the Titanic, but Alice was hoping to prove popular myth wrong. A breakthrough could mean academic success, it could mean the offer of a teaching post when she finished her PhD, it could mean a book deal, a radio series, even TV appearances - and Sebastian wanted her to give all that up for a holiday in Indonesia. Caroline was right. If he loved her, he wouldn't force her to choose. And yet... if he did ask her to choose, would she be able to say no to him? It was easy for Caroline to tell her what to do; she was confident and strong, but Alice was neither of those things, as Sebastian often felt the need to remind her.

As the path wound through the gardens she spotted one of the gardeners with his back to her hard at work, on his hands and knees weeding one of the flower-beds in the rose garden, even though the morning was still early and the dew was still wet on the leaves of the rose bushes.

'Good morning!' she called out, not wanting to pass him without acknowledging his presence, though he hadn't looked up once as she came along the path. Now he looked up, and she noticed that he was much younger – and much better looking – than the head gardener who she had met in her first week at Misterley. This must be the assistant gardener.

'Morning,' he replied, straightening up, brushing the dirt from his hands. 'Going to be another beautiful day, isn't it?' and he flashed her a smile that might not have been as white and even as Sebastian's professional smile, but it felt real and welcoming in a way that Sebastian's smiles never did.

'I think it is,' she replied, smiling back at him, until she felt like the Cheshire Cat, inexplicably unable to stop smiling. He was the first person she had met since she arrived at Misterley who had seemed genuinely pleased to meet her. For Caroline and her family, Alice's presence seemed largely an inconvenience and none of the other garden staff or the tea-room staff had even seemed to notice her.

'I'm Alice,' she said.

'I know who you are. I've seen you before. Saw you in the garden with a bloke, yesterday. Shame about those flowers, mind.'

So he had seen her with Sebastian? 'I... Lilies set off my asthma. I couldn't...' she began.

'It's all right,' he said kindly. 'It's none of my business. Here, I'll tell you what, as you couldn't keep them lilies…' he pulled a pair of secateurs out of his pocket and snipped off a white rose flower from the bush growing beside him. 'A proper Yorkshire rose for you.'

She sniffed it appreciatively, it was heavily scented and rich with honey. 'Thank you!' she whispered, touched by his kindness, finding that the smile was spreading unbidden across her face again.

'No bother. I'm Tom, by the way. Tom Gannon.'

'Nice to meet you, Tom,' she said, holding the rose gently between her fingers as she made her way to the house.

Alice passed through the stable yard at the back of the house which hadn't housed any horses for a very long time. Some builders were at work on Caroline's big project, a wedding venue to be constructed in what had once been one of the stables; she could hear them clattering and banging as well as their radio echoing round the walls of the brick quadrangle, but once she stepped through the door into Misterley Manor, it was like entering another world. Silent save for the ticking of the old grandfather clock at the end of the corridor, shafts of light from the high mullion windows caught fragments of dust floating in mid-air and the musty, damp-smelling corridor with its panelled walls and stone floors took her straight into the heart of the West Wing which Gilbert Fox-Travers had designed and built for Caroline's ancestors.

The West Wing had two principal rooms downstairs, the towering Octagon Library and the long gallery of the Painted Hall which had been designed by Fox-Travers one hundred years ago for the private enjoyment of Sir Edward Lattimore who took great pleasure in a large collection of rather sensuous scantily clad Pre-Raphaelite ladies, including some of Fox-Travers's own works. In the years after Sir Edward's death Lady Isobel, his widow, had often liked to open the building for her charitable functions, but what the members of the Ladies' Association for Moral Welfare must have thought of the jewels in Sir Edward's collection - the notoriously erotic Fox-Travers's Arthurian scenes - was never recorded. Or perhaps that was *why* so many of the ladies had come to visit the gallery.

These days the walls of the Painted Hall were sadly depleted of anything except paint. There were gaps where pictures had once hung, square patches of unfaded paint that were all that was left of the paintings that had once hung there; one-by-one they had been sold to maintain the fabric of the house in recent years. Now the Fox-Travers paintings were amongst the very few that remained, and Caroline had already told Alice that when the estate faced the next lot of death duties on the death of her father, it would be the Fox-Travers Arthurian scenes that would have to pay them.

Alice usually took a small diversion to look at the pictures every morning on her way in to work, feeling a thrill of the connection with the artist who had painted them. *Waiting to receive King Arthur's Sword* was the earliest; a study of The Lady of the Lake, whose flowing, wet robes clung to her in the most revealing of ways, then *The Lady of Shalott* depicted the Lady gazing dreamily into a mirror at an image of Sir Lancelot riding by which looked modest enough, until you looked more closely at the way the Lady's hand disappeared under her skirts. Suddenly the painted image of Lancelot began to make her think of the man she had just met in the garden, with his broad shoulders and dark brown hair. Most notorious of all was *Morgan Le Faye pleads with King Arthur*. If you looked with a knowing eye at the suppliant figure of Morgan kneeling in front of King Arthur, and how her head was positioned, this picture was very suggestive indeed, without showing a single inch of naked flesh. It was Alice's favourite; she told herself that it was Fox-Travers's use of colour in the scene that made it so attractive to her.

From the Painted Hall, Alice stepped into the Octagon Library with the rich, dark reds of the furniture and the carpets, the high arched roof supported by massive wooden beams and shelves and shelves of leather-bound books, all around the octagonal walls of the room. Alice opened the window on the garden side of the room and the fresh air rushed in, the peaty scent of the moors mingling with the scent of old books and wood polish inside the library. She placed the little white rose carefully on the table beside where she worked. Really, she shouldn't have brought it in here... but it was so pretty, it seemed a shame to leave it outside. Her Yorkshire rose, she thought with a smile. Better than all the pre-packaged-plastic lilies in London.

There was a door into the old estate office from which Caroline ran her empire leading directly from the library, a small arched oak door studded with black nails, and this was the door on which Alice knocked.

'Come in.' Caroline's voice was as always crisp, but sometimes, like this morning, Alice could detect a note of weariness. No matter how early Alice arrived at the house, Caroline always seemed to be at her desk.

'I wonder if you could open the cupboard?' Alice said, tentatively. She always feared that she was disturbing Caroline unnecessarily, but Caroline was hesitant to let the key out of her sight and lend it to Alice. She seemed unwilling to let go of anything important.

'Yes, of course. I'll come and open it for you.' She took the key out of the drawer of her desk and they walked back into the library together. 'So, how is the work going?' Caroline asked as she bent down to fit the key into the lock.

'So far there's a lot of important information about the building work and Fox-Travers's design process, and a lot about poetry. Lady Isobel spends most of her time quoting Tennyson.'

'And what about the great mystery? Anything about what happened to Fox-Travers?'

'Oh, I'm not too concerned about the mystery,' Alice said, trying to convince herself as much as Caroline. 'It would be interesting, of course, to know what happened. It's odd, I had expected most of the letters to be between Sir Edward and Fox-Travers, as it was his house that Fox-Travers was designing, but most of them seem to be in Lady Isobel's handwriting. She seems to have led many of the design decisions.' She placed the letters carefully on the huge central table, Lady Isobel's untidy handwriting on the left-hand pile of letters contrasting with Fox-Travers elegant copperplate on the right-hand pile.

'Ah! The "Disdainful Dowager" herself!' Caroline glanced up at the portrait of an elderly and rather formidable looking woman in middle-age that hung above the library fireplace. Oddly for such a stern looking woman, in her hand she held a little white rose, not

———

entirely unlike the one that Tom had given her. Alice looked from the rose in the portrait to the rose on her desk as Caroline continued: 'She was a woman ahead of her time. Quite a forceful character in her later years, from what Daddy tells me. Passionate about this house but didn't suffer fools gladly.' It seemed that Caroline resembled her ancestor in temperament, as well as the physical resemblance that was so striking when Alice looked at Caroline standing in front of Lady Isobel's portrait.

'I've seen nothing yet that would explain why Fox-Travers disappeared,' Alice said.

'My ex-husband had a theory about him getting one of the household into trouble – one of the maids perhaps – and being dispatched in disgrace by Lady Isobel,' said Caroline.

'Was your ex-husband very interested in Fox-Travers then?' Alice asked.

'Yes. It's how we met, after all, when he asked to look at the house. He was particularly interested in the house because he's got family connections to Misterley – not close enough that marrying him was an issue, of course, though from the way Daddy carried on you'd think we were practically brother and sister. My ex-husband badgered us for years to get the solicitor to open those letters early so he could read them, but Daddy wouldn't dream of allowing it – especially at my husband's request. Daddy saw through him from the first. Daddy said we shouldn't let him anywhere near those letters, and since we divorced it has become even more important. That's why Daddy was prepared to allow you to study them first – because you have absolutely no connections to my ex-husband.'

'No, no of course. Am I likely to meet him?' The last thing she wanted was an enthusiastic amateur historian trying to worm his way in to see the letters.

'I'm sure you will. He comes to see Emily every other week. He's due this evening, so keep a close eye on those letters. He is not to be allowed to see them; Daddy has been adamant about that. Don't let them out of your sight even for a minute when he's around.'

'What does your ex-husband look like?' Alice asked, conscious that if she should keep an eye open for him she should know who she was looking for.

'Duncan? He's an ugly little man with glasses that are far too large for his face. Oily grey hair and a stupid beard. You can't miss him.'

'Duncan?' Suddenly, horrifically she recognised the description and the pieces of the puzzle began to fall in to place. 'Not Duncan Russell surely? *Professor* Russell from Ormsborough University?'

'Oh, you've probably come across him professionally, haven't you? At conferences and such like.'

You could say that, thought Alice.

Duncan Russell was the professor she had asked to supervise her PhD. He was the leading British expert on Fox-Travers, based at Ormsborough University, thirty miles away from Misterley over the moors. But he hadn't thought her PhD proposal was worth more than a standard rejection letter. Because of his swift and thoughtless rejection, she privately suspected that Duncan Russell might be a bit of a shit. She wouldn't dream of saying that to Caroline though.

'Yes, I've come across Professor Russell,' she said, as politely as she could.

'Between you and I, he's a bit of a shit,' said Caroline.

Chapter 4

Builders' Bums.

Caroline had been at her desk for nine hours today already. By three-thirty she felt that she had earned a cup of tea and a piece of chocolate cake from the garden tea room, and on a whim Caroline had invited Alice to join her. She still looked as if she needed cheering up. They ordered tea and cake from Sarah, who ran the Garden Tea Room and took a seat at one of the comfortable sofa tables. Caroline let herself sink back into the cushions. However, within two minutes Alice had already launched into one of her painstaking descriptions of Fox-Travers' use of native hardwoods for constructing furniture and Caroline began to regret her offer of tea and sympathy. She changed the subject abruptly.

'How are things going with your young man?' she asked, realising even as she said it that she sounded like Aunty Marjorie. After a decade practically locked in this house with her elderly and eccentric father, and her even more eccentric aunt, she was starting to talk like one of them. Give her another year and she'd be exclaiming "Good gracious!" in a haughty tone like her father did whenever she didn't get her own way, or constantly asking people if they had seen her walking stick, like Aunty Marjorie. Really, Marjorie spent more time wandering around the house looking for her lost walking stick than she did *using* the thing. It was amazing that her hip didn't seem to be getting any worse.

'Sebastian's arriving tomorrow, after his meetings in Edinburgh, to take me to that job interview,' Alice said in a martyred tone.

'You're not going to go, are you? You're not going to let him tell you what to do?'

'I don't know,' she said with a feeble shrug of her shoulders. 'I keep thinking I've made up my mind, and then...'

Caroline wondered if it was legal to shake a visiting PhD student into some semblance of common sense and concluded that probably it wasn't.

They were interrupted by the door of the tea room swinging open and in came Emily, her daughter, and Marjorie, her aunt. They made an odd, but not infrequent double act.

Emily, at seventeen, was striking rather than beautiful. Whenever Emily entered a room, heads would turn. She had long, glossy brown hair, deep blue eyes and a slightly knowing smile. She must have just got back from college as she was still wearing her uniform - well, some of it - her tie and blazer had already been removed, her collar was unbuttoned, and her sleeves rolled up. Marjorie, Sir Henry's younger sister, was nearly 60 years older than Emily with short cropped grey hair, and today she had chosen the most enormous pair of green hooped earrings with a floor-length shocking pink satin skirt and a yellow t-shirt. Although Emily did not share Marjorie's taste for huge earrings, she did have several different piercings of her own, most of which had to be removed to meet the uniform requirements of her sixth-form college. When Caroline looked at her daughter she could instantly see the family resemblance between Emily and her flamboyant great aunt Marjorie. It was harder to see much of herself in her garrulous, untidy daughter.

'Mum, we need the key!' Emily said. 'I forgot mine this morning; must be in my jeans pocket from last night. Marjorie's lost hers again.'

Sarah, the tea room manager, was unloading the tray with the tea and cake for Alice and Caroline.

'Can it wait until I finish my tea?' Caroline asked.

'Not if you want me to finish my art project before Christmas,' said Emily, breaking off a sly chunk from her mum's chocolate cake. Caroline pretended not to notice; she was too tired to start yet another fight with her daughter right now. Before she had even touched her pot of tea Sarah had come back into the tea room and approached the table.

'Caroline, I'm sorry, but the gas has gone off again,' said Sarah. Caroline felt a surge of stress in the pit of her stomach. Suddenly the chocolate cake didn't look quite so appetising.

'Oh, those bloody builders! I'll get the key after I've sorted them out. I *told* Daddy we should have got in that firm from Newcastle, Goldings they were called. Specialist conservation builders, not a local shower like this lot. But Daddy wouldn't have it,' she said to Alice, feeling the need to explain why she had to employ the world's most incompetent builders. 'Don't worry, Sarah, I'll go and have a word with them, see what's going on.'

She dragged her aching body up from the table, feeling like an old woman as she headed across the courtyard to the stable block, where the builders were looking into a drain with puzzled expressions, which was never a good sign. The builders didn't like her. She knew that they called her "Lady Muck" behind her back and they thought she interfered too much – but she had to. They didn't understand the demands of working with a listed building like this, even in the stable block. For the four-hundredth time this week she wished they had employed Goldings.

'The gas has gone off in the tea-rooms. Would that be anything to do with you?' she said brusquely.

'No, love, we're doing nowt with the gas today,' said Derek, the foreman, without looking up from the drain. He was showing an unpleasant amount of "builders' bum". 'Unless... Mikey?' he yelled over his shoulder. 'You've not turned the gas off, have you Mikey?'

'Yeah,' a young lad from the corner spoke up. 'Dazza said to. Said you needed it off.'

'Well, Dazza's a stupid c… a stupid man, isn't he?' The foreman curbed his tongue knowingly in Caroline's presence. 'Go and put it back on again.'

'I'll have to go back inside the house then, won't I? Give us the keys?'

'Guess you will. Get on with it!' There was some muttering from the foreman as, with a swagger, the young lad picked up the keys from his boss. She wasn't sure that she was entirely happy about the foreman handing the house keys over to him like that, but today she was too tired to try and fight that battle. It wasn't as if there was anything much left in the house to steal these days.

She got back to the tearoom to find that Emily had eaten the entire piece of chocolate cake and that Marjorie was drinking her pot of tea. She sighed as Mikey strolled past the tea room window, his defined muscles drawing the attention of several excited lady pensioners sitting near the window – and Emily who gazed at him appreciatively.

'I like having the builders around. Bit more exciting than the old farts who come to the garden centre,' Emily said cheerfully, watching him go past.

'As an "old fart" myself, I resent that!' said Marjorie.

'You might be old, but you're not a fart, Aunty! That's Mikey, he used to go to our college last year. Left to be an apprentice. He's mint.'

'Emily, he's a builder!' Caroline said.

'I know he's a builder, but there's nothing wrong with that, is there?' Emily said, bristling. 'I like him.'

'There's nothing wrong with the builders, of course, but I wouldn't exactly want to invite them to dinner!' Caroline said, with a little laugh. Emily was about to say something, she had her mouth open to speak, but before she had a chance Marjorie cut in hurriedly.

'Some of the finest young men I ever met were manual

labourers,' Marjorie said. 'Nicky who I met in New Zealand... now there was a man who knew what to do with his hands... And Paulo, dear, dear Paulo...' she sighed.

'He reminds me of Tom, you know, Tom who works in the gardens? Phwoar!' Emily rolled her eyes upwards. 'Have you met Tom yet, Alice?' she asked with a wink. 'I used to have a crush on Tom when he split up from his wife,' she continued with relish. 'He's gorgeous AND he gave you a rose. He's been single for a while now, you know. He's about the right age for you – you're about thirty, aren't you? – are you single, Alice?'

'I'm 24 and I'm in a relationship!' Alice flushed visibly under Emily's sharp gaze. 'So, I'm not interested in Tom the gardener – or anyone else for that matter.'

'Emily, I don't think -' Caroline began, before Emily had a chance to ask Alice any more awkward questions about her love life, but Marjorie talked over her.

'Such a shame, Alice, my dear. You look peaky right now and your aura is very murky. A roll in the hay with a nice young gardener might bring some colour to your cheeks! I can thoroughly recommend it as a bit of a pick-me-up. Tom is a fine-looking young man and if I were a younger woman...'

'Aunty Marjorie! You can't say that!' Emily said with all the scorn that a teenager is capable of.

'Why not, Emily?' said Marjorie, raising her carefully plucked and dyed black eyebrows.

'Because you're -'

'Seventy-seven? That makes me elderly, not dead, dear. I can still appreciate a nice bum when I see one!'

'And Tom does have a very nice –' Emily began.

'That will do, Emily!' Oh Lord, Caroline knew she sounded like her father again and Emily rolled her eyes. For once Caroline couldn't blame her.

'Give us your keys, then, Mum, and we'll go and let ourselves in. You finish your cup of tea. I'll bring the key back later.'

It was a tempting offer and it was kind of Emily to notice that she hadn't managed to have anything to drink yet. She should have gone to get the house keys from her desk herself; she didn't entirely trust the pair of them not to lose the keys again, but it would be nice to have some tea at last, even if all the chocolate cake had been eaten. She handed over her own house key to Emily.

'Are you staying here, Marjorie?' Emily asked.

'I'll come along with you. I'd like to see if I can catch a better glimpse of that attractive young builder you're so keen on,' she said, and the sound of their good-natured bickering could be heard all the way along the corridor, growing fainter as they went towards the office.

Caroline lifted the tea pot to pour herself the long-awaited cup of tea only to find that it was empty. Marjorie had drunk the lot.

'Here, there's some left in my pot,' Alice said, pouring her a stone cold, stewed cup of tea.

Caroline looked down at the unappetising cup of tea. It summed up her life really.

Chapter 5

Secret Places.

Sixteen more pages in Lady Isobel's handwriting about stone carvings and Tennyson and a brusque one-page reply from Fox-Travers about stonemasons. Alice sighed. These letters weren't proving to be the insight into Fox-Travers' life and work that she had hoped for. Here, for example, three pages from Lady Isobel about how she thought that section LIX of Tennyson's *In Memoriam* was particularly suitable reading for a Sunday and she hoped that Fox-Travers would also find that it inspired his sabbath thoughts and so on, and so on, and so on, pompous religious musings from the Disdainful Dowager and curt replies from Gilbert Fox-Travers. She wondered what the notorious "bad-boy" of the arts and crafts movement had made of Lady Isobel's pious musings – she was disappointed that his replies weren't more illuminating. Fox-Travers had been renowned for his sharp tongue and here he was being uncharacteristically polite. But she was a client – a wealthy client - so he probably couldn't afford to tell her what he must have *actually* thought about her choice of religious verse. There were no extant diaries of Fox-Travers for this period – perhaps she should look harder at the collected volume of letters that Duncan Russell had published about ten years ago, see if there were any clues that she had previously overlooked there, and then she could always go back to the archives at Cambridge where most of Fox-Travers' papers were kept; there might be more information there.

It wasn't what she had been hoping for. Nothing to indicate what had happened to him or where he had gone, the burning questions that she had hoped to answer. At some point, she supposed she should read some of the Tennyson poetry herself, to find out what Lady Isobel was going on about, but reading worthy Victorian religious verse wasn't her idea of an afternoon well spent, and it wasn't Lady Isobel's state of mind she was interested in. She sighed, lined up the camera and took a photograph of the letter, to be stored in a digital archive for her University. The University had paid Caroline for the privilege and they were paying Alice for the work, so she couldn't neglect the photographic element of her work, boring though it was.

Today she was finding it hard to concentrate on anything with the knowledge that by tomorrow she had to make up her mind about that job interview. She loved Sebastian – of *course* she loved Sebastian – at least she *thought* she loved Sebastian… But what if she didn't? I mean, it wasn't like it once had been with him. When they had first met, they had shared everything with each other; every moment of every day, every thought, every night, and now... sometimes she had thoughts and feelings that she knew he wouldn't understand. He would have done, back then, but now if it didn't have a financial value attached to it, Sebastian didn't care. Once their relationship had been about sharing, now it all seemed to be about giving and taking. If she went back with Sebastian and she got the job with his firm that would be the end of the PhD, and if she chose the PhD that would be the end of life with Sebastian.

It was all very well for Caroline to tell her not to do what a man told her to, but Caroline had the security of a stately home to fall back on, and Alice didn't have enough money even for the deposit on a rental property; she had used all her mother's legacy to fund the PhD. She didn't want to be dependent on Sebastian's superior earning power, but there it was; in a depressingly old-fashioned scenario she had become dependent on him. He had a good job in the city and a nice apartment. She had a tiny bedsit over a chip-shop in Rawscar for four months and then she would be homeless without Sebastian.

She was scared.

She sighed. She would have to wait for Sebastian to get here tomorrow and hope that she could persuade him to see it her way, to let her carry on with things as they were. Either of the other alternatives was unthinkable right now. She stretched her cramped shoulders and turned over a page of the letters.

It was then that she heard a strange noise. A scratching, scuffling noise that seemed to be coming from the floor beside Caroline's office door. There was something moving under the floor – no, not under the floor she realised as she crept closer, but behind the wall! Her first thought was of ghosts, then mice or spiders, or... it could be a rat! Alice's heart was thumping with terror at the thought of encountering a rat in the library – or anywhere else. Moving as quietly as she could, so that the rat wouldn't know she was there and leap out at her, she crept over to Caroline's office door, but Caroline wasn't there. Perhaps she had gone back to see the builders. The door creaked loudly as she closed it and she flinched – but the sound seemed to have scared the rats; they had fallen silent.

So, noise would drive them away, would it? In that case... She started stamping loudly round the floor near the bookcase where the noises had been coming, until she heard a giggle. An unmistakeably female giggle. It sounded like Emily. But where was she?

'Emily?' she asked loudly, and to Alice's amazement, one of the bookcases moved. It moved outwards from the wall as if swinging on a hinge, and in the gap that opened there was Emily's face, peering out from behind a secret door that Alice hadn't known existed.

'Oh! Hi Alice!' she said nonchalantly, as if appearing from a secret doorway in a bookcase was quite a normal thing to be doing. 'I enjoyed your dancing!'

'Oh... thanks...' she said as if stomping around the floor after imaginary rats was also quite a normal thing to be doing. 'What are you doing in the bookcase, Emily? I thought there was a rat!'

'It's Sir Edward's secret room - didn't you know about it?' Emily stepped out of the door, her dark hair loose on her shoulders and her uniform shirt now untucked from her skirt and done up on the wrong button holes. 'He used it to hide from the "plebs" and spy on them when they came to visit the house. Dad reckons he used it for other things too,' she giggled, 'and not many of them had anything to do with literature!'

'Oh, so that's where the secret room is! I thought it was part of the East Wing. Can I see?' The information about the secret room that was out in the public domain was sketchy, to say the least – the Lattimore family had never been very keen to share their secrets with the world outside Misterley Manor.

'Well, I was busy doing some... revising... I was totally revising. I'd forgotten you'd be in here, you see. If you could give me a couple of minutes to... tidy up my books... While you... you could go into the garden and...' Emily had gone scarlet, and there was a movement in the room behind her.

'Your books?' Alice asked, suddenly suspicious.

'Oh. Look, I... it wasn't... You won't tell my mum, will you?' It would appear that, like her renowned ancestor, Emily's pursuits this afternoon had very little to do with literature.

Emily opened the door wider, and behind her stood next to it stood the builder who had walked past them this afternoon. Alice might not have recognised his face, but she certainly remembered his muscles.

'Auright,' he grunted, looking down at the floor.

'Mikey was going to get back to work, weren't you Mikey?' Emily said. 'Now you've had your... um, your tea break.'

There was no sign of any tea mug, flask or take away cup which might have contained any tea.

'Yeah. Later, bae.'

'You're one of the builders?' Alice asked.

'Apprentice.'

Mikey didn't seem to be a master of eloquence, but it was

probably not his conversational skills that had attracted Emily, who picked up his discarded high-vis jacket and hard hat from the floor and handed them back to him.

'Yes, he's very interested in architecture, so I wanted to show him the secret room,' Emily said brightly. 'I'll see you later, Mikey?' she asked, as he headed back towards the back door.

'So, Mikey was helping you to revise?' Alice asked Emily.

'We weren't doing anything, honestly. Well, nothing much... you know... nothing serious. Nothing Mum needs to worry about. We weren't... we haven't... Please don't tell her, Alice! She'll think Mikey isn't good enough for me, but she's totally wrong, you know?'

'So, are the two of you together?'

'We've been in a relationship for about a month now. I've tried to tell Mum, but she just doesn't want to know. Every time I try and bring it up she goes all funny and tells me how she hates the builders. She won't listen!'

'Would you like me to try and tell her? Before *she* finds you in the secret room with him some time?'

Emily's eyes widened with horror. 'Shizz no! I think I'll ask Dad to do it. Then she can take it all out on him, not me.'

'So your father knows?'

'Yes, but he's the only one. Apart from you now. And Aunty Marjorie, of course. And Chelsea from the tea rooms, she's my bestie. And Sarah probably knows if Chelsea knows. And I don't know if Mikey's told anyone, of course. Possibly some of the builders?'

'So most of the people who work at Misterley know but your mum doesn't?'

'When you put it like that...'

'You've got to tell her, Emily!'

'I've tried! Honestly, I've tried, but she just changes the subject or doesn't listen. I tried to tell her in the tea rooms there, but Aunty Marjorie just started going on about Paulo again. And she wouldn't have listened anyway, she never does.'

She turned her huge blue eyes on Alice. Blue eyes and dark hair were a Lattimore trait; you could see the same piercing blue eyes in the portrait of Sir Edward Lattimore that hung in the library. The resemblance between Emily and her great-grandfather was unmistakable, but the blue eyes must have skipped Caroline's generation, Caroline's eyes were an unremarkable shade of brown.

'Mum thinks she can tell me what to do all the time, but she can't,' she said, sounding stroppy. 'I'm nearly 18. I don't want to end up like her, doing whatever Grandad Henry says. She lets him boss her around. I want to make my own decisions and live my own life.'

'I guess I can understand that,' said Alice, thinking of Sebastian.

'Mum says that this house is *a responsibility as well as a privilege and if we let it go then we're letting down future generations.*' She did a wildly inaccurate but wicked impression of her mother. 'That's why she works so much,' she said, rebuttoning her shirt as she spoke. 'She doesn't want to let down the future generations – but you know, I'm the future generation and I don't care. It's only Grandad who gives a shizz about this old place.'

'Really?' Alice sat down on one of the grand library chairs. It still felt wrong to be using furniture like this, rooms that would be roped off and furniture that would have "do not touch" signs in any other stately home.

'She says she's the boss round here, but if you ask me, she's scared of him.' Emily sat down in one of the smaller chairs beside Alice. 'Hell, this place is falling to bits! At the moment we haven't got even a few thousand to fix the holes in the East Wing roof. You should see it when it rains; Mum has to go running with buckets.'

'So why is she paying for work on the stable block, then, not fixing the roof?' Alice asked.

'It's her big plan. It's going be a wedding reception venue, try and make it a proper business because there's lots of money in weddings. It's running behind though. That's why she's so stressed, you know. If it doesn't work...' she mimed a throat cutting motion, '…we're done.'

'I didn't realise she was stressed. I thought she was...' she struggled to find a polite way to describe Caroline's uptight nature.

'High maintenance?' Emily suggested, standing up again as she tidied her hair, using the glossy wood of one of the polished bookcases as a kind of impromptu mirror, tying it back up into a bun with the pony tail band that she was wearing round her wrist. 'I don't ever want to be like her. I want a life of my own, not some stinking old house to run. It's a curse, you know, this place, that's what Mum calls it sometimes.' She spoke vehemently now. 'I mean, have you ever seen my mother smile? Even once? I don't want all this, I don't want my life to be like hers.'

'But it's such an amazing place!' Alice said.

'You don't know half of it. Has she shown you the East Wing yet?'

'Not yet. She wants to wait until Sir Henry has got used to the idea of me being here before she lets me see the family parts of the house.'

'That's rubbish. She doesn't want you to see the East Wing 'cos we shut it up five or six years ago and it's like, half derelict now. She had to choose – East Wing or West Wing and cos we sometimes show people round the West Wing, that's what she chose. One by one she's had to stop heating the rooms cos she can't afford it. There's only Grandad's rooms that get proper heating– and the kitchen from the AGA. You're lucky it's only September – it's freezing by November and we don't get warm until May.'

'I didn't realise.'

'It ruins everything, this place, you know? If Mum and Dad hadn't argued about what to do with Misterley Manor they'd probably still be married. It wasn't an affair or anything that made them split up, it was this house. He thought we should open it to the public. She said we couldn't because Grandad didn't want to. He thought we should work with National Heritage, she said we couldn't because Grandad didn't want to. He thought we should pay for a decent car park... you get the idea?' she said with a shake of the head. 'Woah! You should have heard the fights they had! Grandad said that it's *his* house and he didn't want people poking about in it. He's weird like that. Didn't want *you* coming to work here, you know; he doesn't like strangers in the house. Took Mum months to persuade him.'

Four months, Alice realised. Four months Caroline had kept her waiting for a reply from her father. The image he had in her mind of the skeletal old man became even more sinister; a shotgun laid across his wasted knees, ready to threaten hordes of eager visitors banging on the doors trying to look at his world-renowned interiors. "Get out of my house, you thieving plebs!" the Sir Henry of her imagination would snarl at the hordes of enthusiastic visitors with their guide books and ice-creams.

'Well, I know what I'm going to do when it's mine,' Emily continued, putting her feet up on the huge carved library table like she owned the place, which essentially, of course, she did.

'I'm going to sell it, for like, millions of pounds – though God knows who'd want it. I'll live in London and never worry about holes in the roof!'

'You hate it that much?'

'Yeah. Mum goes on about how it's a responsibility but why does it have to be *my* responsibility? It's such a load of crap. All my friends seem to think I must be dead rich you know, 'cos I live here, but we've got no money for anything. Mum couldn't even afford to pay for me to go on an art trip to London last year with college, I had to ask Dad in the end. Hell, I've just remembered, Dad's going to be here soon, I'm going over to his tonight. He's going to be fuming if

I'm not ready. Do I look OK now?'

By that, Alice supposed she meant *Can you still tell that I've been messing about with one of the builders?* Alice looked her up and down.

'You look fine.'

'Thanks Alice!' And away she went.

Alice turned her attention to the secret room. She had read about it in her research, but all the descriptions in the public domain were vague and had led her to think that it was somewhere in the East Wing. Caroline had never mentioned it to her. Now it stood wide open – surely Caroline wouldn't mind if she had a look inside?

Behind the bookcase was a perfectly round room concealed within a tower that she had believed to be purely ornamental when she had seen it from outside. High trefoil shaped windows shed a dim light that was utterly impractical for reading, and around the walls ran a circular crimson velvet seat, enticingly wide and luxurious; perfect for reclining on the deep cushions. It could have been designed for curling up with a novel, but then again, the seat was more than big enough for two people to lie down in comfort. She wondered who Fox-Travers had designed it for. Was it for Sir Edward and his wife? Or was it one of Fox-Travers' own fantasies?

Alice sat down, and the seat was as soft as it looked, the dim light enticing her to recline on those cushions; a secret place of shadowy desires created by Fox-Travers himself. She stretched out her arms and felt the richness of the velvet beneath her trailing fingertips, closing her eyes for a moment. She imagined Gilbert Fox-Travers standing in the doorway, his dark hair tousled by the wind, his famously wicked dark brown eyes burning into hers, as, closing the door behind him, he loosened his collar and said to her -

'Hi there, Alice, I'm looking for Caroline?'

She snapped her eyes open, to find Tom standing there, his dark hair tousled by the wind and his dark eyes burning into hers.

———

Chapter 6

Duncan's Academic Credentials.

Tom Gannon had spread mud from his work-boots all through the library again.

'How can I help you, Tom?' Caroline asked, as he crossed the library towards her office, every footstep another cleaning job, but she didn't mind cleaning up after Tom.

'I came to tell you we'll have to close off the rock garden tomorrow. Some branches to trim off the trees before the autumn winds start.' Tom had a warm, local accent which Caroline had always found rather attractive – among other things about Tom which were undeniably attractive. There was something about Tom which, despite the fact that he was one of the least outgoing members of her staff at Misterley, always seemed to draw female attention towards him. She had seen him work his quiet magic on woman after woman, all the while totally unaware of the effect that his good looks and thoughtful nature were having on those around him. There was also something that made her think whatever his dark eyes promised his muscular gardener's body could very competently deliver. If she had been twenty years younger...

'Yes, very well, thank you Tom,' Caroline said, shuffling a pile of papers, aware once again that she sounded increasingly like Marjorie. A flustered Marjorie. 'I hope you hadn't been waiting too long for me?' she added.

'I've been talking to Alice,' he said, and Caroline realised that Alice had come out of the secret room behind him and she looked as flustered as Caroline felt. 'I'll get back to work, then. Nice to see you again, Alice.'

When he said her name, it sounded like a caress. No wonder Alice was flustered.

'Nice to see you, Tom,' she said breathlessly.

Both women watched him carefully as he crossed the library, leaving more muddy footprints behind him, and went out through the garden door, which thumped shut behind him. As soon as he was out of the room, Caroline's eyes narrowed.

'Alice, where were you doing in there?'

'I went into the secret room to have a look. Emily... erm, Emily showed me it just now... she was... she was doing homework in there.'

She was stuttering and embarrassed. Something had been going on; what was Alice hiding from her?

'Tom didn't try anything on with you, did he?' she asked, suspiciously.

'No! We didn't even say more than five words to each other, that's all.'

Caroline knew she was being ridiculous. Alice was so shy and self-effacing, she wasn't at all the type for carrying on with the gardener in "Sir Edward's secret shag-pad" as That Man had always referred to it – usually just before he took her hand and pulled her into the little room with him... And thinking of her ex-husband...

'Where were the letters while you and Tom were getting to know each other in the secret room?'

'Oh, they were over there, on the table with the camera, but they were quite safe, I promise -'

'I don't want those letters left, even for a single minute. I've told you that. My ex-husband is due to pick up Emily any time now, if Marjorie had let him in, he could have been in here and you wouldn't have known. Remember, your university is paying for access to these letters – you don't want to just give free access to a rival academic, do you? Please remember to be more careful in future. Otherwise we might have to review the arrangements for your study.'

A look of total panic crossed Alice's face. 'Yes, of course I will. I didn't think, I'm sorry Caroline. But nothing happened -'

'Well, you make sure nothing *does* happen.' Caroline snapped as the door into the library opened, as if fulfilling her prophecy, and her ex-husband walked into the room. 'What a surprise, you're early. I suppose Marjorie let you in?'

'Yes, she did. And I'm not early, Emily's late.' Caroline made a suppressed huffing noise. Nothing, it appeared, was *ever* his fault – it had been like that when they were married, and it was the same now.

'This is Alice Goudge, the researcher from University College Camden. I believe I told you about her. Alice, this is my ex-husband.'

They shook hands, awkwardly.

'I don't believe we've met,' he said.

'We have in fact,' Alice said. 'Three times. Twice at conferences, and once at the Art History Society annual dinner.' Her tone of voice was positively arctic. At least Caroline didn't have to worry about her husband and the researcher becoming too friendly over a mutual love of Fox-Travers, it would appear. 'And of course, you'll remember my enquiry about my PhD – or maybe you won't.'

There was something going on there that Caroline wasn't aware of. Surely Alice was firmly based down in Camden and had nothing to do with her ex-husband's academic department? Wasn't that the whole point of allowing her coming here, that she and her department had no connection whatsoever to him?

'And how are you finding the letters? Lots of useful information?' He gestured at the pile of letters lying before him on the table. An awkward silence fell as Duncan looked up at Alice, who was significantly taller than he was, Alice looked at Caroline, and Caroline looked pointedly down at the letters.

'Absolutely,' said Alice in a non-committal voice as she

carefully placed a brown cardboard folder over the top of the letters, obscuring anything from Duncan's view much to Caroline's relief.

'Emily's on her way. She's getting her things together.' Caroline changed the subject.

'I've told you, she doesn't need to bother. She's got plenty of things at my house,' Duncan said.

'I prefer her to have her *own* things,' Caroline snapped back.

'They *are* her things, Caroline,' Duncan replied, equally snappy. 'I'm not asking her to wear *my* underwear!'

'I should hope not. Though I wouldn't put it past you.' She had never liked his untidy habits; she had tried to cure him of them for all the years they were married, but he remained obdurately untidy.

'Enough, Caroline,' he said, in the same superior tone of voice he had always used to try and end their arguments over the future of Misterley Manor. She hated it then and she hated it now. He turned away from her to speak to Alice. 'So, Alice, how are you finding it working here? My academic credentials weren't good enough for my ex-wife and her father, it would seem, to trust me to work on their precious letters.' Although he purported to be speaking to Alice, still his eyes were fixed on Caroline, waiting for her to respond, goading her with his sarcastic tone. Well, two could play at that game and she and Duncan were old sparring partners.

'That has nothing to do with your academic credentials and you know it; it's because you interfere.' Caroline said. 'My father doesn't want you in this house, meddling with things. Don't you remember how upset he got when you started searching through his old papers without asking him? He's old and he's frail, I can't upset him by putting him through all that, every day. I must put him first, as you are well aware. Alice, I'm pleased to say, is very responsible and does exactly as I have asked her to.' If she chose to ignore visiting lovers bringing lilies and dalliances with attractive gardeners in secret rooms – but she didn't have to mention any of that to him.

——

'Your father is a confused, selfish old man who doesn't want to share what he has with anybody else. But there's no point in going over old ground, you're never going to change my mind and I'm never going to change yours, and in the meanwhile Misterley Manor continues to decay -'

'Decay? We've just invested thousands into the new wedding venue!'

'Yes, well, good luck with that. How many months behind is the project already?'

She didn't have to answer that. She wasn't going to answer that. She wasn't going to let him get to her. 'That is beside the point!'

'Oh no, it's not, and you know it. You can't do all this on your own. The cracks are starting to show, Caroline, and not just the cracks in the East Wing Roof.'

'I don't know what you mean!'

'Oh, come on, Caroline, Emily told me that there's a huge crack in the roof now. You've got to do something, you've got to stop the rot!'

She would not have Duncan lecturing her in front of Alice.

'I think I'll wait outside in the garden,' Alice suggested awkwardly, making for the door.

'No, don't,' Caroline said. 'Look, here's Emily, so Duncan is just leaving.'

'Daddy, there you are!' Emily came flouncing into the room, trailing a suitcase behind her. Caroline instantly winced at the sound of the heavy plastic wheels dragging on the precious old oak floor of the library. 'Let's get going, Daddy. I was thinking, maybe I could meet up with some friends tonight? Or even maybe just... one friend...? You wouldn't mind, would you, Dad?'

'It's fine by me. Can't see a problem with that, can you, Caroline?'

They were both looking at her as if there was some kind of

hidden agenda here. Duncan was up to something, it was obvious. What was he trying to get her to agree with? There was definitely something he wasn't telling her. Well, she wasn't going to make it any easier for him.

'I don't want Emily going out on a college night. She's still only seventeen and that's my rule, as you well know -' Bullseye. She could see her ex-husband swelling up with irritation.

'Well, Caroline, you don't get to tell her who she can meet and what she can do when she is under *my* roof,' said Duncan. 'My word counts for nothing here, so why should yours have any validity in my house? You can meet up with whoever you like, Emily. *I* trust you. You're more than old enough to make your own decisions.'

Ohh, so he didn't like that! Good. Served him right. In reality she knew she couldn't say or do anything that would change Duncan's mind about whatever it was he was plotting with Emily, but she could make him feel as bad about it as she possibly could.

'Yeah, Mum!' mouthed Emily with a grin, behind her father's back.

'Emily!'

'Whatever. Come on Dad, let's go.'

She watched the pair of them leave the library companionably, side by side. It was all gradually slipping away from her. Her daughter paid no attention to anything she said, her ex-husband seemed determined to fight her at every turn, her father was losing his grip on reality and her aunty grew more eccentric every day. Now she had another academic messing things up and getting in her way. One simple instruction – keep the letters away from Duncan – that's all she had asked and already Alice wasn't being careful enough. She didn't want Duncan anywhere near those letters.

'Oh, for Christ's sake Alice, put those letters away for today and go home!' she snapped, as she went back into the estate office and her overflowing inbox.

——

Chapter 7

Grey Marks and Spencer's Pants That Cover Everything.

Where was her camera? This was ridiculous, it should be locked away in the cupboard with the letters. Alice had been using it to take digital images of the letters yesterday and she usually locked it away at the same time as them – but yesterday she had put the letters away in a hurry when Caroline was so cross after Duncan and Emily had left. Had she put the camera away too? She couldn't remember. It must be there somewhere. Because if it wasn't, she was going to be in big trouble with Caroline. The camera contained images of the letters that she had promised to keep safe – especially when Duncan was around. But the cupboard wasn't huge, and there was nowhere a large digital camera could be hidden. Where else could it be? She was just trying to work out where else she might have put it when her phone rang. She recognised the ring tone and didn't even have to look to see who was phoning her. She didn't really want to talk to Sebastian right now, she wanted to find the camera, but she didn't dare leave it in case it was an emergency – or at least, in case Sebastian *thought* it was an emergency. He could get very stressed if he didn't know where she was and what she was doing.

'Ally-Bee! I'm about to leave my hotel room. I've got my last client meeting this morning, then I'll be with you about five this evening.'

'Of course. That'll be great.' Thinking it was a quick call and he had finished she was about to hang up again.

'Is there someone there with you?' He sounded suspicious.

'No, no-one. Why?'

'You sound strange.'

'I'm just really busy right now.'

'Can't you talk for a couple of minutes?' Though he made it sound like a question, it wasn't really - it was a command. Well, she could search for the camera while he talked, she put the phone on speaker and began to look around the bookshelves in case someone had tidied it away for her.

'I guess so,' she said uncertainly, hoping that he didn't want to talk about the job interview right now. 'Is it important?'

'Of course it is! Tell me what you're wearing?'

Oh, so he didn't want to talk. He wanted to *talk*. Usually he left this sort of conversation for last thing at night. It was the last thing she needed right now, a randy Sebastian demanding titillation.

'I'm wearing a denim skirt and a fleece,' she said, in what she hoped was a practical tone of voice, nothing that would encourage him to ask her further questions. 'And I'm looking for my camera –'

'No, underneath. I've got fifteen minutes to myself before my meeting, so tell me -'

'Not now, Sebastian, please! I'm in the library!'

'That makes it even more exciting, doesn't it?' His voice was husky.

'More exciting for you, maybe. Please, not now. I've got to find this camera, Sebastian. All the digital images I've taken are on it. What if someone has stolen it? I'm really worried -'

'But I miss you so much. Come on, Alice, I want to know what you're wearing next to your skin; describe it to me, please?' He wasn't listening to her. She used her best imitation of Caroline's no-nonsense style to crush him.

'Grey Marks and Spencer's cotton pants that cover everything. Not now!'

'Oh, come on Alice!' he groaned. 'Help me out here! I'm going to imagine that you're wearing that red lacy bra that I bought you –'

She heard the creak of the garden door in the corridor behind her and leapt across the desk to turn off the speaker, her face as red as Sebastian's imaginary lacy bra. She had to put an end to it right now, she didn't want Sebastian to start going into any more graphic details – and some of Sebastian's details could be toe-curlingly graphic - of what he wanted to do to her with Caroline or Marjorie hovering in the background listening to every word.

'Please, not now!' she begged. 'It's not convenient! I need to find my camera right now before Caroline finds out I've lost all the images.'

'Right. I see,' he said. 'It's like that, is it?' He sounded grumpy. 'Well, I'll see you tonight. I'll be there about 5-ish, make sure you're home, and put the champagne on ice, because I want to lick it off your -'

'Stop it, Sebastian!' she said, turning off the phone, cringing with embarrassment at the thought that somebody might have overheard him, but when she turned around there was nobody there. Just her imagination after all.

Now, the camera.

She tried to remember the order in which she had packed things away yesterday afternoon. Her whole focus had been on making sure that the letters were safe - which they were – so had she forgotten to lock away the camera? If she had left it out it would be on the table now, and it wasn't there.

What if she had somehow dropped it? Perhaps it could have fallen under the cupboard? She got down on her hands and knees to have a better look.

That's how she was kneeling, face on the floor and bottom in the air, peering under a bookcase when she realised that someone was standing behind her. She straightened up hurriedly, to see Tom leaning against the doorframe watching her with a glint of amusement in his dark eyes.

'Alice? What are you doing?'

'I... oh, well... I... I was looking for... something... Hi, Tom!' She felt herself blushing at his direct gaze, which she was fairly sure had been focussed on her bum until she turned around. She smoothed down her denim skirt, hoping that he didn't think she was as eccentric as Aunty Marjorie and trying not to look as panicked as she felt. His eyes narrowed as if he knew that there was something wrong.

'Are you OK?' he asked.

'I'm fine. I've just… I seem to have misplaced my camera. It must be here somewhere...' she faked a smile which didn't seem to fool him at all. He crossed the room towards her, looking concerned.

'Where did you have it last?'

'I thought it was on the table last night. I should have locked it away, Caroline's so paranoid about her ex-husband finding out what's in the letters,' she said miserably. 'What if he picked it up last night? She'll be so angry with me.'

'Only if she finds out. And I honestly don't think Duncan's the type to go around nicking cameras, don't worry. Look, I'll help you find it, what does it look like?'

'It's a Nikon, green strap with pink roses on it. But you don't need to help, shouldn't you be working?' She already felt guilty about dragging him into her mess.

'George won't mind. I can't leave you like this, you look so stressed.'

'I can't ask you to –'

'You didn't ask. I'm happy to help. Please don't look so worried, Alice. It's going to be fine, we'll find it.' His voice was so calm, so soothing that she believed him instantly. If anyone could help her could find the camera, Tom could...

'Thank you,' she found herself dangerously close to tears of gratitude. 'Can you look around those shelves for me?'

'No problem,' he said and started to search through the library. It was so kind of him to offer to help her, just having his calm, sensible presence made her feel less panicky about the possible implications of losing the camera. With Tom there, everything seemed much more straightforward. But then an awful thought crossed her mind. Sebastian wouldn't have been offering to help her like that unless he wanted something, and there were no prizes for guessing what reward Sebastian would have been seeking. What if Tom was thinking that too?

'Um... Tom?' she said awkwardly. 'You know I've got a boyfriend, don't you?' The last thing she wanted was misunderstandings between them.

'Of course I know – I saw you with him the other day.'

'I just wanted to make sure that you hadn't got the wrong idea,' she said.

'I only offered to help because you needed help,' he said, as if it was the simplest and easiest thing in the world. 'That's OK, isn't it?'

She breathed a huge sigh of relief. The last thing she needed, with everything else that was going on in her life right now, was any further romantic complications with a handsome, kind, assistant gardener. The last thing. The very, very last thing.

Tom looked round the shelves as Alice got back onto her hands and knees to continue peering under the bookcases, moving slowly round the walls, when she heard loud footsteps. From her kneeling position, she could see a pair of bright blue wooden-soled clogs on red-stockinged feet. There was only one person it could be.

'Good morning, Tom. Ah, there you are, Alice, my dear!' said Marjorie, who didn't seem at all surprised to find her crawling round the floor of the library. 'No, don't get up on my account if you're happier down there!'

Alice got to her feet all the same, she didn't think she could talk comfortably to Marjorie whilst peering up at her from the library floor.

'What can I do for you Marjorie? Do you need the spare key again?'

'No, no, nothing like that. I was out for my morning constitutional when I saw this hanging off a bush in the rose garden. I thought it might be yours?' Marjorie was holding out her camera.

'I told you it would turn up!' said Tom.

Alice's mind whirled. How on earth could the camera have got outside into the garden? Even as she tried to think of a logical explanation, she knew that there wasn't one. The only way the camera could have got outside was if somebody had put it there. She felt relief mixed with anxiety.

'Where was it?' Alice asked Marjorie.

'I spotted it hanging off a branch of the climbing rose outside one of the windows. I happened to bump into that attractive young builder, he lifted it down for me. At first, I thought one of the garden visitors might have left it, so I was going to take it to the tea room, but then I recognised the beautiful strap, I remembered seeing it in the library yesterday.'

Indeed, Alice's digital camera did have a very distinctive bright pink and green flowery strap – and no wonder that Marjorie had noticed it, it matched the colours of the Fair-Isle style cardigan she was wearing today.

When she took hold of it the strap felt cold to the touch, but not wet – either it hadn't been out there all night, or the building had protected it from the overnight showers – so did the camera still work, or had it been damaged? And had anybody looked at the images? Alice turned it on as Marjorie watched her with interest.

'Fascinating devices, aren't they?' Marjorie said. 'I remember when I was young, I had one of those Box Brownies, height of technology! Amazing what cameras can do these days.'

The camera still seemed to be working OK, but - surely not - the memory was blank. She had photographed thirty or so of the letters over the last few days and now they were all gone. There was only one picture, an out of focus shot of some gravel and the edge of a flower bed, that seemed to be the one outside the library window.

'Is it OK?' Tom asked.

'No... no it's not... all the images have gone. Marjorie, did you press any buttons on the camera when you found it?'

'Oh, good gracious me no! At least, I don't think I did. I can't be absolutely sure. I wouldn't know where to start with something as technological as that.'

'And Mikey didn't?'

'No, I don't think so. He lifted it down and gave it to me.'

'What was Mikey doing in the gardens anyway?'

'I think he rather likes looking at the architecture,' Marjorie said, vaguely.

'Somebody has deleted all the pictures I'd already taken,' Alice said, looking at Tom.

'Oh, but that doesn't matter, does it, these days? Emily tells me that everything goes up into the clouds, that's right, isn't it?' Marjorie said brightly.

'Well, no, not in this case. I hadn't uploaded them to anything; the wi-fi at my flat is too dodgy and I was going to try yesterday from here, use Caroline's wi-fi, but then Duncan arrived, and then Caroline told me to put everything away,' she said.

'Oh, those two! They used to be inseparable, but they can't say a civil word to each other these days. Such a shame.'

'Yes, I guess,' said Alice, who found it hard to believe that they had ever been a happy couple.

'I really don't think Duncan would have taken it,' Tom said, voicing one of Alice's suspicions. 'I know Caroline thinks he's only out to cause trouble, but I've known him for years. He's a decent man.'

'I have to agree,' Marjorie added. 'And besides which, if Duncan had taken your camera he'd have done it properly! You'd never have seen it again.'

It did seem unlikely that a leading academic would start stealing to further his research like that, but stranger things happened in the febrile world of Fox-Travers scholarship sometimes. One only had to think about what Nathan O'Driscoll had been caught doing in the archives at the University of Cumberland... She shuddered at the thought.

'Perhaps somebody took your camera by accident,' Marjorie said hesitantly, though Alice didn't see how anybody could possibly remove a camera by accident. Then another theory began to occur to her. She knew it had been sitting on the table when she heard Mikey and Emily in the secret room yesterday, and between then and now, *someone* had picked it up and taken it outside or even dropped it out of the reading room window to hang on a branch below. Possibly someone who had been in the secret room yesterday and then had been in the garden this morning "looking at the architecture" when Marjorie spotted the camera. What if *someone* had put the camera out of the window when he was in here with Emily and he had been trying to get back to pick it up?

It must have been Mikey, the more she thought about it, the more it made sense.

She was going to have to break her promise to Emily and she had to tell Caroline about her suspicions. Mikey must have taken the camera.

Chapter 8

False Alarm.

'So you'd take *her* word over mine? I'm telling you, he did nothing. But you never listen to me!' Emily had come barging into Caroline's office in a temper as soon as she was back from college.

'I'm sorry, Emily, but the evidence all points at Mikey. He was in the house – the foreman told me he gave Mikey the keys to turn on the gas again and that Mikey was gone for much longer than he should have been.'

'That proves nothing!'

'I don't understand why you're so upset about it.'

'Because he's… a mate.'

'You've never mentioned that before,' Caroline said.

'Of course I have! I've tried to tell you about me and Mikey but you just don't listen. He's dead upset, Mum. He did nothing!'

'Then what was he doing all that time? If he wasn't sneaking around picking up other people's cameras, what was he doing? And then what was he doing in the garden this morning when he should have been round in the stable block?'

'He was looking for me,' Emily said quietly.

'And why would he be doing that? Don't be ridiculous, you're just making excuses for him now, Emily, and you don't know the first thing about him!'

'But I do! I was at college with him last year, and I said I'd show him round the library –'

'Just because you've met somebody a couple of times doesn't mean you really know them, Emily.'

'But he's... Oh, never mind. You wouldn't understand.'

The teenager's typical defence in an argument that she knew she couldn't win. Implying that Caroline was too old and too out of touch to understand anything. Well, she might be past it as far as Emily was concerned but she could recognise a shifty character when she saw one – and Mikey was, without doubt, one of the shiftiest looking builders she had ever seen. She just didn't understand why Emily would want to stand up for him.

'He wasn't stealing Alice's camera. She should never have said that,' Emily continued.

'She didn't say that. She said she was suspicious that he had been places that he shouldn't have been when her camera went missing, that's all. Who else could it have been? Marjorie, perhaps? Or do you think it was your dad? I'm sorry, Emily, but it must have been Mikey.'

'Oh, yeah. It's so easy for people like you, isn't it?' Emily snapped. 'He's just an apprentice builder from Ormsborough so it must have been him, that's what you think! Well, he's not like that. He really is interested in the architecture; he's been asking me all kinds of things about the place, that's why I was showing him round the library when Alice saw him.'

'You showed him round the library without my permission? You haven't told him about anything important, have you?' Caroline didn't even try to disguise the mistrust in her voice. What if he'd been asking about security? Where the alarms were, the windows with dodgy closures, the voids behind the walls, the doors that were not as secure as she would like...

'Yes. I have,' Emily said defiantly.

'Oh Emily!' She couldn't afford the extensive work that would be needed to improve security; she couldn't afford even a new Yale lock as things stood. What if he had criminal connections? If he was sizing up the house for a burglary? She needed to get him out of here right now!

'I told him all about the history of the house. I showed him the oak panelling because you always said it was unique. He thought it was awesome. I showed him the little gargoyles around the library windows and he loved them. He even thought the way the bricks in the courtyard were laid was interesting. He spent ages trying to copy the pattern with the bricks on the floor of the old stable block. You should have a look; he's done a really good job.'

'That doesn't concern me right now. I don't want that young man anywhere near my house from now on. I've told the foreman and he's being moved to another job. He's lucky they've got another job to send him to. If we could have proved he took the camera he wouldn't have a job at all.'

She put a couple of notes about security on her to do list as Emily continued:

'Well, Alice got it wrong. He was with me the whole time. The *whole time,* Mum do you understand? He never touched her sodding camera.'

'There's no need for language like that,' she said absent-mindedly, as she finished the notes. She was thinking about the broken bolt on the courtyard door – perhaps one of the builders could sort it for her, that would be better than nothing.

Emily was leaning on her desk now, right in her face, disturbing all her carefully arranged piles of paper.

'Why not? At least you bloody well listen when I swear! You know what? Most of my mates complain all the time about how much their parents interfere, how they're never off their backs. I wish you were more like that. It feels like you don't see me or hear me; you never notice things, you never listen! Sometimes it feels like you don't even bloody well care!'

'Of course I care!' Caroline looked up. It was a ridiculous thing for Emily to suggest.

'Then get out of this sodding office sometimes. You take no

time to find out what's going on in my life, you don't know anything about me.'

'I know you shouldn't have brought Mikey into our house without my permission!'

'And why do you think I did that?' Emily yelled. 'Because you'd never have given your permission!'

'And I was right, wasn't I? He couldn't be trusted.'

'That's NOT what I meant!' Emily said, thumping both hands down on the desk, making Caroline jump and several pencils rolled onto the floor. 'Oh, never mind that now. You don't even care. Even Dad's more interested in my life that you are. All you ever think about is this bloody house!'

She had heard it all before, it was Emily's favourite whinge whenever she didn't get her own way, it had been the same ever since her dad left. You don't understand me, not like *Dad* does.

'Emily, I haven't got time for this right now.'

'I KNOW!' she yelled. 'You never have time. I've had enough. I hate this place and I hate you. I want to go and live with Dad. He gets it wrong sometimes but at least he *tries* to talk to me. At least he cares about me!'

'Go to your dad's then. Fine by me,' Caroline said, knowing that it was all teenage posturing. They could sort it all out tonight over supper.

'You can be such a cow sometimes,' Emily called back over her shoulder as she slammed the office door.

'Emily, I'm sorry, but I had to say something...' she could faintly hear Alice apologising through the library door.

'Thanks for nothing,' was Emily's blunt response as the door out of the library slammed as hard as the estate office one had done. It would all have blown over by supper time, Caroline thought as she turned back to her work.

——

Just as she had sorted out the spreadsheet in front of her a siren went off; the fire alarm, shrieking through the antique peace of the old house.

Again.

Since the builders had been there it had already gone off three times, so Caroline was well practised in what to do; she picked up the keys, the house phone and the red disaster folder from its place on the corner of her desk and headed out through the office door. She was pleased to see that Alice was locking the letters away in their cupboard; she had probably already been putting them away for the end of the day when the fire alarm went off as she had mentioned that she was planning to finish early today. The special friend was visiting this evening, of course.

'Probably another false alarm, bloody builders are always setting it off. When you've locked the letters away assemble in the parking area round the back,' she told Alice. 'As quick as you can; don't stop to collect any personal belongings.'

She went straight to the alarm panel – as she expected it was the old stable block sensor that had gone off. She headed straight there, to find dust everywhere from where they had removed some of the old wall panelling. The dust cover that they were supposed to have put in place over the sensor to stop this kind of thing from happening was nowhere to be seen, and neither were the builders. There was no fire. Caroline sighed and phoned the fire station. The alarm had a direct link through to the fire brigade head-quarters, so she had to let them know that, once again, it was another false alarm – many more of these and they'd be reviewing her contract, she guessed. Then back to the fire panel to turn off the alarm. This was becoming a habit; the sound of the alarm no longer sent shockwaves of adrenaline through her, only a sickening feeling of "Oh no, not again" every time it interrupted her.

When she reached the assembly point behind the manor, it was nearly deserted. Alice was there, Sarah and her waitress Chelsea from the tea-rooms and Aunty Marjorie looking puzzled in a gentleman's striped dressing gown. There was no sign of the builders or Emily, her father wouldn't leave his rooms for anything or anyone, and, being a Friday, George the head gardener had already started the weekend early, and Tom was just walking down the path from the gardens towards them.

'Thank you everyone, another false alarm,' she said as if she was addressing a staff of dozens of people. 'The dust cover over the stable block sensor had somehow come off and dust from the building work must have got in. I can't ask the builders as they seem to have left already.'

'They'd gone even before the alarms went off,' Marjorie said with some relish.

Caroline had opened her red folder and was looking at the first page. 'Sarah, you got the tea rooms evacuated OK?'

'There was only me and Chelsea in, we were closing up.'

'Great. You can get back to it, then.' Caroline put a tick on her page. 'Aunty Marjorie, what about Daddy?'

'He wouldn't come. I did try, but as usual he said he hadn't left this house for two years and he wasn't going to leave now.'

Caroline rolled her eyes. 'That sounds like Daddy. What we'll do if there's ever a real emergency I can't imagine. Never mind, another false alarm, no harm done. Now, Emily. Has anyone any idea where Emily is?'

'Last saw her heading up the lawn in the general direction of the Gothic Tower,' said Marjorie. Caroline wasn't surprised; Emily had used the old folly at the top of the rhododendron wood as a den when she was younger, now she used it for sulking as the mobile reception was much better there than in the manor itself. She was probably on the phone to her father right now, demanding that he come and take her away again; that's what she usually did when she was displeased with one of her mother's parenting decisions. It made it difficult to make any punishment stick when the first thing Emily did was go running to her father. She had hoped that by the age of seventeen Emily might have grown out of that habit, but she had more important things than a sulking teenager to worry about right now.

What if the alarm went off like this when she was away at her conference next week? Caroline looked up from her list for a moment and Alice caught her eye, she was chatting to Tom at the far side of the car-park.

'Alice, can you spare a couple of minutes? I'll go through the emergency drill with you. You're going to have to know all about it for when I go to that historic property management conference.'

'Am I?'

'Well, you'll be the closest to the alarm, in the corridor beyond the back door into office. It makes sense if you know what to do. You'll be in charge of the alarm panel in the event of an emergency.'

'I suppose it does make sense,' she said hesitantly.

'I would appreciate it if you would prepare yourself to be on call just in case. I mean, it's the builders. If they weren't here I wouldn't worry, but so many things seem to go wrong with them. At the least, I need you to know how to turn the fire alarms off and contact the fire brigade if they set the alarm off by accident again. Here, keep hold of this, and make sure you've read everything in it.'

She handed Alice the large disaster planning red folder which she had picked up when the alarm went off. It contained instructions on how to deal with every possible calamity that might happen in her absence: fire, flood, bomb threat, Aunty Marjorie locking herself into or out of the house, swarms of locusts, rivers of blood, plagues of boils; you name it, it was there, even though all that Alice was likely to need was the instructions for contacting the fire brigade in case the alarm went off accidentally. In any real emergency George, the head gardener who had been there for over twenty years would be in charge anyway, it was simply that he wasn't always close to the house;

somebody needed to be on hand near the alarm panel while the builders were there. She went through all the basics with her; showed her the alarm panel, the master bunch of keys, the house phone and the list of contacts. She was surprised, when they went back into the library to pick up Alice's bag which had been left behind when the alarm went off, to find how time had flown.

'Half past five already! I'm sorry to have kept you, you wanted to get away early, didn't you?' she said.

She watched as Alice's face turned pale.

Alice felt her face go pale as she realised what she had done. *Half past five already*, Caroline had said. She should have been meeting Sebastian at her flat half an hour ago. A wave of horror swept over her.

'I've got to go! I'm late!' she gasped. 'I'd forgotten all about Sebastian!' She snatched up her bag, sweeping her laptop and notes into their case, and she was heading out of the garden door as she almost bumped into Emily coming the other way.

'Oh, Alice, there you are. There's a man out there looking for you! I said I didn't know where you were.'

'It must be Sebastian.' She tried to get past Emily in the doorway to see if she could see him, but whichever way she moved Emily seemed to be in the way.

'Who's Sebastian?' Emily asked as she finally let Alice get past her.

'My boyfriend,' Alice said, and Emily followed her out of the door.

Sebastian was leaning against his car in front of the grand main entrance to Misterley Manor, fair hair blowing in the wind from the moors. He didn't see her at first because he was busy on his phone – probably sending her a message to see where she was. Oh God, how

———

long had he been there? She had been talking to Tom in the car-park only about half an hour ago, what if Sebastian had seen her with him? If he had seen her and jumped to the wrong conclusions... He would be so upset and unhappy. He could be terribly insecure about her talking to other men, especially when they were as good looking as Tom. But he didn't look unhappy, he looked impatient.

'He's yummy, he looks rich!' said Emily with some relish. 'Nice car.'

His new red BMW was pulled up right in front of the house where even the family didn't park, and Sebastian leaned nonchalantly on the bonnet. He saw them coming round the corner and started to walk towards them, hand raised in greeting. Alice couldn't tell from this distance how unhappy he looked.

'He's not as fit as Tom though, is he?' Emily said, louder than Alice would have liked. Alice hoped that Sebastian wouldn't hear, but she had a feeling that Emily was saying it on purpose to stir trouble for her, because of Mikey.

'Hi! Are you Alice's boyfriend? I'm Emily Lattimore,' she introduced herself to Sebastian, all smiles and innocence as she flicked her hair away from her face.

'Emily, hi. Nice to meet you.' He oozed charm, as if he was talking to one of his clients.

'Alice never told me that she had a boyfriend,' Emily said, as if it was the kind of thing that she and Alice regularly discussed. 'And it's funny, because when Tom Gannon asked me this morning, I told him that I was sure that Alice was single!'

'And who's Tom Gannon?' asked Sebastian, with an edge of hostility in his voice.

'No-one. Just one of the gardeners,' Alice said hurriedly.

'He was asking all about you – and he's gorgeous, isn't he, Alice?' Emily said brightly.

'I hadn't noticed... I wasn't looking...' she stuttered,

awkwardly, even though she *had* noticed, and she *had,* despite her best intentions, been looking.

'Well, I'm off to get some stuff ready for my dad's now, he's on his way to pick me up. He's not as unreasonable as my mum about who I can and can't see. Perhaps it's because nobody's told him that Mikey stole a camera. You have a lovely evening now, Alice.'

Alice couldn't get Sebastian away from Misterley quickly enough.

Chapter 9

Liabilities.

Duncan was standing in her office, waiting for her, when Caroline went back in from explaining the emergency procedures to Alice. His face looked grey and grim. Caroline's office was the old estate office, a strange mixture of traditional panelling and a huge map chest which contrasted with 1980s office furniture and the battered old computer.

'I've come to get Emily. She rang me. She says she can't live here with you.'

'She's being a drama queen. She's got some problem with me because Alice thinks one of the builders has been messing with her camera and I asked him to be transferred elsewhere. It's got nothing to do with Emily, she's making a scene, as always.'

Duncan sat down in the old battered leather armchair in the corner of her office, the one which had been "his" in the old days, making himself at home.

'Caroline, sit down. Can we talk?' He indicated the smaller armchair with the worn floral upholstery that had once been "her" chair. She didn't know why those two chairs were still there – she should have burnt them years ago, but she had never seemed to get round to it.

'I haven't got the time, Duncan, or the inclination to talk to you. Just get Emily and her things and get out. You can bring her back when she's calmed down.'

'Not this time. She really means it this time. Caroline, please sit down and talk to me, we need to discuss this properly.'

'She always really means it until she gets angry with you, then she'll be running back here to me again. She's always played us off against each other, you know that, Duncan.'

She sat down all the same, not in the arm chair he had offered her, but her office chair which gave her a higher seat and the physical barrier of the desk between them.

'I don't think that's what she's doing this time. She's upset.'

'Then fine. Let her live with you if that's what you both want. I can't cope with any of this any more.'

Duncan sat forward in the armchair, elbows resting on his knees. 'Caroline, I'm worried about you.'

'Well, you don't need to worry about me,' she said, organising the pile of papers on the corner of her desk into a neat pile.

'Do you know why Emily was so upset about that business with Mikey?'

'Yes, because she's a teenager and she likes getting upset with her mother. It's what she does.'

'No. Because she's going out with Mikey. She's been going out with him since about three days after he started working here.'

'She's *what*?' Caroline pushed the pile of papers out of the way again.

'She's going out with him.'

She was *not* going to show Duncan that she was surprised by what he said. She would just carry on as normal. Of course, that was why Mikey was hanging round her so much...

'Oh, that. Well, it makes no difference, I still don't trust him. I want him out.'

'Do you know why she didn't tell you?' Duncan leaned in closer towards her.

'Because he's a dodgy character?'

'Because every time she tried you were too busy and then you made it obvious that you didn't like him, so she didn't know how to start.'

'Damn right. I don't trust him, and if I'd known *that* was what was going on I'd've put a stop to it before now.'

'But you can't stop her, Caroline. She's nearly eighteen, she's a grown woman! You can't keep telling her what to do.'

'As long as she's under my roof -' she heard her father's words coming out of her own mouth and stopped herself. 'As long as she's still dependent on me financially, I think I have a right to expect her to live by my rules.'

'She's not, though, is she?'

'Not what?'

'Dependent on you. She's largely dependent on me. I pay for her clothes, her driving lessons, her allowance and I still pay the maintenance to you.'

'Oh, that's right. Rub it in, why don't you?' She swept up a couple of loose pens and banged them down into the pot on her desk.

'Caroline, please, just stop. Just stop being so angry all the time. I want to help you for Emily's sake.'

'But mostly, I would imagine, for your own sake.'

'No. It's not like that, it's never been like that.'

'Really? So you didn't marry me to get your way into this house?' She looked up from the desk.

Duncan stood up and crossed towards the desk. 'Oh, not that again! You know that's not true. That's what your father has told you and it was never *once* about this house. I fell in love with you all those years ago, Caroline, *you* and not Misterley Manor! And now all I want to do is help you and Emily and you are being so bloody unreasonable!'

He glared at her, and Caroline glared right back. No matter what he said, she knew the truth. Her father had opened her eyes to what her ex-husband had been after; peeping and prying around the house into things that didn't concern him.

'Caroline, you spend all day every day stuck in this house, behind your desk. You never stop. You don't spend enough time with our daughter and you certainly don't spend enough time on yourself. Give yourself a break! Please, Caroline, or you're going to make yourself ill.'

'And why do you care?'

'Because there isn't anybody else to care about you.'

'That's rubbish!'

'Is it?' Duncan's eyes met hers, his blue eyes undimmed by the years were still the eyes of the young man she had married.

'Of course!' she said, re-arranging the paperwork in front of her again. 'I've got Daddy and Aunty Marjorie.'

Duncan simply snorted. 'Caroline, you're going to burn yourself out. It's too much for you. You need more help, you need more money, you need more support; you can't run this place on your own any more. Your father is too old and forgetful to help you, and all he does is demand impossible things. I mean, you *know* you should have got in Goldings to do the building work, a proper firm of conservation builders, but your father said Sleightholm's were good enough for his father, so they should be good enough for you and that's what you did.'

'How do you know that?'

'Marjorie told me.'

'Well, Marjorie should learn to keep her mouth shut. She's a liability.'

'Another liability for you to worry about.' He sat down again in the armchair.

'Don't you think you should be getting Emily now? I'm sure you've said enough.' Caroline rose to her feet as if to usher him out of her office, but he sat there, resolutely not moving.

'Caroline, you're making yourself ill, you can't do this all alone. You have no time for your own daughter, and don't you think you should be spending some time with your poor old father too?'

'You hate my father.'

'It doesn't mean that I can't see how quickly he's deteriorated in the last couple of years. He might not have that much longer left.'

'Ohhh, I get it! You don't think I can manage alone, so you're going to offer to help, are you? I know what this is about, it's got nothing to do with me, or Emily or Daddy, it's about getting your hands on those bloody Fox-Travers letters. You can't bear it that Alice gets to read them before you do, and you want to get yourself back in here before *she* makes all the discoveries. It's nothing but academic jealousy!'

'No, it's not that. I think it's time you gave some serious thought to donating Misterley Manor to National Heritage. In another couple of years, unless you make some serious money, the East Wing will start to decay because of the leaks in the roof. You can't let that happen to such an important building.'

Precise, sensible, calculating, cold. He talked as if it was one of his intellectual problems to be discussed not her home to be preserved. How dare he come in here, telling her what to do? It was like it had been when they were married, constantly interfering, constantly arguing with Daddy, crossing him on purpose, as if it was any of his concern what happened to the Lattimore family home.

'This is not your house, Duncan! It's not even my house, it's Daddy's house and he would never – *never* – want to see it given away. It's the family inheritance! We'll find a way. How could you even think we could give it away?'

'Because if you don't, Caroline, your inheritance is going to end up in ruins around you.'

That was the last straw. She would never let that happen, *never*! 'Get out! Get out of here right now. Don't come back. Get your greasy arse out of MY chair in MY house and go away. I don't have to listen to this.'

Now he was angry, spitting white sarcasm to match her blazing red defiance. It was the pattern of every row they had ever had. 'Fine. I came here with the best of intentions, but as usual I shouldn't have bothered. I wanted to help you, but if you won't listen to reason -'

'I'll listen to reason when you talk it. I can manage fine without your help.'

'Yes, yes of course you can. I can see you're managing just *fine.*' He turned her words back on her. 'The house is in great shape, you've got wonderful plans for its future. Carry on doing everything your daddy tells you and your future is rosy.'

'It's got nothing to do with you! We're not married any more, thank God.'

'But it's got everything to do with my daughter and her future. Can't you see that?'

'Are you saying that I'm not capable of securing my own daughter's future?' she yelled.

'Frankly, Caroline, it's beginning to look as if you're not,' he said. She picked up the pile of papers she had tidied from her desk and flung them at his head. It felt great, a release of weeks of tension, to be able to have a real stand up row with someone. Perhaps Duncan had his uses after all.

'Get out, you bastard! Get out!' She picked up another handful of papers ready to throw, but he was already on his way to the door even as the papers fluttered to the floor around him.

'Well, when the whole place is in ruins around you, don't say I didn't try to help!' He said as he turned in the doorway, and as she threw the second pile of papers they bounced off the closing door and scattered all over the floor. She made a strangled sound halfway between a cry and a roar of anger, but there was no-one there to hear. Shaking, she started to pick up the papers again. She was angry and upset. She was angry because of everything he had said to her – and she was upset because he was right, even though she would never, never admit it to his face.

They *should* give the house to National Heritage before it

suffered worse damage... but with Daddy the way he was there was nothing - nothing at all - she could do about it.

‘So, Daddy, how are we this evening?’ she asked carefully, not knowing what her father’s mood would be like tonight.

It was half an hour after she had argued with Duncan, Emily had gone with her father and Caroline had finished work for the day; the fire-alarm had meant she had to work later than she intended. She had calmed down, and it was time to make supper, but today she didn’t feel like eating, and Marjorie had already made herself and Sir Henry some soup an hour ago.

‘Good gracious, girl, don’t talk to me as if I’m an imbecile! I’m as well as can be expected,’ he replied, sounding tetchy but not as full of impotent rage as he would be some evenings. Rain or shine, day or night her father sat in his big old chair facing the window as if he was surveying his domain though his sightless eyes. Everything in her father’s room had to be just right – his glass of water just there, his box of tissues beside it, the footstool to the right, his cardigan on the back of his chair. As long as his glass of water was in the right position, he would never know that everything else was falling to pieces. ‘I heard voices earlier. Raised voices?’

‘Emily’s father came to collect her, we had a disagreement. She’ll be staying with him for a while,’ Caroline said.

‘I don’t want That Man in my house. I’ve told you. Can’t you get that into your head? I do NOT want him coming here.’

‘I’ve told him, but Emily still needs to see her father.’

‘I don’t care. He doesn’t come in my house while I’m in it. You can do what you like when I’m dead and gone; sell the place to the highest bidder, turn it into a pink-gin-party-palace, invite in all the hoi-polloi to run their grubby little fingers over my furniture, but while I’m living and breathing it is *my* house and *my* decision.’

‘I understand that, Daddy, but be reasonable!’ Mild tetchiness could escalate so quickly into blazing anger. She tried to keep things calm. She couldn't shout at Daddy like she had shouted at Duncan, he was so unpredictable these days.

'Reasonable? I've been reasonable. That's the problem. All these foolish ideas of yours, builders in the stable block, pensioners in the gardens, and as for that little academic in the library, prodding and poking into things that don't concern her... it'll all end in tears, you mark my words, Marjorie.'

'Caroline. It's Caroline, not Marjorie.'

'Yes, that's what I said!' His hand was beginning to tremble, he was getting himself worked up, she recognised the signs. 'Shan't have him in the house. Nasty little rat of a man, your husband, never know what you saw in him...' he muttered as if to himself. 'Good for nothing!'

'You're right,' she said, trying to soothe him. 'Of course you're right, Daddy.'

But she did know one thing that Duncan was still good for. It had felt *great* to have a proper fight with someone who was able to give as good as he got.

Chapter 10

Distracting Sebastian.

Alice found herself imagining the dark red velvet of the little side room in the library as Sebastian inserted himself into her later that evening. If she closed her eyes and reached out, she could imagine the sumptuous red velvet beneath her trailing fingers and the cushions soft behind her back, imagine the heady scent from the rose garden on the air and a tall, dark-eyed, masculine figure standing above her in the doorway...

Imagination was better than the reality of the creaking metal-framed daybed in her flat, which smelt ever-so-slightly of fish and chips from the shop at the bottom of the building. She had never noticed it before, but with Sebastian here all the little quirks of her new home no longer felt like quirks but flaws. Sebastian had a way of doing that to her. She sighed.

His rhythmic thrusting suddenly stopped. 'Alice? What are you thinking about?'

She opened her eyes and looked up at his face above her. 'Velvet and roses!' she said in what she hoped was a sensuous way. The last time he had asked her what she was thinking about during sex, and she had replied, quite truthfully "Fox-Travers" he had not been happy and had told her so at great length and in some detail. It had quite spoiled the romantic moment for both of them.

This was the second time they had had sex this evening; he had been so needy when they got back to the flat that he had practically dragged her up the stairs, unzipping his trousers as they climbed, and in five minutes he had finished.

This time he was taking it more slowly and they had made it

as far as the metal-framed day bed that served as both sofa and spare bed.

'I'll tell you what, let's do something special!' he said with a wicked grin as if he was offering her an indulgent treat, but she knew instantly what he had in mind and her heart sank.

'Maybe we could -' she began, but he either didn't hear or didn't listen.

'Turn over, Alice, and I'll go and find my toilet bag.'

She turned over to lie face down on the bed, so that he could have what he wanted. She was still feeling guilty about this afternoon, about letting him down, and she was worried about how the rest of the evening was going to go. He hadn't even mentioned the interview yet, and she hoped he would be distracted for a little while longer, as she could hear him rattling through the contents of his sponge bag behind her. She waited as he made his preparations. Her mind wandered back to the little red velvet reading room as she pressed her face into the coolness of the pillow. When it came to sex Sebastian was easily distracted if she made any noise at all, so she bit her lip as he thrust harder, faster, deeper, until with a loud cry of triumph and a final shudder of effort he was finished. He rolled off her, sweat glistening on his smooth bare chest, gasping for breath.

'Thank you,' he said, tenderly brushing a strand of hair from her face. 'That was amazing!' He was always extra considerate to thank her when she had let him do what he wanted. Sebastian glowed with obvious satisfaction, but Alice felt unfulfilled in every possible way.

Afterwards they sat at her tiny dining table, underneath the skylight where the seagulls circled above them in the pink evening sky. They could hardly see each other for another enormous bunch of lilies that Sebastian had brought for her, she had put them in her bathroom bin which was the only container large enough for them.

'Look, Alice, I know you're not sure about this job, but I've thought of something else,' he said at last.

'I would like to stay here; my PhD is so important to me and I don't want to be a PA, I'd be an awful PA, Sebastian, please don't-'

'I think you should hear what I'm going to say. I think it's going to change everything.'

'OK,' she said, tipping her chair back slightly to catch the evening sun from the skylight on her face.

'I want you to marry me.'

In surprise, Alice nearly tipped her chair right over. She had to grab the table to stop herself.

'What?' It wasn't the immortal moment she had been dreaming of - where was the string quartet, the fireworks or the rose garden? Instead she had empty take away cartons in front of her and a stupidly oversized bunch of lilies in a bin that more-or-less hid his face from her view.

'It's traditional to answer *yes* or *no*, not *wha*t!' He grinned, peering round the lilies, suddenly looking like the cheeky student she had first met, and she found once again her heart starting to curl around the edges with warmth.

'You want us to get married?'

'If you take the job then we can get married.'

'If I take the job?'

'Yes – obviously if you had a wedding to plan and all that, you wouldn't want to be up here would you? With your extra salary we'd be able to afford the wedding we want, and if you can stop focussing so much on Fox-Travers then maybe you'll have some time to put into our relationship instead. It's time you grew up and joined the real world, Ally-Bee. We have to make sacrifices for each other, don't we? I didn't choose my job because I love it, I had to be practical about it. So, when will you come back?'

'Please don't ask me to choose,' she said, quietly, thinking of Caroline's advice.

He didn't answer, he simply slipped a small red box across the table towards her. Inside it was the most enormous diamond she had ever seen; so huge it didn't even look real.

'I didn't think you would need to choose once you saw this,' he said, looking up at her from across the table.

She stared at the contents of the box, trying to disguise her dislike. It was hideous. Large, flashy and ostentatious, quite the opposite of what she would have chosen for herself. Is this what they had come to? Did he know so little about her that he thought *this* was what she would have chosen for an engagement ring? This was all about showing what he could afford to give her, not choosing something she would actually like to wear, something that was suitable for who she was - but maybe that was the point. If she said yes, then she would no longer *be* that Alice, she would be Sebastian's Alice, safe in his little velvet lined box, like the diamond monstrosity he was handing her. It was a symbol of ownership, not love.

'Do you love me?' she asked, suddenly.

'What?' he replied, as if caught off guard.

'It's traditional to answer *yes* or *no*, not *wha*t!' she said. 'So, do you love me?' she repeated.

'I want you. I *need* you.'

'That's not the same thing,' she realised sadly.

'Alice, don't look at me like that! Of course I love you. I've always loved you from the first moment I set eyes on you I knew you were right for me.' For a moment she was back in the college bar the night they had met; the solitary strangers amongst a crowd of old friends. 'Don't you love me any more?' he sounded suddenly lost and sad and she saw again the insecure young man she had fallen in love with – perhaps he was still there after all under the thrusting new Sebastian who had appeared since he had started work at C.C.T. 'Don't you love me, after everything we've been through? Everything we've been to each other? Everything I've done for you?'

The curl of guilt started at the bottom of her stomach and wound its way upwards.

'Oh Sebastian… I know you've been everything to me… when Mum died, I'd never have got through that without you, I know that, but… I can't… I can't...' she couldn't say it. 'I can't give up my PhD for you. I can't try and be what you want, I can't be something I'm not.' If she had any doubts before about what was the right thing to do, it was becoming clearer and clearer. She didn't love Sebastian any more. He was a friend, a good friend – a "special" friend, but she didn't love him like she ought to – like he wanted her to.

'Alice, I need you!' He pleaded.

'Do you need me, or do you just need *someone*?' She surprised herself with the bitter retort that came out of her mouth, unplanned and unpleasant. It was the kind of thing that Caroline would have said.

'No! At work I could have any woman I want – Greta from accounts is always flirting with me. Phaedra and Tamsin would go with me any time, I've seen the way they look at me, and Mollie-Mae on reception tried to get off with me at the office party. I turned them all down because of you!' That old lost look overwhelmed his face and instantly she regretted what she had said. 'I mean, this tiny, smelly flat, this horrible village and that dilapidated old pile you're working in; it's not right. You deserve something better. I know you're afraid to move on, I know how much you loved being a student, but you can't be a student for ever.'

'I'm not afraid to move on,' she said. 'That's not it. I have moved on. I've moved all the way up here to follow my dream. I'm going to find out what happened to Fox-Travers, I know I am, and I'm going to finish my PhD.'

'All this rubbish about Fox-Travers. It's bordering on obsession, Alice, and it isn't healthy for you. I worry, I really do.'

'It's sweet of you to worry, but I wish -'

'Look, Alice, I've given you a simple choice.' He was talking to her like one of his clients, as if she had no choice but to do what he wanted. 'I've shown my commitment to you – there it is, in a box in front of you. All I ask is that you show me the same commitment in return, that's all. Yes or no, it's a simple question.'

'And if I say no?'

'You know the answer to that. If you say no, it's over. I can't have half of you; it's everything or nothing. After everything we've been through I can't believe you'd throw it all away, just like that, would you Ally-Bee?'

Sign on the dotted line. Give yourself to me. Let me manage your assets.

The young man searching for acceptance and approval was long gone, and this new Sebastian had taken his place – and this Sebastian was no longer her soulmate and her equal, this Sebastian wanted to be her boss. She found herself thinking about what Caroline had said to her earlier in the week – if he understood what her work meant to her he wouldn't make her choose, and if he did, then perhaps she should choose her work.

She looked at the box on the table in front of her and she felt sick as she knew what she had to say. She didn't love him, and she didn't want to marry Sebastian and give up her work; not on these terms. She wanted to be asked to marry for love and to say yes because there was no other answer that she wanted to give, not because there was no other answer that she was allowed to give.

'No.' She said it in such a quiet, shaky voice that at first he didn't hear her.

'I'm sorry, what?'

'No, Sebastian.' She said it louder this time, but he still didn't seem to understand what she was saying.

'Ally-Bee?'

'I'm sorry, Sebastian - no.'

Chapter 11

The Ultimate Consequences of the Garden Centre Car-Park.

Alice was walking on the grass so that the sound of her footsteps on the gravel wouldn't disturb Tom at his work right now. She didn't want him to see her like this; eyes puffy and red and her face sore from all the times she had blown her nose since Saturday morning. She didn't want him to see her looking a mess and she didn't want his pity. She just wanted to get into work, lock herself into the library and never, ever see a man again. She nearly made it, but she disturbed a little bird on one of the rose bushes which fluttered upwards and gave her away. He turned. Upon seeing her, his eyes narrowed and he got to his feet, coming straight over to her.

'Alice! What's wrong?'

'Nothing. Nothing, it's just... hay fever. I get very bad hay fever,' she sniffed. But he knew without her having to say anything, that it was a lie.

'I saw you leaving on Friday night with your boyfriend - you looked so unhappy and he looked angry. I've been worried about you all weekend.'

'We split up,' she said, bluntly. 'He told me that unless I left Misterley it was over.'

'I'm sorry,' said Tom, 'that's tough. I'm guessing that you chose to stay here?'

'I've wanted to work here for half my life, I can't just give up my PhD because he wants to go to Indonesia… I told him I didn't want to go home with him, and then he asked me to marry him. I said… I said no. I don't love him; what else could I say? Then he told me that

I'd made a mistake and he walked out. He was so upset. I feel awful – I owe him so much…' She found that the tears were creeping down her cheeks again.

'You can't stay with someone just because you feel you owe them something,' he said with a grim smile, handing her a tissue from his jeans pocket. As she wiped away the tears it was still warm from being next to his body. 'I know how hard it is when a relationship comes to an end,' he added, gently. 'If there's anything I can do, Alice, if you need someone to listen...'

'No… no… I'm fine…' she sobbed, suddenly overwhelmed by his kindness. She didn't deserve it after what she had done to Sebastian. But Tom was divorced, wasn't he? He must know what it felt like at the inevitable end of something which had once been sweet but had turned sour.

He put his hands on her upper arms, gently. 'Alice, can I ask you something?' he said, his eyes locked on hers. 'Tell me honestly - he didn't hurt you, did he?'

Why on earth would Tom think that? And why would he even care?

'No!' she sobbed. 'No, it might have been easier if he had done something like that, then I could hate him for it. He just stopped hearing what I said, that's all. He never listened, he didn't even try to understand things from my point of view.'

'Because if he did – if he had hurt you – then I'll sort it out for you,' and suddenly the grip of his hands on her arms was tighter, more insistent.

'No! He wouldn't lay a finger on me, Sebastian's not like that.'

'If he does give you any trouble, promise me you'll tell me?'

'I promise. But he would never do anything like that!' He let go of her arms and she could still feel the place on her arms where he had held her. For the rest of the morning she felt the ghost of his hands on her skin.

When Caroline found Alice an hour after starting work, staring out of the window, sniffling, Caroline *knew* there was something wrong and she guessed what it must be. Well, no point in beating about the bush, best to get it all out in the open.

'How did things go with Sebastian?' she asked bluntly, striding out of her office and into the library.

'Oh… it was… I…' Alice's voice was heavy with tears.

'You haven't gone to the job interview then?'

'No, no I… he…'

'Do I take it he wasn't very happy?'

'He wasn't.'

'But you did the right thing. I'm sure you did. You can't let a man like that boss you around, tell you what to do, run your life for you. You have to put yourself first! And if he loves you he'll come round to your way of thinking, and if he doesn't, then you're better off on your own.' She sat down at the table in the seat next to Alice.

'Or, perhaps if we really loved each other we would be able to accept that we could think differently and still love each other,' Alice replied, 'but it's too late for that now, he wants it all his own way. He asked me to marry him,' she said quietly.

'What?' Caroline was stunned. That was the last thing she had been expecting to hear.

'He said, if I got the job we could get married.'

'And you said no?'

Alice nodded miserably, crossing her hands in her lap. 'I don't know if I did the right thing,' she said, eyes welling up with tears. This wouldn't do. Caroline knew that she had to help her. Alice needed a little fortitude.

'Of course you did the right thing! A little of our Lattimore *Pride and Strength* wouldn't do you any harm right now. He can't expect you to drop everything to do what he tells you. You've got your own life to live, and marriage is a ludicrously outdated institution anyway. Who wants to be owned by anybody else these days?'

'Hopefully enough people to get your wedding venue off the ground?' Alice commented woefully.

She might be a drip, but this girl wasn't stupid.

'I suppose there has got to be a bit of give and take,' Caroline said. That was something she and Duncan had been bad at. But this wasn't about them, she told herself, it was about Alice.

'But it feels like I've done all the taking, and now he's asked me to give up one thing for him and I wouldn't do it. Maybe I've got it wrong. He was so upset.'

'Then phone him up and tell him. Tell him you've changed your mind, you want him back, you love him,' she challenged Alice. Caroline had her mobile in her pocket and she held it out to Alice. Alice stared at it in silence and then eventually shook her head.

'I don't,' she said feebly, looking down at her feet. 'I don't love him,' she said more firmly, looking Caroline in the eye. Good for her, Caroline thought, that was more like it.

'Then it can't be helped. You get to finish your PhD. That's what you wanted.'

'Yes, you're right. I don't love him like I used to and I'm certainly not convinced that he loves me. I mean, if I loved him, I'd make that sacrifice, wouldn't I? If I'd loved him, I don't think I'd have come here in the first place. And yet...' she looked sideways at Caroline.

'And yet what?' Caroline said kindly.

'I feel like I *ought* to love him. After everything he's done for me, I ought to love him.'

'But sometimes, no matter how much you think you should love someone, you suddenly wake up one day and find you don't.'

'Is that what happened with you and Duncan?'

'Something of the sort. I should never have let anyone tell me what to do.'

'And Duncan kept telling you what to do?'

Caroline nodded, although that wasn't quite how it had been. Caroline had been caught in the middle between two powerful men, both wanting to prove their dominance; Duncan had been the young buck challenging the old stag. She had been caught in the middle whenever they tried to lock antlers.

'This is Daddy's house. My ex-husband seemed to think he knew better than Daddy, and both of them wanted me to take sides. They fought about opening the house to the public and getting National Heritage involved with its upkeep. But it all came down to the garden centre car park in the end. My ex-husband wanted it tarmac because it would last longer and need less maintenance, Daddy wanted ornamental chippings because they would look better.' She thought of the garden centre car park which these days was a rather weedy and dishevelled gravelled space that didn't do the garden centre any favours. 'They wanted me to choose, you see. I didn't realise that my choice of surface for the garden centre car park would have such huge and long-lasting implications,' she said wearily.

'So, Duncan left you because you wanted to put gravel on the garden centre car park?'

'Yes. Essentially, yes.'

She realised how stupid it sounded after fifteen years. She still shuddered to remember the rows that had followed what she had thought to be a simple decision about a car-park. But she had stood her ground with him, as Daddy always encouraged her to do, she had fought her own corner with the Lattimore *Pride and Strength.*

Alice was nodding now, as if what Caroline said made sense, as if she was thinking it all through and comparing her own situation to Caroline's.

'And I've been much happier on my own, much happier,'

Caroline assured her.

There was an awkward pause, as Caroline thought of all the nights she had lain awake wishing that she wasn't on her own. It was all very well Daddy telling her that her ex-husband was up to no good, that she was better off without his interference, but had she really been? It had been fine while Daddy was still capable, but recently… sometimes she wished there was someone; someone else who cared as much about thc house as she did. Just not *That Man.*

'Tom thinks I did the right thing,' Alice said at length.

'Tom? What does Tom have to do with all of this?' She remembered how blind she had been about her own daughter's romantic life – maybe Alice…

'Nothing!' Alice was quick to exclaim. Rather too quick, in Caroline's opinion. 'I just saw him on the way into work this morning. He was… he was very sympathetic…'

But Caroline's attention had been caught by a strange, sweet smell that was drifting through the library. 'What's that smell? Alice, you haven't got lilies in here again have you?' she said, and instantly regretted it as Alice's bottom lip showed signs of an incipient tremble at the thought of Sebastian and his lilies.

'No, I haven't. It smells more like a scented candle?'

And instantly Caroline knew what it must be. Marjorie was up to her old tricks.

'Oh Lord, it's Aunty Marjorie, I'm sure she's burning those awful joss sticks again. She's never got over her hippy phase in the 60's. It's patchouli, I think.' That's what the smell was; it was even more sickly than lilies.

'Yes, I think you might be right,' said Alice. 'The only time I've smelt them was when I was at uni; a girl in my shared house used to burn them to cover up the smell when she was smoking something dodgy.'

'Marjorie will be meditating; says it helps her hip. I'm going to have to ask her to stop; she's getting so absent minded these days, she wanders off and leaves them burning; a few stray embers and the whole place could go up.' As she spoke she was smoothing the letters on the pile, almost reverently. 'It's such a shame, Marjorie used to be such a big help to me when it came to running this place, but these days I've got Daddy unable to leave his rooms and Marjorie forgetting things; then there's Emily who doesn't want anything to do with the house and wants me to sell it off. I try to explain about the responsibility of her inheritance for future generations but she won't listen. There are some days, Alice, where shouldering this burden alone seems unbearable. Absolutely unbearable. There is so much to think of, so much to do. Preserving Misterley Manor is entirely on my shoulders, but at times it feels like I'm trapped in a maze and I can't see a way out of it. I don't care if it is the most important arts and crafts maze in the north of England and that it was designed by Gilbert Fox-Travers, I'm still trapped in it.'

It had all come rushing out. It was a long time since she had been able to tell anyone how she felt about the house. Daddy wouldn't listen, Marjorie would have her mind elsewhere and Emily would tell her to sell it and get rid of the problem. It was ironic, she had sat down to try and listen to Alice's problems and now here she was confiding her own troubles. Alice was a good listener.

'You work so hard, Caroline, and you're doing such a good job.' Alice's voice was soothing, but she had got it wrong.

'I'm not doing a good job, though, Alice. It's falling apart,' she admitted. 'The East Wing is empty and crumbling; it's a disgrace. I don't want anyone to see it the way it is now – I don't want *you* to see it as it is now - but I can't afford to fix it. This wedding venue is my last hope, and if it fails, we'll go under and we'll lose the house. Daddy doesn't understand,' she said with a shrug, 'he doesn't see that we can't afford to keep Misterley going without an income and at the moment our income from the garden centre isn't enough. Maybe

Duncan was right after all; we should move up into the attic and let National Heritage run the place... but Daddy... it would finish him off. There are other times where I think maybe Emily has the right idea.' She sank down into one of the chairs at the library table, and Alice came to sit beside her.

'You mean sell Misterley?'

Caroline sighed. 'I think of what I could have done if I hadn't been tied to this place. I never wanted to be a historic property manager, I wanted to work with horses. I'd have loved to be a vet, or even run stables,' she said, folding her arms across her chest. 'I had the idea of starting a livery business in our stables when I was younger, but Daddy wouldn't let me, and now here I am, too poor to keep horses in my own stables and turning them into some ludicrous wedding factory for Ormsborough people with more money than sense who want to play at being lords of the manor for the day. I look at Emily, and I can't help but think, yes, go for it, do what you want to do and don't let yourself get tied down by this… this… monstrosity.'

'I had no idea you felt like this!' Alice reached out to try and take Caroline's hand, but Caroline shook her hand away impatiently. This would never do! Lattimore resolve was required. She had already admitted too much to Alice.

'How would you know?' Caroline pulled herself to her feet. 'I'm so sorry, Alice. I shouldn't burden you like this. Pay no attention to me; it's not as if I have any of the answers myself.'

She had reached her office door when she remembered that she hadn't told Alice about her change of plans for next week – not that it would make much difference to her, but best to let her know, having spent all that time briefing her on the safety precautions.

'Oh, Alice, I've changed my mind about going to that conference next week. I don't think I can leave the house.' She had booked it six months ago: *Preservation, Conservation and Development: Management of the Historic House in the Twenty-First*

Century. It was so handy, being held in York this year, so close to home, and yet - Marjorie was a liability. Her father was a liability. Emily was a liability too, and as for that Mikey; what if he turned up again whilst she was away? He could potentially be even more of a liability than her father and Marjorie put together. Even though Alice was going to be there and she knew what to do, Alice wasn't enough to stem the rising tide of disorder in the house – particularly if she was still snivelling over Sebastian. No, she couldn't go anywhere. Not even somewhere as close as York.

'Oh Caroline, that's a shame!' Alice said. 'You should go; you were so excited about it.'

Excited wasn't perhaps the word that Caroline would have used, but Alice was an academic. She probably found the very possibility of going to a conference exciting. It wasn't what property managers did, though was it? Property managers had to manage without such frivolities.

'Oh, don't worry, I'm sure I won't miss it.'

'But what about all the networking? All the contacts you could make? And what about all the information you might miss out on? You can't work in a vacuum; if you don't keep up with developments then you'll be left behind. You should go, Caroline.'

'I couldn't. What about Daddy and Marjorie? And most of all, Emily?'

'Emily isn't even living here at the moment, she'll be fine with her dad, and surely Marjorie could look after herself and Sir Henry just for one night? I'll be here during the day to help to keep an eye on the builders, and there'll be Tom… and Sarah and George too.'

'I don't know…' she felt herself beginning to waver.

'Go on, Caroline. You know you'd regret it if you miss those sessions on textile conservation that you told me about!'

Alice was right. She should go. It was only for one night, what were the chances of anything going wrong.

——

Chapter 12

Aflame.

At last Caroline had gone to the conference. She had tried to change her mind about going three more times, but each time Alice had managed to talk her round and finally, reluctantly, she had gone off to enjoy the delights of discussing the management of historic properties for two whole days. Now Alice was able to get back to the letters. Yet more about Tennyson. Lady Isobel was much inspired by "The Crimson Petal and the White" today. She wondered that Fox-Travers should read it for inspiration before he planned the planting of the rose garden, maybe it would inspire him as it inspired her. She directed him particularly to lines 4, 8 and 16 which might be of interest. Alice was not particularly interested, and she imagined Fox-Travers had not been either.

What was in the poem, Alice wondered, was it all about flowers? Perhaps there would be something she could discuss with Tom, go and ask him about whether the flowers in the poem were in the garden somewhere? She didn't even want to admit it to herself, but she had been hoping to see Tom ever since Monday morning, and yet he was elusive. The grounds were large; he could be anywhere, and she had no real reason to seek him out. She turned back to her work. She could look the poem up online, but she still preferred using actual books if she had the chance, and as she was in the middle of an old library, there must be some copies of Tennyson somewhere on the library shelves. She went to the poetry section, and there indeed were three different editions; a large red morocco bound illustrated volume – inscribed from Tennyson himself to Lady Isobel's mother – it was far too nice to use as a reference book. Then one with a beautiful image of flowers on the front – but none of the pages inside had been cut open, they were all still folded shut, so she couldn't read that one. The third was a green cloth-bound volume, plain and ordinary, much more suitable for everyday use. She took it back over to the table and opened it. The smell of musty book dust rose from the yellowing pages – it was a while since this volume had been opened. But wait a minute – there was a name on the flyleaf. Isobel Greenwell. Surely that was Lady Isobel's maiden name? This was her very own copy of Tennyson, perhaps the very one she had been reading when she wrote the letters. It gave Alice a thrill to feel the direct link with the history she was studying.

Alice scanned the contents page. No mention of Crimson petals or white ones. She checked the reference on her phone and found that it was part of a longer poem; a much longer one. So many pages that she didn't stand a chance of finding it easily, so she'd have to use her phone after all... but the book fell open naturally at page 213, because there was something inside it. Pressed flower petals fell out, and there was the poem right in front of her, passages underlined with violet ink, and little pointing fingers drawn beside some of the lines. Lines 4, 8 and 16; none of which had anything to do with plants – or piety.

Oh my Lord. It had been here in front of her eyes all the time and she had missed it!

It was a love poem. Lady Isobel was sending Fox-Travers a message to read a love poem! *The firefly wakens, waken thou with me.... all thy heart lies open unto me... my dearest... be lost in me.*
So, what about the other Tennyson poems Lady Isobel had referenced? Here, here was another letter. Maud Part II, section IV, the XI stanza would inspire him to some spiritual thoughts... here it was, ringed in the same purple ink... *Oh that 'twere possible, after long grief and pain, to find the arms of my true love, round me once again.*

Letter after letter, line after line, poem after poem. It was all there, beating hearts, bleeding hearts and broken hearts and lost hearts and found.

How could she have been so stupid? How could she have been so blind! Here it was at last, the secret that she had hoped she would find. Fox-Travers hadn't seduced a kitchen maid or even Sir Edward's younger sister. It was Lady Isobel herself! It was all here, in coded references to poetry, hidden in the very same letters on which her husband had added terse notes about stone and architraves to the architect. Hidden in plain sight! But had it been a mutual attraction? And how far had it gone, what had happened?

She had to tell someone, right now. She had to share this amazing discovery with someone! She couldn't ring Caroline at her conference, she had promised not to disturb her unless there was a real emergency. Her PhD supervisor was in Prague right now but Duncan… she had to tell Duncan; he was the only person who would understand the significance of all this, she had to ring Duncan - but Caroline had told her not to, and she didn't want to betray Caroline's trust.

She checked the time on her phone, it was after three o'clock. She had forgotten the time as she pored over the letters, it was already after three o'clock, and she hadn't seen the builders once even though she had promised Caroline that she would check them every hour. Her discovery would have to wait. She reluctantly put the letters safely away in the cupboard – so much more important now she knew what they contained; every reference would have to be double checked, and Fox-Travers's replies too – was he responding to her quotes or was he blissfully unaware that she was sending him love letters?

She ran over to the old stable block, where the builders were working – although perhaps not working as hard as they might have been – there were several mugs of tea on the go, the radio was on too loudly and the foreman was reading the *Daily Mail* – but they did appear at least to be doing something with the wall-cladding. It was a filthy job, behind the old tongue- and-groove boarding was the dirt and dust of decades of horses when the room was a stable block, and then cars when it had been used as garages. Four large industrial spotlights illuminated the scene, as there was as yet no lighting installed in the large room, the strong beams of light cut through the dusty atmosphere like headlights through fog. The builders were wearing facemasks to stop the dust getting up their noses, Alice wasn't so lucky and immediately started to sneeze. She wasn't in a hurry to stick around as, with a grin, one of the workers threw another pile of boards down right next to her and a cloud of dust flew up and a host of spiders and other insects scuttled out.

'Everything OK?' she asked, somewhat tentatively.

'Would be better if we still had Mikey to shift the rubbish,' one of them grumbled, but she couldn't work out which of them had spoken.

'Well, I'm not gonna do it,' said a young woman with green hair showing under her hard hat. 'Don't look at me. Not my job.'

Not my job either, thought Alice, hurrying back work. She had no sooner got out the letters and opened the violet-marked volume of Tennyson again when the sound of a siren cut across her study.

The fire alarm was wailing.

The library seemed to pulsate with the sudden harsh sound, bringing Alice to her senses, back from a world of Lady Isobel's throbbing passion to the reality that the builders had somehow managed to set off the fire alarm again. It must be all the dust from those rotten wall panels they were removing, the same dust that had got right up her nose earlier.

Now, what had Caroline told her to do? Oh yes, she had to phone the fire brigade and tell them that it was yet another false alarm and then turn off the alarm. Where was the red emergencies folder? That had the number for the fire station in it. She picked up the folder from the corner of her work table and the office mobile phone (which thankfully she had remembered to charge) and was about to head off to the fire alarm panel, when she thought about the letters. The fire instructions said drop everything and go, but Caroline's instructions were to lock away the letters every time she left the room. She was sure this would turn out to be yet another false alarm, so she took a couple of extra minutes to bundle them up and lock them in the cupboard before she headed out of the library, leaving the volume of Tennyson open on the table. She found the non-emergency number for the fire brigade on the office phone as she walked.

There was the fire alarm panel, beside the staff entrance, and there was the warning light indicating that, as she expected, the source of the alarm was indeed the old stable block where the builders were working. Her fingers were hovering over the phone ready to call the fire brigade and tell them it was another false alarm; she balanced the folder on her knee to find the number, as she glanced out of the little pane of glass beside the staff door and she could see that some of the builders were out in the courtyard, and there was quite a lot of shouting going on.

That wasn't normal.

Why were the builders shouting?

She opened the staff door.

'Is everything OK?' she called out to them.

'Derek's just trying to put it out,' one of the men shouted back.

'Put what out?' she asked, stupidly.

'The fire.'

The fire.

There was a real fire.

It wasn't another false alarm, there was a fire in the old stable block and now she looked closely, there was a tiny amount of black smoke starting to trickle out of one of the high windows at the left-hand end of the stables, where the new wedding venue was supposed to be.

——

Derek the foreman came stumbling out of the door, tearing off his face mask. 'Can't stop it. Used up fire extinguisher. It's going up.' Even as he spoke, the tiny trickle of smoke became a cloud, and the next window along the line, which was closed, began to darken with the smoke inside.

'Is everyone out?' Alice asked.

'Yes, we're all out,' Derek replied.

'I can't see that young lad? Mikey?' one of the men said.

'Lady Muck… I erm, I mean Caroline… didn't want him working her no more. He's over on the job at Saddleton. That's why we had nobody to carry out the wood.'

'But I saw him, he was here about half an hour ago.'

'No, you never. Couldn't have.'

There wasn't time for arguing now, Alice realised. 'Come on, we need to get to the car-park. That's the assembly point.' At least some of Caroline's instructions had stuck. The fire manual. What did it say? Well, even without reading the manual, she knew the first thing she had to do. Dial 999.

'Fire brigade please.' Her voice and her legs were starting to tremble. 'This is Misterley Manor. Yes, it's a genuine alarm this time, there is a small fire in the old stables.'

Two appliances were being dispatched from the fire station at Saddleton, the nearest town, over the other side of the high moors, she was told. They would be here as quickly as they could.

Already Alice could see the light of flames starting to lick at the bottom of that left- hand window. All that old, dry, dusty wood! There was a sharp crack as the window pane shattered, and the smoke began to swirl around the courtyard, catching at her throat and making her cough. Alice ran to the car park clutching the red emergency manual to her chest.

There weren't many people there. Marjorie in a pair of purple corduroy trousers and floral Doc Martens, Sarah from the tea rooms, a couple of her staff. The builders had gone to sit in their vans, watching from a distance. Emily wasn't there; she was living with her dad and Caroline was obviously absent, Tom and George were probably somewhere further away in the gardens.

'Right,' Alice announced, hoping that she sounded more confident than she felt and that her voice wasn't shaking too much, 'there's no need to panic because the fire brigade is on their way. It's a small fire, they'll have it put out in no time at all. Now, I need to find George to take charge -'

'Oh, so it's a real one this time?' Marjorie sounded surprised. 'I thought maybe Caroline had decided to call a fire drill. I suppose it would be out of character for her to call one when she's not even here – she does like a good fire drill, does Caroline. If it's a real fire, perhaps we need to try to get Henry out?'

She was interrupted by a loud crack from the direction of the stable block. The wispy smoke that had been hard to see from the car park was now large black billows of smoke rising from the courtyard. Underneath everything, the sound of the fire alarm still wailed.

Suddenly Tom came running around the corner into the car park, but George wasn't with him. 'I was over by the woodland walk when I saw the smoke – bloody hell – the whole stable block's going up. It's starting to come out under the eaves round the other side!'

This couldn't be happening, it couldn't be more than ten minutes since the alarm had first gone off, surely there couldn't be smoke coming from the roof already?

Another crack, another surge of smoke, another window gone perhaps?

She looked at Tom in horror. This couldn't be happening, this couldn't be real.

'Where's George? He's supposed to take charge, we need him right now!' She gasped. George was the one who would be in charge in an emergency, Caroline had assured her that her only responsibility would be to sort out the alarm panel. 'Sir Henry hasn't come out and the fire seems to be getting a hold.'

'George finished at lunchtime today, he's taken a half day. He's not here.'

'Oh!' Alice said, clutching the fire manual tighter, starting to feel the panic rising. 'Well, if George isn't here, then who's in charge?'

Everyone turned as there was an enormous crash from the direction of the stable block. The builders climbed out of their vans and turned to see what had happened and the tea-room staff gazed in horror in the direction of Misterley Manor. Behind the main building, in the courtyard, flames were suddenly seen licking into the air through a hole in the roof that was getting bigger and bigger every moment.

Misterley Manor was going to burn down.

'Who's in charge, Tom?' she asked again, more urgently, with growing panic as she realised what his answer was going to be before he even gave it.

'You are.'

Chapter 13

A Horticultural Crocodile Dundee.

'I can't! I don't know what to do!' She looked at Tom, who looked like the epitome of the action hero; a kind of horticultural Crocodile Dundee. Tom would save her.

'You've got to,' Tom said tersely. 'Caroline's put you in charge. I haven't got a clue about the house and George isn't here. It's got to be you.'

Tom wasn't going to save her. She felt sick, she couldn't do this on her own. She needed him to help her. If Sebastian was here he would already have snatched the folder from her hands and have told her to wait somewhere safe.

'Please, Tom? Couldn't you do it? Please?' she begged him. 'It's all written here, you've been here so much longer than me!'

'I can't, Alice,' he looked awkward. 'I can't read it.'

'What, you need glasses or something? You could get them, I'll hang on until you get back.'

He looked down at the floor, his face red in the reflected light of the flames. 'No, you don't understand. I can't read. Anything. Not quickly enough,' he said.

'You can't read?'

He looked straight at her, and she saw that he was embarrassed. 'I'm dyslexic. Hated reading, never got the hang of it. I'd need a magnifier and a yellow overlay and a spare day or two to read that folder. It's got to be you, Alice. You're the clever one round here. I'll do anything I can - but you'll have to tell me what to do.'

OK, so she had to get on with it and she had to get on with it now. Hands shaking, she tried to find the correct page in the folder.

She had covered all the *What to do when you discover a fire* section, now she had to move on to *What to do after a fire has broken out* section. She hoped she wasn't going to have to go as far as finding out if there was a *What to do if the entire house burns down with its elderly owner inside it* section of the manual.

'Right. Right, right, right, what do I do first, what should I do?'

Marjorie was standing behind her shoulder. 'It's all right, dear, Caroline's instructions are very detailed. Open the file and start at the beginning, the fire brigade is on their way, so that's the main thing, isn't it? And perhaps I'd better try and persuade Henry to come out?'

Henry. Yes, that was the next important thing. Sir Henry was still in his rooms, somebody had to get him out. But there in big letters across the second page of the file was the instruction that she shouldn't let anybody back in.

'I can't let you go back in there,' she said, decisively, pointing at the manual.

'Well, if you don't let me, my brother will never be persuaded to leave. The fire's a long way away in the stable block, I've got plenty of time, dear. Only I seem to have mislaid my key again.'

'But we can't get the spare keys now!' Alice realised.

'Where's the spare key?' Tom turned to Alice.

'The cupboard in Caroline's desk. But we can't go in there, it's too close to the fire,' Alice said, but Tom had already set off at a run in the direction of the door into the West Wing.

'No! Tom, don't!' Alice called after him, but already he was half way to the door. 'No, nobody must go back in until the fire brigade come, it could be dangerous! DON'T!' she yelled, waving the red file in the air like a warning sign. He wasn't listening. Bloody man, he told her she was in charge and then the first thing - the very first thing - she asked him to do he ignored her. What was he doing? What was he thinking? What was he -

He was back already, Caroline's large bunch of keys in his hand.

'I told you not to go back in there!' she shouted as he came back across the car park towards them.

'And I told you I would help. You do the clever stuff and I'll provide the muscle. OK?'

As he reached her side she could smell the smoke more strongly than ever. It was on his clothes, and there was a streak of soot running up the side of his face. 'No! Not OK! Not if you're going to go running into burning buildings like that!'

'It wasn't burning. Some smoke is starting to get through to the office. I shut the fire door between the tea rooms and the West Wing; that should stop it for a bit longer.'

There was smoke in the estate office. Oh shit, there was smoke from the fire already in Caroline's office and she had forgotten to shut the fire door; she was getting everything wrong – what if she had already made too many mistakes? What if the house did burn down and it was all her fault? She swallowed hard.

'Right, well, I'll go and get Henry, then? Now we've got the key?' said Marjorie, but she showed no signs of moving.

'No, you won't. I'll go,' said Tom, and though he was talking to Marjorie, he was looking at Alice.

'I won't let you. It isn't safe. It says so here, "No-one is to be allowed to re-enter the building"!' She held up the folder with Caroline's instructions in bold red type.

'Well, never mind that, I can't read it, can I?' Tom said, turning towards the main door with the keys.

'No! Wait for the fire brigade!' she said.

'There won't be time. I need to go right now. The sooner I get in there, the quicker I get old Sir Henry out.'

'Don't! You can't go, Tom. I won't let you.' She grabbed his arm, but he easily shook her hand off.

'I'm going. At least that's something I can do.'

'Don't Tom, please don't. What if something goes wrong?'

'Then the fire brigade can get us out when they get here,' he said, turning away from her.

'Tom, no!' she yelled after him, but it was too late, he was already opening the big double door in the centre of the main part of the house.

If only the fire brigade would come. It was about a twenty-minute drive over the moors to Saddleton, how long ago had she phoned? About fifteen minutes. So long, why did it have to take so long?

If only Caroline was here, she would know exactly what to do, whereas Alice felt her knees starting to wobble as she realised exactly what she had to deal with. The fate of Misterley Manor and its contents as well as the safety of everyone here was in her hands. She needed to work out what she was going to do next, and she needed to do it quickly. She couldn't wait and watch for Tom, she had to carry on. There was nowhere to sit so she put the folder down on the ground, knelt beside it and opened the first page.

The fire brigade had been called; everyone except Tom and Henry were safely out of the building. What was next? She turned the page, the words seemed to swim in front of her and she couldn't concentrate as all the while the sound of roaring was growing louder and the smell of smoke stronger. She could see the dancing golden light of the flames starting to reflect off the laminated pages of the fire manual. At last, though, she could hear sirens in the distance, the fire brigade couldn't be far away.

The builders' foreman, Derek, had got out of his van and come over to her. 'Can we do anything to help, love?'

'No… I, erm… I don't know… Wait, we have to put up shelters, it says here, for salvage. You can help with that. Marjorie, do you know where the shelters are kept?'

'I do, they're the square tents that we use for garden events - they're in the big shed. If you come with me, we'll get them. Where should we put them, Alice?'

'I don't know.' There was so much she didn't know. Where was the right page, what should she tell them? 'Oh, here, it says here; not too close to the building. On the Great Lawn.'

'Fine,' Marjorie nodded, and took the builders with her to go and get the tents.

Where was Tom, where was Sir Henry? Surely they should have been out by now? Were they arguing, was Sir Henry's notorious stubbornness proving too much for Tom? If only Caroline was here, she would be able to get Sir Henry out.

But it was going to be OK, because here came the fire brigade now, two solid red fire engines roaring up into the car-park. Alice felt like crying with relief, but she didn't.

'I'm so glad you're here!' Alice said to the man who came out of the fire engine first, he was already on the radio asking for an aerial ladder platform, and additional crews. Six additional crews. That sounded like a lot to Alice.

'Right. I'm the Station Manager, but you can all me Charlie. Who's in charge here?'

'I am,' Alice said quietly.

'Are you the owner?'

'Caroline's the manager but she's in York and Sir Henry – he's the owner - is still in his room. Tom is trying to get him out.'

'You mean the buildings aren't clear?'

'He's disabled; he's blind – someone has to help him. Tom went back in to get him.'

'Tom?'

'The assistant gardener.'

'Right. Priorities. First appliance round the other side of the building, go in through the courtyard, two of you get breathing apparatus on now,' he called out to his crew. 'Second pump, round to the far side where the hole in the roof is, tackle the fire from outside.'

'There's no road, though!' Alice protested

'We take it over the lawns.'

'You can't! It'll wreck the grass!' She couldn't believe that she had said that. What was she thinking? The grass? The grass! When the Manor was burning down, and Tom and Sir Henry were inside it? The fireman rolled his eyes and motioned the driver of the second fire engine to drive straight over the lawn and round the side of the house to the other side of the stable block as if she had never said anything. Alice felt very small and very foolish.

'The two of you with breathing apparatus are to go and find the elderly resident in the main house. You'd better get -' Before Charlie had a chance to say what they had better get, the main door on the south front of the house was flung open, and Tom appeared with a frail-looking man leaning on him, who must be Sir Henry.

Alice ran over towards them, but Charlie pulled her back.

'No. Don't get any closer than that,' he snapped, and she had to wait for Tom and Sir Henry to reach her.

Sir Henry didn't look like she had imagined. In her mind he had become a cross between a character from Downton Abbey and some creature of the night, tall, crooked, angular, perpetually dressed in evening dress with a monocle - not a short balding man with missing teeth and a vivid blue jumper which *must* have been a gift from Marjorie.

'Where's Caroline?' he demanded. Even though she knew he couldn't see her, Alice avoided eye contact. 'Why isn't she here?'

'She's in York.'

'And you are?'

'I'm Alice,' she said.

'Ah yes, the researcher. Well, I hope you know what you're

doing, as Tim here tells me that you are in charge until my daughter gets home.'

'It's Tom. Not Tim,' she said, thinking that the very least he could have done was to remember the name of his rescuer. 'And I know what I'm doing. Caroline's instructions are very clear,' she answered with what she hoped sounded like conviction.

'Alice? Grandad!' A voice called across the lawn. It was Emily.

'Emily, what are you doing here!'

'I saw the smoke from the bus, so I got off. Alice, the house is on fire!'

'Um… yes… it is…' Alice said, unsure how to react to Emily's statement of the obvious. Was she blaming Alice for the fire? Her tone of voice had been almost accusatory.

'Where's Mum? Why have you got the folder?' And Alice realised that under that accusatory tone there was something else. Emily was scared.

'She's in York. She's quite safe,' Alice reassured the younger girl.

'Is she coming back?'

'I haven't told her yet,' Alice confessed. 'I'll ring her when I get a chance. By the time she gets back, it'll probably all be over.'

'You mean the house will have burnt down?' she said, her voice trembled.

'No! The fire brigade will have put the fire out,' Alice said, trying her best to sound like Caroline, pretending a confidence that she didn't feel. At the moment the two fire engines looked woefully inadequate to tackle the flames that were reaching out of the roof of the stable block up into the sky, two, three, four times higher than the fire engines themselves.

'I think I should tell Dad where I am,' Emily muttered, her hands shaking as she got her phone out. Of course, although Caroline was too far away to get back in time, there was someone else who might be able to take charge – or at least help. Duncan knew the house well, Duncan had lived here, Duncan liked telling other people what to do and he was only just over the moors in Ormsborough, not nearly 70 miles away in York.

'Look, Emily, could you ring your dad and ask him to come, right now?'

'I don't want that man setting foot in my house!' said Sir Henry, who had suddenly appeared behind her, and apparently was listening to everything she said. 'You have no right –'

'He won't be setting foot in your house, Sir Henry,' Tom pointed out calmly. 'Nobody will be except the fire brigade. But I think you're right, Alice. Duncan could be very useful.'

'I won't have it!' Sir Henry was getting agitated. He obviously wasn't aware how serious the danger to the house was, or surely he wouldn't be getting this agitated simply about his ex-son-in-law?

'Emily, do you think you could take your grandfather over to the pub? It isn't safe for him to stay here.' Alice realised it would be better if Sir Henry could be taken out of the picture for now, there wasn't time to follow Caroline's instructions and pacify her father. She hoped that Emily wasn't going to choose this moment to be difficult. The last thing she wanted was to have a row with Emily as well as her grandfather right now.

'No, I will not! I will not be -' he was starting to protest, but Emily interrupted, nodding at Alice as she spoke.

'Grandad, I'm scared. I don't want to stay here. Will you take me down to the Lattimore Arms to wait for my dad to come? Please, Grandad?' She was talking in a childlike voice.

'Emily, my dear, I can't. It would be like a captain deserting his ship. Don't ask me. If only your mother was here… but when wanted, she is nowhere to be found.'

'Grandad, please?' Emily's voice trembled as if with tears,

though none were forming in her eyes.

'Oh, very well. If I must. Family must come first. Family must always come first.'

Emily led her grandfather slowly away up the lawn and towards the curve of the main drive, giving Alice a thumbs up gesture behind his back and Alice breathed a sigh of relief as Charlie approached again.

'Right, Alice. We'll need to run the hoses from the ornamental pond over there. We need the electricity off, is that done?'

'Erm...' There had been nothing in the red folder about turning off the electricity.

The fireman rolled his eyes skywards. 'Trev, you were at the last walk-through briefing here, you remember where the electric is? Go and turn it off.' One of his crew disappeared in the direction of the courtyard. She had got it wrong again. She hadn't turned off the electricity before things got out of control, what else had she done wrong?

'We'll handle it from here. You start on assessing your salvage priorities. We've got four more pumps coming from Ormsborough and two from down the coast. Now, get Caroline Lattimore back here, we need her.'

'Salvage priorities. Yes, salvage, of course… and Caroline…'

'Excuse me, do you need any help?' A man in a fleece had appeared beside her. Who the hell was he and where had he come from? 'I was visiting the gardens, I saw the smoke.'

'Please keep away from the building,' she said, automatically.

'How did it start? Do you know?' the man asked.

'Builders in the stable block started it,' she replied tersely, wanting to get on with her jobs.

'Looks pretty big already!'

'Yes, it took hold pretty fast, lots of old wood in there to burn, you see.'

A couple of minutes later her phone started to ping with messages. It had hardly any battery left – why hadn't she charged it properly this morning?

'Seen it on Twitter about Misterley Manor. You OK, hun?' from her Aunty Linda. What did she mean, seen it on Twitter?

Hands shaking, she searched for Misterley Manor on Twitter, and sure enough, there were several tweets on there already with pictures of the stable block and the fire engines.

"Fire at #MisterleyManor. Looks serious. Whole place might go up!" Fifteen minutes ago.

"Fire at #MisterleyManor. Fire brigade in action." Five minutes ago.

"#MisterleyManor fire chaos here!" A picture of her kneeling beside the fire instructions looking panicked – who had taken that? When had they taken it?

"#MisterleyManorfire started by careless builders. *Lots of old wood to burn*!!" Two minutes ago. How did anyone know that? Shit. The man in the fleece. It must have been him, but she didn't have time for that now, it would have to wait, she still hadn't even looked at her salvage priorities yet, that was the next job -

And now the office mobile rang. That was also starting to go flat at an alarming rate.

'Hi, Radio Ormsborough here. Is it true that Misterley Manor is on fire? Do you have a comment?'

She hadn't had time to get anywhere near the "dealing with the press" section of the fire manual, she didn't have a clue what to do. 'No comment. It's an emergency, please get off this line!' she snapped.

Caroline. She had to phone Caroline before Caroline saw it on Twitter. Hands shaking, she tried to find Caroline's number, which went straight to answerphone. She must have turned her phone off while she was in the conference, hell, hell, hell!

―――

Alice flicked over the page now to salvage priorities. Caroline had listed everything, in every room that should be removed, in order of importance. Pages and pages of them. The first page contained the top salvage priorities for the house as on a separate list. How would she ever co-ordinate this? Should she start with the top priorities list, that included things a long way from the fire, or did she start with assigning priorities in the rooms closest to the blaze?

'What can I do?' Marjorie approached her as she studied the file.

Alice looked up, took a deep breath and made a decision. 'You can help with the salvage priorities. I want you to start with the rooms closest to the blaze.' She was buzzing with tension as she began taking the pages out of the folder to give to Marjorie. 'You can help to direct the firemen best as you know the house so well, you need to tell them where to go and what to get.'

'And what about me?' Tom had approached her quietly from the side. 'What can I do now?' She turned to him, speaking with quiet certainty.

'Tom, I'll need you to organise the physical side of the salvage – getting the items up to the tent.'

'OK, I can do that for you,' he said. She would have liked to say more to him – tell him not to do anything dangerous, no more running into burning buildings, make him stay safe – but there wasn't time as the fire chief was heading across the lawn towards her.

'Right, we're ready to start on salvage if you think it's necessary,' she told him.

'It's necessary. We need to get in there quickly, I've raised the emergency call. We've got eight pumps on their way now from all over the county. We can't contain the fire to the stable block, it's spread through the void above the archway and it's already in the roof above the tea room. We're working to contain it for as long as we can, now the aerial platform is here.'

Alice hadn't even noticed the arrival of more fire engines and a cherry-picker which was already rising up regally above the roof of the stable block.

'We have to accept that there is an imminent threat to the West Wing, and from there to the rest of the house. The crew from the third appliance will start salvage there with their breathing appliances, we might only have ten, fifteen minutes at most.'

'Can I send our volunteers into the main house to start getting things out while the fire brigade deal with the West Wing? It will be safe there for a while, won't it?'

'Nobody except fire crews with the correct apparatus to go into the building. Now what are the first salvage priorities for the West Wing?'

'Marjorie, you've got the list.'

'Yes, of course. Library first, then the Painted Hall. Now, the priority for salvage in the library is the shelf of early first editions, on the wall beside the office door.' Marjorie made her way across the lawn with the lead fire-fighter from the salvage crew. 'And we should probably get Caroline's computer out of the office if we can…'

'And everyone who is capable of lifting, you're in Tom's salvage chain, everyone else you're wrapping and packing the salvaged items in the tents.' She took a deep breath. It was all down to her now. 'We can do this. I know we can. We have to, we don't have a choice. It's up to us, all of us, to save this beautiful house and if we can't… if we can't… we have to save what we can. This is our history that's burning, and we need every pair of hands, every one of you. And you -' she was suddenly aware of the brown-fleeced amateur photographer behind her, snapping away again, 'you can put your sodding phone down and help us save things or you can get out of here now, but you are NOT going to hang around taking pictures while this place burns down.'

The man looked startled for a moment, put his phone in his

pocket and joined the salvage chain. Alice was surprised at herself – she wasn't used to giving instructions and she certainly wasn't used to people doing what she said. She wasn't sure that she like it very much, it was easier being the one who did what she was told.

'You got fired up there!' Tom joked as he went past, a handful of builders and staff who had hurried down from the garden centre with him. It wasn't the time, it wasn't the place, the joke was highly inappropriate… so why was she smiling at him?

Now, the next thing she had to do was possibly the worst of all. She started entering the digits into the house mobile phone.

'Halliday Conference Centre, how can I help you?'

'I need to get hold of Caroline Lattimore, she's attending the historic properties management conference? It's a serious emergency, I need her right now.'

'Certainly. Most of the delegates are in the bar, the last session of the day has just finished. Can I tell her who is calling and why?'

'It's Alice Goudge. Tell her to ring me back immediately please.'

Chapter 14

Hurrying Home.

It was Caroline's worst nightmare, a fire at Misterley Manor. Everything at Misterley was old and a little bit dodgy, including her builders. It was only a matter of time before something went wrong, and the session on disaster planning for fires which had just finished had made her realise how badly prepared she was. Her precious red disaster folder hadn't been updated for two years – the list of salvage priorities was out of date for a start, some of the items weren't in the same location, some had been sold and some, like the letters, hadn't even been in the house when she first wrote the plan. She hadn't re-checked the list of contacts recently; she hadn't even remembered to mention turning off the electricity; there was so much that she needed to do. She was still making notes on her handout as she sat in the bar having a drink before the conference dinner when one of the staff from reception came up to her, spotting her name badge.

'Caroline Lattimore?'

'Yes, that's me,' she said, putting down her pen.

'There's been a phone call from a lady called Alice Goudge from Misterley Manor. She'd like you to ring her; she said she couldn't get through to your phone. It's urgent.'

'Thank you.'

She was only due to be away for a single night. One single night away from Misterley, the first she'd had in two years, and Alice couldn't manage without her. She knew she should never have risked it. Her phone had been turned off for the last session and she hadn't turned it on again. It must be the builders. What had they done now? Cut off the electricity or the water to the tea room this time perhaps?

Found dry rot? Death watch beetle? The skeleton of Gilbert Fox-Travers buried under the stable yard? Whatever it was, she was sure it could have waited until tomorrow. Or perhaps Alice had given Marjorie *both* the spare keys and now everyone was locked out of the house. Where had she put the number for the locksmith who she had to call to sort it out last time? She was still trying to remember as she dialled Alice's number.

'Caroline.'

Alice's voice sounded strange and abrupt and there was a lot of noise and interference in the background.

'What's the matter? There's some problem, I understand?' She hoped she could get it sorted quickly, the dinner was due to start in an hour and a half and she wanted to get changed.

'Caroline, you have to come back right now,' Alice said. Caroline had never heard her sound so commanding before; usually Alice was all "If it's all right with you" and "If you're sure you don't mind" not "You have to do it right now". This wasn't normal.

Oh God, perhaps it was her father.

'Is Daddy...?'

'It's fine. He's fine. He's at the pub with Emily.'

This made no sense at all. He hadn't left his rooms in two years, what was he doing at the pub?

'I don't understand. My seventeen-year-old daughter has taken her house-bound grandfather to the pub? Alice, have you been drinking?'

'No, it's... Caroline, there's a problem.' There was something so matter-of-fact about Alice's voice right now that Caroline immediately knew something was very, very wrong.

'What's happening?' and Caroline's voice dropped an octave in sudden fear.

'There's a fire, Caroline. Can you get back here as quickly as possible, please?'

——

Her fingers started to tingle and went numb. She found it difficult to hold the phone, and she began to find her breath coming in short sharp gasps. She dropped the phone and found herself scrabbling on the floor trying to pick it up. This couldn't be happening, she hadn't even finished writing her notes, she wasn't ready for this, everything was wrong.

One of the other delegates sitting at the next table turned round. She looked concerned. 'Sit down, try and breathe more slowly. Is something wrong? Are you ill? Do you need a first-aider?'

'My phone… I dropped it… It was a shock, that's all… I need to speak to Alice…' Caroline was struggling to find enough breath to speak, her chest had gone tight and every breath was an effort.

'Here, I've got it, it's slipped down under here,' the woman said, retrieving the phone which had skidded away under an adjoining table. Distantly on the other end Caroline could hear Alice's voice, tinny and high pitched.

'Caroline, are you there? Caroline?'

'How bad is it?' she asked, though her shortness of breath tried to stop her from speaking altogether.

'I'm so sorry, Caroline.' Alice sounded more like her ineffectual, apologetic self now. It made Caroline feel perversely better. 'But it's not good. It started in the stable block.'

'Those bloody builders!' she gasped. 'So the stable block is on fire? All that work up in smoke! Now we'll never get the venue open on time, all my plans…'

At least it wasn't the main house. At least it was only the stable block. The tightness in her chest started to ease.

'And the fire brigade there, putting it out?' she asked.

'There are five fire engines here, they're doing their best, but…'

'But what?'

'The fire has spread. They're bringing in fire crews from all over North East Yorkshire now, as well as several from Ormsborough.'

'How far? How far has it spread?' The silence at Alice's end of the line said more than her words could have done and Caroline nearly dropped the phone again. 'Alice? Alice? Tell me, what's going on?'

She could hear Alice talking to someone else, voices in the distance, too far from the phone to work out what they were saying, Alice must be holding the phone up against her to deaden the noise, so Caroline couldn't hear properly. It was too long; what was going on now? What was happening? At last she heard Alice raise the phone again.

'Caroline, it's not good. We've seen the flames are in the tea rooms now.'

'The tea rooms? But they're not in the old stable block!'

'No. They're in the West Wing,' said Alice, and Caroline could hear a strange roaring – that must be the fire – and a distant noise of crashing and smashing.

'What's that? What can I hear?'

'I think it's in the tea room – I think it must be the shelves burning, the crockery breaking.'

'You mean they don't think they can save the tea rooms?' Her voice was no more than a hoarse whisper.

'They're working very hard,' said Alice, in that bright, confident tone that was so unlike her, the one that was sending chills right through Caroline's soul. 'Charlie, the fire chief says that if they can form a wall where the original house meets the new part, he's hopeful that we can stop the fire there and it won't spread any further.'

'Where the old house meets the new? I don't understand. The tea room isn't new.'

'Where the West Wing meets the old house. It's an old exterior wall, you see, he's explained it all to me. There are too many voids and connecting spaces in the West Wing, and the fire has too strong a hold. But if they can form a wall of firefighters on the West Wing staircase, just before it meets the main building, then they hope that the fire won't spread any further.'

'But Alice, I don't understand any of this.' Now she was sounding more like the young researcher than Alice herself did. Next she'd be apologising to Alice.

'If the fire brigade can stop the fire at the West Wing staircase, next to the old exterior wall of the house, then they hope that they can save the main building and the East Wing.'

'And the West Wing?'

'Caroline, I'm so sorry...'

'Are you saying that we're going to lose the West Wing? All of it?'

'They're holding the fire back for as long as possible so that we can salvage things. Marjorie and Tom are running the salvage operation right now; there's a human chain going right the way up the lawn to the tents. The garden centre staff are packing things safely away. We found the disaster supplies, so there's plenty of packaging, and at least the weather's dry – that's something.'

'We're going to lose the West Wing? Is that what you're saying?' She found herself repeating the question, hoping that the answer might eventually be "no" if she asked it often enough. Perhaps there was something she was misunderstanding – perhaps Alice wasn't being clear. She would be panicking, that's what it was, Alice was panicking and making things sound worse than they were. Much worse. It would be a little fire, that's all and Alice had got it wrong somehow. A small fire in the old stables. The builders would be able to repair it.

But Alice hadn't answered her question, she was talking to someone else again, and all Caroline could hear was the roar of the flames that were consuming her house, a couple of voices and the sound of radios in the background.

'Alice? What is it? What's happening? Can you put me on Skype, let me see what's happening? Alice?' She heard an enormous crashing sound and knew that there was something very bad happening – but what was it? She heard Alice's voice, distant, as if she had put the phone down and was speaking from a long way away. Alice was swearing.

'Alice? What's happening? Are you OK, is someone hurt? Alice?' She was shouting down the phone in the hopes that Alice would remember she was there and speak to her again – was Alice hurt? Had something crashed down on her? How close was she to the fire? People in the bar were turning to stare, but Caroline didn't care about that right now.

'Caroline, look, I'm going to have to go. Can you get back here?'

'Tell me what's happening. What was that noise?'

'The roof above the tea shop and your office,' Alice said. 'I need to speak to Charlie right now, we need to start pulling out the salvage teams. I'm not sure if everything's clear.'

'Alice, I can't drive. I've had too much to drink, I don't know how I'm going to get back… perhaps I'll risk it…'

'No! No, don't be stupid, Caroline. Can someone there drive you?'

Caroline looked around the bar. She barely knew anyone in the bar, and those she did know were also drinking. She couldn't ask a total stranger to leave the conference dinner to take her home. Then she heard, somewhere close to Alice, a man's voice. Duncan's voice.

'It's OK – we think it's probably best if you don't drive anyway. The shock might affect you. Duncan's going to come and get you,' said Alice.

'What's Duncan doing there?'

'I asked him to come.'

'You had no right!' she protested.

'Probably not, but it seemed like a good idea,' Alice said in a tone of voice that Caroline didn't want to argue with. 'He's on his way to get you now.'

'No! What about one of the garden staff? Tom or George? They could come.'

'I'm coming, Caroline, and please stop trying to interfere.' Duncan must have taken the house phone from Alice. 'Get your stuff together, I'll be there in about an hour. Give you time to sober up – or have another couple of drinks if that's what'll get you through. Don't worry.'

'Don't worry? My house is burning down and you tell me not to worry?'

Now the *entire* bar had turned to look at her.

'*Try* not to worry. I'll be there as soon as I can.'

As she put the phone down Caroline found herself staring at the sheet of notes from the last lecture, still half-finished in front of her.

Make sure that your disaster plan is revised annually and always kept up to date.

Oh shit.

Chapter 15

An Unusual Use for a Stanley Knife.

'We're running out of time, Alice. They're withdrawing the salvage teams; the fire is getting too close now. We can't get everything out. The volunteers are taking the last few items up to the tent now then the salvage teams are moving on to the main house. That's it. They've got everything they can.'

Tom was handing a large vase from the Painted Hall to her as he spoke and walked beside her as she took it up to the next member of the chain. They were both exhausted, sweaty, dirty. Tom looked like an action hero, soot stained and muscular, but Alice looked like she had stepped out of a disaster movie; her shoes were ruined, her hair had gone frizzy and the oversized yellow high-vis waistcoat from the disaster supplies simply wasn't her colour.

'What's been left?'

'The large oil paintings. The little ones are all out, but those three big ones are attached too securely, and the frames are enormous. They're going to have to leave them behind.'

The large oil paintings. That must mean the Fox-Travers Arthurian scenes. Of all the things to have been left!

'They can't! They can't do that, there must be a way,' she thought quickly, desperately and out of the corner of her eye she spotted a solution. 'Wait, we can cut them out!' she said. 'If they cut them out of the frames we can save them all. The frames will burn but the paintings won't. Here, they're using Stanley knives in the tent for cutting the packaging, come with me.' The two of them began to run towards the marquee.

'Are you sure?'

'No. But we're going to do it anyway. Come on!' She found that the best way to carry on was just to try and behave like she thought Caroline would.

She snatched up three knives from the trestle table where the packers were working, Tom grabbed a couple more and they ran back down to the house. Running with knives was probably against all the health and safety guidance in Caroline's red folder but Alice felt empowered to ignore that right now. So much of what was in that precious folder had proved wrong so far – she was lucky that Tom had even found that vase which hadn't even been in the same room it was listed, and why on earth the Fox-Travers paintings weren't right at the top of the list for the Painted Gallery, it was hard to imagine. But at least the basics had been right, and at least there was a plan. She would have been lost without it – even if there were mistakes.

A cordon had been set up beyond which only fire-fighters could go, Alice and Tom were stuck beyond the cordon, shouting to try and get their attention.

'Come on! Come on!' Alice was screaming. 'You need to cut them out! '

'It's no good, they can't hear,' Tom said to her. 'Give me the knives.' He grabbed them from her and ducked under the cordon.

'No! Come back! Tom! What are you doing? Not again!'

Tom was heading towards the burning building. The one rule that Caroline had put in large red letters at the front of the fire manual was "Do not allow anyone to re-enter the building" and now Tom had done it three times. Running down the hill with knives was one thing, but running past the safety cordon was entirely another, and this time with the flames so close that she could feel the heat, he was in real, tangible danger.

She could only wait, a sudden rush of fear constricting her throat until she didn't know if she was going to be able to breathe. He didn't try to go in, he managed to catch the attention of one of the fire fighters, hand over the knives and came back to her.

'You idiot! You total and utter stupid, idiot! I TOLD you not to go back in, what the HELL were you doing!' she yelled at him, furious.

'Saving the pictures for you,' he said with a grin. 'You didn't want me to let them all burn, did you?'

'But you could have died! What if something had fallen on you, what if one of the windows had blown out? You could have been killed!' He could have died, and it wasn't worth it for some paintings. Nobody should be putting their life on the line for that, and this was the THIRD time he'd done it today, as if he was trying to prove something to her; first the key, then Sir Henry what if something had happened, what if… what if he had been killed? 'Don't you *ever* do anything like that again, you could have *died,* Tom.'

'I promised you that I'd help, didn't I?' he said, taking a step towards her.

'And I'm very grateful but –'

'Save that for another time. We need to get on,' he said, because here came Charlie, who had a roll of canvas under each arm. He handed one to Tom and one to Alice.

'There you go. That's it, that's the last, we've pulled back now. The salvage teams are on to the main building, and the rest of the crews are going to concentrate on the stairs. It's time to say your prayers now, that we can stop it.'

In her hands, Alice held the huge canvas that Fox-Travers had painted of Morgan Le Faye and King Arthur. It was ash-stained, covered in sooty hand prints and the edges of the canvas were ragged and jagged where the knife had roughly cut it from the frame. What had she done?

Suddenly the enormity of the situation began to hit her. All this time she had been so busy, following the instructions in the file, delegating, deciding, organising. Now, here she stood, in ruins of the rose garden which was already trampled and hacked away to get to the building, holding in her hands the damaged remains of what had been one of the most powerful and important paintings of the early 20th century.

'Tom, what have I done?' she gasped, breath catching at the back of her throat and not because of the smoke. 'What have I done?'

'You've done what you had to,' he said firmly. 'Stop worrying. Come on, let's get these up to the tent so that they can be packed away.' He deposited his last bundle of salvage, and Alice placed hers carefully beside it.

'Artworks from the Painted Hall,' Alice explained. 'Roll them for now and pack them in something, make sure they don't get crushed.'

'Oh, heavens. That's the Fox-Travers Morgan Le Faye isn't it?' said the woman who was packing away the salvaged items into cardboard boxes from the garden centre. Alice could see tears in the woman's eyes. She tried not to let it affect her, it wouldn't help if she started getting sentimental too, not here, not now. There would be a time for sentiment, but it wasn't right now. She hoped the woman didn't cry all over the paintings, that wouldn't do them any good.

'This are the last things from the West Wing, we're moving on to the main house now.'

'And what's this other painting here? The one behind Morgan Le Faye kneeling, I don't recognise it,' the volunteer asked.

Alice glanced down, and caught a glimpse of another painting, she could only see the very edge of the rolled canvas, it looked an interior of some kind, with a hand holding a jewelled goblet. She didn't recognise it from the Painted Hall, it must have come from somewhere else in the house.

'Don't know; we'll look into it later. Wrap it and store it, please.'

Alice and Tom ducked out of the salvage tent and Alice

looked at the house, as if it was a picture in a film, something that was happening somewhere else to someone else. She could see from where she stood through the trefoil windows of the little tower that contained the reading nook. The velvet cushions, the oak panelling, the light glistening off the brass light fittings, all just as it had been since Fox-Travers created it over a hundred years ago. It was the last time she would ever see that perfect little tower room. Perhaps it was the last time that *anyone* would ever see it as it had been.

She was drained, she needed a break.

She walked to the side of the lawn at the edge of the rhododendron forest, where Tom had already flung himself down in the coolness under the branches sheltered from the heat of the fire and the chaos of the salvage for a few minutes. She hoped he wouldn't mind if she joined him. From where they sat, they could see the Manor in every vivid detail.

An horrendous crash, worse than anything she had heard before, almost like an explosion going off, shook the ground where they sat. Inside the building, the beautiful painted library roof had come crashing down, there across the window she could see one of the huge roof beams where it had fallen to wedge itself on top of the balcony of the library - at least it hadn't crashed right through the delicate metalwork, bringing that down as well – but now flames came out of the space where the roof had been. She hid her face on Tom's shoulder.

'I can't watch,' she gasped, as he put his arm around her and began to stroke her hair.

'It's OK. It's going to be OK. The line of hoses is still holding,' he said, pointing at the join between the old building and the new, where the firefighters were battling with the flames.

Alice had been watching what was being destroyed but Tom must have his eyes on the panelled hallway where the fire-fighters were working to save the rest of the building. Above it two cherrypickers kept the roof soaked with water and inside every hose was trained on stopping the fire. On one side the library was red with flame, to their right the windows of the main house were grey and still, and in the entrance hall a thin line of hoses and firefighters in black and yellow separated the two. The line had to hold, it had to.

Alice didn't know how long she could endure this suspense, waiting and watching for the first flicker of flames in the main building, for the fire-fighters to be withdrawn and come running out to say that the wall of water hadn't worked. Tight panic rose in her throat, this was no good.

'I can't just sit here and watch it burn!' she said.

'You've done everything you can,' Tom said, taking hold of her hands, his eyes locked onto hers, as if he was willing her to be strong. 'You've been amazing.'

And in that moment, Alice did actually feel amazing. Exhilarated. Alive. She had done something real, she had helped to save something from this disaster. She had done the right thing, she hadn't been a spectator, she hadn't waited for someone else to tell her what to do, she had taken charge. Suddenly she felt a surge of freedom. Sebastian had been wrong about so many things, he had been holding her back from achieving her true potential. Now she could do whatever she wanted without Sebastian to tell her she was wrong.

She looked at Tom sitting beside her, his face lit by the glow from the house. It might be wishful thinking but to Alice the flames didn't seem quite so large now.

'You were amazing too. You were so brave,' she said, picturing him running back into the building, not just once but three times. She wasn't angry any more.

'It was the only thing I could do; I didn't want to let you down again.'

'Again?'

'The reading. I wish I could have helped with that.'

'It's no big deal, Tom. I can't swim but I bet you can. It's not anything to be ashamed of!'

'Oh, but I am. There's you with your degrees and all the letters after your name – and me who takes half an hour to read a phone message.'

'And that's why you went back in all those times, even though you knew it wasn't safe. You don't have anything to prove, you know, Tom. Not to me.'

'I had to do something,' he said, turning away from the burning building to look directly at her. 'I don't want you to think I'm useless too.'

'I don't think you're useless, why would I?' she said, her mouth suddenly dry and for a moment they looked at each other. 'I've never thought that, not from the first time I met you and you gave me that rose. You're a good, kind, brave man, Tom.'

'I wish I really was,' he said sadly, and looked away from her.

'You are! You really don't know how awesome you've been today, do you?'

How could she make him see what she saw? How could she make him understand exactly what his help and support had meant to her today when things got tough?

There was one thing she could do… one thing that she suddenly, inexplicably found that she wanted to do very, very much. She was so close to him that all she would have to do was lean her head ever so slightly to one side, close her eyes and brush her lips gently against his. It wasn't a good idea. She was on the rebound after Sebastian, she barely knew him, she didn't know if they had anything in common, it was wrong… and yet… today she could do anything she wanted to.

His lips tasted of smoke and salt. Hers probably did too. She felt her entire body quiver as they touched; a gentle experimental brush of her lips against his wasn't going to be enough for her.

'Tom, I…' she began, her eyes searching his face, but he didn't need words to reply as he reached for her. All she wanted was to taste those smoky lips again and what had been a tentative experiment became something a lot more serious. She pressed her body against his, twining her hands in his hair, pulling him towards her as the kiss deepened. She didn't want to let him go, she was melting inside…

'Are you sure about this?' he murmured, pulling away from her for a moment. 'Are you sure this is what you want?'

She paused for a moment, trying to read the look in his eyes. Was this Tom's way of asking if she wanted to have sex with him? If that's what he wanted her to do for him, she would give him what he wanted... She couldn't deny that she found him attractive – and brave. If he wanted her, she would let him take her; even if the garden of Misterley Manor in the middle of a major fire wasn't the most obvious place to choose to have sex. Perhaps, because he was a gardener, he felt happier outdoors.

'I'm sure,' she said, taking a deep breath, as she tried to sound as if she really was sure and she took his hand, drawing him into the shadows of the rhododendrons where nobody could see them. In his eyes she could see the reflection of the flames from behind them, flickering red, until their kiss deepened again and he closed his eyes with a sigh. His hands on the small of her back were shaking and so were hers. It was all so quick, so new... she hadn't expected Tom to want her like this, so soon, but all her fears and doubts about what would happen next were overwhelmed by one sudden overriding desire, a desire that she had never felt as keenly as this before. It was as if the fire had kindled something inside her, a spark that was going to be very difficult to put out.

She wanted Tom. This was no longer just a favour to him… She wanted him to take her, and she wanted him to do it now. His kisses were hungry but hers were those of a woman starved of desire.

Kissing Sebastian had been about one thing and one thing only – it had always been about Sebastian getting what he wanted - but Tom's kisses promised her the world and everything in it. She took a couple of stumbling steps backwards until her back rested against the trunk of one of the rhododendron bushes where it was dark. Pulling him towards her she flung off her high-vis jacket and her jumper and quickly began to undo the buttons of her jeans.

'No, Alice. Stop, please,' Tom said in a strangled voice. 'What are you doing?'

'Come on, Tom! We don't have long, you'll have to be quick if you want to…'

Sebastian would have been in and out of her and doing up his trousers again by now, he wouldn't have needed asking twice – or even once. Why was Tom pulling away? Had she misread the signals, was he not interested in her after all? Had she done something wrong?

'No. It's not the right time or the right place. I'm sorry Alice, it's too much, too soon. I can't.' He took a step away from her, his breath coming in deep gasps in the semi-darkness, his eyes full of something that wasn't desire and that might easily be mistaken for fear.

Suddenly she felt ridiculous, standing there in just her bra, her jeans half undone, high-vis jacket on the floor, twigs and leaves in her hair. 'But you asked me if I wanted to, and I said yes!'

'I didn't mean… Oh God, I'm sorry, is that what you thought? I was just asking if it was OK to kiss you.'

They stared at each other. He was right, of course he was right. She had got carried away, swept away by all the emotion and because she has assumed that he would want the same as Sebastian. Sebastian liked to take any opportunity that presented itself, but Tom was different. And what was she thinking, trying to seduce him while Misterley Manor was still burning? It was adrenaline; adrenaline, hormones and years of trying and failing to satisfy Sebastian's sudden urges. As the rush of emotion started to drain away, she saw her actions in the cold light of reality. She had just tried to persuade a man who she barely knew to have sex with her in the woods because it was what Sebastian would have done. What had she been thinking? All this time she had been wary of Sebastian's constant and inappropriate appetites… and now… she was no better than he was. She had actually wanted Tom to take her in the rhododendrons. What must he think of her?

'I'm so sorry…' she murmured, mortified, looking down at the ground. She found that she couldn't even look up at him, she was consumed with shame. 'You're right… I got carried away, I'm so sorry. I thought it was what you wanted.'

'You don't need to be sorry… I'm just… I don't think I'm ready. I thought I was, I thought it was going to be OK until… It's just too risky. It's not you, Alice, it's me. I think perhaps you should put your top back on.'

Scarlet with humiliation, she picked her soft green jumper up from the ground where she had dropped it.

'I'll go…' she said, putting her high-vis jacket back on. He tried to help her ease it over her shoulder and she flinched away from him. 'I'd better be getting back. Things to do, fires to put out, you know!'

'Alice… don't be upset.'

'I'm not. No, not at all, no not upset!' she lied, brightly. She had got it all wrong. All of it, Tom, the fire, the pictures… all of it. Though Misterley Manor still burned, her own private fires had been totally extinguished.

Chapter 16

Caroline is Sensible.

Caroline had been waiting on the steps of the Halliday Conference Centre for half an hour. The afternoon was nearly over now, and the evening air was cooler, but there was still some heat left in the concrete steps – she sat down, clinging to the reassuring solidity and warmth of the steps beneath her. If she could stay there the world didn't pitch and swirl around in her mind quite so much. She wished she hadn't had those two glasses of wine; she drank so rarely that it had gone straight to her head and it was muddling her thinking. Several people had asked if she wanted some company, but she found that she didn't. She didn't want to have to chat politely while 70 miles away, Misterley Manor was burning down. She wanted to be left alone. The fear of what she would find when she got back was overwhelming; every time she tried to imagine it, her mind whirled away into fragments that didn't make sense.

For the first time since their divorce, when Duncan pulled up in his battered old black Volvo, she didn't find herself unhappy to see him. She felt numb. His steel grey hair and his beard even seemed reassuringly familiar in a world that didn't make any sense. Nothing mattered now, not old hatreds and divisions, not what they had once been to each other, nothing except what she would find when she got back to Misterley Manor, and the awful knowledge that there was so much she could have done to prevent this, and she hadn't done it. But once again, she found her mind wouldn't go there. The sensible part of her knew that she should be planning, making lists, contingencies, phoning people, sorting things out, *doing* something. But instead she stared blindly out of the window, not even able to focus on the scenery passing her window.

Every now and again Duncan would say something to her and she would nod and agree without actually hearing a word he said. Every time she tried to concentrate on anything all she heard was that awful crashing on the phone and Alice swearing. What was happening?

'Tell me again, where was the fire when you left?'

She had asked before, but she hoped that if she asked again, he might mention something else, something that would give her hope, something that he had overlooked before. But it was always the same story.

'The main house was still untouched by flames. The fire brigade was confident of holding back the fire, keeping it contained to the West Wing. It could be worse, Caroline. Please try not to worry, with the wind direction as it is…'

Duncan was saying something trivial about the weather as he drove, but she didn't have time to listen to that now.

'What do you think is happening?' she said, speaking right over the top of him.

Duncan took a deep breath. 'I was saying, with any luck the wind will be helping the fire brigade, it was blowing away from the house.'

'I should ring Alice.'

'I wouldn't. She's got a lot on her plate right now. If she needs either of us, she'll ring us – or she'll ask someone else to. There's nothing you can do until you get there, Caroline.'

'There has to be something I can do.'

'You could ring the insurance, perhaps, see what they can suggest?'

And her mind fractured into a million thoughts, spinning every which way except ordering themselves into a straight line of action.

——

'No, not now. I can't do that.' She couldn't keep the panic out of her voice. He would know; he would be able to hear it in her voice, he would know what she had done. What she hadn't done.

'OK. It's OK, Caroline. We can deal with that later. I'll help. Let's concentrate on getting there for now.'

If he said anything else she didn't hear it, because they were coming over the crest of the moor road and in the distance, she could see what looked like a tiny, thin wisp of smoke – which must be her home burning. The closer they got, the more smoke she could see, and smell, the acrid fumes catching in the back of her throat, making her feel like retching.

The car crawled down the drive. She couldn't remember anyone being as careful over the speed bumps as Duncan was being today, almost as if he didn't want to turn the corner. Part of her willed him forward, part of her wanted him to turn round and drive away again, back down the drive, away from Misterley, somewhere else, anywhere but here.

When at last he steered around the corner, the car couldn't get all the way along the drive which was blocked with vehicles and people; volunteers and fire brigade and police, and a web of tape to stop people getting too close to Misterley Manor. The car had barely had a chance to come to rest when Caroline clambered out. She was still wearing her smart blue suit and heels from the conference, in stark contrast to the ill-assorted outfits of those around her in high-vis waistcoats and soot stained clothes. Duncan called something after her, but she didn't have time to listen to Duncan right now. He was probably saying that she should have talked to National Heritage before this happened, and he was probably right – but maybe it was already too late for that.

She looked over at the West Wing. All around her people were shouting, telling her things, but she couldn't listen to them right now. She could see flames in the Octagon Library, flames in the Painted

Hall. The little secret tower room was flooded with fire, the windows lit up from inside, and there was a great crashing and smashing as if there was a dragon thrashing about inside. The gallery was coming down, she could see where the stairs had heaved to the left and the walkway was at an angle. The windows were shattered and the panelling was burning. Inside, Caroline could make out the shelves on the walls, still there, as the flames licked at the spines, book by book by book the library was being burnt away. In the Painted Hall a hint of gold flickered on the panelled wall for a moment, she could see the frame of the famous picture of King Arthur and Morgan le Faye still hanging there. Why had they left that behind to burn? Perhaps she could go in and get the paintings herself – if she could still see the frame, there must be a chance to save something of the pictures? But even as she watched, she realised that the corner of the frame she could see glinting in the light was all that was left, the rest was already gone and in a moment the flames reached the last corner and that was consumed too.

She couldn't save the Fox-Travers paintings, but she could save things from the main house which wasn't burning. She could see fire brigade crews working in there, she could go in and help them. She had to do something. It was her fault that things had got this bad, there must be something she could do.

She started to walk straight across the lawn, ignoring the confusion and chaos around her, straight towards the main entrance to the house. She walked straight through the line of helpers up the lawn who were moving the salvaged items. Carved dining chairs were being passed hand-to-hand; there was Emily's friend Chelsea from the tea room struggling under the weight of an oak carver from the dining room. Marjorie was heading towards her, but she didn't have time to deal with Marjorie's problems right now, so she waved her away. She had to be cool, she had to be calm and she had to be organised. They would expect it; everyone would expect it. She had to get on with things, she had to be single minded. She wouldn't think about the West Wing yet; she would do what she could, and she wouldn't think about what she had just seen through the tangled mess of the windows. She would get on with things, as normal.

She could hear Alice shouting her. 'Caroline? Caroline!' she called out and came running after her, but Caroline didn't want to hear her above the roaring of the flames and the cracks and crashes from the inferno. It was strange how quickly Caroline had got used to the noise and smoke, she carried on regardless of both. Alice was right next to her now, but Caroline simply turned away and said:

'Not now, Alice, please.'

Alice ignored her and kept pace with Caroline as one of the firefighters was heading towards them. 'Caroline! Look, that's Charlie, he's in charge. You probably need to speak to him first, he can tell you what's happening, then I'll tell you what we've done. Caroline. Caroline?'

It all felt so unreal. She was in a film; a disaster film, but hers was only a walk-on part now; she was too late for the starring role, to save the Manor. But now she was here, there must be something she could do. She didn't stop at the tape, she reached out, ripped it and carried on towards the inner cordon, the one that no-one other than the fire brigade was supposed to cross. They couldn't keep her out of her own house, could they?

'Stop!' Alice said, grabbing Caroline's arm. 'You mustn't!'

But Caroline didn't turn, she carried on walking and shook Alice's hand off. Alice couldn't tell her what to do and she had no intentions of stopping for anyone.

'Stop! Caroline, stop! You can't go through there!' Alice yelled, trying to get between Caroline and the last line of police tape. Caroline didn't stop, she tried to move Alice out of the way and keep going, but she stumbled as she tried to push Alice, sending them both tumbling through the inner cordon, into the area right around the house which was filling up with debris and fire-brigade equipment. Winded from her unexpected fall, she lay there for a moment, stunned, as she saw the sky above her pulsing orange. One of the firefighters grabbed Caroline, pulling her to her feet and back beyond the cordon. Charlie was over there in an instant.

'You can't come this close to the house,' Charlie said to her.

'But it's my house. It's my house, not yours. Daddy might be in there. Or Emily.'

'But I told you on the phone, nobody's in there!' Alice said. 'They're in the pub!'

Had she said that? Caroline couldn't remember.

'Will you all *please* all get out of my way?' She used her most cool and rational voice. Nobody ever argued with that. Her best Lattimore voice, the one that made people sit up and listen to her.

'No,' Duncan said firmly. He must have followed her once he had parked the car. 'You can't go in there Caroline. Please be sensible.'

'Be sensible? *Sensible*? Can you hear yourself, Duncan? Misterley's on fire and you think I should be SENSIBLE?' She had no idea where that anguished shriek had come from. He deserved it, though.

'Can I help?' A soft voice at her shoulder from a short, dark haired woman with a dog-collar. The vicar of Rawscar, if Caroline was not mistaken. What was the vicar doing here?

'What's going on? Why are you here, is somebody dead?' Caroline asked.

'No! No, of course not. I've asked the ladies of the Women's Institute to open up the Langbarnby village hall, that's closer to here than Rawscar would be, and make some tea so people can take a break up there. I'm here to be a shoulder to anyone who needs one - perhaps we could go for a cup of tea together? We need you to have a clear head, Caroline.'

———

'I should be here,' Caroline said, 'I knew I should be here. I should never have gone away.'

'I don't think it's a good idea to stay here,' said the vicar calmly. 'Look, I know from my own experience – I lost my vicarage in a storm last year, so I know what you're going through. Perhaps you're best not to see this. Let the fire brigade deal with it. Let Duncan help you, and Alice. They can deal with things. You come with me and have a cup of tea and we can chat.' There was something about her quiet authoritativeness that gave Caroline a reason to stop. She needed to talk to the vicar right now; the vicar said she did and it must be true. She couldn't stay here; they weren't going to let her into her own house, so she might as well go with the vicar, get things straight. She didn't want to have to see this. She couldn't do it. The vicar would sort it out. The vicar would tell her what to do, how to cope, and that's what she needed right now; someone to tell her what to do. It was a long time since she had felt so utterly helpless – maybe the vicar could offer her some divine inspiration or even just a cup of tea and a couple of minutes of breathing space.

'Let me help, Caroline. I can sort things out from here. I don't think you're thinking straight right now. You go with Cass – I mean, the vicar,' Duncan said. 'Come back in a little while when you've got things clear in your own mind.'

He was right. For once, Duncan was making sense. She shouldn't stay here right now, she couldn't do it. She needed to get things straight in her head – and she needed to tell her father what she had done before he found out for himself. Once she had done that, she could concentrate on what was going on at the house.

'Thanks, Duncan. I need to see Daddy as a matter of urgency, so if you could take over here?' As he was here he might as well make himself useful.

Duncan nodded, and turned to talk to Alice as they started to plan what would happen next.

——

'Perhaps we could go along to the Lattimore Arms. I need to see Daddy and Emily, and we could talk on the way,' she said to the vicar, allowing her to lead the way along the drive.

'Emily was doing very well last time I called in,' the vicar said, 'but we'll head that way if you like?'

She walked with the vicar along the path, aware that the vicar was talking, but not listening to her. Duncan could take over from here, that was right, Duncan would sort things out while she told Daddy… while she told Daddy…

Chapter 17

Grasping at Gargoyles.

Alice watched Caroline and the vicar walk away across the lawn before she turned to Duncan, handing him the red folder and with it the responsibility for Misterley Manor.

‘Caroline’s not with it, is she?’ Alice asked.

‘No, I think she’s in shock. She made no sense in the car. Hopefully the vicar will be able to help – and at least she’ll keep Caroline out of danger. You’d better fill me in on what has been happening – I take it the fire’s contained to the West Wing?’ Duncan said, flipping through the pages of the disaster manual, laminated pages smeared and grey with soot.

‘It’s still not a certainty but it’s looking hopeful. There’s smoke damage to the main house and the East Wing, but that’s all. It’s amazing that only the West Wing suffered so badly…’ she hadn’t stopped for long enough to think about it until now. ‘And without Caroline’s instructions I would never have known where to start. If it wasn’t for that red folder the whole place would probably be in ashes by now. I should have told her that.’

‘I don’t think she would have listened right now. Give it time,’ he said, running his eye down the pages of *who to contact in case of an emergency*.

‘She’s struggling, isn’t she?’ Alice said.

‘She has been for a long time,’ Duncan said, looking up from the folder with a sigh. ‘Caroline tries to control everything with lists and instructions; but this shows that she couldn’t do it all on her own. I’ve tried to tell her more than once that she should consider giving the house to National Heritage, let them look after it. If she had done, then maybe we wouldn't be here now.' They walked towards the tent, eerily lit by the red glow, and stepped inside. 'This will hit her hard,' he continued. 'Whatever her faults, she put everything she could into Misterley Manor. It was her life as well as her home, but trying to care for it in a way that her father approved of was destroying her. I don't know how much longer she could have gone on with it before something had to give…' his voice trailed off. 'I even wonder,' he said quietly, 'whether if the whole place is destroyed it might be something of a relief to her.'

There was a moments silence as Alice considered the possibility that by tomorrow morning there might be nothing left of Misterley Manor. It was unthinkable. Duncan's thoughts must have been similar, because he added:

'At least there is plenty to be grateful for. No-one was hurt and so many important items have been saved – the paintings, the books, the china, the letters.'

Alice suddenly felt very sick indeed, for a moment she thought she was going to throw up.

The letters.

The key for the cupboard in which she had locked the letters was still in her pocket, nobody had ever asked her for it and she had been so focussed on following Caroline's instructions that she hadn't even thought about the letters.

The list which she had given Marjorie of salvage priorities had a date on it of nearly two years ago. Two years ago, the letters had still been locked up in the family solicitor's safe in Ormsborough, tied up with red tape and brown paper. She felt the colour draining from her face as her hands started to shake with the horror of what she had done – or rather what she had *not* done. The letters had not been on Caroline's salvage list and she had not told Marjorie to add them to it.

'What's the matter?' Duncan asked.

'The letters!' she gasped.

'What?'

'It's too late.'

For a moment they stared at each other in absolute horror.

'You haven't got the letters?'

'They were in the cupboard. They weren't on the salvage list.'

'You don't think the salvage crew might have found them?' he asked, but the tone of his voice implied that he knew it was a slim hope.

'The key is still in my pocket.'

There was a long, long pause before Duncan spoke. 'There's nothing you can do now. It's unfortunate, but it's not a disaster. From what you've told me, the letters were a disappointment and you've made digital copies of some of them, haven't you? So although it's sad, it's not an absolute disaster – if they had held the secret to his disappearance then maybe it would have been different.'

'Duncan, there's something I have to tell you. I know Caroline wouldn't want me to, but if the letters are gone it doesn't seem to matter any more. They had secret messages in them. All those references to religious poetry that Lady Isobel was sending to Fox-Travers? It wasn't exactly religious. They were love poems.'

'Love poems?' There was a sudden note of excitement in his voice.

'Lady Isobel was sending Fox-Travers secret love letters.'

'And was it mutual? Is there any evidence that he returned her feelings, or even understood the secret messages?' he demanded.

'I don't know,' she said, her voice barely above a whisper, as if any of the volunteers in the salvage tent had time to listen to her confession right now. 'There are some that I've digitised, but most haven't been completed, and I only found out today about the code. I didn't have chance to go back through all the letters. I was so close, Duncan. What if all the answers were there in the poems?'

'There'll be a way,' he said, more calmly than she could

possibly have expected for the leading scholar on Fox-Travers. 'We just need to think. Try not to worry right now. It won't help anyone – not you, and not Caroline. Now, why don't you go and have a break yourself? I'll take over from here.' He opened the red folder again and Alice was happy to be dismissed.

'Have you seen Caroline?' Alice asked the vicar. She had taken her break over at the Langbarnby Village Hall where the ladies of the Women's Institute were providing tea, and then come to look for Caroline at the pub.

'I think she headed off towards the Gothic Tower about half an hour ago,' the vicar replied.

'I need to go and talk to her,' Alice said, having come to the decision that she *had* to tell Caroline about the letters. She had to admit her guilt, but she felt sick and she was shaking at the prospect. She would tell Caroline and then she would get back to helping Duncan.

As she wound her way through the dense woodland, stumbling along the path over the twisting roots Alice wished that the walk had been longer, the wood deeper and darker, and that she could have carried on walking until she had stopped feeling sick, but here was the Gothic Tower, hidden in the darkness of the writhing thicket of rhododendron bushes and she had to tell Caroline what she had done.

She opened the door with a creak, using the light from her phone to illuminate the ground floor room and flick the light switch to the right of the door – but the lights were not working; power no doubt being supplied from the main house. The downstairs room which had once been a "banqueting chamber" was empty of everything – furniture and Caroline - but the panelled doorway to the little wooden staircase in the corner was open and someone might have gone up to the room above. Alice climbed up the narrow wooden stairs.

With its floor-length windows pointing away from the house and towards the sea it was easy to think that from here, everything was normal. A half-moon reflected over the water, peaceful and still, and there, sitting on a worn old green sofa lit only by the moonlight, was Caroline. She didn't look up as Alice crept in; she didn't even seem to be aware of her presence, she gazed out of the window towards the sea and the moon. Her face was streaked with tears where her mascara had run down her face and she had made no attempt to clean it away, and she was clutching something tightly in her left hand.

'Caroline?' Alice said, quietly, and only then did Caroline turn towards her.

'Oh, Alice, it's you. I'm coming, just coming,' but she didn't even attempt to move.

Alice crossed the room and sat down on the sofa beside Caroline. For a moment neither woman spoke, until Alice reached out and tried to take Caroline's free hand – it seemed the only thing to do – but Caroline shook her off.

'I can't believe I wasn't here. I can't believe this has happened,' Caroline said after a long while in silence. 'I can't believe I left everything so unprepared.'

'I'm so sorry, Caroline.'

'You needn't be, it wasn't your fault. You did everything you could.'

'But I didn't save everything,' Alice said miserably. 'And it was my fault, Caroline. I took too long. It's all my fault.'

'If it's anyone's fault it's mine. I should never have gone away and left the house without proper arrangements in place. I left you unprepared, it was my fault if it was anyone's.'

'Your instructions were great, but…' Alice said, slowly and hesitantly. '… I've done something stupid. It's the letters. They weren't on the list, so I forgot. I didn't tell Marjorie. The letters got left in the cupboard and the cupboard has burnt away. I'm so, so sorry, Caroline.' Her voice fell to a whisper, she couldn't look at Caroline and side-by-side the two women stared out over the moors.

'I should have kept the list up to date. But it's only one more thing. That's all. Things don't matter, do they? Lives matter, and nobody was hurt,' and yet it sounded as if Caroline was trying to convince herself as much as Alice. 'Things don't matter. They're just things, just things,' she said, and her hand gripped whatever it was she held so tightly that her fingers were going white with the effort.

'Caroline?' Alice said, softly, 'you can talk to me, you know. If you want to talk about anything?'

'You're worrying because you made an error and forgot about the letters. It was an accident, Alice, you didn't mean to do it. What I did was much, much worse, because I knew what I was doing all the time. I knew it was wrong, but I never expected this to happen, I never thought...'

Caroline trailed off into silence, twisting the object between her hands, one to the other and back again. Something that Duncan said came back to Alice - *if the whole place is destroyed it might be something of a relief to her.* Surely Caroline wasn't trying to say that she had been directly responsible for the fire in some way?

'Alice, I don't know how I can go on from this,' she said, brokenly at last. 'It was all my fault. I went to talk to Daddy in the pub and he was so angry. He had every right to be angry; like he said, it's all my fault.' Her voice had dropped to a husky whisper now. 'It would never have happened in his day, as he told me about seven times. Because of me, everything is destroyed, everything is burnt. Our inheritance, our home. *Pride and Strength*? I'm sadly lacking both in Daddy's eyes.'

Had he said that? Alice wondered. It sounded like something out of the pages of a gothic novel, so, yes, he probably had said it, from what she knew of Sir Henry.

'Like you said, though, they're only things,' Alice continued. 'Nobody was hurt, the old part of the house is safe, and the East Wing, and the money from your insurance will sort out everything you've lost.'

'That's just it, Alice, it won't,' Caroline began. 'Because in February when the insurance was due, we were completely stony broke. I didn't renew the insurance, I put all the money into the building project and so we've lost the lot, it's all gone. It's the end for the Lattimores at Misterley Manor, the very, very end,' she twisted the object over-and-over again, without looking at it, 'and it's all my fault. I told my father and he…' she almost couldn't continue, '… he said I was unfit to bear the Lattimore name.'

She dropped the object to the ground in front of Alice as if it was burning her hand; a little carved stone head, a tiny gargoyle-like face, a piece of Fox-Travers's own carving from the library doorway, if Alice was not mistaken. Now she looked at the grinning caricature more closely, she suddenly recognised the features. They had been largely obscured when the little head had been surrounded by leaves up there on the doorway - it was a cruel likeness of the first Lord Lattimore himself, she recognised him from his portrait, glowering in an obvious temper. A small piece of previously unrecognised brilliance burnt and broken but not destroyed – like Misterley Manor itself, burnt and broken but not destroyed.

'No,' said Alice, looking at the brilliant little carving in her hand.

'No?' Caroline looked up at her, puzzled, tearstained.

'No,' said Alice again, 'This is not your fault. It's not your fault, it's not my fault, it's not anyone's fault. It was an accident. You can come back from this, of course you can! You mustn't give up. You're not going to, I'm not going to let you.'

'But -'

'You are not going to give up on Misterley Manor. It's your home and nobody else could care for it like you do. This isn't an end of anything it's a start of something new, something different, that's all.' She felt herself fired up with a sudden wave of optimism; of purpose. Anything seemed possible.

'I wish I had your confidence,' Caroline said shaking her head and looking away from her.

It was the first time anyone had ever said that to Alice.

It was nearly three o'clock in the morning by the time Alice finally made it home to her own flat. She shut the apartment door behind her and breathed a huge sigh of relief. It was cool and calm and quiet in the flat, exactly as she had left it yesterday morning; a magazine open on the dining table where she had been half way through an article, her breakfast pots from yesterday unwashed in the sink, and her landline phone flashing with unanswered messages.

Ten unanswered messages. All of them from Sebastian, each one sounding more concerned than the one before. It was kind of him to be concerned, but she didn't really want to speak to him right now, she didn't want to have to rake over the ashes of their relationship as well as everything else that had happened today.

Everything was such a mess. A week ago she had been a successful researcher working on a substantial new piece of historical evidence, with a rich, successful boyfriend who was planning to give her a diamond bigger than a light bulb. Now look at her. On her own, her clothes dirty and stinking of smoke, her work had just gone up in flames and she had just tried to seduce the gardener in the woods. And worse than that, he had turned her down.

At least with Sebastian she was safe and secure. Sebastian wouldn't have let her make the kind of mistakes she had made today. Had she made the worst mistake of her life when she had handed Sebastian back his diamond ring?

Chapter 18

What a Scorcher!

The Lattimore Arms had kindly offered the family rooms last night, and it looked like they would be staying there for a while yet. In the mirror beside the bed Caroline could see herself; dark circles under her eyes, shoulders slumped, still wearing the same clothes she had come home from the conference in yesterday. On the bed in front of her were spread out several newspapers which Marjorie had brought up for her first thing this morning, all of which featured a very striking photograph of the flaming ruins of her home. It was worthy of a film poster. *Flames of disaster!* read the Mail's headline, *What a scorcher!* read the Sun, *Hot, hot, hot!* was the Express and *Stately home comes close to destruction after devastating blaze* read the Guardian.

Everybody knew what had happened now, everybody would be sympathetic today – but what about tomorrow, when the world began to find out how irresponsible she had been? What was Duncan going to say when he found out? All the help and support that he had given yesterday would disappear in a cloud of anger when he knew this was all her fault and she would deserve his anger. She wanted him to be angry with her; an angry Duncan was easier to deal with than a supportive one; when he was kind like he had been yesterday she no longer knew how to deal with it. She knew how to fight; that was easy, that was normal. In fact her father's anger had been the one thing in all of this mess that seemed normal. Everybody else – Duncan, Emily, Alice, Marjorie, even the Vicar, was being so painstakingly kind that it made her feel worse.

There was a knock on her bedroom door, probably Marjorie again; she had been in and out of Caroline's bedroom this morning like one of those dratted cats of hers – thankfully they were now all accounted for, hiding in various outbuildings – but sooner or later she was going to have to come out of her room and face the world again. There would be things to do, phone calls to make, she had to start working out what to do next, somehow, but right now she didn't have a phone because the battery had run out and she had no charger – that should be the first thing to add to her "to do" list – but she had no list and no clipboard to pin it to because they had burnt yesterday. She was lost without something in her hands to hold her thoughts in place as she opened the door, to find not Marjorie but Duncan standing there.

'Oh, Duncan. You're here. Umm… come in…'

He stepped inside. It was the first time she had shared a bedroom with her ex-husband since the night he had told her that their marriage was over and he couldn't go on.

'How are you this morning?' he asked, but it was a guarded, loaded question. She couldn't answer "I'm fine" because he was searching for a real answer to an entirely different question – "are you fit to face up to things today?" is what she suspected he was asking her.

'I don't know,' was the best answer that she could give him right now. 'How are you? Don't you have lectures or something to give today?'

'I've cancelled the lecture and one of my Post Docs is covering my other teaching for me. I think I need to be here today under the circumstances.'

'No! No, it's fine. I can manage. I can sort things out from here -' she began.

'I don't think you can, not right now. Yesterday you were suffering from shock, it was obvious to everyone, even Alice mentioned it. I don't want to leave you on your own right now.'

'Why?' There was a pause before he answered as he walked over to the bedroom window.

'Because I've got to look out for Emily, haven't I? This is her home, her future. I'm here to help for her sake, so for once please don't push me away.'

She thought about biting back, tell him how she had never tried to push him away, that he had done all of that by himself – but she was too tired for that argument right now. 'OK. Well, I'm going to get some… some paperwork together… and then maybe...'

'Caroline, I know you haven't got any paperwork to get together. I've arranged to meet with the fire brigade investigation team down at the hall, and then I've arranged for one of my colleagues, Dr. Smith, to come and offer her professional help. She's teaching this morning, but she can come this afternoon.'

'I've already got you and Alice. The last thing I need is more art historians sticking their noses in,' Caroline snapped.

'She's not a historian. She's the head of the archaeology department and she specialises in forensic archaeology –'

'Forensic? You think there's been a crime of some kind?'

'No! But she's been called in to help after a couple of major fires at National Heritage properties. She can tell you a lot about what happens next after a fire like this; what needs to be done to preserve as much as possible from the ruins. She said that some of her students might even be able to help you out. She's a good starting point when it comes to working out what to do next; she's seen it all before.'

'I see,' Caroline said, taking a deep breath. 'Then sounds helpful.' Much as she would like to refuse Duncan's attempts to help she knew she couldn't.

'Right. So, let's go down to the Manor and have a look at what's going on.'

'No, I don't think I can right now.' It came out of her mouth before she even had time to think about what she was saying. She didn't want to see the smouldering ruins, she didn't even want to think about it. She couldn't.

'It's nearly half past ten, Caroline. I think it's time -'

'No.'

He couldn't make her. She wasn't ready.

'But Caroline…' He didn't sound angry or aggressive, only puzzled.

'I can't. I can't go down there, I can't.' She knew it sounded ridiculous but she needed more time.

'Look, Caroline, sooner or later you have to. The later it gets, the more difficult it gets. I think that you should come down to the house now; it might not be as bad as you think. I'll come with you, and Marjorie's waiting downstairs, she'll come too.' Duncan was at his most persuasive; usually he would have thrown up his hands and stormed out of the room by now, not tried to persuade her. She had forgotten that he could even be like this, it had been so long. It's amazing what his concern for Emily's future home had brought out of him.

'Duncan, I do appreciate that you think you're helping, but I can't.'

'Caroline – you have to.' He wasn't shouting or yelling, he wasn't even cross, he was simply stating a fact. 'I know it's hard, I do understand, but you have to come with me. You have to see the house, you have to try. This isn't like you.'

'I don't feel like myself any more.'

'If not for yourself, then think about Emily and the rest of the family. They need you to sort this out. Please, Caroline?'

Duncan, for possibly the first time in fifteen years, had said please.

It looked impossible that anything could rise from the ashes of the fire. The West Wing lay in ruins, much of the roof gone, bare bones of the surviving beams etched black against the blue late September sky. The walls were ragged where stone had fallen, and black holes laced with twisted metal gaped where windows had been. Though the fire was out, smoke still rose from the ruins, she could smell it as she walked across what remained of the Great Lawn. The garden too was in ruins, flowerbeds trampled flat in the rose garden, ponds empty of everything but mud and debris, grass worn away to bare mud by the firefighters and their engines. Even the parts of the house which were still standing untouched looked bereft and dirty. Unloved. It was as if Caroline was seeing the house with new cycs, the fire had not made the East Wing and the main house look like that; they had already been decrepit, but the fire had made her see the reality. Without the crowning glory of the magnificent West Wing, Misterley Manor was sad and shabby. She should have listened to Duncan, she should have done something before this had happened. She should have spoken to National Heritage.

They walked closer to the building, and Caroline felt Duncan reach out for her hand as she started to shake with tension. Through the remains of the windows of the Octagon Library, she could see right up to the sky. The walls themselves were still standing, as was the metalwork of the library balcony but everything else; the bookshelves, the pictures, even the carved fireplace and the huge wooden table, were gone. Ash and rubble. The ceiling had collapsed into the centre of the room and all Caroline could see was an unrecognisable tangle of wood, slates and metalwork where at this time yesterday Alice had still been sitting hard at work on those letters.

There, outside what had been the garden doorway, she spotted something, lying forlorn and abandoned beside the path where it had fallen in the salvage effort yesterday. It's covers were stained and buckled with water damage, and the edges of the pages were wet, but otherwise it was intact; the text still legible. It was a miraculous survival from the flames, a volume of Tennyson's poems, annotated in violet ink by one of her ancestors perhaps. Bereft of clipboard and phone to hold on to, Caroline clutched the damaged book. Marjorie had walked down behind them, chattering away about what could and should be happening, what they should do with the house, but now, standing in the late summer sunshine in front of the ruins for a moment even Marjorie was silent.

It was Duncan who spoke first.

'Well, it's got a long way to go,' he said, 'but once the insurance -'

'There was no insurance,' Caroline blurted out. 'I couldn't afford it back in the spring, so I left it. There won't be any money.'

She waited for Duncan to explode, to tell her what an idiot she had been, how she was a failure, inept, a disgrace to the family name. Like Daddy had done yesterday – and he would have been right. But nothing happened.

'I did wonder about that when you were dodging my questions yesterday,' he said calmly. 'Well, it's not the end of the world. I'm sure there will be grants, special funds, something like that that we can apply for. Dr. Smith may be able to advise us better.' For a moment he appeared to be lost in thought, but there was no anger.

'I can help,' said Marjorie, stepping forwards. Caroline had forgotten that she was there, she had been so uncharacteristically quiet.

'It's fine Marjorie -' Caroline began.

'No, no, really I mean it. I have savings. I've worked all my life and saved, not to mention my mother's legacy. It's not a huge amount, but enough for a little while. Enough to tide us over for long enough to get back on our feet, to get a few specialists in. Let me help, Caroline.'

'No. I couldn't –'

'That's a very generous offer Marjorie. We can perhaps make use of some of the money, as a loan, perhaps,' Duncan said. 'Dr. Smith has already stressed to me that we need surveyors as soon as possible. I don't think we can afford to be proud about this. I've got a small amount put away that could be used as well.'

That was the last straw.

'No! No way! I'm not going to let you do that. This is my problem and I'm going to sort it out. I don't need your help and I don't need your money.'

'That's more like it! You *do* need my help, you *do* need my money, at least as a loan, and this is not *your* problem. It's *ours*. You can't deal with all this on your own, I'm going to help you whether you like it or not. I should have helped you out long before now, I've known for a while that you've been struggling,' Duncan said.

'It's not your place. You're not my husband any more.' Caroline felt a surge of the old anger again. He kept saying "we'll do this" and "we'll do that" when it had nothing to do with him.

'Indeed, that's more like it!' Caroline heard Marjorie mutter.

'I'm Emily's father. I'm not doing it as your ex-husband, I'm doing it as her father,' he said with his usual arrogance.

'And very kind of you it is too, Duncan, to offer to help out at this very stressful and difficult time,' Marjorie added.

'Daddy won't like it,' Caroline said.

'Henry will have to lump it,' said Marjorie. 'We need Duncan to help; his university contacts will be invaluable. And besides...'

'What?'

'Arguing with Duncan always brings the colour back to your cheeks and the sparkle back into your eyes, Caroline my dear!'

Chapter 19

Sebastian and the Morning After.

Alice stood by the seaward window of her bedsit, looking out down the little winding street to where the harbour waters sparkled in the late morning sunshine. She didn't know what to do with herself this morning. She didn't want to go back to Misterley Manor until someone told her she was needed – and she didn't want to risk the embarrassment of bumping into Tom - so she had decided to take a day to try and review where she might go next with her work. But she found it difficult to settle to anything without thinking of yesterday – the fire, the letters and Tom – and how it was all her fault. There was one thing that she needed to do this morning, and that was ring Sebastian.

She owed him at least the courtesy of a phone call. Ten messages were a lot, as well as all the missed calls on her phone after it had run out of battery. What did he want? Although it was impossible – it *had* to be impossible – had he somehow guessed what she had tried to do in the rhododendrons with Tom last night? Would he be able to hear the guilt and shame in her voice? Oh God, what a mess she had made of everything, how could she have even thought that was a good idea? She physically shuddered as she thought of what she had done; what she had been willing to do - thank God Tom had stopped her when he did; but how could she ever look him in the eye again? What must he think of her? Perhaps things would be easier for everyone if she took the easy way out, if she packed up and went back to London, leaving behind the mess that she had made. Perhaps it wasn't too late to patch things up with Sebastian, to change her mind, to run away and hide...

'Sebastian. You've been trying to ring me?' she said in what she hoped was a politely conversational way.

'Ally-Bee!' he gushed when he answered the phone. 'You're safe!'

He was speaking to her as if nothing had changed, as if last weekend had never happened.

'What did you want, Sebastian?' she said, cautiously.

'I wanted to know that you were safe. I saw the fire, I was so worried. I hardly slept, I've taken the morning off work.'

'I'm perfectly safe. Thank you for your concern.'

She didn't know quite how to respond to him now. She had half expected him to be ringing to say "I told you so", but he was being so nice, the concern in his voice sounded genuine. Why couldn't he have been so thoughtful when they had still been living together? While they still had a chance to put things right?

'I wanted to tell you how sorry I was.' This was new. Sebastian was sorry?

'Yes, the fire, it's been a huge disaster. I'll pass your concern on to Caroline –'

'No, not that, I'm sorry about our argument last week.' And now he was apologising? Had the world turned totally upside-down? 'It should never have happened,' he continued. 'I should never have got so angry about something silly like a job interview.'

That struck a sour note with her. It hadn't seemed silly at the time; it was her life that they had been arguing about, not just a job interview. 'So, I'm ready to forgive and forget if you are?' he said hopefully. 'If you want to come home now you can,' he said. 'I can forget all the things you said last weekend.'

'I don't know,' she said. What had seemed like a genuine possibility a few minutes ago began to seem much more distant now.

'You've never been any good without someone to look after you, you need me! So, it's time to admit you've made a mistake and

I'm prepared to be generous about it. You can come back and we can start again where we left off, we can forget last weekend ever happened.'

'Forget last weekend ever happened?' she repeated, amazed that he could dismiss it all as easily as that.

'Yes, I'm happy to forgive what you said and you can come back here whenever you want.'

'You're happy to forgive what *I* said?' she echoed. 'It was *you* that asked me to choose. Are you saying that you want me to come back even if I carry on with my PhD? Or only if I give it all up?'

'But you can't without the letters, can you? You'll have pack it in!' He sounded almost triumphant and he hadn't answered her question.

'I still want to carry on with my PhD, even without the letters,' she said. He didn't seem to hear her.

'Can't we try again, Ally-Bee? I miss you so much! Please?' Suddenly his tone made her feel ever so slightly sick. It was the melting tone of voice that she knew all too well - so many times he had used it to talk her into things that she didn't want to do. It was the tone of voice he used when he wanted to join her in the shower. It was the tone of voice with which he had presented her with that horrible red underwear. It was the tone of voice with which he said: "Turn over, Alice." He didn't want her back because he was worried about her, what she had gone through during the fire yesterday – he wanted her back because he wasn't getting any. Maybe Greta from accounts, Phaedra and Tamsin and even Mollie-Mae on reception hadn't, after all, been prepared to offer him the one thing that mattered to Sebastian more than anything else. Sebastian, to put it bluntly, wanted a shag, and he was saying what he thought was necessary to get one. Well, she wasn't going to play that game any more.

'I don't think I can,' she said. 'I'm sorry.'

There wasn't going to be any way back to her old life, she just couldn't do it. She couldn't let Sebastian use her like that any more when she had known last night what it was like to desire someone as much as she had wanted Tom. Sebastian had never made her feel like that. Even if she had got it all wrong yesterday, even if her crass move had appalled Tom and he never spoke to her again, she had known what desire *should* feel like, and this wasn't it. This had never been it, this *would* never be it.

There was a long pause, seconds ticked by in the still air of the flat.

'Is there somebody else?' he asked suddenly. 'That must be it; there must be somebody else. Is that it, Alice?' Guilt shot through her. Did he know? How had he guessed? Could he hear it in her voice? 'I -' she began to say, but the thought of what she and Tom had nearly done last night stopped her mouth; her words dried up. She didn't know how to answer. The unvarnished truth would be "Yes, things got out of control and I tried to shag the gardener in the rhododendrons last night but he turned me down. He had more self-control than you would have done."

But it was none of Sebastian's business what she had – or hadn't – done, and who she had – or hadn't - done it with. Sebastian took her silence and filled it with words.

'Oh God, there is isn't there? Someone else has screwed you. Who is he? What did he do to you?' She prickled with sudden anger at the realisation that he thought she could only have been the passive instrument of somebody else's desire and she realised that he was, as always, far more interested in what she was doing with her body than what she was doing with her research.

'It was just a kiss. It was a heat of the moment thing. And it was me, not him!' She felt guilty as she described it as "just a kiss" because it hadn't been just any kiss. It had been the most amazing kiss she had ever experienced; she still felt a tingle of excitement at the thought of Tom's smoky lips on hers, and then she felt again that awful surge of shame at the thought of what it had nearly led to in the rhododendrons.

'I'm going to find him, whoever he is, this man that kissed you.'

'He didn't kiss me, I kissed him and this isn't about him, or you, it's about me.'

'Has he already had you?' The hurt in Sebastian's voice was obvious. 'Is that what it is? I can't believe you'd do something like that when nothing is even sorted between us. Why would you let him shag you?'

'No! I never said that he "shagged" me. This has nothing to do with him, and as far as I'm concerned, things were sorted between you and me last weekend. You told me that if I didn't want to leave Misterley it was over and *you* were the one who walked out. Now it's none of your business what I do.'

'Of course it's my business! I don't want to see you being used by a man who just wants you for a bit of fun. I just want to look after you, and keep you safe from people like that. Someone who saw you were vulnerable and took advantage.'

She had tried to keep calm, to be kind, but she felt anger welling up inside her. She did the one thing she had been trying not to do. She went full-on Caroline and lost her temper.

'Nobody is "using" me for a "bit of fun"! Maybe for once it was about a bit of fun for *me!* The only man who I've ever allowed to "use" me, as you so charmingly put it, is *you* Sebastian. I haven't had an orgasm for months and I don't think you'd even noticed, had you?'

'Months? But you must have done!' He sounded as if she had physically winded him. She could picture his face, red with surprise and shock.

'Nope.'

'Not that time I surprised you in the shower?'

'What you did with the soap didn't exactly turn me on.'

—

'Or the time I gave you that lacy red underwear?'

'I felt like a slut. An itchy slut in cheap red underwear.'

'Surely last week on your day bed when I -'

'I have never once enjoyed it when you have done that to me.'

'Alice, I never knew!'

'I realise that, and now you do know. I'm beginning to see more clearly, things between us haven't been working for a while and I think deep down we both know that. I'm glad that you made me look at things differently.'

She saw more clearly than ever that Sebastian's kisses had never swept her away. She also realised that Sebastian had never put her needs before his own, Sebastian would never have run into a burning building to impress her and Sebastian would *never* have said no to sex in the rhododendrons, even if it was so clearly the wrong thing to do. Sebastian *never* said no to any sex, anywhere.

'But Alice, I need you!'

'Well, I don't need you. I need my work and I need to find out what I want for myself.'

'I don't know who this man is, but he won't make you happy like I did.'

'This isn't about another man! I don't want any man to "make" me happy, I want to be happy for myself. None of this is about you or him it's about ME!'

'You're making a huge mistake.'

'I honestly don't think I am. And I don't think you wanted me, really wanted me, until you thought I might be with somebody else.'

'I bet he won't be able to satisfy you like I –'

She rolled her eyes in impatience. He still wasn't listening. 'It's not all about sex, Sebastian!' Although he didn't say it, she felt his answer screaming along the phone line in the silence that followed. It *was* all about sex, and without her he wasn't getting any.

'I never said it was all about sex!' he blustered.

He never said it was all about sex, but his actions and his words told a different story.

'If I ever have a relationship again, I want somebody who understands me, someone who is sympathetic, somebody who listens to me. Somebody who makes me feel alive!'

'I can do that. I'm listening now, aren't I?'

'What is my PhD about?' she asked suddenly. She heard him cough and stutter as he tried to frame an answer.

'Why the hell does that matter now? It's got nothing to do with our relationship!'

On the contrary it had everything to do with their relationship.

'No, I want to know. What is my PhD about?'

'Something to do with Gilbert Fox-Whatsit,' he said vaguely. 'You're obsessed with the man. Why exactly are we talking about him again? I want to talk about you and me.'

'You don't know what my PhD is about because you never listen to me!' She should be upset, but after everything that had happened over the last few days this was nothing and she remained calm and cool. She had a point to prove and she could prove it without getting angry.

'Of course I know what it's about! God, you go on about it all the time!'

'Then tell me. Yes, it's about Gilbert Fox-*Travers*. I don't even expect you to remember the title, but just tell me what I was hoping to find out at Misterley?'

'Oh… you want to make some big discovery. Make the other art history nerds notice you!' He made it sound as if it was something trivial.

'And what discovery would that be?' she pressed him further.

'I don't know!' He was sounding angry now. 'How would I know what discovery you were going to make until you made it?'

'Would you run in to a burning building for me?' she asked

suddenly.

'You what? What are you talking about?'

'You heard me! Would you run into a burning building for me?'

'Oh, I see! You want to find out if Fox-Travis saved somebody from a fire, I remember now!'

'No. Fox-Trav*ers* disappeared entirely in 1912, nobody has ever managed to prove conclusively what happened to him. That's what I wanted to find out; what happened to Gilbert Fox-Travers. It's puzzled scholars for years.'

'And that's what I meant! It was you that confused me, talking about burning buildings. I think that fire yesterday has made you confused. Come on, Ally-Bee, stop messing with me. I don't want to talk about Fox-Travers right now. Just say you'll come home?' He sounded tetchy now, the begging hadn't lasted for long.

'No. I'm not messing with you. Last week you made me choose, and I know I made the right choice. I'm staying here at Misterley Manor.'

'Well, you can't, can you? Not without the letters to work on.' There was a certain smug satisfaction in his voice.

'I'm going to find a way.'

'I'm not going to let you go as easily as that. I'll be here waiting when you come to your senses. I want you back, Ally-Bee!'

She took a deep breath, trying to stay calm and sensible. She failed. 'It's too late. Please don't ring me, please don't text me, please don't try and contact me at all. It's over,' she snapped.

'It's not over. It'll never be over, I'm not going to let you say that!' he exclaimed. 'You've had a bad night, you're in shock – you don't know what you're talking about. You'll come to your senses when –'

'I came to my senses last weekend when you asked me to give up my PhD so that you could have a holiday in Indonesia. I shouldn't have stayed with you as long as I did.'

'But Ally-Bee –'

She wasn't going to listen to another minute of his whingeing. 'Goodbye Sebastian.'

She turned the phone off and threw it onto the bed, glaring at it as if it was about to start begging her forgiveness on Sebastian's behalf. She was breathing heavily, her eyes glinting as she stared at it. She felt alive, she felt liberated, she felt powerful. She had stood up to him at last – but she had lied to him about one thing. It wasn't last weekend when she had come to her senses – it was last night when she had kissed Tom in the rhododendrons.

Chapter 20

Let's get to the Catalogue!

The University of Ormsborough was teeming with new students, it was the beginning of October, two weeks after the fire. Term had not long started and shiny-faced students in quirky clothes were everywhere. After two weeks working practically alone in her flat with just the odd visit to Misterley Alice was happy to be back in the familiar buzz of campus life.

Now, where was the library? She checked her phone for directions and took a turn to the left. She was about to turn her phone off to go into the library, when it suddenly started to ring. She knew who it would be, even though she didn't recognise the number. It would be Sebastian. He kept ringing. She had tried telling him to stop. She had tried not answering his calls, she had tried turning off her mobile but still he kept calling, with the same plaintive tone in his voice, asking:

'Ally-Bee, have you changed your mind yet? I need you.'

She had explained, she had protested, she had yelled, but still he kept calling. She had blocked his number, so he borrowed other people's phones to contact her; this was getting embarrassing – if not a little bit creepy. Did he not understand the words "please leave me alone and stop ringing me all the time?" Angrily, she turned off the phone without answering.

The University Library and Archive was an ugly grey-brick and glass building that dated from the 1970s, it could have been any academic library on any campus university in Britain, they all seemed to look the same to Alice who had seen a few in her time. She walked up to the enquiry point inside the main door.

'I've got an appointment with Professor Duncan Russell in the archives, I wonder if you can tell me where I might find him please?'

'Yes, certainly. The Fletcher Room in the basement. If I can see some ID, please, I'll sign you in.'

Alice pulled out her campus card for her home university in Camden, catching sight of her photograph on the front - she had it taken when she started her PhD last year. She wasn't sure that she even recognised the bewildered young woman looking back at her from her own photograph, the last two weeks had changed everything so completely. The woman on the entrance desk let her through the barriers and into the library. It even smelt like every other university library that she had ever been into, new books, photocopier toner, sweaty students and cheap carpet mingled into eau-de-library. It made a change from the smell of smoke that still hung over everything at Misterley, or yesterday's fish and chips in her flat. The Lattimores had been allowed to move back into the undamaged part of the house and Alice went over to help them reinstate some of their salvaged possessions into the main building but still the smell of smoke overwhelmed everything, even seeping into her clothes, until Alice began to find anything that *didn't* smell of smoke quite strange.

'Alice. Good of you to come.' Duncan met her half way down the main staircase.

'Thank you for asking me.'

'I've booked a study room so that we won't be disturbed.'

The departmental secretary had fitted Alice into Duncan's diary as a matter of urgency. Alice couldn't quite see why. Fires were urgent, she had thought, or even his own PhD students with a crisis, but meetings with a visiting academic from another university? What was Duncan up to?

Duncan went down the stairs before her and opened the heavy door into the Fletcher Room that held the university archives – a fire door, Alice noted, nice and heavy. It was like stepping into an entirely different library; instead of neat cloth-bound books and rows of students with laptops, down here old leather-bound books and huge wooden map chests filled the room, immediately reminding her, with a pang, of the library at Misterley. Even the "old book" smell was reminiscent of the Octagon Library. Her eyes fell first on the wooden shelves, and second on the position of the fire exits - just in case. Duncan led her to a small door at the far side of the room and into a private study room where a large table was covered with foam book supports and there were two comfortable-looking chairs, which, when Alice sat down, were nowhere near as comfortable as they looked.

'I've been giving things some thought over the last couple of weeks. About what I can do to help Caroline - I mean, to help her with the problems at Misterley, that is. And there are two things I wanted to talk to you about.' His blue eyes shone with purpose; she had never noticed how vividly blue his eyes were before – just like Emily's.

'Caroline found this the morning after the fire.' He pushed a water-damaged volume of Tennyson towards her, instantly recognisable as the volume she had been reading when the fire alarm went off.

'Lady Isobel's Tennyson!'

'Complete with annotations. I realised what it was as soon as I saw it. The paper conservators here at the university have dried it out for us. Now, between this, and the digitised letters and what you remember, can you put together a rough idea of Lady Isobel's correspondence with Fox-Travers?'

'A rough idea, yes definitely. I don't know how academically rigorous -'

'I'm not suggesting you make it your PhD. I'm suggesting something more commercial. A joint work. *Flames of Passion* or some such populist title, partly telling the story of her infatuation with Fox-Travers, and the letters and partly the story of the fire at Misterley. I have a publisher interested already.'

—

'You do?'

'So, if you'd be interested I can investigate further. There will be an advance – not a large one, but sufficient, perhaps to pay your rent for a few more months while we work on the book together.'

'That's an amazing proposition!'

'I had always hoped after I had to turn your PhD proposal down that we might get to work together one day.'

'What? I thought you didn't like my PhD proposal?'

'Quite the opposite. But I didn't think that my involvement would help you. Fox-Travers scholarship needed someone to see those letters, but the minute Sir Henry found out that I had any involvement that would have been the end of your PhD chances and the end of your access.'

'Why didn't you explain?'

'Well, it was all a bit too personal. How could I say I didn't want to take you on because my ex-father-in-law wouldn't like it?' He raised his eyebrows.

'I guess I can understand that,' Alice said.

'You'd be interested in working with me, then? You'd have to do a lot of the day-to-day research, of course, I'd be more of a consultant than anything else.'

'Yes! Yes, I'd be interested.' Which Fox-Travers scholar *wouldn't* be interested in working on something with Professor Duncan Russell? She was quite glad that Caroline had been proved wrong about him – he wasn't such a shit after all. Tempting visions of guest appearances on late night Radio 4 programmes danced through her head. It was all she had ever dreamed of!

'It's a good idea,' Alice said, 'if Caroline –'

'You can leave Caroline to me. I think I can persuade her.'

Alice thought that since the fire, ironically, much of the spark had gone out of Caroline. She spent much of her time with an assortment of cleaning materials in the old servants' hall below stairs washing soot-stained china, drying out water damaged books or brushing off debris from soft furnishings. She had set up a temporary office down there, and rarely seemed to leave it. She sat behind the enormous old scrubbed pine servants' table, looking smaller, diminished and grey as if the smoke had seeped into her skin and hair.

'And then there is something else that has occurred to me.' He was fiddling with a pencil as he spoke with nervous energy. 'From what you have told me, the letters were not what I expected. I understood the package to contain the entire correspondence between Lady Isobel and Fox-Travers.'

'Her correspondence appears to be more or less complete, but some of his appear to be missing. For every seven or eight letters of hers, there is only one of his.'

'And yet with all his other correspondents he was a profuse letter-writer. If, as it seems, there was a romance of sorts occurring between them, does it seem likely that he would be writing fewer letters than he did, say to William Morris or even to his brother?'

Duncan raised an eyebrow and then suddenly she realised what he was implying. 'So you think the missing part of the correspondence might still exist somewhere?'

'It's possible. I mean, it is also possible that there were no responses to her letters in the first place because he didn't want to reply, or that Lady Isobel had destroyed the missing letters herself? Perhaps, knowing Fox-Travers, they were scandalous?' suggested Alice, imagining the kind of things Fox-Travers might have been capable of writing in a love letter.

'Or,' Duncan said with a gleam of hope in his eyes, 'because she might have treasured them and kept them hidden safely away from her husband.'

'So, you think they might be hidden somewhere?' Alice realised what he was thinking.

'It's possible that they are somewhere in the family archive, which is here in this very library, or they might still be somewhere at the house.'

'And because all the correspondence was believed to be in the parcel with Lady Isobel's letters, nobody has ever looked for them,' Alice added.

'Neither in the archives or the house. They could be hidden in plain sight, as it were,' Duncan said.

'It's a thought…' Alice murmured. 'It's a real possibility… so how do we find them?'

'This is where you come in! Let's get to the catalogue!' He flung open the door and crossed the reading room with such obvious purpose that students looked up angrily as he disturbed them. At the other side of the room was a shelf with three old leather-bound ledgers, gold-tooled spines reading *Lattimore Archive.*

'Aren't they on-line?' Alice asked.

'They've never been digitised. There are cursory online records from the 1990s. The detail is in the original shelf list, that's why the collection has never been thoroughly studied. Even I don't know everything that's in there. A minor collection of a minor local family archive has never been top of anyone's list and because nobody realised that these other letters might exist, nobody has been looking for them!' He noisily blew the dust off one of the old handwritten ledgers as if to prove his point.

'So, the answer might be in here!' Alice whispered, more conscious than Duncan was of the other archive users around her.

'That's right! And you can be the one to find it!' Duncan said loudly with absolutely no consideration at all.

'But I don't understand why you *want* to help!' Alice said. 'I thought you and Caroline hated each other!'

'I want to help because of Emily, first and foremost – it's her future too – and because *somebody* has got to help Caroline, because she sure as hell isn't helping herself right now. The fate of Misterley

Manor is in her hands, and her fate is in our hands.'

'So, it's about the house?'

She could understand that. Misterley was a special place that would inspire devotion for its own sake.

'The house and Emily.'

She looked at him, a sudden realisation came to her. 'The house and Emily and Caroline,' she said. 'You're still very fond of Caroline, aren't you?'

'Nonsense! This is purely an academic interest,' he said firmly, looking away from Alice towards the exit. 'Now, if you'll excuse me I must be getting on. I'll be in touch when I have more information.'

When he had left her, she sat down with the shelf-lists at one of the long tables and opened the first one. The writing was tiny and the paper yellowing.

Box One, folder one, document one. Estate management papers concerning the sale of estate property; Beckside Cottage at Langbarnby to Mr. H. Herring. Plans of the cottage, including the drainage, and the garden attached...

Alice was going to be here for a while.

Chapter 21

Too Much Yellow Highlighter.

'Arson?'

It was the last thing Caroline had expected. Careless builders, electrical faults, spontaneous combustion, even a lightning strike from the Almighty seemed more likely than *this* conclusion. Duncan had read the preliminary fire brigade report which Caroline had been unable to bring herself to look at. She had printed it out and it sat on the corner of her table in the old servants' hall, waiting. Duncan had read it within an hour of receipt and he had turned up to discuss it with her whether she wanted to or not – and on the whole, she found that she didn't want to discuss it, and yet here she was, cornered in the servants' hall.

'They can't rule it out. They've found the where the fire began, in the old coal store, and there is no electricity or gas supply to it, so that rules out the most obvious cause. The builders weren't working there, but it was piled high with boards ripped out from the old panelling.' Duncan waved the paper of the report at her – his copy had post-it notes and yellow highlighter pen all over it.

'That shouldn't have been there. It should all have gone to the skip outside the courtyard,' she said, standing up. She wasn't going to be able to get Duncan to go away by feigning that she was too busy to talk to him; he was ignoring her attempts to carry on at the computer keyboard.

'So, the most obvious conclusion is that the wood was put there on purpose, and then lit on purpose,' Duncan continued, putting the report down on the table beside her, open at a page which was almost feverishly covered with bright yellow highlighter.

'That can't be right. Arson? Who would want to…' Caroline tailed off, running through all the possibilities in her head, trying not to look at the report with its damning lines of dayglo yellow.

'They can't say for certain. It could have been a careless builder having a sneaky cigarette, or it's even possible that one of the planks was already smouldering when it was put in there; sparks from a saw or something –'

'It could have been, that sounds feasible.'

'But they can't rule out arson. There's going to have to be some further investigation, police involvement. They'll need to talk to everyone, find out who put the wood there – and why - and how the fire might have started.'

'Mikey,' said Caroline. 'It must have been Mikey.' It was the obvious conclusion. He had motive and opportunity. And she didn't like him. 'He was the one who stacked a lot of the wood in there.'

Duncan was flicking through the pages of the report again. 'Mikey seems a decent enough lad. I like him. You've got no reason to suspect him, you can't say that.'

'I can. He was angry with me because of the camera business. He knew the house, he knew about the wood. It must have been Mikey.' She turned her back on him, hoping to end the conversation. She should have known that Duncan wasn't that easy to put off, he simply walked around her and continued the conversation leaning against the huge old dresser that ran along one end of the servants' hall.

'I think you should let the police get on with what they do best. You don't know it was Mikey and from the few times I've met him, I'd say that he genuinely cares about Emily – and he's genuinely interested in the house. He even asked me about Fox-Travers and his architecture a few times.'

'Oh, well, he's *got* to be a good lad if he's asking questions about Fox-Travers,' Caroline said. Duncan was so easy to fool sometimes, Mikey had bad news written right through him, anyone could see that.

'It could have been anybody, Caroline, you shouldn't rush to conclusions.' Now he sounded like he was lecturing her again. In a minute he would be trying to get her to write a 2000-word essay on who were the likely culprits to have tried to burn down Misterley Manor with bonus credit for investigation of their possible motives.

'Alice? Or Marjorie? Perhaps Daddy staggered out there with a can of petrol and a box of matches?' she suggested wryly.

'Well, perhaps not any of them, but what if Emily was having a sneaky cigarette?'

'Emily doesn't smoke!' Caroline was appalled at the suggestion.

'Emily wouldn't want us to know if she smokes. She's nearly 18, it's not impossible, and Chelsea from the tea-rooms does, and they're friends.'

'So, you think Emily and Chelsea were out there having an illegal smoke and accidentally burnt down the house?'

'Possibly. Or one of the builders. Or if you're looking for a suspect for arson, what about one of your local rivals?'

'The wedding co-ordinator for Harthorne Hall came over and started a bonfire in the coal shed? Don't be so ridiculous, Duncan! It can't have been arson. Unless, of course, it was *you*!' She let her voice drip with sarcasm.

'What?' He sounded genuinely shocked that she would even consider it. Good. He was so certain of everything, he deserved a shock every now and then.

'Professional jealousy. You heard that Alice found something in the letters, didn't you, and you couldn't stand it and so you set fire to Misterley Manor?' She was only partly joking but she knew that he wouldn't have done that to Emily. Or Fox-Travers's beloved Misterley Manor. No, it wouldn't have been Duncan.

'Give me some credit!' he said, walking away from her. 'If I'd wanted those letters I'd have bribed Alice. Offered her a conference paper to present or a journal article to write; she'd have leapt at the chance and told me everything.'

'I think it might have taken more than that to bribe Alice. She's an upstanding young woman, you know!'

'She's a poverty-stricken PhD student,' he quipped back. 'You don't really think I did it, do you?' he said, turning back towards her and now she knew he wasn't joking with her any more.

She thought for a moment. No, she didn't think he had done it. Duncan was the last person who would have harmed Misterley Manor on purpose, and the last person who would have made any kind of stupid mistake that might have led to its destruction. He was probably the only person left who she could trust absolutely when it came to the house. Daddy and Marjorie were both too eccentric to be trusted implacably, Emily was too young, Alice was too unconfident, the builders were plain incompetent, and Mikey was quite clearly on the wrong side of the law. Even she herself might have made some crucial mistake that had led to the fire, any of them could have done something stupid, but Duncan?

'Honestly, Duncan? You're the last person I'd suspect. You're the only one who loves this place more than I do. You probably love this house more than anything else in your life.'

'You know that's not true,' he said and now he looked hurt rather than shocked and for a moment she felt remorseful. She liked to wind him up, but she hadn't even realised that she still had the power to hurt his feelings; she thought he had become immune to her scorn long ago. 'You and your father always said I loved the house above everything else, but that's never been true. I love our daughter more than anything else in the world, and I… Oh, never mind, it doesn't make any difference now. What's done is done, and we can't turn back time.'

He glanced over his shoulder towards where the burnt-out ruins were, even though from down here there was no way of knowing the desolation that lay outside, and she knew that he was thinking about the fire. If he could turn back time to stop it, she knew that he would do, and so would she, in a heartbeat.

'It's too late,' she said with a sigh. 'It won't make any difference, will it? Not now. Look, Duncan, I wanted to tell you something. You were right. There's something I should have done a long time ago. You were right, and Daddy was wrong about one thing.' She sat back down again, and a took a seat at the other end of the table, so far away that she nearly had to shout down to him.

'So, you admit that we *should* have put tarmac on the Garden Centre car-park?' he said with that look she knew so well – that little quirk of an eyebrow that always gave him away. He was joking.

'Not that! I've been on the phone to National Heritage this morning about the house.'

'You phoned National Heritage?' He sounded amazed, and he got up and walked up around the table towards her. 'Does your father know?'

'Not yet. I'd rather keep it a secret for a while longer, just between the two of us. I should have paid more attention to what you said a long time ago and I'm sorry, Duncan. I never gave you a chance, and I never gave you credit. You were only looking out for Emily all along,' Caroline said. It wasn't something that came easily to her, apologising to Duncan.

'Well, I suppose I didn't exactly make it easy. I turned everything into a fight,' he said sitting down in the chair next to her. She didn't think they had been this close in the last fifteen years.

'No, you didn't. It was me, it was my fault,' she said.

'It wasn't! Don't be ridiculous!' She heard the snap of a quarrel in Duncan's voice and Caroline laughed. She couldn't help herself, and she knew that Duncan would understand why she was laughing. He understood her sarcastic sense of humour better than anybody else. 'Listen to us,' she said. 'We're even trying to turn an apology into a fight!'

'Well, we were always good at fighting, weren't we?' He said it with a rueful smile. He didn't snap, he didn't argue, he didn't even try and contradict her for once.

'We were,' she said, just as an idea came to her. 'Look, I'm going to a meeting next week down in London with someone from National Heritage. I don't want to leave the house, but I wondered, given the circumstances, if you might come and look after things for a couple of days while I'm away?'

'Not Alice?'

'Alice has her own work to do. She's lovely and she did her best, but I'd rather have you, Duncan. I trust you. You won't want to let Emily down and you won't want to let Misterley down.'

'And I won't let you down, either, Caroline.'

There was something in the way he said it that made her think of the old days, before the fire, before Daddy got so angry, before the arguments started.

'I know you won't.'

Chapter 22

Forbidden Doors.

Alice had never been into the East Wing before. Today Caroline was in London for a meeting with National Heritage which nobody was supposed to know about, but in fact everybody did. Everybody except Sir Henry, of course. It gave Duncan several hours to organise a search for the letters whilst she was away and they would be undisturbed. It wasn't that he feared her disapproval, he told Alice several times, very loudly, until he had obviously convinced himself that he was telling the truth. It was simply that he didn't want her to worry about them going into the East Wing. Marjorie was on side to get them into the East Wing as she had access to the keys, a huge bunch of old iron keys with a fading brown paper label.

The doors to the East Wing were always kept locked and the shutters closed. What could lie beyond the door, in the forbidden part of the house? Whereas Fox-Travers had designed the West Wing with spectacular rooms for public display the East Wing had been designed with the family in mind. Alice knew from her studies that there was a Billiard Room, a garden room, a small drawing room, a winter dining room and above them several bedrooms and a bathroom, but she had never seen any of them.

She felt like she was stepping into the pages of a fairy tale – Beauty and the Beast, perhaps, or Bluebeard, where unknown terrors awaited her beyond the locked door. Either that, or rooms frozen in time, furniture festooned with cobwebs, treasures of the past covered in dust just waiting to be rediscovered. Alice's heart was beating faster as Marjorie fitted the forbidden key into the forbidden lock of the forbidden door.

It wasn't just the secrets of the East Wing that were making her heart beat that little bit faster. Tom stood beside her; Marjorie had insisted on his presence – to help with the heavy lifting, so Marjorie said. She had barely seen him since the night of the fire, and when they did run into each other there was a lot of embarrassed coughing and staring at the ground. Alice wasn't keen to make any kind of move, even so much as to speak to him, in case he thought she was going to leap on him again, and Tom seemed equally unsure, so they largely avoided eye contact. But today, it seemed, that wasn't going to be an option.

'I think we should split into two,' said Marjorie. 'Tom and Alice, you can look in the bedrooms whilst Duncan and I take the downstairs rooms.'

'Wouldn't it make more sense if Duncan and I –' Alice began.

'No. You and Duncan are the experts, so it makes no sense for you to work together, otherwise Tom and I will be at a disadvantage - don't you agree, Duncan?' She didn't actually give Duncan a chance to agree but carried on. 'It makes *much* more sense for you and Tom to go upstairs with each other. You don't have a problem with that, do you?'

Alice nearly exploded with embarrassment, but to make any protest would just make the situation worse. 'Of course not!' she said, just as Marjorie opened the prohibited door with a loud, menacing creak that reverberated around the entrance hall. Slowly, slowly the door swung open, to reveal…

….A corridor, stretching away to the end of the East Wing. Its peeling pale blue paint was dingy and greying, the floorboards were bare and dusty, and the walls were devoid of any decoration. No sinister portraits, no candelabras draped with cobwebs, no mouldering wedding banquets. Nothing. It looked more like an abandoned hospital than one of Fox-Travers's masterworks.

'Come on then everyone!' said Marjorie with relish. 'Let's

split up and search for clues. Duncan, we'll go and check out the garden room first, that was one of Lady Isobel's favourite rooms in later life. Go on, you two! What are you waiting for? Get upstairs to the bedroom!'

Alice was beginning to get a vague feeling that Marjorie was trying to set her and Tom up.

Alice and Tom climbed the wide staircase. Light flooded in from a large un-shuttered window half way up the stairs; Alice was tempted to stop and examine the design but there wasn't time for that now.

'Where do we start?' Tom asked, and for a moment Alice wasn't sure whether he was talking about the hunt for the letters or something else. Alice opened the nearest door. It was the bathroom; magnificent tiles with an ugly 1960s suite – whoever ripped out the original Edwardian fittings to replace them with these powder-blue monstrosities should have been shot. They had a quick look, but the bathroom didn't really seem like a possible hiding place for precious letters for many reasons, so then they moved on to the bedrooms. Lady Isobel's room was the obvious place to start. Duncan had told her that Lady Isobel's room was the last door on the right, overlooking the gardens, and she opened the door gingerly.

'Oh no!' she gasped as the door swung open.

'What's the matter?' Tom was right behind her. Even though the shutters were closed they no longer fitted the windows properly, so light filtered in through the gaps and in that dim half-light Alice could see that Lady Isobel's bedroom was no longer the room it had once been. It was cold, damp and decaying and there were water stains and black mould in the far corner.

'Look at it! It's awful.'

All the furniture had been removed except for the four-poster bed and an enormous wardrobe which were presumably too big to move anywhere else. The bed was simply the wooden frame with a bare, stained mattress. If Marjorie had thought she was sending Alice and Tom upstairs with an eye to a romantic liaison between the two of them she obviously hadn't considered the unwholesome state of the mattresses.

Tom opened the shutters and light flooded in, making the damage and decay all the more obvious. There was no carpet on the floor, just bare boards, and in the corner of the room there was an assortment of buckets ready for when it rained. The windows were ornately carved, but ivy was creeping in through a gap where the wood had rotted through and every time the autumn wind blew outside the frames rattled.

'It's a bit of a mess,' Tom agreed. Understatement of the year, thought Alice. How could Caroline and Sir Henry have allowed this beautiful room to crumble away like this? No wonder Caroline hadn't wanted her to see the East Wing; it was almost as bad as the destruction by fire, the slow silent decay of years of neglect.

'There aren't even many places to search. We're looking for voids behind the panelling or loose floorboards, maybe hidden recesses in the furniture, things like that,' Alice said.

Tom was tapping the wooden panels, many of them warped and buckled where the water had got in, and Alice was investigating the wardrobe. Nothing there but a pile of moth-eaten blankets and a pile of yellowing old newspapers from the time of Charles and Diana's wedding. No letters and no secret places to put them.

Eventually both Tom and Alice found themselves inspecting the large ornate four poster bed at opposite sides. It was a Fox-Travers original, Alice could tell immediately even under a film of dust and grime; the carving was so vital. Sensuously entangled branches looked like limbs; caressing, stroking, intertwining up the bedposts, impossible to tell where one branch ended and another began. The blowsy carved roses that bloomed at the bed's head and swarmed with bees ready to probe the flowers seemed to say only one thing –

"pollinate me". It was a bed designed for lovers.

Tom was examining the carved flowers with care and attention. 'That rose there,' he said, 'that's an old rose. The carver's caught it perfectly. Might even be Monsieur Daniel.'

Alice didn't know who Monsieur Daniel was. 'No,' she said, 'It wasn't carved by Monsieur Daniel, I'm pretty sure that Fox-Travers himself carved this.'

Tom laughed. 'No, I mean the rose. The name of the rose is Monsieur Daniel. It's the white one that's planted all over the rose garden – your Fox-Travers bloke must have really liked it. It's an old French climbing variety, very hardy.'

'You can tell that without even knowing what the colour is?'

'Pretty much,' he said with a shrug.

'That's amazing!' she said, and she remembered the little white rose that he had given her the day they first met. Her Yorkshire rose. Had that been Monsieur Daniel? She looked at him for a moment, then looked straight down at the mattress again when his eye caught hers.

'Here, I'll give you a hand with that,' he said, helping her lift the heavy old mattress so that she could search underneath for pockets or other hiding place, but there was nothing but wooden slats below the mattress. 'No. Nothing there,' she said as he let the mattress drop back and a cloud of dust flew out of it. When they had finished coughing and sneezing there was a moment's silence as they glanced around the room wondering where to look next. They had searched all the obvious places and found nothing.

'So, what next?' Tom asked, and for a moment Alice wasn't sure if he was talking about the letters, or the way things were between them after the fire. She didn't know how to answer either question. There was still an awkward hesitation there between them that she couldn't deny, a sense that neither of them quite knew what to do. Perhaps it was better to talk about it, get it over with now before it got any more difficult. She wanted to apologise for her behaviour that night; she needed to explain herself to him. Perhaps if she could do that things could get back to normal between them, they could start again; they could be friends.

'Can we stay here a couple more minutes before we start looking somewhere else? Can we talk?' she asked nervously.

'If that's what you want,' he agreed, though now he walked away from the bed and turned his back to her, which made it simultaneously easier to apologise when she couldn't see the possible disapproval on his face, but harder to know if that disapproval was actually there.

'How are you doing – since the fire?' she asked politely, holding onto the smooth carved wood of the bedpost as if it could anchor her safely to normality.

'Oh, OK. And you?' he replied equally politely.

'I've been working over at Ormsborough University quite a lot. I've looked for you when I've been here.'

'I've been out and about in the van helping Caroline,' Tom said.

'Oh, I see…' There was a pause as she gathered herself, tracing the sinuous stem of the carved rose on the bed as she began to speak. 'Look, Tom, I want to apologise. How I behaved that night… I don't know what came over me.' She couldn't look at him, she focussed all her attention on the sensuous flow of the carvings beneath her fingers. She could even feel the thorns of the roses, the detail was incredible… but now was not a moment to get distracted by Fox-Travers. Tom deserved her full attention.

'I can understand that things got out of control. Things weren't normal.' He was still looking at the opposite wall, avoiding eye contact with her.

'It was all my fault. I just got myself all mixed up. I wanted to do the right thing – I wanted you to be…' she searched frantically for a word that didn't make it sound like she had been offering her services to a client. *On a scale of one to five, where one is "disappointed" and five is "completely satisfied", how did you rate Alice's performance in the rhododendrons that night?* 'I just wanted you to get what you wanted,' she said, lamely.

'And I did want to - you know I did. You're a very, um, a very attractive woman, Alice.' He shifted awkwardly, showing a sudden overwhelming interest in the panelling to his left. 'But I knew it wouldn't be the right thing to do, I'd be taking advantage of a crappy situation, I could see how messed up things were for you that day. I knew if we'd done it – it would have made everything worse, and I couldn't let you make that mistake because of me.'

'It was the fire… no, it wasn't just the fire,' even as she started saying it, she realised why she had really tried to get him to go with her into the rhododendrons. 'It was partly the fire, and partly how I felt about you – and partly how I felt about Sebastian. I didn't even stop to think that you might not be like him; that going with you might mean something different.'

'I'm not sure I understand quite what you mean,' he said, turning back towards her with a spark of anger in his eyes.

'He would have seen it as a kind of… payment…' she said, realising as she spoke how crazy and wrong it sounded – how crazy and wrong it made the whole of her relationship with Sebastian sound. 'No, not a payment. A reward. For good behaviour; for bravery. That's what I wanted to do, I can see it now, though at the time things were confused – I wanted to reward you.'

Tom made a strange sound that was half way between a snort of disdain and a laugh. 'I'm not Sebastian!' he said. 'And you shouldn't do something just to keep someone else happy. You deserve better than that.'

She looked at him for a moment. 'I don't even know how long things had been like that between me and Sebastian. It's taken a while

- it wasn't like that at first... but lately... it's been all about keeping him happy.'

'And you? Have you been happy?' He took a step towards her.

She couldn't speak, she shook her head, looking down at the floor. 'I can't honestly say that I have. I don't know when we stopped being happy together, but we haven't been happy for months... possibly years,' she said with a sigh.

'It's not the way to have a relationship, is it? Doing things that somebody else expects you to do, always trying to be what they want you to be.' There was such bitterness there that it was obvious that he was talking about more than just her relationship with Sebastian. There was something else on his mind right now, and she could guess what it was.

'Is that what is your ex-wife was like?' she asked, looking up at him again – this time it was Tom who turned away.

'Oh yes. She liked to have things all her own way too. I know what it's like to never be quite good enough for someone.'

For a moment neither of them spoke. He crossed the room, coming to sit beside her on the bed, but not too close. Their hands were only inches apart, but it could have been hundreds of feet, so scared did she feel about crossing that gulf and touching his hand with her own.

'Tell me about it – about your wife?' she asked softly.

'You really want to know?' he replied, raising an eyebrow.

'Only if you want to tell me.'

There was a long pause before he spoke. 'There's not much to tell, really. We got married too young, I guess. She wanted different things, we realised it wasn't working. I moved out, she got what she wanted – the house, the car and all that. All the "stuff" that she had ever wanted. We went our separate ways.'

That was it? That was all that had happened? In her head she had created a tragic and heroic past for Tom, and hoped that he needed a gentle guiding hand to bring him back to love and life, but this was prosaic. He sighed and continued.

'But the way things ended with Chloe… it makes it difficult for me. I find it hard to get past all that, makes it hard to open up to anyone in case…' He looked down at the floor. '…in case it happens again. I can't go back. Oh, come on, look, I don't really think we should be talking like this right now. Shouldn't we be getting on with looking for these letters?'

She longed to ask what he was scared of. What did he think she would do to him? What had Chloe done? There was a secret there; she knew it. What was Tom running away from?

'I'm sorry, Tom.' He had his hands clasped in front of him now, shoulders slumped. He looked lost, and surely a comforting hand on his shoulder wouldn't be too much too soon? She moved tentatively towards him, but as if he sensed her movement he got up and walked away.

'It was a long time ago now. Don't worry about me – but if *you* need any help – well, I've been there, I know what it feels like, all this crap. If you ever need somebody to talk to…' He stood in front of her, looking down at her. 'I can always be a friend. If nothing else, I can always be a friend.'

'Thank you,' she whispered. 'I appreciate that, Tom.'

'Perhaps we could –' he began, moving closer to her as she held her breath, wondering what he was going to say, but there was a sudden loud clatter in the room beside them which made him spring away again.

There was someone else in the East Wing.

Chapter 23

Too Many Trollops.

The noise had come from the room next to them, a room that had once been a dressing room but was now empty of everything except some old metal clothes rails hung with empty wire hangers, which must have been the rattle that they had heard.

'What was that?' Alice whispered, snatching her hand back from Tom.

'It must have been Duncan or Marjorie,' Tom said, walking to the door.

'Why would they be in the dressing room?' They looked at each other.

'Perhaps I'd better go and make sure everything's OK,' said Tom, heading for the adjoining room, and Alice followed him.

The room was empty of everything except a couple of metal rails full of empty coat-hangers, a few of which had fallen onto the floor. Perhaps that was the noise they had heard.

'I think there was someone here!' Alice said quietly, picking up the coat-hangers. 'Unless it was a ghost.'

Tom looked at her strangely. 'No such thing. Just the wind, I expect,' he whispered back.

'Maybe. Look, that door's open, that could create a through draft if Duncan or Marjorie opened the door downstairs. It's been enough to make the coat-hangers rattle, that's all.'

'I don't think a breeze would be enough to knock them off the racks, though?'

'It must have been. If it wasn't Duncan or Marjorie, Caroline's out and Sir Henry won't leave his rooms. Unless there's a burglar or something, it must have been the wind,' she hissed.

'It doesn't make sense,' Tom whispered.

'Why are you whispering?' asked Duncan loudly from behind them, making them jump. He must have come silently up the East Wing staircase behind them, the worn carpet on the stairs, one of the few still left in the East Wing, softened the sound of footsteps – perhaps it had been him in the dressing room after all?

'Thought we heard someone moving about in the dressing room. But there was no-one there,' said Tom, back at his normal volume.

'Unless it was you?' Alice suggested.

'Not me. The outer doors are all locked, no-one could have got in,' Duncan assured them. 'And Marjorie's been with me. The wind, perhaps?'

Now Marjorie came clumping up the stairs behind him, jangling the huge bunch of old keys. The sound of her heavy walking boots could not be silenced even by the softest of carpets – it certainly hadn't been Marjorie creeping around up there.

'Right, come on then!' she boomed. 'Let's have a look at the mysterious locked cupboard in old Sir Edward's room. I've always wondered what was behind that door!'

None of the keys fitted. It wasn't surprising, otherwise why would the door have remained so firmly locked for so long? Sir Edward's bedroom felt entirely different to Lady Isobel's room. Even with the shutters open this room felt heavy, closed in and stale when hers had felt airy despite all the dust. The one window was smaller and looked out on the twisting darkness of the conifers in the rock garden, the walls were a heavy dark mahogany and the half-tester bed made of a similar dark wood was hung with navy blue velvet which seemed to soak up all the available light. Even the mirrors seemed to reflect darkness rather than light it made Alice feel uneasy. It was easy to imagine this room as a place for dark deeds; anger and coldness.

'What do we do now?' asked Alice.

'Let's have a look. I'll see if I can get it open,' said Duncan, setting to with a screwdriver to take off the handle, as Marjorie and Alice sat on the bed at the other side of the room and Tom crouched beside him offering advice.

'Do you know,' said Marjorie to Alice, 'I've often thought that if any room in the house were to be haunted - not that I think any of them are – it would be this one. It has an oppressive atmosphere. I would never be able to sleep in here.'

'I know what you mean. It's so dark in here, and cold.'

'That locked cupboard has always disturbed me too. I never remember it being opened, even when I was a child. It's because of its shape too. Just the right size for a person to hide. Whenever people used to use that expression, you know, about "skeletons in the closet" I always used to think about that cupboard. I still do. What if there is something in there?'

'What do you mean?'

'Well, nobody knows what happened to that architect, the one who wrote your letters, do they? What if he -'

'You think Fox-Travers is in the cupboard?' Alice could imagine Fox-Travers's mouldering skeleton, locked behind the heavy cupboard door for all eternity and she shuddered.

'Although you'd think someone would have noticed a funny smell,' Marjorie said with a wrinkle of her nose.

'Did you ever mention your theory to Duncan?' Alice asked, nodding in the direction of the two men who crouched together over the lock, oblivious to the women's quiet conversation.

'Duncan thought it was nonsense,' she said with a grin. She sighed, meditatively. 'You know it's strange. Obviously, things ended badly between Caroline and Duncan, and I know Henry hated him from the first time they met, but I've always rather liked Duncan. Very forward thinking, decisive. Lots of good ideas. He was good for

Caroline too.'

'I thought they did nothing but argue?' Alice asked.

'He encouraged her to think for herself, instead of blindly doing what family tradition dictated. Even if sometimes he did it by making her cross, starting arguments, which in the long run were the downfall of their marriage; still, there was a spark between the two of them from the moment they first met. Ah, it was love at first sight. I could see it in their auras when I first saw the two of them together. Like you and Tom.'

'Me and Tom aren't...' Alice spluttered.

'Well, you should be!' Marjorie proclaimed. 'I knew it from the first moment I saw you together on the night of the fire. Never mind that drip of a man from London, the one who came looking for you that day. Tom's the man for you, my dear. I could read it in your auras. That's why I asked him to help you today. There's only one way to get what you want, Alice my dear!'

'I don't want –' she began to protest, but before she had a chance to say anything else, there was a shout of achievement from Duncan.

'Got it!' he announced.

'What secrets will it yield?' said Marjorie with glee, crossing over the room.

'Well, let's find out,' he replied, pausing. Perhaps he feared the possibility of skeletal remains too? But he turned the handle and pulled the door, which was stuck and didn't want to open. Duncan pulled harder, and the door budged slightly but still didn't open.

'I'll give you a hand,' Tom said, and between the two of them they yanked the door open. Alice closed her eyes and braced herself for the dusty rattle of Fox-Travers's skeletal corpse, but all she heard was Marjorie's disappointed:

'Oh. Is that it?'

She opened her eyes again. Inside the door was a void about

2 metres deep, which led to another door. It didn't look exciting – but there, on one side were shelves stacked with old grey boxes; this could be it! Duncan stepped forwards and opened one.

'Are there letters?' Alice asked, breathless.

Duncan didn't reply. He held up a pair of old men's shoes.

'It's a shoe cupboard,' said Tom. 'Only a shoe cupboard.'

'But why would it have been locked up?' asked Marjorie. 'A secret shoe cupboard? It makes no sense!'

'Perhaps it was locked by accident. If the key was lost and there was nothing important in there, it explains why nobody ever tried to open it, just for a few pairs of old shoes,' Duncan suggested.

'And what about the door at the other side, where does that go?' asked Alice.

Duncan and Marjorie looked at each other.

'I've no idea,' said Duncan, 'I don't remember seeing another locked door anywhere. Marjorie?'

'It must come out somewhere near the servants' stairs, the ones that they used for emptying chamber pots and such like. They lead down to the family kitchen now.'

This door was bolted from the inside, but once the bolts were undone, like the outer door it would not open.

Tom put his shoulder to it and pushed.

'Are you sure –' Alice began, but before she had a chance to add "that it's a good idea?" with an almighty ripping noise, the door burst open. It had been wallpapered over and hidden, many years ago, and now the wallpaper was torn apart. There was no way they were going to be able to hide what they had done now.

'Oh Lordy, that's torn it!' said Marjorie with a huge grin. 'But a secret door! How exciting. Our old housekeeper, who had been with the family since she was a girl, once told me that old Sir Edward had a secret entrance for his trollops – this must be it - but I didn't realise that it was anything more than gossip!'

'An entrance for his what?' Alice exclaimed.

'His trollops, my dear. Renowned for them! That's why his poor, long suffering wife had to found the Ladies Association for Moral Welfare, too many trollops. He died riddled with venereal disease. Dreadful old man.' She shrugged as if it was nothing, but Alice's mouth hung open with surprise at her candour and Tom was having a coughing fit. 'Now, what are we going to do about hiding the door?'

And then they all heard it. A noise in the family kitchen at the bottom of the stairs, the sound of a door opening, and a beam of light from the bottom of the staircase. They froze. They had been discovered. Had Caroline come home early?

'Hello?' Marjorie called out.

'Marjorie? What the hell are you doing up there?' shouted Emily.

They unfroze.

'I forgot I told her to meet me here after college,' said Duncan to the conspirators before he called out, 'Emily, look, promise you won't tell your mother?'

'There you are, Dad, I've been looking all over. I didn't think when you said you were at the Manor that I'd find you up in a bedroom with Aunty Marjorie.' Emily appeared, running up the stairs two at a time. 'Oh! And Alice and Tom. What *are* you all doing?'

'Academic investigations,' Duncan said hurriedly, but Emily had seen the doorway.

'A secret door! Oh my God! That's totally amazing! How did you find it, where does it go?'

'It's the other side of that locked cupboard in old Sir Edward's room.'

'You know, I spent years when I was a kid looking for secret passages. Never found one though. This is amazing! How did you know it was here?'

'We didn't. We were looking for letters,' said Duncan. 'The other half of the letters that Alice was working on. They might still be somewhere in the house and we hoped that we might find them in that locked cupboard.'

'But all you found was a door. What about those boxes though? They might be letters, mightn't they?'

'Sadly,' said Alice, stepping back into the cupboard and picking up another of the boxes, 'they're only shoes.'

As she lifted the box to show Emily it seemed surprisingly heavy to contain shoes, and the bottom gave way. It wasn't gentlemen's shoes that came cascading out of the crumbling cardboard box, it was old photographs. Photographs, some of them hand-tinted in colour, of Edwardian ladies of various sizes, various states of undress and various compromising positions with men and other women. There were naked breasts and bare buttocks everywhere, lace and leather and feathers, and - what *was* going on in that photograph, surely that must have been illegal?

Emily grinned. 'That's not shoes,' she said, giggling. 'That's my great-grandad's porn stash!'

'You did *what*?' Caroline couldn't believe her ears. She had left Duncan in charge for one day, that's all, and aided and abetted by her dotty old aunt, her self-effacing PhD student and her rather hunky assistant gardener, not to mention her grumpy teenage daughter, they had ransacked the house in search of non-existent letters without her permission. She should never have trusted him; Daddy had been right, he was up to something.

'We found Edwardian pornography. A lot of it. Some of it is very interesting. It seems to include photographs that Alice and I believe were taken by Fox-Travers himself as studies for the Arthurian paintings. Look, here's Morgan Le Faye...' He pushed a black and white photographic study of an entirely naked model kneeling in front of a man who appeared to be enjoying the whole experience rather more than was strictly necessary for photographic purposes.

'You've been studying these in some detail then, while I've been away?' Caroline said with her usual sarcasm.

'We all have. Such fun!' exclaimed Marjorie who as always was totally immune to her niece's cynicism. 'Who know the extent of the perversions of the Edwardian gentry?' she added with relish. 'The things that those men got up to with their top hats on! I never knew academic work could be so stimulating.'

'I took the liberty of getting the original paintings out of the storage at the university to compare with the photographs,' Duncan added. He had asked the university's archaeology museum to help store the most precious and fragile items after the fire, including the Fox-Travers paintings, and now they were carefully placed on the pine table at the centre of the servants' hall, where he had been waiting for Caroline to get back before they looked at them. He must have been pacing the floor waiting for her to return, she thought. Caroline tried not to look too closely at the ragged edges where the paintings had been cut from their frames. The cutting had been necessary to save the paintings, but still, she didn't like to see it.

'There's something else wrapped up here, behind it,' Caroline muttered as she carefully unrolled the canvas. 'Alice, give me a hand, would you? There seems to be another canvas here.'

'Oh yes, I remember seeing it now, on the night of the fire. I think it's come from somewhere else in the house, it was wrapped up with this one in a hurry,' said Alice.

'I don't think it's from the house; I don't recognise it,' said Caroline.

Alice looked at the canvas Caroline held. Her breath caught in her throat when she saw what it was. She didn't recognise the painting, but both women instantly recognised the subject from the portrait that had hung at the side of the library fireplace. Reclining naked on a green day-bed was a young Lady Isobel. Her blonde hair hung loose but it concealed very little, not her plump breasts, nor the shadows between her thighs. The rumpled bed in the corner of the room behind her and the luminous glow on her face spoke of a night of passion, and over the day-bed trailed a red and white heraldic banner and outside the window was a knight on a horse. It was an utterly exquisite painting. There was no question that anyone other than Fox-Travers could have painted it.

It appeared that Alice had been rendered temporarily speechless.

'Oh… A… It's… Oh!'

'Is this what I think it is? Duncan? Did Fox-Travers paint this?' Caroline demanded.

Alice pointed to the instantly recognisable monogram at the corner of the painting, which, when Caroline looked closely, she could make out as "GFT". Gilbert Fox-Travers.

'It's Lady Isobel!' Alice managed to say at last.

'Hidden away for all this time the colours were still as fresh and clean as the day they had been painted,' Duncan added with reverence.

'Who is it on the horse then?' Caroline asked, thinking what a fine-looking horse it was, and what a fine figure of a man was astride it.

Duncan leaned in, and Alice peered over his shoulder. 'A young Sir Edward Lattimore, do you think? He was dark haired before he went grey; quite a stylish man in his younger days, I believe?' Duncan suggested.

'Or Fox-Travers himself, he had that long dark hair too,' Alice said. 'It could be... Oh my Lord. Oh. My. Lord. We've found an unknown Fox-Travers.'

'Is it a good one?' Caroline asked. She didn't like to reveal her ignorance of such things to Duncan, but perhaps the reason it had been hidden was because it was an inferior work.

'A masterpiece!' Alice breathed. 'An absolute masterpiece! And what a subject! What a story! Oh. My. Lord. It's proof, absolute proof of the love affair that was in the letters.'

'It's astounding,' breathed Duncan with reverence, as if he were in the presence of a minor deity. 'And the family resemblance is so strong – she really looks like you did at that age, Caroline.' He looked her up and down for a moment as if mentally comparing the likeness for himself.

Given the pose of the subject and the lack of clothes, Caroline found herself blushing but Duncan was quite unaware of what he had just said.

An hour and a half later and the servants' hall was full. Word had got around about the discovery, and everyone had started to appear, one by one. Marjorie had told Emily, Emily had told her friend Chelsea from the tea rooms, and Chelsea had told Sarah. Duncan had summoned two colleagues from the university. Alice had told Tom, who had told George the head gardener, George didn't care about art, but he liked the idea of the nudity. He told several of the garden centre staff who came too.

'A masterpiece,' Duncan was saying. 'Undoubtedly a masterpiece. Possibly his best work – the composition, the way he has caught the light, the delicacy of the portraiture -'

'The enormous tits on her!' George was heard to mutter.

'It's quite clearly a fourth Arthurian piece. Lady Isobel is Guinevere, the dark-haired man is her Lancelot, riding away after a night of passion.'

'So why did anybody want to hide it?' Sarah from the tea room asked the obvious question that Caroline had been considering all this time, but she hadn't wanted to interrupt Duncan who couldn't stop talking about the quality of the brushwork, and then examining

Lady Isobel's nipples with a magnifying glass.

'Well, the subject matter - had it been known back then would have been rather scandalous. It's probably been hidden since it was painted.' Duncan had been talking all afternoon as if he was delivering a masterclass. 'There's no doubt after you've seen this painting but that it was painted from the life, and it leaves very little to the imagination. A gift from Fox-Travers to his lover, Lady Isobel perhaps? He hid it for her, perhaps hidden away for some future time when they could be together, who knows? But the portrait couldn't be seen publicly without her utter disgrace. Astounding that such a painting exists, astounding that it should have remained secret so long.'

'I recognise that sofa thing she's lying on,' said Emily, who had been lurking around in the background. She wasn't exactly *talking* to Caroline, but at least she was there. 'It's the scummy old one in the Gothic Tower.' Emily reached out towards the picture to point.

'Don't touch it, please!' Caroline snapped, and Emily shrugged and withdrew her finger.

'She's right, isn't she?' said Marjorie. 'So maybe it was actually painted somewhere in the house.'

'Do you think she actually posed naked so he could paint her?' Alice asked Duncan, 'or is it his fantasy, do you think?'

'It looks as if they'd been indulging in something other than painting to me!' Marjorie said with a guffaw of laughter. 'The dowager doesn't quite so disdainful with no clothes on!' Caroline shot her a look and Marjorie stopped laughing.

'Is it going to be worth a lot of money, then?' asked Emily, getting straight to the point; the point that Caroline had been burning to raise.

'It could be worth a *lot* of money,' Duncan said. 'The other three Arthurian paintings were worth a fair amount, but this one is going to be worth more. Significantly more.'

'If we sold it, would it be enough to rebuild the library and all that?'

Duncan's face fell. 'Emily, you'd need about a hundred of these to rebuild the library, but it would be a start.'

'I'm going to go and tell Grandad,' Emily said.

'Thank you, Emily, that's a kind thought,' Caroline said. 'It might cheer him up. He's been very low spirited, since the fire.' But Emily had already gone, without listening to what Caroline had been saying.

'Has he been giving you a hard time again?' Duncan said with a quirk of his eyebrow.

'Of course not,' Caroline said. She felt like she should defend her father, though this time she was less inclined to defend him than she had used to be.

His blazing sightless eyes as he had brandished his white stick at her, calling her a disgrace to the Lattimore name was branded across her memory. She tried to shake it away, Duncan was watching her carefully.

'Ignore him, Caroline,' he said kindly and Caroline shrugged, turned her head away and didn't answer.

Chapter 24

Gilbert Fox-Travers. La-Di-Da.

The police report sat on her desk, unread. It had sat there for two days, while she did other, more important things, but she couldn't put it off any longer. She knew the main conclusions; she had spoken to the officers in charge of the investigation several times, but she still hesitated to look at it in black and white. The police had interviewed everyone, even Mikey, and had concluded that it wasn't arson, that the fire was purely accidental, but if it wasn't arson, then somebody might be to blame for the accident. What if the findings were that it was her fault?

It was easier not to read the report, she thought with a shudder, and pushed it to one side again. There must be something else she should be doing. She could do some work to sort out the Bonfire Night celebrations. She hadn't been able to cancel the fireworks, the insurance company wouldn't take "I don't want to have any fireworks anywhere near the burnt-out shell of my stately home" as sufficient reason to cancel the event which was to be held in the show field, well away from the house. She was stuck with either abandoning the event and losing a lot more money or persevering with the possibility of further disaster. Neither option appealed. Perhaps, compared to the stress of planning for Bonfire Night, she should read the report after all.

She opened the printed copy of the report. She still liked to read things in hard copy; she was old fashioned like that. Emily laughed at her, but Emily wasn't here right now. It was pretty much what she expected. There were many contributary factors: builders had been lazy and instead of putting the wood in the skip it had ended up in the old coal shed. Then somebody - possibly Chelsea from the tea rooms or one of the builders - had been having a sneaky cigarette and hadn't disposed of either their cigarette or a match properly. The floor had been covered with old coal dust, the wood had been dry and burnt easily. The builders hadn't checked the store room, Alice had assumed it was another false alarm; Caroline hadn't been present, the instructions had been out of date – so many little things came together. Caroline didn't think she wanted to know exactly who had caused the fire; it wouldn't make any difference, and it would only make the smoker feel guilty for what had been nothing but a moment's carelessness. Probably no-one would own up to it anyway, and she still couldn't shake her suspicions about that Mikey. He had been up to something, she was sure of it, even if it was just pursuing her daughter.

There was to be a planning meeting this afternoon and everyone was coming, including George and Tom who had been working hard to minimise the damage to the garden, and Alice and Duncan whose contributions to the restoration effort were rather less practical, but nonetheless important. Every other day one of other of them was there working on their book, asking strange questions or poking about in corners looking for letters. She had got quite used to one of other of them appearing where they were least expected. She had found Duncan lying on her bathroom floor the other day inspecting the tiles. Caroline sighed. If there was to be a progress update at the meeting she was going to have to be on top of what progress had been made. It was time to look at the ruins for herself; she hadn't been out there for a while. At least she wouldn't have to go by herself because just as she was about to set off Alice arrived.

'Come with me to look at the ruins?' she suggested. She hoped Alice wouldn't notice how edgy it made her.

'I've seen the report,' she said, as they walked slowly around the outside of the house – the longest possible way to reach the ruins.

'And I was wrong about Mikey. He wasn't even there on the day of the fire, so it seems he's blameless after all.'

'But he had been there. When I saw the builders not long before the fire broke out, one of them said they'd just seen him. I'd forgotten all about it,' Alice said.

'Are you sure?' Caroline was onto it like a shot. 'Why didn't you mention it to the police?'

'They didn't ask me about Mikey. They just asked me the procedural stuff – when did the alarm go off, what did I do first, where everybody was at the time. I'm sure it wasn't Mikey, it's just a coincidence. Even if the builders did see him, he had probably gone long before the fire started. He probably just came to pick up some tools or something… I shouldn't have mentioned it, I'm sure it isn't important…'

Alice was making excuses for him, Caroline could see it in her face.

'We'll see about that,' Caroline began to say, but as they rounded the corner and saw the metal fence ahead she fell silent. All her willpower was needed to keep walking forwards right now, as she walked closer to the metal fence surrounding the ruins and Alice followed her, until they could see into the rubble of the library. Last week, Dr. Smith had come with a structural engineer from the university to have a look at the ruins, and now Caroline could tell Alice what the engineer had told her. 'See that beam there? The one that's fallen onto what's left of the balcony?'

'The huge one?' Alice asked.

'That's the crucial one. If that falls then it will bring the remains of the balcony down, and as it's still attached to the remains of the roof at the top, probably those other two beams, the ones right up there, do you see?'

'The ones at the far end?'

'No, these ones closest to us, just there, see, if you look up through the gap like this, you can see them.' She pointed, trying to pretend to herself that this was a purely academic exercise. This wasn't her home, this wasn't the ruins of the Octagon Library, she was showing Alice something for her PhD, it was an essay in disaster recovery, that was all. Purely academic. She looked for a moment in silence, telling herself that none of this was real.

'I see them,' Alice said, prompting Caroline to continue.

'They have to stay in place because without those beams…' Just pieces of wood, that was all. She tried not to imagine them as they had once looked, painted with stars and leaves and supporting the arched roof above her head. 'Without those beams, what's left of the roof will come down, it will come crashing down and… and… the balcony…'

'Caroline, are you OK?' Alice said, concerned as she tailed off, unable to speak.

Then she heard a loud cough behind her. Duncan. 'Good morning!'

'Duncan, good morning. Are you here for the meeting?' Alice said politely, as if it was a normal state of affairs to be standing in the middle of the remains of the rose garden, staring at an empty, burnt out shell that had once been one of the finest libraries in the north of England.

'I am. Shall we head in?' he said, but he was addressing Caroline, not Alice. It was almost as if he was steering her away from the ruins, back to the safety of the servants' hall where things remained the same as they always had been, and nothing could be seen of the world outside. It was almost as if he understood.

When they arrived, the servants' hall was already full, with Sarah from the tea rooms and Marjorie, and George and Tom there in the corner. They all found seats at the long pine table, peering at each other over and through the forest of drying literature which Caroline had propped open on the table in an attempt to save the water damaged books that had been pulled from the library. The whir of a dehumidifier made it difficult for Caroline to be heard as she started the meeting, trying to keep things as normal as possible.

'Right, first of all, we have a suggestion from Duncan,' said Caroline.

'I think,' said Duncan getting to his feet, 'that before we start to discuss Bonfire Night, that we could give some consideration to running more events at the Manor. I mean, we have the show field, which is used for the village show, but what about holding other events there? Concerts, car boot fairs and the like? Plenty of other places do it, and it would have a minimal impact on the house and it could bring in some more money.'

There was a murmur of agreement from most of the staff.

'We do already do the Easter Egg hunt and the fireworks,' Caroline pointed out, 'but maybe the time has come to look at other events too. I'd like everyone to give this some thought over the next few weeks, please. Events that we could stage with minimal effect on the house itself – and minimal effect on Daddy.'

'What about a haunting event?' said Sarah. 'I know the one over at Harthorne Hall is really popular. We could do something like that here too, we've got the rock garden and the follies that we could use, without bringing people anywhere near the house itself, if that might bother your father.'

'What exactly does a haunting event consist of?' Caroline asked.

'Well, I'm not entirely sure. I've never been myself, but I think it's actors,' said Sarah. 'It's on next week, perhaps someone could go and find out? It's more of a young persons' thing, I think…' She looked sideways at Alice.

'Oh, yes, Alice, why don't you go and check it out for us?' Marjorie suggested. 'And perhaps Tom could go with you? It might not be very nice to go on your own.'

'Excellent idea!' said Caroline before Alice had a chance to say anything. It was about time that those two got their act together, if they were going to. She had got rid of that awful Sebastian weeks ago, and they were so obviously drawn to each other, it was a crime for them not to have got together. 'Yes, if you two could do that it would be marvellous. Now, let's come back to this another time and get onto the plans for Bonfire Night – the one event we *do* have planned in a couple of weeks. I had hoped to cancel but that would mean a massive loss – a loss we can ill afford right now – we need to make sure that all the normal arrangements are in place. I suspect with all the adverse publicity that it will be quieter than in previous years –'

'I'm sorry, Caroline, I can't agree with you there.' Duncan spoke up. 'I think you'll find that this year will be busier than ever. People will want to come and see the ruins, there will be a curiosity…'

'Well they can't,' Caroline snapped. 'The show field will be used, as usual, and the gardens will not be open. I don't want the public to see *that*.' Her upper lip trembled as she spoke, but soon she had it firmly under control again. She was not going to let Duncan – or anyone else - see anything but a stiff upper lip. *Pride and Strength* that's what she needed right now.

'But if it makes some money? That could go towards restoration? Perhaps it would be an idea to let them see, to encourage generosity,' Duncan pressed her.

'No. No, nobody comes any closer to the house than the garden wall. I will not have it.'

'Do you mean *you* won't have it, or your father won't let you?' Duncan said.

'Oh, for heavens' sake!' Caroline stood up and walked away from the table for a moment, back to them all, struggling to stay composed. 'Leave my father out of this!'

'Which is exactly what you have all been trying to do,' said a voice from the doorway. 'Why was I not told about this meeting?' Her heart sank. The last thing she wanted was for Daddy to start interfering; for a start it would soon become clear to everyone around the table how out of touch with reality he was becoming, and there was a chance that he might discover some of the things that she carefully hadn't told him about – like her visit to National Heritage in London last week.

'But evidently you *were* told about the meeting!' said Marjorie.

'Emily happened to mention it to me. She came all the way from her father's house to visit me, you know. At least *she* doesn't appear to have forgotten about me, even though thanks to *your* mismanagement, the poor girl feels unwelcome in her own home and –'

'Why aren't you at college, Emily? Who gave you permission –' Caroline cast an accusatory glance at Duncan.

'Chill Mum, it's a PD day. Didn't you know?'

'Oh. Yes, of course, of course I did.'

Of course she didn't. Since Emily had moved out she didn't know where she was and what she was doing. Another thing that seemed all wrong, the things that had been certainties crumbling away to ash.

'Never mind that. Help me to a chair, please, Emily,' said Sir Henry, and she guided him down the steps and into the nearest seat. 'Thank you, you can go now.'

'No, I'd like to stay, if that's OK. Everybody else is here, I don't want to miss out!' Without waiting for an answer, she sat down beside her grandfather. 'So, what's going on?'

'Arrangements for Bonfire Night,' Duncan answered shortly.

'Duncan Russell, is that you?' Sir Henry turned his head in the direction of where Duncan was sitting even though he couldn't see him. 'Nobody told me you were here. Popping up like a bad penny, I thought we were shot of *you* when my daughter saw sense and got rid of you.'

'How do you think Emily got here to visit you? And I'm here to represent Emily's interests.' He spoke calmly and sensibly. He hadn't always been that restrained with her father when Henry was being unreasonable. If there was one thing wilder than her arguments with Duncan it had been Duncan's arguments with her father. She didn't think she could face all that today, so she was grateful to Duncan for his restraint.

'She's a Lattimore. The last of the Lattimores. This house is *our* house and it has nothing to do with *you*.'

'She's Emily Russell, Henry, not Emily Lattimore. And you need me. I am an expert on –'

'Gilbert Fox-Travers. La-di-da, we all know that. But it is not your house and your opinion does not matter to me. Get out. Go on, get out!'

She sensed, rather than saw Duncan count to ten and reply calmly and professionally:

'I can't do that, Henry, and I won't. Whatever your personal opinion of me might be, you need me. Emily needs me,' Duncan said.

'Caroline never needed you. Caroline shouldn't have taken up with you in the first place, all you wanted was to get your grubby little hands on this house right from the start and -' Thankfully whatever insults Sir Henry was throwing now were drowned out by a particularly loud rumble from dehumidifier, and Caroline took up the reins of the meeting once again. She had to take control.

'Daddy, not now! Shall we get back to the point? Bonfire Night.'

'Yes, good idea Caroline,' said Duncan.

'The future of our home doesn't need input from every Tom, Dick and Harry – or Duncan,' Sir Henry said scathingly. 'Who else is here, by the way? If he's here, you've included the cleaning staff, the waitresses from the tearoom and the illiterate second deputy under

———

gardener, I presume? I wouldn't like to be discussing important arrangements without any of them!' She could see from the look on Tom's face that he had taken offence – as no doubt her father had intended. Tom had saved his life and that was the thanks he got. Caroline sighed. Her father probably didn't even remember what Tom had done. She would have to explain it to Tom later and hope he would understand that Daddy wasn't himself at the moment.

'The *assistant* gardener is here, Daddy. I'm so sorry, Tom,' Caroline apologised for her father.

'It's fine,' Tom muttered. But from the grim look on his face it clearly wasn't.

'But the housekeeping staff and the catering assistants aren't here. There's me, Duncan, Marjorie, Alice, George, Tom from the gardens and Sarah the tea room manager. And now you and Emily.'

'Alice? Alice? Who the heck is Alice?'

'The researcher, remember? She's been a great help.'

'Ah yes, where would we be without researchers?' That comment was thrown in Duncan's direction, but thankfully he did not rise to the bait.

'Now, shall we get on? Leave things to me, please, Daddy.' She tried to take a leaf out of Duncan's book, staying cool and calm, taking a deep breath.

'It was leaving things to you that got us into this mess in the first place! I left things to you and the bloody house burnt down! You're inept, girl!'

She stood stock still, unable to say a word for fear that her voice would crack. He had called her things like that in private before now; he had called her all the names under the sun and expressed his disappointment in her managerial ability in no uncertain terms, but never, like this, in front of all her staff – and her ex-husband. Duncan would be loving this. She didn't dare look at him. She looked down at the ground, at the cracks between the flagstones, and wondered how many generations of servants had done the same when admonished by the butler or the housekeeper in this very room.

'Henry, that is grossly unfair!' She heard Duncan's voice, and she heard him scrape his chair back as he stood up.

'That's *Sir* Henry to you.'

'It's still grossly unfair, *Henry*, Caroline has done nothing wrong. The fire was not her fault.'

'Please, sit down. It doesn't matter,' Caroline said softly to him.

'I don't like him talking to you like that.'

'It doesn't matter,' she said quietly, although there was nothing wrong with Sir Henry's hearing and he tutted.

'Good God, it's as if the pair of you were married again. Bicker, bicker, bicker all day!'

'Why don't we get back to Bonfire Night?' Marjorie said cheerily as always. 'I hope I won't be needed, you know how much I hate fireworks.'

'Of course, Aunty. We will plan for a reduced number of attendees – it was over seven hundred last year, so maybe, what, four hundred this year?' Caroline got a grip and Duncan sat back down again.

'Can't understand why you didn't cancel the whole shebang,' Sir Henry muttered. 'Bloody plebs crawling around the estate, gawping at our misfortune.'

'Daddy!'

'Henry, I don't think you understand how much Misterley needs the money from this event, you need to stabilise and protect the ruins right now, even before you can start to think about restoration,' Duncan pointed out.

'We have plenty of money!'

'No, you don't –' Duncan began to say, but Caroline cut him short.

'Please don't! Not now!' She shot an anguished look in Duncan's direction that her father couldn't see, and she changed the subject. 'Sarah, do you have all the plans in place for the catering?'

'Yes, the marquee is booked for the tea tent, and I've confirmed the same mobile catering vans as last year.' Sarah spoke quickly and quietly, without looking at either Caroline or Sir Henry.

'George, are you and Tom set up to deal with the parking?'

'Yes, we've got volunteers coming in to help park, and a couple of local farmers lined up with tractors in case anyone gets stuck in the mud like last year.'

'The fireworks display firm are ready and waiting. They're going to take extra care to keep well away from the house, and all the permits are in place. That leaves the security, which I wanted to increase this year. The last thing I want is curious members of the public trying to get near the ruins.'

'Security? Well, if you need more security, why did we pay for those bloody great fences and cameras to keep people out? I won't have you throwing good money after bad. You told me the cameras and fences would do the job.'

'Ordinarily they would, but Daddy, it's a sensible precaution with an event.'

'Extra security would be a sensible outlay in the circumstances,' Duncan added.

'So it's *your* idea is it?' asked Sir Henry.

'No, it was Caroline's idea. She's in charge. I'm saying I think she's right.'

'Daddy, you're not helping.'

'You were always keen to tell us what to do, if I remember. It was why you married Caroline, after all, wasn't it? So, you could tell us what to do with our own house?'

There was an outcry as several people spoke at once – Duncan as well as Marjorie, Caroline and Emily all protested.

'If you'd had your way, you'd have given our home – our *home* to those awful National Heritage people, and the bloody plebs would be swarming all over it right now while we lived, like starving artists, in the garrets.' Sir Henry had got to his feet and was waving his stick in Duncan's general direction, causing him to duck out of the way several times.

'And maybe if you had let National Heritage take charge the West Wing wouldn't be a burnt-out shell.'

'Maybe not, but at least it is still my home. *My home.* You have no right to be here. We don't want you. Get out.'

'I have every right to be here because of Emily. It's her future.'

'My future? I don't want anything to do with this horrible place. I wish it had burnt to the ground. I hate it.' She turned and left the room. Sarah and Alice, looking awkward, excused themselves and followed Emily out of the room.

'She doesn't want your help,' Sir Henry said. 'And neither do we.'

'I want to hear that from Caroline,' Duncan said, his voice no longer angry but controlled and cool. 'I want Caroline to tell me that she doesn't want my help.'

'Well, girl?' Sir Henry turned towards where Caroline had been sitting, but she was no longer in her seat, she had crossed the room to stand between the two men. 'Tell your odious ex-husband that we don't need him to interfere.'

'No,' said Caroline, taking a deep breath.

'I beg your pardon?'

'I can't tell him that, because I do need him. I wish I had listened to him when we were still together, because he was right then and he's right now and we were wrong. We should have given the house to National Heritage then when it was still intact. Because I tried to do it all myself we've lost the West Wing. I couldn't do it. I can't do it. And he's the only person in this whole, stupid, awful mess who's trying to help me. I'd like to ring National Heritage right now and beg them to take this place.'

'Over my dead body!' Sir Henry said grandly.

'If you were dead then the inheritance tax would cripple us anyway. Let's stop pretending, shall we, Daddy? It's over; we've got no money, we've lost the West Wing and the new wedding venue. That was our last hope. It's the end of the line for the Lattimores at Misterley, and, as you so graciously keep telling me, it's my fault.'

'Should never have let a woman take charge. Maybe that husband of yours would have done a better job after all.' There was a moment's silence as Caroline tried to convince herself that her father didn't mean it. Then Duncan spoke.

'I doubt it,' he said. 'Caroline has given everything to this place. Everything. No-one could have done more.' He moved to stand beside her. He didn't take her hand, but he was close enough that he could have done.

'Right. So that's how it is? The two of you against me again? I thought those days were long gone. Take me back to my room, Emily.'

'Emily's not here,' said Caroline.

'Then you can do it, Marjorie,' he said to Caroline.

'I'm not Marjorie. I'm Caroline.'

'You both sound the same. Both of you nagging women.'

'I'll go,' said Marjorie, stepping forwards and taking her brother's arm. 'Come along Henry.'

'Thank you. I don't know what it's coming to, unwelcome in my own house!' The sound of his complaining faded with the tapping of his stick as he and Marjorie made their way back upstairs.

'Something's wrong with your father, isn't it?' Duncan turned to her, the light of realisation dawning in his eyes.

'We think he's in the early stages of dementia. The blindness doesn't help, but sometimes he thinks mother is still alive and he's forever confusing me and Marjorie and Emily with each other. It's not just the blindness.'

'Then why are you still trying to do what he tells you?' Duncan asked bluntly, but not unkindly. She thought about lying, she thought about pretending that everything was all right, that life was going just fine, but she couldn't do it any more.

'Because… he's the only one who still seems to care about *what* I do…' she said.

'Oh Caroline, that's not true!' he replied. 'Emily and Marjorie both care very much. They might not tell you, but they do. And I know that we've had our differences over the years, but so do I.'

He reached out and took her hand, and rather than slapping him away or telling him to leave her alone, she squeezed his hand in return. It felt good to have someone on her side at last – even if it was Duncan.

Chapter 25

The Haunting of Harthorne Hall.

She had to keep reminding herself that it was not a date, as she sat beside Tom in his van in her tightest jeans and her warmest jacket, although Caroline and Marjorie both seemed to think that a trip to "The Haunting of Harthorne Hall" with Tom could be a romantic way to spend the evening, Tom wasn't interested in anything like that. Friends, that's all. She also had to keep reminding herself that it was for the good of Misterley Manor.

Alice did not like scary movies, she did not like blood and ghosts and vampires and anything that might jump out at her. She knew it was pathetic – Sebastian frequently told her how pathetic it was when she refused to look out from behind her hands in the cinema – but she couldn't help it.

Today, she was determined to remain cool, calm and detached. She wasn't going to let anything scare her; she had her phone, she had a checklist from Caroline and she had Tom to hold her hand if it was frightening. But she wasn't going to get frightened, she told herself firmly.

The Haunting of Harthorne Hall had excellent road signage, she would give it that; the yellow signs directing them to the stately home had started once they had passed Ormsborough and brought them right to the entrance gates. She awarded "Road signage" five stars out of five on the sheet that Caroline had given her.

'There's no way you could get lost, is there?' she said to Tom, several times with increasing desperation as she found she hoped that Tom *would* get lost. They could just keep driving until they reached County Durham and miss the whole event. The closer they got the more scared she became. What if there were snakes? She hated snakes. What if there were spiders? Creepy-crawly legs and wispy webs; she shuddered at the thought. Zombies and werewolves and things she could handle – just about – because she knew they weren't real, but bats and snakes and worst of all, rats…

'Oh look, there's the car-park!' she announced brightly, strangely reassured by the stewards in their high-vis tabards. Caroline was very fond of a high-vis tabard, there was a whole cupboard full of them back at Misterley Manor and for Alice it was a symbol of normality, security, stability – the very opposite of werewolves, zombies and rats. Another five stars went on the checklist for car-parking arrangements. High-vis jackets very much in evidence, all health and safety precautions adhered to.

'Alice, are you scared?' asked Tom.

'Me? No, no, not at all, not even slightly. Well, maybe a little bit…' he looked at her questioningly. 'Oh all right. Yes. I'm scared. I'm sorry Tom, I should have said, I'm a coward when it comes to scary things. I can't watch a horror film without crying. It used to drive Sebastian mad!'

'Then why did you say you would come?'

'I didn't exactly have an option. Marjorie made me.'

'Why, if you're scared?'

'Well… I want to help Caroline,' she said. 'Shall we go in?'

'What about a quick drink first? Maybe a gin or something would make you a bit less stressed?'

'And Caroline wants us to check out the catering facilities too,' Alice added.

'Oh well, we'd better have a drink then!' Tom said, walking beside her, so close that their hands almost touched. Almost, but not quite. Should she reach out for him? Would he mind if she did, or would he pull away?

'Tickets please,' demanded a steward, and the moment was

lost as Alice delved into her pockets for the tickets.

Several points on the checklist later (ticketing arrangements, event signage and toilet facilities all got four or five stars) they found themselves in the bar area. It was a marquee at the edge of the parkland where the "haunting" took place, Alice could hear screams echoing out from the woods. There were a lot of excitable teenagers running around which made Alice feel old, even at 24 she felt considerably older than most of them. There was no box on her checklist to grade "age appropriateness of event" so Alice added one. She gave it two stars.

Tom had bought her a "Ghost gin" which was a weird milky-white colour, and she was sitting at a table in the corner trying to hide from Tom the fact that she was shivering uncontrollably, partly from fear, and partly because of Tom's proximity. That's when they heard a well-known voice.

'At least have a proper drink. Mikey'll get you one, he's nineteen, they'll serve him,' said Emily, loudly.

Alice and Tom looked at each other.

'No way! My mam will kill me if I come in smelling of vodka,' said Emily's friend.

'My mum wouldn't care; she wouldn't even notice,' said Emily, with a note of defiance in her voice. 'And anyway I'm living with my dad now and all he ever thinks about is art. But I don't think I'll bother. Not worth it.'

'Do you think she's seen us?' Alice mouthed to Tom.

'Nope.'

'Do you think we should say something to her, so she knows we're here?'

'Nope. Why ruin her evening? We've got other things to do.'

'Yes, I suppose we'd better go and look at the haunted woods now,' Alice said, her heart sinking.

They were half way along the dark trail that lead to "Camp

Zombie Apocalypse" when they heard Emily again, out of sight now along the trail ahead of them. She was screaming loudly, and they could hear Mikey laughing. She came running out of a hut in a clearing ahead of them, but she didn't see them in the darkness.

'You are such a freak, Emz! You're scared of everything!' They heard Mikey shout. 'Emz? It's just a zombie, stop being such a wuss. Come here and I'll protect you.'

Emily went back to Mikey and he put his arm protectively around her as she slipped a hand into his back pocket, and they set off down the path away from Alice and Tom again, further into the woods.

'Let's give them a bit of space. Feels a bit like we're spying,' said Tom.

Alice agreed. Loitering behind trees with Tom was much more appealing than encountering zombies in wooden huts. There wasn't a place on the score sheet for "quality of secluded spots behind trees" on her list, but if there had been, this spot would have definitely warranted the full five stars. No-one could see them, it was dark and she was shivering. Maybe if she shivered a bit more loudly he would put his arm around her– or maybe he wouldn't even notice, and although she found his proximity exciting, she had no plans to throw herself at him in the woods again. Though she could always hope that he might decide to throw himself at her…

'Alice…' he began to say something, but he changed his mind. 'Never mind, let's get on. Have you got that checklist?'

'I've got it,' she replied, and the opportunity slipped away.

Every now and then a zombie cheerleader would lurch towards them, dripping gore and groaning, Alice would jump and Tom would almost, but not quite, hold her hand. Then Alice would nervously make notes about the quality of the make-up and the acting, and then it was on to the next area. After Camp Zombie Apocalypse they found themselves on the path to Transylvania between towering pine trees, the path was lined with sinister red glowing lights. Alice gave it five stars for atmosphere but a paltry 3 for health and safety considerations, there were so many trip hazards in the dark. Caroline would never approve.

It had started to drizzle now, and it was colder than ever.

'Something's going to jump out at us along here, isn't it?' she said nervously. There was definitely something rustling in the trees beside the path just ahead of them.

'Probably. Are you OK?' Tom asked.

'I think so,' Alice said, anxiously, and finally, finally he reached out and held her hand.

'It'll be fine!' he said with a comfortable smile.

Now *this* was more like it. She was ready to face anything that might be lurking in the undergrowth with Tom finally holding her hand. It didn't last. The rustling in the trees became louder, and there was a sudden shout and laughter.

'Get off me, Mikey! Stop it!'

In an instant everything changed. Tom let go of Alice's hand and lunged into the undergrowth after the sound of Emily's voice, fists clenched. Alice tried to follow him, stumbling over tree roots and brambles in the darkness.

'Tom? Emily? Where are you?' she called out, unable to see much under the dense canopy of the fir trees.

'Get your hands off her, you bastard!' Tom was yelling, no more than a few paces ahead of her. Someone or something crashed off through the bushes and then she heard Tom thrashing around too.

'Tom! What the...' she heard Emily call out. 'It's nothing Tom, just leave it!'

Alice stumbled into the clearing where Emily stood, looking utterly confused. She could hear Tom in the bushes, but she couldn't see him.

'Are you OK?' Alice asked breathlessly.

'I'm fine. What are you two doing here? Did you follow me?'

'No! We heard you shouting and Tom... well, he just took off.'

'Can't see where he's gone,' said Tom, stumbling back into the clearing. 'I can't catch him. Did he hurt you? If he laid a finger on you I'll knock his bloody head off his shoulders.'

'No! he hasn't done anything. Please just leave it, Tom. I'm fine.'

'I heard you shout out. Did he hit you?' He was breathless with anger.

'No, Tom, really!' Emily seemed more scared of Tom's anger than she had been of whatever it was Mikey had done. Alice could understand her fear – Tom was fierce when he was angry and Alice was unnerved too. She had never seen him like this before; he had always been so calm, so restrained in his responses. Even during the fire he had been in control of his emotions that now blazed out wildly in every direction.

'What did he do to you?' His fists were still clenched by his side.

'He tickled me, Tom. That's all. He just tickled me.' Tom looked at Emily, who was practically quaking. 'Mikey didn't do anything. Please, Tom, don't be like that. He didn't do anything!' she begged.

Alice watched Tom. The anger was slow to drain away from him, he unclenched his fists but his shoulders still showed the tension.

'He tickled you?'

'Yes. We were just messing on – you know – and he tickled me. That's all. He's a decent lad, honestly Tom, there's no need to be so angry...'

'Well, no harm done,' said Alice, as cheerfully as she could, pretending that there was nothing wrong, that she wasn't shaken by Tom's response.

'Yeah, except now I've lost my date!' Emily said, a bit of her typical sass starting to return as Tom calmed down.

'I'm sorry, Emily. I probably over-reacted a bit,' said Tom as they walked back towards the path.

'Just a bit.' Emily sounded more like herself now. 'The way you went after Mikey I thought you were going to kill him!'

'As long as you're OK.'

'I'm fine. But maybe you need a bit of anger management, Tom. And I wish everybody would just leave Mikey alone. I'm going to find him.' She ran off down the path, leaving Tom and Alice alone in the woods.

'I'm sorry…' Tom said. He and Alice stood in the middle of the path, watching Emily run in the general direction that Mikey had gone. He was breathing hard and he looked like he was a million miles away from her right now.

'I don't believe it was just tickling her. Do you?' Tom turned to Alice.

'Of course not! But I'm fairly sure Emily wasn't in any danger. Just young people doing what young people do in the woods…' she said, and found herself blushing. It was a good job that it was dark – Mikey and Emily had probably been doing exactly what she had wanted to do the night of the fire, that was all. She was all too aware of the irony of her situation with Tom right now and she didn't think she should say too much more about it. And she didn't want to press him any further to find out why he had been too upset; it had been more than just Mikey and Emily. She found herself wondering exactly what had happened when Chloe and Tom split up – what had she done? And perhaps she had she done it in the woods with someone who wasn't her husband?

'I thought he was hurting her,' Tom said at last.

'I realise that. But he wasn't.'

'I sometimes over-react a bit,' he admitted.

'It's fine, Tom, don't worry.' Tom's hands were thrust into his pockets now, his shoulders still taut with tension. He didn't reach for her hand again.

They went round the rest of the haunting, taking in ghost pirates, vampires and werewolves along the way, and Alice made her notes. They talked about event management and autumn leaf cover, but it wasn't the same. He appeared lost in thought, distant, withdrawn. At the end of the night he drove her all the way down the village to her front door, driving all the way down Quay Street even though it was forbidden. He had been quiet and subdued all night ever since the incident with Emily.

'Would you like a cup of coffee?' she asked, half fearing, half hoping that he would say yes, but feeling that she had to offer. He had driven her all the way to Harthorne Hall, after all.

'No, it's fine, thanks. I'll get back home. Another time, perhaps.' His shoulders were slumped and he didn't look at her.

'OK, I'll hold you to that!' she said more cheerfully than she felt. She watched him drive away up the street. What a terrible evening. She had been really hoping that it would be a way to get to know Tom better, and perhaps that was exactly what she had got. She hoped that she never, ever saw him get as angry as that again.

She opened the door at the bottom of the flight of stairs leading to her attic flat. Just inside there was a huge bunch of flowers with a note from her landlord who had taken them in for her. A huge bunch of white lilies. She didn't even have to look at the card to know who they were from and what they were for. She sighed. Sebastian, again. Why couldn't he get the message, that it was over? She picked up the card, and as expected the message read, *I forgive you, Ally-Bee. Can we talk?*

'No!' she said firmly to the empty village street.

She felt a sudden wave of rage. She had had enough. She picked up the lilies to fling them straight into the rubbish bin, but somehow that didn't seem to be conclusive enough. She wanted rid of

Sebastian and everything to do with him, especially his stupid, sickly white lilies. She marched down Quay Street to the harbour and with all the strength she was capable of, she threw them as far out into the sea as she could. The waves picked them up and smashed them to pieces against the harbour wall.

'No!' she said again. 'No, no, no, NO!' she screamed out to sea.

Chapter 26

Fire Damage.

'What do you mean, run out of space?' Alice had heard the radio crackle into life and though she could tell it was Duncan's voice at the other end, but she could only hear Caroline's side of the conversation. 'Well, open up the next field for a car park too, then. What do you mean that's already full too?'

Alice and Caroline were in the servants' hall, watching the security monitors. It was Bonfire Night; the crowds were arriving thick and fast – and in huge numbers. As Duncan had predicted, people had come flocking to support the Manor rather than staying away – already it looked like there were many more cars than last year and the bonfire wasn't due to start for half an hour yet.

Alice had come down from the catering tent where Sarah was doing a roaring trade in hot chocolate and parkin. Alice was Caroline's runner for tonight as Caroline was glued to the monitors. In the end she had employed two security guards in addition to the garden staff, but she would have liked more – many more.

'Well then, bring them down the drive and put them on the Great Lawn.' She turned the radio off and said to Alice: 'I can't believe it. George is on the main gate and he's let in so many people that we've run out of parking space. Even the overflow has overflowed. They'll have to park on the lawns. We've only just started to sort out the mess that the fire-engines made so it's the last thing I wanted to do.'

'But think of all the money that will be raised,' Alice said, as Caroline noticed the first cars appearing on the monitors of the front drive.

'Oh hell, there are no parking staff here yet, they must all be over in the far field. I'll go and direct them for now,' she said, snatching up a high-vis jacket from the pile by the door which she flung on over her jumper. 'Alice, go and ask the security men to come and help until the parking people get here.' And Caroline set off out onto the Great Lawn. Alice could see her waving frantically at the first car to try and direct the string of cars in the right direction.

Now, where were the security guards? She had a quick check on the monitors to see if she could spot them patrolling the perimeter of the metal fence that was all that kept the public away from the ruins. Already people were gathering at the fence and even though Caroline had wanted them kept out of the gardens people had wandered in. They were queueing to look up at the ruins outlined against the night sky, pointing, murmuring, exclaiming, and there were the security guards, keeping an eye on the crowds, arms folded rather enjoying their position of power at the other side of the security fence. Alice had to push her way through a throng of curious public to get to them, before she was able to direct them to help Caroline. She was heading up the lawn to tell Caroline that security were on their way, when she saw a familiar face amongst the crowd.

'Mikey!' she said. 'What are you doing here?'

'Come to see my girlfriend, haven't I?'

'Are you and Emily still going out?'

'Course. And I thought I'd have a look at the house, like. Sad about them letters, mind. Duncan told me you were looking for some others.' Oh, so Mikey and Duncan were on first name terms, were they?

'That's right. We think his letters to her might still exist somewhere.'

'Hidden away, like?'

'Yes. But we've tried all the likely places. So, it seems that if they *did* still exist – which is a long shot anyway – they were probably in the bit that burnt.'

'In that little tower, Duncan said.'

'Well, it's possible,' Alice said. Duncan's pet theory, from a passing mention of a "special place in the tower" in one of Fox-Travers's other letters, was now was that the letters had been hidden in the little round reading room and that they were gone like everything else.

'I was dead sorry, like. If I was there to shift that wood…'

'That wasn't your fault,' Alice said.

'Don't mean I'm not sorry. This house was something special before the fire, wasn't it? Anyway, I'm going to find Emz. As long as that crazy gardener isn't around to chase after us again. See ya later,' and he slipped away into the crowd.

Alice found Caroline at the top of the lawn.

'It's chaos. Utter chaos. *So* many people. God alone knows what Daddy's going to make of all this. Oh Lord, it's a disaster!' The radio crackled again, and Caroline listened. 'Why can't they come down here? Oh. Yes, you've got to get that sorted, that's the last thing we need.'

'What's wrong?'

'The main car park staff can't come down – people are starting to park all over the village, they're blocking the roads, so Duncan has asked them to stop people parking there and direct them into the drive.'

'Does it matter, for one night?'

'Of course it does, Alice – what if something goes wrong? What if there's an accident; someone is ill, a trip, a fall, a burn… a fire out of control… what if the fire brigade can't get through?'

Alice heard the dictatorial tone in Caroline's voice but saw the panic in her eyes.

'You're right. They've got to keep the roads clear. Good job Duncan thought of it.'

'He's good like that. For someone with an excessive amount of education, he's actually got a fair amount of common sense too.

——

Like you.'

It was possibly the first time she had heard Caroline say anything pleasant about her ex-husband, these days things seemed to have changed. She was relying on Duncan in a way she hadn't before; asking him questions, listening to his views, following some of his instructions. It was unheard of! She had even started referring to him as "Duncan" in public rather than her more normal "Emily's father" or "My ex-husband" or even "that bloody man".

'Right. I've got to get back to the monitors. Double lines of cars down the lawn please, facing the house.'

Alice was still helping to park the cars, with the two security guards, when she heard an enormous cheer from the show field beyond the lawn. There was a huge safety cordon keeping the public well away from the fireworks, and inside the cordon Alice could make out Tom's figure, along with George and a couple of others, keeping an eye on the crowds. It was a still, damp night and the first fireworks shot upwards with a loud bang and the whiff of gunpowder in the air. There were "ooohs" and "aaahs" from the crowd as a sparkle of silver and gold exploded across the sky. Alice couldn't help but think of the night of the fire, the sparks flying upwards and the smell of burning from an entirely different kind of conflagration, and she knew she wouldn't be the only one thinking about that night as she cast a glance behind her at the burnt-out shell of the West Wing. The crowd that had been gawping at the ruins had now drifted away to watch the fireworks and the building stood deserted and black against the night sky.

Then she saw a quick flash of something moving. A light, like a torch or a phone behind the empty hole where the library window had been. Surely, she must have imagined it? The security guards should be back at their posts now; if there was something wrong they'd spot it straight away. If there was someone in there, surely Caroline would have seen it on the monitors by now too. Caroline's recent insecurities were starting to affect her too; she was seeing problems and potential disasters where there weren't any. She needed to get a grip!

She was heading back to the servants' hall to see what Caroline needed her to do next when all hell broke loose. First, Caroline came racing out of the garden door and heading straight for the ruins.

'There's someone moving in there! On the monitor!' she yelled to the security guards. Oh hell, it hadn't been her imagination; there *was* somebody moving inside the library. A figure could be seen quite clearly now in the big gaping holes where once there had been windows. It was madness, one false move would bring that enormous roof beam crashing down. Whoever was in there could be seriously injured – killed even – and the remains of the roof would fall. Alice was weaving her way through the parked cars to get down to the house, when she spotted Emily doing the same thing from the direction of the catering tent where she had been working with Chelsea and Sarah.

'Mikey! Mikey!' she was shouting, 'don't be such an idiot, get out of there!'

Mikey was in the ruins.

'Emily? What's the matter?' Caroline called out when she saw her daughter. All three women reached the edge of the safety cordon at the same time.

'Oh Mum. I'm so sorry, it's Mikey. He wouldn't listen to me.'

'It's Mikey in there?'

'He thinks he can get the letters out. I can't believe he'd do something like this! I've messaged Dad, he's coming down too.'

'The letters?'

'I told Mikey that Dad has the idea that those priceless letters might be hidden in the little tower room and that they might have survived the fire if they're in the walls behind the stones. I told him not to go!'

'That's ridiculous!' said Alice. 'The letters probably aren't even there. It's just a hunch of Duncan's, there's no proof...'

'Mikey's gone in to try and steal the letters? It wasn't enough for him to burn down the house, now he's trying to steal things from the ruins? I want the police, I want him arrested –'

'Burnt down the house? You think Mikey set fire to the house?'

'It's crossed my mind.'

'He wouldn't do that. He wouldn't, Mum, he loves this house and he loves me. He wouldn't do that.' Tears were forming in her eyes. For a long moment Caroline watched her daughter.

'And you love him, don't you?' she asked. Unable to speak Emily nodded vehemently.

Now they were close enough to hear the security guards warning Mikey to get out, the bright beams of their torches shone into the ravaged interior, the huge fallen beam hanging over his head, Mikey stood transfixed in the beams of light. All the time, fireworks were bursting over their heads in showers of sparks, lighting up the ruins and Mikey in their multicoloured reflections.

'Mikey! Be careful!' Emily yelled. It seemed a bit late to be giving him that piece of advice.

'Just stand still. Don't move. Don't touch anything or you'll bring the whole lot down,' Caroline called out, clear and commanding. Another piece of unnecessary advice as Mikey was already frozen to the spot.

'Emz, help us!' Mikey called back. 'I can't get back. A bit of the floor's gone.'

'I'll get some hard hats and then I'm going to go in and get him,' said Caroline.

'No, Mum! Don't! You'll get hurt!' Emily tried to grab her mum, but it was too late. She was already heading in the direction of the house to pick up the hard hats.

—

'What the hell did you think you were doing?' Emily shouted to Mikey, sounding rather like her mother when she talked to Duncan.

'Your Dad said that there might be those letters hidden in that tower room where we... you know... and nobody dared come and get them. So I thought -'

'You thought you'd steal them?' Emily demanded. 'Was my mum right about you all along?' Like her mother in a moment of crisis she sounded stern and commanding, but Alice could hear the quiver of fear in her voice beneath it all.

'No! I thought if I got them out it might make up for it.'

'For what?'

'Cos it was my fault, the fire. I'm sorry, Emz. I was supposed to clear that scrap wood, the pile of wood in the store-room, but cos they were moving me on I was pissed off and I didn't do it. It started the fire, didn't it? I'm dead sorry and I thought if I could get them letters for you, you know, it might make everything OK again with your mam. Emz, I'm dead sorry.'

'It wasn't your fault. It wasn't the wood that started the fire, it was whatever set light to it. And that wasn't you, I know it wasn't.'

'Of course I never. I wanted to make it right, Emz, so that your mam might let me come back here. I didn't realise how bad it was in here, like. There's big bits of floor burnt away and like, piles of burnt stuff. Then some of the floor just fell away, there's a massive hole underneath and I can't see how to get out again.'

'Did you get to the tower?' Alice found herself asking.

'Everything's burnt. Just the bare walls, there's nowt there. No hidden things.'

It had all been for nothing.

Caroline came back, one hard hat on her head, another in her hand for Mikey. She held an enormous torch. 'Open the barriers, will you? And give me some light. The floor will be most solid at the edge, I'll stick to that.'

'No, Mum! Don't!'

'Nobody knows their way round that building as well as me, I could go in there blind and know where I was. It's got to be me. Now Mikey, stay where you are. I'm coming in with a hard hat, and then we'll find a way out for you.'

'The floor looks OK behind me…' he started to say.

'No! That's right under the balcony, don't move Mikey. You'll have to come round the edge, that'll be safer. There's still bits of the bookcases left to hold onto. Don't go backwards whatever you do, that balcony could come down any minute. You're not to move until you've got this hard hat on,' she was talking to him as she edged around the wall, her face suddenly lit red or green or golden by the grand finale of the fireworks above her, the beam of the torch cutting through the darkness.

'Alice, I can't watch.' Emily shrank into Alice's arms. 'This is all my fault. I wish I hadn't told him about the letters. I wish Dad would come.'

And almost before the words were out of her mouth, Duncan was there. 'What the hell… Caroline, get out of there!'

'Please don't shout at me Duncan. It doesn't help.'

'Where did she find those hard hats? I've got to help her.'

'Back in the hall.'

He had turned to head to the hall when there was an ominous clattering from inside the Octagon Library. Emily screamed and buried her head further into Alice's shoulder, and Alice flinched.

'I dropped the torch. It's OK, I can get it back, it didn't fall all the way down into the cellar. Mikey, can you catch this if I throw it?'

'Yes.'

As Caroline gently threw the hard hat, Alice held her breath as she watched through the twisted remains of the window. If he dropped it, it could crash into the fragile supports of the balcony… it didn't. He caught it and put it on.

'Got my steel toe caps on, so at least that's something,' Mikey said, almost as if he was reassuring himself.

'Right, now, stay at the edge of the room. Round this edge, near the windows. Do you see? There's that one bit that you need to avoid, step over it… no need to panic, just one big step; this is quite firm here where I am, see? Here, take my hand... that's it, that's it… well done…'

Mikey had made it across the gap to the firmer piece of flooring. He was OK. The fireworks were into their finale now, the bangs and pops getting louder, the colours brighter as the sky was lit up. It was helpful, because it cast enough light for Mikey and Caroline to see more clearly.

'Right, follow in my footsteps now. Round the edge here, it's much easier…' and gingerly they carried on, hugging the soot-blackened stone walls, the remains of the panelling and shelving still visible in places. They could be seen first in the furthest window then the middle one. If only all the frames had burnt away, instead of leaving the twisted metal remnants in the windows like prison bars then they could have easily made it out through the window.

'That's it. That's it.' Alice could barely breathe. They were past the windows now and it was impossible to see them behind the solid bit of wall between the windows and the door. She could hear Caroline keeping up her running commentary though, telling Mikey where to step, how to move. Duncan was on his way back, Alice could see him running along the path in the purple light above them.

'Now, slowly, slowly… mind that piece of the balcony stairs that's sticking out there…'

They couldn't see what happened, but there was a crack, a sharp almost metallic crack, and Caroline cried out, Mikey shouted something incomprehensible, as the noise became louder, like the fireworks going off above them. They could see the balcony, as if in slow motion, begin to crumble, starting at the right-hand side where

Caroline and Mikey were, and moving round to the far side where the immense beam rested so precariously. For a moment it hung there, and Alice hoped that the walls were strong enough to hold it without the balcony to prop up the other end, but with a final burst of fireworks, and the sound of applause and cheering from the bonfire field the beam began to fall. First the beam, then the other roof beams, and finally what remained of the ceiling and then the wall on the far side started to tumble down into the ruins, crashing through the burnt floor into the cellar below. Ash and dust flew upwards in a cloud as if the library was on fire again, and they could hear nothing from behind the wall where Caroline and Mikey had last been seen. A terrible silence followed, and a hubbub from the bonfire field as the gathered crowd realised what had happened.

'Mum!' Emily screamed out, an utterly terrifying sound, and Alice had to hold on to her to stop her running headlong into the ruins. 'Mikey!'

'Phone a bloody ambulance!' she yelled to the security guards who were standing there looking bemused. 'Now!'

And the next thing she knew, Duncan was crashing through the gap in the barriers and into the ruins. She didn't have enough arms to stop him as well as Emily. Then Mikey stumbled out of the ruins, he looked like a chimney sweep covered in ash and soot.

'Where's Mum? Where's Mum?' Emily wailed.

'She's OK. It's going to be OK, Emz. She's got her foot stuck, under something but your dad's going to get her out. I promise. It's going to be OK, I promise. It's going to be OK.'

Chapter 27

Mikey's Muscles Are Put to Good Use.

From where she lay, Caroline could see the sky. She tried to look at the stars and not the chaos around her; she tried to concentrate on the constellations and not on the pain in her leg.

'I can shift that, get your leg out,' said Mikey, his face looking pale and young and scared even under the black covering of soot and ash.

'No, if you try and move that then it might fall,' she said tightly. 'Just leave me here. Go and make sure they're phoning the emergency services please.'

She didn't want to be responsible for something else happening to Mikey. He had already saved her life once, she didn't want him to put himself in any further danger; he was so young. And Emily loved him.

They had been so close to getting out of there, only a few steps away from the doorway when the back of her high-vis safety jacket had caught on a jutting out bit of the twisted metal of the fallen balcony. It had pulled down the rest of the balcony and then the beam had started to fall. With all the strength he was capable of Mikey had pushed her out of the way and he had fallen on top of her. If he hadn't, she would have been right under that fallen tangle of metal, instead of which it was just her left foot caught by the debris. Mikey had saved her life.

'No way. I'm not going to leave you on your own in this,' said Mikey stubbornly.

Just then there was movement in the doorway behind them, the main entrance which had scaffolding planks that had been propped up there by the fire brigade investigators to allow them to go in and out.

'Duncan!' she heard Mikey say, though she couldn't see for herself who it was, she didn't dare move in case she did any more damage.

'It's OK, lad. You go and find Emily. Tell her that her mum's going to be fine, she'll be worrying,' he said softly. 'I'll stay with Caroline.'

'OK,' he said, and he was gone. There were only a few paces between where she lay and the doorway, they had so nearly made it. If it hadn't been for that bloody high-vis tabard.

'Duncan? What are you doing, you shouldn't be in here!'

'The fire brigade and the ambulance are on their way. Good job we made sure the roads were kept clear!'

'Yes, I suppose so. But I don't need you. Wait outside with the others, there's no point in you putting yourself at risk too,' she said through gritted teeth. Her foot wasn't hurting as much as it had done, or perhaps she was getting used to it. She could manage, she would be fine without him, waiting for the ambulance.

'Perhaps if rather than trying to move the metalwork from the top of your foot, perhaps if I crumbled away some of the charred wood from underneath, that might give you the space to get your foot safely out.'

'No. Leave it, Duncan. I don't want you to get hurt too. What would Emily do if we were both… well, if something happened to both of us?'

'Nothing's going to happen, Caroline. I won't let it. You were brave coming in here after Mikey.'

'I had to.'

'No, you didn't. But you still came.'

'And so did you.'

Duncan had set to work, and she found that, after all, she

thought she would let him carry on trying. The ambulance and the fire brigade might take as much as half an hour to get here, and it would seem a long time in the darkness on her own. Like all those long nights after Duncan had left when she had been too proud to admit that she might have made a mistake. *Pride and Strength* could only get you so far in life. She winced as Duncan jarred her foot as he pulled a large piece of charred wood away.

'Sorry,' Duncan muttered, without looking up or stopping. Caroline found she didn't like the silence as he worked, so she asked another question.

'Could you see from outside? Could you see what else has gone?'

'It's not looking good. The last remnants of the roof are gone and three of the walls, right down to the cellar.'

'Then there's not going to be anything left to save, is there? We're not looking at restoration any more, are we, if the roof has gone completely.'

'Please don't think about that right now,' he said, through gritted teeth. She could hear, but strangely not feel, his hands scrabbling about underneath her foot, breaking away chunks of the charred wood.

'How's it going, Duncan?' Caroline said, a tremor of fear in her voice.

'Don't worry, love,' Duncan said through gritted teeth. 'I'm going to get you out.'

'Duncan, I wish we had been nicer to each other, back then. I wish I had been nicer to you.'

'We could both have done things better,' he agreed.

'If... If things don't go right, then I wanted you to know, these last few weeks, since the fire, I have appreciated your support and your help. Things have been hard and without you they would have been a lot harder.'

His hands must be raw by now from scrabbling at the burnt wood. She glanced up at the balcony again as one of the remaining metal struts above them was starting to make a creaking noise. They didn't have long.

'I wanted to say I was sorry for everything,' it came out in a rush. 'I'm sorry for the way I treated you, I'm sorry for not listening to you. I'm sorry that things ended the way they did; you didn't deserve any of it.'

'Oh, I think I did. I wasn't exactly reasonable either. I couldn't stand seeing you do what your father told you when we both knew it was wrong.'

'I know,' she said. This might be the only chance she ever got to explain herself, to put things right between them. 'But Daddy had no-one but me. The last of the Lattimores. He had always been so proud of this house, *his* house, and he chose not to see what it was coming to. I helped him deceive himself, I suppose.'

'I understand why you did it. I could have helped, perhaps, instead of fighting you every step of the way.'

'But you did that because you loved the house too. That's the one thing that united us; you, me and Daddy, we all love Misterley.'

'That's never been all it was about. Whatever Henry told you it wasn't just the house that -' he didn't finish what he was saying because there was an ominous creak from the last section of the balcony right above Caroline's head.

'I know. I know, Duncan.' She couldn't reach for his hand as he was still busy frantically crumbling away the wood; there was only one small section to go, but there wasn't going to be time, the balcony was creaking again. 'Duncan, please go, leave me here.'

'No way. I'm staying with you until I can get you out. I'm not going anywhere.'

'Thank you,' she whispered, closing her eyes as all she could hear was the creaking of the balcony above her, the cracking of the burnt wood, and growing ever closer, the sound of an approaching siren.

'Mum, I'm sorry... I'm so sorry...'

Duncan had carried her out of the ruins, an unlikely action hero, straggly grey beard blowing in the wind and his sensible green raincoat flapping behind him as he tried not to stagger under her weight. It was a good job that she was so skinny these days. He set her down on one of the garden benches and she winced with the pain as Emily flung herself at her mother.

'It's fine Emily, you don't have to be sorry... I'm sorry. Mikey saved my life. He might be a bit... a bit...' A bit rough was what she wanted to say, how could she put it without hurting Emily's feelings? '... a bit of a rough diamond, shall we say? But he was trying to do the right thing.'

'Do you believe me now that he didn't take the camera?'

Well, Caroline wasn't quite prepared to go that far, even if he had just stopped the library gallery from falling on her head.

'Even if he did, I'm prepared to forgive him. He did save my life.'

'Why did you go back in after him, Mum? You didn't have to.'

The flashing lights of the ambulance could be seen heading down the drive, Caroline could see her daughter's face pulsing blue in the darkness, as if the fireworks were still exploding above them.

'I know I didn't have to. But... you said you loved him. And no matter what I think of him – I mean, I *thought* of him – you're my daughter.' She thought of her father and his irrational hatred of poor Duncan, and she knew that she could never bring herself to be like him. If Emily really loved this Mikey then she would have to at least *try* and accept him or risk Emily having to make the same agonising choice that she had to. It wasn't a choice she was prepared to force

Emily to make – because Emily was more than likely to choose Mikey, and then Caroline might never see her daughter again. She reached out for Emily's hand. 'If you love Mikey – if you *really* love him, then I guess I'll give him a chance. But if he does anything to upset you – anything at all – he'll be out of here so fast that his feet won't touch the ground. OK?' She tried to sound fierce, but she could hear her voice wavering. It was the pain, she told herself, the pain and the shock, that's what it was.

Emily nodded tearfully, burying her face in her mum's rather ash-stained high vis jacket. Caroline felt a reassuring hand on her shoulder and she didn't have to turn round to know that it was Duncan. It was almost like they were a proper family again.

Alice and Tom headed back towards the family car park where her car and his van were parked once the ambulance had taken Caroline to A and E for x-rays and stitching. On one side of them the house slept, huge and dark, save for the light glimmering up from where Marjorie had just switched it on in the basement kitchen. On the other side, they knew but could not see the eerie twisting trees of the monolithic rock garden stretch up to the dark sky. They could barely see each other as they followed the light from Tom's phone.

'Would you like to… would you like to come back for a cup of coffee, or anything? Nothing… you know, just a coffee, that's all…' Alice offered, wanting to ask him for more than coffee but not daring to.

'Not tonight. I don't think it would be a good idea,' said Tom. 'I know what you're saying, and I wish I could say yes, but I just don't think it would be a good idea. You and me – we're just too different.'

Alice stopped in the darkness of the pathway. 'That's not necessarily a bad thing, though.'

'I can't see a single example where it's gone well – you and Sebastian, perhaps? Me and Chloe? Duncan and Caroline? Even

Mikey and Emily, that's all going to fall apart…'

'How can you know that?'

'It's just how things are. You know it.'

'And what makes you think we're so different? I'd say we've got quite a lot in common.'

'You're an intelligent, talented, gifted young woman. You'll be a professor before you know it – and I'm just a gardener.'

'You're an intelligent, talented, gifted young man,' she said. 'And you'll be Head Gardener before you know it!'

'That's just it, isn't it? You want me to be Head Gardener and I'll never be Head Gardener because I can't read. You must think I'm stupid.'

'Of course not! Tom, of course I don't. It doesn't matter if you can't read, that doesn't make you stupid.'

'That's not what Chloe thought.'

'Well, I'm not Chloe, am I?' she challenged him.

'Chloe wasn't half as clever as you are and Chloe thought I was stupid. She wanted me to start my own business and be my own boss. Nothing I did was good enough for her, and if I wasn't good enough for someone like her, how could I ever be good enough for someone like you?'

She didn't know what to say. She didn't quite know what *he* was saying.

'Are you saying that you think that I think that…' she began. It was all too complicated. There was only one thing to do. She took a deep breath and addressed the issue directly, like Caroline would. 'Look, Tom. Honestly? I like you a lot. I thought you might like me too, but it all seemed to go wrong. I don't understand. One minute you're kissing me and it's like… wow…'

She practically kicked herself. Years of education, and when it came to trying to tell Tom how she felt the best she could do was "it's like… wow…" as if she was a starstruck thirteen-year-old who had just been kissed for the first time. She didn't feel intelligent, talented and gifted right now, she felt utterly tongue tied. 'You kiss me and then the next minute, you don't want to know. If you don't want me, that's fine – I didn't behave normally that night of the fire, I can understand that, but it was a one-off and I know I got it wrong. I won't do anything like that ever again, I promise. I'm not going to try and jump on you. Oh God, Tom, just tell me what's going on?'

There was a long pause as she tried to read the expression on his face in the darkness.

'It's not that night. It's me…' he said at last. 'It's me and Chloe.'

'Is that it?' she snapped. 'Is that the best excuse you can give me? I thought you and I might have a chance of something special. Seems like I was wrong again.'

She started walking briskly back towards the carpark so that he wouldn't see how upset she was. He followed her.

'I'm so sorry, Alice. I never wanted to hurt you, but it just won't work. I know it won't.'

'Because it didn't work with Chloe it won't work with me?' she asked angrily, stopping under the one rather feeble floodlight which lit the staff car park. Her car and Tom's van were the only vehicles left, in opposite corners of the carpark, parked as far away from each other as they could be. It seemed symbolic.

'I'm sorry, Alice. It won't work.'

'We can make it work! Let's just try!' She kissed him, standing together in the white beam of the floodlight as if they were in the spotlight of some romantic drama. She kissed him as hard and as long as she could, but his lips didn't yield, he didn't want to kiss her back.

'I'm sorry, Alice,' he said, his voice muffled with emotion. She looked him full in the face and she saw something there that she didn't expect.

———

'You're not sorry,' she said, 'you're scared! I can see it in your eyes. I don't know why you're scared but the possibility of being in a relationship with me scares you.'

'That's not true,' he said. 'It's late. We should be getting home. I can't talk about this any more; not now.' He had turned away from her and was walking towards his van.

'I don't understand, Tom. What have I done?' she called after him.

'Nothing,' he said, over his shoulder as he opened the door and climbed in. 'It's me, Alice, it's not you.'

She stood alone in the solitary white beam of the floodlight watching him drive away from her then she climbed miserably into her own car and drove back over the brow of the hill to Rawscar. She left her car in the village car-park and walked down Quay Street to her flat. She didn't like it when it was dark and late like this and she was on her own, no noise but the sea pounding against the harbour wall. Even the seagulls were asleep.

That was when she heard movement in the little yard at the side of the Fish and Chip shop. Probably a cat, she thought as she fumbled in her pocket for her door key; but her hands were cold from the walk down the hill, and it was difficult to get hold of.

'Alice. Alice, why did you do it?'

Either the cat in the alleyway had learnt to speak, or it wasn't a cat. She spun round and there in the mist behind her, a bunch of wilting lilies in his hand, was Sebastian.

Chapter 28

Alice Doesn't Like Lilies.

'Where were you?' He was in her face, in her space, closer than she wanted him to be.

'I've been at work. Bonfire Night,' she said, trying to sound calm and taking a step backwards. 'What are you doing here?'

'You wouldn't answer your phone. I was worried. I had to see you.'

'Well, now you have, you can see that I'm fine. I didn't answer my phone because I didn't want to talk to you – and I don't really want to talk to you right now.' She tried to move purposefully past him, to get to the front door but he was blocking her way.

'Have you been with that man? Have you been with him all night?'

'No. I've told you, I was working over at Misterley Manor – they had a firework display and I was helping out.'

'Until nearly two in the morning?'

'There was an accident. Caroline had to go to hospital, so I was there late. And I don't see why I should have to explain myself to you.' She tried to sidestep him, but he moved right back in front of her again, face to face with her and she could smell the gin on his breath. Sebastian must have spent quite a lot of tonight in the pub.

'Who is he?'

'I don't know what you mean.'

'Of course you do. The other man. The one you kissed, the one you were with tonight, your new shag. Who is he?' He managed to sound needy and angry at the same time.

'No-one. I'm not with anyone right now. We're just friends,

that's all.' Well, that at least was true.

'I can smell him. I can smell him on you.' Now that was just a weird thing to say; he must be even more drunk than she had first thought.

'Stop being ridiculous, Sebastian. I'm tired and I'd like to go to bed now. If you want to talk, we'll meet in the morning. You go back to wherever you're staying, please.'

'It's right up the top of the hill. I want to come in, just let me in. I won't try and touch you or anything like that…'

'I'm not going to let you in. I don't want you in my flat, Sebastian. You need to understand that I don't want you here.' She tried to move past him to the door, but he stood right in her way.

'Let me in. I want to talk, I need to make you understand,' he said, and when he was close to her like this she could smell the tang of vodka on his breath.

'No, Sebastian!' she said. 'It's over. I don't want you to come in, I want you to go away.'

'But I still want you,' he said pathetically. 'Look, if you want you can still do your PhD. I won't make you get a job. We can forget all that. Just let me come upstairs with you and we can talk. Just talk. That's all I want to do.'

"Come upstairs and talk" – she had heard that one before. Talking was almost certainly the last thing on Sebastian's mind right now, he was so transparent, especially when he was drunk.

'No,' she said brusquely, 'We agreed that it was over. I don't want you to come in.' She pushed past him, physically pushing him out of the way to get into the door at the foot of her stairs which she slammed and locked behind her. But he didn't go away; she watched him through the patterned glass walk up and down for a while, then he came and started knocking on the door. Two times, three times, then a steady pounding when she didn't answer. He wasn't going away. She waited but the banging didn't stop.

There was nobody else in the building. The fish and chip shop had closed hours ago, the holiday cottage offices long before that. Her nearest neighbours were all holiday cottages, she had no idea if any of them were occupied. She went upstairs to her flat and tried to ignore him but the banging continued. She wondered about calling the police, but as they would probably have to come from Ormsborough there was one other option – Tom. He was only in Langbarnby, a couple of minutes' drive away, and he had told her that if she ever had any trouble from Sebastian she should tell him. Well, now she was having trouble, real trouble. She hesitated. She couldn't ask him. But who else was there?

The banging suddenly stopped and she breathed a sigh of relief. He was going away, and she wouldn't have to call anyone. But when she looked out of the corner window, she could see he hadn't gone anywhere, he appeared to be relieving himself down the alley at the side of the shop opposite. Then the banging started again – Sebastian wasn't going away. The banging went on and on until she heard a crash – it sounded like one of the panes of glass in the door shattering. Now there was only a Yale lock and a flimsy bolt between her and Sebastian, what if he could reach the lock through the broken pane of glass?

'I'm coming in, Ally-Bee,' he declared, and she shut herself into the flat, bolting the inner door, sitting down and leaning against it with her full weight. For the first time she was genuinely scared of what he could do next. What if he smashed his way in?

There was only one thing she could do. Her hand shaking, she called Tom.

'Alice?' Tom's voice sounded wary when he answered.

'I'm sorry to even be asking you after everything else, but I couldn't think who else to call. I've got a problem. Sebastian's here, he's drunk and he's banging on my door. He's trying to get in. He won't go away, he won't listen to me.'

'It's OK, I'm coming. It'll only take me five minutes to get there at this time of night. Don't let him in, and don't go out. Promise you won't put yourself in any danger.'

It was a long five minutes until she heard a van screech to a halt on the street outside, she heard a door slam and she heard Tom's voice, low and dangerous.

'OK, Sebastian, mate, I think that's enough. Come on, leave it.'

'Who are you?' Sebastian said.

'I'm Tom. I work with Alice up at Misterley Manor.'

'Well, this has nothing to do with you. Go away!'

Alice came tiptoeing down the stairs, hoping that she could hear better what was going on without being seen through the frosted glass door – but that was the wrong assumption. Sebastian had seen her through the broken pane.

'Ally-Bee! Ally-Bee! Just let me in! I want to talk, that's all!'

'Alice, go back upstairs. I'll sort this out,' Tom said. 'Now, come on mate, you're making a scene. She doesn't want to talk to you.'

Alice didn't go back upstairs, she sat half way up the stairs where she couldn't be seen, listening.

'Are you the one who's screwing my girlfriend?' Sebastian's voice was high-pitched and shaky.

'I'm not screwing anybody.' Tom's voice was resolutely smooth and calm. 'Look, can't this wait until tomorrow morning? Everything will be clearer in daylight.'

'I want to hear it from her. Not you. I want to talk to Alice.'

'Alice doesn't want to talk to you.'

'She might have said that, but she doesn't mean it. I know she wants me.' It was the casual tone of dismissiveness in his voice that enraged her, the ease with which he discounted everything she had said in favour of what he wanted her to say, and she raced down the stairs angrily flung open the door.

'I did mean it. Go away, Sebastian.'

Sebastian laughed.

'Stop it!' she yelled. 'Of course I meant it. I was blind to stay with you for so long when we've had nothing in common since you left the university. I loved you once, but I don't love what you've turned into. And you don't love me, you only love your own idea of what I am!'

'You don't know how to put another person first, do you? You should have put *me* first but all you ever think about is yourself.' He jabbed at the air with his finger. 'It's all about Fox-Travis this and Fox-Travis that! What do you think it felt like for me? Always coming second to some dead dumb-fuck.'

Angrily she took a step forwards, and he took a step backwards, slipping slightly on the damp cobbles. Tom was staying out of the way, standing back, arms folded, but his large, reassuring presence in the background emboldened her to say exactly what she wanted – exactly how she should have said it from the first.

'It's not like that! But you don't want me, do you? You want this ideal woman you've created in your mind, but that's not me; it's never going to be me. You can't turn me into her. I don't want your executive penthouse and your BMW and your suits from Harvey Nick's and your flashy diamonds. I want to carry on with my research. That's all I want and you never once bloody well bothered to ask me.' Well, I… I never needed to… Any woman would… I thought…'

Something on the ground caught her attention, as he floundered with surprise and shock at her sudden anger. The wilting bunch of lilies that he had brought. He had propped them up beside her door when he started banging. She picked them up and shook them at him.

'Do you know something? I HATE lilies, Sebastian. I've never liked them. The smell makes me feel sick and they remind me of funerals, and yet you keep giving me lilies because they're *your* favourites!' She thrust the bunch of flowers at him. 'It kind of sums up our relationship, don't you think? Take your lilies and get out. I don't want them and I don't want you, Sebastian.'

She thought he was going to grovel and beg but he drew himself up to his full height, and with a sudden clarity and dignity he said to her:

'I wouldn't have kept giving you lilies, Alice, if you had ever *once* told me you didn't like them.' He cradled the drooping flowers in his arms. 'How am I supposed to know you don't like my gifts if all you ever say is "thank you"?'

There was a silence, save for the sound of the sea in the distance, as Sebastian and Alice looked at each other, and Tom took a step backwards, getting out of the way. Alice's anger had subsided – there was some truth to what he had said. If he had treated her without consideration, perhaps it was because she had let him – but she would never make that mistake again.

'Well, now you do know,' she said, breathing heavily. 'I'm sorry if I gave you the wrong idea. Thank you, but *no* thank you.'

She felt strong, she felt successful, she felt powerful. She had told him in no uncertain terms exactly how she felt, and now she didn't need to be angry any more. 'Go home, Sebastian. It's over. I don't want to see you ever again.'

There. She had done it. This time there was no apologising and no appeasement. He could be in no doubt; their relationship was over. All she had to do was turn and walk away in a calm and dignified manner. But Sebastian wasn't going to make it that easy.

'No, Alice, listen,' he began, and he grabbed hold of her arm.

'Get off me!' she hissed, angrily, trying to shake his hand off, but he kept tight hold. 'Sebastian, let go of me!' His fingers tightened around her wrist.

'Get your hands off her.' Tom stepped forwards from the

shadows. 'I think it's time you left.'

'Don't interfere. This has nothing to do with you, Mr. Friend-Zone. We're talking, that's all.' He was like a puffed-up pigeon, sticking out his chest in front of the other cock-birds.

'You can talk without touching her. Let go, Sebastian.'

Sebastian's fingers gripped her tighter than ever as she tried to prise his fingers off.

'Ow! Sebastian, you're hurting me!'

Alice raised her arm, Sebastian's hand still gripping tight, and bit him. It wasn't hard enough to draw blood, but it was hard enough to shock him into letting go.

'You little bitch!' he gasped, and before either of them had a chance to think about what was going on, Sebastian raised his bitten hand and went to slap her across the face. The blow never landed, because in two steps Tom was beside her, and he punched Sebastian so hard that he reeled over backwards and down onto the cobbles of Quay Street, with a sickening thump.

'I told you not to touch her!' Tom roared. 'See how you like it! See how you like it, you little shit!'

She recognised the blazing anger in Tom's voice.

'You…' Sebastian spluttered through blood that was already oozing from a cut to his mouth 'You… you dumb fuck… So that's what you like now, is it, Alice? A bit of rough?'

'Better a bit of rough than a shrivelled little prick like yours…' Tom began.

'Tom, don't! He's not worth it!' said Alice, feeling increasingly like she was in a soap opera. This couldn't be happening, in the middle of Quay Street at two o'clock on a November morning, she should be somewhere on a dingy London side street with a signature tune and end credits about to roll.

'You'd better shut that stupid mouth of yours now, before you start something you can't finish!' Sebastian was climbing to his feet again.

'Sebastian, stop it!' She had never seen him roused like this. It wasn't pretty. They were fighting; properly fighting. They were fighting in the street, over her, as if she was some prize to be lost and won. She was appalled, and yet at the same time… Tom was fighting for her honour in the street.

'No, no, you show me. Come on, dumb fuck, show me what you've got!' Sebastian danced out of the way as Tom swung at him.

'Please don't. Please stop it, both of you!' she pleaded, as this time when Tom swung again, his fist connected with Sebastian's jaw, a glancing blow that knocked him sideways but did not knock him over.

'Do you want some more? Do you? Do you?' Tom was challenging him. 'Come on then, come here. I'll give you some more.'

'No, please stop. Tom!' She was scared of what Tom might do to Sebastian. He was stronger, he was sober, and he was so very, very angry.

Sebastian was hunched over, eyeing his opponent sideways. He was beaten, he must have had enough. He was half the size of Tom, and he wasn't a natural fighter. But suddenly he lunged at the bigger man, ramming his shoulder right into Tom's stomach, winding him. Now Tom reeled backwards, gasping to catch his breath and Alice caught his arm to stop him from stumbling.

'Please, Tom, it's not worth fighting about. Please don't, please stop, I don't want you to get hurt, I should have phoned the police, I should never have got you involved.'

'He was hurting you, Alice. I'll show him what happens to people who do that. People like that shouldn't be allowed to get away with it.' Suddenly she was reminded of the crusading anger with which he had gone after Mikey on Halloween night.

'But he's drunk, Tom. He's not normally like this.'

'I don't care what he's normally like. I care that he tried to hit you tonight. I'll make him sorry he ever touched you.'

With a growl, like a cornered animal, Sebastian was rushing at Tom again, shoulder down ready to charge. This time Tom was the one who neatly sidestepped his onrushing shoulder, and he blundered into the wall of the fish and chip shop behind Tom.

'You bastard. You think you can steal her from me,' he growled, rubbing a bruised shoulder.

'I stole nothing!' Tom snapped back, swinging round, panting. 'Don't talk about her like she's some piece of meat!'

'You wouldn't know what to do with her if you had her. I know how to treat a woman properly,' Sebastian said, with an arrogant little cock of his head.

'That's enough. said Tom. 'You heard what she said, she doesn't want you. Time to go.'

'Doesn't want you either though, does she, mate? Just friends, that's what she said you were. Well, good luck with that. Not even a particularly good shag anyway, can't honestly recommend it, but at least she never says no.'

For a moment Alice thought she was going to be sick.

'Get out,' said Tom, low and menacing.

'OK. OK, I'm going,' he said. 'And as for you - you're welcome to her,' he said to Tom, and he swayed away up the street, in the direction of his bed and breakfast. Alice just wanted to crawl back into her flat and never come out again.

'Tom... I... I'm so sorry...' She sank down onto the doorstep of the fish and chip shop, her own was covered in broken glass from the door.

'It's OK, Alice. It's OK.' His voice was hoarse.

'I just feel so...' She couldn't even begin to put into words how used and useless his parting shot had made her feel. She shook her head vehemently. 'He made me feel so dirty.'

'Don't let him make you feel like that.' He sank down beside her, the anger that had consumed him a few minutes ago had died away to nothing – he seemed exhausted, defeated, as if Sebastian was the one who had won the fight. 'Look, there's something I haven't told you about. Maybe it's time I was honest with you – now I've seen what you and Sebastian were like, perhaps I owe you the truth about me and Chloe. About why I don't want to take things any further with you – why I *can't* take things any further.'

The look on his face was suddenly grim and cold. A shiver overwhelmed her; his dark eyes looked darker than ever. Something must have gone very wrong between him and Chloe. Was he trying to atone for something he had done? The sudden vicious anger that he was capable of, did that mean that their relationship had disintegrated into violence, was that what he was trying to protect her from? Was he scared of his own anger and what it might lead to? Had he lost his temper like that with Chloe? Had he hurt her in some way?

'What is it?' she whispered, not wanting him to answer.

'When I was married to Chloe…' he began, not looking at her, looking away down the street to the sea. 'Chloe was difficult sometimes. She could be very difficult.'

'I understand that. Sebastian could be difficult too. Tom, did you… was there violence involved?' She asked it very, very quietly, as if she hoped that if he couldn't hear the question he wouldn't give her an answer, but he had heard.

'Yes,' he said, even more quietly.

'You hit your wife?' she said, feeling a chill right through her body. She wanted to sympathise, but she couldn't. She didn't think she was managing to hide the distaste in her voice.

'No!' he said, as if she had stung him. 'Oh my God, no!' and now he was looking at her; his eyes burning into hers with a ferocity that made her look down. She wasn't afraid of him, exactly but… 'It's not just women, you know,' he continued. 'It's not just women like you who get themselves into bad situations in a relationship. It's not just women who get manipulated and shamed and hurt by men. Sometimes…' and he couldn't say any more, and suddenly she understood why Tom had gone for Mikey and Sebastian when he thought they were out of line.

'Your ex-wife abused you?'

'My ex-wife, after three years of making me feel useless started to slap and kick me when she lost her temper. Sometimes she'd throw things. Then she would call me a coward because I wouldn't fight back.'

'Tom… I…' She was overwhelmed with remorse. How could she even for a moment have thought that he might be capable of something like that?

'How can I tell anyone that? That I let her make me feel worthless, but I stayed? How weak and pitiful does that make me?'

'You're not weak or pitiful. You went back into that burning building three times. You tried to help Emily when you thought Mikey was hurting her – and you came to help me. That's not pitiful. The weak thing would have been to hit her back – that makes you the strongest person I know.'

'But do I have to spend the rest of my life proving it?'

'I don't know, Tom. Do you?'

'Perhaps I do,' he said, and hauling himself to his feet, he walked away from her up the hill.

———

Chapter 29

The Solid Thrust of the Shaft.

Duncan drove carefully along the main drive towards Misterley. Caroline knew he was doing it to protect her from the bumps; he was usually careless of his car which was an old workhorse of a Volvo, used to jolting in and out of potholes without a moment's thought from the driver. Duncan always focussed on the destination rather than the journey, but today was different, he was driving as if he had a boot full of fragile china. He had followed the ambulance over to the A and E in Ormsborough and he'd got there only about ten minutes after she had, and then they had sat and waited together. It was a long wait, being the Saturday closest to Bonfire Night, and Caroline's injury was only painful, not life-threatening. She had a bad cut where the metal had pierced her shoe, it needed several stitches and the doctors warned her that her whole foot would swell and turn all the colours of the rainbow over the next few days – she probably wouldn't be able to wear anything but slippers on her feet - but nothing was broken.

Caroline had watched burn victims being brought in; the smell of bonfires and fireworks seemed to hang on the air in A and E, and every time a new patient arrived in a wheelchair or stretched out on a trolley Caroline had thanked her lucky stars that no-one she loved had ended up like that in the fire at Misterley. Eventually, in the early hours of the morning, they had stitched her up and allowed Duncan to take her home, and now he was driving the car along the main drive to Misterley as if the slightest bump might break her.

'Stop!' she said, as Duncan was about to turn the corner to head down to the main house. She didn't think she was ready to see it right now; the gap where the remains of the West Wing had collapsed into the cellar. She had just about got used to the sight of the ruins over the last few weeks; it had taken a long time, but she had got used to the ribs of the roof outlined against the sky. Now to see it without even that... she wasn't ready. 'Look, can you take me up to the Gothic Tower? I told Marjorie and Emily to go to bed, I don't want to disturb them.'

He'd never know the real reason, she didn't have to tell him that she was scared to look at the remains of her home. Maybe by the time it was daylight she might feel more positive. She didn't want him to know how pathetic she had become since the fire.

'At least now it will be dark,' Duncan said, 'if that would make it any easier. You wouldn't be able to see the ruins.'

He knew. Somehow he knew; damn him!

'I don't know what you mean! That has nothing to do with it,' she tried to protest, but he looked at her quietly for a moment. 'Oh, fine. You're right,' she admitted. 'I don't want to see it. Let's go to the Gothic Tower, I've got some blankets and a kettle stowed away up there, I'll be fine until daylight.'

'I'm not leaving you on your own,' he said as he steered the car along the little track that the gardeners used to get to the Gothic Tower in the estate van.

'Don't be ridiculous. I'll be fine!' she protested, but once again, he said nothing, opening the door and helping her out of the car, using the light from the headlights to help them. She allowed herself to lean on him as the Gothic Tower loomed above them, comforting in its solidity. In about another minute Caroline knew that Duncan would be reiterating his theories about the Gothic Tower and Fox-Travers's phallic symbolism. It wasn't even a minute.

'There's something about the solid thrust of the shaft that makes this a peculiarly masculine building -' he began, and Caroline smiled to herself. 'What is it? Why are you smiling like that?'

'I knew you were going to say that,' she said with a grin. There was something comfortingly solid about the predictability of Duncan as well as the tower itself.

'Here, let me get the door for you,' he said as she limped in. The stairs were daunting, but the downstairs room was unfurnished so she couldn't stay there. She had often thought what a lovely little house this would make with the cellar for a bathroom, this ground floor for a kitchen-diner and the magnificent upstairs room for a living and sleeping area, with its huge floor to ceiling windows looking out over the moors and down to the sea. Maybe one day, when she was older. When she didn't have to worry about her father and Marjorie and Emily too.

'Duncan, before you go, would you do me a favour and fill the kettle from the outside tap? I can't face going all the way down again right now.'

'I've told you,' he said as he picked up the kettle from the table in the window, 'I'm not going anywhere. I won't leave you on your own like this.'

'There's no need -' she began, but he had gone with the kettle. She sighed as she sank down onto the old rattan sofa, with its cosy throw. Sometimes she wished she could stay here forever, looking out over the heather. Tonight she could see nothing from the window, it was still too dark, but in another few hours the light would begin to dawn and she would hear the birds up on the moors. By then she might feel strong enough to face the day and the ruins, but not now. Not yet. For now, she was happy here where she could pretend that everything was fine, that she was in control. Sometimes she found herself wondering if any of that Lattimore *Pride and Strength* she had told Alice about had been more than just a façade. Underneath she had no more *Pride and Strength* than the self-effacing PhD student – although these days Alice seemed so much more assertive, while she herself was going to pieces. She closed her eyes for a moment, and heard Duncan come back up the stairs and plug in the kettle. He made tea.

———

She had teabags, chipped mugs and a stash of UHT milk from the tea rooms; it didn't make the world's nicest cup of tea, but she wrapped her hands gratefully around its warmth as Duncan handed it to her sat down beside her. She should tell him to go; she didn't need him here, but even as she told herself that in her best Lattimore voice, the one that Daddy would be proud of, she knew that she wanted him to stay. Like an old coat, Duncan's presence beside her was comfortable and she was too exhausted to fight any more.

'Thank you,' she whispered, almost as if she was afraid that thanking him out loud would somehow be a betrayal of her father.

'Tomorrow,' said Duncan, 'We'll start sorting all this out. You don't have to do it on your own, we'll do it together.'

'But Daddy...' she began, but even as she started the old argument that Daddy wouldn't like it, Daddy wouldn't stand for it, Daddy would make her life hell if she let him help, she knew that argument was over and gone. Daddy wasn't the man he had once been, and there was only one man who might help her to prevent the total annihilation of her family home. Not her own father, but her daughter's father. Duncan. 'Oh, never mind,' she said. 'Never mind that now. Let's forget about that until tomorrow. I don't want to think about the ruins or my father or grants or National Heritage or anything else. Not right now.'

'Then let's not think about it,' he said, and she felt his arm slip protectively around her shoulder. She thought about protesting; that's what she *should* do... but it felt warm and it was a long time since any man had touched her like that. It was rather nice, even if it was Duncan - or perhaps *because* it was Duncan. Duncan who had risked his own life to get her out of the ruins tonight, Duncan who had driven her across the moors as if she were an unbearably precious thing.

Before she knew what she was doing, she found her head was resting on his shoulder. This is how they had used to sit together in the evenings when Emily was small, and they were both exhausted from the sleepless nights that came with a small baby. Those had been good times, she remembered. It had been a long time since she had allowed herself to think about the times before the arguments began, before Daddy took against Duncan, when things had been good… And before she had a chance to think too much about it, she was aware of Duncan's lips on her hair, softly kissing the top of her head as it rested on his shoulder – and still she didn't pull away from him. He gave a long drawn out shuddering sigh, as if he was releasing some pent-up emotion that had been waiting inside him for years. Perhaps, for these few hours while they waited for the dawn, they could pretend that the years in between didn't exist and for a couple of hours they could pretend… just pretend…

'Duncan,' she murmured, 'Duncan, kiss me?'

And she found that Duncan didn't need asking twice. She no longer saw the academic's beard and the greying hair, she saw his piercing blue eyes and felt the warmth of his lips as they met hers. Duncan had always been a good kisser, and the years had not diminished his skill; he knew exactly how to make her feel loved. When Duncan kissed her, there was no yesterday to worry about and no tomorrow to fear, only a here and now that filled her with a warmth she hadn't felt for a long time. A warmth which was rapidly growing into something more…

'I'm sorry, I should stop,' Duncan said, pulling away from her. 'I don't know what came over me.'

'I do,' said Caroline firmly, pulling his head back down to her own, 'and don't even think about stopping!'

And so he didn't. He didn't stop until she fell asleep in his arms afterwards, their clothes scattered around them on the floor, her foot propped carefully on a cushioned box and a smile of contentment on her face that was only outshone by the one on Duncan's as he watched over her while she finally drifted off to sleep.

The next thing she knew was the sound of the dawn chorus

outside the tower, and the old familiar sound of Duncan's snoring within it which woke her. She was lying on the sofa where they had made love, naked except for the red and white patterned throw that Duncan had placed over her at some point while she slept, and for the first time in a long while she felt… happy.

'I've told you,' said Sir Henry, when Caroline found him in his rooms the next morning, 'that I will not have THAT MAN in my house.'

'But I want him here.'

'I don't care what you want. You are not the master here, I am.'

She took a deep breath and tried to explain it nicely to him. 'I'm afraid we need him, Daddy. My foot isn't broken but I'm not going to be able to drive for a while. Now Emily is living back here, she'll need him to get her to and from college.'

'Can't she get the bus?'

'Not every day, it depends on her timetable.'

'Then can't Marjorie do it?'

'Daddy, Marjorie hasn't driven for over four years now.'

'Well, I'm sure she could make an exception for Emily.'

'I don't want Marjorie driving Emily anywhere. It wouldn't be safe.'

'Safer than having That Man in the house,' he muttered.

'I don't understand why you hate Duncan so much,' Caroline said. 'I always thought it was because you were worried about him taking advantage of me –'

'I am.'

'Daddy, I'm nearly fifty-three. I'm not some naïve teenager to be taken advantage of, and Duncan was never like that. It was only when you started picking and disagreeing with him that the problems started. I can't believe I didn't see it at the time.'

'What's he been saying to you?' Sir Henry snapped back,

sharp as ever. 'What's he been doing? Been sniffing around again, eh?'

She wasn't about to tell her father what Duncan had been doing last night in the Gothic Tower – it was none of his business. She began to see his bluster for exactly what it was – her father was scared of Duncan. There was something about him that absolutely terrified Sir Henry, it was written all over his face whenever Duncan's name was mentioned these days. Perhaps losing his sight had made him less cautious about how his expressions might be read, because there was no mistaking it. Perhaps Duncan's intellect intimidated him? Perhaps he had realised that some of Duncan's more practical ideas might have saved the house? Or was it simply that Duncan had always been the thin end of the wedge which would allow other people into his beloved home?

Well, things had changed. Fifteen years ago, it would have been easier to agree with her father to keep the peace – this time, she wasn't going to let Duncan down. Sir Henry was the past, and she had to preserve him, like the house – but Duncan was going to help her find her way into the future. She took a deep breath.

'He hadn't done anything other than try to help. He never did. Why are you so afraid of him?' Caroline asked.

'Afraid of him? Afraid of That Man? Honestly, girl, I do wonder sometimes where you get these ideas. Preposterous. The idea of it! Me, afraid of that man?'

But his laugh was hollow.

Chapter 30

Sex on the Beach. Or Then Again, Not.

'You don't look your normal chipper self today!' Marjorie announced when she saw Alice on her way into work on Monday morning. If she was honest, Alice didn't feel particularly 'chipper' either. Even the sight of Marjorie in a petal-pink satin skirt and cropped fuchsia cardigan with what looked like a pair of Emily's trainers and some green ankle socks didn't cheer her up.

'Bad weekend,' she said.

'Yes, Bonfire Night was such a disaster,' Marjorie agreed. 'But Caroline's not badly hurt and that's the main thing isn't it?'

'It is. But it's not just Bonfire Night, I'm afraid,' Alice admitted.

'Ahhh... I see... boyfriend trouble, eh?' Marjorie said, nodding wisely.

'Something like that,' Alice said and turned to go into the old servants' hall.

'Wait a minute. Would it help to talk?'

'I don't think so, Marjorie. There's nothing to talk about.'

'I'm sure there is. There's always something. Come on, I'll make us a cup of tea. There's no-one else about this morning. Caroline is over at the hospital, Duncan has taken her, Emily's at college so there's just us. Is it Tom, is he the problem? I've known Tom a long time and even though I haven't known you that long I do think that you'd be perfect for each other. Twin souls, I felt it the moment I first saw you together. Your auras were in complete alignment. I'm a great believer in auras. And tea and sympathy.'

Alice found herself following Marjorie into the family

kitchen, which was a glorious symphony of original Victorian features, like the clothes airer and the magnificent cream and green tiles, mixed with ugly orange 1980s pine kitchen units.

Marjorie made a couple of mugs of tea, painstakingly using a tea pot (properly warmed on the Aga), loose leaf tea and strainer, while Alice started to wonder why she had thought talking to Marjorie might be a good idea.

'So, tell me all about it. What's gone wrong?'

'Everything,' Alice said as she sipped her tea; Earl Grey - or was it Lady Grey? 'Tom told me that he didn't think we could make it work. Then Sebastian turned up drunk in the street outside my flat and he wouldn't go away. The next thing, there's Tom, who couldn't even look at me half an hour earlier fighting Sebastian in the street.'

'Oooh, how exciting! I remember back in '68 when Paulo and Herbie came to blows over me on a beach in California; such a thrill! Two red-blooded males fighting over you! I'm surprised you didn't drag him off to bed then and there – your knight in shining armour!'

'It wasn't like that. It was awful. I wanted them to stop. It was like being a piece of meat.'

'Oh, how terribly feminist of you! Good for you! Your sisters salute you!' Marjorie raised her cup of tea. 'So, who won the fight?' There was a certain amount of inappropriate enthusiasm in Marjorie's question.

'Well, Sebastian was the one who went away.'

'I saw that weedy little ex of yours, he'd be no match for our Tom! If I'd been twenty years younger… or thirty… I'd be fighting you for that young man myself. His muscles might not be quite as good as Mikey's, but he has the look of a man who knows how to use them. Mmmm…'

'No. Sebastian was no match for Tom,' said Alice hurriedly, pulling Marjorie back onto the topic.

'So, Tom beat off his rival for your affections. And the

problem is?'

'Tom doesn't want me.'

'Is that all? I thought it was something much worse. I thought at the very least you'd pulled him down into the sand and seduced him after the fight, like I did with Paulo, and that you were regretting it.' There was an unashamed twinkle in Marjorie's eyes.

'We weren't even on the beach!' Alice protested.

'No, but I was when I was with Paulo,' she sighed. 'I couldn't recommend sex on the beach, to be fair, and Rawscar in November isn't conducive to romance of that kind. And sand gets in all kinds of uncomfortable places. I can still remember the scratchy feeling even now when I –'

Alice didn't know what to say and she tried to hide her embarrassment with a loud cough. She knew her face was scarlet.

'Oh dear, aren't you feeling well?' Marjorie asked as Alice tried to regain her composure and steer the conversation away from sandy sex.

'Perhaps it's for the best that things haven't gone anywhere between us. Sebastian was always telling me that I was hopeless.'

'And you believed him, didn't you?'

Yes, of course she had always believed him. It hadn't occurred to her not to. 'Not always.'

'But when it mattered, you hear Sebastian's voice in your head. I'm right, aren't I?'

'No, you… I… oh. Yes. I suppose…'

'And Tom's ridiculous ex-wife – I always disliked that woman - he can't get her out of his head either. You're both dwelling too much on the past, and what other people, who are no longer a part of your life, might make of what you are doing now. Don't let past unhappiness ruin your chance of starting again. Let it go – let *them* go. Trust each other. Move forward. Don't let your pasts ruin your future.' Marjorie sounded like a talking box of fortune cookies.

——

'It's easier said than done.'

'Granted. But you've got to try! For the sake of your auras!'

'Well, I –'

'You must fight for him, my dear, and your strongest enemy might well be Tom himself. You mustn't give up. You mustn't let him get away. I can still never forgive myself for giving up on Paulo all those years ago. Don't make the same mistake I did.'

'I'll be very careful with the sand,' Alice promised hurriedly, shaking her head as if trying to shake the image from her mind.

'No, no! I mean don't stop trying. He likes you, Alice, I can see it in his aura – as well as the way he looks at you. No mistaking it. And you like him, don't you?'

Alice nodded. It felt wrong admitting it to Marjorie, but she did. She liked Tom; she liked him a lot, but she was scared. What if she had got it all wrong again? She had been wrong with Sebastian, what if she was wrong for Tom too? It was as if Marjorie could read her mind.

'The pair of you were made for each other. He just needs a bit of help to see it. A bit of encouragement, perhaps?' She winked at Alice. She actually winked. 'I know! Perhaps I could be your fairy godmother?'

'No!' Alice was horrified at the thought. What if Marjorie started talking to Tom about sex on the beach? 'No, I think I need to talk to him again. I need to try and explain; get him to see that I'm not like her.'

'Or,' said Marjorie, thoughtfully, 'you could just take all your clothes off and worry about all the talking later. That always worked for me…'

Alice bolted down her cup of tea and made a run for it before Marjorie could give her any more advice.

Alice had come to work up at Misterley this morning as Duncan and

Caroline were both away. She was trying to concentrate on transcribing the letters from the images that she had taken before the fire, but it was easy to be distracted because in front of where she was working, on the vast scrubbed pine table, lay the painting of Lady Isobel waiting for the expert from the auction house who was coming to see it this afternoon. She glanced at it every now and then; even with ragged edges the painting, hidden away and protected from the dust and light of the library for so long shone with a transcendent luminous beauty; the sensuous brushstrokes, and the exquisite detail with which he had depicted her luxuriously naked body – it took Alice's breath away whenever she looked at it. She was so busy looking at it that she didn't hear Sir Henry enter the room until he coughed. She spun round in surprise. How had he managed to get there so silently? Where was the tapping of his white stick? Where *was* his white stick?

'Good morning,' she said formally, always worried about saying the wrong thing to him and bringing his wrath down on herself. Surely even Sir Henry couldn't object to being wished "good morning"?

'Oh, it's you. That girl. Is my daughter here?'

'No, she's at the hospital this morning.'

'With him?'

'With Duncan? Yes, he's taken her to the hospital. It'll be a while before she's able to drive.'

'Couldn't you have done it?'

'She wanted Duncan.'

'Always interfering where he's not wanted.'

'I think Caroline asked him to take her, not the other way around.'

Sir Henry sniffed.

'Can I help with anything?' Alice asked politely.

'I doubt it. I came to see when the valuer was going to arrive about that picture.' The disdain in his voice was palpable. 'I want to make sure it's all done properly.'

'He's due this afternoon, I believe. Caroline got out the old boxes of photographs we found and the painting before she left in case she got delayed at the hospital.'

'Oh, so the painting's here too is it?'

'On the table in front of you.'

'I wish I could see it. Damned eyesight.'

'Would you be able to feel anything from the brushstrokes?' Alice suggested. He raised an eyebrow roughly in her direction.

'No. I don't think I could do that.'

'Well, perhaps I could describe it for you?'

'Why don't you do that. Can you get me a chair?'

She helped him to sit down in the big chair that Caroline usually occupied at the head of the table. He sat upright and forbidding with his stick clasped in one hand, as if he was about to start beating out rhythm for an orchestra.

'It's an oil painting, isn't it? A substantially sized oil painting?'

'Yes, it was behind the Morgan Le Faye painting, so it's the same size and shape.'

'And it features the young lady Isobel *in flagrante* before she became a moral crusader.'

'We believe so. She's reclining on a sofa thing.'

'Do better than that please. Less vague. I thought describing works of art was your job?' If he had a moustache he would have twisted it like a Victorian villain at that point with a condescending sneer.

Alice ignored him. 'On a green velvet chaise-longue. She's lying there and there's a red and white banner draped over the foot of the couch. I can't tell what it's meant to be. There might be a rose on it there at the edge of the painting.'

Alice leaned further over the image to try and catch what the picture might be. 'Yes, I think it's a rose. She's lying on her right side, she has her head propped up on her elbow. Her hair is loose and trailing over her body, but it isn't doing much for her modesty. I can go into more detail if you would like?' She tried to hide her grin at his pompous discomfort.

'No - tell me about her expression, her face.' He stared forwards, as if creating the image in his mind from her words.

'Well, she looks…' She looked as if she had spent a night in the arms of her lover. Her heavy eyes looked relaxed and fulfilled and content – and alive with possibilities. 'Tired,' was the best she could do. 'There's a knight on a horse outside the window,' she continued. 'He's wearing a long cloth coat; it's red and white striped like the banner, and his face can't be seen clearly; he has long dark hair. She's stretching out her hand after him as if she doesn't want him to leave.'

'How touching,' he said, but he didn't sound as if he meant it. 'And That Man believes there is a possibility that the knight could be Fox-Travers himself?'

'Well…' Alice and Duncan had already noted the similarities of stature and colouring between the knight and the remaining portraits of Fox-Travers – but that wasn't enough to say for definite, was it? Well, not enough to tell Sir Henry for definite anyway. 'His face can't be seen. There's no way of knowing.'

'Ah. Good, good. What about the setting? What does that look like?'

'Well, it's a bedroom in a castle. On the right-hand side, in the corner, you can see a dark four-poster bed with the bedclothes on the floor. Next to it is a small table, and above that a cupboard in the panelling with a golden chalice in it; maybe it's meant to be the Holy Grail? You can make out the jewels shining there; diamonds and rubies, red and white like Lancelot's colours. Then there's a great leaded oriel window at the left-hand side of the picture, floor to ceiling, with trefoil shapes at the top. The sun's rising outside, and it's what gives the whole painting a rosy glow.'

'Floor to ceiling with trefoils at the top, you say?'

'Yes, that's right. It's plain glass, not coloured, so the light -'

'Yes, yes. You've told me that. What shape is the room?'

'What shape? It's an…' she was about to say that it was an ordinary room when she noticed something. It wasn't ordinary at all – it appeared to have multiple sides, like the Octagon library. All of a sudden, she knew what Sir Henry was driving at. 'It's hexagonal, I think.'

She had only been in the Gothic Tower once, and it had been dark and she had other things on her mind that night, but the Gothic Tower had windows like this one and it was hexagonal. 'It could be the Gothic Tower! I think it is. The window is just like the upstairs window in the Gothic Tower, the one that looks out to the sea, but a lot of other things are different.'

The view from the window, the furnishings, the colours were all different which had possibly hidden the obvious conclusion from them all and it had taken the insight of a blind man to reveal it – Lancelot and Guinevere must have been painted in the Gothic Tower.

'Tell me more about the picture; the horse?'

Alice knew nothing about horses. She couldn't estimate its height in hands, she couldn't even tell what gender it was as it was painted. There was only one thing she could tell Sir Henry accurately.

'Well, it's brown.'

'Bay or Chestnut?'

'Yes, that's right.'

Something had occurred to her. The picture had been painted in the Gothic Tower. Duncan reckoned that Lady Isobel and Fox-Travers had a special secret place in a tower- what if it wasn't the secret library tower, as they had all assumed, but the Gothic Tower that they referred to?

——

'Oh. My. Lord!' Alice said.

'What is it, what's the matter?'

'I've realised something!' She could hardly speak from excitement. 'If Lady Isobel had a hiding place, as Duncan suspects, here it is, in the painting. A cupboard in the wall of the Gothic Tower with a jewelled cup inside!'

'Duncan thinks she kept the Holy Grail in a cupboard in our Gothic Tower?' he said in a disdainful tone.

'No, not the Holy Grail. Not the real, actual Holy Grail… but I think… I think I might know where the letters are hidden! I've got to go, sorry, Sir Henry. I've got to go right now!'

She would have phoned Duncan and Caroline if they hadn't been at the hospital with their phones turned off. Marjorie kept talking about her mobile phone, but she never seemed to know where it was and certainly never answered it. There was only one person she could phone to tell the news - Tom. She wanted to talk to him anyway following her chat to Marjorie this morning. His phone went straight to answerphone, he was probably up a tree or thigh-deep in a pond right now. She tried not to dwell on the image of Tom thigh-deep in a pond. It wasn't helping her concentration at all. She left him a brief message.

'Tom, hi, it's Alice. I think I know where the letters might be, the lost Fox-Travers letters. I'm going to see if I can find them, I think they're in the Gothic Tower.'

As she raced up the lawn towards the rhododendron forest, her heart thumped in her chest. This was it, the last chance. The letters had to be there, they had to!

She imagined telling Duncan and Caroline when they got back, how pleased they would both be, and Marjorie, after all her efforts to help them. "Oh, jolly good show!" she'd say, or something like that. It was a shame that there was nobody to come with her and help her find the letters, but if she could find them right now she might know the end of the story before it got dark. She might finally know what had happened to Fox-Travers all those years ago.

She ran faster than ever, along the twisting path through the rhododendrons, and there was the tower, like something out of a fairy tale. She flung open the door and thudded up the stairs. There, in the tower room, was the immense oriel window, looking out over the tops of the rhododendrons over the moors to the sea in the distance. If the window was *there*, Fox-Travers's easel must have been *here*. She paced out the distances. That would put the bed over against the far wall, and the cupboard would be over here.

She practically threw herself against the wall. It was one of four frames of the panelling. The first two sounded dead and dull, the wood up tight to the stone wall behind them but the third rang hollow. That was it! There was a cupboard! But how did it open? There was no sign of a handle or a hinge, nor even any line where the cupboard door met the frame… unless… yes! It must slide. In the painting it had looked like an alcove in the wall, there wasn't a door standing open, she if she used her fingers and tried to move it… yes! The panel had slid along an inch to the right. It was a cupboard and it was going to open... she couldn't see well enough yet to see if there was anything in there – it was so stiff, perhaps she would have to get some tools… but now she had got it open a little way she was able to get her fingers in and pull, the door slid further. There was something inside. There was something, no Holy Grail but there were some boxes.

She pulled and pushed even harder at the panel of oak. The edges were smooth, as if hers was not the first hand to have pushed it open. It needed to be a little bit wider… there! It wasn't quite fully open, but it was wide enough to reach in and slide the two little cardboard boxes out. Plain, small grey boxes, almost like the ones they had found in the shoe cupboard. Her hands started to shake as, kneeling on the floor she opened the first one, praying that it wasn't going to be more pornography. She took a deep breath and opened the lid. There, inside the box was exactly what she had hoped for. Two bundles of letters tied with blue ribbons and a sketchbook.

She untied the ribbon. It was old and difficult to wriggle it apart, but at last it came free, and into her lap fell letter after letter, on blue paper and white and cream, in carefully flowing writing, black ink spilling words across her knees, the same name over and over again. Your Gilbert, Your loving Gilbert, Your most devoted Gilbert. Oh. My. Lord.

She opened the old sketchbook, edges yellowed with age and musty smelling, but the sketches all clear and flawless. Lady Isobel in various poses, various expressions, various states of dress and undress – all of them signed with "G. F-T."

She really had found treasure.

Chapter 31

Lady Isobel Reveals Her Essence.

Alice tried to ring Duncan and Caroline, but their phones were still turned off, so she left a message for Caroline. She tried to ring Tom, but his phone went straight to voice-mail again. It was almost as if their phone silence gave her the permission she needed to read the letters – there was nobody to interfere, to tell her not to do it, and so she sat down, hands trembling.

Perhaps these letters would contain the secrets that Lady Isobel's carefully coded missives had only hinted at – and perhaps here she would find the end of the story. The letters were in rough order, with the odd one out of sequence, and some missing; the ones that had been with Lady Isobel's correspondence, perhaps.

As she turned over page after page there was certainly *plenty* of evidence of the depth of their relationship. They had both fallen in love, that much was clear. Here. *Burn after reading...* He had not been as discreet as she had, he had not even tried to write in code and had relied on her destroying the evidence, which she clearly hadn't. She had treasured the evidence and kept it safely hidden – until now.

I dream of you nightly, I think of you constantly, I imagine how you are spending your days without me and I imagine you sit alone at night and think of me...

She read on. Fox-Travers's writing was clear and easy to read, unlike Lady Isobel's which it had taken her a while to make out. She was used to Fox-Travers's writing in her previous research after all. *Burn after reading... I would lie with you, I wish we could be as one, as husband and wife are together. I burn for you, I burn and I feel I would know you and understand you so much better if you would reveal to me your very essence in the act of love... Your husband is absent so much or busy with his own pleasures... he would not miss you for one single evening so that I could show you the heights of my devotion and desires...'*

And yes! Here again... *Burn after reading... Having known what it is to lie with you I cannot live without you. Your lips are as essential to me as breathing, your touch is as precious as gold, your nether parts as...* Oh! He might have been an artist, but Fox-Travers was certainly no poet – *that* wasn't quite how Tennyson might have put it! And more and more, letter after letter as he spoke of their meetings in their special place, their secret hideaway – here, in the Gothic Tower – where he described how she had "revealed her essence."

She needed to sit down; her legs had gone numb with kneeling on the floor and so she took the letters over to the green velvet chaise leaving the sketchbook on the mantlepiece next to the cupboard.

More of the same, much, much more, and plans. Plans to go away to Italy or Spain, plans to be together, all she had to do was to pluck up courage to leave him. He was a lecher who brought mistresses into his house, he didn't deserve her, Sir Edward was immoral, dissolute and probably diseased.

What had happened? Had they quarrelled? No, here it was: *Dear Lady Isobel, I am requested by your husband to write to you to put an end to all that has gone between us. I have been foolish beyond everything and I have led you to believe what is untrue. I have used you for my pleasure and I regret my part in our little affair. You will not see me again. I regret the pain I have caused you. Your husband is a good and worthy man and I suggest that you do as he recommends.* No! No, no, no, no! Why would he do that? How could he? No, it couldn't be true! This was almost the last letter, signed so coldly "Fox-Travers" and written in such a formal style. He had found out, her husband had found out, and he had done something - what had he done? And why had Fox-Travers let him do it? Why hadn't he fought for the woman he loved?

She read on:

The child, when it is born it must seem your husband's. I see that now, I cannot acknowledge it is mine, it has been made clear to me. For your sake, I have returned your letters as he requests so that your honour can be protected.

The child when it is born must seem your husband's. Did that mean… Sir Henry's father, he must be the child, Lady Isobel's only child. The child, when it is born *must seem* your husband's – but wasn't.

The child was Fox-Travers's son, which meant that Sir Henry, Caroline and Emily were all direct descendants of Fox-Travers! *There* was a story to catch people's interest, a story that would sell books, and perhaps there were tests, DNA tests, that would prove it. She couldn't wait to tell them the news, it was so exciting!

But first there was one more letter, totally different from the others, but Fox-Travers's unique handwriting was still instantly recognisable. The paper was cheaper and thinner, dirty, torn and folded and unfolded many times. It was also much later in date, almost four years later, and it was written from Arras in 1917.

She knew even before she read the letter that in her hand she finally held the answer to the final mystery of Fox-Travers's disappearance. He had gone to fight in the Great War and he had never come home. There was another letter, in another hand with it; a less carefully formed note.

'This paper was found amongst the papers of the deceased at Vimy Ridge with instructions that in the event of his death it was to be forwarded to you.' It was signed, but the signature was almost impossible to read; only one thing stood out – Fourth Canadian Division. Canadian. What was Fox-Travers doing at Vimy Ridge with Canadians?

Hands shaking, she knew she was about to find out.

My dearest Isobel,

Allow me to call you what you are one last time, my love, my one and only love. If you are reading this letter, then I am, as seems likely, already at my final peace with God. It seems unlikely that any of us shall come home again from this awful place, and I shall join so many of my comrades. I want nothing else, for my life has been dark and empty without you.

That day when you did not come to me as we had planned to go to Italy I finally knew that it had all been a dream and that you would never be strong enough to leave him. I saw it in your face, the fear of our future, the hesitation to take that final step with me and I knew that you would not come to me. I cannot be angry because you were afraid, only sad that I was not able to banish those fears for you.

I want you to know the truth before I take it to the grave with me. Your husband, who played the wounded party in all this was not innocent. He employed me for one purpose and one purpose only; he did not care about architecture or art, but he knew of my reputation with ladies, and knowing that he himself would never father a child, he bought me to give him the heir he needed to keep the estate from his brother's family, who he despises. He paid me handsomely for my services, and he gained his son. He sold you to me, Isobel, and when my purpose was fulfilled he made me leave you with threats. If he had threatened me I would have borne his anger for your sake, no matter what he threatened, but he made threats against you and against our child and I knew I could not put you into such severe jeopardy. He is a man of dark desires and I believe him possible of many sinister things. Do not forget that he paid me to get him an heir.

He never expected that I would fall in love with you. My reputation preceded me, perhaps, but I never once lied to you, my darling Isobel, and everything I told you was true. I loved you beyond words. I wish I had braved the consequences and been courageous enough to rescue

you. I wish I had known our son. Do you think of me when you look at him? I cannot forget you and I cannot live without you. I wish I had been braver. Forgive me, my beloved Isobel and know that my last thoughts will be of you.
Gilbert.

He wished he had been braver. and she was too afraid. They had both done what they were told by Sir Edward, he of the dark desires, the rampant venereal disease and the countless trollops.

Suddenly all she could think of was Tom and she knew that she wasn't going to make the same mistake as Lady Isobel. Marjorie was right, she had to fight for him, even if her worst enemy wasn't going to be an enraged husband or a jealous ex-wife – it was going to be the voice in Tom's head that told him it wouldn't work.

Footsteps on the stairs behind her, was it Tom? Had he got her message? No, they were slow faltering footsteps and the tap, tap, tap of approaching crutches. It must be Caroline, back from the hospital! Alice sprang to her feet and turned to face the door as it slowly opened, but it wasn't Caroline, it was Sir Henry who entered the room, his stick tap, tap, tapping in front of him.

'How did you get out here?' Alice asked, amazed.

'I know my own land, Emily. Contrary to popular belief I can still find my way around. I see more than anyone thinks, even without my sight.'

'It's not Emily, it's Alice,' she said. He must have mistaken her voice for Emily's. 'Sir Henry, I found the letters - it's amazing, they were there all along, a sketchbook and two boxes full of the most amazing letters from Fox-Travers. Love letters. They all say "burn after reading" at the top, but thankfully she didn't - she kept them in the little secret cupboard after all. It's the most amazing story – the last letter came from France in the First World War, so that's where he died. He'd gone to Canada, you see, after the affair was found out

– well, not exactly found out, because apparently Sir Edward knew all along; he wanted an heir and Fox-Travers was employed to provide one! But he didn't expect them to fall in love, you see – it's an amazing discovery!'

She was aware that she was babbling with excitement, but she couldn't keep it all in. *This* would change everything in Fox-Travers scholarship; *this* would sell copies of the book, *this* was her ticket to appear on Radio Four! And how pleased was Sir Henry going to be to find that he was actually descended from such an amazing artist?

'Here, come and sit down.' She helped him to sit on the rattan sofa which creaked as he sat down – he must be heavier than he looked. 'I'll read them to you if you like. The letters reveal that Sir Edward couldn't father children, but he wanted an heir. Of course, Fox-Travers had the same colouring and build – except of course his eyes were brown, not blue - it wouldn't raise suspicion if the child looked like him, and so all your family is actually descended from Gilbert Fox-Travers! Isn't it amazing? It means that Fox-Travers did have descendants after all, and that you and Marjorie and Caroline and Emily – you've all got Fox-Travers's blood running through your veins! Can you believe it!' She sat down beside him, the bundle of letters on her knee, the precious final letter on the top. The answer to the mystery that she had been seeking.

'After all, it's as simple as that. An unmarked soldier's grave at Vimy Ridge for your artist chap. But without those letters there is no proof of any of this. Where are the letters?'

'I've got them here.'

'Can I have them?' he asked her as a question, but the tone of voice was commanding. He held out his hand like a man used to being obeyed, but something in his manner made Alice pause. What if he decided to lock these letters in the solicitor's vault and away from scholarship forever?

And then she realised something. He had said "An unmarked

——

soldier's grave at Vimy Ridge" – but she had never mentioned Vimy Ridge to him.

He had known what happened to Fox-Travers before she told him.

And if he had known that, what else did he know without needing to be told?

Suddenly Alice found that she did not want to hand over the letters to him right now.

'Where are the letters? Give them to me!' He stood up, and despite his age, he was still quite a formidable figure and she found herself wishing that he really had been the spindly skeletal figure of her gothic imagination.

'I'll need to sort them out, they're all mixed up…' she prevaricated. 'Why do you want them?' Alice asked, looking up at him.

'Because they were never meant to be found,' he said, tapping away from her, towards the open cupboard. 'My father told me they were gone, or I would never have let them be recovered. You should never have found them, Caroline. Now I need to do the right thing. I need to get rid of these ridiculous letters once and for all.'

He stood up and made his way to the table which thankfully only held the empty boxes in which the letters had been stored. He pushed them to the floor when he realised that they were empty. It was amazing the way he found his way about. Had he been following her all this time? Was it Sir Henry who interrupted her and Tom that day in Lady Isobel's bedroom? Is that how he seemed to know so much without being told?

'It's Alice, Sir Henry, not Caroline,' Alice reminded him, 'and these letters are massively important to art history scholarship, and to this house! Think what they might be worth to a library or a museum!'

'Ah, my dear. Yes indeed, they may be important, but the

point is, they are *my* letters and *I* shall decide what to do with them. You have them there, don't you? Now give them to me.' He started groping his way towards her using the table for support.

'No,' said Alice, firmly. 'I won't. I want to let Caroline see them first, I want her to help decide what happens to them. Let's not make any hasty decisions that we might regret, let's take them to Caroline now, shall we?'

'Oh, don't be so ridiculous! Caroline won't know what to do, she's merely a slip of a girl. I am the master here, and I demand that you give me my letters now!' He sounded like a spoilt child, demanding sweets; he didn't sound reasonable or rational. Sir Henry took another couple of hesitant steps towards her voice.

'No,' said Alice again, firmly.

'Give them to me, you little bitch!' he yelled, and in a single fluid motion that Alice would not have believed him capable of, he raised his stick and slashed out savagely at her face.

Chapter 32

Burn After Reading.

'Daddy! What are you doing?'

Caroline and Duncan had got Alice's message, they had come straight over the Gothic Tower. Caroline had needed Duncan to help her up the steps, but she was so excited to see what Alice had found there was no holding her back. She was shocked by the sight that met her eyes.

It was easy for Alice to dodge out of the way of Sir Henry's stick; he couldn't see her, and he was distracted by the sound of Caroline and Duncan opening the door which caused him to flail wildly and inaccurately.

'Don't do that!' Caroline said, breathless with shock while his cane clattered uselessly to the floor. For a moment there was a stunned silence. Duncan and Alice looked utterly amazed by what they had seen; sadly, for Caroline it didn't come as any surprise. He rarely hit his target, but recently Daddy had become rather prone to sudden violent outbursts of anger. It was frustration; losing his sight and his frequent bouts of confusion had meant that Daddy was… unpredictable… these days.

'How dare you! These are my letters, how dare you! Give them to me!' he shouted.

'Daddy, stop it!'

'You found the letters?' Duncan got straight to the point with Alice.

'These letters are amazing. The whole story is here!' Alice said.

'No. No, no, no!' Sir Henry staggered towards her again, but

Duncan grasped his arms and held him back.

'Stop it! I can do what I want. They are my letters!' Caroline watched as Sir Henry tried to lash out at Duncan.

'I should have known you were involved, Duncan Russell.'

'I don't think Sir Henry is thinking quite straight at the moment,' said Alice, tactfully glancing at Caroline.

'He hasn't been thinking straight for several years now, Alice,' Caroline said quietly. 'I've tried to protect him, but it's quite clear that he's not... well, he's not what he used to be.'

'I can hear you! I can hear what you're saying. Get off me, Russell! I should never have let you marry her; never. Never should have let you in the house. Not one of our sort. Not at all.'

'You couldn't have stopped me. I loved him,' Caroline said.

'Love. Such nonsense. Where did *love* ever get any of us? Fuss and nonsense. If it wasn't for Lady Isobel's misguided idea of *love,* then we wouldn't be in this ridiculous mess in the first place.'

Alice and Duncan looked at each other for a moment.

'Alice, what have you found?' Duncan asked, and but Sir Henry suddenly stopped her replying:

'Look here, I'll give you one of the paintings, girl. One of the Fox-Travers paintings. Whichever you like. It's yours. Give me the letters now, quietly, and I'll give you a painting.'

'What?' she said, and the room was suddenly so quiet you could hear the birds singing outside.

'You heard me. I'll give you one of the paintings. Give me the letters you have in your hand and I'll give you a painting. It's not too late.'

'You mean, you'll give me a painting if I keep what I know to myself?'

'That's it. A painting. Your own Fox-Travers.'

'Daddy, you can't say that. Those paintings belong to the house.' What was he thinking? Caroline was appalled.

'And the house belongs to me!'

'What do you know? What's in the letters?' Duncan asked. Caroline watched her father as Alice answered. He seemed to crumple further into himself with every word from Alice's mouth.

'I read the letters and it's an amazing story.'

'Don't tell him! Please don't tell him! Not that man, don't tell him,' and the commanding tone was replaced by a pathetic wheedling one.

'Fox-Travers was Sir Henry's grandfather all along,' Alice continued, 'and Sir Edward *paid* him to get Lady Isobel pregnant and give him an heir.'

'He did *what*?' gasped Caroline.

'He had to have an heir or his title – and the estate - would have had to go to his brother's family when he died,' Duncan said thoughtfully.

'But Fox-Travers fell in love with her,' Alice continued. 'And I know what happened to him. He was paid off – he went to Canada, and he fought in the First World War. He's an unknown soldier lying somewhere near Vimy Ridge.'

'It all makes sense – though who would have thought the Disdainful Dowager had such a scandalous past!' said Caroline, sinking down awkwardly onto one of the chairs; her foot was hurting, and she was feeling light headed from the pain – and the shock.

'This means nothing. Nothing is proved. Don't get any ideas that this means anything to you, Duncan Russell.'

'To me? Why should it mean… Oh! I see! So that's what's been bothering you!' Duncan's eyes widened. 'Now I understand.'

'What has any of this got to do with Duncan?' Alice asked. Sir Henry did not answer, but Caroline did, slowly and carefully.

'It means that if Fox-Travers was our ancestor, then Sir Edward Lattimore wasn't. It means that the inheritance was illegitimate. Misterley Manor should not, by rights be ours.' She was looking up at Duncan as she spoke, because she knew exactly what this meant.

'I'll fight it. Every inch of the way I'll fight it. You'll get nothing that belongs to my family!' said Sir Henry.

'I don't want anything of yours,' Duncan said. He was magnificent: calm, controlled, utterly in charge of the situation.

'Of course you do. You've always wanted it. That's why you married her, wasn't it, for her prospects – for her property. Good God, man, I'm not stupid!' Her father, in contrast to Duncan, was blustering with anger, red faced, desperate. Caroline felt sorry for him, struggling to protect the last tattered vestiges of an inheritance that it seemed had never been his to begin with.

'I married your daughter because I loved her and that was the *only* reason,' Duncan snapped. 'But now I see why you were so desperate that I should keep my distance.'

'What's going on? I don't understand?' Alice said.

'You see, if Sir Henry's father was the illegitimate son of Fox-Travers, then he wasn't a Lattimore, and neither is Daddy. Or Marjorie or I for that matter,' said Caroline.

'I can't have that. I can't have the Lattimore name sullied. Misterley belongs to me, to my family.' Sir Henry sounded even more desperate, and with a sudden movement that Caroline would hardly have believed possible from a man so frail and sightless, stood up and he pushed the old sofa up against the door to the staircase. Alice and Duncan were still standing by the table at the other side of the room, Caroline was still seated on the chair by the wall and struggling to get up. Now he pulled something from his pocket, something small and silver which caught the light from the windows. Something small and silver which opened with a loud click. A cigarette lighter.

There was only one door to the room, and he stood between them and the door with the lighter in his hand, clicking it open and shut, feeling his way round the trigger. 'Now, give me the letters.'

——

'Come on, Daddy. Sit down, have a little rest,' Caroline suggested.

'Move out of the way,' added Duncan.

'No. not until one of you gives me my letters. They are MINE.'

'Please, Sir Henry, don't. These letters are so important to Fox-Travers scholarship; you can't imagine!' Alice pleaded with him. He ignored her.

'Then I only have one option left,' Sir Henry said, and before any of them realised what he was doing he had bent down, flicked on the lighter in his hand and touched it to the cheap throw that was draped over the old sofa, which flickered then flared and began to burn. 'Burn after reading. That's what you said.' He flinched as the flames licked at his hand, looking surprised at the sudden pain, and shocked.

'Don't be so stupid!' Duncan yelled, and snatching the throw of the sofa he stamped on it, Alice helped him, and between them it only took seconds to tread out the flames, but the smoke hung in the tiny room, making them all cough, Sir Henry worst of all.

Caroline heard footsteps on the stairs – somebody must have heard all the shouting. The door rattled but the sofa was still blocking it, so the door wouldn't open.

'What's going on?' Tom's voice shouted from outside the door. 'Alice? Alice are you there? Are you OK?'

The young gardener seemed very concerned about Alice's wellbeing, Caroline noticed. He had come running to protect her, which was good; she had always liked Tom and increasingly she liked Alice. Marjorie was right; he would be better for her than that awful young man with the lilies.

'I'm fine, Duncan and Caroline are here. It's Sir Henry, he's…' Alice glanced towards Caroline as if asking for her permission to continue.

'Sir Henry is having a bad day,' Caroline said. It was the best she could do right now.

'Wait a minute, I'll move the sofa,' said Duncan, shoving it out of the way.

Tom tumbled into the room and with him a breath of fresh air as the smoke started to disperse. Typical, Caroline thought. She had only just managed to get the smell of smoke out of these clothes after the first fire.

'I got your message, Alice. I heard shouting. What's going on? Why can I smell smoke?'

'Alice found the letters and Sir Henry doesn't think they should have been found. We were persuading him not to burn them,' said Caroline.

The fight had gone out of Sir Henry; he had sat on the sofa where Duncan had pushed it into the corner; his head was down, his shoulders slumped, and he was muttering to himself.

'Come on, Daddy, I wonder if we need to get you to a doctor,' Caroline said, seeing that his hand was reddening from the burn.

'No, no I'm fine. No doctors, I've told you, no doctors. There's nothing wrong with my mind, I don't need a doctor. I'm tired, just tired that's all. There's nothing wrong with my memory, I can recall everything perfectly, I can't see so well, that's all. Stop nagging me, Marjorie.'

'It's not Marjorie, it's Caroline. At least let Sarah from the tea room look at your burn. She's a first aider.'

'A burn? Don't be ridiculous, the fire was weeks ago!' he said. 'Nonsense! I haven't burnt it.'

Alice and Duncan looked at each other while Caroline tried to look anywhere but at Alice or Duncan.

'I'll come with you, Caroline,' Duncan said.

'Tom, why don't you stay here and help Alice pack up the letters?' Caroline suggested. 'Then bring them down to the house when you're finished.'

'There's no need,' Alice said quickly.

'I think Tom's the best person to help you,' Caroline said, as Duncan firmly steered a protesting Sir Henry out of the room, leaving Alice and Tom alone in the Gothic Tower.

Chapter 33

Blame the Women's Institute.

Between Caroline's foot and Sir Henry's sight, it took a while for them to get back to the house, and to get Sir Henry settled back in his room after Sarah had dressed his burn. Then there was something that Caroline knew she had to ask her father – she hadn't wanted to bring it up in front of Alice and Tom, but there was something that had been nagging at her since her father had started waving the cigarette lighter about.

'Daddy, was it you?' she asked.

'I'm sorry, Caroline, to what are you referring?' he said archly. At that moment the door to his rooms opened.

'Henry, do you want a cup of tea? Just putting the kettle -' Marjorie stuck her head round the door, for some reason she was wearing a flowery knitted hat on it. 'Sorry, is this a bad time? I'll come back later.'

'No, you stay, Marjorie,' Caroline said, and her voice was low. 'I think it would be better if you were here too.'

'Oh! Oh, very well. I'll come in then, shall I?' She cast an inquisitive glance at Duncan and walked over to stand beside him. 'Is it something I can help with? What has happened?'

'Daddy has tried to set fire to the Gothic Tower.'

'Well I had to stop her, didn't I? Had to stop her and that husband of yours prodding and poking into things that didn't concern them. I had to stop the girl.'

'Alice? You mean you had to stop Alice?' Marjorie asked.

'Alice. Yes, her. That girl. You mustn't listen to her. She steals things. Like That Man. You should get rid of her.'

Caroline had something else on her mind. 'So, Daddy, was it you?' She swung round, dangerously calm.

'I don't understand you.'

'I think you do. Was it you? Did you do it? It was you, wasn't it?' Caroline stood stock still, her face grey and rigid with anger.

'I suppose I must have done,' said Sir Henry, looking utterly perplexed and downcast. 'Yes, yes… I suppose it must have been me.'

'You did it? You set fire to Misterley Manor?'

'No, not that. The other thing, with the camera, I did that. I didn't set fire to Misterley, why would I do that? It's my *home*.' He sounded suddenly frail and sad.

'Because you're a half-crazy old fool who doesn't remember *what* you've done half the time!' Caroline shouted, her patience with her father at an end. 'You –'

'It wasn't Henry,' said Marjorie, firmly, her voice cutting across the rant that Caroline was about go into. 'I think I know who started the fire, but it wasn't Henry. I promise you.'

'Then who was it?' Caroline demanded. 'Was it Mikey after all?'

Marjorie held out her hand and took a step towards her niece. 'I'm so sorry, Caroline… I can't be sure, but I've a terrible feeling that… Oh Caroline, I'm so sorry, and I do hope it was one of the builders after all… it was an accident… I should have told you, I'm so sorry, but it might have been me.'

'It was *you?'*

For a few moments there was the longest, loudest silence that Caroline had ever heard in her entire life.

'I'm so sorry.'

'Tell me exactly what happened.'

Marjorie sighed, and began to speak. Her voice was quiet, suppressed, most unlike her usual exuberant self. 'I was having a joint in the little store room about half an hour before the fire.'

'I'm sorry, *what*?' Caroline was barely able to speak.

'In the sixties I became partial to the odd spliff, now and again. When my hip became particularly troublesome last year Pat from the Women's Institute recommended that perhaps I might consider taking up old habits again; purely in a medicinal way, for the pain in my hip, you understand. So, really, I suppose we should blame the Women's Institute. I've been smoking the odd tiny little bit of medicinal marijuana. That's what the joss sticks were for.'

'Marjorie, why didn't you say anything?'

'Because I knew you'd worry. When you told me to stop burning them in the house, I started going outside, to the little old store room next to the old stable block. But my hip has been so much better since –'

'*Drugs?* But how on earth… where have you been buying it from? Have you been getting pot delivered to the house? To *this* house?' She tried to catch Duncan's eye, but he was looking away from them both. Caroline had a feeling that he might, just possibly, be laughing.

'Mikey delivered it. His brother gets it for me from a friend of his girlfriend who knows someone. Pat from the W.I. gets her marijuana from him, and the vicar's husband does too, so he's terribly respectable… for a drug dealer…'

'So, when we thought Mikey was acting suspiciously the day that camera disappeared…' Caroline said slowly, tailing off and waiting for Marjorie to continue.

'He was bringing me my… well, my "stash" as Mikey likes to call it. I'm sure the camera wasn't anything to do with him.'

'Daddy?' Caroline swung round 'When you said you had done "the other thing with the camera", what exactly did you mean?'

'Shouldn't have had it in there, quite unnecessary,' Sir Henry said. 'Looking at the letters was one thing, photographing them quite another. I told you, I told you, Caroline. But she would insist on having that bloody camera in there.'

'What did you do, Daddy?'

'I threw it out of the window. I pressed all the buttons I could feel, and I threw it out of the window.'

'Right,' said Caroline, picking up her stick and hobbling around the table away from him. 'Why did you do that, Daddy?' She was exhausted. All this was too much.

'I didn't want that girl here. We don't need any of that; this is *our* house. Ours and nobody else's and I wanted to see that it stayed that way. We don't need other people, we don't need National Heritage and we don't need Duncan. That's all I ever wanted. Our house, our home, our inheritance.'

'And you let me get Mikey removed even though he had done nothing wrong?'

'Who is Micky, when he's at home?'

'Mikey, not Micky… Oh, never mind.' He probably wouldn't remember the conversation by tomorrow morning. But she owed Emily a big apology, she should never have doubted her – and Mikey. He might be a small-time drug delivery mule, but he hadn't stolen the camera.

'Well, I might have tried to persuade you not to; I knew he hadn't been anywhere near that camera because he had been with me at the time,' began Marjorie, 'but I assumed that you'd sacked him not because of the camera but because he was getting it on with Emily that time.'

'Good God, what else is going on that I don't know about?' Caroline was absolutely stunned. 'My daughter is "getting it on" with a drug dealer, my ancestors have been concealing pornography in shoeboxes, my father attempted to burn down the Gothic Tower to destroy some letters, letters which show that the house isn't actually ours at all, and my aunt has been smoking pot and accidentally burnt down the West Wing… what else? What next?' And she glared round the room at Marjorie who was opening his mouth to speak. 'Marjorie, what else have you got to add?'

'What do you mean, letters that prove the house isn't actually ours?'

'Oh, of course, you missed that. We're descended from Fox-Travers. He had an affair with Lady Isobel and he fathered her child – your father, Marjorie. You're not really a Lattimore, by birth, but a Fox-Travers.' She said it in a matter-of-fact tone of voice. Marjorie gaped at her.

'A Fox-Travers?'

'Sir Edward knew all about it,' Caroline added. 'It would appear that he knew that he would never have children and he employed Fox-Travers, not simply as an architect but as a potential method of getting an heir and stopping his estate passing to his brother.'

'His brother?' Marjorie echoed. 'Is this true, Henry?' Sir Henry had gone very quiet, unfocussed and he didn't answer her.

'His brother,' Duncan confirmed 'would have been the male heir, not Lady Isobel's son.'

'You mean,' said Marjorie loudly and proudly, 'the good-for-nothing brother who gambled away his own inheritance and married that housemaid?'

'That's the one.'

'The one who changed his name because he hated his family so much? What was it, what did they call him... Joseph... Joseph...'

'Russell,' said Sir Henry.

'Oh yes, that's it! That was it, of course, Russell! Any relation of yours, Duncan?'

An awkward silence as everybody looked at Duncan and Duncan looked alternately at the floor, the walls and the ceiling.

'Great-grandfather,' Duncan confirmed reluctantly.

'Well I never! Does that mean that the house should belong to you then?' Marjorie asked with total innocence. There was an even longer pause as Duncan looked at Caroline and she looked back at him.

'I suppose it does,' Caroline said. 'I suppose that's exactly what it means. The Lattimore inheritance should be yours, Duncan.'

'Not after all this time, I doubt,' said Duncan, looking at Sir Henry who had gone very quiet. 'And even if it legally could be mine, I wouldn't want it. It's yours, Caroline. It's part of your flesh and blood, this place.'

'Right now, I'd give you it if you'd have it,' she said quietly.

'Don't be so ridiculous. It's not the house I want, Caroline. It's never been about ownership.'

'I know. I know that now,' she whispered, looking at him and seeing again the man with the sparkling blue eyes who had proposed to her in the Gothic Tower all those years ago. 'And there's something I've put off for too long,' she said, 'Daddy, we've got to start looking at what to do to help you. You need some proper help. You need to see a doctor.'

'There's nothing wrong with me! I don't want to see a doctor!' he protested, but even as he said it the defeated bend of Sir Henry's shoulders told her another story.

'Well, whatever next!' Marjorie was saying as there was a knock on the door. Duncan opened it and George ushered in a little man with a large moustache that seemed to have a life of its own.

'He was looking for you downstairs,' George said before he went back downstairs, muttering.

'Hello? I'm Mr Sowerby, the valuer, come to see your nude?'

Caroline began to laugh. If they had been in a stage farce the little man's entrance could not have been timed more perfectly. She caught Marjorie's eye, but Marjorie was also trying not to laugh. She thought Duncan would be serious, she turned to him, but no, Duncan was also suppressing silent mirth.

'Ah yes, the painting,' Caroline said, a tinge of hysteria in her voice. 'It's so good of you to come and value the painting Mr. Sowerby. It's downstairs in the servants' hall. The painting of my ancestor, the admired and virtuous Lady Isobel Lattimore, the upright doyenne who founded the Ladies' Association for Moral Welfare, lying stark naked on a sofa, in the midst of an affair with a notorious artist who fathered her illegitimate child, throwing the inheritance of our family fortune into doubt. I *knew* there was something I'd forgotten!'

'So, what happens next?' asked Emily. She had come in from college and gone straight to find her mother. Emily had moved back into Misterley Manor and hadn't gone back to her father's house since the accident - mind you, neither had Duncan, Caroline thought with a secret smile to herself. After what had happened on Saturday Duncan had stayed over every night – just to make sure that Caroline could manage with her injured foot. That's what they had told everyone, but every night once the rest of the house were all in bed, Duncan would tiptoe along the corridor from one of the spare bedrooms and into Caroline's room. It felt like being a naughty teenager again. If Emily knew what was going on she would probably be utterly disgusted. A smile spread over Caroline's face as she pictured her daughter's possible reaction to what her mum and dad were doing every night in the four-poster bed - sometimes more than once every night.

'Mum? Mum! I asked you what you were going to do with the paintings. You were miles away!' Emily said, and Caroline recognised an echo of her own nagging tone in her daughter's voice.

'Sorry, darling. I'm going to sell the paintings. I'll have copies made first, but I'll sell the originals. It's not fair to keep such amazing works locked away in private, they should be somewhere where everyone can see them. I'd like to come to an agreement with one of the national museums if I can – or possibly even one of the big

———

American ones. Unless I can come to an agreement with National Heritage about taking over the whole property, then they'll stay in the house.'

'But what about having her… you know… her lady bits on public display?' Emily asked primly.

'Well, if our renowned lady ancestor hadn't wanted to have her "lady bits" put on public display she shouldn't have let Fox-Travers paint them in such detail, should she?'

'Like sexting, then?' Emily said.

'Yes, a bit, I suppose. Oh Lord, Emily, you haven't!' Caroline sounded concerned.

'No, Mum! Oh my God, no! Urgh, why would you even *think* that?' She shook her head.

'It'll be quite nice for history to see her as something other than an uptight moral campaigner, I suppose. The young Lady Isobel was amazing,' Caroline continued.

'Are you going to sell Misterley to National Heritage then?' Emily asked.

'Good Lord no! But I am in talks with National Heritage to see if we can find a way forwards together. Why, do you think I should sell it?'

'No,' Emily said hesitantly. 'Not any more.'

'So, you do care about it after all? What made you change your mind?'

'It was what Mikey said, about our kids growing up here. I'd like them to have the same kind of childhood I did,' and she smiled.

'*Your* kids? Is there something you're not telling me, Emily?' Caroline managed to sound stern, amused and worried both at the same time.

'Mum! No! I think this place… well, it's a responsibility isn't it? It doesn't belong to us, we look after it for our kids and their kids.'

'Oh, do you think so?' Caroline raised her eyebrows, hearing her own words coming back to her from her daughter's mouth.

'Yeah, that's what Mikey said.'

'And if Mikey said it then it's got to be true,' said Caroline with a wry smile. 'I'm beginning to think that perhaps Mikey has something going for him after all.'

'He loves this place, Mum. He was dead upset when the West Wing burnt. He says when he's done his apprenticeship he'd like to learn to work with old buildings; maybe work for Goldings up in Newcastle, perhaps. You said they were the best for old buildings. Not that there's anything wrong with Sleightholm's, but Golding's would have been so much better, Mikey says.'

'Well, do you know what, Emily? I think on this occasion Mikey might be right. Perhaps having a decent builder in the family wouldn't be such a bad thing. Come on then, give your old Mum a hand to get outside. I wanted to have a look… a good look… at the ruins before I make any decisions about what to do next.'

'And the paintings?' Emily said as she helped her mum back towards the door. 'You never said how much the paintings were worth, Mum.'

Caroline paused, enjoying the moment of suspense. 'Five million,' said Caroline, watching with pleasure the mixture of emotions that flooded Emily's face.

Chapter 34

Alice Reveals Her Essence.

Evening was already falling; since the clocks had gone back the evenings were darker and wetter and the leaves were being blown from the trees tonight by a blustery wind that swept down from the moors and the air outside the Gothic Tower was cold with the promise of the first frost of the year.

Tom and Alice had tidied up the mess and disposed of the burnt remnants of the throw. They had left all the doors open to lessen the smoky smell, as they checked round the room to make sure that all the letters had been found, and now it was nearly as cold inside the tower as it was outside. Alice eyed the fireplace.

'I wonder if we could light a fire. It would be cosy up here if we could.'

'I think I've had enough of fires for a while,' Tom said.

Although the afternoon was wearing on, neither of them seemed to want to leave the tower quite yet. Alice sat down on the battered old sofa, and Tom, after a moment's hesitation, sat down beside her.

'I wonder how the valuation is going?' Alice said brightly, making conversation. She wanted to talk about other things – about how they might move forwards together – but she didn't know where to start without risking him walking away again. Had the fight changed anything for him? She felt she understood him better, that she knew what the demons were that he had to fight, but she wasn't sure how to help him defeat them, she only knew that she wanted to try.

'I doubt those paintings will be worth enough to restore the ruins, mind,' Tom said, looking out at the moors in the dusk, the heather blowing in waves like the sea.

'You know what…' an idea suddenly struck Alice, '… if they can't be restored, perhaps you could turn them into a garden. Flowers that Fox-Travers would have planted; roses and things climbing over the ruined walls.'

'Ay, you've got an idea. If the walls could be stabilised and we could create a system of raised beds… it could incorporate some of the damaged building; some of the architecture and carved stonework that's been saved.'

'I could help you research what plants Fox-Travers used; he describes the planning of the gardens in the letters,' Alice added enthusiastically.

'It could even have some shelter, a pavilion thing for weddings; make it part of Caroline's wedding business if she wants to go on with it,' Tom said.

'A summer house covered in climbing roses. What was that French rose called that Fox-Travers liked?'

'Monsieur Daniel? It's not a bad idea that. I'll have to have a word with Caroline, see what she thinks.'

'We could put some ideas down on paper,' Alice suggested, and Tom didn't tell her it couldn't be done. 'You can do the sketches, I'll add the details for you.'

'We'll have a good look in daylight. It's too dark to start now.' It felt like they were the only two people for miles, marooned in their tower, surrounded by the heather sea. Although the lights had been restored to the tower since the fire, the dusk seemed more natural.

'I'll check the cupboard one more time. In case we've missed anything,' Alice said, trying to delay the moment when they would head back to the house.

'So, how do you feel now you know the secret?' Tom asked, watching her feel around inside the cupboard, making sure that there was nothing else in there.

'I feel sad. It was such an unexceptional end for such an exceptional man. An unknown soldier in France. No, can't feel any more letters.'

'So why didn't they get together, if they were that obsessed with each other?' Tom asked.

'As far as I can tell from the letters they were scared. They planned it, they thought about it, but when it came to it she was afraid to take that final step to leave her husband and he was afraid to try and make her. He simply accepted her decision.'

'Sad, that.'

'Perhaps sometimes it's worth taking a risk,' she said, looking at him out of the corner of her eye. 'Perhaps what happened to them shows that sometimes the difference doesn't matter. Lady Isobel and Sir Edward should have been just right for each other when you look at it – rich and educated from the right kind of families to make a perfect match – and yet they were miserable too. And perhaps Fox-Travers could have been the one to save her from that misery. But they were too scared, so we'll never know what it could have been like.'

She had one final check of the cupboard and as she was about to shut it again, her fingers reached something at the back corner; something dry and dusty, that she didn't want to touch.

'Oh! There is something else,' she said. She shone the torch in and swept it out with a piece of paper. Withered and dry and brown they fell into her hand crumbling as she touched them - petals.

'Roses,' she said softly, brushing the dust off her fingers.

'There could still be more of a story for you to find; what might have happened to him in Canada?' Tom said.

'I don't know if I want to know.'

'Perhaps he loved her faithfully until he died,' Tom said.

'You're a romantic at heart, aren't you?' Alice looked at him.

'I guess I am. I spend too much time in the gardens not to think every now and then about the people who first made them grow.'

'We could create the garden together in the ruins, like them, maybe, do you think?' Alice suggested softly. 'The Fox-Travers Garden.'

'The Phoenix Garden, more like. Something rising from the ashes.'

'I like that. Something beautiful growing out of a disaster.'

For a moment she caught his eye and she wondered if he was thinking the same thing as her – that perhaps the garden wasn't the only thing that might grow from the wreckage of the past. Alice took a deep breath.

'I don't want to make the same mistake they did.'

'Who? What do you mean?'

'Lady Isobel and Fox-Travers. They were scared to move forwards, but I don't want to be scared any more. And I don't want you to be scared. I'm not Chloe and you're not Sebastian. We have to trust each other.'

'I know. But it's not that easy, is it? I don't know whether I can go through all that again. It's not you, Alice –'

'I know! It's not me, it's Chloe. But what about us, Tom? Isn't it worth trying? I'm not going to treat you like she did. And you won't treat me like Sebastian did, I know you won't because it's not in your nature.'

'I want to, I just don't know if I can,' he said, looking away.

She thought for a moment about Marjorie's wise advice, pondering those wise words in her heart: "Trust each other. Move forward. Don't let your pasts ruin your future… or just take all your clothes off and worry about all the talking later."

'Come on, let's take these letters back to the house,' said Tom, turning to leave, and Alice knew what she was going to do. She took off her jumper and dropped it onto the floor. She shivered, partly with anticipation and partly because the Gothic Tower was draughty and cold.

'I trust you, Tom,' she said, and he turned back towards her. His eyes, widening rapidly with surprise, were fixed on hers. 'I trust you to do the right thing.'

He put down the letters on the table, coming back across the room towards her. 'Alice, you don't have to do this if you don't want to. I'm not like Sebastian.' He picked up the jumper and tried to hand it back to her.

'The difference is that this time I want to,' she said, and began to unhook her bra. 'I'm not doing this because I think *you* want me to, I'm not here because I'm trying to please you, I'm doing this because *I* want to and I think you feel the same. Do you?'

She took a step forwards, dropping her bra to the floor, and an involuntary groan escaped him as his gaze slid downwards over her body – she could almost feel the heat of his eyes on her skin.

'Yes!' he said, as if she had forced the word from 'Yes… but what if -'

She touched a finger to his lips. She felt bold, alive, resolute. 'Don't give me any what ifs,' she said. 'I want us to move forward together. Forget about Sebastian, forget about Chloe, we're not going to let our pasts ruin the future. It's not going to be easy for either of us, but –'

Tom softly kissed the finger that she held to his lips, then the palm of her hand, her wrist, her arm, her naked shoulder blade. She took that as a sign that he was prepared to give their relationship a try. She reached out and began to unbutton his shirt, but as if her touch had stung him he took a step backwards. Her heart sank. He was going to turn away from her again, wasn't he?

He took hold of her upper arms and held her at arm's length, his fingers hot on her cold, bare skin, gazing at her as if he could read the future in the pattern of goosebumps on her flesh.

'I promise you, I'll never let anyone hurt you, Alice,' he said, his eyes fixed on hers.

'And I'll never let anyone hurt you,' she whispered. 'Do you trust me?'

He stood still, his breathing ragged, still holding her away from him at arm's length, looking at her as if he was trying to make up his mind. Then he bent his head and breathed a single word in her ear, pulling her towards him.

'Yes,' he whispered.

He was still tense as she began to kiss him, but soon he was kissing her back just as passionately as he had done on the night of the fire, but this time he didn't tell her to stop and put her clothes back on and there was no look of disgust or fear in his eyes: this time she could read something altogether different there.

Hands shaking, she began to undo the belt of his trousers, as he struggled with the button on her jeans. It was then that she remembered.

'Oh! Oh no!' she gasped.

'What is it?' He sounded concerned. 'Have you changed your mind? Look it's fine if you have, I completely understand –'

'No! It's just… I'm sorry… I'm wearing my ugly grey cotton pants…'

'The Marks and Spencer's ones that cover everything?'

How did he know about that? Of course, the day she had been on the phone to Sebastian in the library, she thought somebody had been there. It had been Tom?

'You heard that? I knew there was somebody there that day!'

'I practically had to go and have a cold shower,' he admitted. 'But I don't care about your underwear right now. I'm more interested right now in what you've got underneath…' and his hands slipped gently downwards to prove it.

She drew him over with her to the old, battered green sofa, sinking down she felt the velvet beneath her trailing fingers and the cushions soft behind her back. She watched Tom's masculine figure standing tall above her as he made his final preparations and moved in towards her.

'No!' she whispered, as he laid her down beneath him.

'What is it?' He pulled back and suppressed a groan of frustration. 'What's wrong?'

'Nothing's wrong!' she said. 'I just want you to do something for me.'

'Anything,' he murmured. 'What do you want me to do?'

Her eyes glinted. 'Turn over, Tom!' she whispered and with a deep groan at last his body sought hers as she took her place on top of him.

'Oh… God… Alice… I'm going to…'

'Tom!'

And head thrown back, her tall slender body arching above him, with a high, keening cry of satisfaction Alice revealed her essence to Tom in the Gothic Tower.

The End.

Acknowledgements

Firstly to Lisa Hall and all the team at Manatee Books for having faith in me as a writer. It means a lot! Thank you for your tireless efforts on my behalf.

Secondly to everyone on the "Writers Block North East" course 2017 -2018, without whom this would have been an entirely different book – and especially Laura Degnan for being my writing mentor.

Thirdly, as always, to my "Beta Buddies" who discussed with the utmost seriousness daft questions like: "Would you say September 25th was late summer or early autumn?" and to the Romantic Novelists' Association, whose members are always inspirational and generous with their support.

And especially to everyone who has read my books and offered their support; people who I know who helped me to sell books and share news, who pestered their friends to buy my books and also to the amazing bloggers who took the time to review and support me even though they didn't know me at all. There are too many of you to mention each by name but I am truly grateful.

And as always, thanks to my friends and family, particularly this time to my teenage children to whom this book is dedicated – the character of Emily (and her vocabulary) owe a lot to both of you.

16921756R00173

Printed in Great Britain
by Amazon